CW01547172

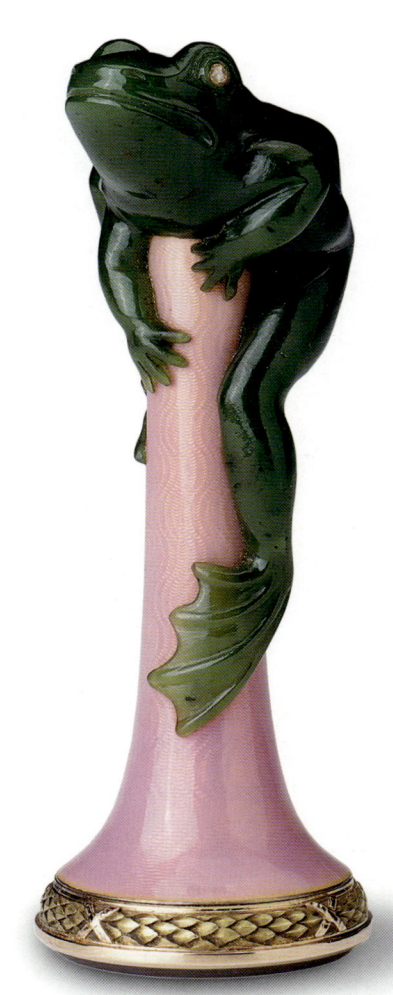

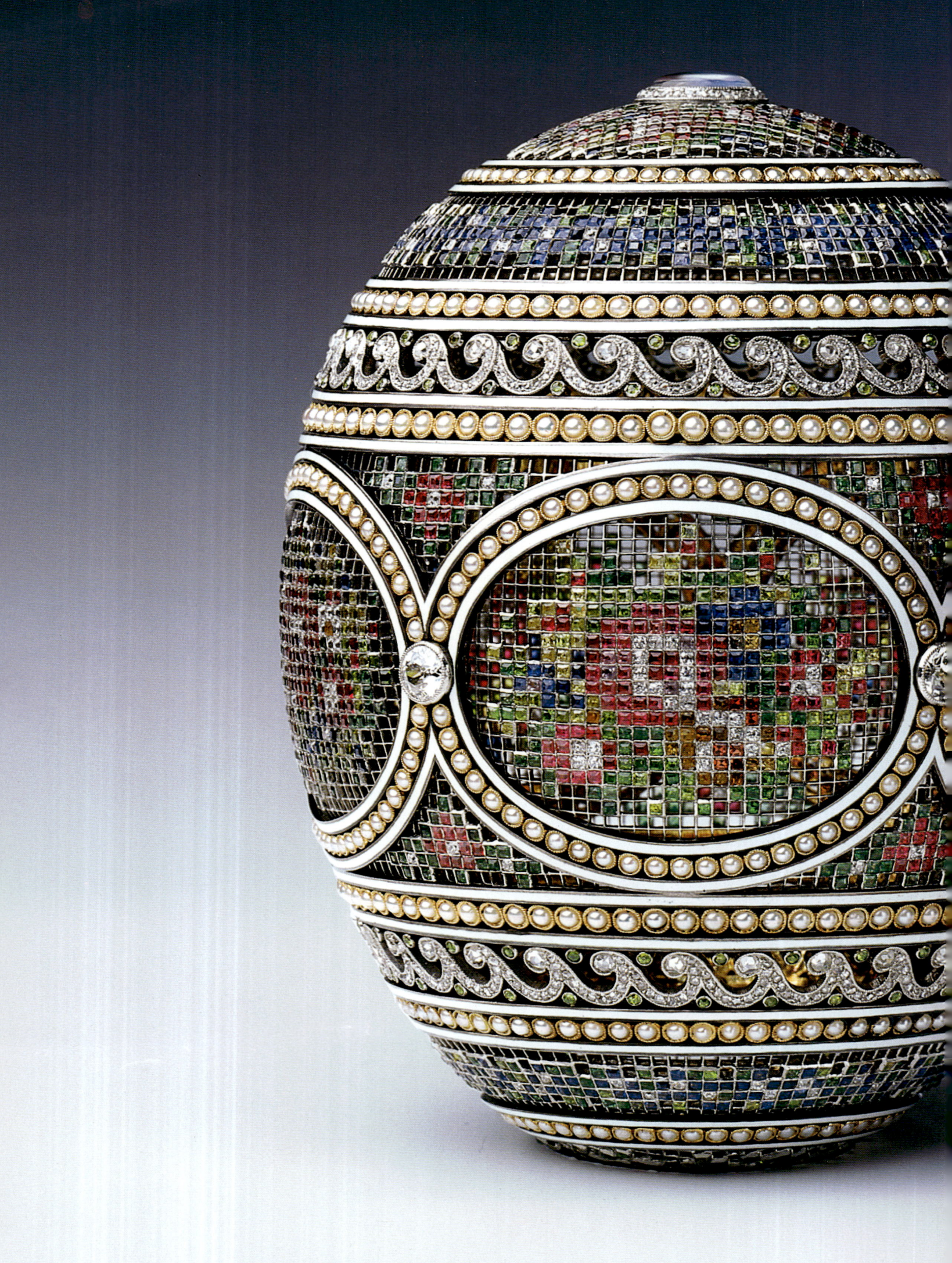

FABERGÉ

IN THE ROYAL COLLECTION

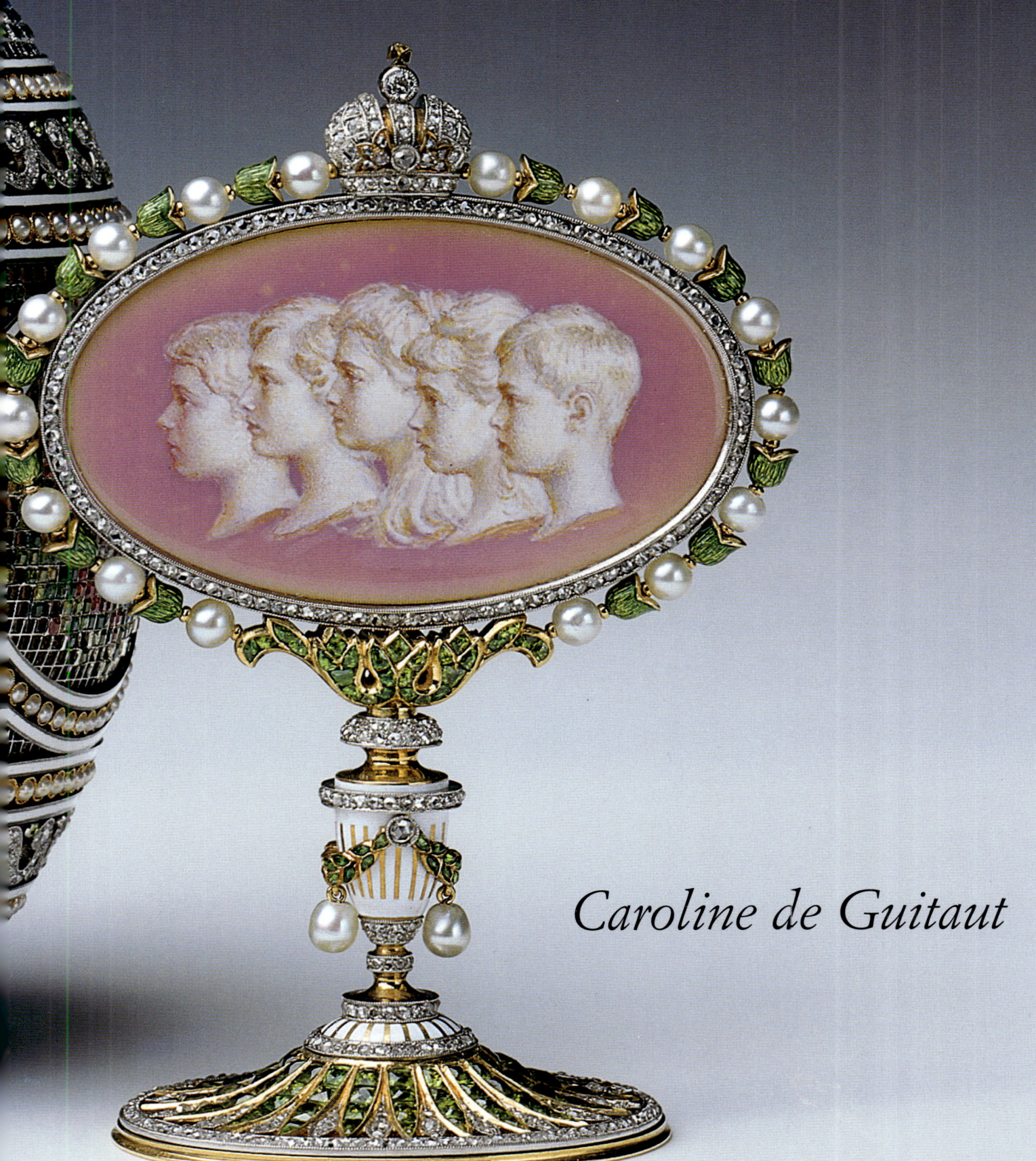

Caroline de Guitaut

Published by
Royal Collection Enterprises Ltd
St James's Palace, London SW1A 1JR

For a complete catalogue of current publications, please write to the address above, or visit our website on www.royal.gov.uk

© 2003 Royal Collection Enterprises Ltd
Text by Caroline de Guitaut and reproductions of all items in the Royal Collection © 2003 HM Queen Elizabeth II.

121178 (hardback)
121186 (paperback)

ISBN (hardback) 1 902163 66 4
ISBN (paperback) 1 902163 83 4

British Library Cataloguing in Publication Data:
A catalogue record for this book is available from the British Library.

Designed by Karen Stafford
Produced by Book Production Consultants plc, Cambridge
Printed and bound by Graphic Studio, Verona

Front and back cover: Cigarette case, 1908 (cat. 187)
Page 1: Seal, 1903–17 (cat. 301)
Title pages: Mosaic Egg and Surprise, 1914 (cat. 3)
Page 5: Kovsh, 1908–13 (cat. 324, detail)
Page 6: Cornflowers and buttercups, *c.*1900 (cat. 133, detail)

PICTURE CREDITS
All works reproduced are in the Royal Collection unless indicated otherwise below. Royal Collection Enterprises are grateful for permission to reproduce the following:

pp. 10, 12, 15, 19: Courtesy of Wartski, London; p. 24: © A LA VIEILLE RUSSIE, reproduced by permission; pp. 52, 175: Drawing from U. Tillander-Godenhielm, P.L. Schaffer, A.M. Ilich and M.A. Schaffer, *Golden Years of Fabergé: Drawings and Objects from the Wigström Workshop*, New York, 2000, A La Vieille Russie and Alain de Gourcuff Editeur. © A LA VIEILLE RUSSIE, reproduced by permission; p. 54 (lower right): Royal Archives © Her Majesty The Queen; pp. 104, 127, 129, 154, 214; Courtesy of Ulla Tillander-Godenhielm, from an unpublished album of drawings by Henrik Wigström; p. 210 © Christie's Images Limited 2003

Every effort has been made to contact copyright holders; any omissions are inadvertent, and will be corrected in future editions if notification of the amended credit is sent to the publisher in writing.

This publication has been generously supported by Sir Harry Djanogly, CBE

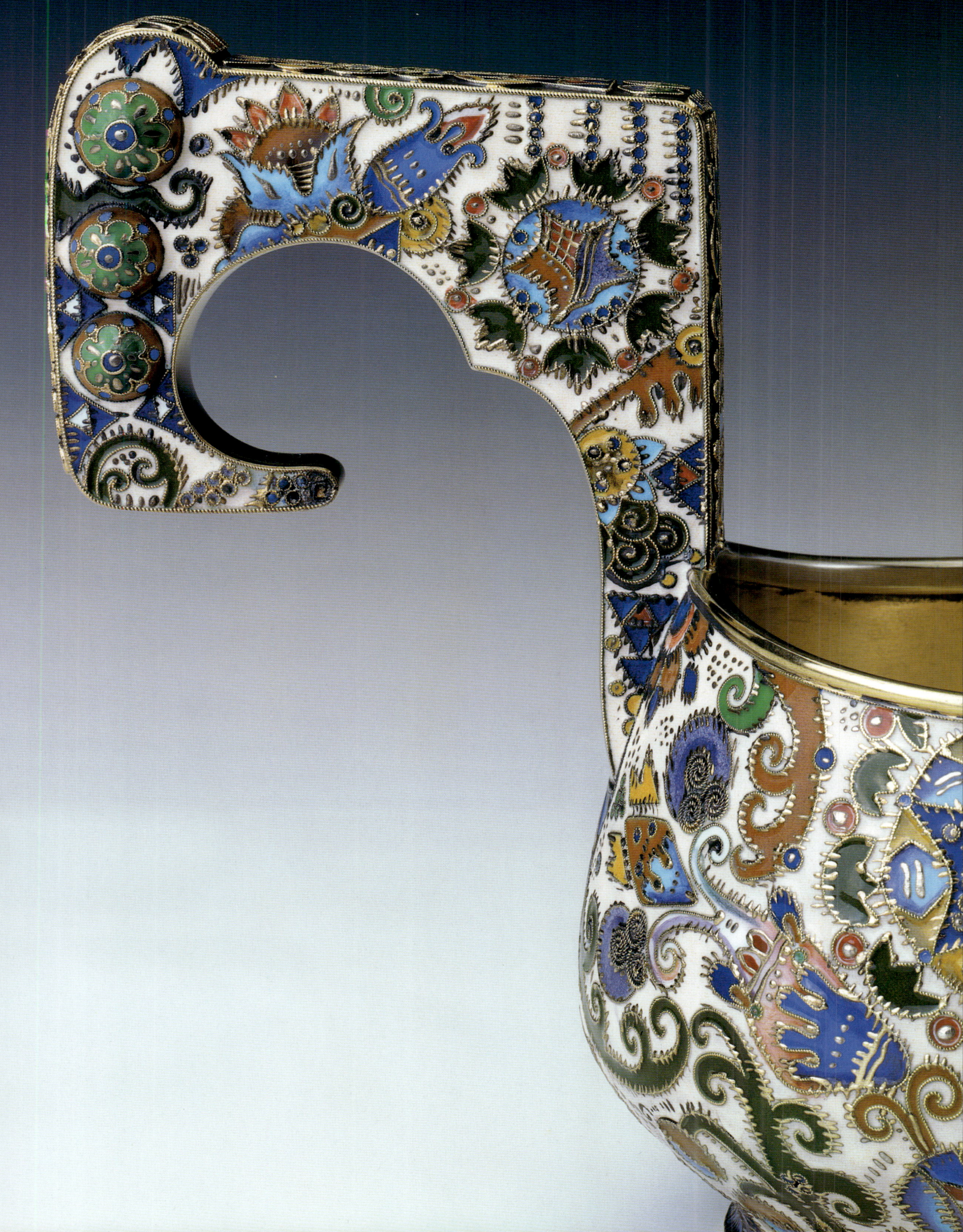

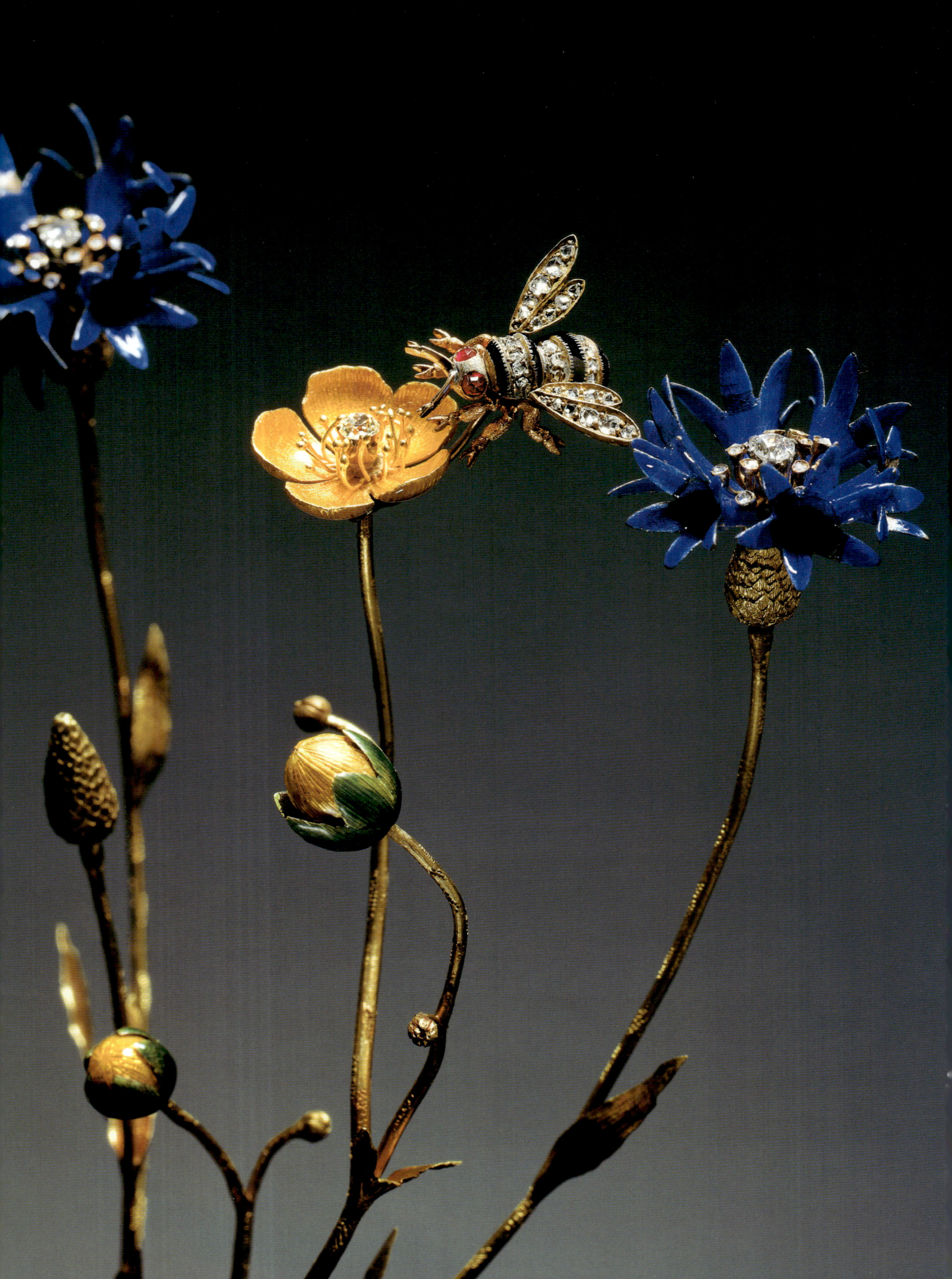

CONTENTS

AN INTRODUCTION TO THE ROYAL COLLECTION AND TO CARL FABERGÉ

THE BRITISH ROYAL COLLECTION of works by the great Russian goldsmith and jeweller Carl Fabergé (1846–1920) is unique. Widely recognised as one of the finest Fabergé collections in the world, it has several features that set it apart from others and that give it an outstanding and remarkable character.

Firstly, its size has no equal, for the collection numbers almost six hundred pieces. Size is not necessarily indicative of importance, but the other most notable attributes of the collection are the quality and the variety of the objects it encompasses. It is well known that Carl Fabergé had exacting standards that were rigorously applied, and pieces from his workshops are inevitably of exceptional quality, made from the best materials by the most talented designers and craftsmen of the time. The Royal Collection includes some of the finest examples of almost every type of object made by Fabergé's workshops – from Easter eggs to animal sculptures, from flowers to cigarette cases, from presentation boxes to bell pushes and from cuff links to miniature furniture.

Secondly, of all collections of Fabergé, that in the Royal Collection is perhaps the best known. Works from it have been lent to almost all the major retrospective Fabergé exhibitions held in the United Kingdom and abroad from the 1930s to the present. Two major exhibitions featuring the collection were held at The Queen's Gallery, Buckingham Palace, in 1985–6 and in 1995–6. However, undoubtedly the single most significant feature of the collection is the manner in which it was formed. Almost all the items in it were acquired prior to the Russian Revolution, during the period when Fabergé's business was at its most successful and its most prolific, c.1885–1917. A large proportion of the other notable 'public' Fabergé collections – such as those at the Cleveland Museum of Art (Cleveland, Ohio) and the Hillwood Museum (Washington) – and most of the substantial private collections, such as the Forbes Collection, were formed from the 1920s onwards when works of art by Fabergé began to appear in the West. Some were smuggled out of Russia by émigrés and sold on the open market; others were acquired from the Russian state-run sales organisations by dealers and industrialists from the West such as Emanuel Snowman, Armand Hammer and Alexander Schaffer. They brought the pieces to a new audience of collectors in the United Kingdom and the United States.

The royal collection of Fabergé is inextricably and uniquely linked to the Romanov dynasty. Many pieces were given personally to members of the British royal family by their relations in Russia, notably the last two tsars and their consorts: Alexander III and Marie Feodorovna, and Nicholas

Laurits Tuxen, *The marriage of Tsar Nicholas II and Alexandra Feodorovna, November 1894*
Oil on canvas, 169.4 x 139.9 cm (66³⁄₄ x 55")
RCIN 404465

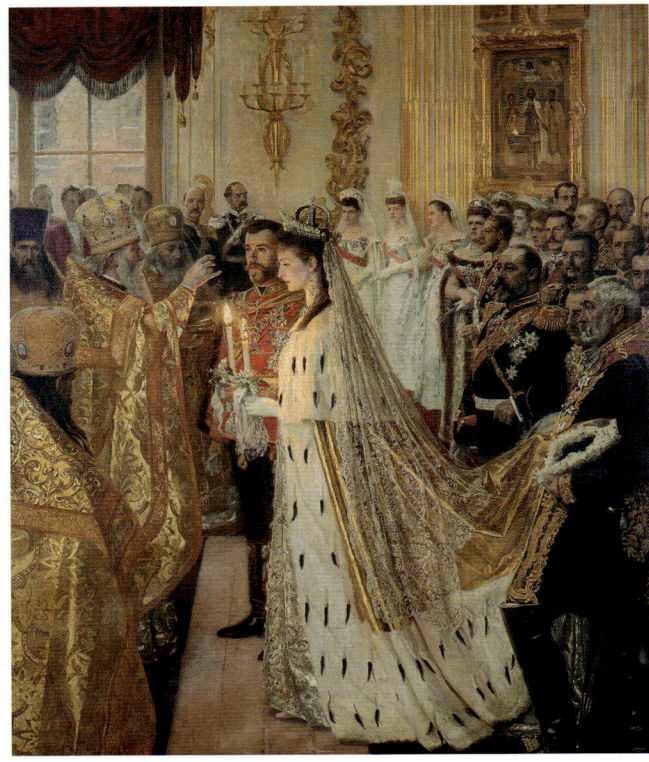

II and Alexandra Feodorovna. The only collections comparable in terms of scale and content were those of the Russian imperial family themselves, which in total ran to thousands of objects. These were confiscated and dispersed after the Russian Revolution, although there are still notable holdings in both Moscow and St Petersburg.[1] The family links were doubly significant. The combined patronage of two Danish princesses, Dagmar (1847–1928), who became on her marriage Tsarina Marie Feodorovna, and her sister Alexandra (1844–1925), who became Queen Alexandra, consort of King Edward VII (1841–1910), effectively established Fabergé as an international figure. In fact, the two Danish princesses became the greatest publicity machine that Fabergé could have hoped for, resulting in patronage from most of the royal houses of Europe.

There was a constant exchange of gifts between the families for Easter and Christmas, for birthdays and other notable anniversaries, and to commemorate occasions when the families met in Russia, England or Denmark. As a result, many of the works by Fabergé in the Royal Collection are intimately connected to people, places and even animals of significance to the royal family. The passion for collecting Fabergé started by Queen Alexandra and shared by King Edward VII was inherited by two of their children, Princess Victoria (1868–1935) and King George V (1865–1936). The latter acquired with Queen Mary (1867–1953) the three Imperial Easter Eggs now in the Royal Collection. These had been commissioned by Tsar Nicholas II a few decades earlier. The collection continued to expand with the next generation. King George VI (1895–1952) added numerous cigarette cases and Queen Elizabeth (1900–2002) a variety of pieces including flowers and presentation boxes. No pieces have been added to the collection during the reign of Her Majesty The Queen but other members of the Royal Family, for example The Prince of Wales, have acquired some works.

From the time when King Edward VII and Queen Alexandra first became aware of Fabergé's work, the size and scope of the collection was dictated by the pieces received as personal gifts from their Russian and Danish relatives, their immediate family and their friends. They also purchased pieces for each other from Fabergé's London branch, which opened in 1903. There was no attempt by the royal family to form a representative thematic collection of Fabergé's work, as certainly happened with other collections made in England and, especially, in the United States after the Russian Revolution. Possibly the sole exception was King Edward's commission of hardstone carvings of the animals at Sandringham for Queen Alexandra. The royal family's love of Fabergé was well known in Edwardian circles and as a result of numerous gifts the collection grew rapidly in the first decade of the twentieth century. This helps to explain why there is such a wide variety contained within it. In addition to the largest known holdings of Fabergé's animals and flowers, there are Imperial Easter Eggs, boxes, frames, bibelots, desk accessories, cigarette cases, traditional Russian objects and all manner of practical items, luxurious women's accessories, jewellery and even one of the rare hardstone human figures. The only types not well represented are the everyday silverware that Fabergé produced in large quantities – which formed the core of his business – and fine jewellery.[2]

The earliest exhibition of works by Fabergé to include pieces from the Royal Collection was the *Exhibition of Russian Art* held in London in 1935.[3] A considerable number of objects were lent to two exhibitions in 1949 and 1953 at Wartski, the jewellery dealer established by Emanuel Snowman, who brought many pieces of Fabergé out of Russia from the 1920s onwards. The first celebrated the publication of H.C. Bainbridge's book on Fabergé;[4] the second The Queen's Coronation. In 1977 Kenneth Snowman (son of Emanuel) organised the first major retrospective exhibition of Fabergé's work, held in London at the Victoria and Albert Museum in celebration of The Queen's Silver Jubilee. It included pieces from the Royal Collection supplemented by other loans. This exhibition captured the imagination of museum visitors and as a result, from the early 1980s, exhibitions of Fabergé's work to which many pieces from the Royal Collection have been loaned have been regularly organised in the United States, Russia and all over Europe. Two of the Imperial Easter Eggs, the Colonnade Egg and the Mosaic Egg (cat. 2 and 3), have each been exhibited no fewer than sixteen times.

The enthusiasm of the British royal family for Carl Fabergé's work undoubtedly helped to ensure his international success, but there were many other factors that contributed to his rise to become the greatest jeweller and goldsmith of the late nineteenth and early twentieth centuries. Fabergé was fortunate in undertaking his apprenticeship in the three major European centres of goldsmiths' work, Frankfurt, Florence and Paris. This gave him an invaluable insight into the materials and techniques particular to the artistic traditions in those cities. It later became evident from his work that he had been deeply influenced by the variety of styles in the decorative arts that he had seen during his formative years. He was to draw on this knowledge for the rest of his career, during which he produced modern-day objects in a range of historic styles using his own reinterpretation of earlier techniques. This important experience, coupled with his knowledge of the Russian decorative arts and of traditional Russian techniques such as hardstone carving and cloisonné enamelling,[5] provided Fabergé with a substantial advantage over his competitors and explains why so many of them sought to imitate his products (see pp. 243–64).

Within a few years of taking over his father's modest goldsmith and jewellery business in St Petersburg in 1872, Fabergé had transformed it into a large enterprise consisting of separate workshops, each headed by a workmaster responsible for ensuring quality, production and the recruitment of the best-trained craftsmen. In return the workmasters were allowed to mark their products with their own initials. Certain of the workshops specialised in particular products; for example the workshops of Holmström and Thielemann in jewellery, that of Kollin in gold revivalist pieces and Hollming's in enamelled boxes. There were separate workshops dedicated to the production of enamel and to the silk- or velvet-lined fitted boxes of holly, sycamore and maple in which each piece of Fabergé was sold. Carl Fabergé promoted the best workmasters to head workmaster and from 1872 to 1886 this post was held by Erik Kollin. Michael Perchin held the post from 1886 to 1903 and Henrik Wigström from 1903 to 1917. The head workmasters collaborated with Fabergé on matters of design and each had a range of distinctive styles, but Fabergé also recruited designers such as Franz Birbaum (1872–1947), active between 1893 and 1917, and his own brother Agathon (1862–95), who were to be influential in the artistic direction of the firm's products. Other designers were involved in specific projects; for example Alma Pihl (1888–1976)

designed two of the Imperial Easter Eggs, one of which, the Mosaic Egg, is now in the Royal Collection (see p.40). There were also specialist sculptors such as Boris Frödman-Cluzel (b.1878) who specialised in animal and figure sculpting, stonecarvers such as Derbyshev and Kremlev and enamellers such as Petrov and Boitzov. Many of the craftsmen, sculptors and designers were trained at the Baron Stieglitz Central School of Technical Drawing in St Petersburg. The number of craftsmen employed by Fabergé seems very high – at its peak around five hundred – but it must be remembered that with a few exceptions each object was entirely made by hand. This involved a range of techniques and skilled craftsmen and the objects were therefore very labour intensive to produce.

Fabergé was able to keep ahead of the considerable competition in his field by constantly developing new products in new styles and designs. If objects in a particular style did not sell well, he had no compunction about destroying them to make way for new ranges.[6] He insisted on selecting only the very best materials. He acquired Karl Wöerffel's stonecarving workshop – one of his main suppliers of nephrite, jasper, rhodonite, bowenite and all the naturally occurring

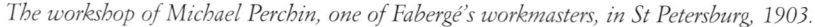

The workshop of Michael Perchin, one of Fabergé's workmasters, in St Petersburg, 1903.

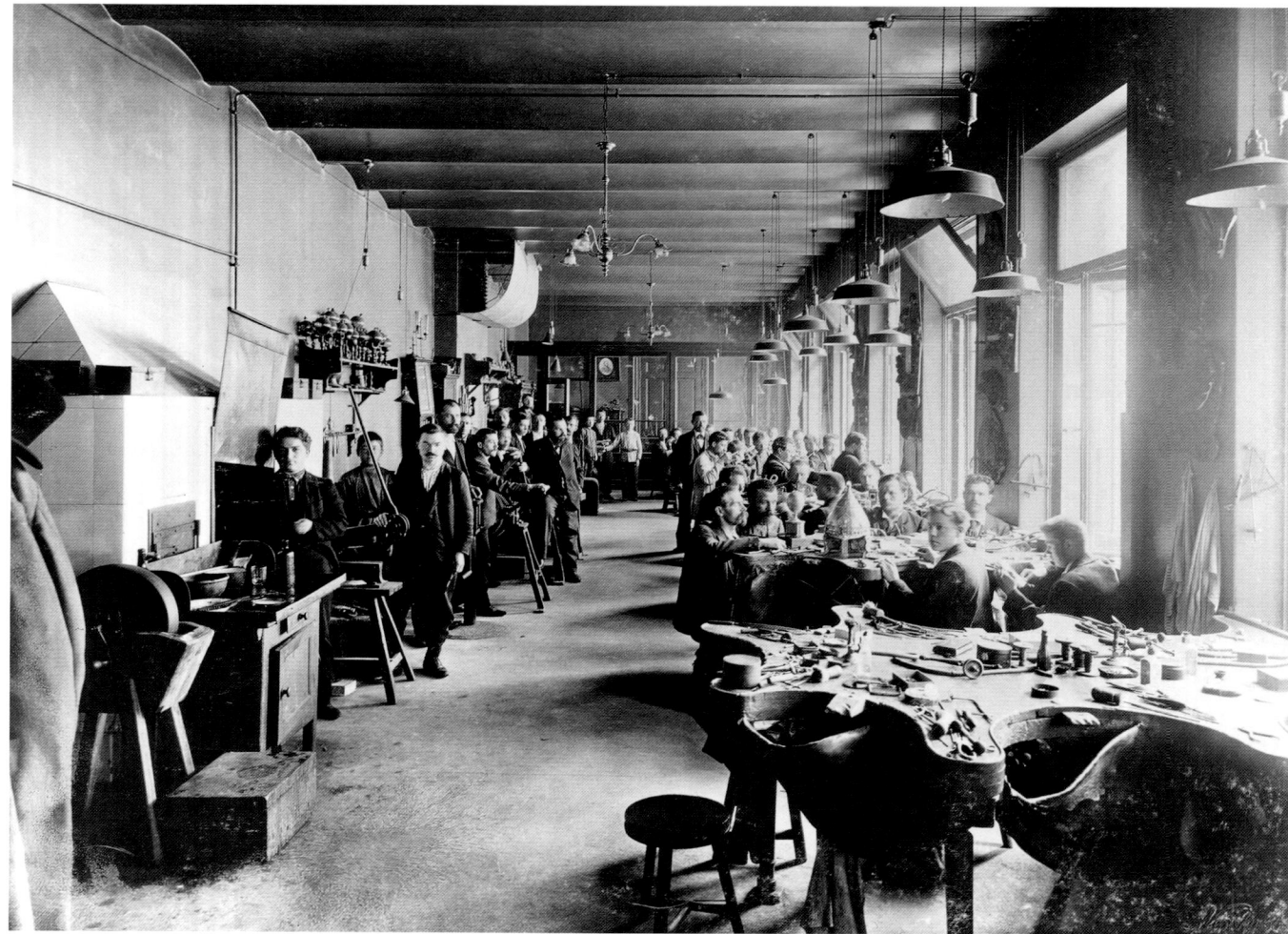

stones that he regularly used – to ensure that the quality of supply was maintained.

Works made by Carl Fabergé himself are difficult to identify, but he would certainly have been closely involved in the production of the most important commissions such as the Imperial Easter Eggs and also in the more complex objects such as the flowers and hardstone figures.[7] His managerial and administrative role within the company was central to its success and he would have dealt personally with orders from the imperial family and other important clients. In 1908 he visited King Chulalongkorn of Siam (now Thailand), who had appointed him an official court supplier, but in spite of King Edward VII and Queen Alexandra's obvious admiration of his work he was never to meet his greatest English clients.

The firm of Fabergé had supplied the Russian Imperial Cabinet (the department of the Tsar's household dealing with the official gifts bestowed by the Tsar) with various objects since the 1860s but it was not until 1885 that the firm was granted an appointment as supplier to the court of Tsar Alexander III. This was also the year in which the Tsar commissioned Fabergé to produce the first Imperial Easter Egg. Three years earlier he had been awarded a gold medal at the 1882 Pan-Russian Exhibition in Moscow. Presumably in response to the growing number of official commissions from the imperial family, Fabergé opened a branch in Moscow in 1887 which specialised in producing silver objects. Wider recognition of his work came with the award of the Grand Prix at the Exposition Universelle in Paris in 1900 and from that date his business became an international concern. Branches were opened in Odessa (1900), London (1903) and Kiev (1905). The London branch served primarily as a showroom for the British royal family and their circle, but it was also from this branch that lucrative selling trips were undertaken to the Continent and further afield to India, Thailand, China and Japan between 1908 and 1917.

Given the meteoric success of Fabergé's business, it is noteworthy that the quality of the objects and the ingenuity and originality of their design never suffered. This serves as a remarkable testament both to Carl Fabergé personally and to the skill and dedication of his craftsmen, and helps to explain why his work continued to be sought after in the West following the closure of his business by the Bolsheviks in 1918. No new pieces were made after 1918 but many works by Fabergé began to appear on the open market in the 1920s, brought out of Russia by émigrés Auction houses began to organise sales of Fabergé and other Russian works of art in the late 1920s. The first in London was held at Christie's in 1927 and included part of the Russian crown jewels. A second sale of Fabergé was held at Christie's in 1934, but the prices realised were low. Gradually, over the next decade, more and more pieces appeared and an enthusiasm for collecting Fabergé began all over again, stimulated by the early exhibitions already mentioned and undoubtedly by Queen Mary's passionate interest.

This book accompanies the third major exhibition of Fabergé from the Royal Collection, drawn entirely from the Collection's own holdings.[8] Its aim is to display some of the finest pieces, including important examples of the various types and styles of object for which Fabergé is renowned. The exhibition has also afforded the opportunity to include recent research from Russian archives into the provenance of these pieces and to give a detailed account of the formation of the collection through an analysis of the key collectors and their tastes. A selection of pieces by contemporary makers, also drawn from the Royal Collection, is included for the first time. This is intended to place Fabergé in the context of other goldsmiths and jewellers, such as Cartier, Boucheron and Hahn, who were active in the same period in Russia and Europe, many of whom were profoundly influenced by his work.

1   The Kremlin Armoury Museum, the State Historical Museum, Moscow, and the State Hermitage Museum, St Petersburg, contain significant holdings of works by Fabergé.

2   The Fabergé jewellery in the Royal Collection is of the more modest type produced, i.e. enamelled and set with semi-precious cabochon stones. There are some examples of table silver by Fabergé in the Royal Collection but they are not included in the exhibition.

3   London 1935; see cat. 22, 55 and 226.

4   H.C. Bainbridge was manager of Fabergé's London branch from 1907 until its closure in 1915.

5   From 1867 Fabergé began to repair antiquities voluntarily at the Hermitage Museum. He also acted as an appraiser of metalwork and jewellery acquisitions at the Museum, thereby enriching his knowledge of Russian art.

6   Von Solodkoff 1984, pp. 35–6.

7   Bainbridge (1942a, p. 937) states that Carl Fabergé oversaw each stage of the making of the flower studies.

8   Those held at The Queen's Gallery, Buckingham Palace, in 1985–6 and 1995–6 showed 341 and 543 pieces respectively.

CHRONOLOGY OF THE HOUSE OF FABERGÉ

1814 Fabergé's father Gustav born of Huguenot origin in Pernau on the Baltic

1841–2 Gustav Fabergé becomes a master goldsmith in St Petersburg and opens a shop at 12 Bolshaya Morskaya. He marries Charlotte Jungstedt

1846 Peter Carl Fabergé born in St Petersburg, 30 May

1857 August Holmström (1829–1903) joins Gustav Fabergé's business as head jeweller

1860 Gustav Fabergé and his family move temporarily to Dresden

1861–4 Carl Fabergé travels through Europe as part of his apprenticeship in Frankfurt, Florence and Paris

1862 Fabergé's brother Agathon born in Dresden

1864 The Fabergé family return to St Petersburg and Carl Fabergé joins his father's business

1866 Gustav Fabergé starts to supply the Imperial Cabinet

1867 Carl Fabergé works voluntarily at the Hermitage Museum, repairing antiquities and acting as an appraiser of metalwork and jewellery acquisitions

1872 Carl Fabergé takes over his father's business. Erik Kollin (1836–1901) becomes head workmaster. Fabergé marries Augusta Jakobs (1851–1925)

1874 Birth of son Eugene Fabergé (d.1960)

1876 Birth of son Agathon Fabergé (d.1951)

1877 Birth of son Alexander Fabergé (d.1952)

1882 Fabergé awarded the gold medal at the Pan-Russian Exhibition, Moscow. Carl's brother Agathon joins the firm

1884 Birth of son Nicholas Fabergé (d.1939). All four sons later join the family firm

1885 Fabergé appointed Supplier to the Court of Tsar Alexander III. The Tsar commissions the first Imperial Easter Egg. Fabergé awarded a gold medal at the Nuremberg Fine Art Exhibition for his copies of the Scythian Treasure (discovered at Kerch in the Crimea in 1867)

1886 Michael Perchin (1860–1903) becomes head workmaster

1887 Fabergé's Moscow branch opens and is managed by Allan Bowe

1894 Eugene Fabergé joins the firm

1895 Death of Agathon Fabergé. Carl's son Agathon enters the firm

1897 Carl Fabergé is awarded the royal warrant for the courts of Sweden and Norway

1900 Fabergé exhibits at the Exposition Universelle in Paris and is awarded the Grand Prix. He is decorated with the Légion d'Honneur. The Odessa branch of the firm is opened

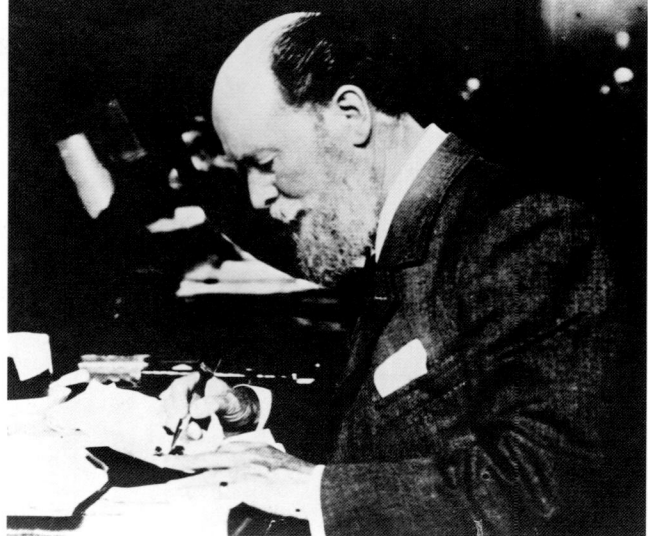

Peter Carl Fabergé, photographed c.1905 by H. Oeburg

1901 Fabergé supplies the Imperial Easter Egg known as the Basket of Flowers Egg (now in the Royal Collection) to Tsar Nicholas II

1902 Exhibition of 'artistic objects and miniatures' at the Von Dervis Mansion, St Petersburg. The Basket of Flowers Egg is among the exhibits

1903 The London branch of the firm, managed by Arthur Bowe, is opened at Berners Hotel. Henrik Wigström (1862–1923) succeeds Michael Perchin as head workmaster

1904 The London branch moves to Portman House, Duke Street

1905 The Kiev branch of the firm is opened

1906 The London branch moves to 48 Dover Street

1907 H.C. Bainbridge takes over as manager (with Nicholas Fabergé) of the London branch

1908 Fabergé is appointed court jeweller and enameller to the King of Siam

1910 Fabergé supplies the Imperial Easter Egg known as the Colonnade Egg (now in the Royal Collection) to Tsar Nicholas II

1911 The London branch moves to 173 New Bond Street

1914 Fabergé supplies the Imperial Easter Egg known as the Mosaic Egg (now in the Royal Collection) to Tsar Nicholas II

1915 The London branch is closed

1918 Fabergé's St Petersburg headquarters is closed and he emigrates to Switzerland

1920 Carl Fabergé dies in La Rosiaz, Switzerland, 24 September

THE FORMATION OF THE COLLECTION: A HISTORY OF ROYAL COLLECTORS

THE CHARACTER OF THE Royal Collection of Fabergé was almost entirely shaped by the close relationships between the Russian, Danish and English royal families, all of whom exchanged gifts when they gathered for family occasions, anniversaries such as birthdays, and at Easter and Christmas. A large proportion of the collection was formed in this manner, mainly during the reign of King Edward VII, whose consort Queen Alexandra had been introduced to Fabergé's work by her sister Marie Feodorovna, wife of Tsar Alexander III of Russia. Once Fabergé's London branch had opened in 1903, the King and Queen and two of their children, Princess Victoria and George, Prince of Wales, purchased many pieces, as gifts for each other or for their friends. The clientele of the London branch included friends of the King and Queen who, well aware of the royal couple's admiration for Fabergé's wares, bought them many gifts to add to their collection. Later Queen Mary, consort of King George V, acquired many pieces by gift, her enthusiasm for Fabergé also being well known. Further she made her own purchases, particularly in the late 1920s and 1930s when pieces of imperial provenance began to appear for sale in the West. Many of these were given to King George V. Through the 1940s, 1950s and 1960s King George VI and then Queen Elizabeth acquired a range of pieces which were among the last to enter the collection.

Queen Alexandra (1844–1925) was undoubtedly the most significant influence in the history of the formation of the royal collection of Fabergé. It is not known when her sister, Tsarina Marie Feodorovna, first introduced her to Fabergé's work. It may have been as early as 1881 when, as Princess of Wales, she attended the funeral ceremonies of the assassinated Tsar Alexander II in Moscow and St Petersburg with her husband, later King Edward VII. The Princess of Wales stayed on after the funeral with her sister, whose apartments certainly contained works by Fabergé and other court suppliers. It should be borne in mind that Gustav Fabergé (Carl's father) had begun supplying the imperial court from 1866. At annual family holidays in Denmark, when the Prince and Princess and Tsar and Tsarina would spend time together with the King and Queen of Denmark, gifts were always exchanged. Documents in the Russian State Historical Archives reveal examples of Marie Feodorovna's expenditure with Fabergé prior to her trips to Copenhagen.[1] These are evidence of the considerable number of pieces she took with her on such occasions, some of which were no doubt given to her sister.

Queen Alexandra's visits to Russia were in fact rare. After the funeral of Alexander II she returned, as Princess of Wales, for the wedding of Grand Duchess Xenia (1875–1960) in August 1894, and in November of that year she attended the funeral of her brother-in-law Tsar Alexander III

Queen Louise of Denmark with her two daughters, Queen Alexandra and Tsarina Marie Feodorovna at Amalienborg, 1893.

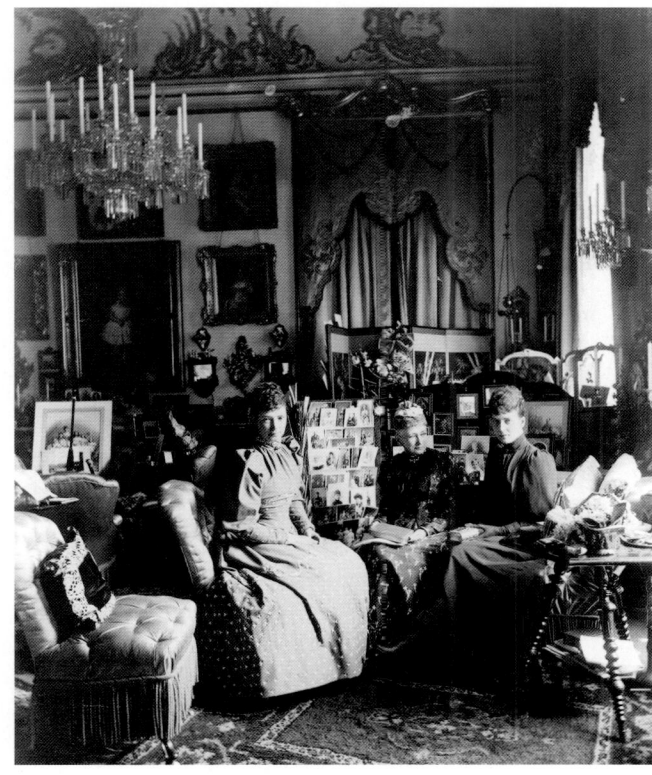

with the Prince of Wales and with George, Duke of York (later King George V). The funeral was swiftly followed by the marriage of Alexander III's heir Tsar Nicholas II to Princess Alix of Hesse. There is no personal account by Queen Alexandra of this prolonged visit but those of Prince George and Charlotte Knollys (her Woman of the Bedchamber) survive.[2] Prince George describes a visit to Fabergé's shop with his father on Tuesday 20 November[3] and Charlotte Knollys one with the Princess of Wales on 22 November.[4] The visit to Russia coincided with the Princess's birthday and the Duke of York reports in his diary, on seeing his mother's presents set up as a birthday table at the Anichkov Palace, 'motherdear's birthday . . . saw all the presents, she has got half Fabergé's shop'.[5] It is therefore clear that Queen Alexandra was acquiring many pieces of Fabergé as presents from her family from at least the 1880s. She also began to purchase pieces before the London branch was opened for business. Her accounts reveal two payments from her presents account to 'C. Fabergé' for jewellery in May and December 1902.[6] She was, however, not the first member of the royal family to purchase works from Fabergé. Queen Victoria's accounts list two payments to 'C. Fabergé' for presents purchased in 1897 for 'brooches etc.' and in July 1898 for jewellery.[7] Queen Victoria is not known for her interest in Fabergé's work but she owned several pieces, including a red and oyster guilloché enamel visitor's book given to her by Tsar Nicholas II and Tsarina Alexandra Feodorovna in 1896, signed by those who attended her Diamond Jubilee the following year (cat. 331).

Queen Alexandra and King Edward VII were the *raison d'être* for the opening of Fabergé's London branch in 1903. By this date they already owned a large number of pieces by Fabergé. Their collection was to grow considerably in the following decade. The London branch was initially established by Arthur Bowe, one of three brothers involved in Fabergé's business in Russia. Allan Bowe managed the Moscow branch and sent his brother to set up an office in Berners Hotel with stock from Moscow. The office moved briefly to Portman House, Duke Street, before the business arrangement between Bowe and Fabergé was ended. In 1906 Carl Fabergé established a branch of his St Petersburg business at 48 Dover Street under the joint management of H.C. Bainbridge and Nicholas Fabergé, his youngest son. In 1911 this branch moved to 173 New Bond Street where it remained until its closure in 1915.

Queen Alexandra made regular visits to the branch, usually timed to coincide with the arrival of new stock from the workshops in Russia, which she often insisted on viewing before anyone else.[8] Carl Fabergé's own awareness of the particular tastes of the King and Queen combined with Bainbridge's role as a go-between for the craftsman and his British royal patrons meant that the branch was always stocked with pieces that appealed to them. Bainbridge records how

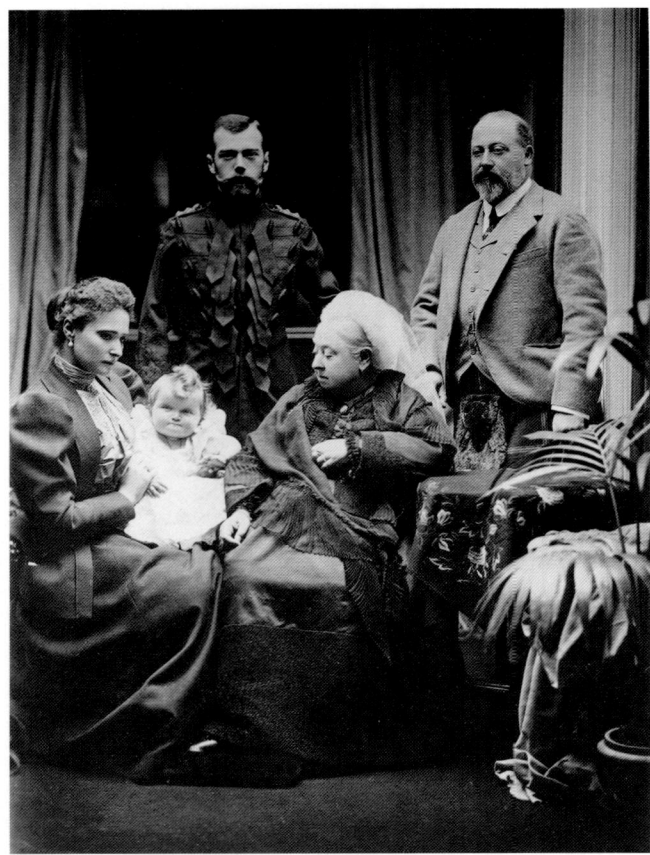

Queen Victoria and Prince Albert Edward (later King Edward VII) with Tsar Nicholas II, Tsarina Alexandra Feodorovna and their eldest daughter, Grand Duchess Olga, at Balmoral, 1896. Photograph by Robert Milne.

he would 'ransack the Petersburg stock' once a year. Carl Fabergé would then examine his selection and comment 'the King and Queen won't like any of them,' and Bainbridge would return to the drawing board.[9] Clearly, not only were both men eager to please their best customers, but Fabergé had a shrewd understanding of the objects which would be most attractive to them.

Queen Alexandra's taste was always for the more modest of Fabergé's products. Her adoration of his animals and flowers mirrored her preference for the simpler things in life. She loved animals and was almost as devoted to her dogs and horses as she was to her children. She was happiest at Sandringham House in Norfolk, where she was surrounded by a menagerie of animals and where a cheerful and informal spirit was the hallmark of her style of entertaining. She enjoyed life at Marlborough House during the London season, but it was at Sandringham that she kept her treasured collection of works by Fabergé – in two cabinets in the Drawing Room that were lit up with electric light each evening. Thus the collection became known from this time as the Sandringham Collection. Queen Alexandra was the recipient of many gifts of Fabergé animals and flowers, not only from the King

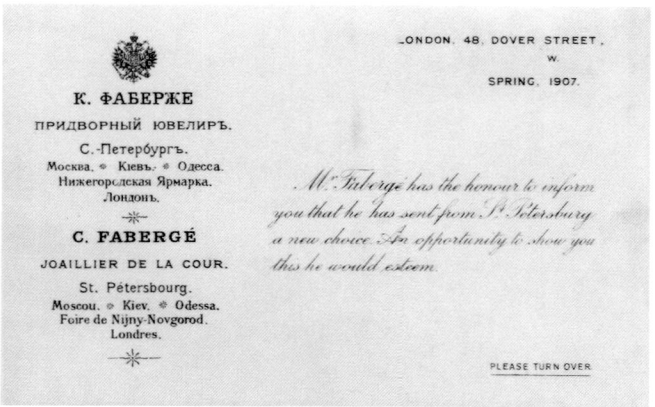

Invitation to Fabergé's London branch, 1907.

but from her many friends. Bainbridge describes how objects within a strict price bracket, not exceeding £50, were her preference, although occasionally this limit was exceeded. An example is the chrysanthemum (cat. 140) purchased by Stanislas Poklewski-Koziell from the London branch in 1908 for £117 and presented to Queen Alexandra; another is the crow (cat. 32) purchased by the Queen herself in 1914 for £75.

There are two sources of information for Queen Alexandra's purchases from Fabergé from which it is possible to build up a picture of her buying habits. These are her own accounts, a proportion of which survive in the Royal Archives, and the sales ledgers from the London branch which are held in the Fabergé Archive in Geneva. Queen Alexandra's own accounts reveal that between 1902 and 1914 a total of £3,197 was spent with Fabergé. Of that total £2,614 was paid from the Queen's presents account, indicating that many of the objects were given away rather than kept by her.[10] The remaining £583, paid from a 'miscellaneous' account, must relate to objects she kept.

The London ledgers are an invaluable source of information as they indicate the types of objects purchased by Queen Alexandra as presents. It is reasonable to assume that any of these objects which do not now form part of the collection were paid for from the presents account. The ledgers run from October 1907 to January 1917. There are no entries in the ledgers between October 1906 and October 1907, probably due to reorganisation following the end of Fabergé's business arrangement with Allan Bowe. Fabergé was obliged to close the London branch in 1915 to comply with the imperial order that all capital abroad should be returned to Russia in order to finance its war effort, but H.C. Bainbridge carried on the business privately for another two years.

At first there were no import taxes on objects brought into England by Fabergé and the laws on hallmarking gold allowed for wide interpretation. Fabergé refused to have his objects hallmarked in England for technical reasons. As a result

the Goldsmiths' Company brought a court case against him in 1910 which took more than a year to settle and which Fabergé lost. Birbaum describes how, following the case, the process of sending objects to be sold in the London branch became complex. Each silver or gold object had to be sent to London to be hallmarked and then returned to Russia to be finished before being sent back to London to be sold. The reason for the double journey was that when enamelled objects were hallmarked, some separation occurred between the enamel and the metal. It was therefore necessary to carry out finishing back in Russia. According to Birbaum, it was deemed that this process would lead to losses for the firm; the closure of the London branch was therefore hastened, rather than initiated, by the First World War.[11]

Queen Alexandra made the majority of her purchases at the London branch in the Easter and Christmas seasons, which underlines the fact that many were intended to be given away. She purchased most frequently between 1906 and 1911, the largest number of objects (thirty-three) being bought in 1909. Her acquisitions ranged from animals and cigarette cases to miniature eggs and frames. She also bought a number of pieces of jewellery, very few of which remain in the collection. While there is no record of any direct commission, the special relationship that the Queen had with Bainbridge must have resulted in some objects being specially designed for her. One such example is the frog cigar lighter (cat. 82) which she purchased for King Edward VII in 1906. It is so much in keeping with his taste that she is likely to have ordered it specially for him.

The most notable exhibition of Fabergé during the early years of the twentieth century was held in St Petersburg in 1902 and included several of the Imperial Easter Eggs, among other treasures. The only exhibition held during the same period in England, in fact the first ever to be staged there, was organised by Lady Paget, wife of General Sir Arthur Paget. It was held in June 1904 at the Albert Hall and took the form of a charity bazaar in aid of the Royal Victoria Hospital for Children. Queen Alexandra gladly lent her support, apparently purchasing a jade scent bottle and an enamel and diamond cigarette holder, both made by Fabergé.

Queen Alexandra had often expressed to Bainbridge a wish to meet Carl Fabergé. In January 1908 an opportunity arose when he came to London, but as soon as Bainbridge put forward the Queen's suggestion Fabergé seemed to be overcome by modesty and – according to Bainbridge – caught a train back to Paris almost immediately. They were never to meet. Even in later life Queen Alexandra and her sister Marie Feodorovna continued to surround themselves with works by Fabergé at Hvidøre, the villa outside Copenhagen which they shared.

Queen Alexandra's passion for Fabergé's work influenced many in her circle who became his customers, not least the majority of the crowned heads of Europe. This point is particularly well illustrated by a recollection of Bainbridge. On one visit which the Queen made to Fabergé's premises in Dover Street, she was accompanied by her father the King of Denmark, the King and Queen of Norway, the King of Greece, and her own daughter Princess Victoria.[12] But her greatest influence was to be over King Edward VII.

King Edward VII equalled and in some ways surpassed Queen Alexandra in enthusiasm for Fabergé's work. He placed the only documented British royal commission with Carl Fabergé, through H.C. Bainbridge in 1907, when he ordered a series of models to be made of the favourite horses and dogs kept at Sandringham, as birthday presents for Queen Alexandra. This grew into the largest order for animal sculptures ever placed with Fabergé and is the reason why the Royal Collection today contains the largest surviving group of Fabergé animal sculptures in existence. Full details of the commission are set out on pp. 21–4.

Apart from this most significant order, the King purchased many pieces from the London branch and formed a distinct taste for certain of Fabergé's products. The London ledgers provide an insight into his buying habits. In addition to the animals he bought the figure of a Chelsea pensioner (cat. 234), the sole example in the Royal Collection of the rare group of hardstone figures of people, of which Fabergé produced only about sixty in total. He purchased several cigarette cases and may have encouraged his friends to copy him in carrying these elegant accessories. He also received them as gifts. One example is the coloured gold case made to commemorate his fortieth wedding anniversary (cat. 163), which was given to him by his sister-in-law, Marie Feodorovna. The most outstanding case he owned, however, was the exquisite blue enamel piece decorated with a diamond snake which the Hon. Mrs George Keppel, his favourite mistress, bought for him in 1908 and which to this day contains the stub of one of his cigars (cat. 187).

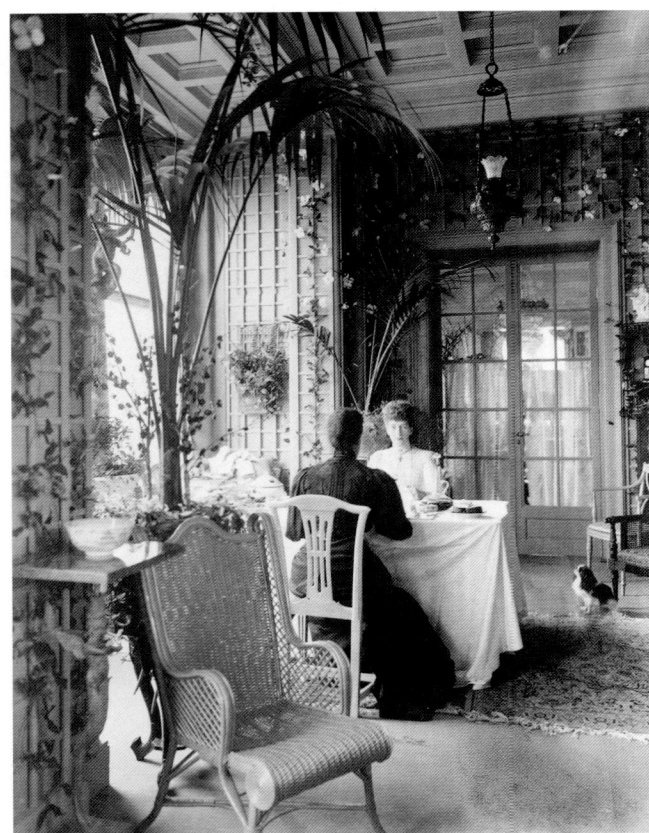

Queen Alexandra and her sister, Dowager Empress Marie Feodorovna, at Hvidøre, Denmark c. 1908. Photograph by J. Danieleen.

Although he vied with his consort to be the first to view new stock from St Petersburg,[13] the King's acquisitions reveal his interest in objects closely associated with his family life. The frame enamelled in his racing colours and containing a photograph of his most successful racehorse, Persimmon (cat. 224), was probably made at his personal suggestion and may have been a prototype for other objects, for example frames in the racing colours of the King's friend Leopold de Rothschild. The series of frames and boxes with sepia enamelled views of Sandringham, the estate King Edward VII acquired in 1862 and where he had a new house built, was also no doubt produced with his involvement – particularly as he purchased several of them himself (see p. 157). The King would have been well aware of Fabergé's work from his visits to Russia with his family. He was the recipient of two presentation objects from his wife's nephew Tsar Nicholas II, one to commemorate his attendance at the Tsar's coronation in 1896 and the other presented during a diplomatic meeting in Reval in 1908 (cat. 317 and 326).

For his own purchases, the King sometimes asked Bainbridge to leave a selection of items at Buckingham Palace from which he could make a choice.[14] Like Queen Alexandra, he was also the recipient of many gifts and he made his preference for certain of Fabergé's products very clear. He apparently suggested that, instead of giving him a print, someone who wished to purchase a present for him should 'go to Fabergé's they have a hippopotamus cigar lighter in nephrite . . . besides the lighter, I am sure, is half the price and it is amusing.'[15]

The King's knowledge and clear enjoyment of Fabergé's work encouraged many of his friends and contemporaries to become clients of Fabergé. These included some of the best customers of the London branch, such as Stanislas Poklewski-Koziell, a councillor at the Russian Embassy in London, Leopold de Rothschild, Sir Ernest Cassel, Lord Revelstoke, the Duke of Norfolk and the Marquis de Soveral. The London ledgers are full of the names of royalty and aristocrats from every corner of Europe and the Indian sub-continent. While many of Queen Alexandra's Fabergé objects were intended to charm and delight and were arranged in her cabinets at her whim, the more practical items acquired by the King were regularly used. They sometimes required repair, and there are several entries in the London ledgers for re-enamelling cigarette cases owned by King Edward VII and later by King George V.

Princess Victoria (1868–1935), the second daughter of King Edward VII and Queen Alexandra, inherited her parents' interest in Fabergé. She was a good customer of the London branch and purchased many pieces both for her own collection and as gifts. She often accompanied Queen Alexandra on visits to the London branch, where they would enjoy examining pieces newly arrived from Russia in what was in effect their private showroom. Her own small collection was principally of animals and flowers, but she purchased a range of objects including several pieces of jewellery, such as tie-pins, pendants and brooches. She also bought cigarette cases and an unusual frame with miniature views of St Petersburg (cat. 229). Princess Victoria inherited several pieces from her mother, such as parasol handles, flowers and animals. As she did not marry, these were bequeathed to King George V after her death.

Possibly an even greater admirer of Fabergé than his sister, King George V acquired many pieces both as Prince of Wales and later as King. He was particularly enamoured of the animal sculptures and bought many of those originally commissioned by his father in 1907. Several of the portrait sculptures from Sandringham were of dogs owned by him and kept at the kennels there, such as the Clumber spaniel Sandringham Lucy (cat. 20). He describes in his diary numerous visits to Fabergé's London branch. On 3 May 1903 he reports some early purchases, either at the branch or on a visit by Fabergé to Marlborough House: 'he [Fabergé] has just come over from Russia, we bought about 43 of his lovely things.'[16] As Duke of York, he had visited Fabergé's St Petersburg headquarters with his father in 1894 while attending the funeral of Tsar Alexander III and the marriage of Tsar Nicholas II and Princess Alix of Hesse. During this time he also visited the Baron Stieglitz School in St Petersburg where many of Fabergé's designers and craftsmen were trained. King George V describes with great affection the occasions on which he met his Russian cousin, notably at Cowes in August 1909 when the imperial family arrived aboard their yachts the *Standart* and the *Pole Star*. He recalls that he had not seen the Tsar and Tsarina for twelve years. Nine years later, in July 1918, after the brutal murder of the Tsar and his family, the King wrote in his diary, 'I was devoted to Nicky, who was the kindest of men, a thorough gentleman, loved his Country & his people.'[17] Just as happened among his parents' generation, gifts were exchanged on occasions such as the meeting at Cowes. There are letters from the King to the Tsar, held in the Russian State Archive which record the King's thanks for gifts at Christmas in 1906, 1908–10 and 1912. The gifts described include a stick handle, some vases, a match box, a cigarette case and a bust of the Tsar. At least some of these would have been supplied by Fabergé.[18]

In addition to the animal sculptures which King George V particularly liked, he also added to the collection desk accessories, cigarette cases and frames. He used such items as the desk clock (cat. 276) and the pen rest (cat. 285) at Buckingham Palace.[19] His most notable acquisitions were, however, made long after the London branch had

Tsar Nicholas II (left) and George, Prince of Wales (later King George V), at Barton Manor, Isle of Wight, August 1909.

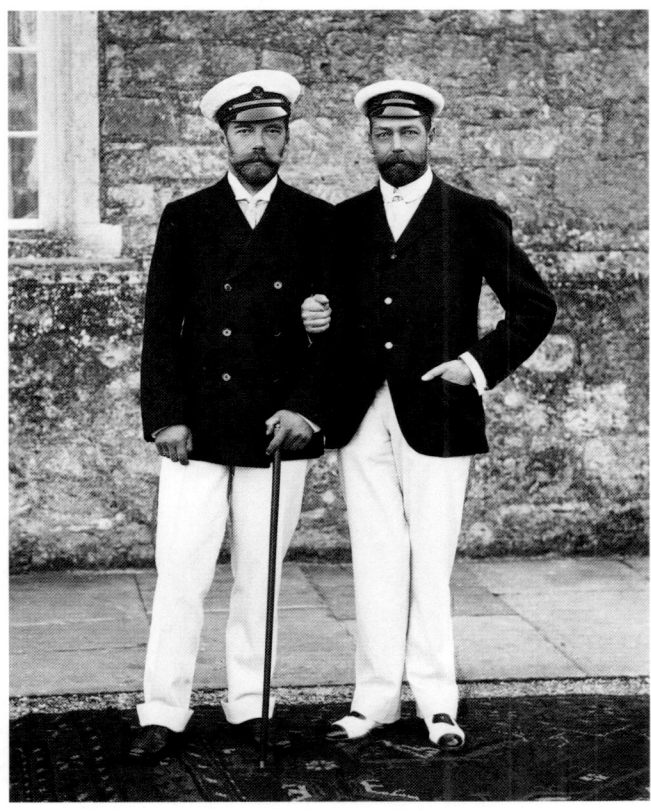

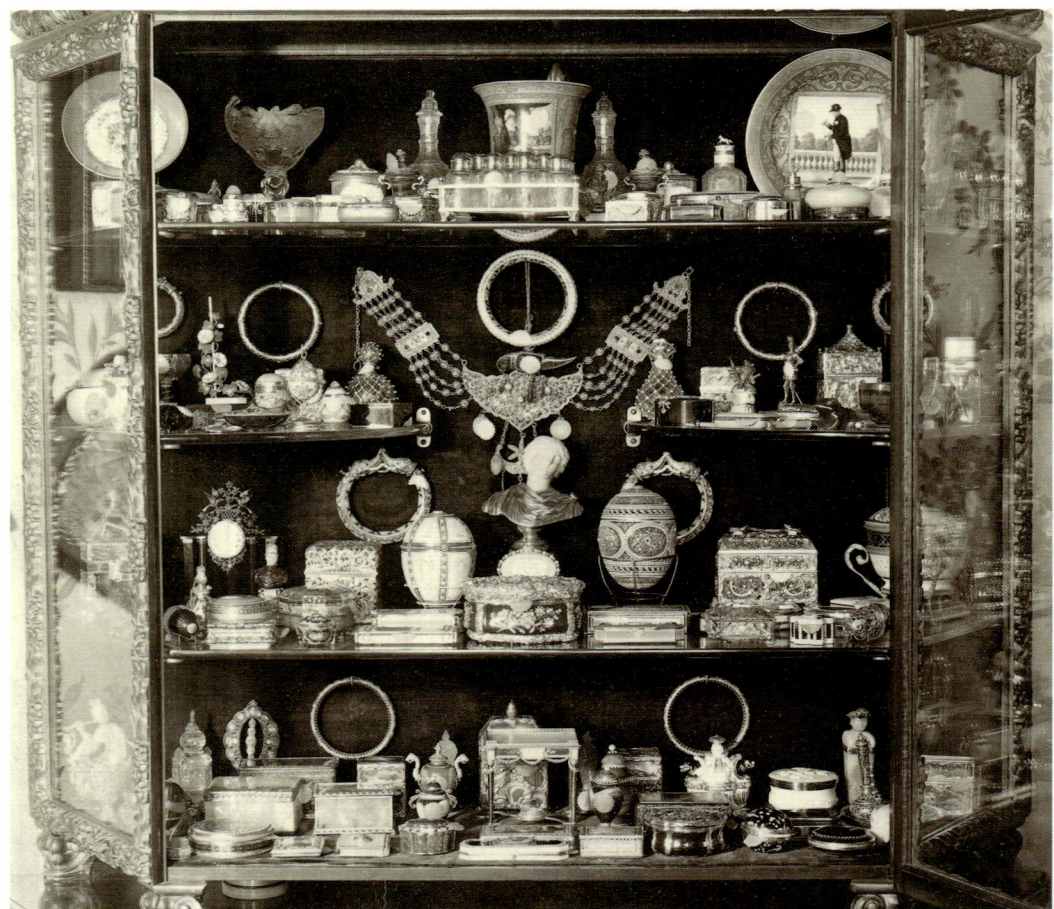

Part of Queen Mary's Fabergé collection in a display cabinet at Buckingham Palace, c. 1950.

closed. In the 1930s, together with Queen Mary, he bought the three Imperial Easter Eggs now in the Royal Collection. They both continued buying works by Fabergé from a number of different sources after 1917, including the dealer Wartski and Goode's Cameo Corner. The firm of Wartski had been established in London from 1911 by Emanuel Snowman, one of the first Western dealers to bring works by Fabergé out of Russia after the Revolution. Queen Mary acquired numerous pieces from the firm, notably the Easter egg made for the Kelch family (cat. 4).

Queen Mary acquired a large number of pieces for the collection, mainly in the form of cigarette cases and snuff boxes given to King George V, who owned many such objects. She also received many gifts from the imperial family, such as the nephrite box given to her in 1912 by the Dowager Tsarina Marie Feodorovna (cat. 150), and from her friends, many of whom were noted Fabergé collectors. Two examples are the bonbonnière with views of Balmoral Castle and Windsor Castle which was given to her for her birthday in 1934 by Sir Philip Sassoon and the imperial presentation box given by the Maharaja of Bikanir for her birthday in 1937 (cat. 177 and 142).

Pieces purchased by Queen Mary from the London branch included miniature eggs, animals, bell pushes and flow-

ers, but it seems the majority were intended as gifts, as many of them no longer survive in the collection. As a renowned collector of *objets d'art* of all kinds, Queen Mary kept fastidious records of all the pieces she acquired for the Royal Collection, which were listed by year of acquisition and by type of object, and for each of her acquisitions she made a record of the provenance of the piece as given to her.[20] Her taste ranged from eighteenth-century gold snuff boxes to lacquer and jade, but she had a particular fondness for Fabergé. In many respects she may be regarded as the first serious collector of his work in the British royal family. It was not without reason that Bainbridge described Queen Mary in 1949 as 'the greatest surviving connoisseur of Fabergé's craftsmanship',[21] and among King George V's papers in the Royal Archives is a list of all the Fabergé workmasters annotated in her hand, noting how useful the document was.[22]

Queen Mary was instrumental in influencing a whole generation of collectors who sought to acquire pieces with imperial provenance. Her own most notable acquisitions were the three Imperial Easter Eggs purchased with King George V in the 1930s, but in addition to her collecting, she stimulated interest in the subject of Fabergé by attending sale views and exhibitions and paying regular visits to West End dealers. She twice visited the Russian exhibition held in Belgrave Square in 1935, on 30 May and again on 14 June, when she recorded: 'went to the Russian Exn. again at 7 (when the public had left). Met by Mr C. Fabergé's son & Mr Bainbridge. Looked at the china, silver, & the Fabergé things, most interesting'.[23] Sir Owen Morshead, the Librarian at Windsor Castle, went to the same exhibition and wrote to Queen Mary on 4 June, encouraging her to attend the exhibition and to meet, through Lord Herbert, Fabergé's son.[24] *Connoisseur* magazine gave a lively review of the exhibition, which had been opened by the Duchess of Kent and to which Queen Mary had made several loans.[25] On 31 January 1949 Queen Mary visited Sotheby's to view 'some Fabergé things and very pretty trinkets'[26] which had belonged to Sir Bernard Eckstein, the noted collector and Fabergé enthusiast. One of the objects sold at the series of six Eckstein Collection sales was the Imperial Easter Egg known as the Winter Egg, which sold in New York in 2002 for $9.5 million. In 1949 it had realised £1,700. Another of the pieces included in the same sale was the convolvulus plant, now in the Royal Collection (cat. 123), which was given to Queen Mary by the royal family on her birthday in May 1949.[27]

Queen Mary's visits to Wartski were listed in the Court Circular; for example on 15 November 1947 she visited the dealers at their premises at 138 Regent Street to inspect 'some rare examples of the work of Fabergé'.[28] Earlier in the year, according to the *Daily Telegraph*, she caused a traffic jam when she visited the same premises to purchase pieces by Fabergé; when she emerged the crowd, who had waited two hours, 'surged forward, cheering and waving'. Queen Mary also began to make loans of Fabergé from the Royal Collection. The 1935 Belgrave Square exhibition has already been mentioned, and in 1948 she lent the miniature Louis XVI table (cat. 245) to the Antique Dealers' Fair and Exhibition at Grosvenor House. Six years later, after the Queen's death, an exhibition devoted to her art treasures from Marlborough House was staged at the Victoria and Albert Museum. Among the exhibits, arranged to correspond to the rooms in which the Queen had carefully placed them, were three of her most notable Fabergé acquisitions: the Mosaic Egg, the miniature piano and the carnet (cat. 3, 236 and 334).

Queen Mary's successor in the royal family as a true collector and connoisseur of Fabergé was her daughter-in-law, Queen Elizabeth, consort of King George VI. Queen Elizabeth formed a remarkably broad-ranging collection of paintings and works of art of all kinds and her Fabergé collection, like many of the things she acquired, was intensely personal. King George VI had shared her enjoyment of Fabergé and formed a large collection of cigarette cases which he used throughout his life. Several examples from his collection are included in this catalogue (see p. 124). Queen Elizabeth's taste was more diverse, ranging from flowers, animals and bibelots to superb examples of imperial presentation boxes

and some of the larger silver-mounted pieces made in the Moscow workshops such as the magnificent decanters (cat. 336). She began to form her collection in the early 1940s, primarily through purchases from Wartski and Spink. Queen Elizabeth also purchased a gold cigarette case from H.C. Bainbridge, who wrote to her in 1944 suggesting that she might be interested in acquiring it.[29] She received several pieces as gifts, notably in 1944 the charming study of cornflowers and oats (cat. 132). Her last purchase of Fabergé was the pair of decanters mentioned above, which were bought in 1973.

In some ways Queen Elizabeth's personal collection can be regarded as the epitome of the vast range of styles seen in Fabergé's work. She owned frames made of guilloché enamel, hardstone and coloured gold desk accessories, clocks in Fabergé's typical strut form and hardstone animals. She also owned a number of pieces in the Pan-Slavic or Old Russian style, such as the *kovshes* (drinking bowls), a small *bratina* (ornamental bowl) and a charming box (cat. 183). Queen Elizabeth also collected a variety of pieces by Fabergé's contemporary St Petersburg jewellers and goldsmiths, some of which are shown here for the first time. Her collection was for the most part displayed in an elegant cabinet in the first-floor Corridor at Clarence House, but in the same tradition as her royal forebears she used many pieces on a daily basis. Queen Elizabeth was always a generous lender to exhibitions and many of the

Queen Elizabeth at Wartski, 1971.

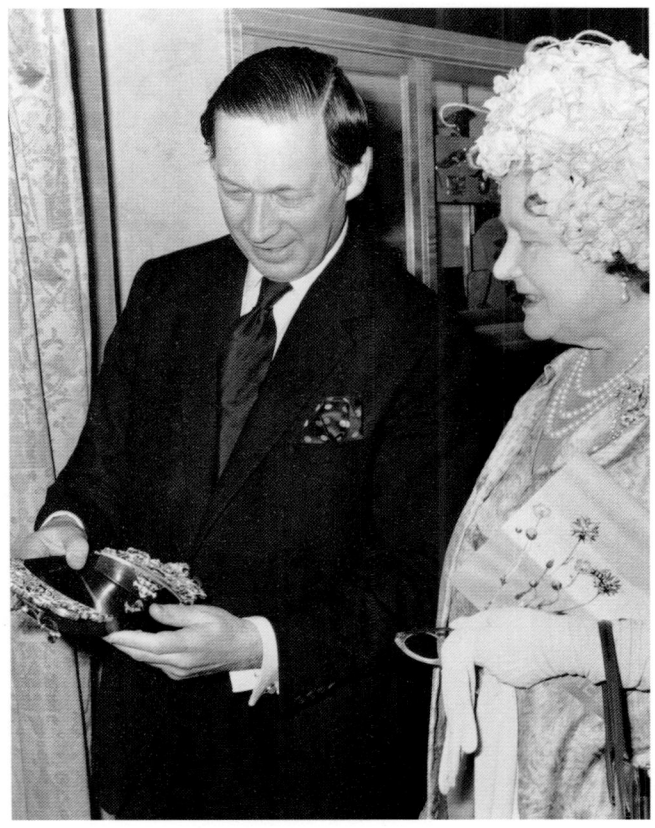

pieces from her collection – notably the imperial presentation boxes and the two magnificent flower studies – have been lent to a wide variety of exhibitions over the last fifty years. One of the earliest loans was to Wartski's 1949 exhibition; the King lent three cigarette cases and the Queen a gold box and the spray of cornflowers and oats. Her acknowledgement of Fabergé's work is perhaps best summed up in something she apparently said to H.C. Bainbridge when he was received by the King and Queen at Buckingham Palace in 1948: 'there is one thing about all Fabergé pieces, they are so satisfying.'[30]

Although no new pieces have been added to the Royal Collection during the present reign, the traditional royal interest in Fabergé has been maintained by The Queen and other members of the Royal Family, including The Prince of Wales, whose unusual desk seal is included in this catalogue (see cat. 301). The present reign has been marked by increased accessibility to the collection in the form of articles, books and, principally, exhibitions in which pieces from the collection have been included. A large number of loans were made to the *Great Britain USSR* exhibition at the Victoria and Albert Museum in 1967, at the height of the Cold War; a major

part of the collection was lent to the exhibition *Fabergé, Jeweller to Royalty*, held at the Cooper Hewitt Museum, New York, in 1983; and over twenty pieces were included in the major touring exhibition *Fabergé: Imperial Jeweller* held in St Petersburg, Paris and London in 1993–4. In addition to the many loans to exhibitions from the 1930s to the 1970s mentioned in earlier pages, the two most popular exhibitions to be held at The Queen's Gallery, Buckingham Palace, were of Fabergé – in 1985–6 and 1995–6, together attended by over 350,000 people.

The importance of the Fabergé collection in the context of the Royal Collection as a whole has been underlined by the inclusion of representative selections in several general exhibitions: *Sovereign*, held at the Victoria and Albert Museum in 1992 to commemorate the fortieth anniversary of The Queen's accession to the throne; *Princes as Patrons*, which was held at the National Museum and Gallery of Wales, Cardiff, in 1997; and most recently a display of over seventy pieces in *Royal Treasures, A Golden Jubilee Celebration*, the inaugural exhibition held at the new Queen's Gallery, Buckingham Palace in 2002–3.

1   Muntian 1997, p. 330.
2   Queen Alexandra ordered that all her private papers should be destroyed after her death.
3   RA GV/GVD: 20 November 1894.
4   RA VIC/QAD: 22 November 1894.
5   RA GV/GVD: 1 December 1894.
6   RA VIC/Add A 21/200A, pp. 122, 134.
7   RA PP/VIC/Personal and Extraordinary Expenditure, 1894–8.
8   Bainbridge 1949, p. 101.
9   Op. cit., p. 100.
10   RA VIC/Add A 21/200A–C.
11   Habsburg & Lopato 1993, p. 456.
12   Bainbridge 1949, p. 28.
13   Op. cit., p. 101.
14   Op. cit., pp. 82–3.
15   Op. cit., p. 83.
16   RA GV/GVD: 3 May 1903.
17   RA GV/GVD: 25 July 1918.
18   RA GV/DD 2/Acc1578.
19   Bainbridge 1949, pp. 108–9.
20   These were assembled at the Victoria and Albert Museum under the direction of Sir Cecil Harcourt Smith and bound in leather volumes. They are entitled *Queen Mary's Bibelots*.
21   Bainbridge 1949, p. 109.
22   RA GV/CC 55/243.
23   RA GV/QMD: 14 June 1935.
24   RA GV/CC 48/504.
25   *Connoisseur*, June 1935, vol. 95, no. 406, pp. 358–60.
26   RA GV/QMD: 31 January 1949.
27   Sir Bernard Eckstein Sale, Sotheby's London, 8 February 1949, lot 119.
28   *The Times* Court Circular, 15 November 1947.
29   RA QEQM Papers. Letters between H.C. Bainbridge and Arthur Penn, Acting Private Secretary.
30   Bainbridge 1949, p. 110.

THE SANDRINGHAM COMMISSION

IN 1907 KING EDWARD VII made the single most important contribution to the royal Fabergé collection. He decided to commission Carl Fabergé to produce portrait sculptures of his and Queen Alexandra's favourite dogs and horses kept at their beloved Sandringham. He was well aware of the Queen's enjoyment of Fabergé's charming animal sculptures; indeed by this date both King and Queen owned many examples. This commission, which was extended at the King's wish to include a whole menagerie of domestic, farm and wild animals found on the Norfolk estate, resulted in the formation of the largest assemblage of Fabergé's hardstone animal sculptures. It was also by far the largest order ever placed through Fabergé's London branch.

The commission involved two of the key influences on the King where Fabergé was concerned: Mrs George Keppel, who shared his enthusiasm for Fabergé's work and with whom he made visits to the London branch; and H.C. Bainbridge, manager of the London branch and the go-between for King Edward VII, Queen Alexandra and Carl Fabergé. Bainbridge describes in his usual effusive manner how the idea for models of pedigree animals to be made in different stones had already occurred to him in conversation with one of Fabergé's other customers. On Mrs Keppel's next visit to Fabergé he mentioned the idea, and it was apparently she who put the suggestion to the King. The very next day, Bainbridge reports, he received a telegram from Sandringham informing him that the King agreed with the plan. In some respects it is surprising that the King concurred so rapidly but, as already mentioned, he more than anyone understood the Queen's fondness for Fabergé's animals. Not only that; her devotion to all her dogs, horses and other animals kept at Sandringham and Marlborough House was obvious to all who knew her. The Queen was almost constantly surrounded by as many as ten dogs while at Sandringham, her favourite breed being Pekinese. There was a huge assortment of dogs kept in the twenty-six kennels on the estate all of which the Queen knew individually and regularly fed with cubes of bread. These ranged from borzois, Great Danes, bulldogs, Clumber spaniels,

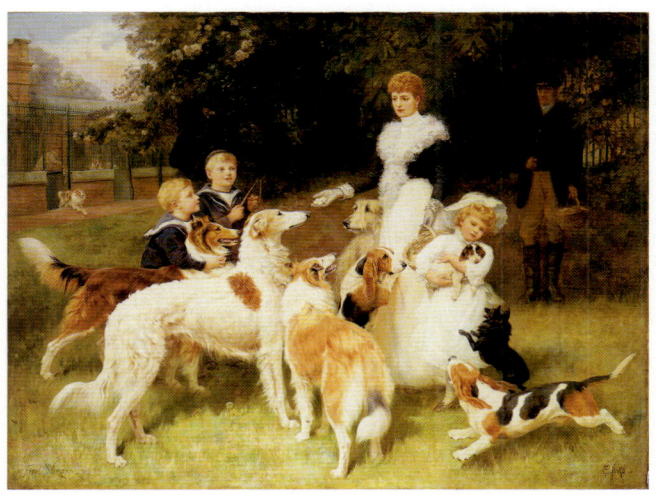

Frederick Morgan and Thomas Blinks, *Queen Alexandra with her grandchildren and dogs,* 1902
Oil on canvas, 166.6 x 204.5 cm (65$\frac{1}{2}$ x 80$\frac{1}{2}$")
RCIN 402302

Japanese spaniels, dachshunds, pugs, terriers, Chinese chows and Pomeranians, basset hounds and St Bernards to an assortment of stray mongrels. The more unusual breeds included a Samoyed, known as Jacko, from an Arctic expedition and a Siberian sledge dog called Luska. The keeper of the kennels, Brundson, often had as many as sixty dogs in his charge at any one time. In a letter from Sir Dighton Probyn (Equerry to King Edward VII and later Comptroller and Keeper of the Privy Purse) of 30 May 1914, written in reply to an offer from a Mr Phillips to replace the Queen's beloved dog Togo, Probyn sums up Queen Alexandra's attitude: 'The Queen is such a regular Dog-worshipper that Her Majesty likes <u>all</u> dogs – Dogs of any breed or description.'[1] Queen Alexandra loved horses as much as dogs. She enjoyed driving about the estate at Sandringham, particularly as riding had become difficult for her after the attack of rheumatic fever she suffered in 1867. Later, in 1916, she became very distressed at the thought of having some of her old worn-out horses put down as an economy at Probyn's suggestion, as the staff of the stables were likely to be reduced to between six and twelve during the First World War.[2]

The King shared the Queen's devotion to animals, and was very attached to his own numerous dogs and horses – many of which were to be modelled by Fabergé's sculptors as part of the commission. Prince George and Princess Victoria, together with the King and Queen's other children, had grown up at Sandringham surrounded by animals of every kind. Following King Edward VII's visit to India when Prince of Wales in 1875–6, he returned to Sandringham with an extraordinary cargo of gifts – including a miniature Indian pony called Nawab which the royal children used to ride upstairs to Queen Alexandra's dressing room, a Himalayan bear and an aviary of ninety birds.[3] The children were equally enthusiastic about dogs and horses; several of Prince George's own dogs were amongst those to be modelled by Fabergé's sculptors.

According to Bainbridge, no sooner had the King's telegram arrived and Bainbridge himself 'taken the next train to Wolferton' to meet Mr Beck, the land agent of the Sandringham Estate, than the King decided to include 'the whole farmyard'.[4] In reality the King's decision to extend the commission undoubtedly came about more gradually. The sculptors were dispatched by Fabergé from St Petersburg and would have taken at the very least several days to reach Norfolk.

The commission must have been somewhat daunting for Fabergé. He sent over his best animal sculptors, who were based on the estate for several months. There are no records of the precise length of their stay, where they were lodged or how they were paid, or even of how the wax models of each animal were dispatched back to St Petersburg. Bainbridge played a major role in these administrative details but did not include any of this information in his 1949 book. It must be assumed that with the destruction at their own request of the private papers of both King Edward VII and Queen Alexandra some interesting references to the commission were lost. Surprisingly, given his interest in Fabergé's work, there is no mention of the Russian sculptors or the work they carried out in King George V's diary entries of the relevant period, nor in those of Queen Mary. However, from Bainbridge's scant descriptions, information from the London ledgers and the physical evidence presented by the sculptures themselves, a picture of the commission emerges.

The number of sculptors sent from St Petersburg is not clear, although at least two are named by Bainbridge, Boris Frödman-Cluzel and Frank Lutiger. Frank Lutiger was of Swiss origin and was attached to the London branch. Bainbridge reports that Lutiger joined the other sculptors sent from St Petersburg to work at Sandringham and that he later worked on sculpting Leopold de Rothschild's animals at Ascott in Buckinghamshire. There has been much debate about the role of an English sculptor, Alfred Pocock. According to

Bainbridge, he produced several hardstone animals for Fabergé and worked for the London branch in addition to working independently, but there is no reference to any involvement by him with the Sandringham commission.[5] One sculpture of a dog is consistently ascribed to him: the Pekinese in fluorspar, a material not otherwise used in Fabergé's hardstone animals (cat. 70).

One important source, which has recently come to light, is the account of the work undertaken by Boris Frödman-Cluzel. The information has been gathered by Mr Valentin Skurlov, a leading Fabergé scholar, who has kindly allowed it to be included in this catalogue.[6] Frödman-Cluzel (b.1878), of Swedish origin, trained at the Baron Stieglitz School in St Petersburg. His association with Fabergé began between 1903 and 1906. He was regarded as an exceptionally talented sculptor, as a review of an art exhibition held in St Petersburg in September 1907 records: 'his figures of dogs and bulls, as well as people . . . are equally alive.'[7] Two months later the sculptor was already in London, according to a letter dated 15 November 1907 to his friend Olga Bazankur. He indicates that he has been summoned to work for the King and that he will be engaged for at least two months, which gives some idea of the duration of the initial part of the Sandringham commission. On 24 December he wrote to her again, apparently on headed paper from Sandringham House. He explains with great excitement that his client is King Edward VII, that he is living in a 'hall' on the estate, and that he is working well under the personal supervision and praise of his client, who has supplied him with a list of animals to be sculpted. 'My zoological range has been added to by twenty new models that I have made here', he adds.[8] Frödman-Cluzel describes the animals as 'my friends' and 'his [i.e. the King's] favourites'. An article which appeared in the *St Petersburg Gazette* on 20 December 1907 gives further details, explaining that Frödman-Cluzel had been warmly welcomed by both the King and the Queen and that he and the other sculptors had been treated as guests of honour and even invited for a day's shooting with the King. Amongst the people Frödman-Cluzel met at Sandringham were the Kings of Norway and Spain, the Emperor of Germany and George, Prince of Wales, 'for whom he worked just as conscientiously as he did for his father'. The article goes on to explain that Frödman-Cluzel would not return to Russia before the middle of January as he would be working for the Rothschild family, modelling their famous racehorses, following his success in modelling the King's horse Persimmon (cat. 18).[9]

This account accords with Bainbridge's description of events at Sandringham. The most important moment came when it was time for King Edward VII to inspect the wax models of all the animals that the sculptors had prepared, in the Queen's Dairy. This event took place, according to Bainbridge, on Sunday 8 December 1907, seven days after Queen

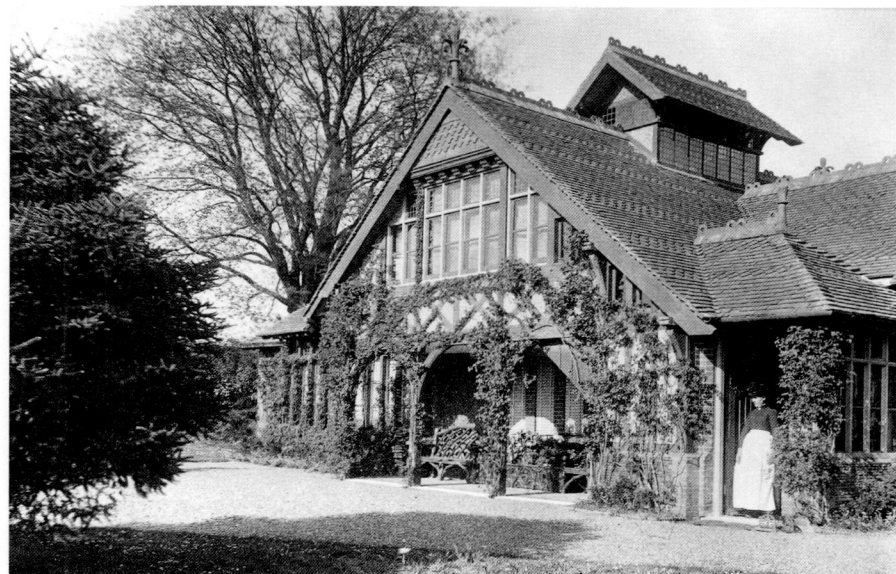

The Dairy at Sandringham, c. 1900.
Photograph by H. P. Robinson and Son.

Alexandra's birthday. (It had apparently been the King's intention to present at least some of the animals to her for her birthday that year.) Accompanied by his guests and by his favourite dog, Caesar, the King made his way after lunch to the Dairy, where the sculptors had been working and where they waited nervously for the King's approval of their labours. Bainbridge describes how he watched the scene from a distance, hiding behind a hedge – presumably fearing that his client might not be entirely happy with the results.[10] Fortunately, the King appeared to be delighted: 'Will you please tell Mr Fabergé how pleased I am with all he has done for me. I have pointed out to the artists one or two places where some little alteration can be made, but otherwise I think the work splendid.'

With this seal of approval, Bainbridge was free to arrange for the delicate wax models to be sent to St Petersburg for the stonecarvers and workmasters to begin production. The exception was the model of Persimmon, which was sent to the Moscow silver workshops to be cast. Back in Russia, Carl Fabergé oversaw the careful selection of the appropriate hardstones in which each animal was to be carved. The models would then have been passed to the sculptor-stonecarvers, as Birbaum referred to them.[11] Those who carved the models were probably Kremlev and Derbyshev. Again, this process would have taken some time, particularly as the carvers would have been working on a number of objects simultaneously. The carvings were then returned to the workshop of the head workmaster, Henrik Wigström, for polishing and for the fitting of gold parts, such as feet for the studies of birds. Surprisingly few drawings survive in the published design album from Wigström's workshop, given that many of the animals from the Sandringham commission were finished there. One drawing that does relate to the commission is that for the goose (cat. 42).

With King Edward VII's extension of the commission it is impossible to be sure how many of the more than three hundred animal carvings in the Royal Collection were modelled from life at Sandringham. Nonetheless, approximately one hundred of the Fabergé animals can be directly related to the commission, of which fifty-seven are included here. The variety of animals is surprising, encompassing a bear (cat. 46) and several rare breeds of dog. A family of monkeys was apparently kept among the menagerie on the estate but it is not possible to say which of the examples in the Royal Collection represent the Sandringham monkeys. An elephant was even reputed to have lived on the estate, but again it is impossible to know which of the many elephants in the collection might be its likeness.

There are, however, many identifiable portraits among the group, including the dogs Caesar, Sandringham Lucy, Vassilka, Jacko and Bobeche; and the horses Persimmon, Iron Duke and Field Marshal. The unnamed turkey is a Norfolk Black, a breed indigenous to East Anglia, and is therefore likely to have been modelled from life at Sandringham. Other well-known personal pets of King Edward VII, Queen Alexandra and King George V are also likely to be among the group but are now difficult to identify for certain. Among these are King Edward VII's bulldog Paul, Queen Alexandra's Pekineses Togo and Little Billie, her Japanese spaniels Facie and Punchie and King George's Labradors and his Cairn terriers Snip and Bob. Also kept at Sandringham were an Italian donkey, a miniature pony, prize-winning sheep, Dexter bulls and numerous doves and pigeons housed in the aviaries, some or all of which should undoubtedly be included in the group.

Bainbridge misleads his readers when he recalls that the finished animals were sent to London and all of them were acquired by King Edward VII and given to Queen Alexandra for her Fabergé collection.[12] While King Edward did acquire

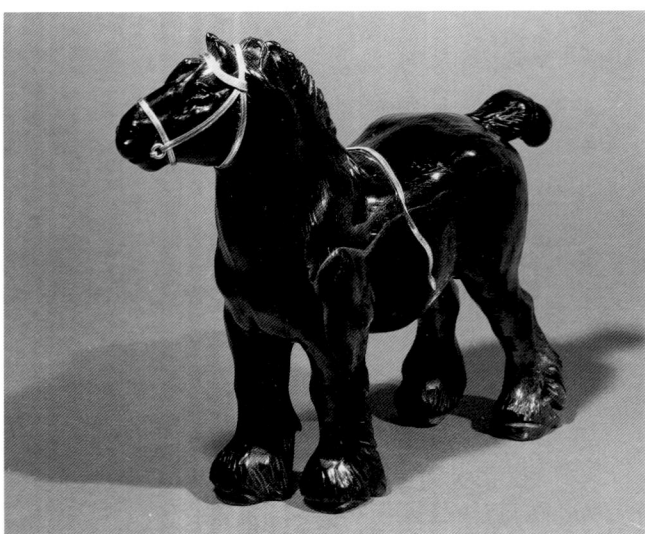

Obsidian Shire horse, modelled from life at Sandringham, formerly the property of Henry, Duke of Gloucester.

a number of the sculptures for the Queen, the ledgers of the London branch (through which all the Sandringham animals were sold) reveal that there were plenty of other purchasers, not least Queen Alexandra herself and King George V. Examples of the Queen's purchases include the model of Iron Duke, bought in 1909; the dormouse, bought in 1912; and a bulldog and a goose bought in 1911. Those of the Prince of Wales include the turkey and the portrait of his own Clumber spaniel Sandringham Lucy, bought in 1909. Others who bought pieces originally commissioned by the King and presented them to him were Princess Victoria, Grand Duke Michael of Russia and the Hon. Mrs Greville. The last named bought the sculpture of Caesar, the King's favourite dog. Sadly, it did not join the collection until after the King's death.

Given the variety of purchasers and the five years or more over which the animals were bought from the London branch, it is very difficult to calculate the exact cost of the commission. Most of the animals cost in the region of £30

to £50, in keeping with Queen Alexandra's wish for modest presents. Some were considerably more expensive; Sandringham Lucy, for example, cost £102, Iron Duke £70 and Persimmon £135.[13]

Some of the animals that were part of the original commission have subsequently left the collection and others were not in the end purchased for it. Notable among these is an obsidian Shire horse which belonged to the Duke of Gloucester (1900–74) and which was included in a sale at Christie's in 1954. The catalogue records that the horse was modelled from life at Sandringham for King Edward VII. A horse listed in the London ledgers as having been purchased by Queen Alexandra on 27 June 1909 and described as the King's Shire stallion Hoe Forest King is not now identifiable in the Royal Collection; the Shire horse traditionally referred to as Field Marshal (cat. 27) may have been wrongly identified and could represent Hoe Forest King. In 1914 Mrs Keppel purchased from the London branch a nephrite frame with a silver bas-relief of King George V's Sealyham terrier Happy. This no longer survives in the Royal Collection, although it may not have been part of the original Sandringham commission. In 1912 Queen Alexandra purchased a sculpture of Sandringham Dido, a smooth-haired basset hound which had won best of breed at Crufts in 1907. It has not been possible to identify this dog among the portrait sculptures now in the Royal Collection.

Given the scope of the commission, it was of the utmost importance that none of the sculptures was repeated and King Edward VII is known to have expressed his concern that 'we must not make any duplicates' with regard to the Queen's collection of Fabergé animals. Carl Fabergé would generally have concurred with this view; any suggestion of copying or multiple production would have been frowned on. Even so, one of the models from the Sandringham commission does have an identical twin: a replica of the turkey (cat. 25) was sold at Christie's in 1964 and is now in a private collection in the United States. There is no evidence that this particular model ever formed part of the Royal Collection.

1   RA VIC/Add A 21/228/115.
2   RA VIC/Add A 21/228/162–166.
3   RA GV/AA 28/38; Cathcart 1964, p. 105.
4   Bainbridge 1949, p. 102.
5   Bainbridge 1949, p. 137.
6   Some of Mr Skurlov's research was published in Stockholm 1997.
7   Pushkin House, Archive 15, inventory 1, file 668.
8   Ibid., sheet 15.
9   Ibid., sheets 16–17.
10 Bainbridge 1942b, p. 985.
11 Habsburg & Lopato 1993, p. 451.
12 Bainbridge 1949, p. 104.
13 Habsburg & Lopato 1993, p. 126. Von Habsburg cites a payment in the London ledgers on 14 October 1907: 'Purchases to St Petersburg. Note 49. Cost of goods sold in London to date £5,240/5/3.' The sculptors had barely started their work by that date and none of the wax models could have been carved in hardstone and returned to London for sale before early 1908, so this figure cannot be related to the Sandringham commission.

FABERGÉ IN CONTEXT: CONTEMPORARIES AND COMPETITORS

THE NAME OF FABERGÉ is synonymous with luxury objects and jewellery made to exacting standards from the finest materials. It should be noted that while his work was eclectic by nature, drawing on a wide range of design sources, it encapsulated the style of a whole period at the end of the nineteenth century and beginning of the early twentieth century. Supported by Fabergé's international reputation, this style proved deeply influential on goldsmiths and jewellers based in Russia and encouraged others abroad to imitate his products. He counted not only the Russian imperial and British royal families as his best clients, but most of the royal houses of Europe, along with aristocrats and wealthy businessmen around the world. The importance of the British royal family among Fabergé's clients has already been outlined and their contribution to his success is evident, but they did not confine their patronage to him. Similarly, the Russian imperial family bought from other jewellers and goldsmiths, with the result that objects by other makers were given as official presents and in some instances entered the Royal Collection as gifts (e.g. cat. 357). The works of art by other makers included here provide a representative rather than a comprehensive overview of both Russian and European competitors of Fabergé and give an insight into the acquisition of works in Fabergé's style by members of the royal family.[1]

Although Gustav Fabergé had begun to supply the Imperial Cabinet in 1866, it was not until his son Carl received the official title of Supplier to the Court of His Imperial Majesty Tsar Alexander III in 1885 that the firm became a major supplier. Ten years later the death of Alexander III, followed by the wedding and coronation of his heir, Nicholas II, brought an overwhelming number of commissions to the jewellers and goldsmiths of St Petersburg and Moscow. While Fabergé was awarded many of the most important commissions and was eventually to become the most prolific royal jeweller, there were several other firms that were already well-established suppliers to the court.

The firm of Bolin was established by Carl Edvard Bolin in St Petersburg in the 1830s and was the main supplier of presentation orders and decorations to the court. From 1839 Bolin was appointed official jeweller to the imperial court and the firm became the foremost jewellery business in Russia. It was not until the 1890s that Fabergé emerged as Bolin's main competitor. In spite of the originality of its jewellery, much of which was in the art nouveau style, Bolin's firm took inspiration from Fabergé for certain products. They made fine gold and jewelled cigarette cases, but in general their work lacked the refined elegance and sophistication of Fabergé's designs. Given the longevity of Bolin's firm and the close links between the Russian and English families, it is surprising to find that there are now no works by Bolin in the Royal Collection. Queen Alexandra's accounts reveal that she made only one purchase from the firm, in January 1904, of a brooch costing £41;[2] the brooch has not been identified. Between 1912 and 1932 Queen Mary acquired the only recorded Bolin piece to enter the Royal Collection, a green enamel cigarette case very reminiscent of Fabergé's style. Sadly, this object cannot now be traced.[3]

Another major competitor of Fabergé, but not represented in the Royal Collection, was the firm of Tillander. Established by Alexander Tillander in St Petersburg in 1860, from the 1890s the firm supplied the court with presentation items such as brooches, cuff links and tie-pins incorporating the imperial emblems. The firm also made jewellery, miniature Easter eggs, cigarette cases and picture frames – often in the style of Fabergé – and had a loyal following among the nobility and industrial magnates of St Petersburg. In April 1911 the firm moved to 26 Nevsky Prospect, taking over the premises formerly occupied by the court jeweller Hahn. Tillander established a long-lasting and lucrative collaboration with the Parisian jeweller Boucheron (also a competitor of Fabergé) after the assassination of the latter's Moscow representatives in 1911.

Karl August Hahn established his firm in St Petersburg in 1873. In 1896 Hahn was commissioned by Tsar Nicholas II to produce a diadem to be worn by Tsarina Alexandra Feodorovna at her coronation. Hahn was subsequently appointed

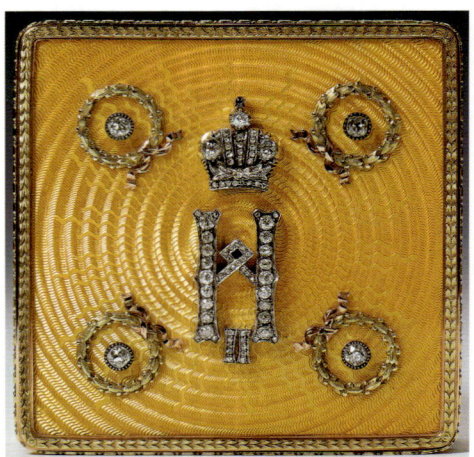

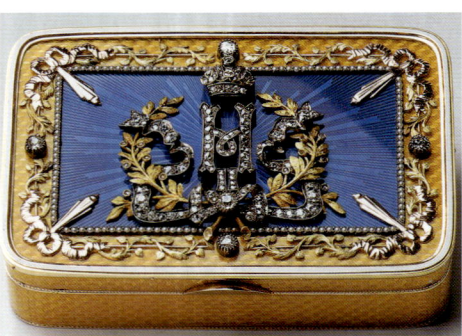

Imperial presentation box by Fabergé, 1896–1908 (cat. 145) and (below) an imperial presentation box by Fabergé's competitor Hahn, c.1900 (cat. 354).

supplier to the court and provided a range of objects including presentation boxes, cigarette cases and frames. Presentation boxes were the traditional gift of the tsar to foreign high-ranking dignitaries and a prestigious award to Russian subjects of high merit. In general, Hahn's presentation boxes, while suitably opulent, are less up-to-date in style and the enamelling incorporates a more limited colour palette than that used by Fabergé. A comparison of a presentation box by Hahn (cat. 354) and one by Fabergé (cat. 145) reveals the differences between the two makers. The Hahn box is a little old-fashioned in shape and the guilloché enamelling, while finely executed, shows a limited range of patterns. The Fabergé box by contrast is engraved with an exciting variety of patterns which are almost three-dimensional in quality when seen through the translucent yellow enamel. From 1892 Hahn employed as a head workmaster the independent goldsmith and jeweller Carl Blank, who became a partner in the business from 1911. He produced work of a very high standard, most evident in the objects that bear his mark in conjunction with that of Hahn. The presentation cigarette case (cat. 355) is a fine example of guilloché enamelling by Blank and compares well with Fabergé's work, except for the large hinge and clumsy closing mechanism. In spite of the quality of Blank's enamel, it is generally accepted that Fabergé was producing the finest enamelling of the period; no other maker approached, for example, the enormous range of colours he produced. Although competitors, the two firms sometimes collaborated. Hahn was responsible

for remounting Fabergé's presentation boxes, which were occasionally returned to the Imperial Cabinet by their recipients for a variety of reasons. The boxes would then be recycled and presented to another recipient. This often involved removing the portrait miniatures applied to them and replacing these with the diamond-set cypher of the Tsar. After the death of Dimitri Hahn (Karl August's son), the business premises were taken over by Tillander and Carl Blank returned to working independently. According to Valentin Skurlov, Blank continued to fulfil commissions for the Imperial Cabinet for orders and decorations.[4]

The firm of Ovchinnikov was founded by Pavel Ovchinnikov in Moscow in 1853. The business expanded quickly to become a major supplier of silver and enamel objects in the Pan-Slavic or Old Russian style. In 1873 Ovchinnikov opened a branch of his business in St Petersburg, run by his son Michael. Ovchinnikov's success rested on his cloisonné enamelling, which was widely recognised as being of excellent quality. The firm became known in the rest of Europe when its work was exhibited at the Exposition Universelle in Paris in 1900. A set of salts in the Royal Collection (cat. 364) demonstrates Ovchinnikov's use of cloisonné enamelling in jewel-like colours and is a good example of the firm's traditional Russian-style objects. Fabergé was also producing pieces in the Old Russian style from his Moscow workshop from the 1890s onwards. These were mainly enamelled by Feodor Rückert, who produced the highest-quality cloisonné enamelling for the firm (see cat. 325). The date of acquisition of the set of salts is unknown but they are likely to have been acquired by King Edward VII and Queen Alexandra. Queen Alexandra's accounts reveal that she was a customer of Ovchinnikov; she made purchases from the firm of jewellery and 'Russian *objets d'art*' between 1905 and 1911 amounting to £1,000, paid for from her miscellaneous account, but none of these objects appears to survive in the Collection today.[5] King George V was also a customer of the firm, as an invoice in the Royal Archives reveals. It appears that the King purchased two cigarette cases, a squirrel and a rabbit both in purpurine, two aquamarines and three amethysts in July 1911. The invoice was issued from Paris, indicating that Ovchinnikov made further selling trips to the Continent, but the items were purchased in England.[6]

There are two works in the Royal Collection by the St Petersburg goldsmith Ivan Britsin. Britsin's workshop specialised in the production of guilloché enamel objects in the style of Fabergé. The frame and seal included in this exhibition (cat. 348 and 366) are enamelled in Britsin's characteristically limited palette of colours in which white featured heavily. According to Von Habsburg, Britsin occasionally supplied Fabergé, whose mark appears in combination with his own on a number of pieces.[7] The frame and seal in the Royal Collection were acquired at an unknown date by Queen Elizabeth.

It is interesting that Queen Elizabeth added to her collection of Fabergé several pieces by other makers in the same style. These included a further piece by Britsin: a white enamelled cigarette case that she purchased from Wartski in 1951 but which is no longer in the Collection.

Easter eggs in Fabergé's style were produced by a number of his Russian competitors including Hahn and Bolin; these were invariably made of gold and enamel. The firm of Köchli, established in St Petersburg in 1864 by Friedrich Köchli, who was of Swiss origin, was particularly known for its jewellery, presentation boxes and cigarette cases. Queen Alexandra's accounts reveal that she was a customer of the firm: one purchase of jewellery was made in April 1901, paid for from her presents account in the sum of £63.[8] Köchli apparently also produced Easter eggs, including a magnificent rhodonite example now in the Royal Collection (cat. 337), acquired by Queen Mary in 1947. The egg bears the imperial eagle, implying that it was perhaps originally supplied to a member of the imperial family. Köchli had supplied Tsarina Marie Feodorovna with jewellery and the egg may originally have belonged to her, particularly as it was made before 1896.

In the late nineteenth and early twentieth century several artels of goldsmiths and jewellers established themselves in St Petersburg and Moscow. The artels were independent co-operatives of craftsmen, some of whom had worked for Fabergé. Two of the best known are represented in the Royal Collection. The Eleventh Artel was based in Moscow and specialised in cloisonné-enamelled objects. A *kovsh* in this style was acquired by Queen Elizabeth (cat. 359), complementing the Old Russian-style pieces by Rückert that she owned (cat. 323 and 324). The Third Artel, also direct competitors of Fabergé, was based in St Petersburg and produced guilloché enamel objects such as clocks, frames, miniature eggs, bowls and dishes. The gum pot in the Royal Collection (cat. 367), produced between 1908 and 1917, compares closely with Fabergé's work in the same vein. The provenance of the gum pot is unknown but the Third Artel apparently supplied the imperial family and it may therefore have been a gift.[9]

Several smaller makers in St Petersburg, some known only by their marks, were producing *objets d'art* in imitation of Fabergé. These included the maker Astreyden, whose pencil holder (cat. 368) is very much in Fabergé's style. Astreyden was active in St Petersburg between 1908 and 1917 and specialised in the production of small guilloché enamel objects of this kind. There is another almost identical pencil holder in the Royal Collection (cat. 369), marked by the maker *AR*. Very little is known about this maker, except that he was active in St Petersburg in the early twentieth century. In addition to guilloché enamel accessories in Fabergé's style, the maker *AR* produced silver-mounted ceramic objects, illustrated by the small bowl included here (cat. 370). While this bowl cannot be regarded as a direct imitation, Fabergé did produce

many silver-mounted objects, including porcelain and glass vases supplied by other makers such as Tiffany, Gallé and Royal Doulton.

There are a number of Russian objects in Fabergé's style in the Royal Collection which are included in this catalogue but which are either unmarked or cannot be identified with a particular maker. These include a combined paper-knife and pencil holder (cat. 365) stamped with the name Johann Faber. The model is very much in keeping with Fabergé's work, his firm having made several paper-knives in this shape. Two guilloché enamel frames demonstrate the impact of Fabergé on other St Petersburg makers. One (cat. 350) contains a photograph in a pink guilloché surround of Tsarina Marie Feodorovna, but the quality of the frame is far removed from anything produced in Fabergé's workshops, having a wooden back and plain support rather than Fabergé's highly finished ivory backs and elaborately scrolled struts. The pencil holder and frame were both acquired by Queen Elizabeth. A miniature frame (cat. 349) in blue guilloché enamel contains a photograph of Tsar Nicholas II and in scale and style is entirely in keeping with Fabergé's miniature frames. However, the heavy gold mount and lack of applied vari-coloured gold decoration set it apart from those frames produced by Fabergé's workmasters – particularly Viktor Aarne, who made some of the finest miniature frames for the firm (see p. 157). The frame is marked with the initials of the maker, *OB*, by whom other objects are known but about whom very little information has been established. The date and means of acquisition of the frame are unknown but, given that it contains a photograph of Tsar Nicholas II, it is assumed to have been a personal gift from the Tsar and Tsarina either to King Edward VII and Queen Alexandra or to King George V and Queen Mary.

There are a number of other examples by unknown Fabergé imitators. A green enamel miniature Easter egg (cat. 361) is very close to Fabergé's own in style and design; Queen Mary recorded it as being by Fabergé, but it is entirely unmarked and has therefore not been attributed to him. The elegant white guilloché enamelled and rhodonite cigarette case (cat. 357) was given by Grand Duchess Xenia to Queen Mary in 1912. The case does not bear a maker's mark but the design has all the characteristics of Fabergé's work. Cigarette cases were supplied to the imperial family by a selection of other goldsmiths, and it is impossible to identify the maker here. Fabergé's range of practical objects included match holders formed of bricks made in the Gusareva factory in Moscow and applied with mounts in gold and silver (see cats. 318 and 322), transforming them into elegant, functional pieces. One unmarked match holder in the Royal Collection is in a different style from the other two (cat. 358); the brick was made in the Gusareva factory but the cloisonné enamelling in Old Russian style – while reminiscent of the work produced by Rückert for Fabergé – is unmarked. It may have been produced in the Moscow workshops of Ovchinnikov, famous for their cloisonné enamelling.

The importance of indigenous hardstones to Fabergé's work cannot be overestimated for he used them in a remarkable variety of applications. His supplies were drawn from both Russia and Germany. Kolyvan, Ekaterinburg and Peterhof were the traditional centres for lapidary carving in Russia and they supplied a vast range of hardstones cut and carved to the orders of jewellers and goldsmiths both in St Petersburg and Moscow and from abroad. The Kolyvan workshop had supplied Fabergé with some ready-made objects, according to Birbaum's memoirs.[10] They may also be seen as competitors producing their own objects and supplying other makers. The rhodonite dish (cat. 363), for example, was presented by the employees of the Kolyvan lapidary factory to Tsar Nicholas II and Tsarina Alexandra Feodorovna on the occasion of their coronation on 9 May 1896. This dish is well crafted, particularly considering the difficulty of carving the relatively friable rhodonite, but the style is very traditional, based on Russian presentation dishes produced from the 1870s onwards. (Birbaum had described the ready-made pieces supplied to Fabergé as technically well made but old fashioned.) The dish was acquired by Queen Mary in 1938.

The examples of works by Fabergé's Russian competitors, whether from St Petersburg or Moscow, demonstrate how influential his style was and how many of his contemporaries attempted to emulate his designs. In general, however, Fabergé managed to keep ahead of the competition, both in terms of the number of orders fulfilled and, more importantly, by producing a far greater range of innovative designs than any other maker at that time.

Fabergé's influence extended not only to goldsmiths in Russia but also to those based much farther afield. The international reputation of his firm was keenly felt in London and, particularly, in Paris. Several important makers decided to compete in the same market, undoubtedly encouraged by the wealth of important commissions and the apparently insatiable appetite of Fabergé's clientele.

Chief amongst these foreign competitors was the firm of Cartier, which by the late 1850s was the most important retailer of jewellery and *objets d'art* in Paris, having been founded in 1847 by Louis François Cartier (1819–1904). Initially the firm retailed works made by other suppliers including Falize and Boucheron but from 1900 it began to design and manufacture its own products. These were made in a series of workshops run by different makers who worked exclusively for Cartier. This paralleled the organisation of Fabergé's own workshops. A further comparison can be made between the expansion of the two firms: Fabergé opened branches in Moscow (1887), London (1903) and Kiev (1905); Cartier opened branches in London (1902) and New York (1909).

Furthermore, the reason for the opening of the respective London branches appears to have been the same: Fabergé's branch was designed primarily to serve as a private showroom for King Edward VII and Queen Alexandra. It seems that almost exactly the same reason prompted Cartier to open its London branch. The number of orders placed in London in connection with the King's coronation in 1902 was so great that the firm responded by opening premises at 4 New Burlington Street. The Cartier vesta case (cat. 346) appears to have been a coronation souvenir as it incorporates a gold coronation crown. It may have been acquired by Queen Alexandra, who spent £210 on 'coronation souvenirs' at Cartier on 30 December 1902.[11] Another comparison can be drawn between the clientele of the two firms; both had an international outlook including, for example, clients in India. Cartier produced objects linked with the Delhi Durbar for the coronation of King George V in 1911. In addition, a number of Fabergé's most important Russian clients, including Grand Duchess Xenia and Tsarina Marie Feodorovna, became patrons of Cartier's branches in London and Paris. Indeed, many of the same names appear in the sales ledgers of the two firms.[12]

In 1904–5 Pierre Cartier travelled to St Petersburg and Moscow to sell Cartier jewellery and also to buy enamelled objects and hardstone carvings in which the Russian workshops specialised. After this visit, Cartier began to use a number of Russian suppliers. These included Svietchnikov, Lagoutiev, Sourovi and Wöerffel, the last named being one of Fabergé's suppliers of hardstone. In 1904 Cartier also requested two palettes of enamel colours from the Moscow workshop of Yahr, and the firm began to produce enamelled items including cigarette cases and frames for Cartier.[13] By 1906 Cartier began to make its own Russian-style objects rather than relying on suppliers from Moscow and St Petersburg.

It is clear that the objects produced by Cartier at this time were inspired by Fabergé's object types rather than being slavish copies. The possible exceptions are some of the hardstone animal carvings. The Pekinese, pug and penguins (cat. 341, 342 and 343) are very close to Fabergé's examples of the same animals and must have been inspired by them. There are distinctions to be drawn between Cartier and Fabergé animals, however, notably in the choice of stone and style of carving. The flamingo, giraffe and rabbits (cat. 338, 339 and 340) are all carved from rose quartz, a stone that Cartier used a great deal but that Fabergé did not favour. Cartier's animals were mainly produced in the lapidary workshop of Berquin-Varangoz, which was taken over by Aristide Fourrier from 1918 (see cat. 344). Their style of carving is different from Fabergé's in two ways. The first is that, whereas Fabergé's animals are essentially as true to nature as possible, Cartier's are for the most part more decorative and have much less detail, for example in the carving of feathers or fur. The minute attention to detail of Fabergé's animals – largely attributable to his deep interest in nature, the skill of his animal sculptors and the influence of Japanese netsuke carving – is not evident in Cartier animals. The other major difference is in the choice of stone; the preference for rose quartz has been mentioned but, in addition, Cartier's lapidaries did not take advantage of any natural striation in the stones they used to indicate the markings or colouring of an animal or bird, whereas Fabergé's carvers consistently did.

The other object types which Cartier produced in competition with Fabergé were functional pieces such as the box, frame and dish (cat. 345, 347 and 353). These all bear some comparison with Fabergé's work but are essentially in a style quite apart from his, incorporating different stones, a more limited palette of enamels, and colour combinations distinct from his. A greater divergence between the styles of the two firms is seen in the flower studies Cartier produced. It is almost certain that Cartier was inspired to produce hardstone flowers by the success of Fabergé's own models, but the firm began almost at once to make flowers in a different style. This is clearly illustrated by the lilac flower (cat. 344) which, while not marked by Cartier, is entirely consistent with the firm's flowers – notably in the arrangement of the flower and vase on a plinth in the manner of Japanese flower arranging, known as *ikebana*, and in the use of the glass case in which the lilac is enclosed. This flower was acquired by Queen Mary in 1924.[14] In 1934 Mrs Meyer Sassoon gave Queen Mary two further flowers, a lily and a study of daisies, both in Cartier's style.[15] King Edward VII's patronage of Cartier has already been mentioned and Queen Alexandra was also a good client. In addition to the amount she spent on coronation souvenirs in 1902, she spent a further £1,572 with Cartier between 1907 and 1911, all paid for from her presents account (which helps to explain why there are now so few objects by Cartier in the Royal Collection).[16]

The second most notable foreign competitor of Fabergé was the French jeweller Boucheron. The firm had been established in Paris by Frédéric Boucheron in 1855, and in the early 1890s began to exhibit jewellery in Russia, establishing a branch in Moscow in 1893. Tsar Nicholas II and Tsarina Alexandra Feodorovna were to become good customers of the firm.[17]

Like Fabergé and Cartier, Boucheron opened a branch in London, initially in Sackville Street, moving in 1915 to Piccadilly. In 1911 the Moscow representatives of the firm, Georges and Henri Delavigne, were murdered and the Moscow premises were closed down. Although renowned for jewellery, Boucheron made objects inspired by Fabergé's products. At the 1900 Exposition Universelle in Paris, Boucheron exhibited opera glasses, parasol handles and cigarette cases in the manner of Fabergé.[18] Boucheron's objects in Fabergé's style led some to believe that the Basket of Flowers Egg (cat. 1) had been made by the firm, rather than by Fabergé. Records of the royal family's patronage of Boucheron are limited to Queen Alexandra's accounts and Queen Mary's lists of bibelots. Queen Alexandra made one small purchase in 1913 amounting to £12, which was charged to her presents account.[19] It was Queen Mary who acquired the cigarette case (cat. 356) in 1928 and presented it to King George V.

A further source of Fabergé-inspired articles was the antique dealer Edouard Henry Dreyfous. Based in 1897 at 104E Mount Street, Dreyfous moved to Grosvenor Square in 1899 and to 30 Old Bond Street in 1913. Queen Alexandra was a good customer of the business and her purchases included 'antique articles' as well as pieces in Fabergé's style. An enamelled rose in a rock crystal vase (cat. 362) engraved with Dreyfous's mark was mistakenly identified as being by Fabergé when it was included in Wartski's 1953 exhibition.[20] In spite of its passing similarities with Fabergé's flowers, it is clearly quite different in style and execution. Queen Mary was given a miniature Easter egg enamelled and jewelled like Fabergé's in 1927 by her children, but this too is stamped by Dreyfous (cat. 360).

The examples in the Royal Collection of works by some of Fabergé's competitors demonstrate the wide-ranging influence that he exercised over other goldsmiths and jewellers, not only in Russia but also farther afield. They also provide a valuable insight into the history of acquisitions by members of the royal family and show that, while purchases were made from other firms, their predilection for Fabergé's work remained paramount, mirroring the pre-eminence of Fabergé amongst his contemporaries.

1   The competitors described in the text are restricted to those whose work is represented in the Royal Collection, with the exception of the makers Tillander and Bolin.
2   RA VIC/Add A 21/220B, p. 33.
3   QMPP I, no. 207.
4   Christie's 2002a, p. 67.
5   RA VIC/Add A 21/220B–C.
6   RA PP/GV/3/3/179.
7   Habsburg 1987, p. 339.
8   RA VIC/Add A 21/220A, p. 103.
9   Habsburg 1987, p. 338.
10 Habsburg & Lopato 1993, p. 460.

11 RA VIC/Add A 21/220A, p. 131
12 Habsburg 1996, pp. 339–54.
13 Nadelhoffer 1984.
14 QMB II, no. 98.
15 QMB III, no. 200–201.
16 RA QA/Add A 21/220 B–C.
17 Neret 1988.
18 Habsburg 1987, p. 336.
19 RA VIC/Add A 21/220C, p. 93.
20 London, 1953.

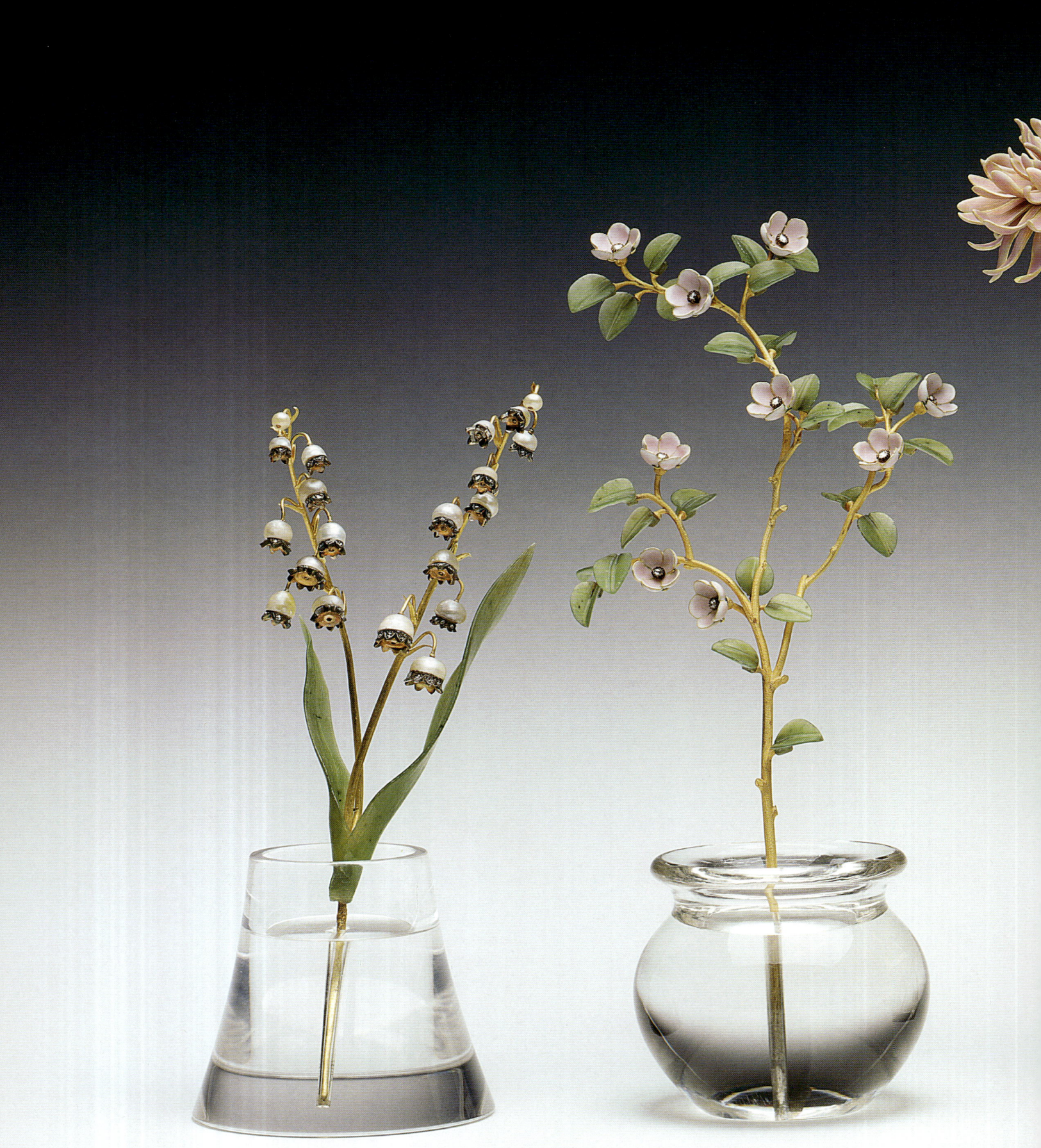

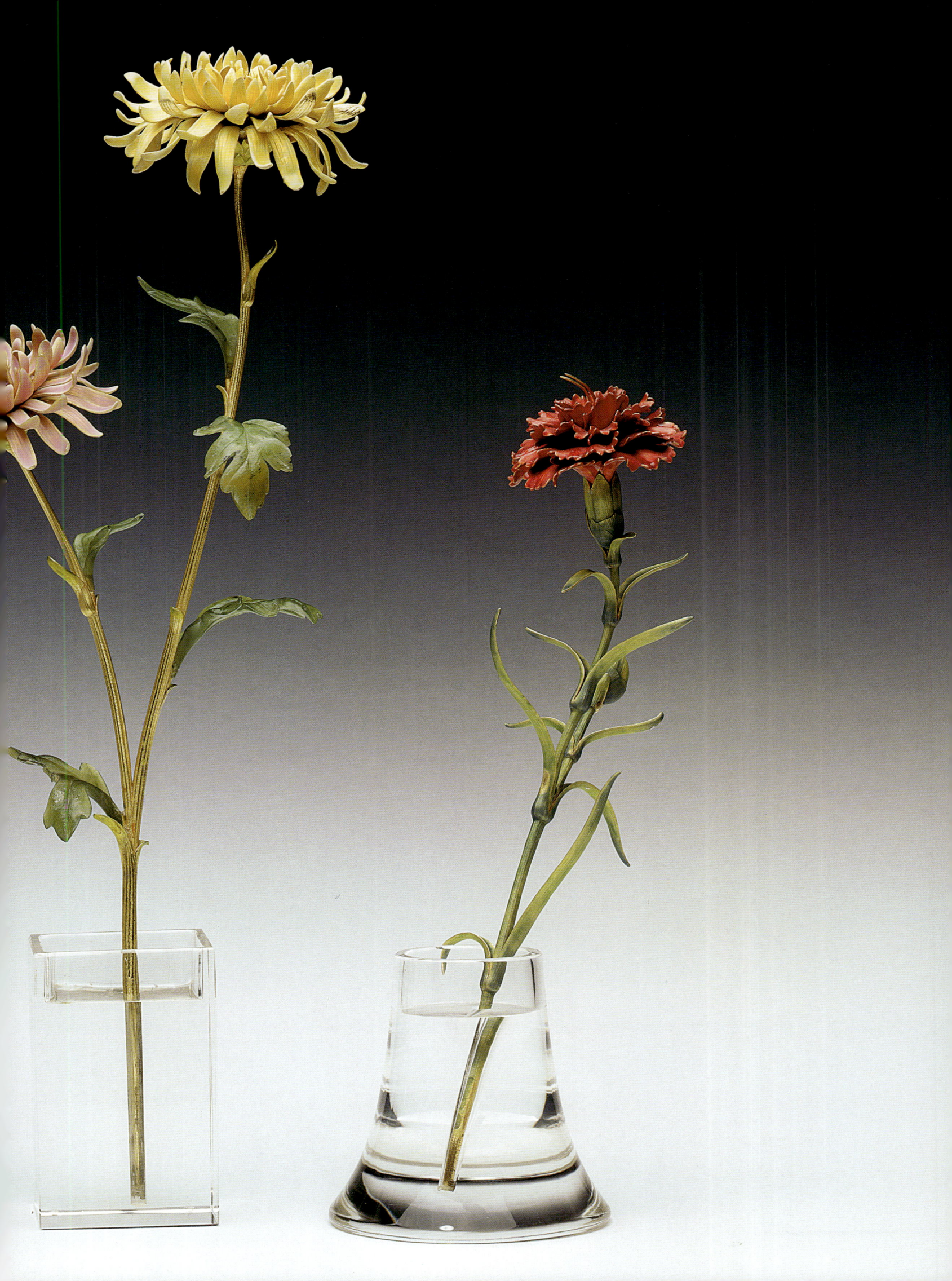

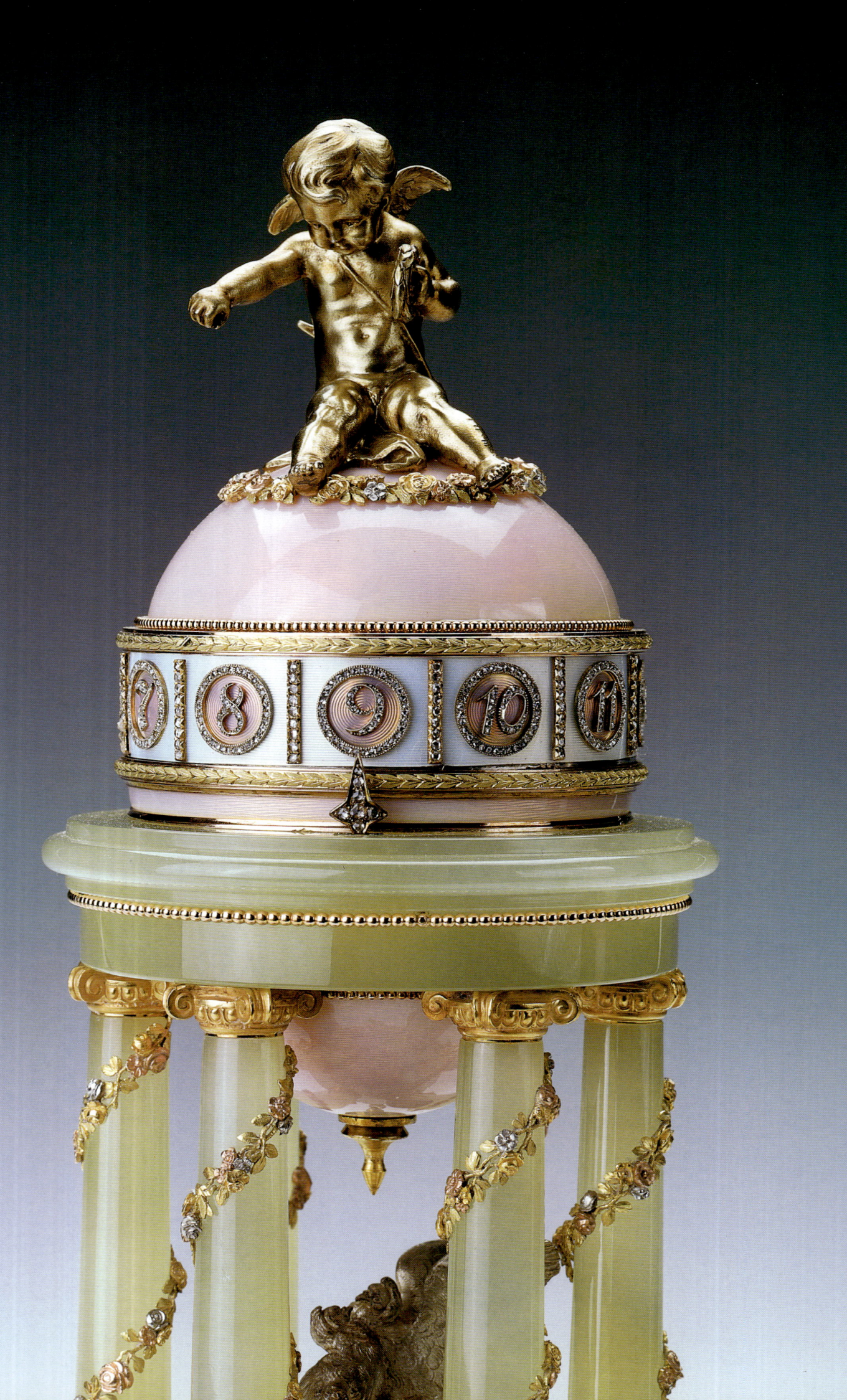

EGGS

THE BEST KNOWN and most admired of all Fabergé's creations are the Imperial Easter Eggs. These costly creations were somewhat atypical of Fabergé's production but they are the greatest expression of his ingenuity in design and above all of his technical ability as a goldsmith and jeweller. Many of the eggs have themes drawn from the natural world, for example birds and flowers, constant sources of inspiration for Fabergé's works of art. The eggs show to advantage his imaginative use of materials such as hardstones, coloured golds, enamel and precious stones; and as a group they demonstrate the wide variety of styles encompassed in his work, from neo-rococo to art nouveau. He also produced many other egg-shaped items, from miniature egg pendants to boxes and gum pots.

Eggs had a special significance in Fabergé's work, and more broadly in Russian life. Easter was the most important celebration in the Russian Orthodox calendar and during the Easter celebrations hand-dyed hen's eggs would be brought to church to be blessed and presented to family and friends. This practice evolved in the late nineteenth century into the exchange of costly gifts, including richly decorated eggs, among the St Petersburg aristocracy. The eggs made by Fabergé were undoubtedly the most lavish and expensive of such presents.

The first Easter egg made by Fabergé was commissioned by Tsar Alexander III in 1885, the same year that Fabergé was appointed Supplier to the imperial court. The egg was intended as a wedding anniversary present for Alexander III's consort, Tsarina Marie Feodorovna. This egg was the first in a series of fifty produced by Fabergé for the Russian imperial family between 1885 and 1916. The tradition of presenting the Tsarina with an Imperial Easter Egg was continued by Tsar Nicholas II following his father's death, and between 1895 and 1916 two were produced each year, one for Tsarina Alexandra Feodorovna and one for the Dowager Tsarina Marie Feodorovna.[1] The cost of the eggs was considerable, averaging 10,000 roubles each. It has been calculated that at today's prices the cheapest egg made for the imperial family would have cost £76,000 ($120,000) and the most expensive more than £900,000 ($1,440,000).[2]

Although the designs for most of the eggs had a theme, generally drawn from the year's important events and achievements in the imperial household, Carl Fabergé was given freedom by the Tsar to approach them as *objets de fantaisie*. Within the firm the design process was usually a collaborative effort; Fabergé worked with several of his designers including Franz Birbaum, Alexander Ivaskev, Gustav Shkilter (1874–1954) and Alma Pihl, the last of whom designed the Mosaic Egg (cat. 3). The production of the eggs, which was carried out in great secrecy, was a complex and lengthy business, each one taking approximately one year to make. Many craftsmen were involved –

stonecarvers, gem cutters and setters, goldsmiths, enamellers, engravers and polishers, and miniaturists. The production
of each egg was overseen by a head workmaster; of the thirty-
three marked by a workmaster, seventeen were made in
Michael Perchin's workshop, thirteen in Henrik Wigström's,
two in August Holmström's and one in Albert Holmström's.
Most of the eggs, such as the Mosaic Egg, contain a 'surprise'
of some kind; the majority open to reveal miniature models,
sometimes with mechanical parts, and images of people,
places and events of importance to the imperial family.

During the Revolution in 1917 many of the Imperial Easter Eggs were confiscated from the apartments of
the Dowager Tsarina Marie Feodorovna and of Tsarina Alexandra Feodorovna at the Anichkov Palace and at Gatchina,
and taken to the Moscow Kremlin Armoury for storage.
In the chaos of the period, eight of the fifty eggs disappeared
and have never been recovered. Others, such as the Basket
of Flowers Egg (cat. 1), suffered damage and several lost
the surprises they had originally contained. Fourteen of
the eggs from the Kremlin, including two now in the Royal
Collection, were sold in 1930 and 1933 by Lenin's gov-

ernment bureau – the Antikvariat – which was established
in 1921 to sell Russian state treasures to the West. The American industrialist Armand Hammer bought several of the
eggs, as did the dealer Emanuel Snowman. They were
later sold to collectors and museums in the West. The three
in the Royal Collection were acquired by King George V and
Queen Mary in the 1930s.

In addition to the fifty Easter eggs made for the
imperial family, Fabergé was privately commissioned to produce eggs for the nobility and wealthy members of society,
including Dr Emanuel Nobel and the Duchess of Marlborough. Financiers, industrialists and businessmen formed
an important part of Fabergé's Russian clientele. Their new-
found wealth, a result of the dynamic industrial growth of
St Petersburg and Moscow in the early twentieth century,
enabled them to emulate the imperial family and members of the nobility by placing large orders with Fabergé. The
most significant private commission came from Alexander
and Barbara Kelch, who in 1898 ordered the first in a series
of seven eggs from Fabergé. These were comparable to
the Imperial Easter Eggs in design and in the richness of the

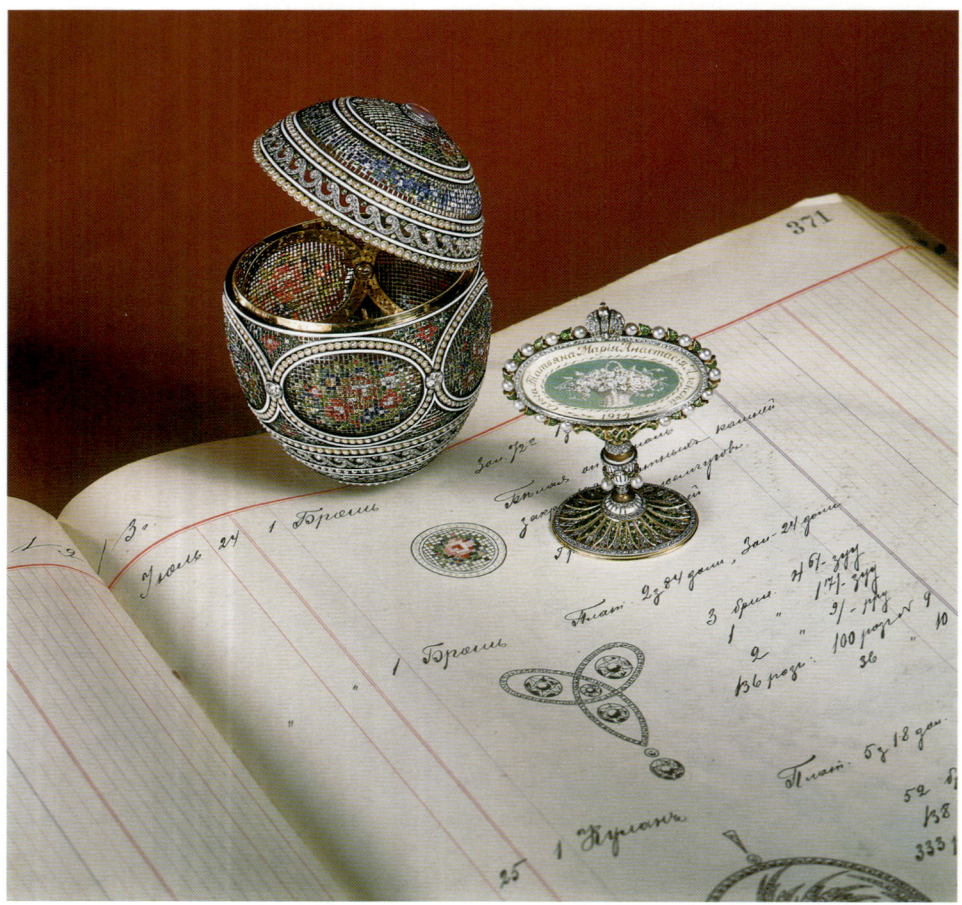

*The Mosaic Egg and Surprise (cat. 3)
on a page dated 24 July 1913 from the
stock book of Albert Holmström,
showing a design for a brooch using a
similar* petit-point *technique.*

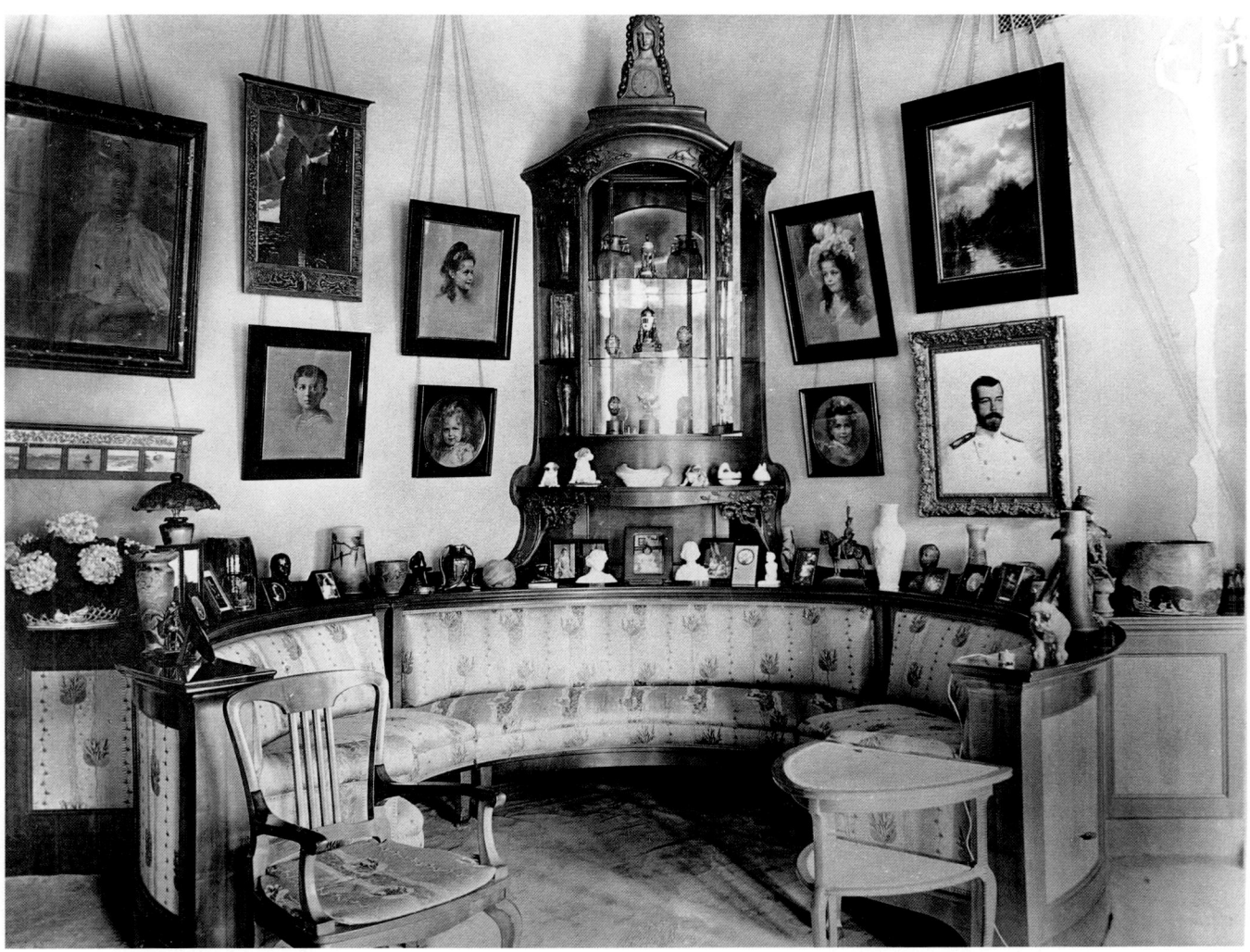

Tsarina Alexandra Feodorovna's Mauve Room at the Alexander Palace, Tsarskoe Selo, c.1911. The Colonnade Egg (cat. 2) is clearly visible on the top shelf of the cabinet.

materials used. One of the Kelch eggs is now in the Royal Collection, having been acquired by King George V and Queen Mary in 1933 (see cat. 4).

Hundreds of miniature Easter eggs in an incredible range of designs and materials were made in Fabergé's workshops. A small number of surviving design albums have been published; one from the Wigström workshop features pages of miniature eggs. They appear to have been one of the most popular gifts, reinforcing the importance of Easter in the Orthodox calendar. They were worn as pendants and were occasionally designed to open, revealing miniature surprises. The eggs were given as presents by the imperial family

to the grand duchesses every Easter, so that by their coming of age they would have had an entire series. They were consequently of great sentimental value. Both Tsarina Marie Feodorovna and Tsarina Alexandra Feodorovna kept in their apartments at Gatchina wooden showcases with bronze fittings that were filled with miniature Easter eggs.[3] Many miniature eggs were purchased from Fabergé's London branch at Easter time by King Edward VII, Queen Alexandra, King George V and Queen Mary. For example, on 1 April 1912 King George and Queen Mary purchased eleven eggs during one visit. They were clearly intended as presents as relatively few of them remain in the Royal Collection today.

1   It should be noted that no eggs were produced during the years 1904–5 because of the Russo–Japanese war.
2   Fabergé, Proler, Skurlov, 1997, p. 47.
3   According to the research of Tatiana N. Muntian. See Muntian 1997, p. 314.

1 BASKET OF FLOWERS EGG, 1901

For many years the imperial provenance of the Basket of Flowers Egg was doubted. The Imperial Easter Eggs were created in the utmost secrecy and, once delivered, kept in the private apartments of the imperial family. Only on one occasion during the reign of Tsar Nicholas II was the Russian public able to view some of them. This was at a charity exhibition held under the patronage of Tsarina Alexandra Feodorovna in March 1902 at the mansion of Baron von Dervis in St Petersburg (see below). The Basket of Flowers Egg was exhibited on this occasion, and photographs show that the egg-shaped vase was of oyster-coloured enamel throughout. The base of the vase was replaced and enamelled in blue some time between Queen Mary's acquisition of the egg in 1933 and the photograph of it published in Bainbridge's book in 1949. This was owing to damage sustained after the Revolution. No trace of payment for the repair has been found.

The recent discovery of Fabergé's invoice for 6,850 roubles, dated 16 April 1901, has confirmed that the egg was ordered by Tsar Nicholas II for Tsarina Alexandra Feodorovna. In 1917 the egg was confiscated from the Anichkov Palace by the provisional government. It was sold for 2,000 roubles by the Antikvariat in 1933. The identity of the purchaser is not given on the official receipt but it is likely to have been the American industrialist Armand Hammer.

The profusion of wild flowers enamelled on gold in the Basket of Flowers Egg is evidence of Fabergé's interest in nature. Each flower, leaf and husk is painstakingly modelled and enamelled to look as realistic as possible.

Silver, parcel gilt, gold, oyster guilloché and blue enamel, diamonds, 23 x diameter 10 cm (9^1/$_{16}$ x 3^{15}/$_{16}$")
Unmarked
RCIN 40098
PROVENANCE: Commissioned by Tsar Nicholas II for Tsarina Alexandra Feodorovna, 1901 (6,850 roubles); confiscated by the provisional government, 1917; sold by the Antikvariat, 1933 (2,000 roubles); (?)Armand Hammer; acquired by Queen Mary, 1933 (QMB, III, no. 88; QMPP VII, no. 187)
REFERENCES: Bainbridge 1949, pl. 3 (opposite p. 53); Fabergé, Proler, Skurlov 1997, p. 156
EXHIBITIONS: St Petersburg 1902; Munich 1986–7, no. 620; QG 1995–6, no. 136; QG 2002–3, no. 204

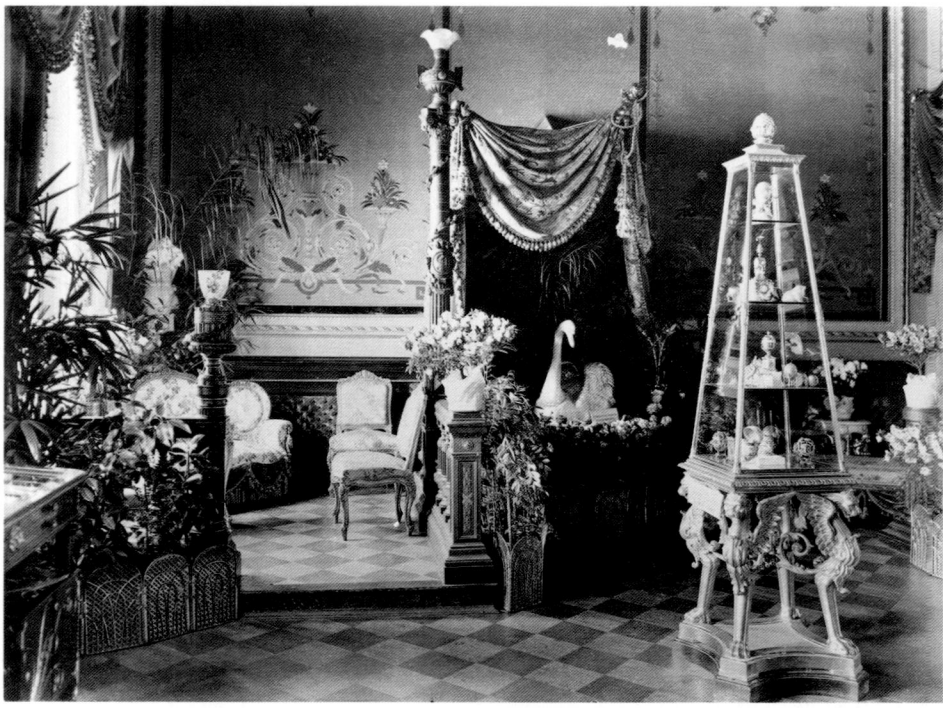

A view of the Charity Exhibition of Fabergé Artistic Objects, Old Miniatures, and Snuff-Boxes. *Held at the von Dervis mansion, St Petersburg 1902.*

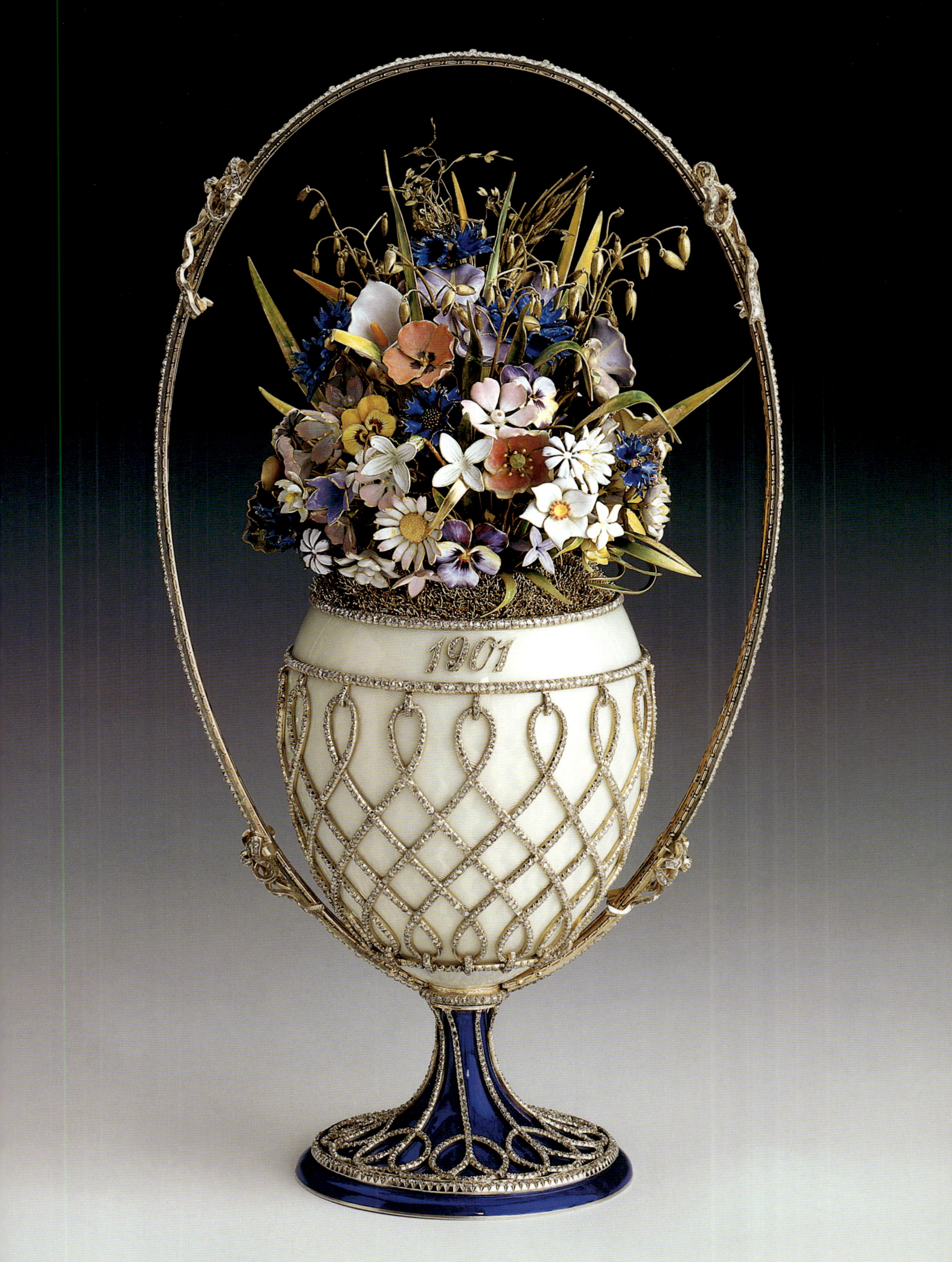

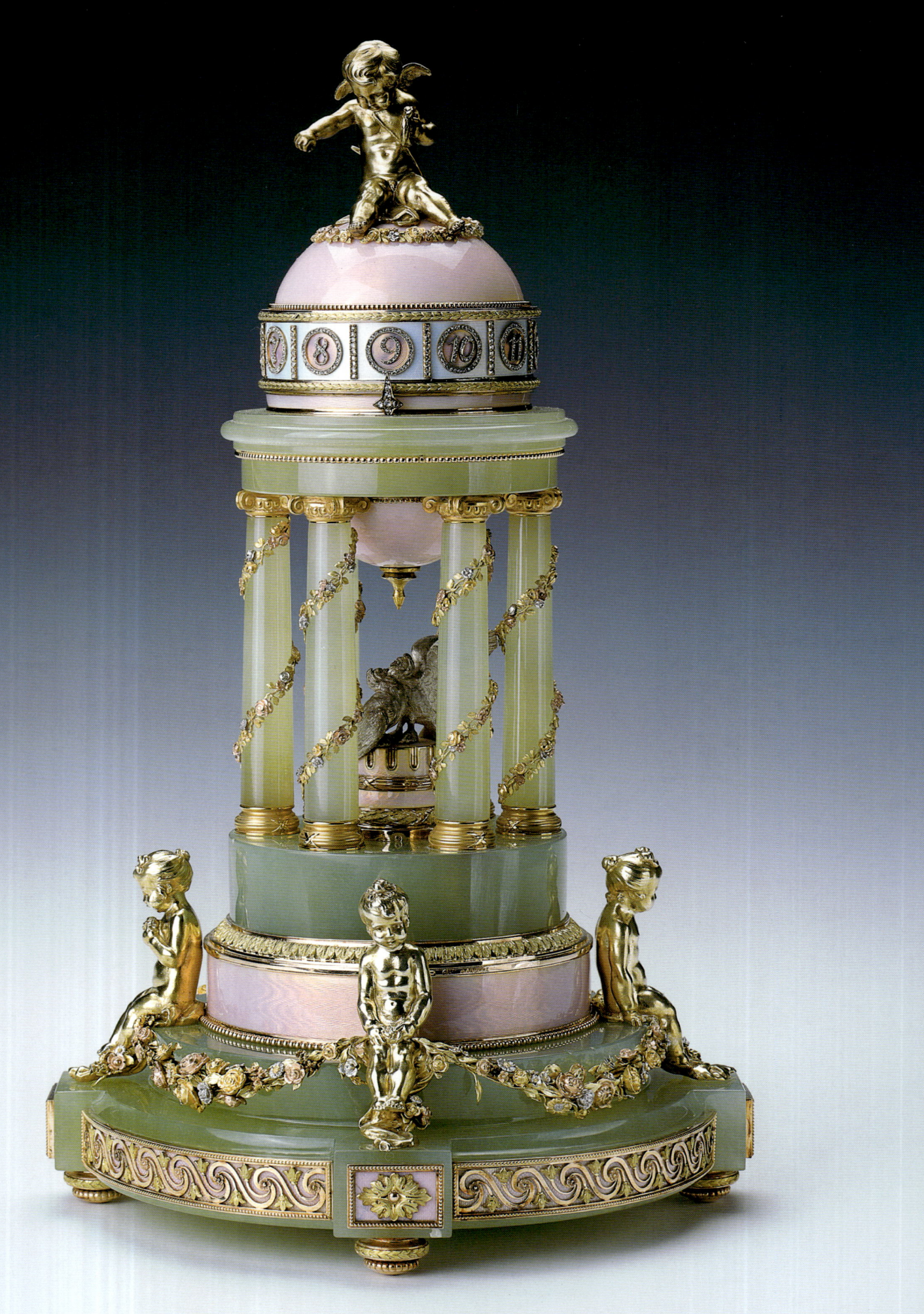

2 COLONNADE EGG, 1910

Four of Fabergé's Imperial Easter Eggs incorporate clocks in their designs, thereby giving them a practical rather than purely decorative or commemorative purpose. In this example a rotary clock by the Swiss firm of Henry Moser & Cie, who supplied the majority of movements for Fabergé's clocks, forms the Easter egg. The symbolism behind the design of the egg is, however, its most important feature, for it represents a temple of love. The pair of platinum doves symbolise the enduring love between Tsar Nicholas II and Tsarina Alexandra Feodorovna. The silver-gilt cherubs seated around the base represent their four daughters, Olga (b.1895), Tatiana (b.1897), Maria (b.1899) and Anastasia (b.1901); the silver-gilt cupid surmounting the egg symbolises the long-awaited heir to the throne, Tsarevitch Alexis (b.1904); all five children died with their parents in 1918. Fabergé produced a second Easter egg which has the Tsarevitch as its central subject; known as the Tsarevitch Imperial Easter Egg, it was presented to his mother in 1912 and commemorates his recovery from a severe attack of haemophilia.

The description of the Colonnade Egg in the memoirs of Franz Birbaum states that the Tsarevitch held a silver-gilt ribbon-tied staff or rod in his right hand to indicate the time. This is confirmed by early photographs of the egg and by a description of it in a Fabergé album of the Imperial Easter Eggs presented to Alexandra Feodorovna between 1907 and 1916. By the time Bainbridge's book was published in 1949 the staff had been replaced by an enamelled rose. Both the rose and the staff have since been lost.

This egg bears the mark of Henrik Wigström, Fabergé's head workmaster from 1903 to 1917, who supervised the production of twenty Imperial Easter Eggs. Its design is indicative of the predominantly classical style of Wigström's work.

The recent discovery of Fabergé's invoice for this egg has confirmed that it was ordered for Tsarina Alexandra Feodorovna by Tsar Nicholas II for Easter 1910. In 1917 it was confiscated by Kerensky's government from the Anichkov Palace. The egg appears on a list dated 1922 of confiscated treasures transferred from the Anichkov Palace to the Sovnarkom, a state-run organisation 'for the collection and conservation of treasures', headed by a special plenipotentiary. It was acquired in Russia and brought to Europe by the dealer Emanuel Snowman.

Bowenite, four-colour gold, silver-gilt, platinum, guilloché enamel, rose diamonds, 28 x diameter 17 cm (11 x 6¹¹/₁₆")
Mark of Henrik Wigström; gold mark of 56 *zolotniks* (1908–17); FABERGÉ in Cyrillic characters
RCIN 40084
PROVENANCE: Commissioned by Tsar Nicholas II for Tsarina Alexandra Feodorovna, for Easter 1910; confiscated by the provisional government, 1917; transferred to the Sovnarkom, by 1922; Emanuel Snowman; acquired by Queen Mary and given to King George V, 1931 (according to a manuscript annotation by Queen Mary in her copy of Bainbridge 1933, pl. V)
REFERENCES: Fabergé, Proler, Skurlov 1997, pp. 194–6
EXHIBITIONS: London 1953, no. 46; Australia 1977, no. 100; London 1977, no. F3; London 1981; New York 1983, no. 57; QG 1985–6, no. 32; San Diego/Moscow 1989–90, no. 14; London 1992; St Petersburg/Paris/London 1993–4 no. 20; QG 1995–6, no. 257; Stockholm 1997, no. 5; London 1999, no. 1; QG 2002–3, no. 205

3 MOSAIC EGG, 1914

The *petit-point* flower motif repeated on the five oval medallions of this Imperial Easter Egg was designed by Alma Theresia Pihl, who came from a distinguished family of jewellers employed by Fabergé. She was the granddaughter of August Holmström, Fabergé's principal jeweller, and her father Knut Oscar Pihl was head of the jewellery workshop in Moscow from 1887 to 1897. Her uncle Albert Holmström took over August's workshop and was the workmaster responsible for the production of this egg.

In 1909, at the age of 20, Alma joined her uncle's workshop as an apprentice draughtsman responsible for making accurate drawings of each object made in the workshop. She began to design objects herself and became an assistant designer, her first major project being forty small brooches commissioned by Dr Emanuel Nobel in 1912. In 1913 she was asked to design the Imperial Easter Egg for presentation to the Dowager Tsarina Marie Feodorovna. This egg is known as the Winter Egg. Her design was so successful that she designed the Mosaic Egg the following year. According to an interview given by Alma Pihl to her niece before her death in 1976, the inspiration for the design of the Mosaic Egg came to her during a quiet evening with her husband Nikolai Klee and her mother-in-law, early in 1913. Alma sat reading a book and looked up to see the light catching the embroidery that her mother-in-law was working. The idea of translating the *petit-point* into metal and precious stones occurred to her immediately. The workshop began experimenting with this idea and there were at least two prototypes: a watercolour design for a circular brooch appears in Albert Holmström's stock book dated 24 July 1913. It is not known whether the circular brooch was ever made but an octagonal brooch with a similar floral mosaic motif was executed and is in the Woolf family collection.

Each of the tiny precious stones had to be precisely cut and calibrated to fit into the curving platinum cagework that holds them in place. The skill required to do this well illustrates the exacting levels of craftsmanship of Fabergé's workshops. At one end of the egg, the initials of Alexandra Feodorovna are set beneath a moonstone. Concealed within the egg is an enamelled medallion surmounted by the imperial crown. This is the 'surprise', held in place by two gold clips. It is decorated on one side *en camaïeu* with the profile heads of the five imperial children and on the reverse in sepia with their names and the date 1914 surrounding a basket of flowers (see p. 34). The curious mark on the pedestal of the surprise is thought to represent Carl Fabergé's tribute to his father, Gustav, as 1914 marked the hundredth anniversary of his birth.

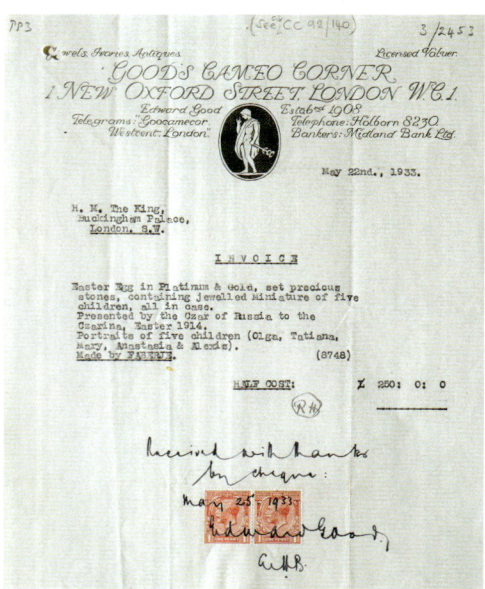

Gold, platinum, enamel, rose and brilliant diamonds, rubies, emeralds, topaz, quartz, sapphires, garnets, moonstone, egg 9.5 x diameter 7 cm (3³/₄ x 2³/₄"); surprise 7.9 x 5.5 x 2.9 cm (3¹/₈ x 2³/₁₆ x 1¹/₈")
Engraved on the egg *C. Fabergé*; engraved on the pedestal of the surprise *G. Fabergé*
RCIN 9022
PROVENANCE: Commissioned by Tsar Nicholas II for Tsarina Alexandra Feodorovna, for Easter 1914; confiscated by the provisional government, 1917; sold by the Antikvariat 1933 for 5,000 roubles, probably to Armand Hammer; purchased by King George V from Cameo Corner, London, 22 May 1933 for £250 'half cost', probably for Queen Mary's birthday 26 May (QMB, 1932–7, p. 30; QMPP vol. VII, no. 164)
REFERENCES: Snowman 1987, p. 150; Fabergé, Proler, Skurlov 1997, pp. 219–21
EXHIBITIONS: London 1954; QG 1962–3, no. 61 (10 & 10a); London 1977, no. F5; New York 1983, no. 105; QG 1985–6, no. 79; Munich 1986–7, no. 544; London 1987; San Diego/Moscow 1989–90, no. 23; London 1992; St Petersburg/Paris/London 1993–4, no. 29; QG 1995–6, no. 252; Stockholm 1997, no. 8; QG 2002–3, no. 206

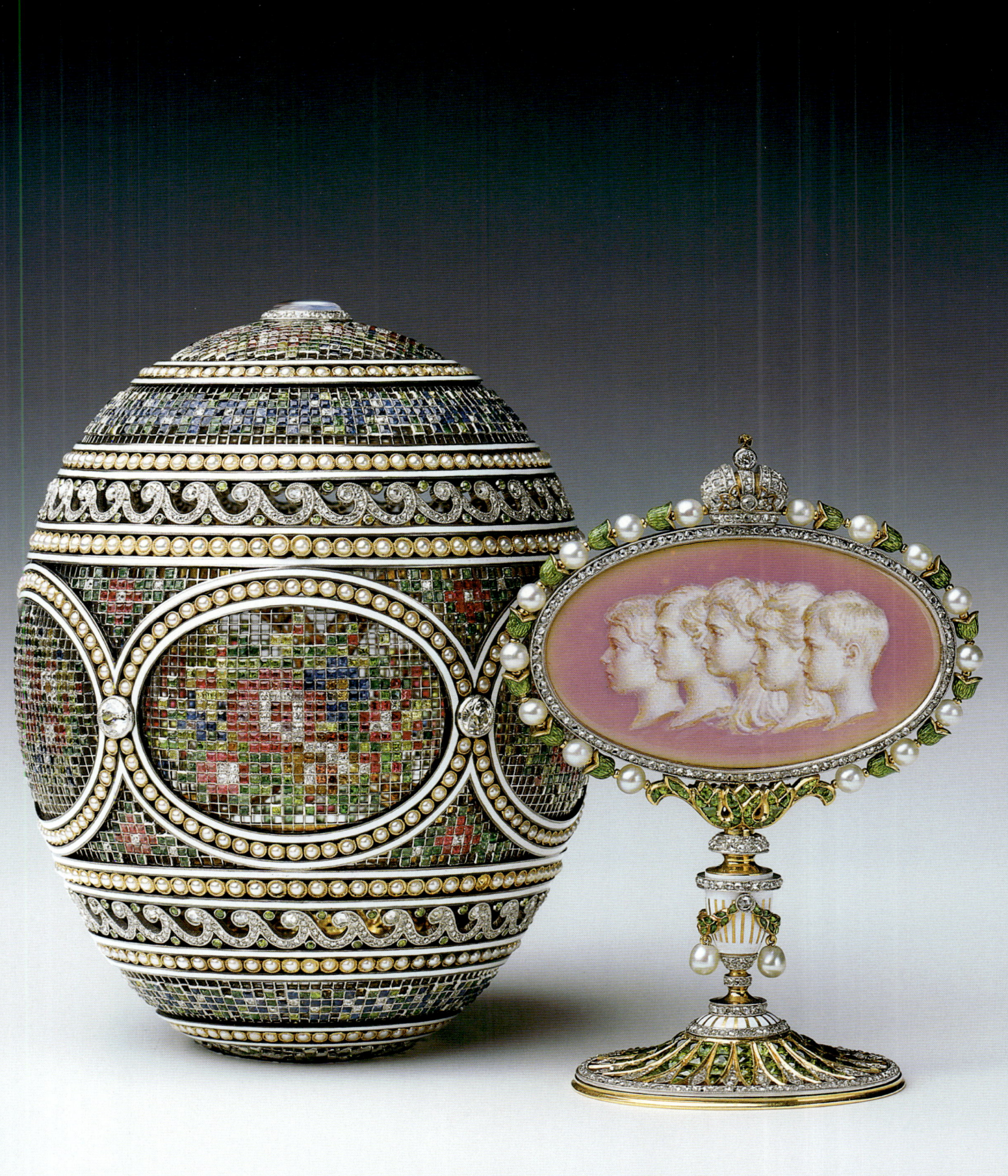

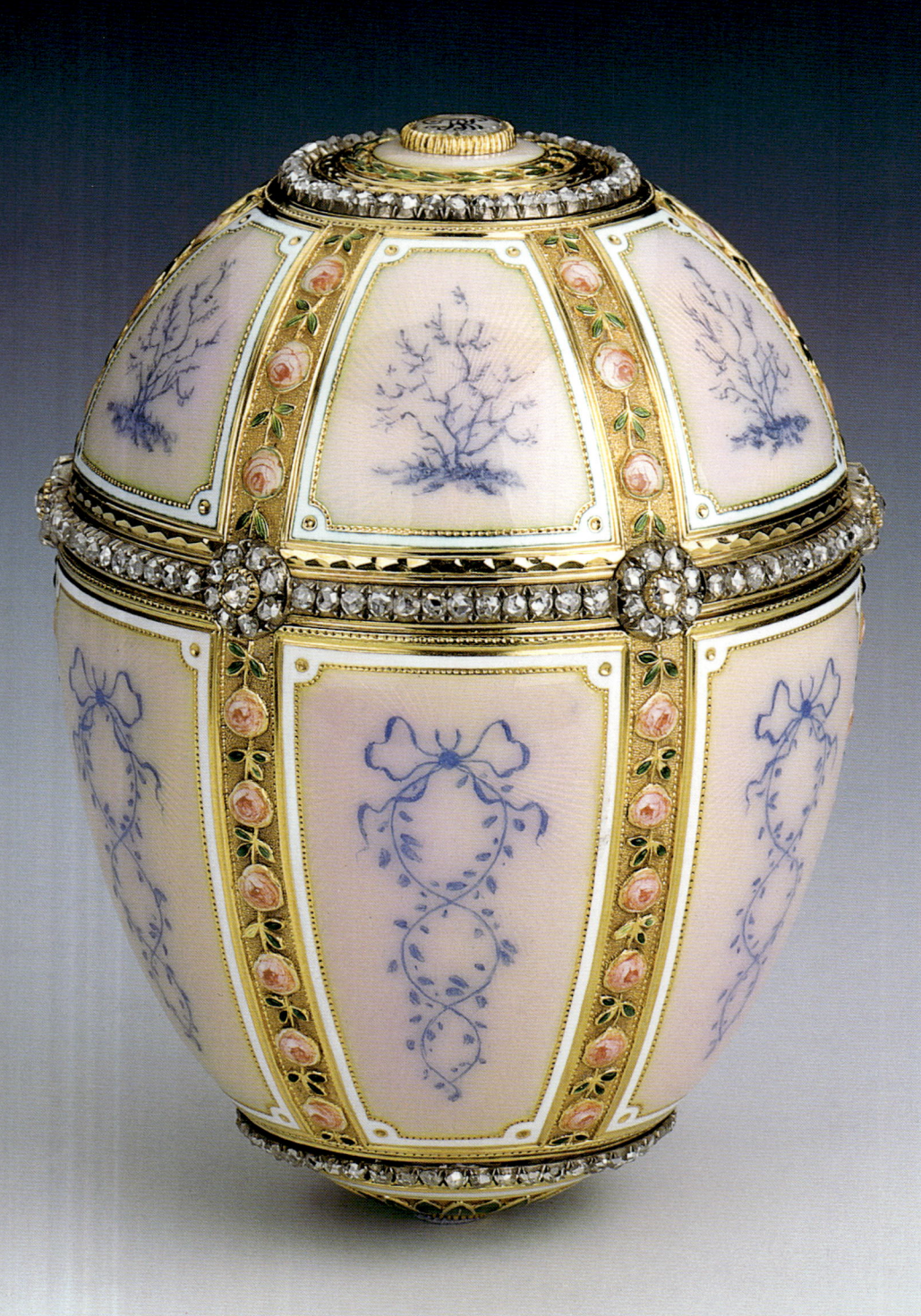

4 EASTER EGG, 1899

Barbara Petrovna Bazanova came from a wealthy Muscovite family, which owned gold mines, railways and shipping companies. In 1894 her marriage was arranged to Alexander Kelch, who came from a noble St Petersburg family and who, among other business concerns, was involved in mining enterprises in Siberia and is thought to have supplied Fabergé with gold and other raw materials. They lived in a Gothic-style mansion designed by Shene and Chagin at 28 Sergeevskaya Street (now Tchaikovsky Street) in one of St Petersburg's most fashionable districts.

In 1898 Kelch commissioned the first of a series of seven Easter eggs from Fabergé which were as lavish as those made for the imperial family. Indeed, four of the eggs were incorrectly catalogued as missing imperial eggs in early documentation. Michael Perchin, Fabergé's head workmaster until his death in 1903, is the documented workmaster of all the Kelch eggs. This egg is the second in the series and bears Barbara's initials under a portrait diamond at the top and the date 1899 at the bottom. The egg, often referred to as 'The Twelve Panel Egg', is divided into twelve translucent pink and blue enamel panels, six with moss agate motifs, by chased gold borders overlaid with enamel decoration of roses and foliage. Fabergé had used a similar division of the decoration on two earlier Imperial Easter Eggs, the Danish Palaces Egg of 1890 and the Twelve Monograms Egg of 1895. A preliminary design reputed to be for cat. 4 was published in 1984. Some of the later eggs in the Kelch series were certainly inspired by those in the possession of the imperial family – such as the Bonbonnière Egg, which Barbara Kelch would have seen at the 1902 exhibition, to which she lent her so-called Pine Cone Egg.

The surprise this egg once contained is missing and was not with it when it entered the Royal Collection in 1933. It is possible that it was sold separately from the egg when it left Russia, as appears to have happened with some of the surprises now missing from Imperial Easter Eggs.

Barbara and Alexander Kelch separated legally in 1905 and Barbara left Russia to live in Paris. It is not clear exactly what happened to the eggs at that time, but they were offered for sale by the Parisian jeweller Morgan in about 1920 and were acquired by Zolotnitzky of A La Vieille Russie in Paris who sold six of them to an American collector around 1928. Cat. 4 was apparently not among these six and is believed to have been brought out of Russia by Wartski. Paul Schaffer stated that the egg was sold in 1933 for $850, but the names of the vendor and purchaser are not given.

Gold, guilloché enamel, diamonds, 9.5 x diameter 7 cm (3³/₄ x 2³/₄")
Mark of Michael Perchin
RCIN 9032
PROVENANCE: Commissioned by Barbara and Alexander Kelch, for Easter 1899; Wartski; purchased by King George V, 2 December 1933 (£275) and given to Queen Mary for Christmas 1933 (QMB, 1932–7, no. 89); (QMPP, 1936, vol. VIII, no. 59)
REFERENCES: Schaffer 1984, p. 134; Snowman 1984, p. 123; Fabergé, Proler, Skurlov 1997, p. 77
EXHIBITIONS: QG 1962–3, no 61 (13); London 1977, no. F1; New York 1983, no. 112; QG 1985–6, no. 71; Zurich 1989, no. 198; St Petersburg/Paris/London 1993–4, no. 185; QG 1995–6, no. 278; QG 2002–3, no. 207

5 EGG-SHAPED BOX, *c.*1900

Fabergé produced boxes, pendants and even cups in the form of eggs and there are numerous examples of these objects in the Royal Collection.

Two-colour gold, pink guilloché enamel, rose diamonds, moonstone, cabochon emerald, 4 x diameter 2.7 cm (1^9/$_{16}$ x 1^{11}/$_{16}$")
Gold mark of 56 *zolotniks* (1896–1908); initials of Carl Fabergé in Cyrillic characters
RCIN 8960
PROVENANCE: Acquired by Queen Mary, before 1920
REFERENCES: QMB, I, no. 248; QMPP, I, no. 245
EXHIBITIONS: QG 1995–6, no. 249

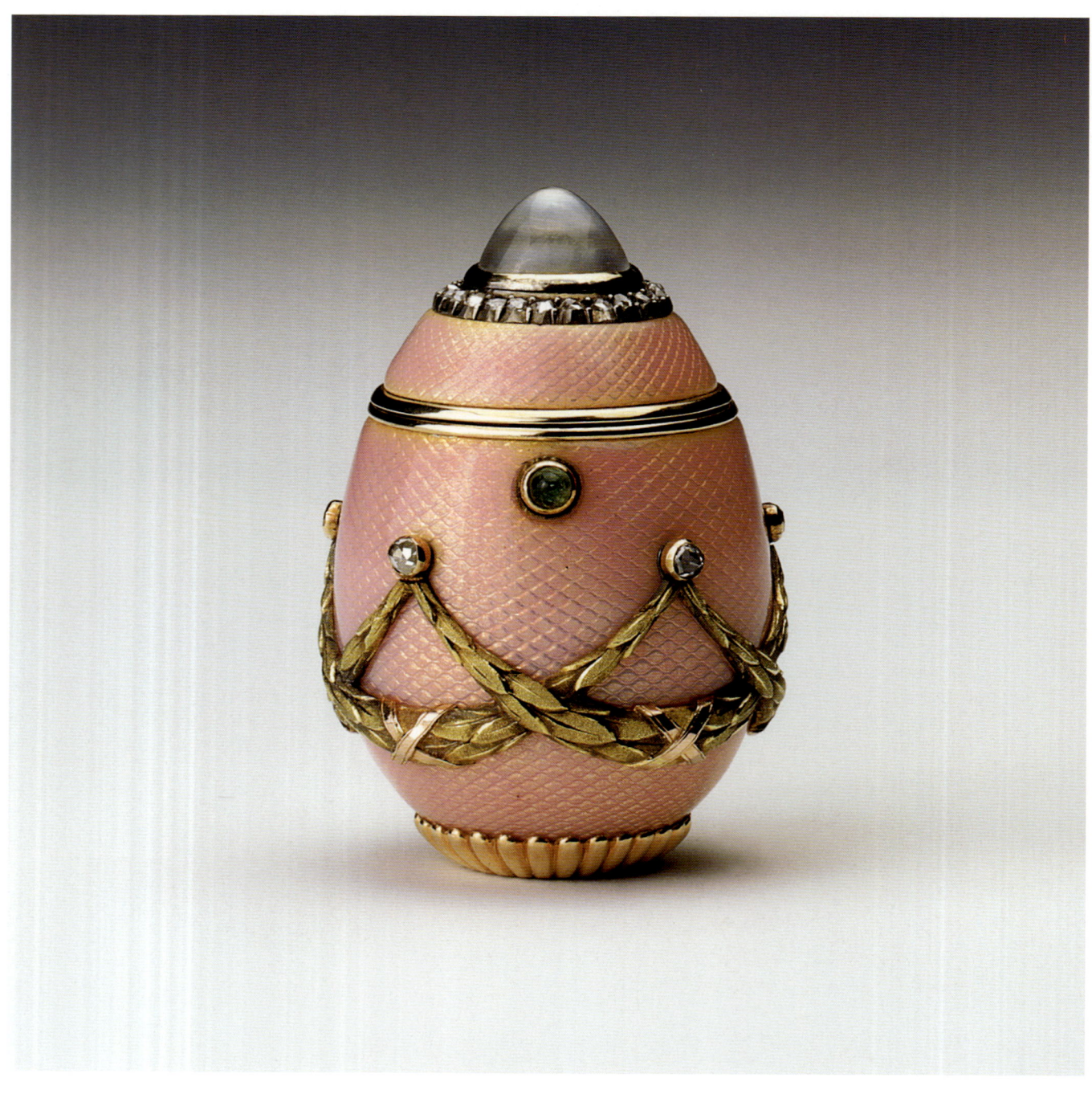

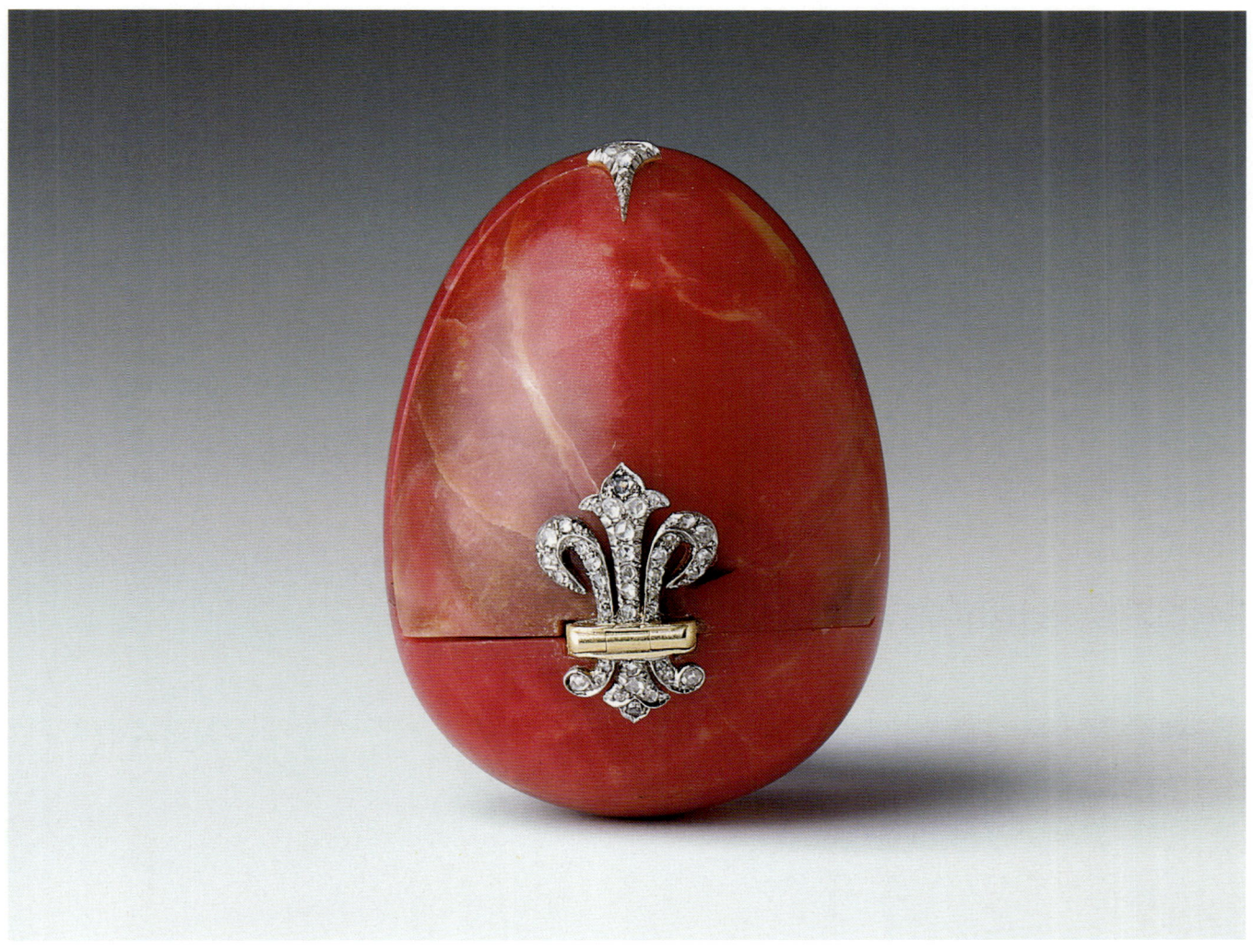

6 EGG-SHAPED BOX, BEFORE 1903

Fabergé was strongly influenced by the tradition of hardstone carving in Russia, which was centred on Ekaterinburg in Siberia. He exploited the full range of naturally occurring hardstones for all manner of objects, from animals and flowers to practical and decorative objects. Rhodonite, a form of striated pink marble, was one of the stones he used most frequently.

Rhodonite, gold, rose diamonds, 5.8 x diameter 4.3 cm (2⁵/₁₆ x 1¹¹/₁₆")
Mark of Michael Perchin; gold mark of 56 *zolotniks* (1896–1908); *FABERGÉ* in Cyrillic characters
RCIN 8973
PROVENANCE: Purchased by Grand Duchess Xenia of Russia (155 roubles); presumably a present to King Edward VII and Queen Alexandra
EXHIBITIONS: QG 1995–6, no 52

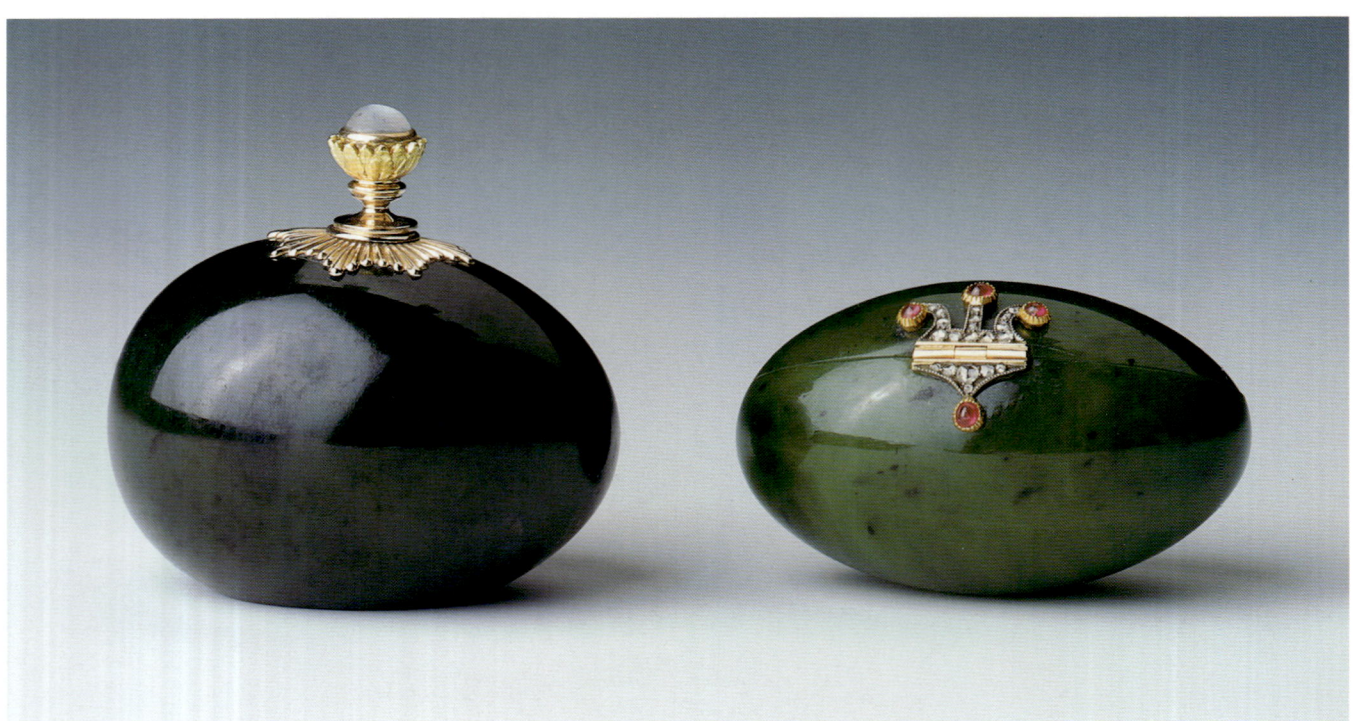

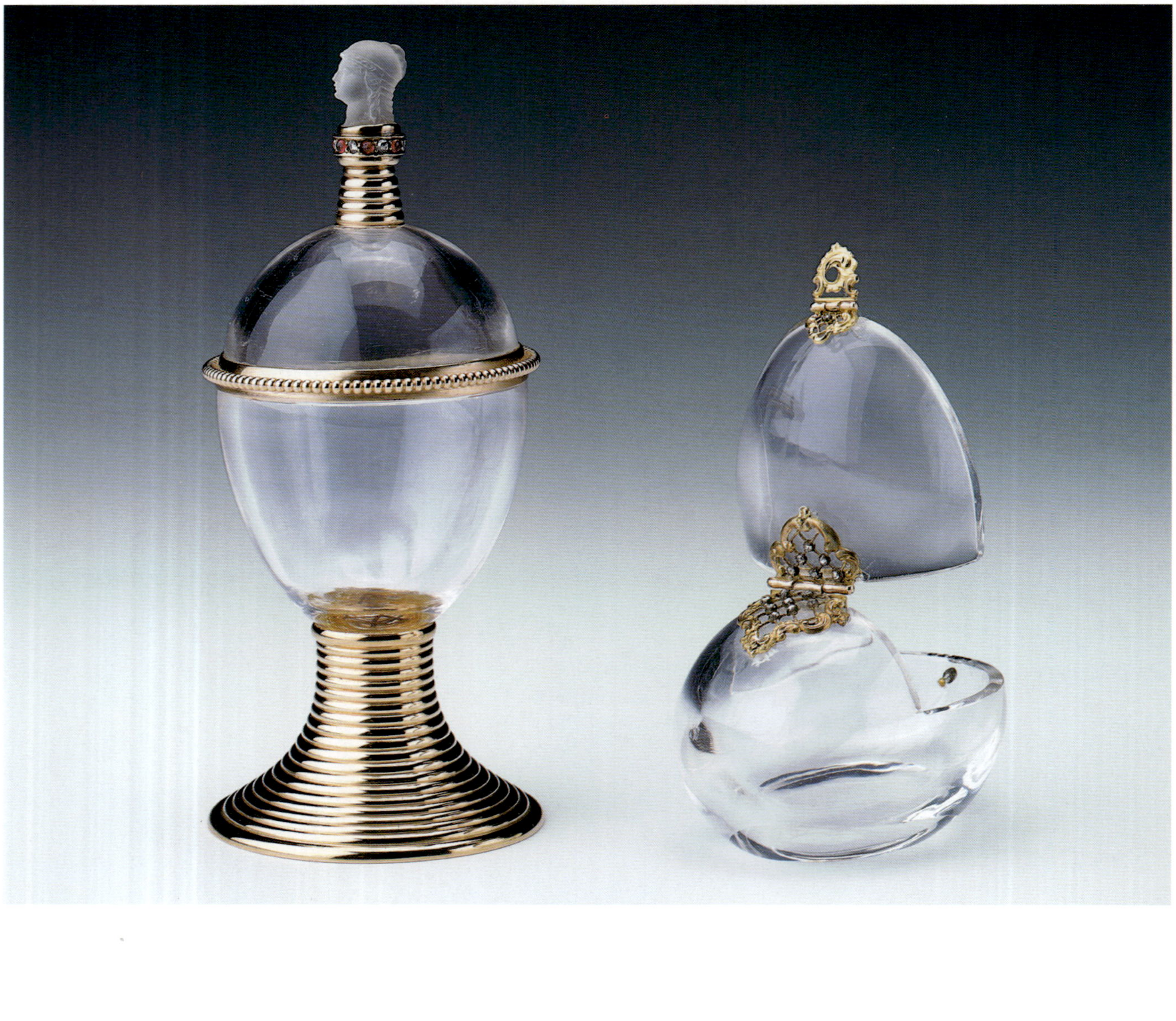

7 GUM POT IN THE FORM OF AN EGG, 1896–1903

Fabergé made practical objects, particularly gum pots, in a variety of different shapes including those of fruit such as apples and pears (see cat. 314). This example is in nephrite, a stone which Fabergé used extensively and particularly successfully for a wide variety of desk accessories.

Nephrite, two-colour gold, moonstone, 4.5 x 4.5 x 3.5 cm (1³/₄ x 1³/₄ x 1³/₈")
Mark of Michael Perchin; gold mark of 56 *zolotniks* (1896–1908)
RCIN 40148
PROVENANCE: Probably acquired by Queen Alexandra; Royal Collection by 1953
EXHIBITIONS: London 1977, no. G17; QG 1995–6, no. 377

8 EGG-SHAPED BOX, *c*.1900

Nephrite, gold, rose diamonds, cabochon rubies, 2.3 x 4.6 x 2.9 cm (⁷/₈ x 1¹³/₁₆ x 1¹/₈")
Unmarked
RCIN 40150
PROVENANCE: Probably acquired by Queen Alexandra; Royal Collection by 1953
EXHIBITIONS: London 1953, no. 52; London 1977, no. G19; QG 1995–6, no. 478

9 EGG-SHAPED CUP, 1896–1901

A cup and cover in the antique style, the finial of a carved moonstone in the form of Minerva's head. The foot is enamelled with the letters *X.B* for *Christoss Voskress* ('Christ is Risen'). The cup was specifically intended to be used for the traditional presentation of an egg on Easter morning. It was produced in the workshop of Erik Kollin (1836–1901), who specialised in revivalist pieces in gold.

Rock crystal, gold, rose diamonds, cabochon rubies, moonstone, 11.1 x diameter 4.5 cm (4³/₈ x 1³/₄")
Mark of Erik Kollin; gold mark of 56 *zolotniks* (1896–1908); FABERGÉ in Cyrillic characters
RCIN 40181
PROVENANCE: Probably acquired by Queen Alexandra; Royal Collection by 1953
EXHIBITIONS: London 1977, 13; QG 1995–6, no. 198

10 EGG-SHAPED BOX, 1896–1903

Fabergé used rock crystal mainly for the vases in which his flower studies appear to be held in water (see pp. 110–21). Birbaum, Fabergé's chief designer, describes how rock crystal was difficult to carve because it was prone to crumbling and says that it was worked on only by the most experienced workmasters. As it could not tolerate heat from soldering, any settings, such as the gold and diamond clasp on this box, had to be assembled with clips and pins.

Rock crystal, two-colour gold, rose diamonds, 3.5 x 5.6 x 4 cm (1³/₈ x 2³/₁₆ x 1⁹/₁₆")
Gold mark of 56 *zolotniks*
RCIN 40170
PROVENANCE: Probably acquired by Queen Alexandra; Royal Collection by 1953
REFERENCES: Habsburg & Lopato 1993, p. 457
EXHIBITIONS: London 1953, no. 76; London 1977, no. 17; QG 1995–6, no. 472

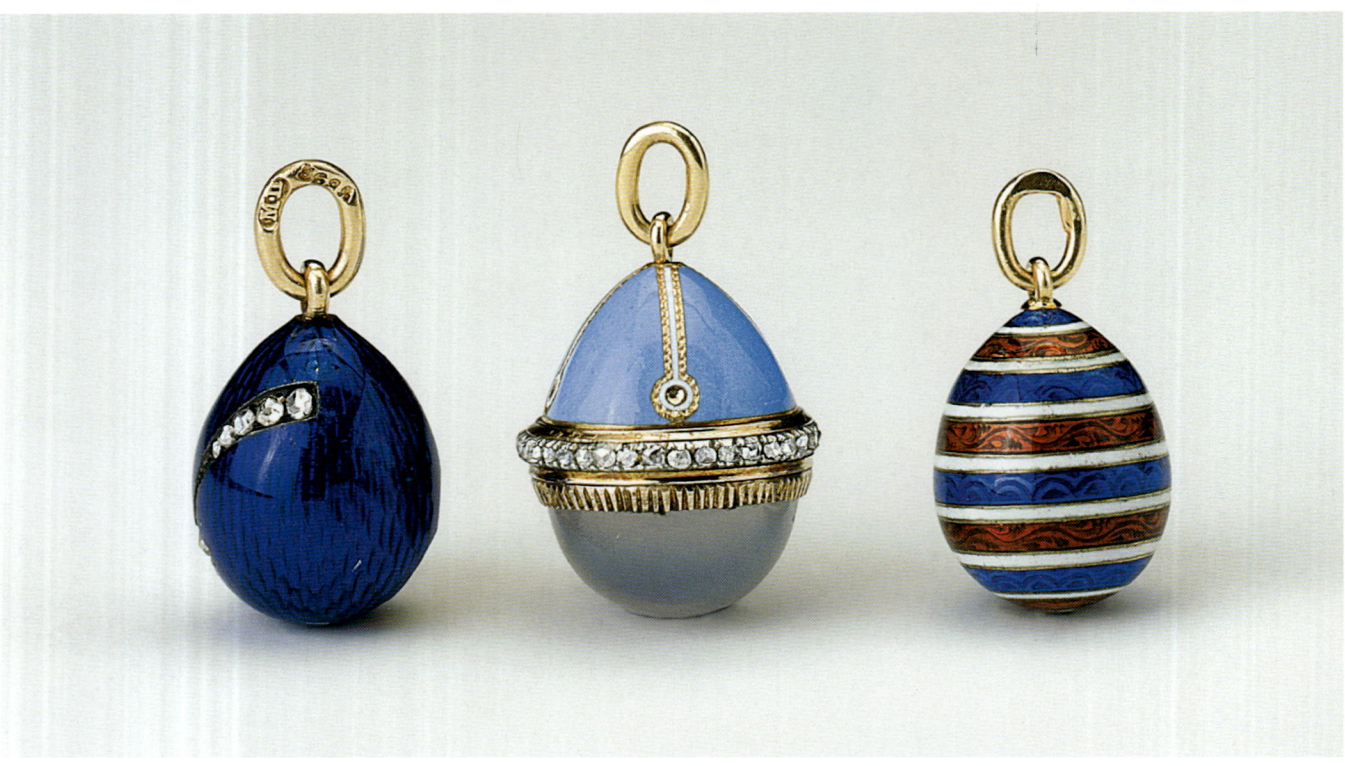

11 EASTER EGG PENDANT, 1896–1903

This amusing design was undoubtedly among the miniature Easter eggs purchased by members of the royal family from Fabergé's London branch, but the purchases were so numerous that the ledgers often do not describe the eggs individually.

Gold, guilloché enamel, rose diamonds, 1.6 x diameter 1.2 cm (⁵/₈ x ¹/₂")
Mark of Michael Perchin; gold mark of 56 *zolotniks*
RCIN 18351
PROVENANCE: Probably acquired by Queen Alexandra; Royal Collection by 1953

12 EASTER EGG PENDANT, 1896–1903

Gold, enamel, cabochon moonstone, rose diamonds, 2.2 x diameter 1.4 cm (⁷/₈ x ⁹/₁₆")
Mark of Michael Perchin; gold mark of 56 *zolotniks* (1896–1908)
RCIN 18835
PROVENANCE: Probably acquired by Queen Alexandra; Royal Collection by 1953
REFERENCES: Tillander-Godenhielm *et al.* 2000, pls. 187 and 191
EXHIBITIONS: QG 1995–6, no. 142

13 EASTER EGG PENDANT, BEFORE 1886

Made by Fabergé's first head workmaster Erik Kollin.

Gold, enamel, 2 x diameter 1.1 cm (¹³/₁₆ x ⁷/₁₆")
Mark of Erik Kollin; gold mark of 56 *zolotniks*
RCIN 18846
PROVENANCE: Probably acquired by Queen Alexandra; Royal Collection by 1953
EXHIBITIONS: QG 1995–6, no. 144

14   EASTER EGG PENDANT, 1903–1917

Quartzite, gold, rubies, rose diamonds, 1.9 x diameter 1.5 cm (³/₄ x ⁹/₁₆")
Mark of Henrik Wigström; gold mark of 56 *zolotniks*
RCIN 18845
PROVENANCE: Probably acquired by Queen Alexandra; Royal Collection by 1953
EXHIBITIONS: QG 1995–6, no. 153

15   EASTER EGG PENDANT, 1896–1903

This egg was made in the workshop of August Holmström (1829–1903). There are relatively few
works by him in the Royal Collection.

Jade, gold, rose diamonds, 2 1 x 1.7 x 0.7 cm (¹³/₁₆ x ¹¹/₁₆ x ¹/₄")
Mark of August Holmström; gold mark of 56 *zolotniks* (1896–1908)
RCIN 24747
PROVENANCE: Probably acquired by Queen Alexandra; Royal Collection by 1953
EXHIBITIONS: QG 1995–6, no. 233

16   EASTER EGG PENDANT, *c*.1900

Bowenite, guilloché enamel, cabochon sapphire, 2.1 x diameter 1.1 cm (¹³/₁₆ x ⁷/₁₆")
Initials of Carl Fabergé in Cyrillic characters
RCIN 24726
PROVENANCE: Probably acquired by Queen Alexandra; Royal Collection by 1953
EXHIBITIONS: QG 1995–6, no. 232

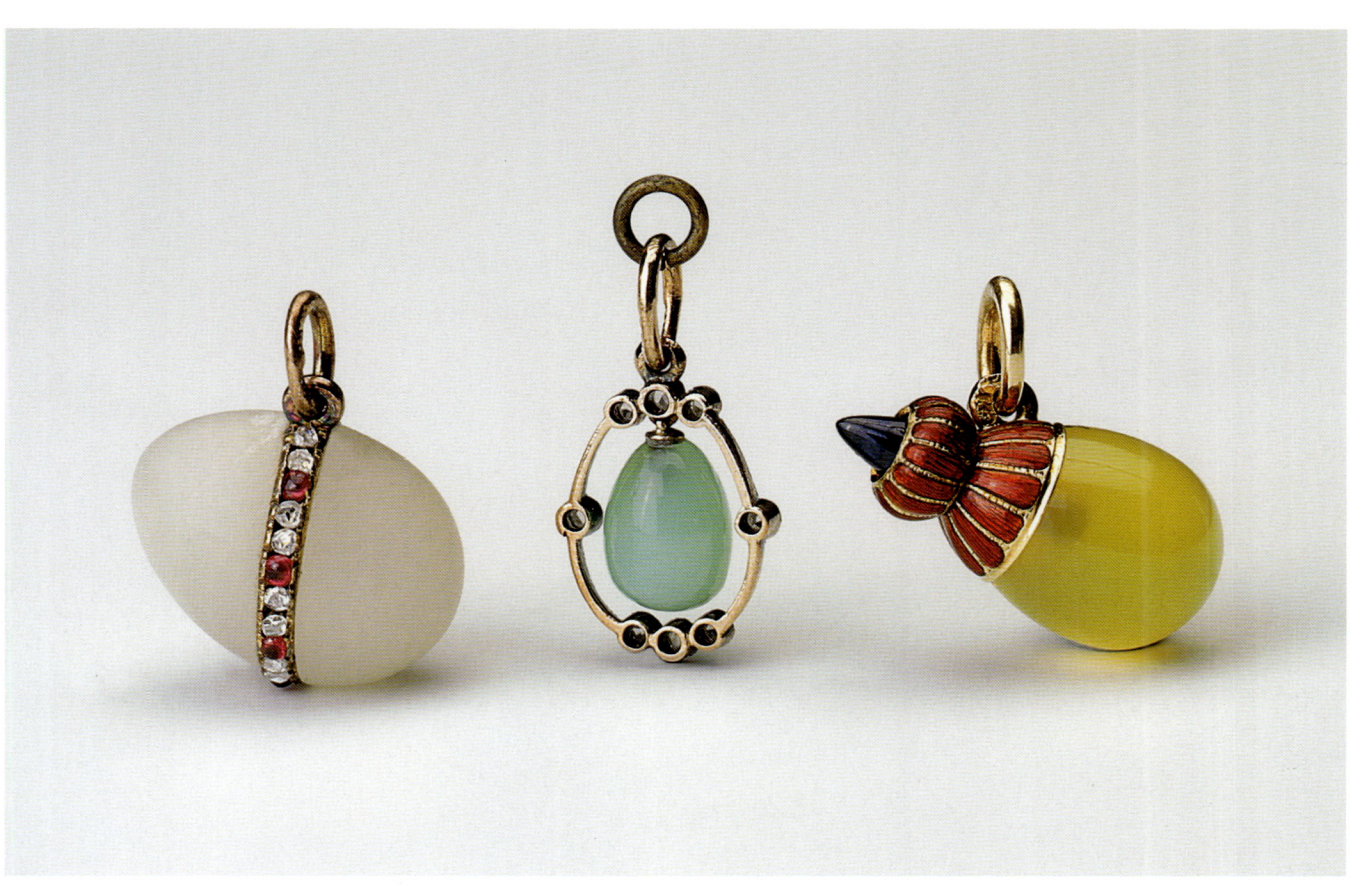

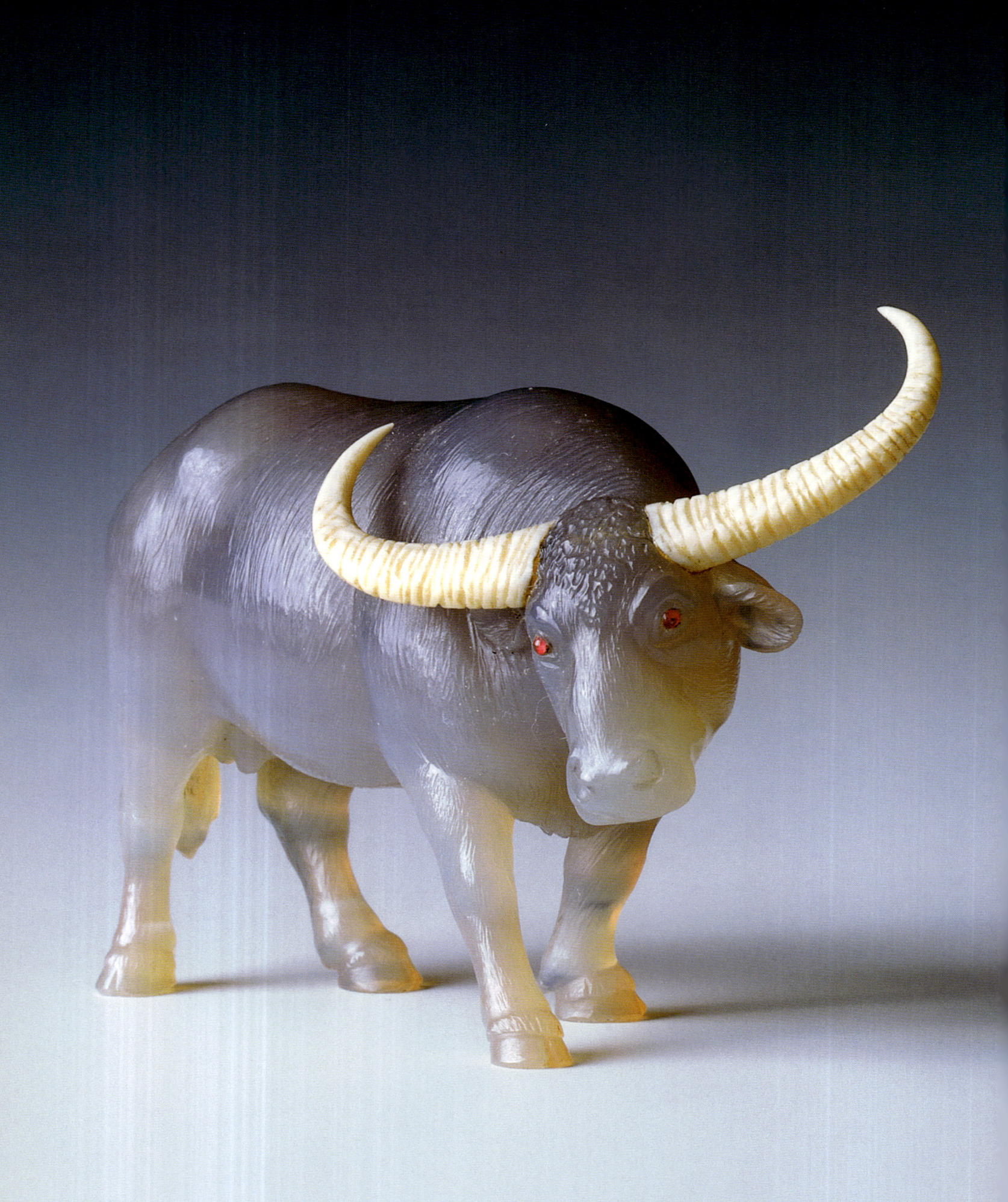

ANIMALS

I T IS KNOWN THAT Carl Fabergé was passionately interested in the natural world and in particular ornithology, which may account for the very large number of birds of all breeds produced by his sculptors. Photographs of his workshops show animal models of every type (including some wax models produced by his own sculptors),[1] which his designers used as a resource for their work. Many of Fabergé's animals are so realistic that they must have been modelled from life, perhaps at the zoo in St Petersburg which had been established near the Peter and Paul Fortress in 1865. Fabergé's sculptors, like many of his artists, were for the most part trained at the Baron Stieglitz Central School of Technical Drawing in St Petersburg. The training was rigorous and unhurried, students often studying for up to ten years. Several specialised in sculpting animals. These included Boris Frödman-Cluzel, whose particular skill in modelling horses was due to time spent working on models for the Pavlosky Guards Regiment. Skurlov has suggested that Frödman-Cluzel's attendance at the summer camps of the guards regiment in 1907 may have been in preparation for the work that he would undertake later that year at Sandringham (see p. 22). His letters from June 1907, including one to his friend Olga Bazankur, reveal his fascination with the horse: 'I want to sculpt an equestrian statuette and they [the regiment] have offered me a mar-

vellous model in one of the cavalry regiments.'[2] He was to go on to model the statuette of Persimmon as part of the Sandringham commission (cat. 18). Fabergé's other animal sculptors included Malyshev and Ilinskaya, who produced animals and birds for the firm from 1910 onwards.

In addition to the natural world, Fabergé was greatly interested in Japanese netsuke carving. He owned a large collection of netsuke, which was incorporated into the Hermitage in 1917.[3] The particular appeal of netsuke to Fabergé will have been the densely carved style and minute attention to detail, which are directly replicated in some of his animal carvings. Some of them are based exactly on known netsuke types (see cat. 97 and 98). The main distinction was the materials used: Japanese netsuke were usually carved from ivory, wood or bone, whereas Fabergé used stones from the huge range of natural mineral resources in Russia.

There was a long tradition of hardstone carving in Russia, particularly in Ekaterinburg, with which Carl Fabergé would have been familiar. However, during his apprenticeship Fabergé's horizons were broadened not only by the objects he saw across Europe but also by the hardstone carving he saw at Idar Oberstein in Germany (where he was later to have some of his own supplies cut at Stern's workshops) and by the *pietra dura* workshops in Florence. Much of Fabergé's hardstone was cut at Karl Wöerffel's workshop in St Petersburg, which Fabergé later bought to ensure the quality of supply and production. The two most distinguished hardstone carvers in his employ were

LEFT: *Water buffalo, c.1913 (cat. 80).*

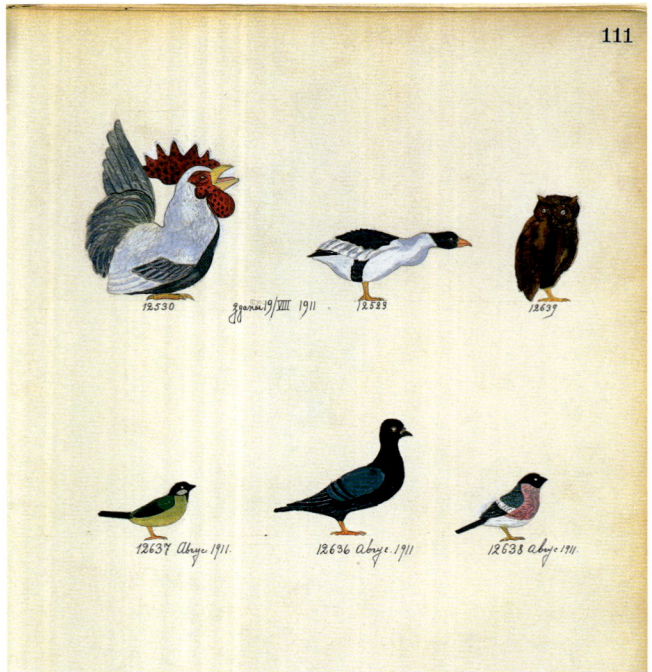

Plate 111 from an album of watercolour designs by Henrik Wigström, 1911, showing a goose (see cat. 42).

Derbyshev and Kremlev. According to Tillander-Godenhielm, Kremlev had twenty carvers at his workshop, an indication of the level of demand for hardstone objects during Henrik Wigström's period as head workmaster (1903–17).[4] The stonecarving workshops would prepare the pieces to the specification of Fabergé's workmaster and the carved stone would then be sent to Fabergé's workshops for polishing and for any metal components to be fitted, for example the gold legs of certain birds.

Fabergé's sculptors carefully selected the correct stone to emulate the colouring of a particular animal or to give an impression of its texture in real life. Some of the best examples of this technique in the Royal Collection are the snail (cat. 55) and the seal (cat. 86). There are, however, occasional humorous departures from realism, such as the red elephant (cat. 94) and the green bulldogs (cat. 38 and 39). For the most part, the carefully observed poses and intricately carved details of Fabergé's animals – with every feather and hair described – set them apart from those produced by his contemporaries and competitors (see pp. 28–9).

There are in the region of three hundred animals by Fabergé in the Royal Collection and this constitutes the largest collection of his animals anywhere in the world. It seems that the British royal family's love of animals was greater even than that of the Russian imperial family. In an inventory of the possessions of Marie Feodorovna and Alexander III, compiled after the Revolution of 1917 by Major General Yerekhovich, chief director of the Anichkov Palace, approximately a hundred stone animals were listed.[5] It should be borne in mind that Marie Feodorovna, like her English relatives, bought many of Fabergé's animals as gifts for her family and friends.

An exceptional variety of animals and birds is included in the Royal Collection, which was formed during the production period of two of Fabergé's head workmasters, Michael Perchin from 1886 to 1903 and Henrik Wigström from 1903 to 1917. The majority of the collection, as already mentioned, was formed by King Edward VII and Queen Alexandra in connection with the King's commission of 1907 (see pp. 21–4). Other animals were acquired both earlier and for many years afterwards.

The earliest royal purchase of animals from Fabergé's London branch was made by Queen Alexandra on 29 October 1906, when she bought a rabbit and an owl, both in agate. On the same occasion she purchased the frog cigar lighter (cat. 82). Her famous collection of animals may have already been started before that date, through gifts from her family and friends. It was well known that of all Fabergé's products she preferred animals and flowers.

Once the Sandringham models began to be carved in St Petersburg and dispatched back to the London branch, the collection grew rapidly. Many additional animals were purchased by King George V and by his sister Princess Victoria, such as the owl on a perch (cat. 58) and the kangaroo (cat. 85). Even after the closure of the London branch in 1917 King George V and Queen Mary continued to acquire animals from other sources, notably from the dealers Wartski (cat. 68) and from Prince Vladimir Galitzine, from whom Queen Mary acquired two parrots, a duck, a cockerel and an agate bird between 1928 and 1930.[6] In more recent years, Queen Elizabeth acquired two elephants (cat. 111 and 113) and a sparrow (cat. 98) amongst other animals.

1   Nationalmuseum, Stockholm 1997, p. 14.
2   Pushkin House. Archive 15, inventory 1, file 668.
3   Snowman 1979; Habsburg & Lopato 1993, p. 31.
4   Tillander-Godenhielm *et al.* 2000, p. 36.
5   Muntian 1997, p. 330.
6   Archives of Princess George Galitzine.

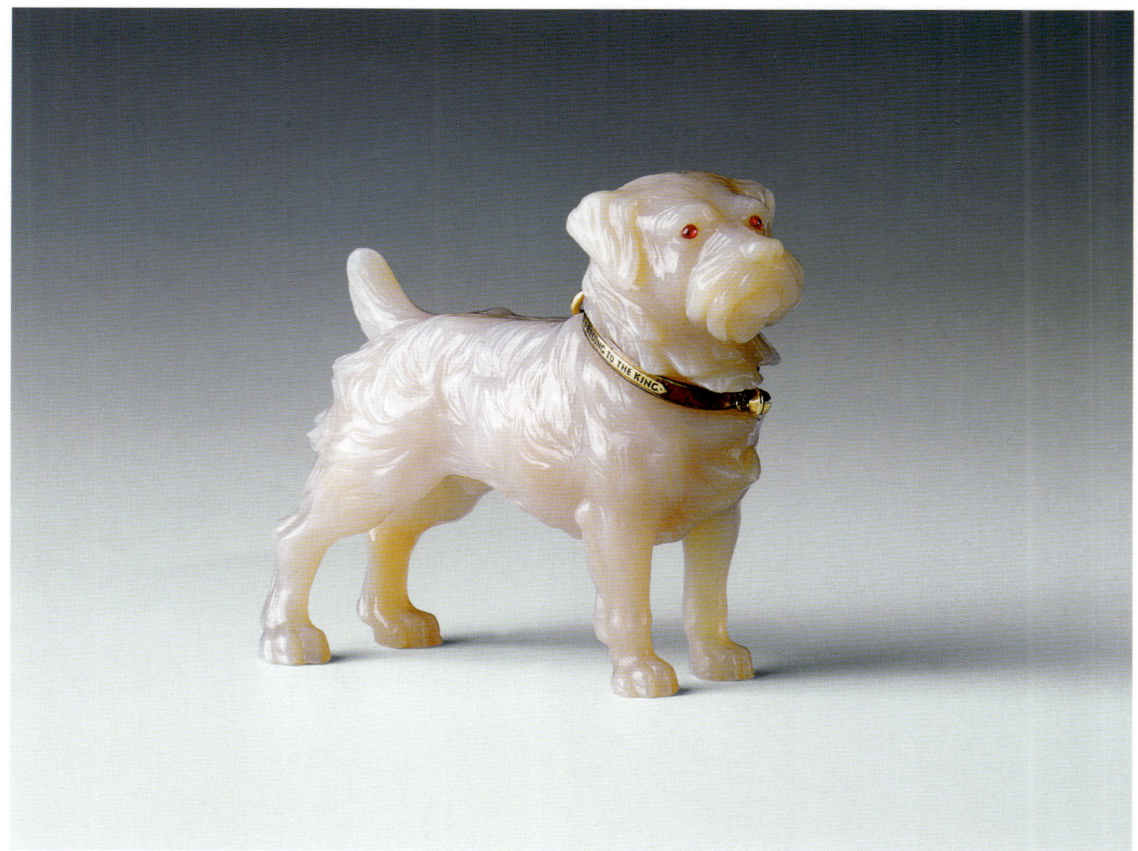

17 CAESAR, *c.*1908

King Edward VII's initial idea for the 1907 commission was for the favourite royal dogs and race-horses to be immortalised by Fabergé. Caesar, the King's beloved Norfolk terrier, would certainly have been one of the most important subjects to be modelled. Caesar was bred by the Duchess of Newcastle *c.*1895 and of the many dogs that King Edward owned – basset hounds, Clumber spaniels, chow-chows and French bulldogs – he was the King's favourite.

The King clearly doted on Caesar, who accompanied his master almost everywhere, even to Biarritz and Marienbad. On one occasion Caesar was taken ill abroad and the King even contemplated summoning his vet from London to treat him. On 8 December 1907 the King unveiled the animals modelled in wax to Queen Alexandra and the assembled guests at Sandringham, and Caesar accompanied the party to the Dairy, where his own likeness, wearing a collar inscribed *I belong to the King*, was among the waxes.

Fabergé and his workmasters had the ability to imbue their models with personality and this expressive portrait certainly matches contemporary descriptions of the way Caesar would wag his tail and 'smile cheerfully' up into his master's eyes when King Edward scolded him for misbehaving. Such was their mutual devotion that Caesar wandered the corridors of Buckingham Palace in search of his master in the days following the King's death on 6 May 1910. Caesar's final duty was to walk behind the King's coffin, led by a Highlander, in the funeral procession from Westminster to Paddington on 20 May 1910. A portrait by Maud Earl painted at this time and entitled *Silent Sorrow* was reproduced in the *Illustrated London News* of 21 May 1910. Caesar died in 1914 and is buried in the grounds of Marlborough House in London. A carving of him in marble sits at the feet of the King on his tomb in St George's Chapel, Windsor.

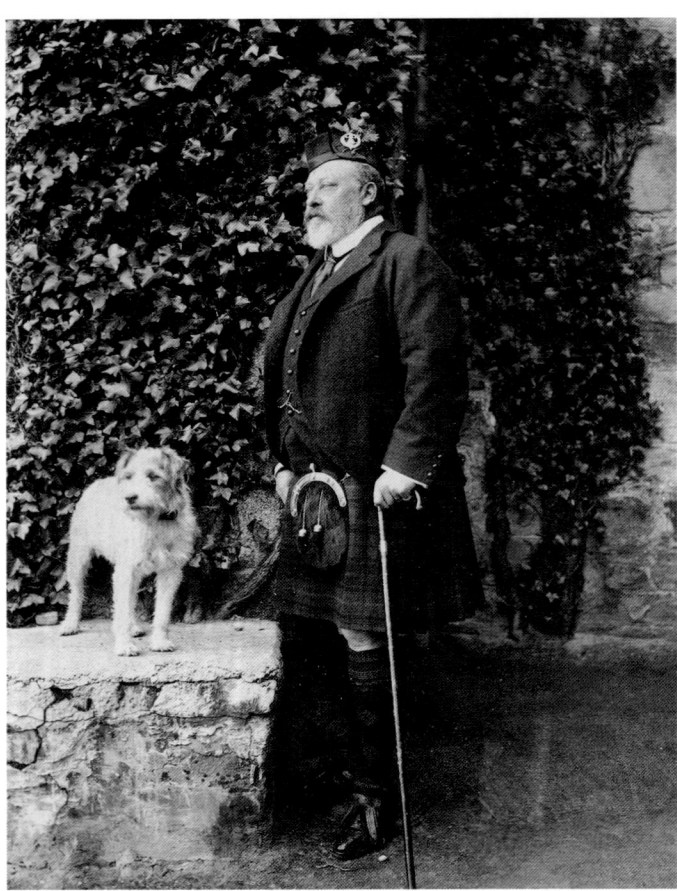

King Edward VII with Caesar, c.1906.

Chalcedony, gold, enamel, rubies, 5.1 x 6.5 x 2.2 cm
(2 x 2⁹/₁₆ x ⁷/₈")
Unmarked
RCIN 40339
PROVENANCE: Commissioned by King Edward VII,
1907; bought by the Hon. Mrs Greville at Fabergé's
London branch, 29 November 1910 (£35); by
whom given to Queen Alexandra
REFERENCES: Hough 1992, p. 328; Habsburg &
Lopato 1993, p. 129; Skurlov 1997, p. 35
EXHIBITIONS: London 1953, no. 21; London 1977,
no. A16; New York 1983, no. 70; QG 1985–6,
no. 246; Munich 1986–7, no. 380; London 1992;
QG 1995–6, no. 354; QG 2002–3, no. 209

18 PERSIMMON, 1908

Persimmon was King Edward VII's most successful racehorse. He was the winner of the Derby and
the St Leger in 1896 and of the Ascot Gold Cup and Eclipse Stakes in 1897. King George V describes
in his diary the great excitement surrounding Persimmon's
Derby success: 'it was a splendid victory & it was only won
by a head, Papa led "Persimmon" in, he got a tremendous
ovation, I never saw such a sight & I never heard such
cheering. I won £300 on the race.'

Persimmon was among the animals modelled
from life as part of the Sandringham commission in 1907.
Boris Frödman-Cluzel prepared the model from which
the silver statuette was made by Henrik Wigström in 1908.
The statuette was bought by King Edward from Fabergé's
London branch in November 1908 and, according to the
ledgers, a further six bronze copies were purchased by the

*Extract from the diary of George,
Duke of York (later King George V)
for June 1896, describing Persimmon's
victory at the Derby.*

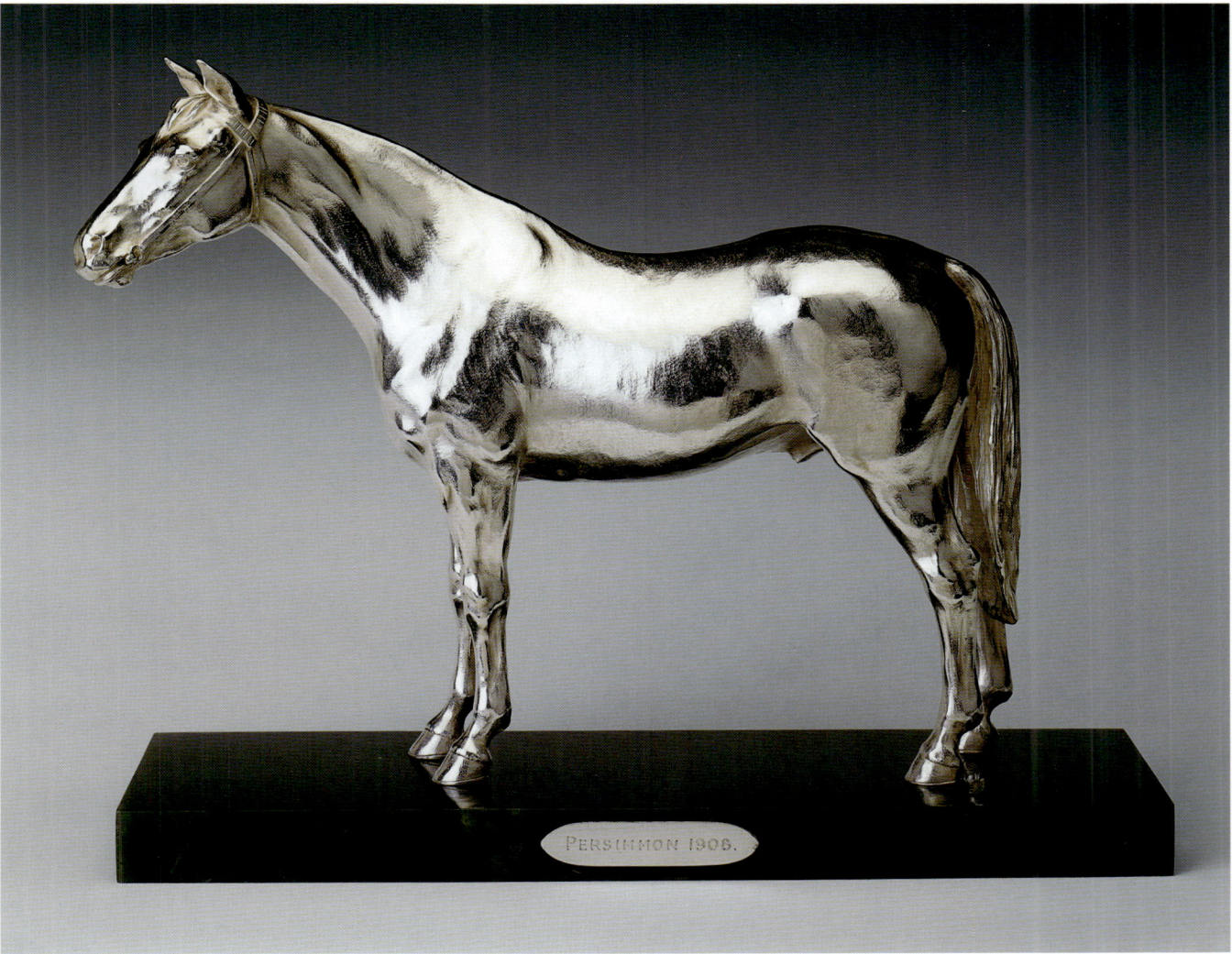

King on 21 December 1908. These were obviously intended to be given away as none survives in the Royal Collection. Bainbridge describes how he successfully persuaded Mrs Leopold de Rothschild to have her husband's racehorse St Frusquin, which Persimmon had beaten into second place in the Derby, modelled in silver by Fabergé in imitation of the King's commission. Bainbridge adds that later Leopold de Rothschild had between six and twelve bronze models made of the sculpture; those he also gave away. Fabergé made a photograph frame in the King's racing colours which is in the Royal Collection and which contains a photograph of Persimmon (cat. 224).

     Persimmon was retired to stud at Sandringham where he had been bred and where he was champion sire on four occasions. In 1908 he slipped in his box and fractured his pelvis; despite every effort to save him he had to be put down. A bronze statue of Persimmon by Adrian Jones, commissioned by King Edward VII, stands on the lawn outside the stud.

Silver, nephrite, 24.3 x 31.2 x 9.6 cm (9⁹/₁₆ x 12⁵/₁₆ x 3³/₄")
Mark of Henrik Wigström; silver mark of 91 *zolotniks* (1908–17); *FABERGÉ* in Roman letters; English import marks for 1908
RCIN 32392
PROVENANCE: Commissioned and bought by King Edward VII from Fabergé's London branch, November 1908 (£135)
REFERENCES: RA GV/GVD: 3 June 1896; Bainbridge 1949, p. 89
EXHIBITIONS: London RA 1977; QG 1995–6, no. 346

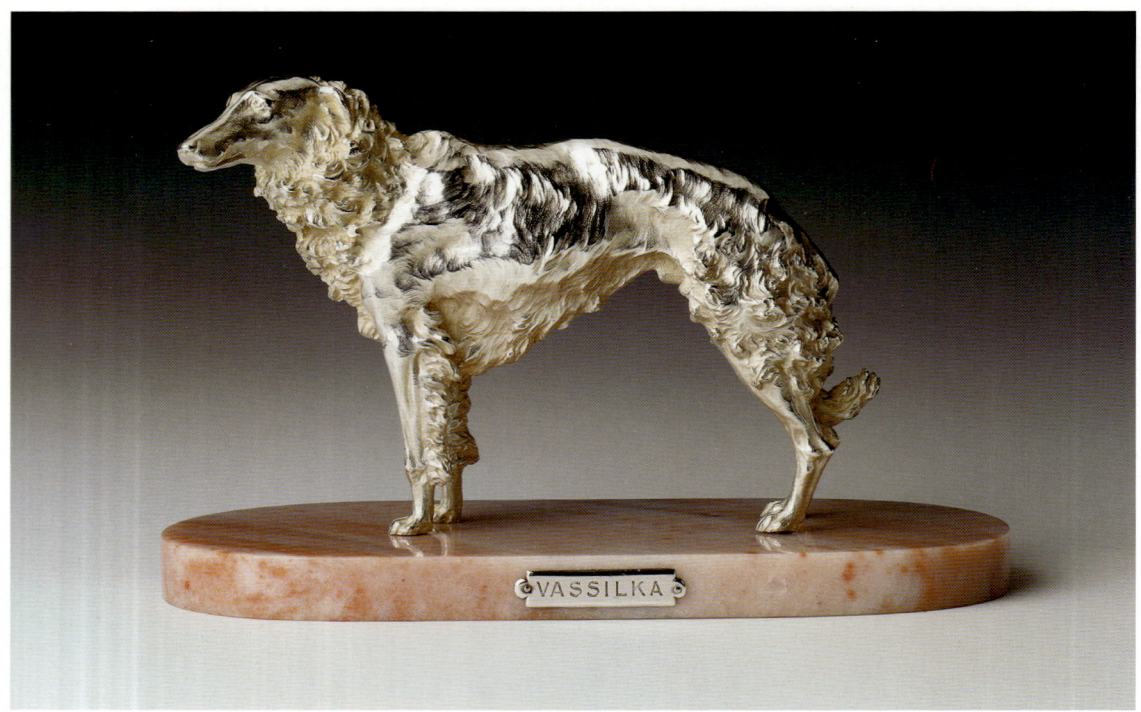

19 VASSILKA, 1908

The borzoi Vassilka was a gift from Tsar Alexander III and Tsarina Marie Feodorovna to King Edward VII and Queen Alexandra. Kept at Sandringham, Vassilka won more than seventy-five prizes. The silver statuette of Persimmon (cat. 18) and this statuette are the only two works from the Sandringham commission produced in Fabergé's Moscow workshops.

Silver, aventurine quartz, 13.4 x 21.1 x 9 cm (5¼ x 8⁵/₁₆ x 3⁹/₁₆")
Moscow silver mark of 91 *zolotniks* (1908–17); *C. FABERGÉ* in Cyrillic characters; English import marks for 1908
RCIN 40800
PROVENANCE: Commissioned by King Edward VII, 1907
EXHIBITIONS: QG 1995–6, no. 358

20 SANDRINGHAM LUCY, *c.*1908

A charming and remarkably realistic portrait model of King George V's Clumber spaniel Sandringham Lucy. The breed originated in France in the eighteenth century and was first bred in England by the Duke of Newcastle at Clumber Park, Nottinghamshire. This figure was modelled from life as part of the 1907 commission at Sandringham, where there were Clumber spaniels from the late nineteenth century, as seen in the painting by T. Jones Barker entitled *A big shoot at Sandringham 1867* (RCIN 402303). Both King Edward VII and King George V used them for shooting.

Chalcedony, rubies, 4.4 x 10.5 x 3.6 cm (1¾ x 4⅛ x 1⁷/₁₆")
Unmarked
RCIN 40442
PROVENANCE: Commissioned by King Edward VII, 1907; bought by the Prince of Wales (later King George V) from Fabergé's London branch, 1909 (£102)
EXHIBITIONS: London 1953, no. 53; London 1977, no. A24; New York 1983, no. 67; QG 1985–6, no. 255; QG 1995–6, no. 319; QG 2002–3, no. 213

21 BORZOI, *c.*1908

Traditionally referred to as a collie, this model seems closer to a borzoi. There were certainly examples of both breeds at Sandringham during the late nineteenth and early twentieth centuries. Queen Victoria had owned collies, notably one called Sharp, while Queen Alexandra kept both collies and borzois (also referred to as deer hounds) with the larger breeds in the kennels at Sandringham. Borzois were exclusively bred for the Russian court. The two most famous borzois owned by King Edward VII and Queen Alexandra (to whom they had previously been given by Tsar Alexander III) were Alex, of whom there is a painting in the Royal Collection by Benjamin Firth (RCIN 402320) and Vassilka, who was modelled and cast in silver by Fabergé (cat. 19).

The painting *Queen Alexandra with her grandchildren and dogs*, by Frederick Morgan and Thomas Blinks (RCIN 402302, see p. 21), shows the Queen outside the kennels at Sandringham in 1902 surrounded by a variety of dogs including a borzoi and two collies. Contemporary accounts of the kennels by Lady Dorothy Nevill and Lord Knutsford describe how Queen Alexandra fed the dogs with bread from a flat basket and knew each of the dogs' names and characters well.

Agate, rubies, 5.4 x 6.8 x 1.5 cm (2¹/₈ x 2¹¹/₁₆ x ⁹/₁₆")
RCIN 40030
PROVENANCE: Commissioned by King Edward VII, 1907
EXHIBITIONS: London 1977, no. A20; QG 1985–6, no. 233; QG 1995–6, no. 354; QG 2002–3, no. 210

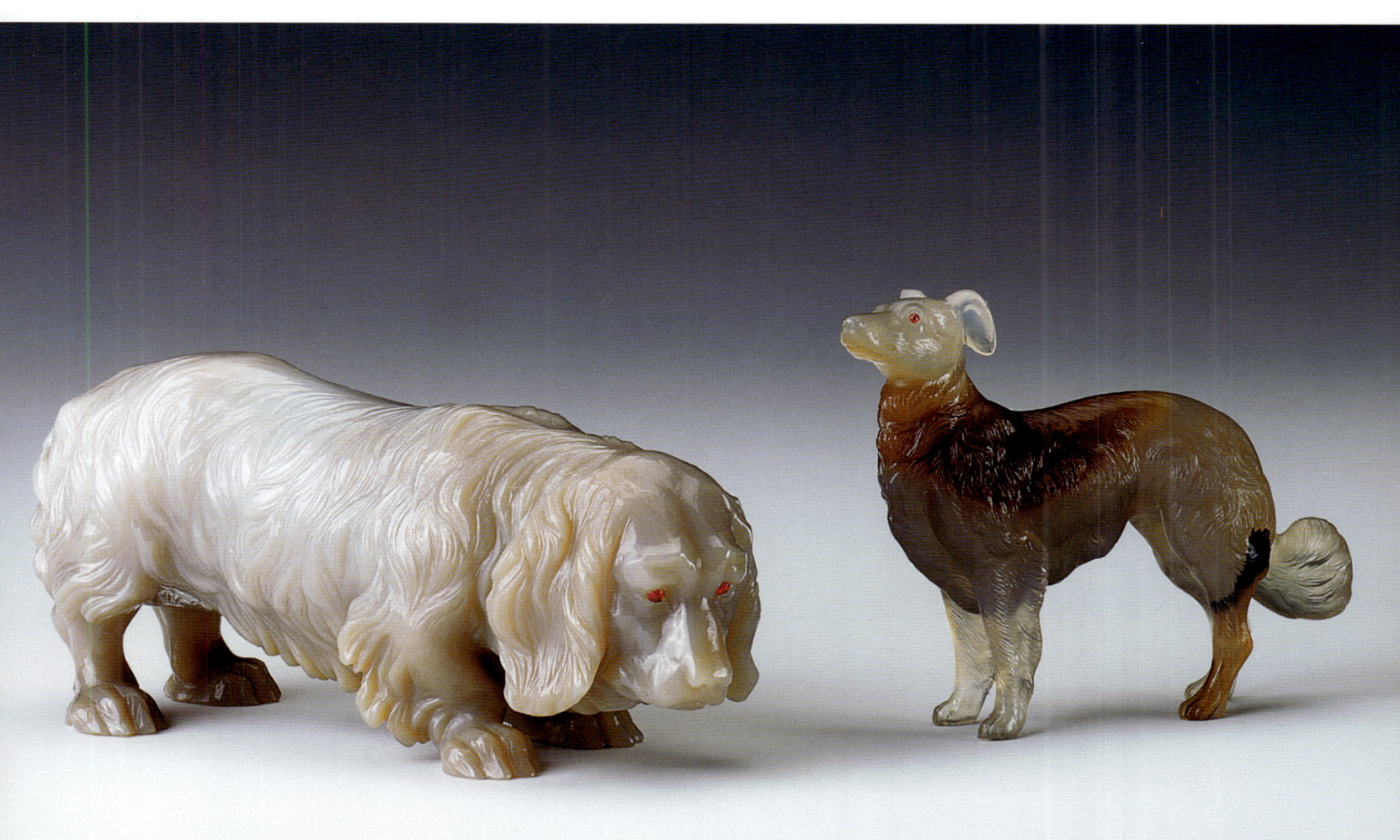

22 SOW, *c*.1907

The recumbent pose of this sow was acutely observed from life by one of the team of sculptors working at Sandringham. The carving formed part of Princess Victoria's collection and is possibly the one she herself purchased from the London branch in 1912, although the relatively small cost for an animal of this scale (£14 10s) may indicate the purchase of a different pig. Unfortunately the description in the ledger is not sufficiently detailed. This sow was exhibited at the exhibition of Russian art in Belgrave Square, London in 1935.

Aventurine quartz, rose diamonds, 7.2 x 14.7 x 7.5 cm (2^{13}/$_{16}$ x 5^{13}/$_{16}$ x 2^{15}/$_{16}$")
Unmarked
RCIN 40041
PROVENANCE: Commissioned by King Edward VII, 1907; Princess Victoria; possibly the pig bought by Princess Victoria from Fabergé's London branch, 25 November 1912 (£14 10s)
REFERENCES: Bainbridge 1949, pl. 96
EXHIBITIONS: London 1935; London 1977, no. A35; QG 1995–6, no. 72

23 SOW, *c*.1907

Modelled from life at Sandringham as part of King Edward VII's commission. In total twenty-two pigs were produced and remain in the collection today, of which three are included here. However, the London sales ledgers mention only eight purchased by members of the royal family between 1907 and 1916. The others are therefore presumed to have been gifts.

Aventurine quartz, rose diamonds, 3.9 x 7 x 3.1 cm (1^9/$_{16}$ x 2^3/$_4$ x 1^1/$_4$")
RCIN 40003
PROVENANCE: Commissioned by King Edward VII, 1907
EXHIBITIONS: London 1977, no. A40; QG 1995–6, no. 71

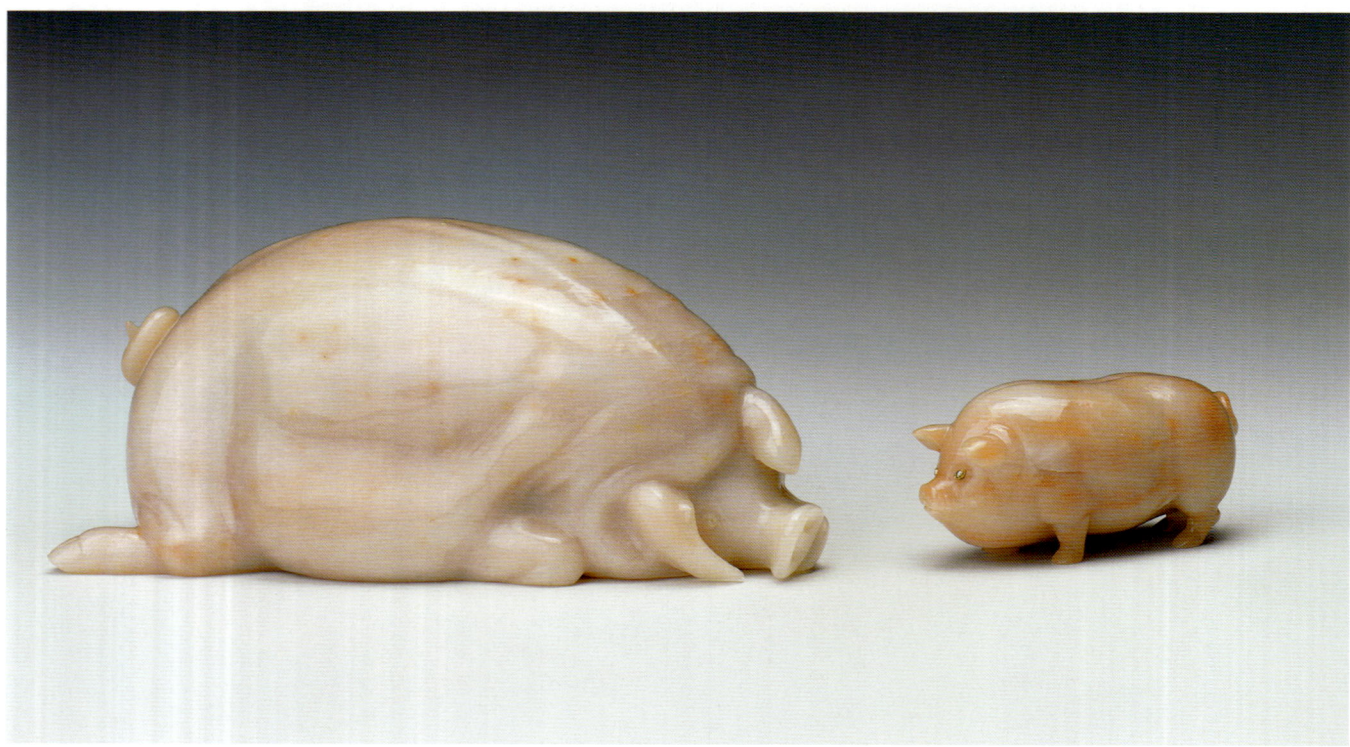

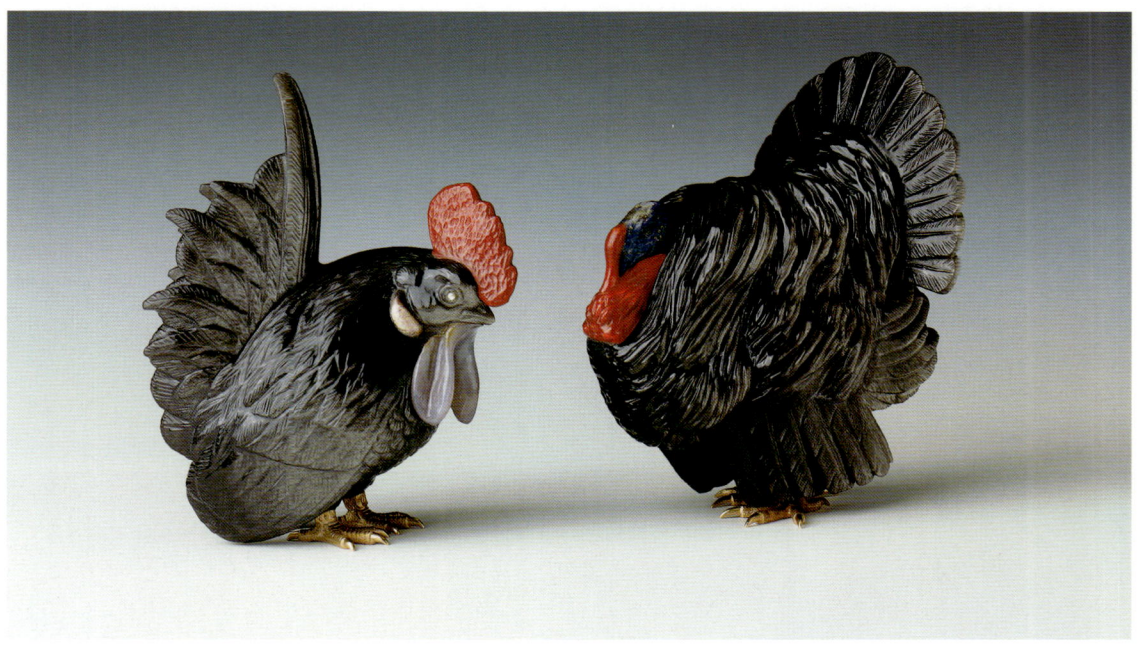

24 COCKEREL, *c.*1908

This magnificent cockerel, on a larger than usual scale, is one of nine modelled from life at Sandringham. Like most of the birds fitted with gold feet, it was made in Henrik Wigström's workshop. A plate from the album of designs produced in Wigström's workshop shows a drawing of a cockerel on a similar scale to this one, although it was apparently executed in different hardstones (see p. 52). It is assumed that this cockerel was the one purchased by Queen Alexandra from Fabergé's London branch in 1909. The price of £113 10s is one of the highest paid for an animal forming part of the King's commission.

Obsidian, purpurine, jasper, rose diamonds, gold, 9.9 x 7.8 x 4.7 cm (3⁷/₈ x 3¹/₁₆ x 1⁷/₈")
Mark of Henrik Wigström; gold mark of 72 *zolotniks* (1908–17)
RCIN 40454
PROVENANCE: Commissioned by King Edward VII, 1907; bought by Queen Alexandra from Fabergé's London branch, 1909 (£113 10s)
REFERENCES: Bainbridge 1949, pl. 95; Tillander-Godenhielm *et al.*, 2000, p. 159
EXHIBITIONS: London 1953, no. 3; London 1977, no. D34; QG 1995–6, no. 67

25 TURKEY, *c.*1908

Part of the Sandringham commission and modelled from life, this is a breed of turkey known as a Norfolk Black and found only in East Anglia. A second turkey of identical design and proportion was made at the same time, but was apparently not purchased by the royal family (see p. 24).

Obsidian, lapis lazuli, purpurine, rose diamonds, gold, 9.7 x 8.5 x 7.3 cm (3¹³/₁₆ x 3³/₈ x 2⁷/₈")
Mark of Henrik Wigström; gold mark of 72 *zolotniks* (1908–17)
RCIN 40446
PROVENANCE: Commissioned by King Edward VII, 1907, bought by the Prince of Wales (later King George V) from Fabergé's London branch, 1909 (£55)
REFERENCES: Bainbridge 1949, pl. 95; Snowman 1962, pl. 273
EXHIBITIONS: London 1953, no. 7; London 1977, no. D21; New York 1983, no.122; QG 1985–6, no. 262; QG 1995–6, no. 66; QG 2002–3, no. 214

26 IRON DUKE, *c.* 1907

One of several portrait models of the horses kept at Sandringham, including Field Marshal (cat. 27) and Persimmon (cat. 18), modelled as part of King Edward VII's commission. Iron Duke was the King's shooting pony.

Aventurine quartz, cabochon sapphires, nephrite, silver-gilt, 10.5 x 13.8 x 5.4 cm (4^1/$_8$ x 5^7/$_{16}$ x 2^1/$_8$")
Engraved on plaque *IRON DUKE*
RCIN 40411
PROVENANCE: Commissioned by King Edward VII, 1907; bought by Queen Alexandra from Fabergé's London branch, December 1909 (£70)
EXHIBITIONS: QG 1995–6, no. 366

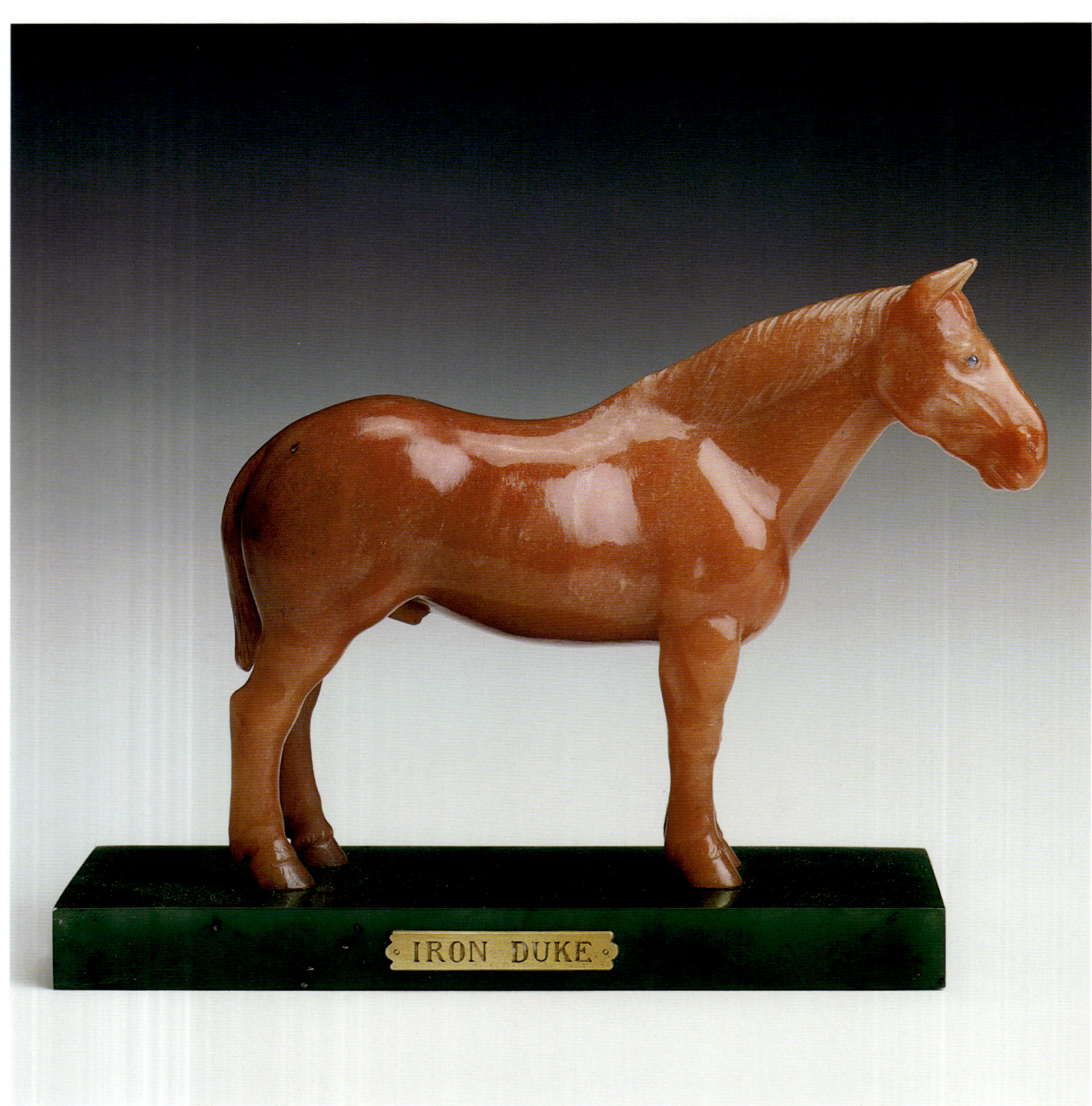

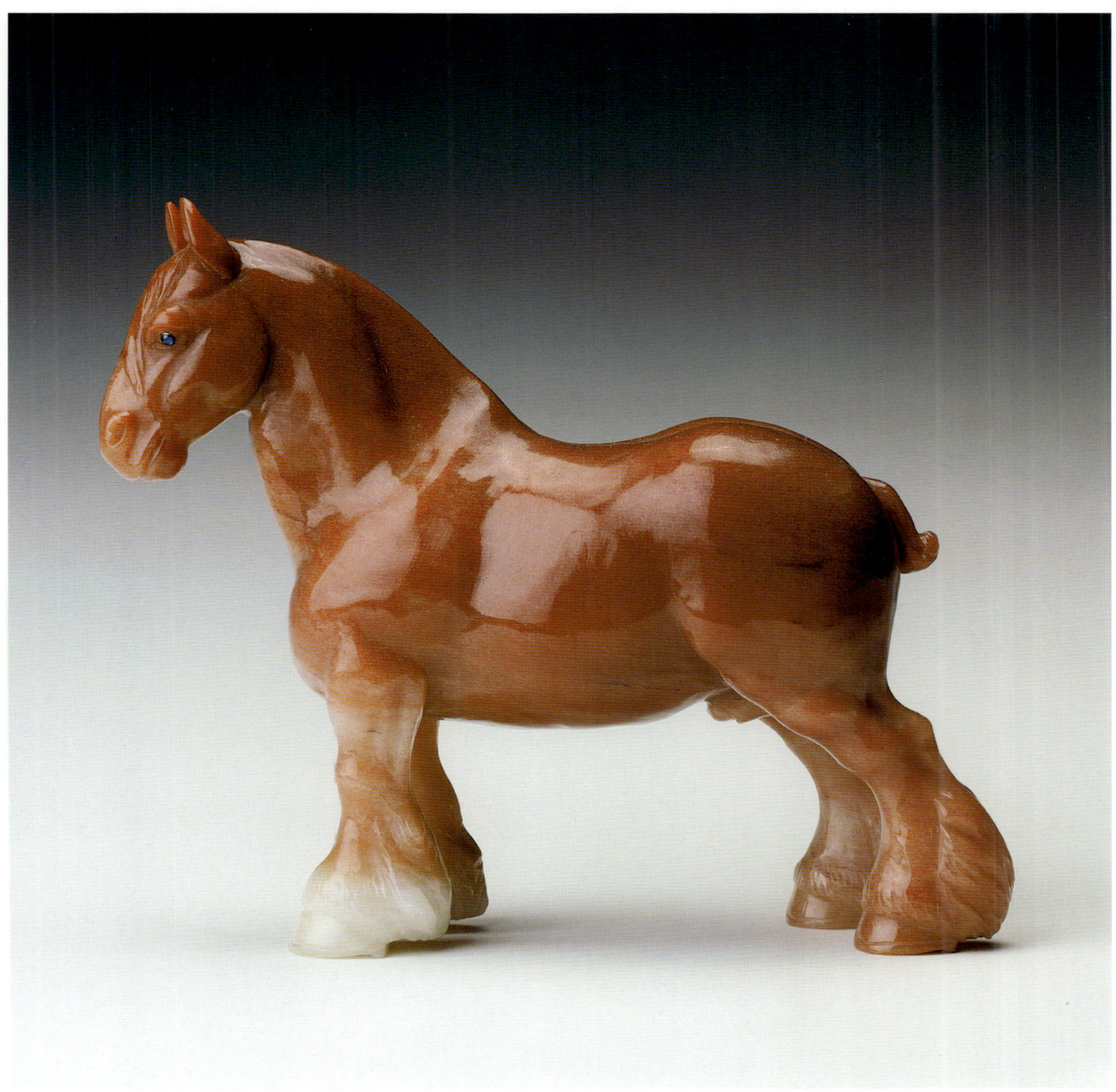

27 FIELD MARSHAL, *c.*1907

One of at least three Shire horses modelled as part of the Sandringham commission. Thought to be a portrait model of the champion Field Marshal, it could represent another Shire stallion named Hoe Forest King, a model of which was purchased from Fabergé's London branch in 1909 (see p. 24).

Aventurine quartz, cabochon sapphires, 14.5 x 17 x 5.7 cm (5¹¹/₁₆ x 6¹¹/₁₆ x 2¹/₄")
Unmarked
RCIN 40412
PROVENANCE: Commissioned by King Edward VII, 1907; given to Queen Alexandra for her birthday, 1 December 1908
EXHIBITIONS: London 1953, no. 35; London 1977, no. B14; New York 1983, no. 73; QG 1985–6, no. 256; St Petersburg/Paris/London 1993–4, no. 87; QG 1995–6, no. 367

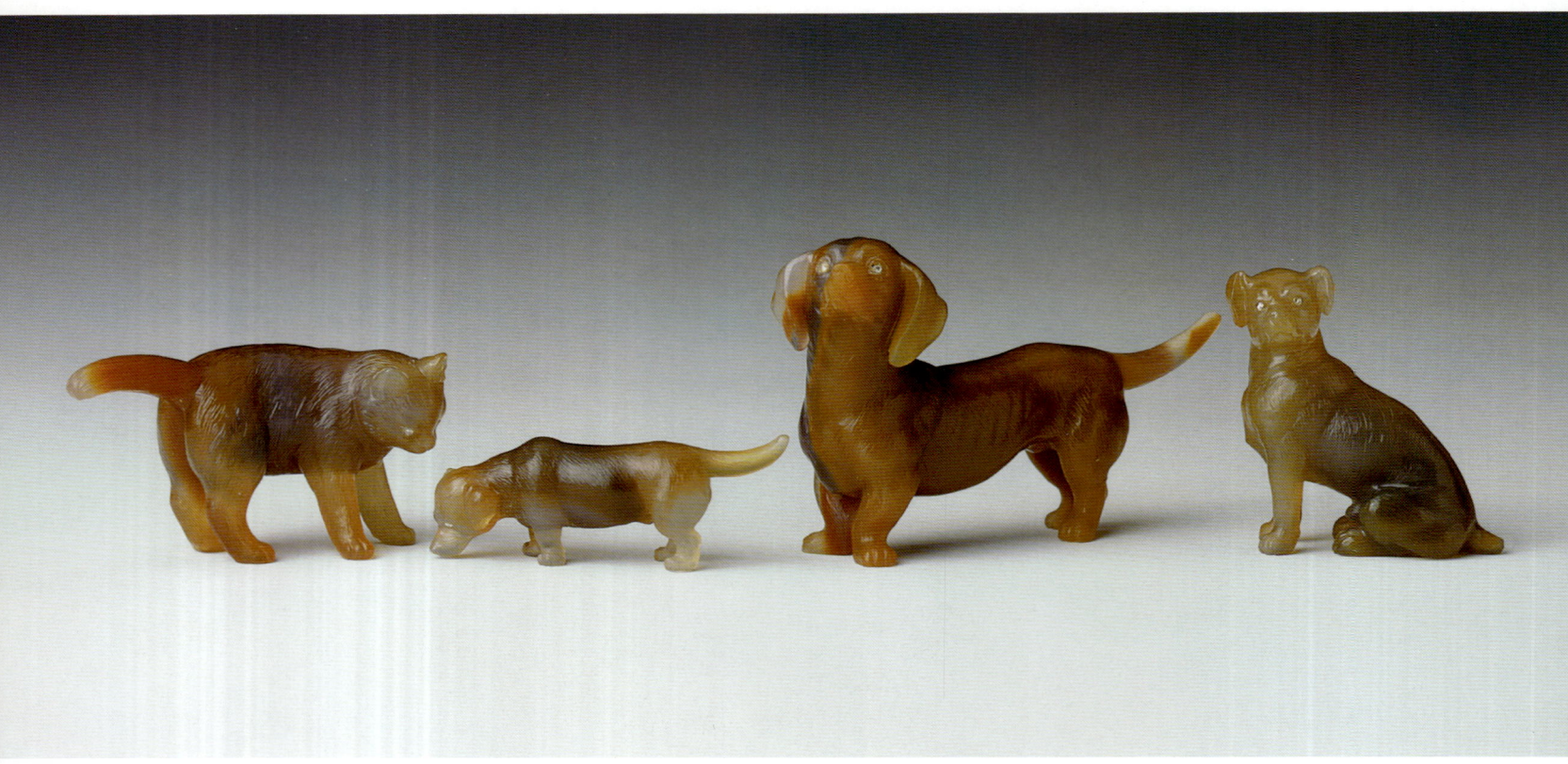

28   KITTEN, *c.*1907

There are three cats and kittens by Fabergé in the Royal Collection and it is certain that his sculptors, while employed on the estate at Sandringham, would have seen many such animals.

Agate, rose diamonds, 2.7 x 5 x 2.3 cm (1^{1}/$_{16}$ x 1^{15}/$_{16}$ x ^{7}/$_{8}$")
Unmarked
RCIN 40037
PROVENANCE: Commissioned by King Edward VII, 1907
EXHIBITIONS: London 1977, no. A13; QG 1995–6, no. 322

29   DACHSHUND PUPPY, *c.*1907

Dachshunds were among the dogs kept at Sandringham. Grand Duke Michael of Russia (1878–1918), brother of Nicholas II, purchased a Fabergé dachshund from the London branch in November 1908, but it is not now possible to establish whether it was this model or a second one also in the Royal Collection (cat. 30).

Agate, rose diamonds, 1.8 x 4.3 x 1 cm (^{11}/$_{16}$ x 1^{11}/$_{16}$ x ^{3}/$_{8}$")
Unmarked
RCIN 40059
PROVENANCE: Probably commissioned by King Edward VII, 1907; possibly the dachshund bought by Grand Duke Michael from Fabergé's London branch, November 1908 (£14 10s)
EXHIBITIONS: London 1977, no. A29; QG 1995–6, no. 356

30 DACHSHUND, c.1907

Agate, rose diamonds, 4.3 x 7.3 x 2.1 cm (1^{11}/$_{16}$ x 2^7/$_8$ x ^{13}/$_{16}$")
Unmarked
RCIN 40392
PROVENANCE: Commissioned by King Edward VII, 1907; either this or cat. 29 may have been bought by Grand Duke Michael from Fabergé's London branch, November 1908 (£14 10s).
EXHIBITIONS: London 1953, no. 27; London 1977, no. A25; QG 1995–6, no. 351

31 SEATED LABRADOR, c.1907

This dog is believed to be a Labrador, many of which were kept at Sandringham during the reign of King Edward VII.

Chalcedony, rose diamonds, 3.7 x 3.5 x 1.8 cm (1^7/$_{16}$ x 1^3/$_8$ x ^{11}/$_{16}$")
Unmarked
RCIN 40026
PROVENANCE: Commissioned by King Edward VII, 1907
EXHIBITIONS: London 1977, no. A30; QG 1995–6, no. 352

32 CROW, c.1907

This magnificent carving is on a much larger scale than the other animals which formed part of the Sandringham commission.

Kalgan jasper, obsidian, acquamarine, silver-gilt, 7.8 x 15.7 x 5.7 cm (3^1/$_{16}$ x 6^3/$_{16}$ x 2^1/$_4$")
Mark of Henrik Wigström; silver mark of 88 *zolotniks*, undated
RCIN 13756
PROVENANCE: Bought by Queen Alexandra from Fabergé's London branch, 25 November 1914 (£75)
EXHIBITIONS: QG 1995–6, no. 1

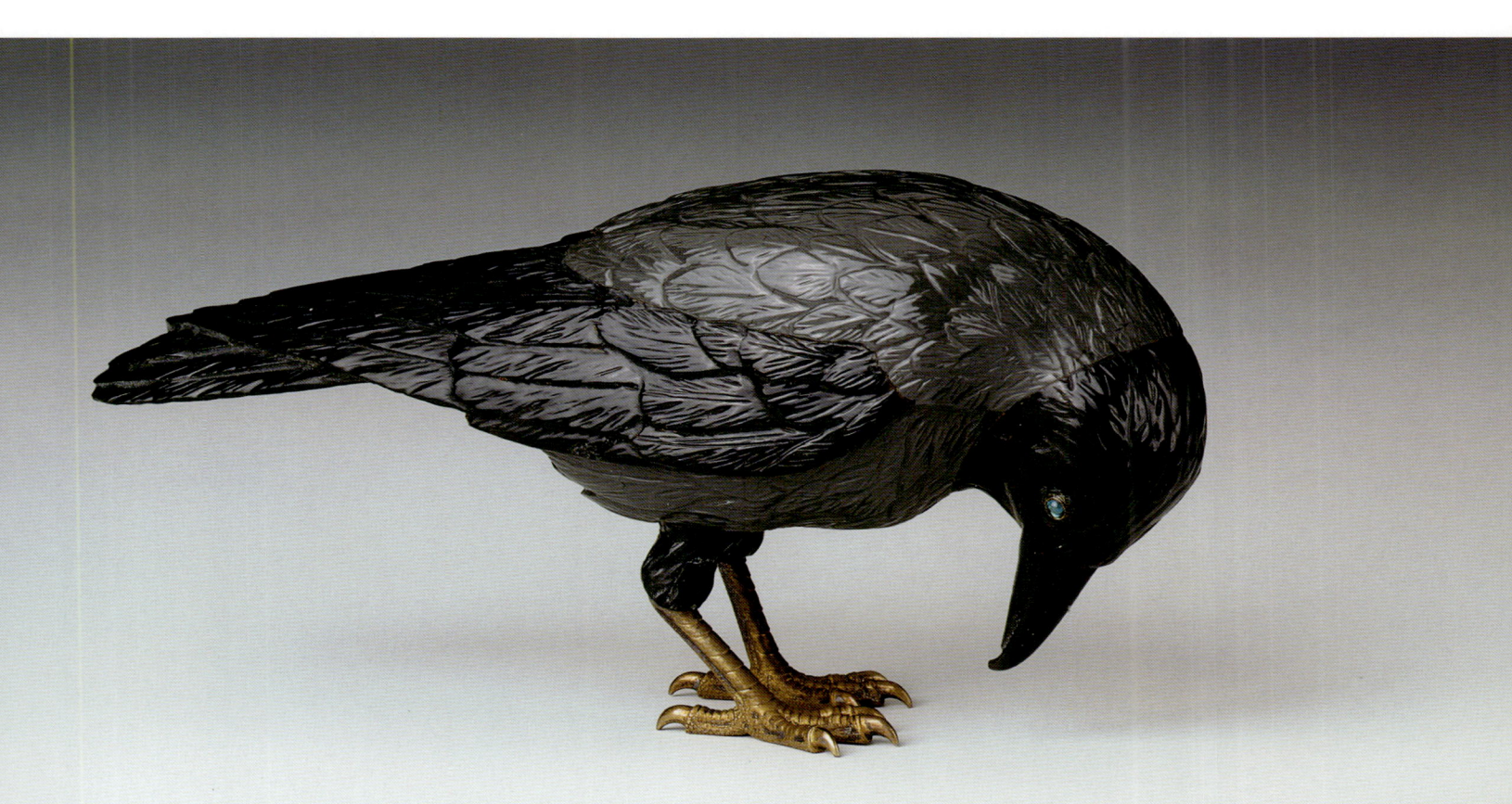

33 WEST HIGHLAND TERRIER, *c.*1907

The West Highland terrier is closely related to the Cairn terrier, examples of which were kept by King George V in the kennels at Sandringham.

Agate, rose diamonds, 4.5 x 6 x 1.8 cm (1³/₄ x 2³/₈ x ¹¹/₁₆")
Unmarked
RCIN 40047
PROVENANCE: Commissioned by King Edward VII, 1907; possibly the dog listed as a 'Welsh Terrier' bought by Queen Alexandra from Fabergé's London branch, November 1908 (£14 10s)
EXHIBITIONS: London 1977, no. A28; QG 1995–6, no. 353

34 GRIFFON, *c.*1907

The griffon is one of the more unusual breeds of dog represented in the Fabergé collection. It is possible that the griffon was among the many dogs to be found at Sandringham.

Agate, rose diamonds, 5 x 4.7 x 2 cm (1¹⁵/₁₆ x 1⁷/₈ x ¹³/₁₆")
Unmarked
RCIN 40046
PROVENANCE: Commissioned by King Edward VII, 1907
EXHIBITIONS: London 1977, no. A26; QG 1995–6, no. 350

35 SAMOYED, *c.*1907

Among the exotic breeds of dog kept at Sandringham by King Edward VII and his family were Siberian sledge dogs, schipperkes and Pomeranians. This dog, previously thought to be a Pomeranian, is now believed to be a portrait model of Jacko, a Samoyed presented to Queen Alexandra in 1899 by Major F.G. Jackson, leader of the Jackson–Harmsworth Expedition to Franz Josef Land (1895–8).

Chalcedony, rose diamonds, 4.6 x 5.2 x 1.5 cm (1¹³/₁₆ x 2¹/₁₆ x ⁹/₁₆")
Unmarked
RCIN 40067
PROVENANCE: Commissioned by King Edward VII, 1907
REFERENCES: Dutt 1904, p. 105
EXHIBITIONS: London 1977, no. A21; QG 1995–6, no. 323

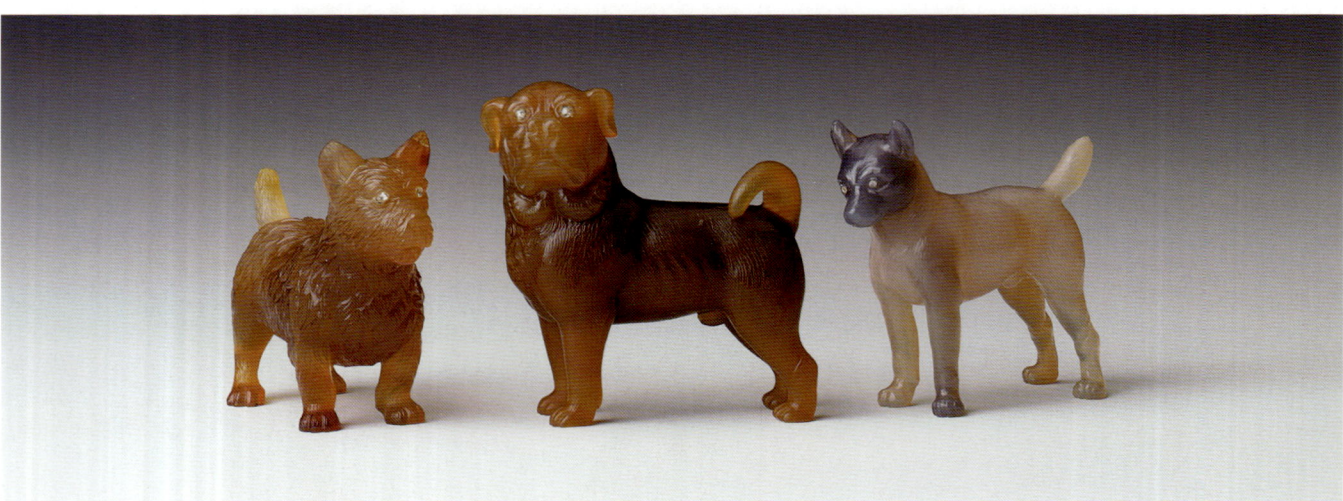

36 PEKINESE, *c.*1907

Queen Alexandra's love of Pekinese dogs is well documented and she owned many throughout her life. In April 1905 the Empress of Japan sent Queen Alexandra a gift of four pairs of Pekinese dogs. Unfortunately, during the long and arduous journey all but one of the dogs died. A further hardstone model of a Pekinese is included here (cat. 70) and there is also an example of a Pekinese in the style of Cartier's animal carvings (cat. 341).

Agate, rose diamonds, 3.6 x 4.4 x 1.9 cm (1⁷/₁₆ x 1³/₄ x ³/₄")
Unmarked
RCIN 40390
PROVENANCE: Probably acquired by Queen Alexandra
REFERENCES: RA VIC/Add A 21/228/3–12
EXHIBITIONS: London 1977, no. A18; QG 1995–6, no. 326

37 POODLE, *c.*1907

George, Prince of Wales, later King George V, had a favourite French poodle named Bobeche. As this is the only example of a poodle among the Fabergé animals in the collection, it may be a portrait model of his dog.

Agate, crystal, 6.5 x 7.8 x 2.7 cm (2⁹/₁₆ x 3¹/₁₆ x 1¹/₁₆")
Unmarked
RCIN 40389
PROVENANCE: Commissioned by King Edward VII, 1907
REFERENCES: Snowman 1962, pl. XLII
EXHIBITIONS: London 1953, no. 26; London 1977, no. A19; QG 1995–6, no. 327

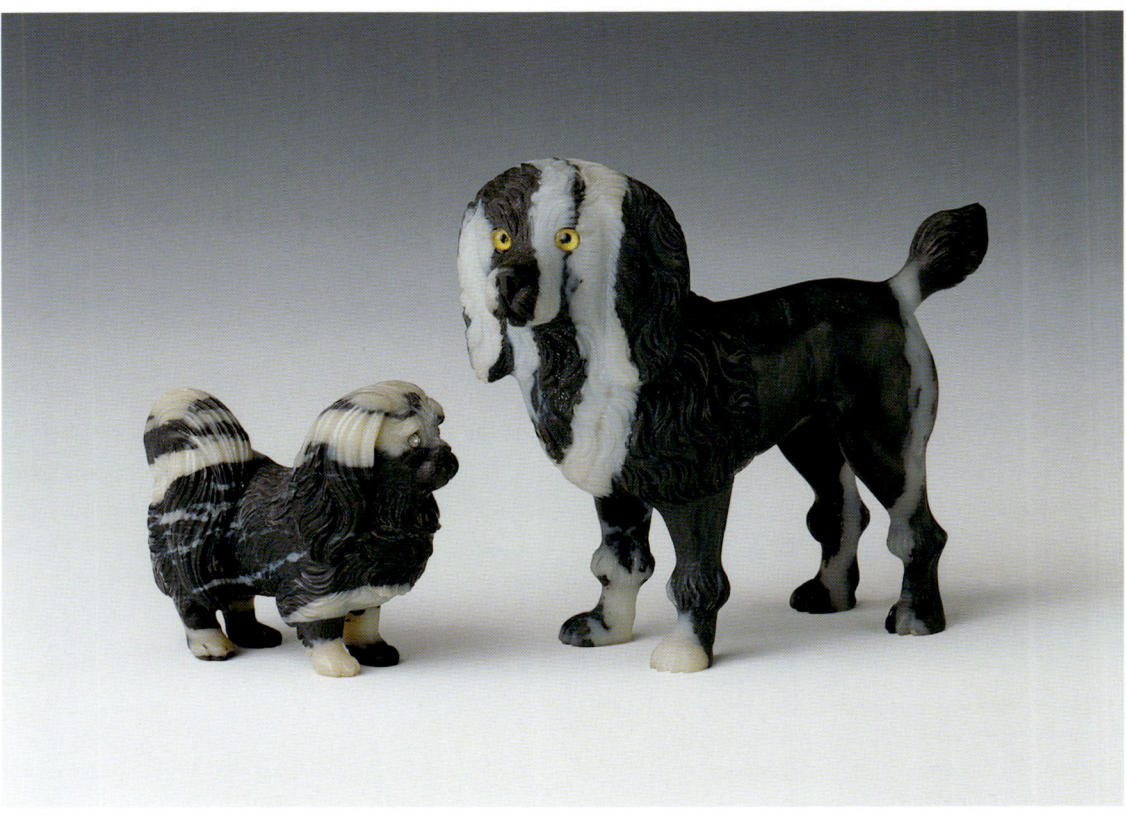

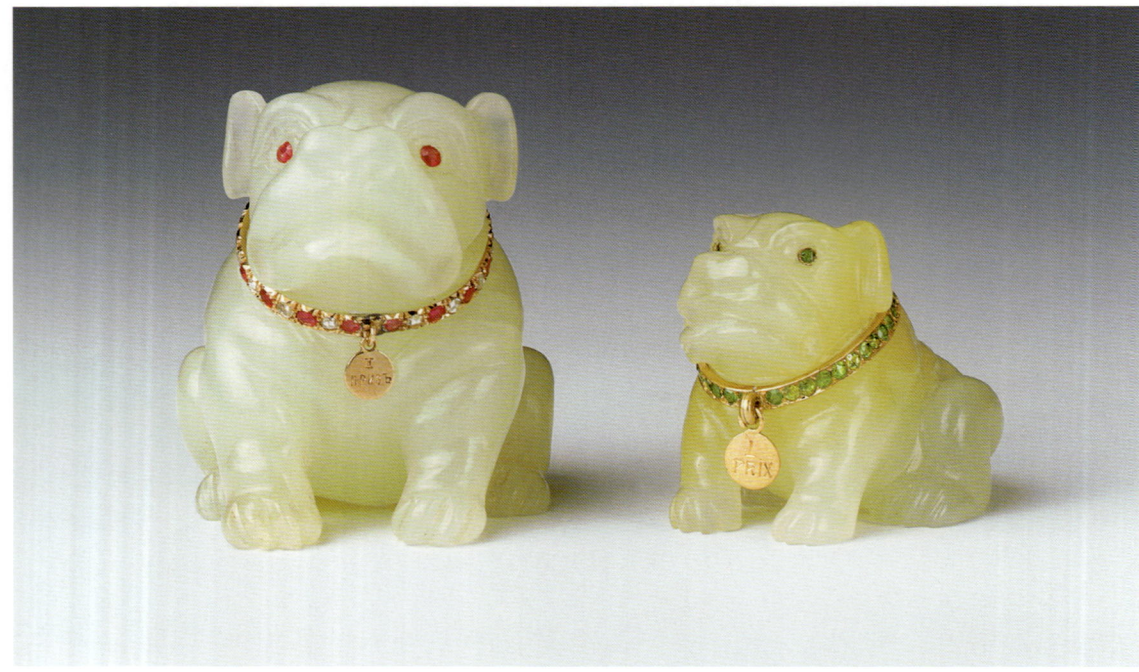

38 SEATED BULLDOG, *c.* 1900

Bowenite, rubies, diamonds, gold, 4.3 x 4.9 x 3.7 cm (1¹¹/₁₆ x 1¹⁵/₁₆ x 1⁷/₁₆")
Engraved on gold disc *1st Prize* in Cyrillic characters
RCIN 40431
PROVENANCE: Probably acquired by Queen Alexandra
EXHIBITIONS: London 1977, no. A23; QG 1995–6, no. 341

39 SEATED BULLDOG, *c.* 1900

Bowenite, emeralds, gold, 3 x 3.7 x 2.5 cm (1³/₁₆ x 1⁷/₁₆ x 1")
Engraved on gold disc *I PRIX*
RCIN 40052
PROVENANCE: Probably acquired by King Edward VII
EXHIBITIONS: QG 1995–6, no. 338

40 HEN, *c.* 1908

This portrait study from the Sandringham commission combines the talent of the sculptor in captur-
ing the inquisitive nature of the hen with the skill of the hardstone carver, both in selecting the
perfect stone and in carving and polishing it to simulate the sheen of the hen's feathers. Birbaum
notes that the Sandringham carvings were generally made from naturalistically coloured stones that
matched the colouring of the bird or animal.

Agate, rose diamonds, gold, 5.9 x 5.1 x 2.9 cm (2⁵/₁₆ x 2 x 1¹/₈")
Unmarked
RCIN 40450
PROVENANCE: Commissioned by King Edward VII, 1907
REFERENCES: Habsburg & Lopato 1993, p. 457
EXHIBITIONS: London 1977, no. D35; New York 1983, no. 118; QG 1985–6, no. 268; London 1992; QG 1995–6,
no. 76; QG 2002–3, no. 216

41 DUCKLING FLAPPING ITS WINGS, *c.*1908

Aventurine quartz, rose diamonds, gold, 6 x 4.4 x 5 cm (2³/₈ x 1³/₄ x 1¹⁵/₁₆")
Mark of Henrik Wigström; gold mark of 72 *zolotniks* (1908–17)
RCIN 40419
PROVENANCE: Commissioned by King Edward VII, 1907
EXHIBITIONS: London 1977, no. D27; QG 1995–6, no. 92

42 GOOSE, 1911

The design for this goose, exactly as executed – with the date 1911 – appears in the album from the workshop of Henrik Wigström (see illustration on p. 52). A similar model of a goose from the Sandringham commission, made by Wigström's workshop, is also exhibited (cat. 65).

Quartzite, obsidian, rose diamonds, gold, 3 x 7 x 2.3 cm (1³/₁₆ x 2³/₄ x ⁷/₈")
Mark of Henrik Wigström; gold mark of 72 *zolotniks* (1908–17)
RCIN 40323
PROVENANCE: Commissioned by King Edward VII, 1907
REFERENCES: Tillander-Godenhielm *et al.* 2000, p. 78
EXHIBITIONS: London 1953, no. 93; London 1977, no. D7; New York 1983, no. 120; QG 1985–6 no. 272;
QG 1995–6, no. 116; QG 2002–3, no. 219

43 DUCKLING, *c.*1907

Aventurine quartz, cabochon sapphires, gold, 4.8 x 5.3 x 2.8 cm (1⁷/₈ x 2¹/₁₆ x 1¹/₈")
Mark of Henrik Wigström; gold mark of 72 *zolotniks* (1908–17)
RCIN 40468
PROVENANCE: Commissioned by King Edward VII, 1907
EXHIBITIONS: London 1977, no. D26; QG 1995–6, no. 94

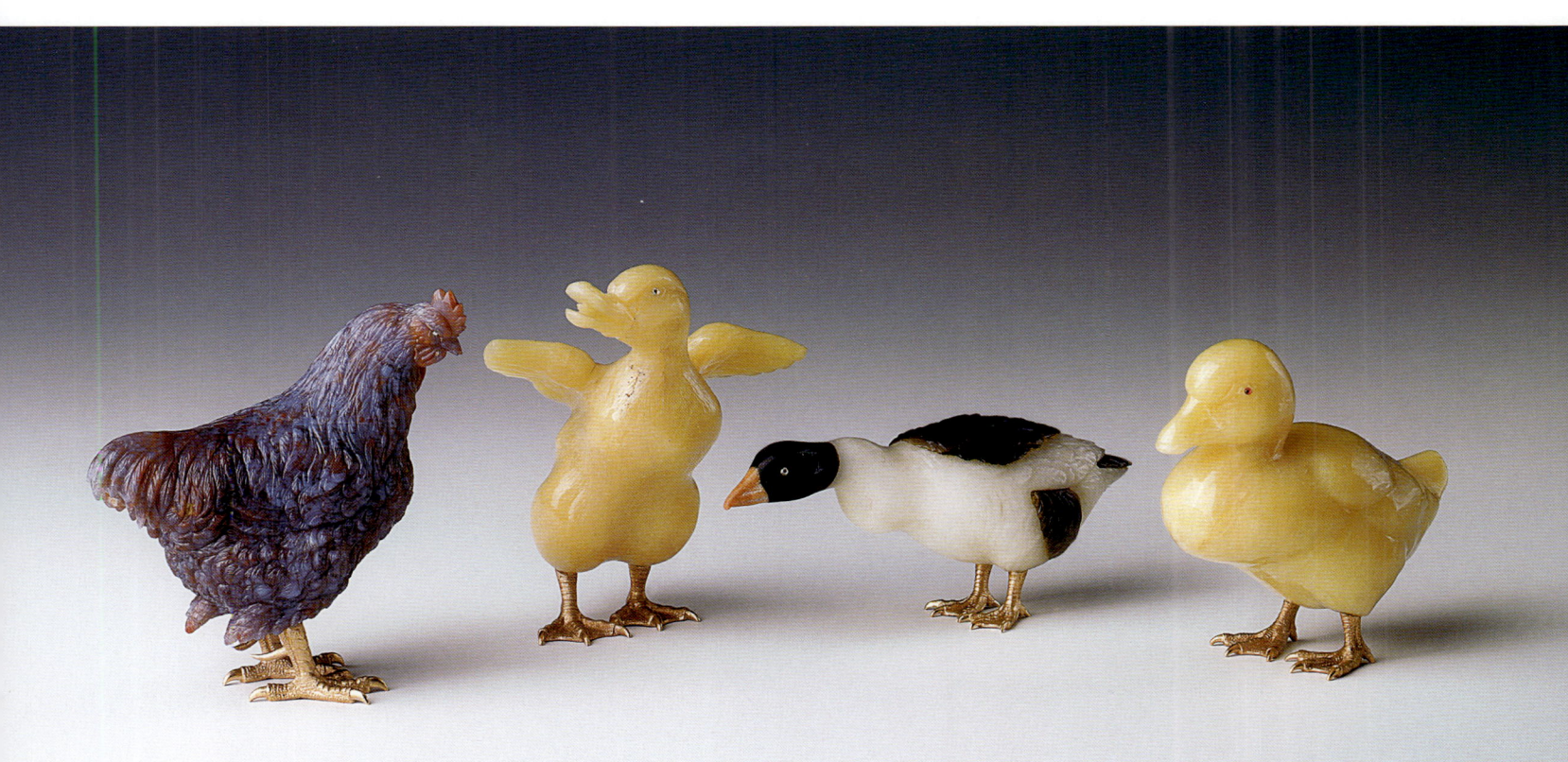

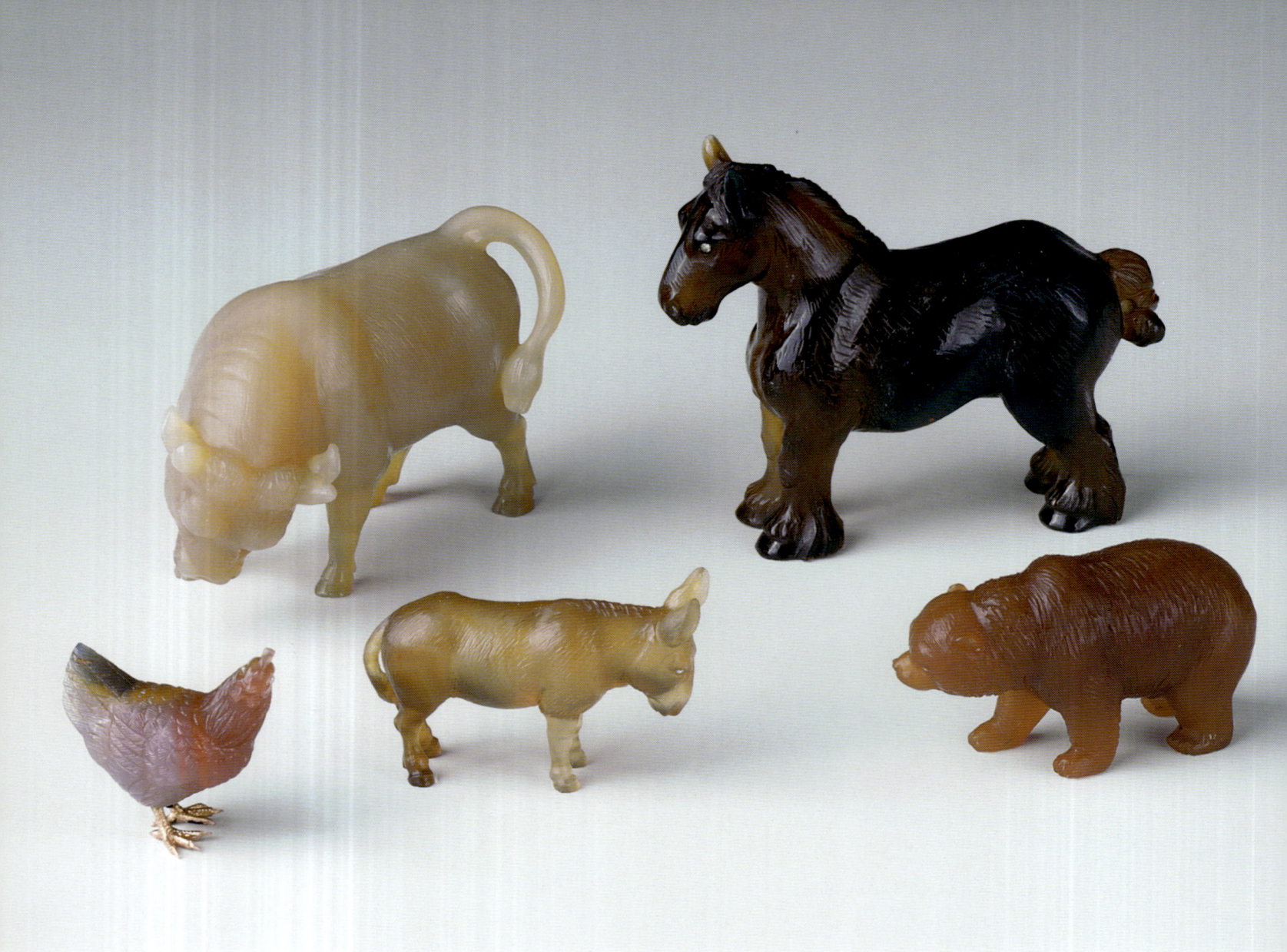

44   BULL, *c.*1907

One of three bulls and cows modelled from life as part of the Sandringham commission.

Chalcedony, cabochon rubies, 3.8 x 6.2 x 3.1 cm (1½ x 2⁷⁄₁₆ x 1¼")
Unmarked
RCIN 40043
PROVENANCE: Commissioned by King Edward VII, 1907
EXHIBITIONS: London 1977, no. B18; QG 1995–6, no. 294

45   SHIRE HORSE, *c.*1907

One of two Shire horses forming part of the Sandringham commission which are on a smaller scale than Field Marshal (cat. 27).

Agate, rose diamonds, 5.5 x 6 x 2.5 cm (2³⁄₁₆ x 2⅜ x 1")
Unmarked
RCIN 40441
PROVENANCE: Commissioned by King Edward VII, 1907
EXHIBITIONS: QG 1995–6, no. 298

46 BROWN BEAR, *c.*1907

Although the majority of the animals forming the Sandringham commission are either of a domestic or farmyard origin, it is possible that it might have included bears. It appears that bears were kept on the Norfolk estate as late as the 1880s. Mrs Herbert Jones described how 'two big bears in a pit, indifferent to spectators, calmly climb their accustomed pole'. According to Helen Cathcart, the bear pit was adjacent to York Cottage. It contained two bears called Charlie and Polly who 'were dreaded by their keeper when he had to wash them every day'. They were eventually sent to London Zoo by the Prince of Wales (later King George V).

Agate, rose diamonds, 2.5 x 3.9 x 1.7 cm (1 x 1⁹/₁₆ x ¹¹/₁₆")
Chiselled on one paw *C* and on the other *F*, the initials of Carl Fabergé
RCIN 40301
PROVENANCE: Commissioned by King Edward VII, 1907
REFERENCES: Jones 1883; Cathcart 1964, p. 139
EXHIBITIONS: London 1977, no. C31; QG 1995–6, no. 441

47 DONKEY, *c.*1907

One of a group of animal carvings on a miniature scale, of which there are several in the Royal Collection. Even with these proportions, the quality of the carving, choice of naturalistically coloured stone and attention to the characteristics of the animal were paramount for Fabergé's sculptors and stonecarvers. According to contemporary accounts, an Italian donkey kept at Sandringham around 1900 was driven in a carriage by the young princes and princesses.

Chalcedony, rose diamonds, 2.6 x 3.3 x 1.2 cm (1 x 1⁵/₁₆ x ½")
Unmarked
RCIN 40033
PROVENANCE: Commissioned by King Edward VII, 1907; possibly the donkey bought by King George V from Fabergé's London branch, 7 November 1910 (£11 15s)
REFERENCES: Dutt 1904, p. 102
EXHIBITIONS: London 1953, no. 16; London 1977, no. B23; QG 1995–6, no. 299

48 HEN, *c.*1907

There are five hens, nine cockerels and six chicks by Fabergé in the Royal Collection.

Agate, rose diamonds, gold, 2.3 x 2.2 x 1 cm (⁷/₈ x ⁷/₈ x ³/₈")
Unmarked
RCIN 40132
PROVENANCE: Commissioned by King Edward VII, 1907
EXHIBITIONS: London 1977, no. D15; QG 1995–6, no. 108

49 FOUR PIGLETS, *c.*1896–1903

Although the carver has not marked the stone, this piece bears the maker's mark of Michael Perchin on a gold support underneath. Many of the animal carvings in the Royal Collection were made during Wigström's period in charge of the workshops, but this group is one of an apparently small number made in the workshop of Michael Perchin, Fabergé's head workmaster between 1886 and 1903. It cannot, therefore, have formed part of King Edward VII's 1907 commission. Another similar group of piglets is known, carved in a different stone but by the same workmaster.

Chalcedony, gold, 0.9 x 5.2 x 3.8 cm ($^3/_8$ x $2^1/_{16}$ x $1^1/_2$")
Mark of Michael Perchin; gold mark of 56 *zolotniks* (1896–1908)
RCIN 40038
PROVENANCE: Probably acquired by Queen Alexandra; Royal Collection by 1953
EXHIBITIONS: London 1953, no. 110; London 1977, no. A36; New York 1983, no. 131; QG 1985–6, no. 292; London 1992; QG 1995–6, no. 84; QG 2002–3, no. 218

50 PIG, *c.*1907

Modelled from life at Sandringham.

Agate, rose diamonds, 2.1 x 4.4 x 1.6 cm ($^{13}/_{16}$ x $1^3/_4$ x $^5/_8$")
Unmarked
RCIN 40011
PROVENANCE: Commissioned by King Edward VII, 1907
EXHIBITIONS: London 1977, no. A41; QG 1995–6, no. 80

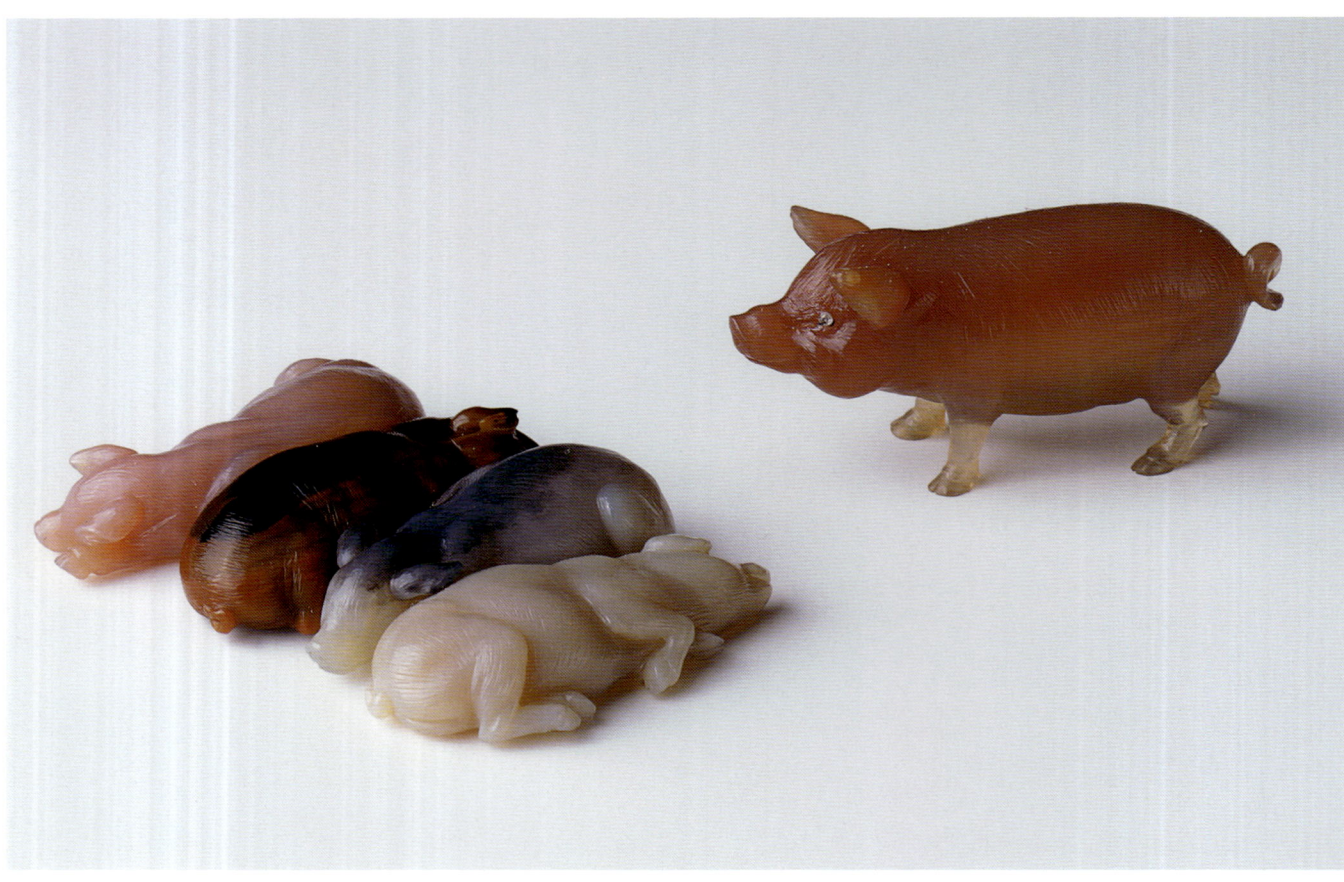

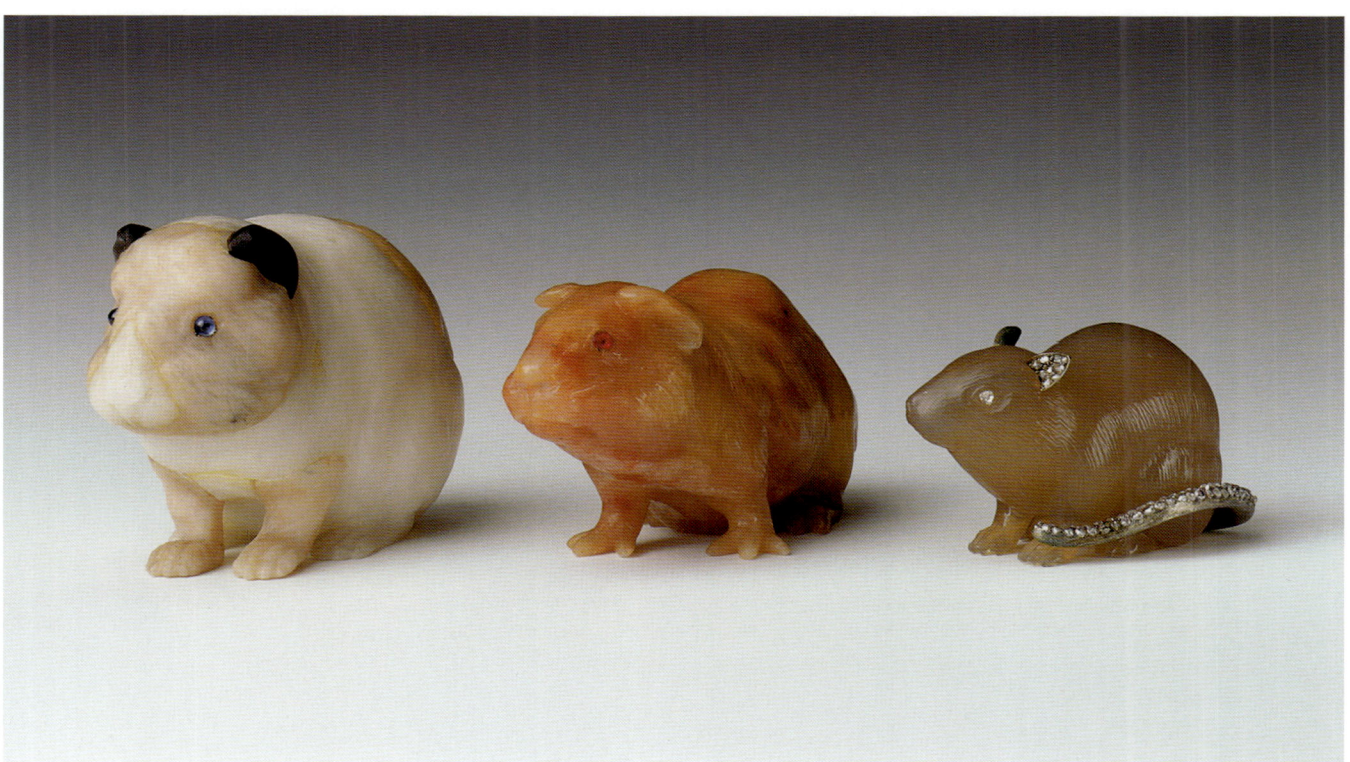

51 GUINEA PIG, *c.*1900

This is one of two guinea pigs in the Royal Collection, both included here.

Quartzite, aventurine quartz, obsidian, cabochon sapphires, 3.6 x 5.6 x 3.1 cm (1⁷/₁₆ x 2³/₁₆ x 1¹/₄")
Unmarked
RCIN 40449
PROVENANCE: Probably acquired by Queen Alexandra; Royal Collection by 1953
EXHIBITIONS: London 1953, no. 79; London 1977, no. B27; QG 1995–6, no. 317

52 GUINEA PIG, *c.*1907

Agate, cabochon rubies, 3.2 x 6.2 x 2.8 cm (1¹/₄ x 2⁷/₁₆ x 1¹/₈")
Unmarked
RCIN 40396
PROVENANCE: Probably acquired by Queen Alexandra; Royal Collection by 1953
EXHIBITIONS: London 1977, no. B24; QG 1995–6, no. 318

53 MOUSE, *c.*1907

Chalcedony, rose diamonds, silver, 2.5 x 3.8 x 2.2 cm (1 x 1¹/₂ x ⁷/₈")
Unmarked
RCIN 40045
PROVENANCE: Bought by the Duchess of Westminster from Fabergé's London branch, 11 November 1907 (£25 5s); presumably given to King Edward VII or Queen Alexandra
EXHIBITIONS: London 1977, no. B26; QG 1995–6, no. 453

54 DORMOUSE, *c.*1910

Chalcedony, platinum, gold, sapphires, 6.2 x 5.2 x 5.8 cm (2⁷/₁₆ x 2¹/₁₆ x 2⁵/₁₆")
Unmarked
RCIN 40261
PROVENANCE: Bought by Queen Alexandra from Fabergé's London branch, 5 November 1912 (£33)
REFERENCES: Snowman 1962, pl. XLII
EXHIBITIONS: London 1953, no. 92; London 1977, no. B25; New York 1983, no. 168; QG 1985–6, no. 263;
St Petersburg/Paris/London 1993–4, no. 88; QG 1995–6, no. 315; QG 2002–3, no. 220

55 SNAIL, *c.*1910

Occasionally different stones were combined by the carvers to give the most realistic effect, a technique described by Birbaum as 'mosaic sculpture' (see also cat. 51). Here the carving and polishing of
the hardstones immediately evokes both the shiny hard surface of the snail's shell and the soft flesh of
its body. This snail is one of the group of animals that formed part of Princess Victoria's collection
and that she lent to the 1935 exhibition in Belgrave Square.

Chalcedony, jasper, 4.5 x 10 x 3.7 cm (1³/₄ x 3¹⁵/₁₆ x 1⁷/₁₆")
Unmarked
RCIN 40254
PROVENANCE: Probably commissioned by King Edward VII, 1907; Princess Victoria
REFERENCES: Habsburg & Lopato 1993, p. 457
EXHIBITIONS: London 1935; London 1953, no. 98; London 1977, no. B8; New York 1983, no. 155; QG 1985–6,
no. 259; QG 1995–6, no. 8; QG 2002–3, no. 221

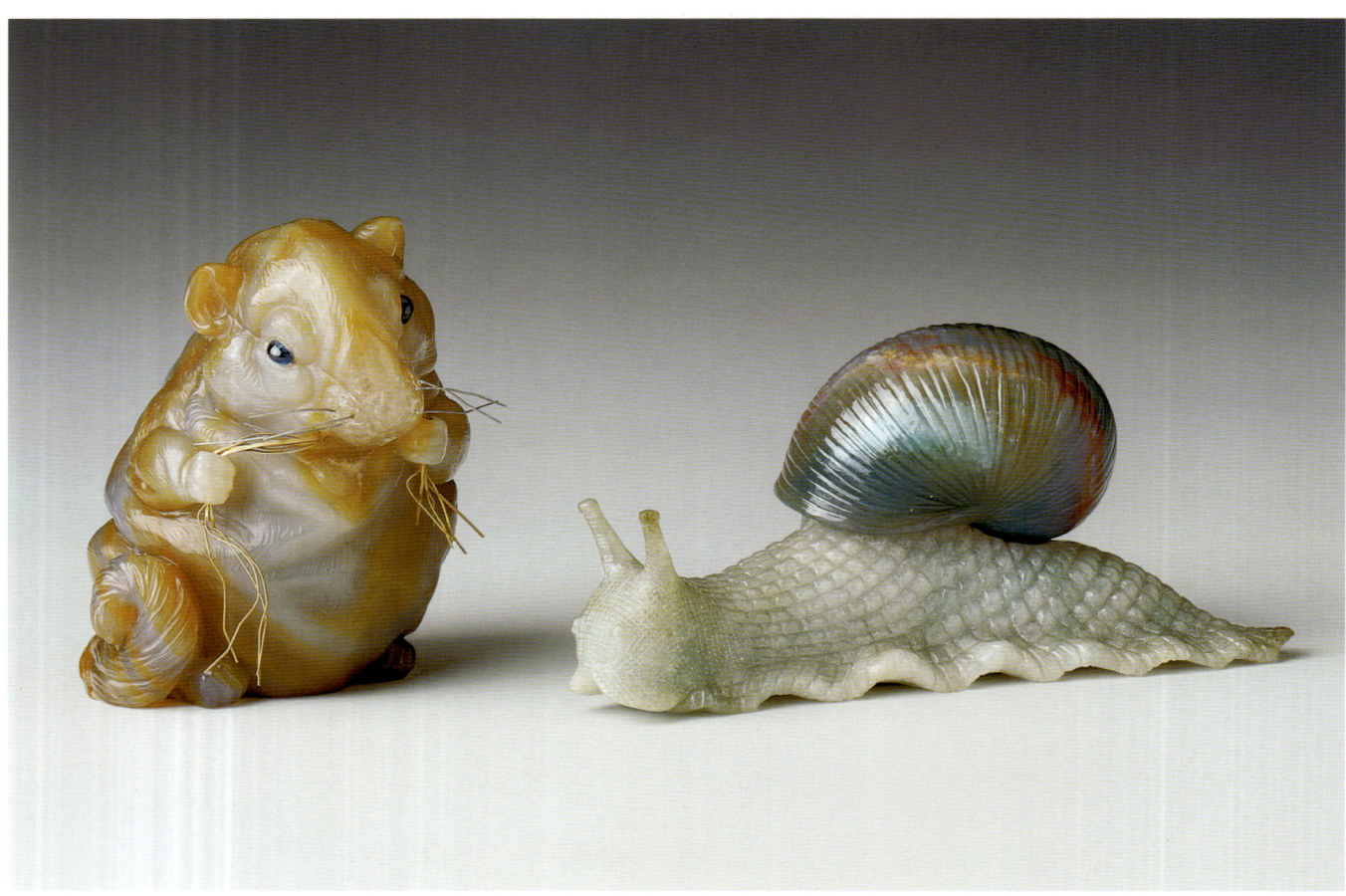

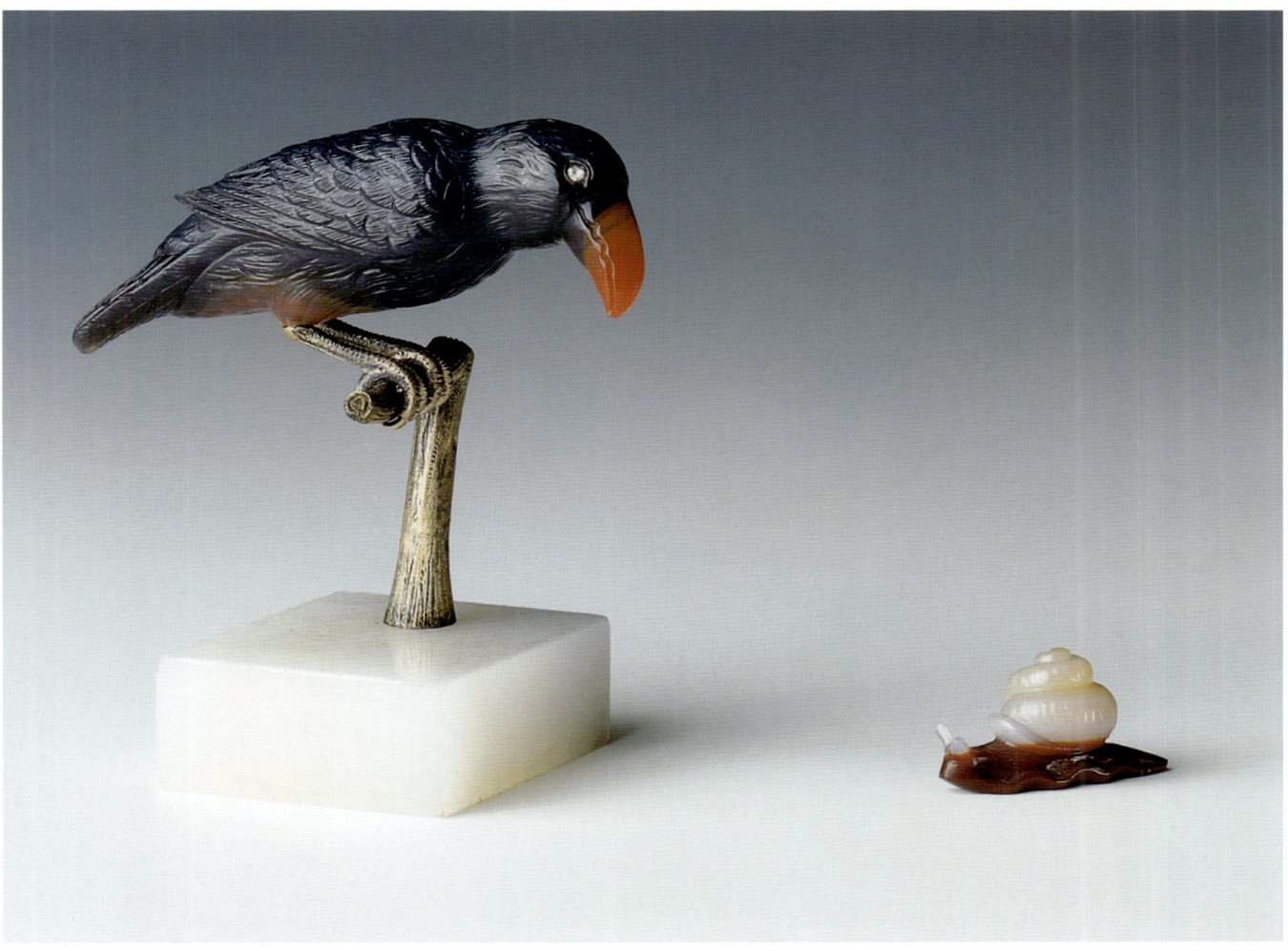

56 RAVEN, *c.*1900

In total there are seven Fabergé birds on perches or in cages in the Royal Collection.

Agate, rose diamonds, gold, onyx, 5 x 4.3 x 3 cm (1¹⁵/₁₆ x 1¹¹/₁₆ x 1³/₁₆")
Unmarked
RCIN 40284
PROVENANCE: Probably acquired by Queen Alexandra; Royal Collection by 1953
EXHIBITIONS: London 1977, no. D59; QG 1995–6, no. 444

57 SNAIL, *c.*1907

One of the group of miniature carvings, this snail is unusual because it has been carved in the manner of a cameo, with the different strata of the stone used to define the tips of the snail's tentacles and distinguish its shell from its body.

Agate, 1.9 x 2 x 0.9 cm (³/₄ x ¹³/₁₆ x ³/₈")
Unmarked
RCIN 40089
PROVENANCE: Probably commissioned by King Edward VII, 1907; bought by the Prince of Wales (later King George V) from Fabergé's London branch, December 1909 (£3 10s)
EXHIBITIONS: London 1953, no. 73; London 1977, no. B10; QG 1995–6, no. 2

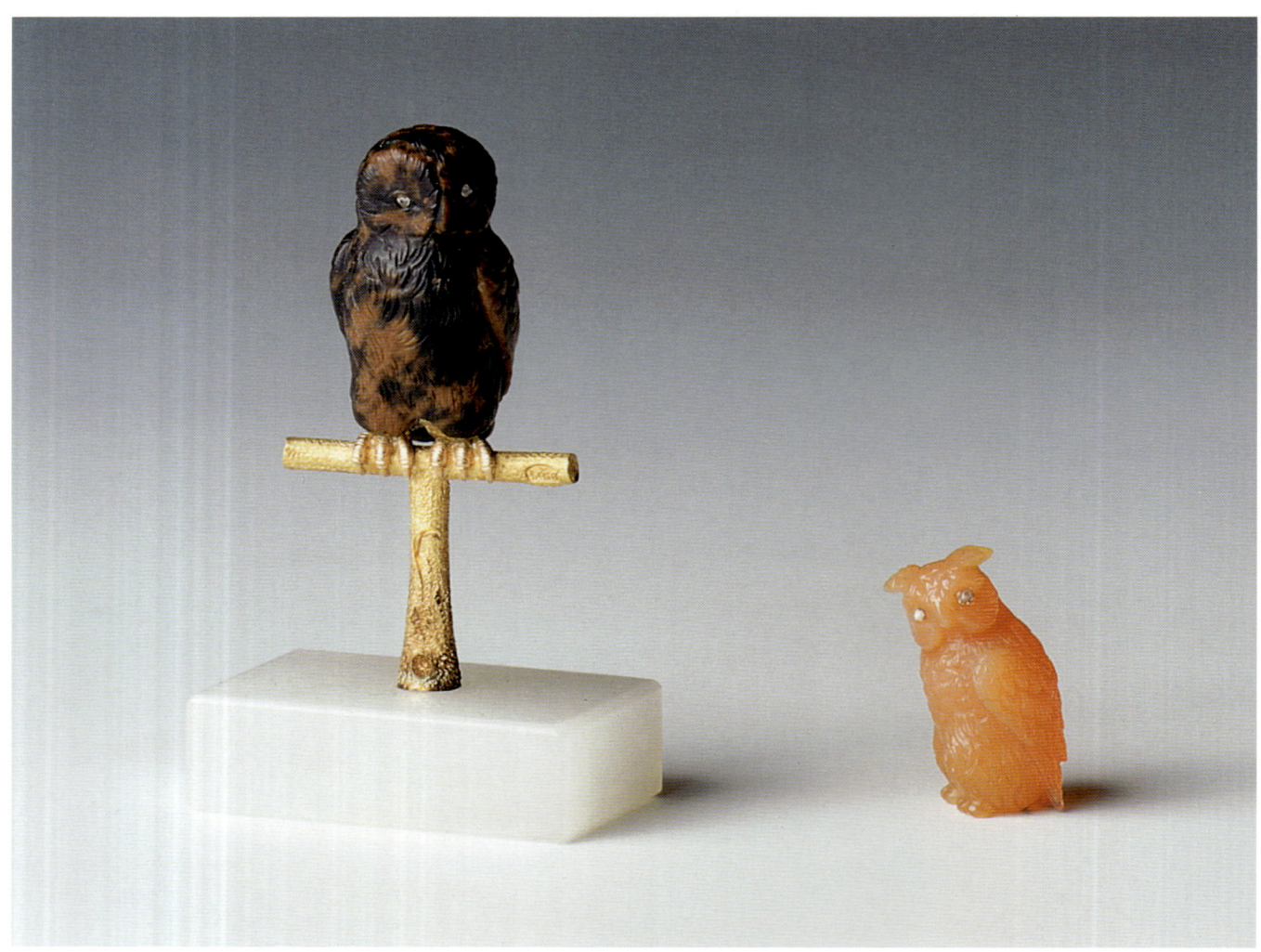

58   OWL ON A PERCH, 1903–1908

Together with cat. 22 and 55, this owl formed part of Princess Victoria's collection. She purchased two owls on the same visit to the London branch.

Jasper, rose diamonds, gold, onyx, 4.4 x 2.4 x 1.6 cm (1³/₄ x ¹⁵/₁₆ x ⁵/₈")
Mark of Henrik Wigström; gold mark of 72 *zolotniks* (1896–1908)
RCIN 40324
PROVENANCE: Bought by Princess Victoria from Fabergé's London branch, 8 November 1911 (£10)
EXHIBITIONS: London 1977, no. D57; QG 1995–6, no. 428

59   OWL, *c*.1907

The extraordinary detail of the carving on such a small scale vividly demonstrates the skill of Fabergé's hardstone carvers.

Agate, rose diamonds, 1.7 x 1 x 0.6 cm (¹¹/₁₆ x ³/₈ x ¹/₄")
Unmarked
RCIN 40140
PROVENANCE: Probably commissioned by King Edward VII, 1907
EXHIBITIONS: London 1977, no. D38; St Petersburg/Paris/London 1993–4, no. 86; QG 1995–6, no. 30

60 RABBIT, *c.* 1907

One of the more humorous of Fabergé's animals, the shape of the rabbit accentuating its comical appearance.

Aventurine quartz, olivine, 3.6 x 1.7 x 1.7 cm (1⁷/₁₆ x ¹¹/₁₆ x ¹¹/₁₆")
Unmarked
RCIN 40040
PROVENANCE: Probably commissioned by King Edward VII, 1907
EXHIBITIONS: London 1977, no. A5; QG 1995–6, no. 445

61 DOE AND THREE BABY RABBITS, *c.* 1907

Fabergé produced a number of charming animal groups including monkeys (cat. 104) and piglets (cat. 49).

Agate, rose diamonds, 4.6 x 3.4 x 6.7 cm (1¹³/₁₆ x 3⁵/₁₆ x 2⁵/₈")
Unmarked
RCIN 40409
PROVENANCE: Bought by Grand Duchess Vladimir of Russia (1854–1920) from Fabergé's London branch,
20 November 1913; presumably given to Queen Alexandra, King George V or Queen Mary
EXHIBITIONS: London 1977, no. A4; QG 1995–6, no. 300

62 HARE, *c.* 1907

Translating the typical characteristics of an animal into hardstone to achieve the most realistic representation was usually the primary concern of Fabergé's sculptors and explains why his animals have both a freshness and an enduring charm. Although always recorded as being a rabbit, this particular carving has more the proportions of a hare. Several rabbits were purchased by members of the royal family from the London branch, and a hare was purchased from Wartski in 1928. In total, there are nineteen rabbits and two hares in the Royal Collection.

Agate, rose diamonds, 4.5 x 3 x 2 cm (1³/₄ x 1³/₁₆ x ¹³/₁₆")
Unmarked
RCIN 40069
PROVENANCE: Commissioned by King Edward VII, 1907
EXHIBITIONS: London 1977, no. A12; QG 1995–6, no. 89

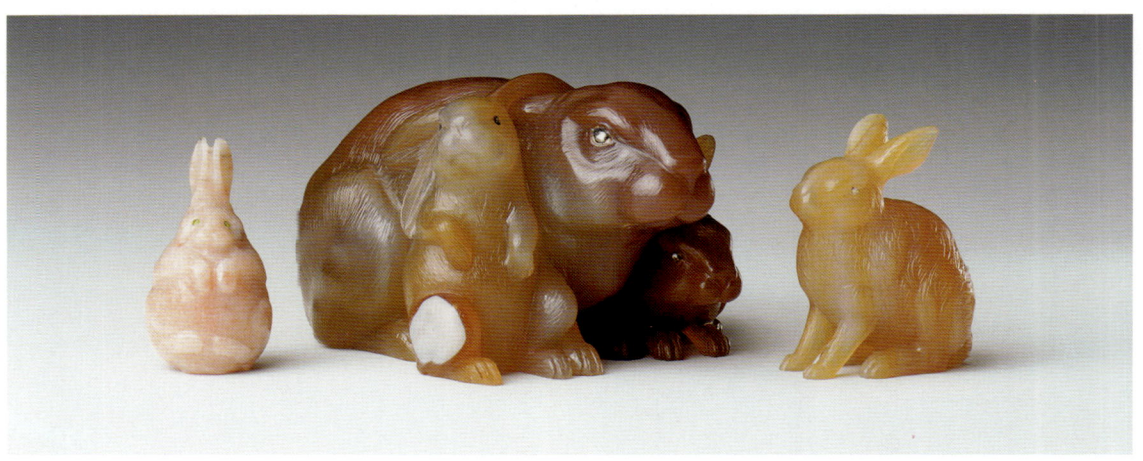

63 PIGEON, *c.*1907

Both King Edward VII and the Prince of Wales (later King George V) kept homing pigeons at Sandringham next to Queen Alexandra's dove-house. According to contemporary accounts, most of the pigeons were of famous Belgian breeds. This is one of six examples of pigeons and doves that are part of the wide range of birds by Fabergé in the Royal Collection. The banded agate realistically emulates the varying grey and white tones of the bird's feathers. Although cat. 63 is unmarked, a similar pigeon was completed in Wigström's workshops in 1911 and is illustrated on a page from the design books of his workshop (see p. 52).

Banded agate, cabochon rubies, gold, 4.4 x 5 x 2 cm (1³/₄ x 1¹⁵/₁₆ x ¹³/₁₆")
Unmarked
RCIN 40032
PROVENANCE: Commissioned by King Edward VII, 1907
REFERENCES: Dutt 1904, p. 106; Tillander-Godenhielm *et al.* 2000, p. 78
EXHIBITIONS: London 1977, no. D49; QG 1995–6, no. 100

64 DEXTER BULL, *c.*1907

Among the herds of cattle kept by King Edward VII at Sandringham were pedigree shorthorns, red-polls, Jerseys and Irish Dexters. The Dexter herd was reputed to be one of the finest in England and won many prizes. The herd was mainly kept at Church Farm, Wolferton, and continued to be bred by King George V. This magnificent carving is made of obsidian, a natural volcanic glass which when highly polished has a velvety sheen, particularly suited to replicating the shiny quality of the coat of a well-groomed bull.

Obsidian, cabochon rubies, 8 x 11 x 4 cm (3¹/₈ x 4⁵/₁₆ x 1⁹/₁₆")
Unmarked
RCIN 40428
PROVENANCE: Commissioned by King Edward VII, 1907; bought by Queen Alexandra from Fabergé's London branch, November 1908 (£44)
REFERENCES: Dutt 1904, pp. 223–4; Bainbridge 1949, pl. 94; Cathcart 1964, p. 167
EXHIBITIONS: London 1977, no. B15; QG 1995–6, no. 293

65 GOOSE, *c.*1907

Unlike many of Fabergé's animal carvings, which are cut from a single piece of stone, this goose is a composite sculpture made of different hardstones to give the most accurate rendering possible of the bird's natural colouring.

Quartzite, obsidian, rose diamonds, gold, 5.5 x 5.6 x 3 cm (2³/₁₆ x 2³/₁₆ x 1³/₁₆")
Mark of Henrik Wigström; gold mark of 72 *zolotniks* (1908–17); English import marks for 1908
RCIN 40340
PROVENANCE: Probably the goose purchased by Queen Alexandra from Fabergé's London branch, 13 November 1911 (£16)
EXHIBITIONS: London 1977, no. D6; QG 1985–6, no. 271; QG 1995–6, no. 115

66 MOUNTAIN SHEEP, *c.*1907

Bainbridge recalls how by 1907 almost every animal imaginable had been produced in hardstone by Fabergé and that Queen Alexandra had been given such a wide variety of these animals that there were hardly any breeds left to cover. Several breeds of sheep were farmed at Sandringham during this period, but this is the only Fabergé sheep in the Royal Collection.

Agate, rose diamonds, 4 x 7.1 x 3.6 cm (1⁹/₁₆ x 2¹³/₁₆ x 1⁷/₁₆")
Unmarked
RCIN 40017
PROVENANCE: Commissioned by King Edward VII, 1907
EXHIBITIONS: London 1977, no. B19; QG 1995–6, no. 292

67 DUCKLING, *c.*1908

Eight ducks were modelled as part of the Sandringham commission by Fabergé's sculptors. Four were purchased by members of the royal family from Fabergé's London branch between 1907 and 1916.

Chalcedony, cabochon rubies, gold, 3.4 x 3.3 x 2.2 cm (1⁵/₁₆ x 1⁵/₁₆ x ⁷/₈")
Mark of Henrik Wigström; gold mark of 72 *zolotniks* (1908–1917)
RCIN 40328
PROVENANCE: Probably the duck bought by Queen Alexandra from Fabergé's London branch, 1909 (£11 15s)
EXHIBITIONS: QG 1995–6, no. 93

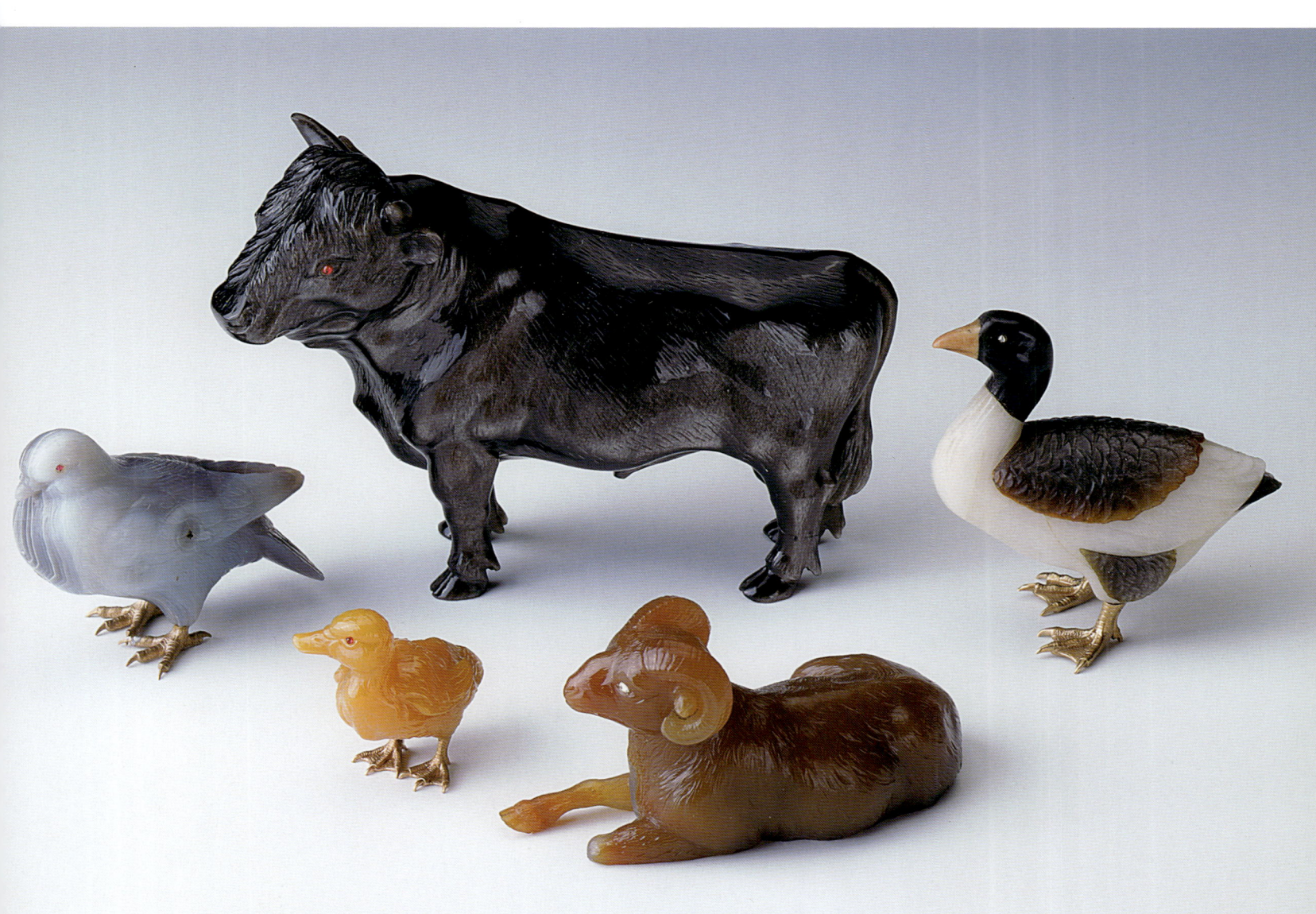

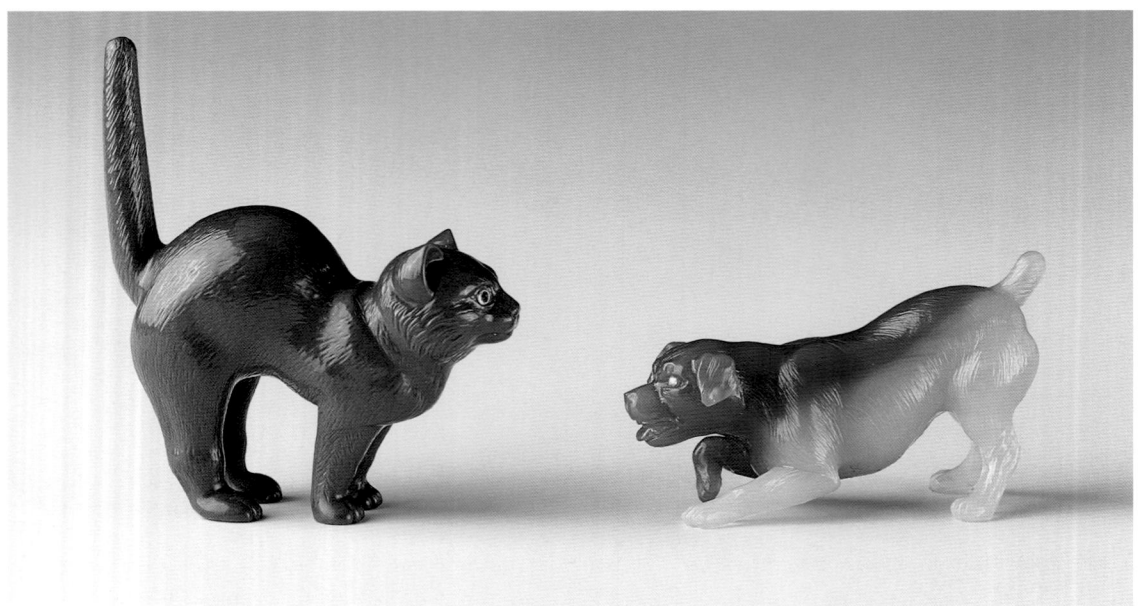

68 CAT, *c.* 1910

Jasper, emeralds, gold, 5.6 x 5 x 1.9 cm (2³/₁₆ x 1¹⁵/₁₆ x ³/₄")
Unmarked
RCIN 40294
PROVENANCE: Probably the cat bought by King George V from Wartski, 31 December 1929 (£15)
REFERENCES: RA PP/GV/3/3/2143
EXHIBITIONS: London 1953, no. 81; London 1977, no. A14; New York 1983, no. 234; QG 1995–6, no. 321;
QG 2002–3, no. 212

69 BORDER TERRIER, *c.* 1908

The Border terrier, a breed that originated along the border between England and Scotland, was used
as a working terrier until the early twentieth century. It was certainly to be found among the many
dogs kept at Sandringham during King Edward VII's reign.

Chalcedony, rose diamonds, 3.1 x 4.9 x 2.3 cm (1¹/₄ x 1¹⁵/₁₆ x ⁷/₈")
RCIN 40444
PROVENANCE: Commissioned by King Edward VII, 1907
EXHIBITIONS: London 1977, no. A31; New York 1983, no. 71; QG 1985–6, no. 239; QG 1995–6, no. 320;
QG 2002–3, no. 211

70 'QUEEN ALEXANDRA'S PEKINESE', *c.* 1907

This has been credited to Alfred Pocock, an English modeller and sculptor who worked for Fabergé's
London branch and produced animal carvings independently. Bainbridge asserts that Pocock was one
of the sculptors who worked at Sandringham in 1907 alongside Boris Frödman-Cluzel and Frank
Lutiger. He adds that prior to this, in 1905 or 1906, Queen Alexandra had asked to see models for
two animals and that it had been necessary for Fabergé to find a modeller in London at short notice.
Pocock, a scholarship pupil at the Royal Academy Schools, was selected and produced the models to the
Queen's satisfaction. He continued to model and sculpt animals, apparently for Fabergé and for his own
production.

The choice of stone – fluorspar – for this dog, consistently referred to as Queen Alexandra's favourite Pekinese (although there is no documentary evidence to suggest that this is a specific portrait model), is quite different from anything used in other Fabergé animal carvings. The modelling and carving are also less assured and lack the refined detail and polishing for which Fabergé's models are renowned. In style it is reminiscent of animals known to be by Cartier (see cat. 338, 339 and 340). A drawing for a similar dog does exist in the Cartier Archives, but it is for a smaller version with cabochon sapphire eyes. It is difficult to be certain that this dog was produced entirely independently of Fabergé's output, particularly as Bainbridge records that it was modelled at Sandringham and cut in St Petersburg.

Fluorspar, rose diamonds, 11.4 x 6 x 12 cm (4^1/$_2$ x 2^3/$_8$ x 4^3/$_4$")
Unmarked
RCIN 40268
PROVENANCE: Commissioned by King Edward VII, 1907
REFERENCES: Bainbridge 1949, pp. 137–8, pl. 96
EXHIBITIONS: London 1977, no. A17; QG 1985–6, no. 253; St Petersburg/Paris/London 1993–4, no. 91

71   FRENCH BULLDOG, *c.*1910

One of a large group of Fabergé bulldogs in the Royal Collection. This dog, which is referred to as a French bulldog, was modelled from life at Sandringham. King Edward VII kept French bulldogs among the many dogs he owned, of which one was a prize-winner called Paul. This carving was purchased by King George V in 1910, together with a box (cat. 179), two macaques (cat. 104) and a donkey (cat. 47).

Agate, guilloché enamel, rose diamonds, 9.8 x 13 x 6.1 cm (3^7/$_8$ x 5^1/$_8$ x 2^3/$_8$")
Unmarked
RCIN 40008
PROVENANCE: Bought by King George V from Fabergé's London branch, 7 November 1910 (£38)
REFERENCES: RA PP/GV/3/3/128
EXHIBITIONS: QG 1995–6, no. 329

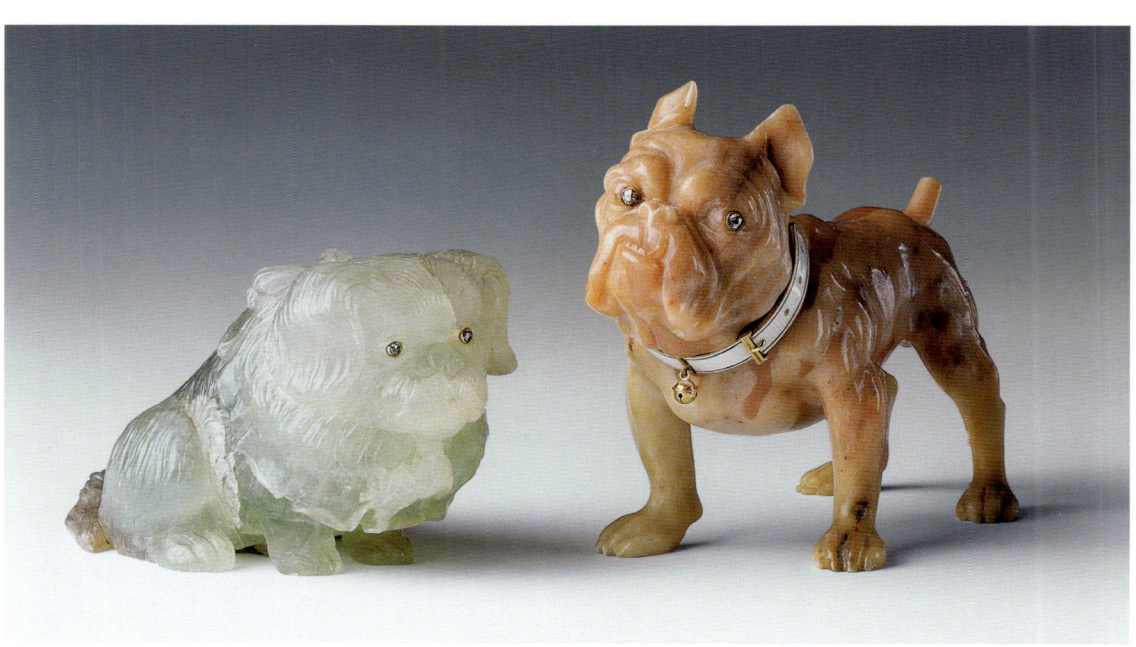

72 CORNCRAKE ON A WHEATSHEAF, 1907

This bird and wheatsheaf are carved from a single piece of chalcedony.

Chalcedony, rose diamonds, 3 x 7 x 4 cm (1³/₁₆ x 2³/₄ x 1⁹/₁₆")
Unmarked
RCIN 13737
PROVENANCE: Commissioned by King Edward VII, 1907
REFERENCES: Snowman 1955

73 CAPERCAILLIE, c.1907

Agate, rose diamonds, gold, 3.5 x 4.1 x 2.1 cm (1³/₈ x 1⁵/₈ x ¹³/₁₆")
Mark of Henrik Wigström; gold mark of 72 *zolotniks* (1896–1908)
RCIN 40061
PROVENANCE: Presumably acquired by King Edward VII and Queen Alexandra
EXHIBITIONS: QG 1995–6, no. 96

74 JUNGLE FOWL, c.1903–1908

The carver has chosen an exotically marked hardstone with a fluorescent quality to emulate the markings of this bird.

Tiger's eye quartz, rose diamonds, gold, 4.3 x 7 x 2.1 cm (1¹¹/₁₆ x 2³/₄ x ¹³/₁₆")
Mark of Henrik Wigström; gold mark of 56 *zolotniks* (1896–1908)
RCIN 40315
PROVENANCE: Probably acquired by Queen Alexandra; Royal Collection by 1953
EXHIBITIONS: London 1953, no. 83; London 1977, no. D17; QG 1995–6, no. 33

75 COCK PHEASANT, c.1907

Thousands of pheasants were bred for shooting on the Sandringham Estate during King Edward VII's reign. According to the account of Boris Frödman-Cluzel, he and the other sculptors were invited to spend a day shooting with the King. This model was probably produced from life as part of the commission.

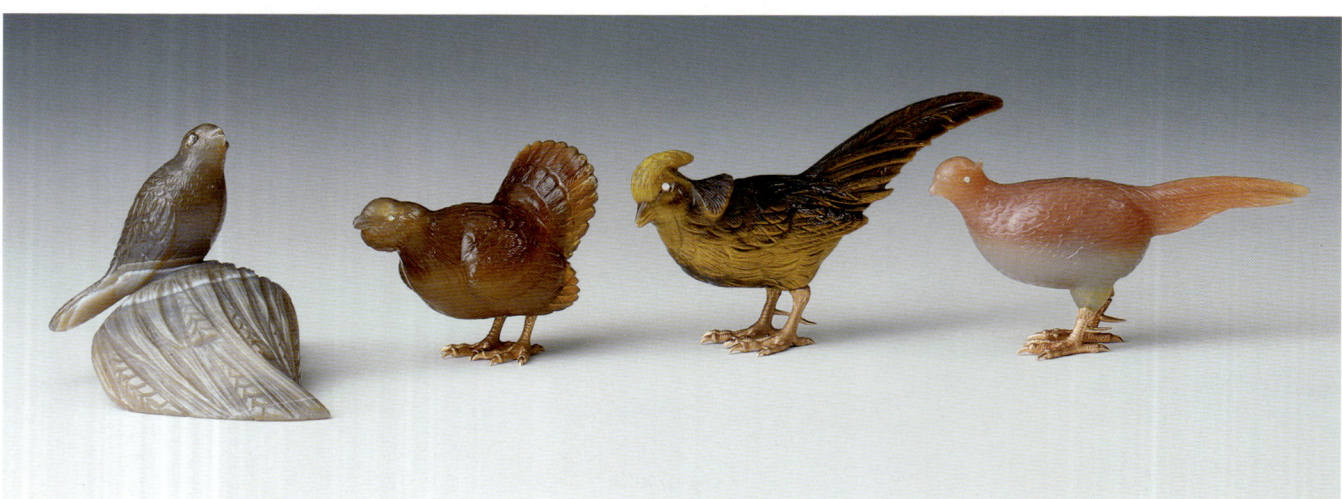

Agate, rose diamonds, gold, 3.3 x 6.2 x 2.1 cm (1⁵/₁₆ x 2⁷/₁₆ x ¹³/₁₆")
Unmarked
RCIN 40314
PROVENANCE: Commissioned by King Edward VII, 1907
EXHIBITIONS: London 1977, no. D16; QG 1995–6, no. 34

76 COCKATOO ON A PERCH, BEFORE 1896

Queen Alexandra kept a cockatoo in her apartments at Marlborough House and her fondness for birds was noted by the contemporary author Arthur H. Bevan. He records that she had in her boudoir 'several canaries, bullfinches and other songsters'. He also notes that King Edward VII kept a green parrot in his room; it was moved to Sandringham, where it later died.

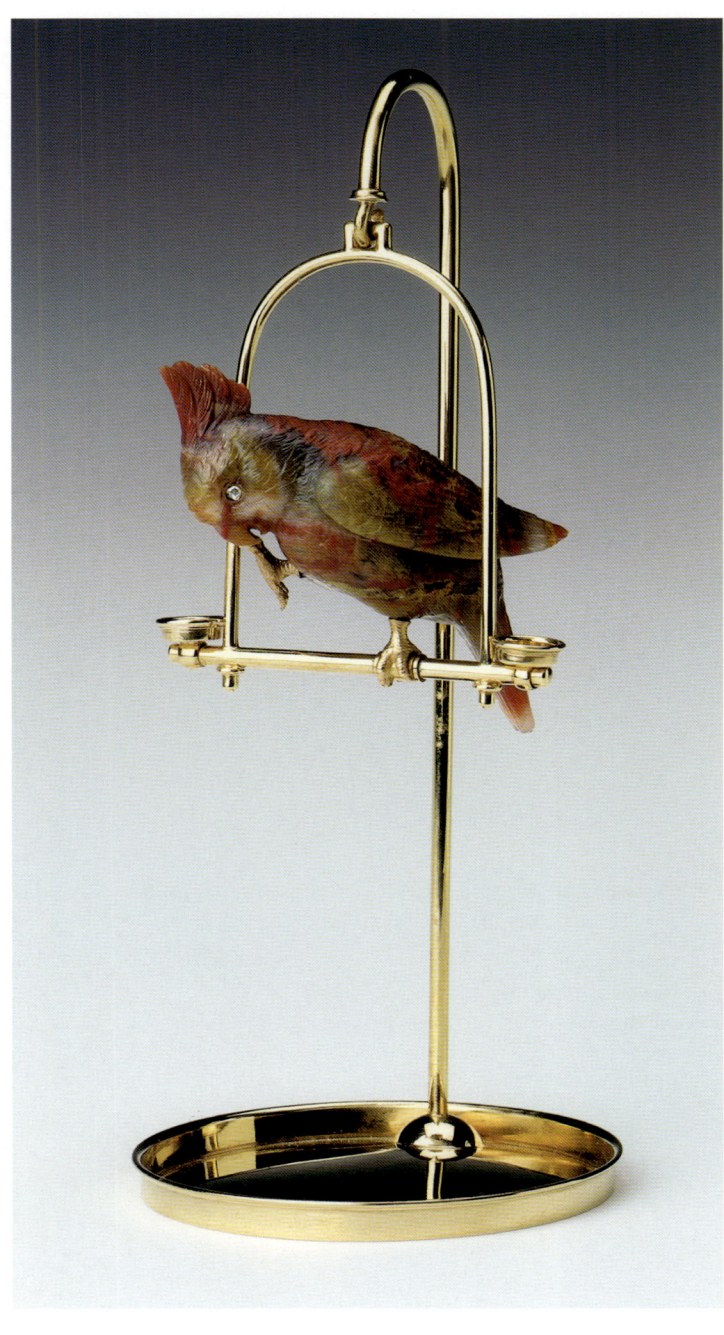

Agate, rose diamonds, gold,
13 x 5.3 cm (5¹/₈ x 2¹/₁₆")
Mark of Michael Perchin; gold mark of 56 *zolotniks* (before 1896); *FABERGÉ* in Cyrillic characters
RCIN 40478
PROVENANCE: Probably acquired by Queen Alexandra
REFERENCES: Bevan 1896, p. 78
EXHIBITIONS: London 1977, no. D4; QG 1985–6, no. 91; QG 1995–6, no. 451

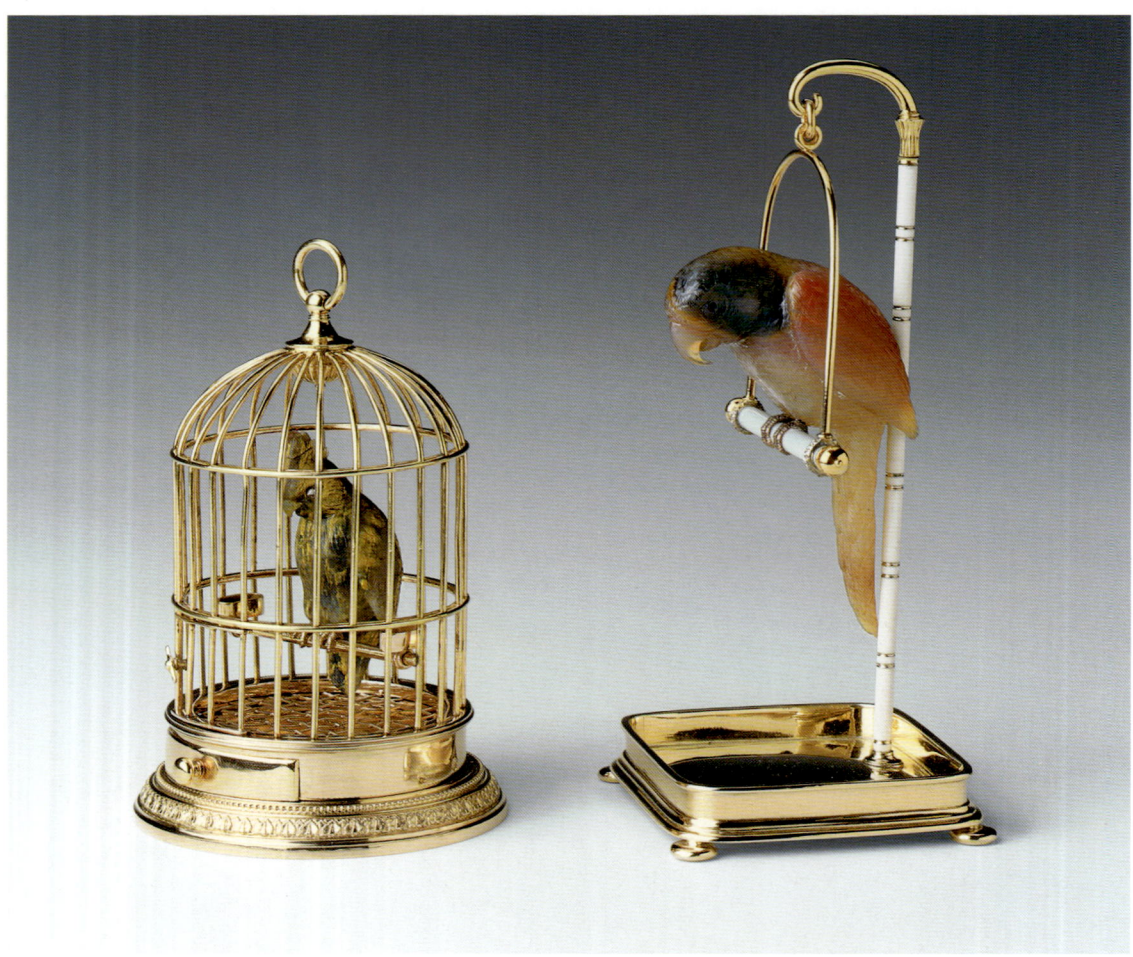

77 COCKATOO IN A CAGE, 1896–1903

Tiger's eye quartz, rose diamonds, gold, silver-gilt, 10.4 x 7.1 cm (4$^{1}/_{8}$ x 2$^{13}/_{16}$")
Mark of Michael Perchin; silver mark of 88 *zolotniks* (1896–1908); *FABERGÉ* in Cyrillic characters
RCIN 40480
PROVENANCE: Probably acquired by Queen Alexandra
EXHIBITIONS: London 1977, no. D19; QG 1985–6, no. 94; QG 1995–6, no. 448

78 PARROT ON A PERCH, 1896–1903

Other examples of parrots on perches are known, for example in the India Early Minshall Collection, Cleveland Museum of Art, Ohio.

Agate, rose diamonds, gold, silver-gilt, guilloché enamel, 14.5 x 7.2 x 6.2 cm (5$^{11}/_{16}$ x 2$^{13}/_{16}$ x 2$^{7}/_{16}$")
Mark of Michael Perchin; silver mark of 88 *zolotniks* (1896–1908); *FABERGÉ* in Cyrillic characters
RCIN 40481
PROVENANCE: Probably acquired by King Edward VII
EXHIBITIONS: QG 1995–6, no. 449

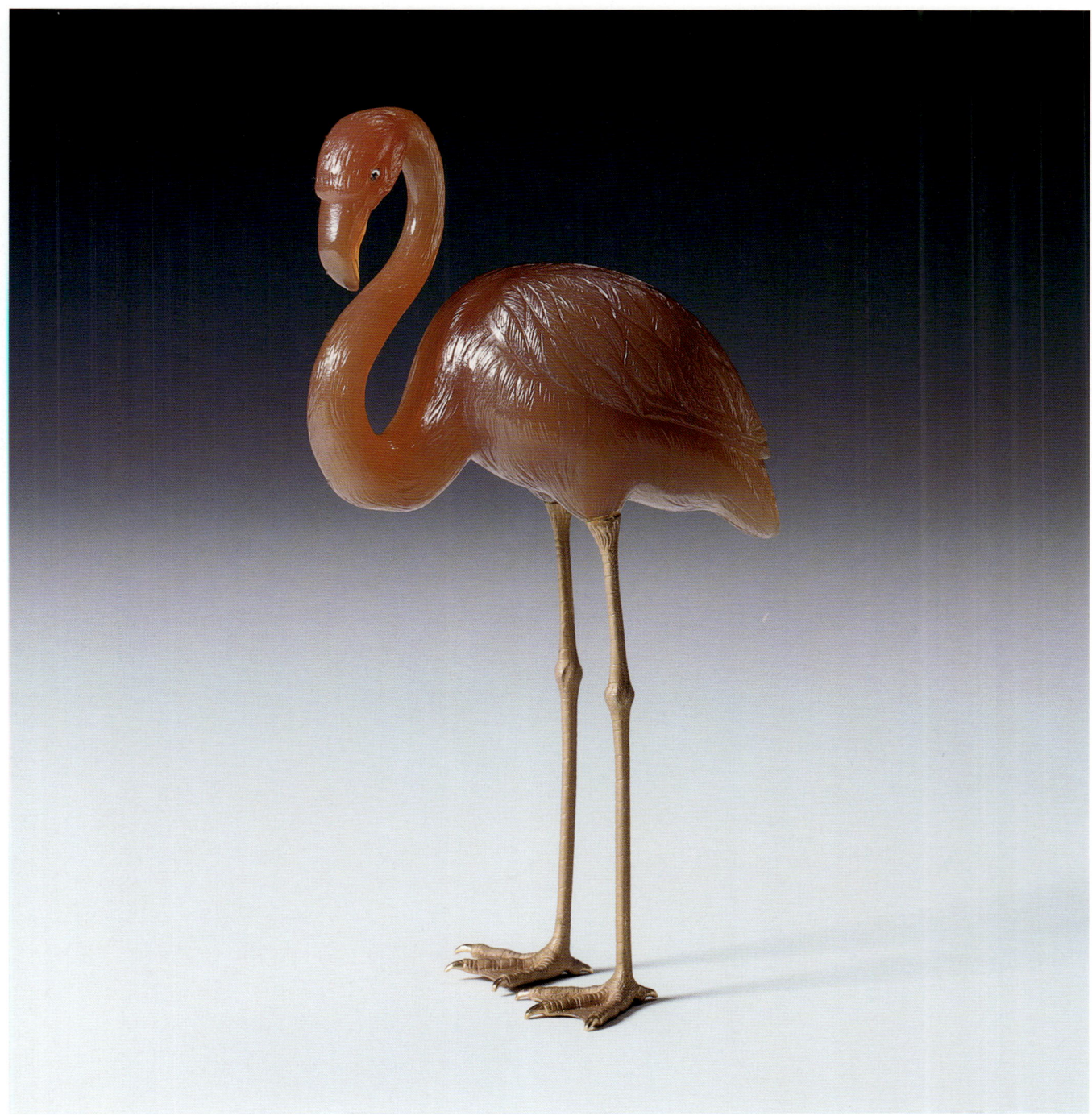

79 FLAMINGO, 1903–1908

Cartier, one of Fabergé's competitors, chose to produce hardstone flamingos inspired by Fabergé's work.
The Royal Collection contains an example (cat. 338) which appears stylised and unnaturalistic by
comparison with this skilfully executed model.

Agate, rose diamonds, gold, 10 x 5.2 x 2.4 cm (3¹⁵/₁₆ x 2¹/₁₆ x ¹⁵/₁₆")
Mark of Henrik Wigström; gold mark of 56 *zolotniks* (1896–1908)
RCIN 40465
PROVENANCE: Probably acquired by Queen Alexandra
EXHIBITIONS: London 1977, no. D46; QG 1995–6, no. 4

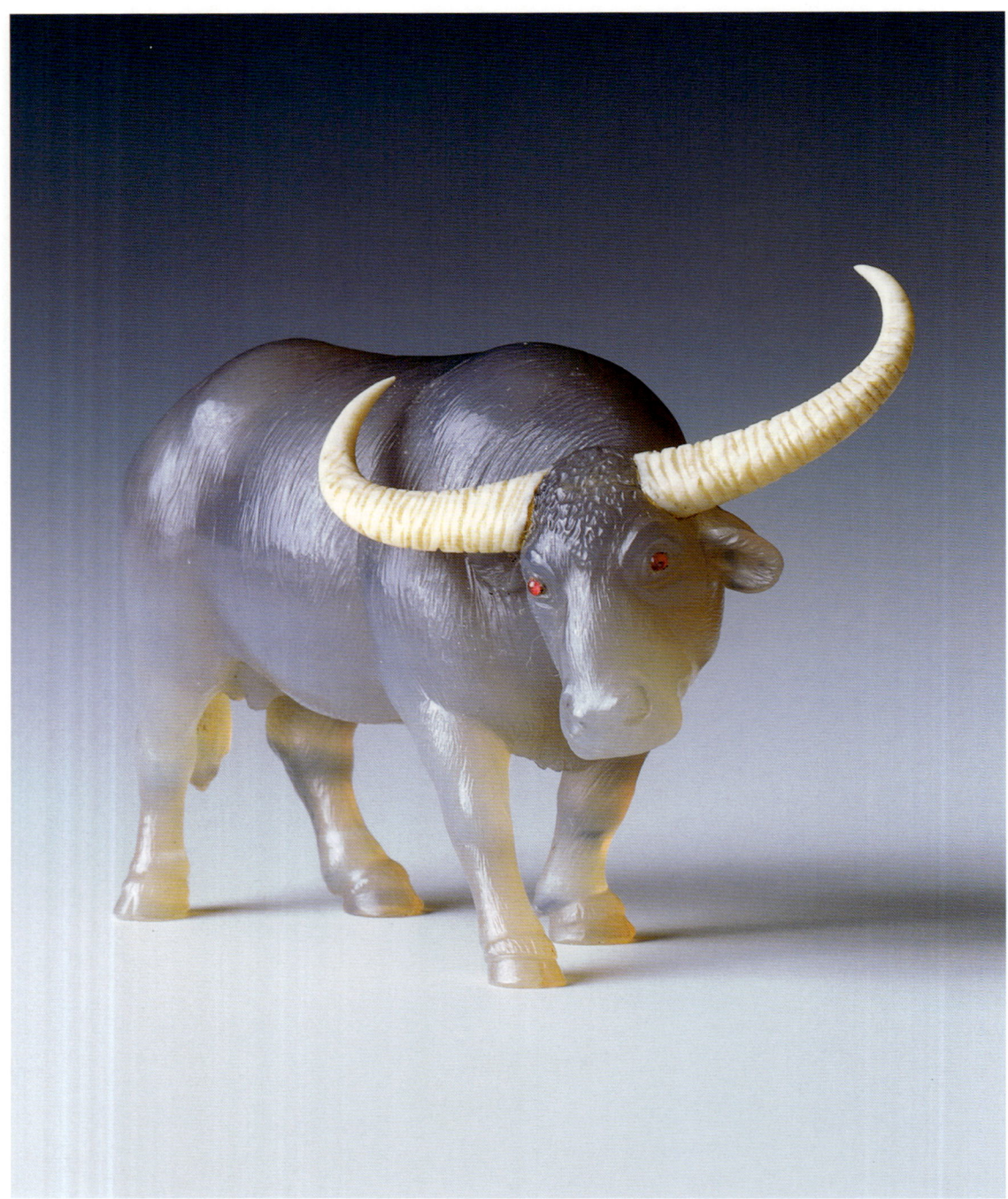

80 WATER BUFFALO, *c.* 1913

This is one of the most successful of Fabergé's wild animal carvings, taking full advantage of the exceptionally translucent qualities of the stone.

Chalcedony, ivory, cabochon rubies, 5.9 x 8.4 x 3.3 cm (2⁵/₁₆ x 3⁵/₁₆ x 1⁵/₁₆")
Unmarked
RCIN 40388
PROVENANCE: Bought by King George V from Fabergé's London branch, 13 November 1913 (£41)
REFERENCES: RA PP/GV/3/3/588
EXHIBITIONS: London 1953, no. 11; London 1977, no. B16; QG 1985–6, no. 171; QG 1995–6, no. 291; QG 2002–3, no. 227

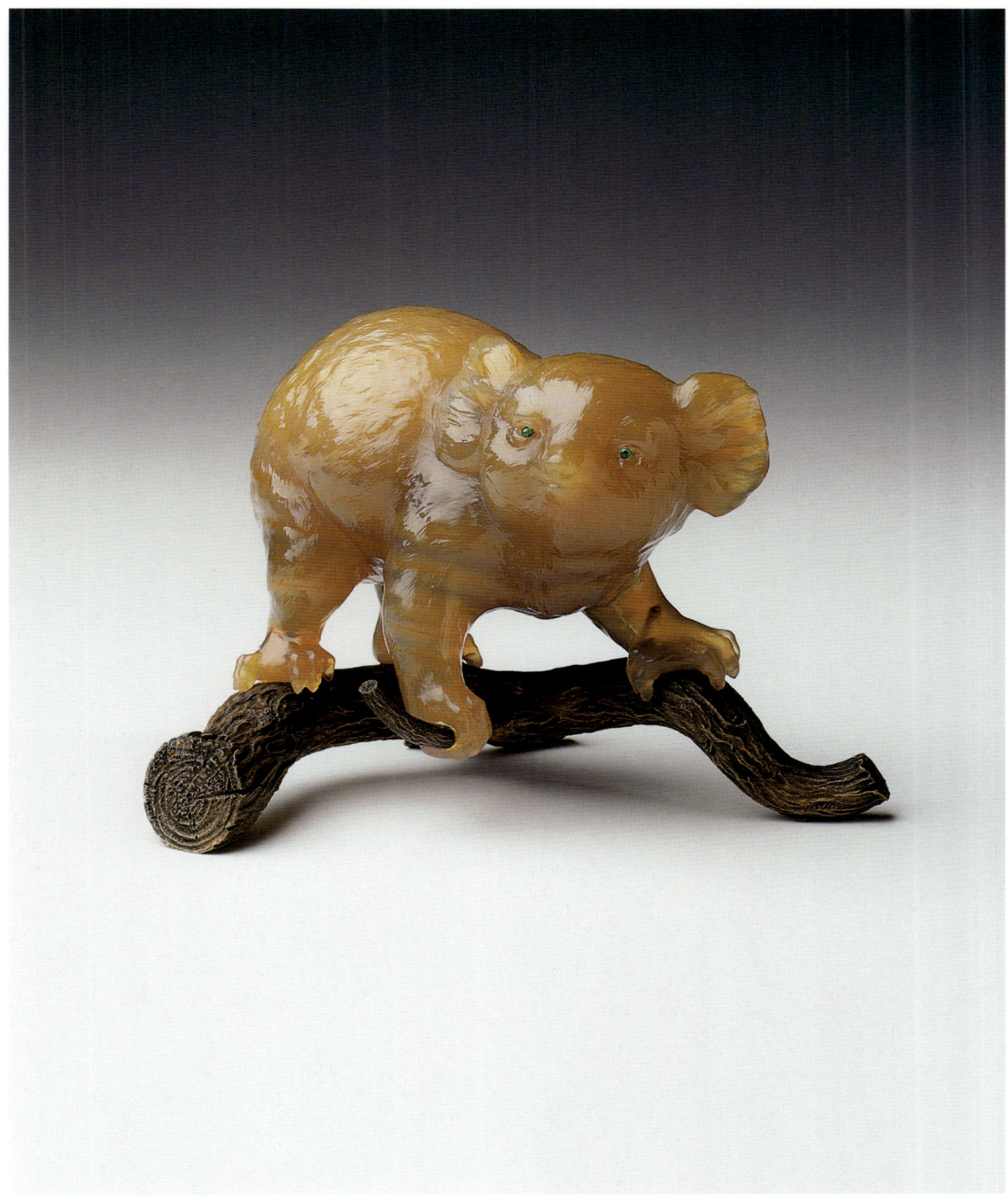

81 KOALA BEAR, 1908–1913

King George V's Fabergé collecting encompassed a large number of the exotic animals which now form part of the Royal Collection. He purchased this koala, the water buffalo (cat. 80), the kangaroo (cat. 85) and a camel (not shown) on the same visit to Fabergé's London branch in November 1913.

Agate, cabochon emeralds, silver, 6.6 x 8.2 x 7.3 cm (2⁵/₈ x 3¹/₄ x 2⁷/₈")
Mark of Henrik Wigström; silver mark of 88 *zolotniks* (1908–17); *FABERGÉ* in Cyrillic characters.
RCIN 40407
PROVENANCE: Bought by King George V from Fabergé's London branch, November 1913 (£38)
EXHIBITIONS: London 1977, no. C27; New York 1983, no. 99; St Petersburg/Paris/London 1993–4, no. 84;
QG 1995–6, no. 303

82 FROG CIGAR LIGHTER, *c.*1906

Together with cat. 83, this is an example of an animal carving which also has a functional purpose. It is thought to have been specially made for King Edward VII at Queen Alexandra's instruction. Queen Alexandra purchased a silver cigarette lighter in the form of a pig and another in rhodonite, described in the London ledgers as 'a new model'. Neither of these now forms part of the collection and they are therefore presumed to have been given away.

Nephrite, brilliant diamonds, silver-gilt, 9.7 x 7.3 x 7.2 cm (3¹³/₁₆ x 2⁷/₈ x 2¹³/₁₆")
Mark of Henrik Wigström; silver mark of 88 *zolotniks* (1896–1908)
RCIN 40413
PROVENANCE: Bought by Queen Alexandra from Fabergé's London branch, 29 October 1906 (£75 10s)
EXHIBITIONS: QG 1995–6, no. 363

83 FROG-SHAPED BOX, BEFORE 1896

Bowenite, cabochon garnets, rose diamonds, nielloed gold, 3 x 6.7 x 4.1 cm (1³/₁₆ x 2⁵/₈ x 1⁵/₈")
Mark of Michael Perchin; gold mark of 56 *zolotniks* (before 1896); *FABERGÉ* in Cyrillic characters
RCIN 40359
PROVENANCE: Probably acquired by Queen Alexandra; Royal Collection by 1953
REFERENCES: Snowman 1962, pl. 273
EXHIBITIONS: London 1953, no. 6; London 1977, no. B3; QG 1995–6, no. 536

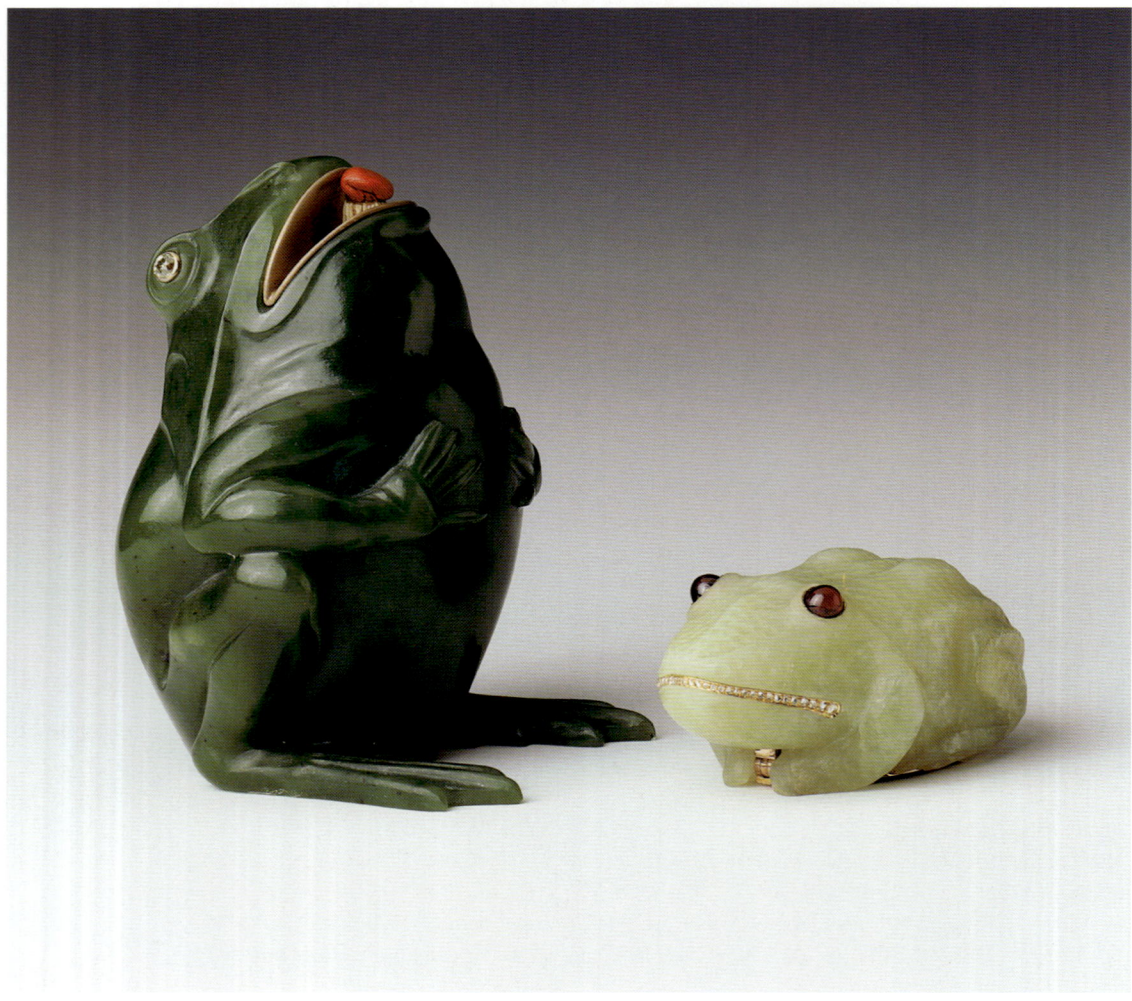

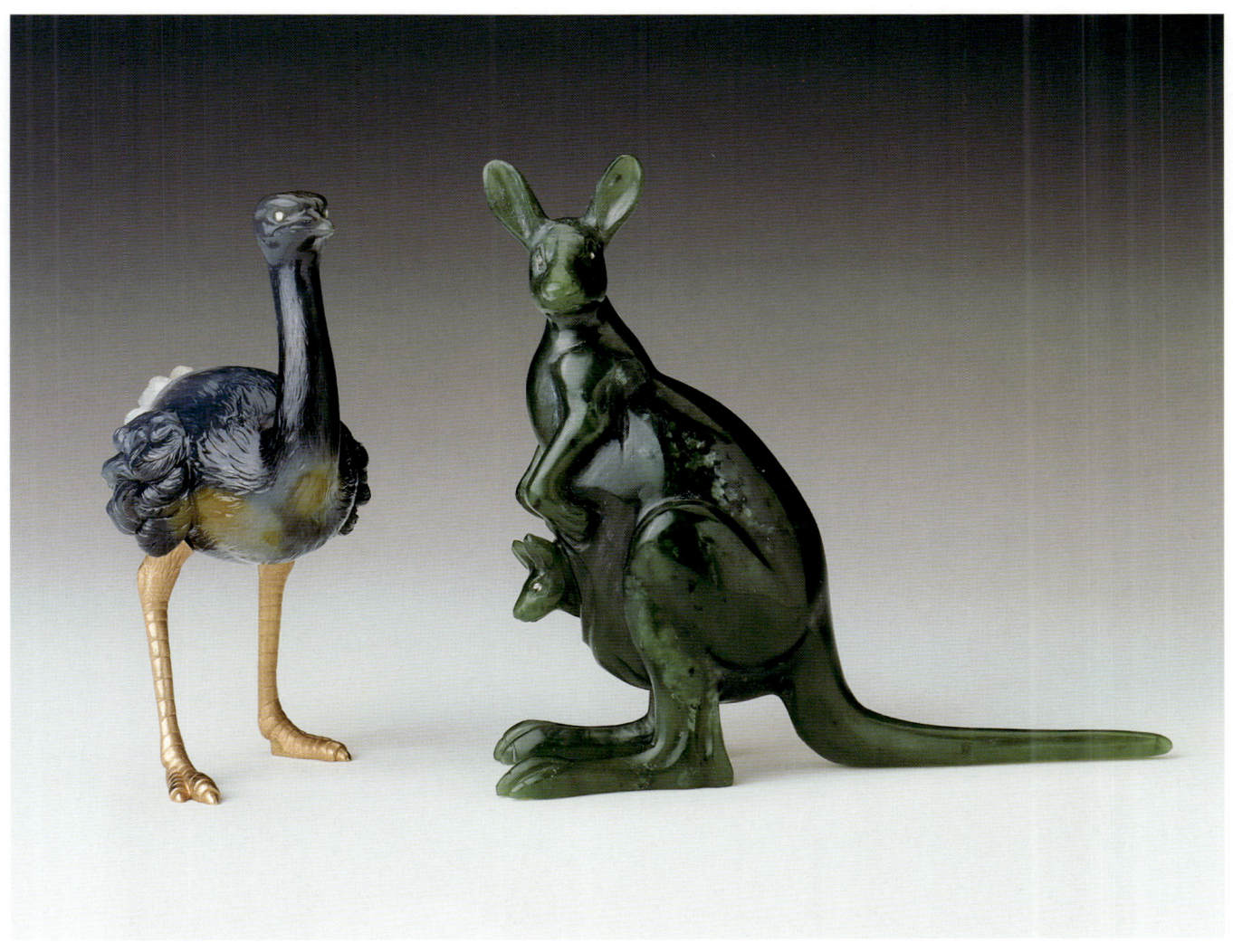

84 OSTRICH, *c.*1900

Chalcedony, red gold, rose diamonds, 8.5 x 5.4 x 3.5 cm (3³/₈ x 2¹/₈ x 1³/₈")
Unmarked
RCIN 40277
PROVENANCE: Probably acquired by Queen Alexandra; Royal Collection by 1953
EXHIBITIONS: London 1953, no. 72; London 1977, no. D50; QG 1995–6, no. 37

85 KANGAROO AND BABY, *c.*1913

Nephrite, rose diamonds, 8.8 x 9.7 x 3.1 cm (3⁷/₁₆ x 3¹³/₁₆ x 1¹/₄")
Unmarked
RCIN 40269
PROVENANCE: Bought by King George V from Fabergé's London branch, November 1913 (£23)
EXHIBITIONS: London 1977, no. C36; Melbourne 1979–80, no. 115; QG 1995–6, no. 304

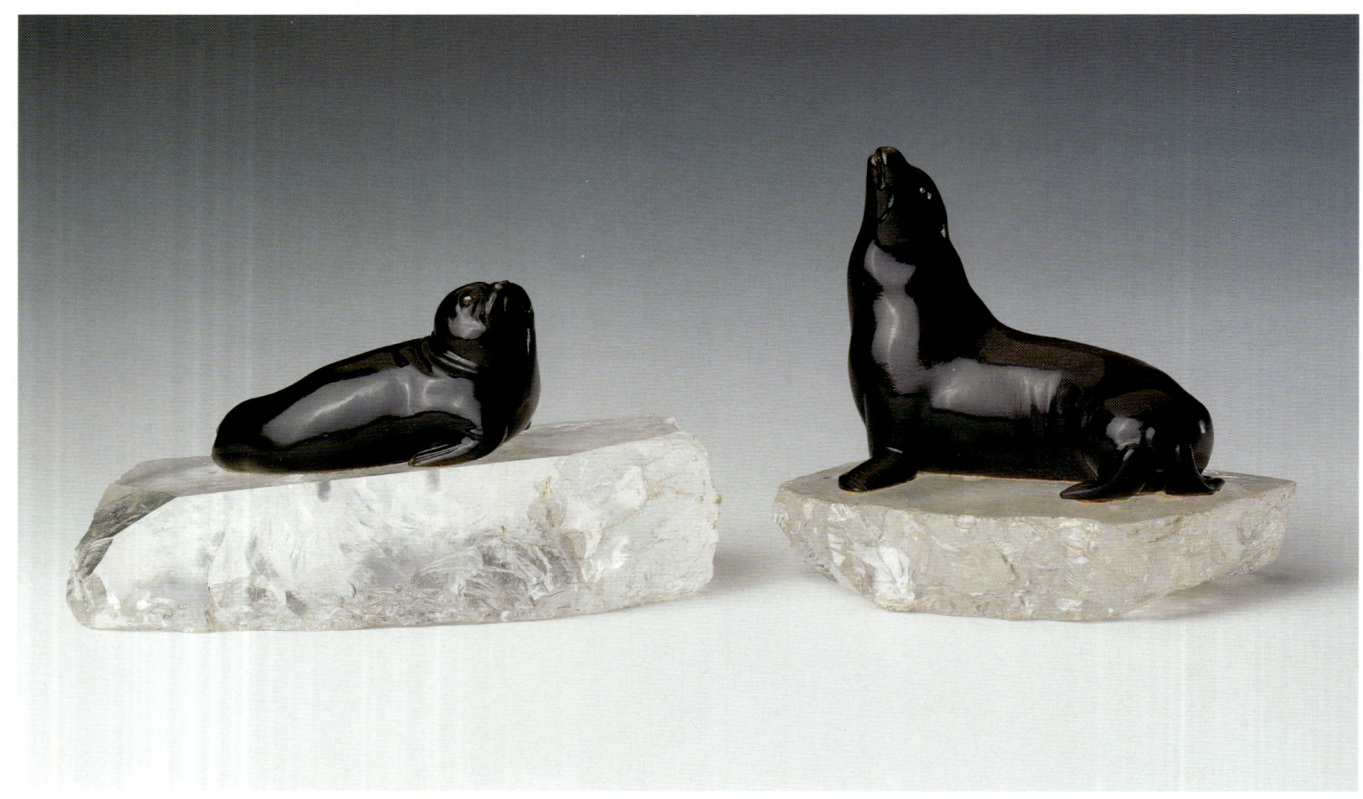

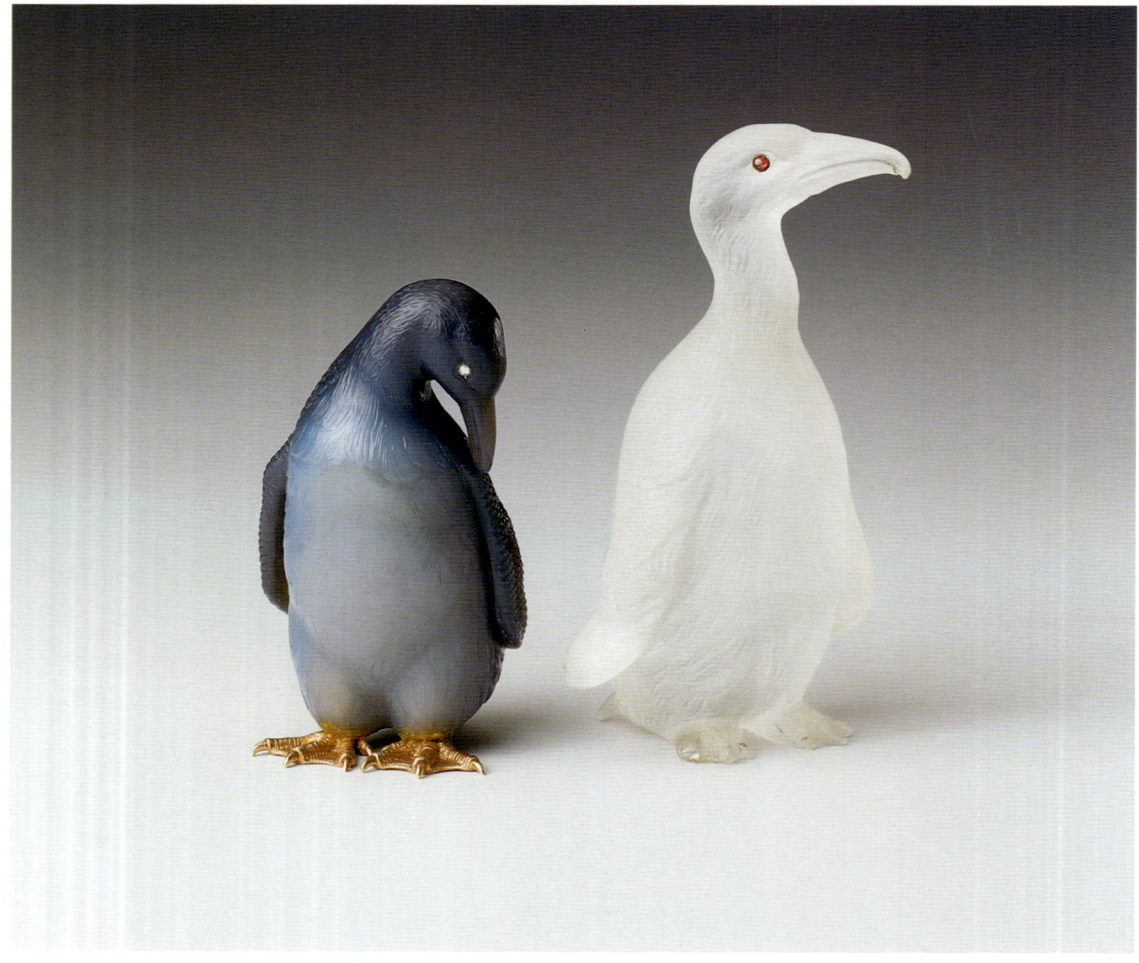

86 SEAL ON ICE FLOE, *c.*1900

This is one of the most successful combinations of hardstones used by Fabergé's sculptors. Birbaum describes how the obsidian perfectly captures the wet sheen of the animal's skin, while the rock crystal represents an ice floe. Fabergé repeated the successful combination of rock crystal and obsidian for sea lions on ice floes (cat. 87 below). There are four Fabergé seals and sea lions in the Royal Collection, and a further model is known in the De Grigné Collection. It is not known who purchased this example, but a seal on an ice floe was bought by the Maclaine [sic] of Lochbuie from Fabergé's London branch in July 1911 and could have been presented as a gift to King George V or Queen Mary.

Obsidian, rock crystal, 6.4 x 12.3 x 7.8 cm (2¹/₂ x 4¹³/₁₆ x 3¹/₁₆")
Unmarked
RCIN 40811
PROVENANCE: Probably acquired by King George V and Queen Mary
EXHIBITIONS: QG 1995–6, r.o. 18

87 CALIFORNIAN SEA LION, *c.*1900

Obsidian, rock crystal, rose diamonds, 8.5 x 10.3 x 8.2 cm (3³/₈ x 4¹/₁₆ x 3¹/₄")
Unmarked
RCIN 40364
PROVENANCE: Probably acquired by Queen Alexandra; Royal Collection by 1953
REFERENCES: Habsburg & Lopato 1993, p. 459
EXHIBITIONS: London 1977, no. C29; QG 1995–6, no. 24

88 PENGUIN, 1896–1908

Queen Alexandra purchased 'penguins agate orletz' from the London branch on 13 November 1911. The penguin was a model which Cartier also produced as part of their range of hardstone animals, inspired by Fabergé. A pair of penguins believed to be by Cartier is included in the exhibition (cat. 343).

Chalcedony, gold, rose diamonds, 5.4 x 3.5 x 2.7 cm (2¹/₈ x 1³/₈ x 1¹/₁₆")
Mark of Henrik Wigström; gold mark of 72 *zolotniks* (1896–1908)
RCIN 40285
PROVENANCE: Bought by Queen Alexandra from Fabergé's London branch, 13 November 1911 (£21 10s)
EXHIBITIONS: London 1953, no. 58; London 1977, no. D5; QG 1995–6, no. 36

89 GREAT AUK, *c.*1900

A rare example of an animal carved in rock crystal, which although used extensively by Fabergé for other objects – notably the *trompe-l'oeil* flower vases (see pp. 103–21) – was sparingly used for animals and birds.

Rock crystal, cabochon rubies, 3 x 5 x 2.7 cm (1³/₁₆ x 1¹⁵/₁₆ x 1¹/₁₆")
Unmarked
RCIN 40280
PROVENANCE: Probably acquired by King Edward VII and Queen Alexandra; Royal Collection by 1953
EXHIBITIONS: London 1977, no. D3; QG 1995–6, no. 26

90 COCKATOO ON A HANGING PERCH, *c.*1900

Agate, olivines, gold, enamel, silver-gilt, 13.5 x 6.3 x 6.2 cm (5⁵/₁₆ x 2¹/₂ x 2⁷/₁₆")
Mark of Michael Perchin; silver mark of 88 *zolotniks* (1896–1908); *FABERGÉ* in Cyrillic characters
RCIN 40483
PROVENANCE: Probably acquired by Queen Alexandra; Royal Collection by 1953
EXHIBITIONS: London 1977, no. D39; New York 1983, no. 188; QG 1985–6, no. 93; QG 1995–6, no. 450;
QG 2002–3, no. 231

91 PAIR OF BUDGERIGARS ON A PERCH, 1896–1903

Nephrite, rose diamonds, silver-gilt, guilloché enamel, 16.5 x diameter 8.6 cm (6¹/₂ x 3³/₈")
Mark of Michael Perchin; silver mark of 88 *zolotniks* (1896–1908); *FABERGÉ* in Cyrillic characters
RCIN 40482
PROVENANCE: Probably acquired by King Edward VII and Queen Alexandra
EXHIBITIONS: London 1977, no. D20; QG 1985–6, no. 92; QG 1995–6, no. 348

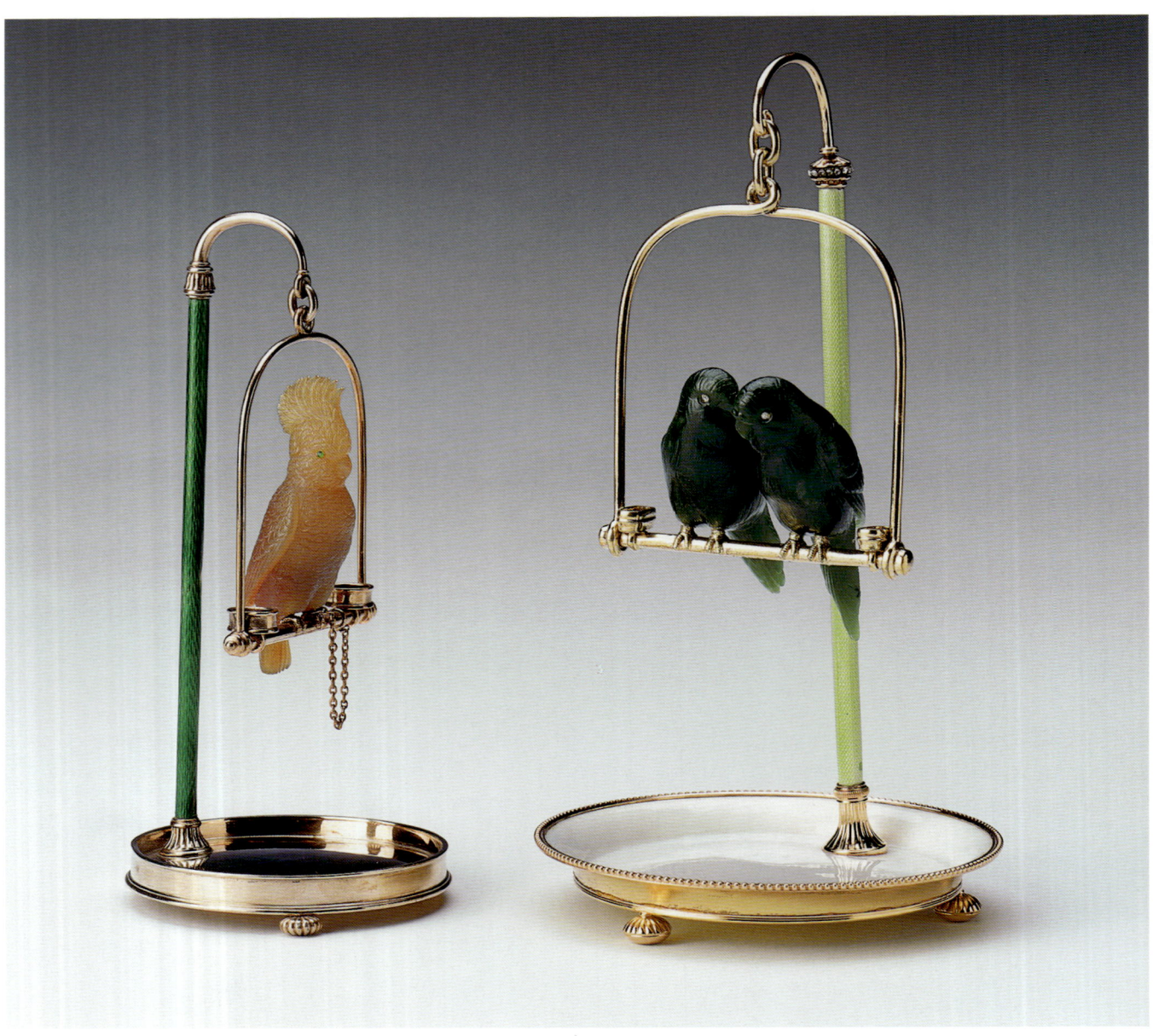

92 BEAVER, *c.*1907

Nephrite, rose diamonds, 5.5 x 3.7 x 8 cm (2³/₁₆ x 1⁷/₁₆ x 3¹/₈")
Unmarked
RCIN 40383
PROVENANCE: Bought by King Edward VII from Fabergé's London branch, 30 November 1907 (£25 5s)
EXHIBITIONS: London 1977, no. C28; St Petersburg/Paris/London 1993–4, no. 85; QG 1995–6, no. 296

93 KINGFISHER, *c.*1900

One of several models of kingfishers in the Royal Collection, one of which was purchased by the Prince of Wales (later King Edward VIII), in July 1913. Fabergé apparently referred to kingfishers as ice-birds and the London ledgers recall that King Edward VII purchased an icebird on 30 November 1907 for £25 5s. The stylised geometric design of this bird is similar to the type of netsuke carving known in Japan as *itobon*.

Nephrite, rose diamonds, gold, 5.6 x 3.5 x 5.4 cm (2³/₁₆ x 1³/₈ x 2¹/₈")
Mark of Henrik Wigström; gold mark of 72 *zolotniks* (1896–1908)
RCIN 40387
PROVENANCE: Purchased either by King Edward VII in 1907 or the Prince of Wales (later King Edward VIII) in 1913
REFERENCES: Munn 1987
EXHIBITIONS: London 1977, no. D53; QG 1995–6, no. 22

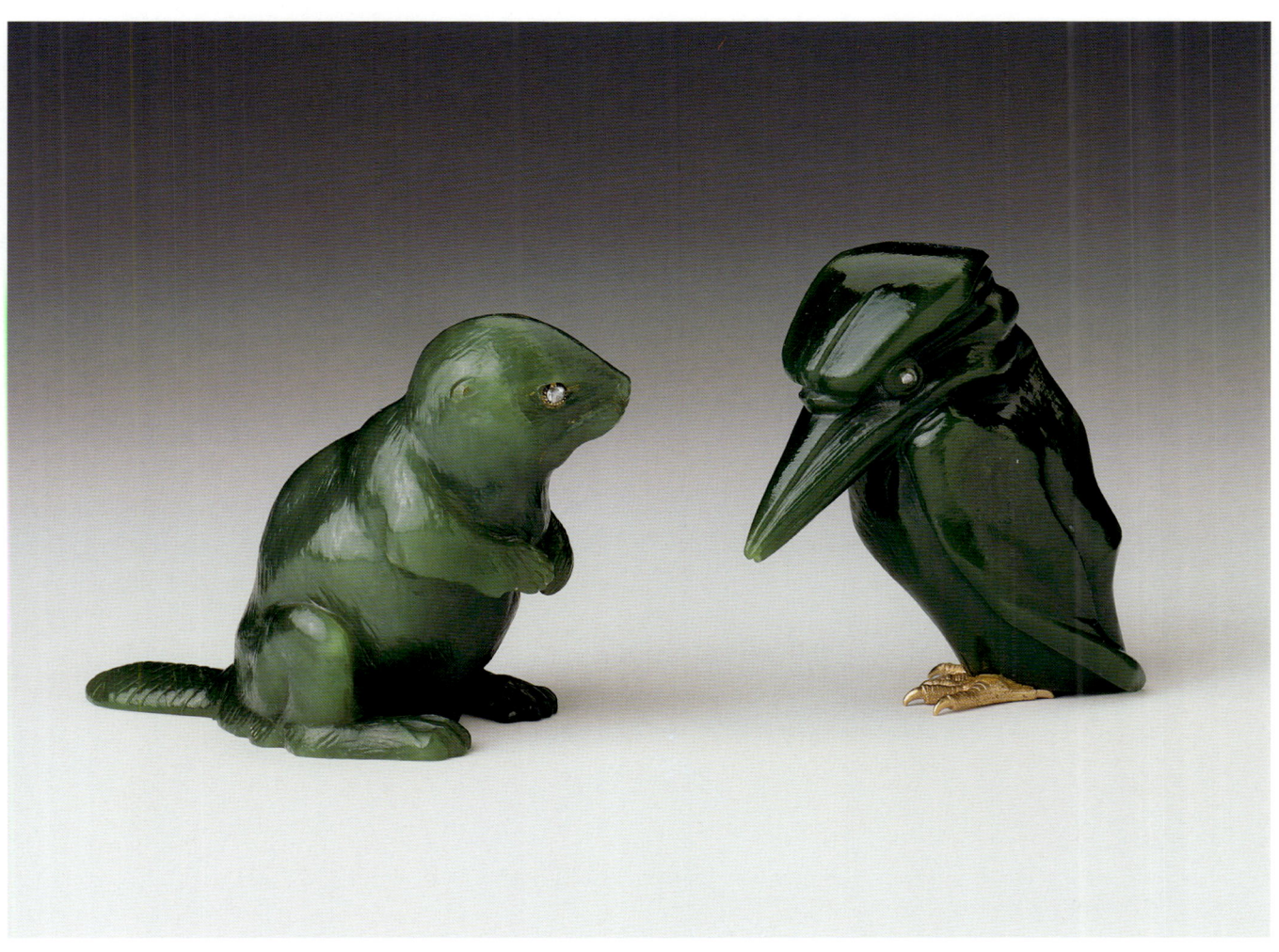

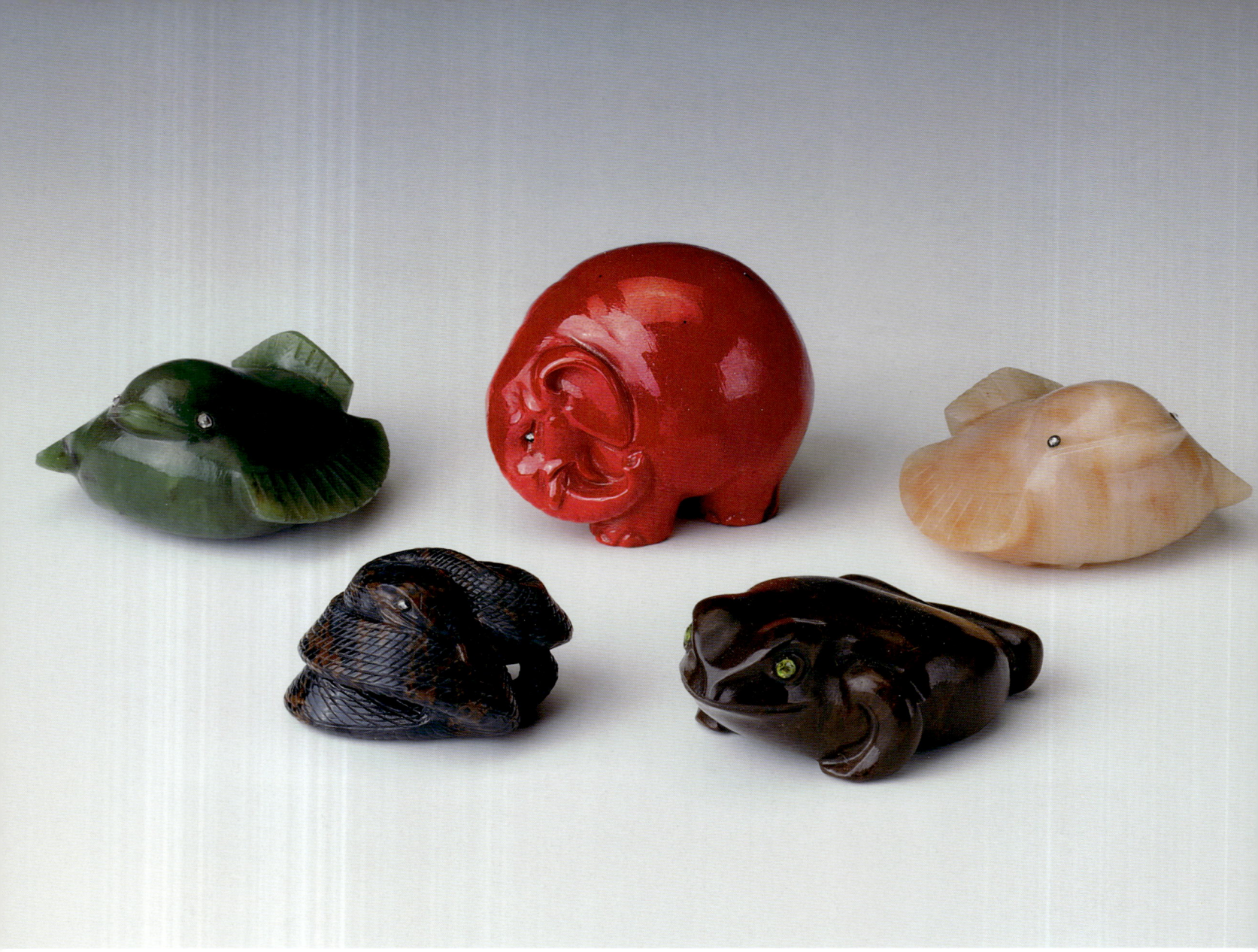

94   ELEPHANT, *c.*1910

The stylised low-relief carving of this elephant, together with cat. 93 and 105, particularly demonstrates Fabergé's interest in oriental art and in Japanese netsuke carving. It was necessary for Fabergé's sculptors to keep the carving dense to ensure that the fragile stone did not fracture. Birbaum notes when describing the animal carvings, 'it should be said that the pose was always as compact as possible, as dictated by the technique of the material'. Departures from naturalistic-looking animal carvings were not uncommon. The choice of stone colour – red elephants, blue rabbits and green dogs – was intended to add a humorous touch.

Unlike the majority of his animals, Fabergé occasionally repeated his elephant models. Countess Torby, the morganatic wife of Grand Duke Michael of Russia (1861–1929), formed a collection specifically of Fabergé's elephants.

Purpurine, rose diamonds, 3.7 x 3.9 x 4.5 cm (1⁷/₁₆ x 1⁹/₁₆ x 1³/₄")
Unmarked
RCIN 40270
PROVENANCE: Bought by Queen Alexandra from Fabergé's London branch, 24 December 1912 (£11)
REFERENCES: Habsburg & Lopato 1993, p. 459
EXHIBITIONS: London 1977, no. C15; QG 1985–6, no. 187; QG 1995–6, no. 514; QG 2002–3, no. 224

95 SPARROW, *c.*1900

Together with cat. 93, 94, 96, 97, 98 and 105, this stylised bird is an example of the direct influence of Japanese netsuke carving on Fabergé's animals.

Aventurine quartz, rose diamonds, 2.3 x 4.3 x 3.9 cm ($^{7}/_{8}$ x 1$^{11}/_{16}$ x 1$^{9}/_{16}$")
Unmarked
RCIN 40330
PROVENANCE: Probably acquired by Queen Alexandra; Royal Collection by 1953
EXHIBITIONS: London 1977, no. D43; QG 1995–6, no. 529

96 TOAD, *c.*1900

Birbaum describes the different types of jasper used in Fabergé's workshops. This toad, carved in the manner of a netsuke, is of what he describes as Orskaia jasper, which is typically warm brown in colouring.

Jasper, olivines, 2.2 x 4.5 x 3.7 cm ($^{7}/_{8}$ x 1$^{3}/_{4}$ x 1$^{7}/_{16}$")
Unmarked
RCIN 40370
PROVENANCE: Probably acquired by Queen Alexandra; Royal Collection by 1953
REFERENCES: Habsburg & Lopato 1993, p. 457
EXHIBITIONS: London 1977, no. B4; QG 1995–6, no. 539

97 COILED SNAKE, *c.*1900

This snake appears to have been copied directly from a netsuke, having much in common with examples from the Nagoya School. Carl Fabergé owned a collection of five hundred netsuke which was incorporated into the Hermitage Museum, St Petersburg, in 1917.

Jasper, rose diamonds, 2.3 x 3.7 x 3.1 cm ($^{7}/_{8}$ x 1$^{7}/_{16}$ x 1$^{1}/_{4}$")
Unmarked
RCIN 40404
PROVENANCE: Probably acquired by Queen Alexandra; Royal Collection by 1953
REFERENCES: Davey 1982, no. 577; Habsburg & Lopato 1993, p. 31
EXHIBITIONS: London 1977, no. C10; QG 1995–6, no. 523

98 SPARROW, *c.*1900

Carved in the style of a common netsuke type from the Kyoto School known as a *fukura suzume*.

Nephrite, rose diamonds, 2.5 x 4.5 x 3.6 cm (1 x 1$^{3}/_{4}$ x 1$^{7}/_{16}$")
Unmarked
RCIN 100303
PROVENANCE: Acquired by Queen Elizabeth, date unknown
REFERENCES: Snowman 1962, pl. 248; Davey 1982; Munn 1987
EXHIBITIONS: London 1991

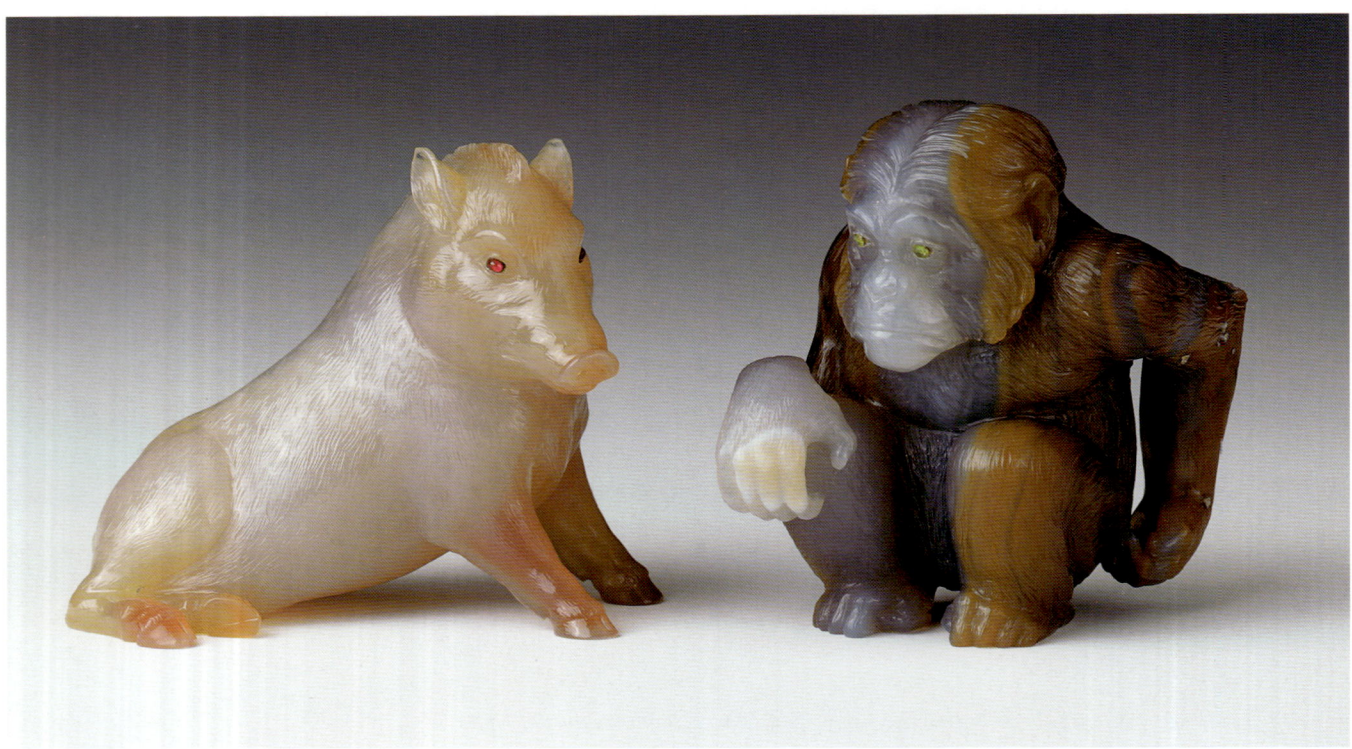

99 WILD BOAR, *c.*1908

Fabergé cleverly incorporated tiny precious stones for the eyes of his animals and birds. These range from diamonds, sapphires and rubies to olivines and were added not to increase monetary value – they are in themselves worthless chips – but to enliven the sculptures. Frödman-Cluzel recalls how he saw a statue of a wild boar in Geneva during his training in Europe. It is possible that he may also have seen the famous statue of a boar in the Medici collection in Florence.

Chalcedony, cabochon rubies, 6.7 x 8.6 x 5 cm (2⁵/₈ x 3³/₈ x 1¹⁵/₁₆")
Unmarked
RCIN 40260
PROVENANCE: Bought by the Prince of Wales (later King George V) from Fabergé's London branch, December 1909 (£31)
REFERENCES: Skurlov (unpublished research)
EXHIBITIONS: London 1977, no. B13; QG 1985–6, no. 213; QG 1995–6, no. 331; QG 2002–3, no. 222

100 CHIMPANZEE, *c.*1910

One of a number of carvings of apes in the Fabergé collection, this one has a pose that is particularly expressive. The stonecarver has made best use of the natural striations in the single piece of agate to suggest variations in the texture of fur and the animal's colouring. The fine carving and polishing of the stone is characteristic of the high standards maintained by Fabergé and his craftsmen.

Agate, olivines, 7.5 x 6.2 x 7.6 cm (2¹⁵/₁₆ x 2⁷/₁₆ x 3")
Unmarked
RCIN 40377
PROVENANCE: Probably acquired by King Edward VII; Queen Mary by 1949
EXHIBITIONS: London 1953, no. 5; London 1977, no. C1; New York 1983, no. 177; QG 1985–6, no. 167; QG 1995–6, no. 196; QG 2002–3, no. 223

101 AARDVARK, *c.* 1910

Agate, rose diamonds, 4.3 x 6.8 x 2.8 cm (1¹¹/₁₆ x 2¹¹/₁₆ x 1¹/₈")
Unmarked
RCIN 40471
PROVENANCE: Bought by King George V from Fabergé's London branch, 25 November 1914 (£18)
EXHIBITIONS: London 1977, no. C32; QG 1985–6, no. 194; London 1992; QG 1995–6, no. 330; QG 2002–3,
no. 225

102 DUCK-BILLED PLATYPUS, *c.* 1900

This exotic animal is an extremely rare example of a marked animal carving. Fabergé's hardstone animals in general were not marked, except in the case of birds with gold feet. One further animal in the
Royal Collection is marked, the brown bear (cat. 46).

Agate, rose diamonds, 2.9 x 7 x 3 cm (1¹/₈ x 2³/₄ x 1³/₁₆")
Chiselled on back left paw *C. FABERGÉ*
RCIN 40298
PROVENANCE: Probably acquired by Queen Alexandra; Royal Collection by 1953
EXHIBITIONS: London 1953, no. 114; London 1977, no. C35; QG 1995–6, no. 305

103 WARTHOG, *c.* 1900

Described by the late Kenneth Snowman as being of 'authentic repulsiveness', this is nonetheless a
fine example of realistic modelling by Fabergé's sculptors.

Agate, rose diamonds, 3.9 x 6.9 x 2.7 cm (1⁹/₁₆ x 2¹¹/₁₆ x 1¹/₁₆")
Unmarked
RCIN 40380
PROVENANCE: Bought by King George V from Fabergé's London branch, 14 December 1915 (£8 2s)
REFERENCES: Snowman 1955; RA PP/GV/3/3/810
EXHIBITIONS: London 1977, no. B22; QG 1995–6, no. 333

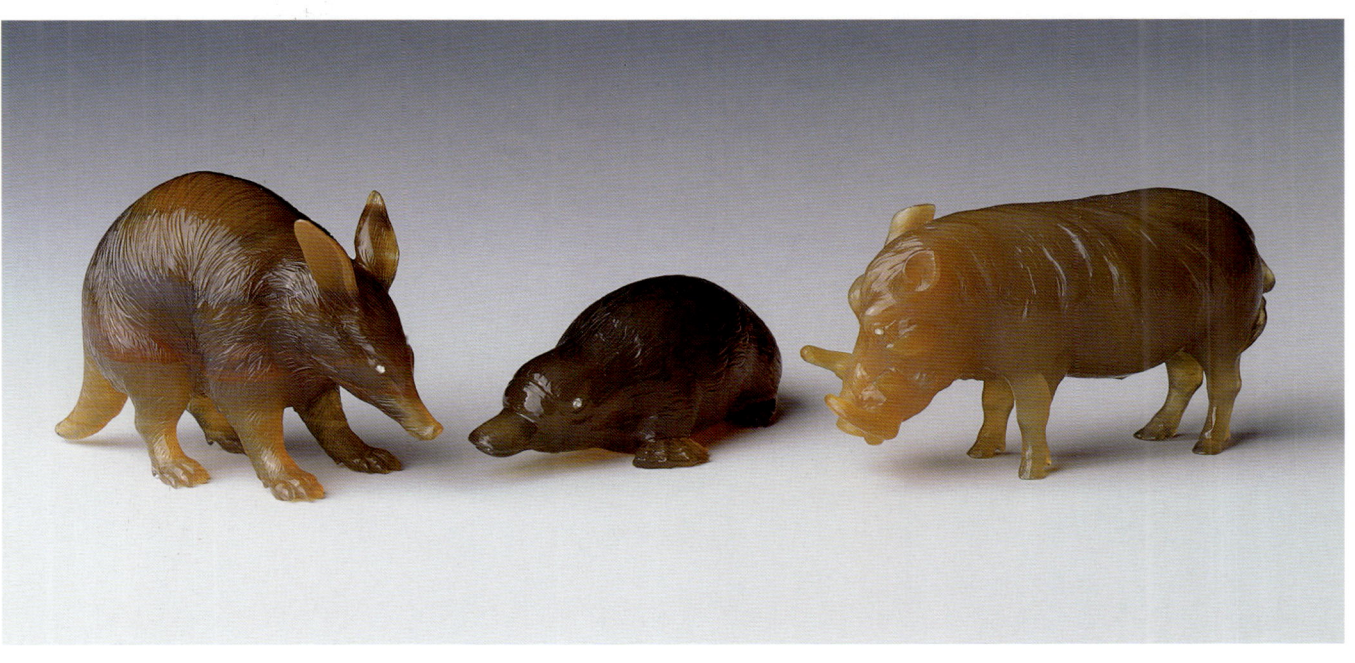

104 PAIR OF MACAQUES, *c.*1900

Monkeys of all varieties, in a range of poses, were produced in Fabergé's workshops and were clearly popular with his customers. Four were purchased by the royal family from the London branch between 1907 and 1916. There are now seven monkeys, four chimpanzees and one baboon in the Royal Collection, of which five are included here. This charming and realistically modelled study of macaques, carved from a single piece of chalcedony, is an example from the large number of animals purchased by King George V.

Chalcedony, rose diamonds, 4.4 x 5 x 4.7 cm (1³/₄ x 1¹⁵/₁₆ x 1⁷/₈")
Unmarked
RCIN 40049
PROVENANCE: Bought by King George V from Fabergé's London branch, 7 November 1910 (£41 10s)
EXHIBITIONS: London 1977, no. C5; QG 1995–6, no. 185

105 CHIMPANZEE, *c.*1900

An extraordinarily dense carving in the style of a netsuke.

Agate, rose diamonds, 3.5 x 2.5 x 2.5 cm (1³/₈ x 1 x 1")
Unmarked
RCIN 40394
PROVENANCE: Probably acquired by Queen Alexandra; Royal Collection by 1953
EXHIBITIONS: London 1977, no. C4; QG 1995–6, no. 524

106 RHESUS MONKEY, *c.*1900

Agate, rose diamonds, 2.4 x 5 x 2 cm (¹⁵/₁₆ x 1¹⁵/₁₆ x ¹³/₁₆")
Unmarked
RCIN 40074
PROVENANCE: Probably acquired by Queen Alexandra; Royal Collection by 1953
EXHIBITIONS: London 1977, no. C8; QG 1995–6, no. 176

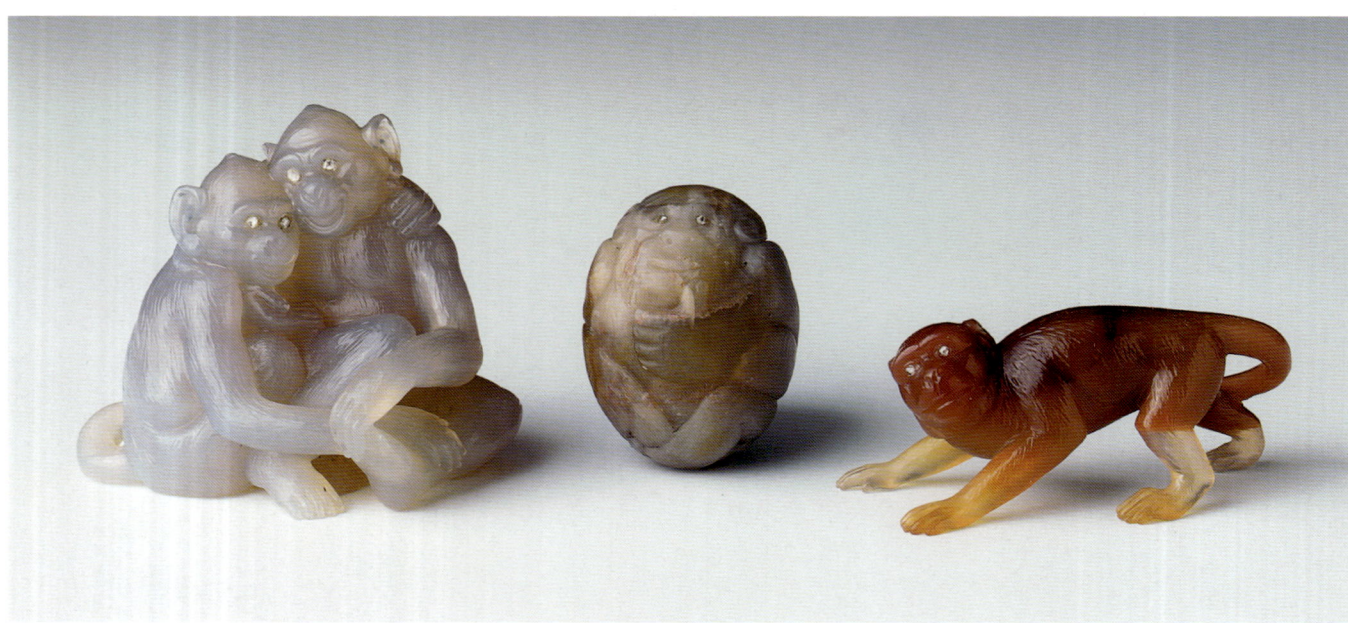

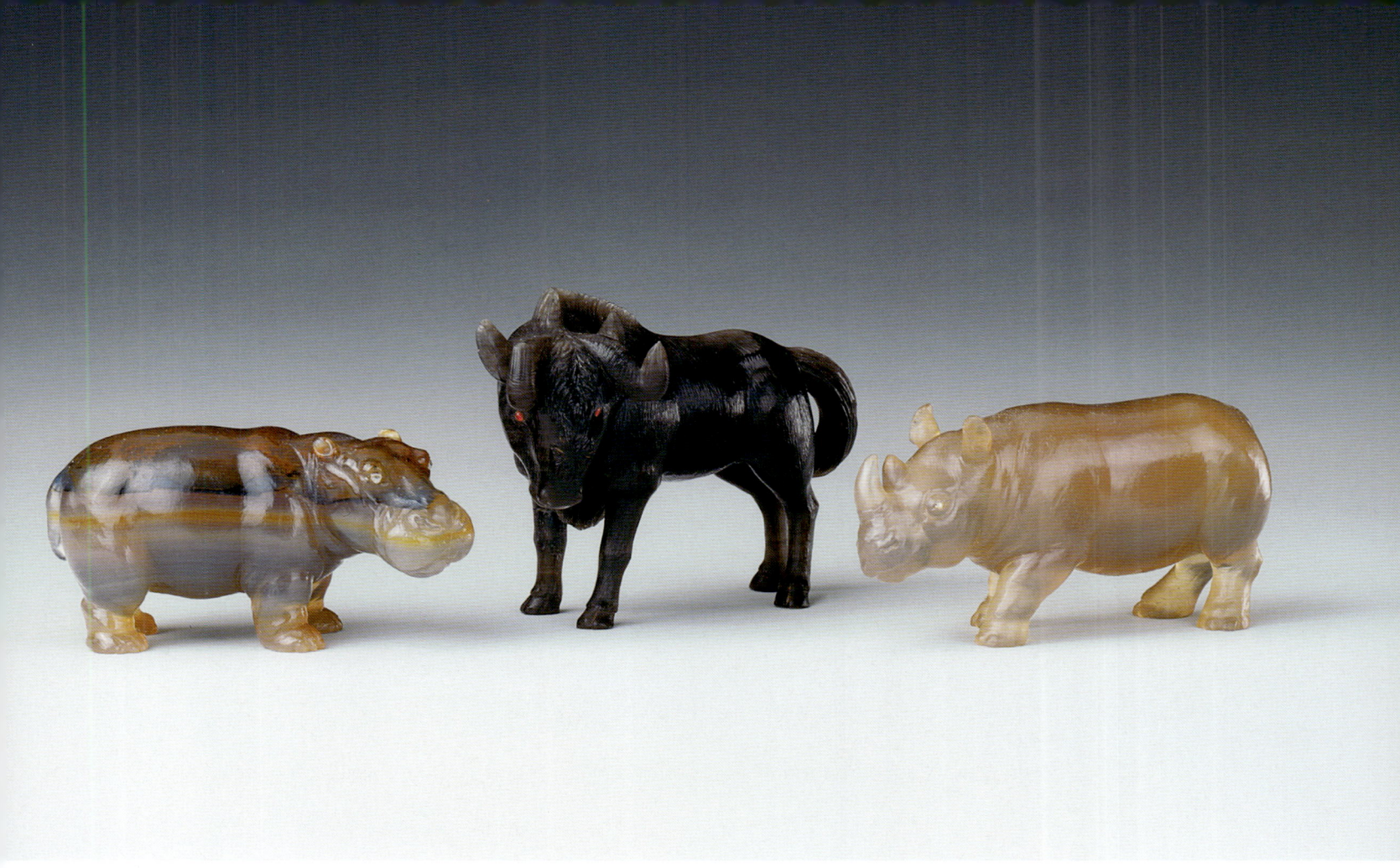

107 HIPPOPOTAMUS, *c.*1900

One of eight examples in the Royal Collection.

Agate, rose diamonds, 3 x 5.9 x 2.9 cm (1³/₁₆ x 2⁵/₁₆ x 1¹/₈")
Unmarked
RCIN 40337
PROVENANCE: Probably acquired by Queen Alexandra; Royal Collection by 1953
EXHIBITIONS: London 1977, no. C22; QG 1995–6, no. 287

108 BUFFALO, *c.*1900

Obsidian, cabochon rubies, 4.7 x 7.1 x 3.1 cm (1⁷/₈ x 2¹³/₁₆ x 1¹/₄")
Unmarked
RCIN 40267
PROVENANCE: Probably acquired by King George V; Royal Collection by 1953
EXHIBITIONS: QG 1995–6, no. 335

109 RHINOCEROS, *c.*1900

One of three rhinoceroses by Fabergé in the Royal Collection.

Chalcedony, 3.2 x 6 x 1.9 cm (1¹/₄ x 2³/₈ x ³/₄")
Unmarked
RCIN 40018
PROVENANCE: Probably acquired by Queen Alexandra; Royal Collection by 1953
EXHIBITIONS: QG 1995–6, no. 285

110 ELEPHANT, *c.*1900

The elephant is one of Fabergé's most popular and most often repeated animals; the Royal Collection alone contains forty-nine examples. In this instance, the use of rhodonite to create a pink elephant adds a humorous quality to the carving. The compact pose, influenced by Fabergé's interest in netsuke carving, is particularly evident in the purpurine elephant (cat. 94). Bainbridge asserts that Fabergé exaggerated particular characteristics of animals. For elephants, he played upon their bulk, reduced the length of the back and 'pushed them together concertina fashion' to make them even more appealing.

Rhodonite, olivines, 4.5 x 7.6 x 3.3 cm (1³/₄ x 3 x 1⁵/₁₆")
Unmarked
RCIN 40020
PROVENANCE: Possibly the rhodonite elephant bought by King George V from Wartski, 24 November 1928 (£15)
REFERENCES: Bainbridge 1938
EXHIBITIONS: QG 1995–6, no. 312

111 ELEPHANT, *c.*1900

It has been suggested that the kneeling pose of this elephant is derived from a well-known Japanese bronze type.

Nephrite, rose diamonds, 14.5 x 5.5 x 12.5 cm (5¹¹/₁₆ x 2³/₁₆ x 4¹⁵/₁₆")
Unmarked
RCIN 100302
PROVENANCE: Bought by Queen Elizabeth from Wartski, 7 April 1949 (£260)
REFERENCES: Snowman 1962, pl. 248; Munn 1987
EXHIBITIONS: London 1991

112 ELEPHANT, *c.*1900

At least six of the elephants in the Royal Collection are carved from nephrite, in this instance on a slightly larger scale than the rest. This particular animal was purchased by King George V in 1912.

Nephrite, brilliant diamonds, 7.8 x 11.5 x 6.5 cm (3¹/₁₆ x 4¹/₂ x 2⁹/₁₆")
Unmarked
RCIN 40048
PROVENANCE: Bought by King George V from Fabergé's London branch, 28 October 1912 (£76)
EXHIBITIONS: London 1977, no. C14; QG 1995–6, no. 179

113 ELEPHANT, *c.*1900

Nephrite, rose diamonds, 7.6 x 6 x 10.2 cm (3 x 2³/₈ x 4")
Unmarked
RCIN 100301
PROVENANCE: Bought by Queen Elizabeth from Wartski, 2 February 1947 (£150)
REFERENCES: Snowman 1962, pl. 248

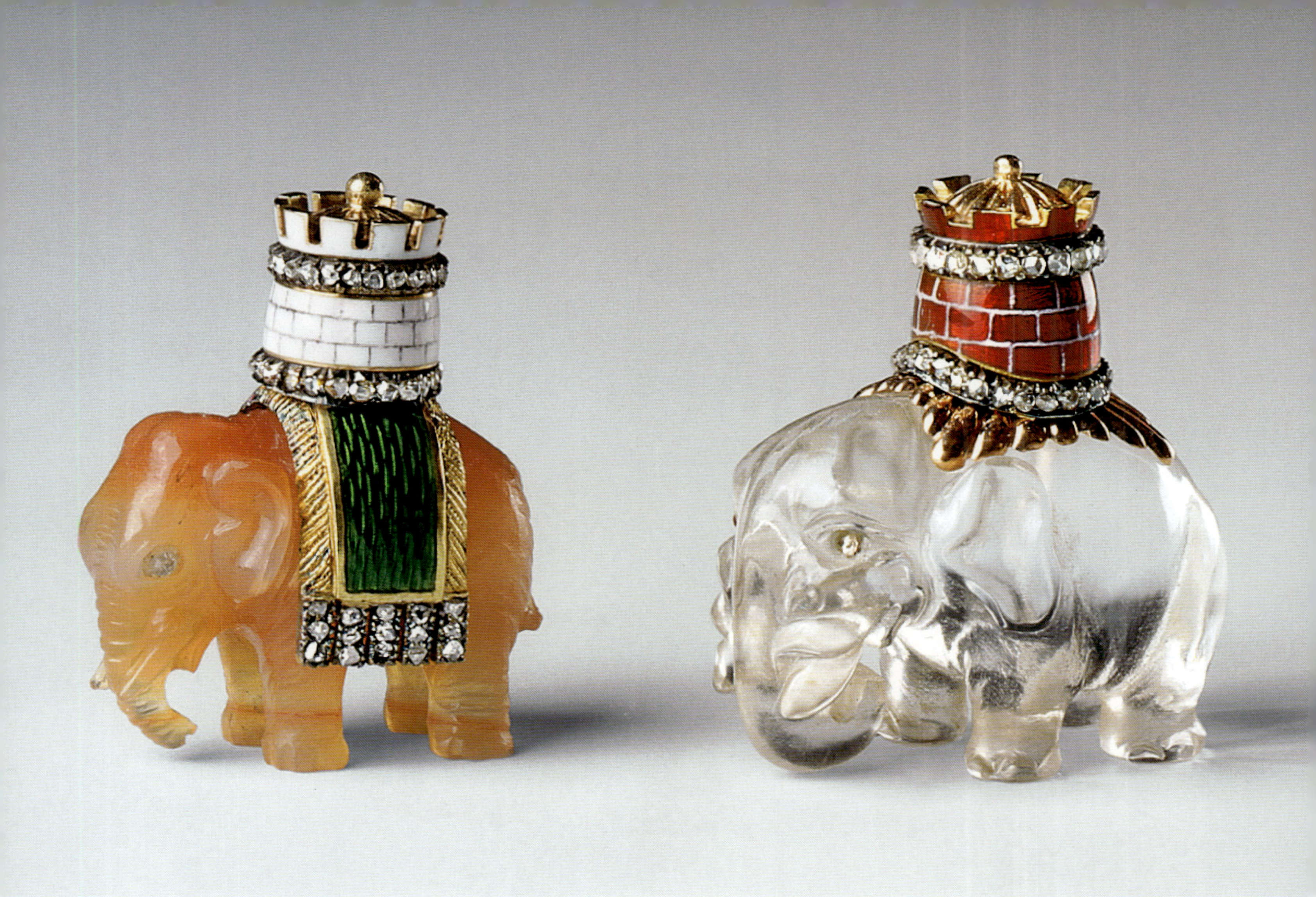

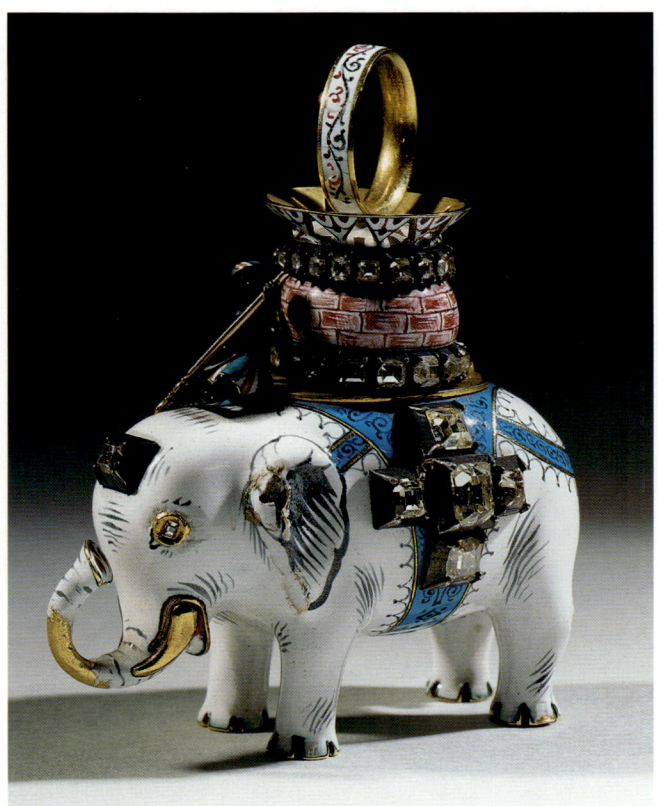

Gold and enamel badge of the Order of the Elephant of Denmark, 1884–5.

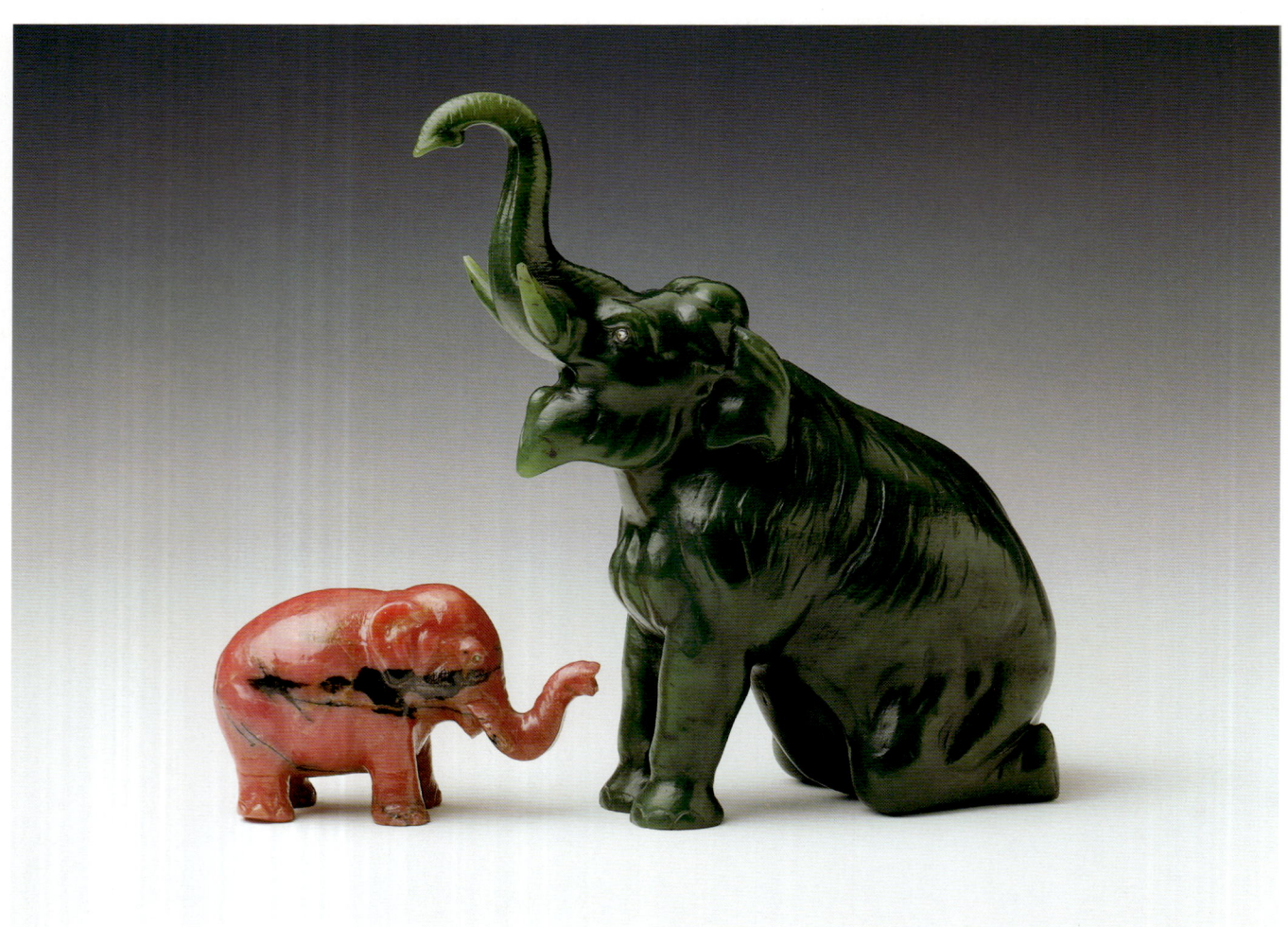

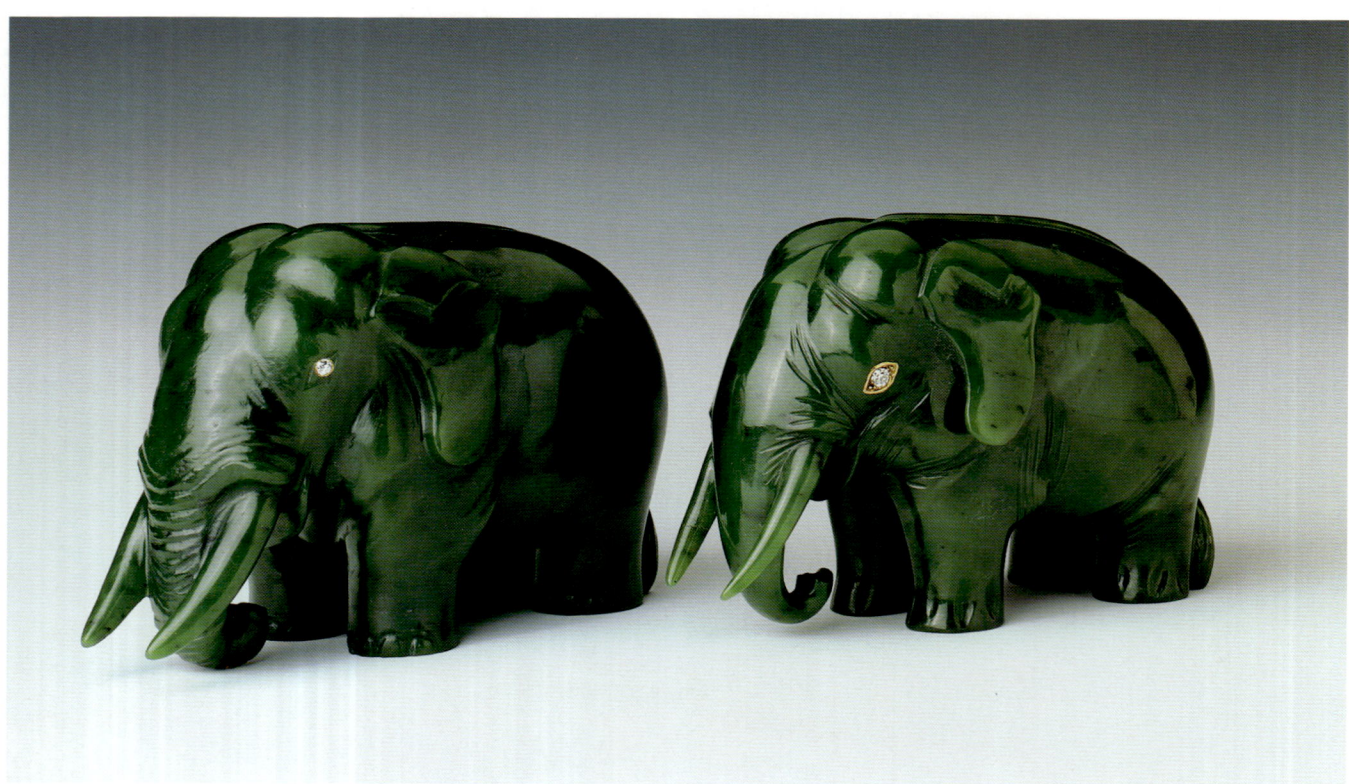

114   ELEPHANT AND CASTLE, *c.*1900

The highest Danish order of chivalry was the ancient Order of the Elephant, believed to have been founded by the Danish King Knut IV in the twelfth century. It was a symbol of absolute rule in Denmark. The order was re-established by King Christian I in 1464, and after the marriage of the future King Edward VII to Alexandra, daughter of King Christian IX of Denmark, in 1863, it was awarded to several members of the British royal family. The badge of the order was formed by an elephant and castle; the elephant symbolises chastity and defence of the Christian faith.

Direct commissions for objects incorporating the elephant and castle were placed with Fabergé in 1892 when Tsar Alexander III and Tsarina Marie Feodorovna commissioned the firm to produce a large *kovsh* surmounted by an elephant and castle to commemorate the golden wedding anniversary of King Christian IX and Queen Louise. In 1903 Tsar Nicholas II commissioned Fabergé to produce an Easter egg for Marie Feodorovna; known as the Danish Jubilee Egg, it is surmounted by an elephant and castle. Fabergé's two greatest patrons were Alexandra and her sister Marie Feodorovna, and he shrewdly introduced miniature elephants and castles to his range of products, perhaps at their suggestion. Two are included here and a third by Fabergé, which reputedly belonged to Marie Feodorovna, was acquired by Queen Mary and given to King George V.

Agate, rose diamonds, gold, enamel, 2.5 x 1.9 x 1.3 cm (1 x ³/₄ x ¹/₂")
Unmarked
RCIN 40198
PROVENANCE: Acquired by Queen Alexandra
REFERENCES: GV Boxes, Vol. VI; Patterson 1996
EXHIBITIONS: London 1977, no. C19; QG 1995–6, no. 149

115   ELEPHANT AND CASTLE, *c.*1900

Rock crystal, two-colour gold, enamel, rose diamonds, cabochon rubies, 2.6 x 2.2 x 1.3 cm (1 x ⁷/₈ x ¹/₂")
Unmarked
RCIN 40199
PROVENANCE: Probably acquired by Queen Alexandra, date unknown
EXHIBITIONS: London 1977, no. C20; QG 1995–6, no. 150

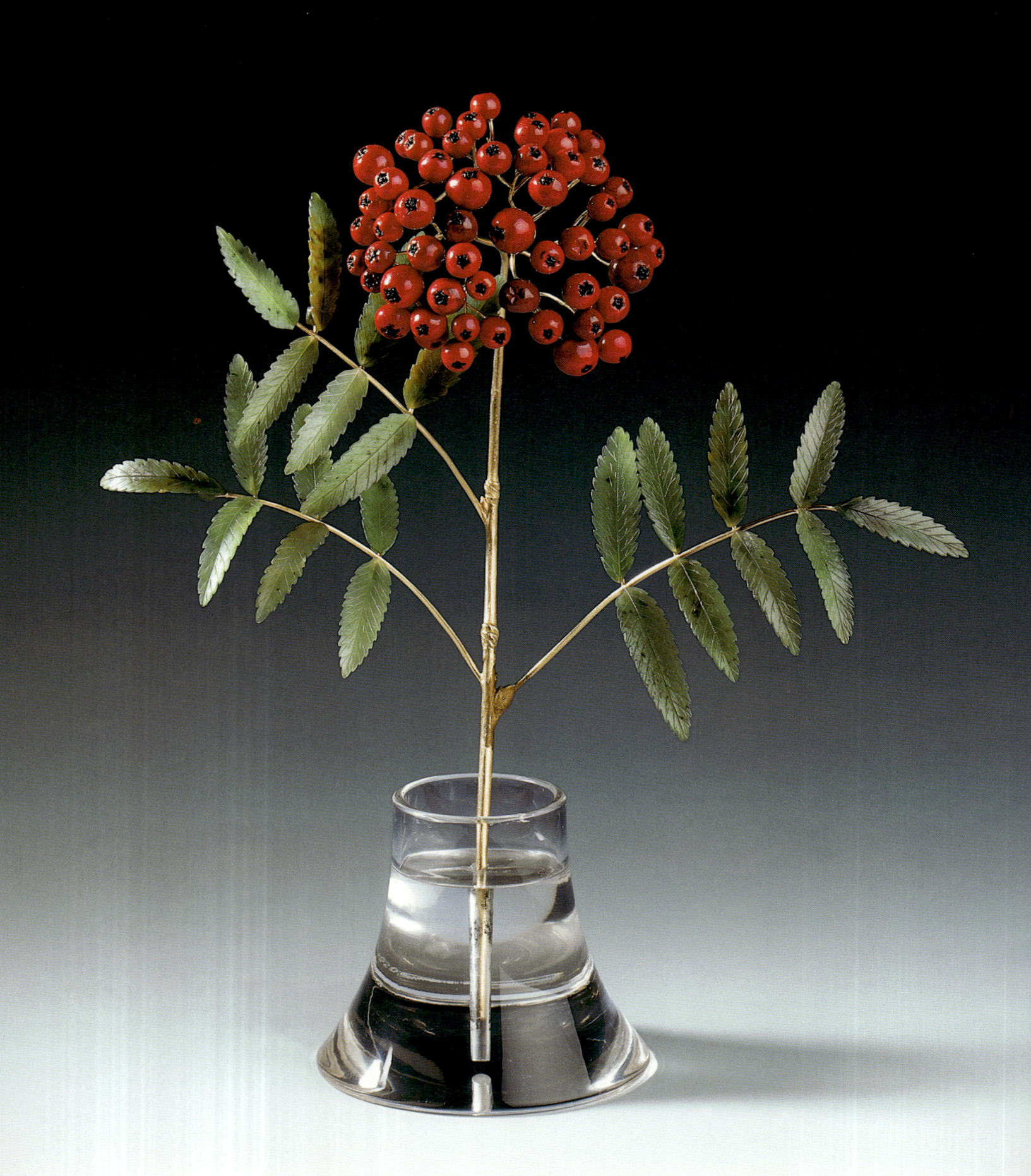

FLOWERS

FABERGÉ'S FLOWER STUDIES are probably his most exquisite objects. They incorporate all the painstaking techniques and expensive materials usually seen in his work, and their chief purpose is to delight the eye with a decorative reminder of the short Russian spring and summer.

Their inspiration is rooted in several different artistic traditions. Firstly, there is the lapidary carving tradition in Russia, the importance of which has already been mentioned in connection with Fabergé's animal sculptures (see pp. 51–2). In her essay on the Kremlin's collection of Tsarina Marie Feodorovna's belongings, Tatiana Muntian points out that the imperial Ekaterinburg and Peterhof factories made bunches of amethyst grapes, flowers and berries of semi-precious stones and that these were collected by the Tsarina.[1] According to a history of the state Peterhof lapidary works, the factories were 'burdened with orders from the court for their private requirements, presents and exhibitions abroad'.[2] Fabergé would have been well aware of the work produced by these factories and that of the firm of Pavel Ovchinnikov, who supplied a betrothal bouquet in silver, gold and enamel for Marie Feodorovna's marriage in 1886. It should be noted that Marie Feodorovna also owned several of Fabergé's flowers.

Secondly, examples of stone and jewelled bouquets were to be found across Europe, made by court jewellers in the eighteenth century. Carl Fabergé would undoubtedly have seen such objects during his apprenticeship, particularly in France. Fabergé had also repaired a flower bouquet

in the Hermitage made by Catherine the Great's court jeweller, Jérémie Pauzié.

The influence of oriental art is also seen in Fabergé's botanical pieces, particularly in the pine tree (cat. 121). Birbaum records how Fabergé first became aware of Chinese hardstone carvings of flowers when a bouquet of chrysanthemums was brought to him for repair. The chrysanthemums were made entirely from different stones and other natural materials such as coral, although Birbaum dismissed Chinese flower carvings as 'curiosities of the stone carver's skill rather than works of art'.[3]

The natural beauty of flowers strongly appealed to Fabergé, and this explains why his flower studies are so realistic and, for the most part, botanically accurate. Their naturalism enhanced their popularity with his clients in Russia, where the short spring and summer months meant that home-grown flowers were seen only very briefly. Wealthy members of society were able to afford flowers imported from the south of France, which were kept on ice to preserve their freshness during the long journey to Russia, but they clearly also enjoyed the charming and decorative hardstone alternatives. Moreover, the intrinsic decorative quality of the flowers was perfectly in keeping with the bibelots and *objets d'art* displayed in great numbers in the apartments of Tsarinas Marie Feodorovna and Alexandra Feodorovna as well as their contemporaries.

The retail cost of the flowers was considerable because their manufacture was so expensive. Birbaum

LEFT: Rowan tree, c.1900 (cat. 136).

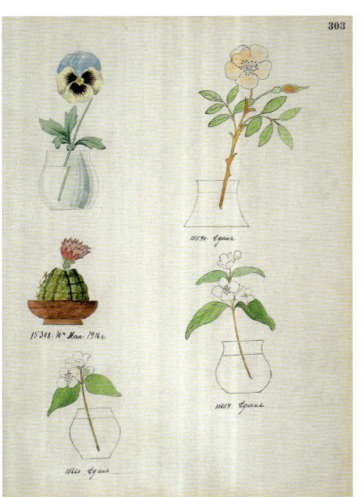

A plate from a previously unpublished album of watercolour designs by Henrik Wigström, showing various flowers including a philadelphus (cat. 116), a pansy (cat. 120) and a rose (cat. 128).

acknowledges that the cost of the flowers was sometimes 'as much as several thousand roubles' each.[4] The most expensive flower bought through the London branch was the chrysanthemum (cat. 140), which cost £117.

The first stage of production involved the designers. According to Bainbridge these were Carl Fabergé himself, assisted by Franz Birbaum. The enamelling was carried out by Alexander and Nicholas Petrov and by Boitzov. The stone leaves were cut by Kremlev and Derbyshev, and the precious stones set by August and Albert Holmström. Finally the gold stalks and grasses were added and the flowers assembled in the workshop of Michael Perchin and later in that of Henrik Wigström. The whole process was apparently carefully monitored by Carl Fabergé at each stage.[5] Fabergé's flowers are often not marked, mainly because the stems were too fragile to stamp, but occasionally marks are found which help to determine when they were made and by which workmaster. Of the twenty-six flowers in the Royal Collection, eight are marked: one is stamped *FABERGÉ* alone, one is marked by Feodor Afanassiev and six by Henrik Wigström. Drawings for some of the flowers by Wigström have recently been discovered in an unpublished album; some relate to the flowers now in the Royal Collection (see cat. 116, 120 and 128).

Birbaum states that Fabergé's flowers were first exhibited at the Exposition Universelle in Paris in 1900, at which time they were immediately copied by German and Austrian factories which produced poor-quality imitations using cheap materials. Other makers in Europe would also have seen them. These include Cartier, who began making flowers in a similar vein at around this time, although Cartier soon developed its own particular style of flower models which was quite different from Fabergé's (see cat. 344). In fact, it appears that Fabergé began making flowers well before 1900. A raspberry plant was apparently given to Queen Victoria in 1894 by her Lord Chamberlain.[6] According to Muntian, the earliest acquisition of a flower by the Russian imperial family was in 1895, when Tsarina Alexandra Feodorovna acquired a yellow rose.[7] Dr Marina Lopato has cited an even earlier example: a hibiscus flower that was among the objects exhibited by Fabergé at the Pan-Russian Industrial Exhibition in Moscow in 1882.[8]

The greatest Russian collectors of Fabergé's flowers were Tsarina Marie Feodorovna, Tsarina Alexandra Feodorovna and Grand Duchess Maria Pavlova. In England Queen Alexandra was the most prolific collector. Princess Victoria and Queen Mary also added to the Royal Collection and Bainbridge identifies the Marchioness of Ripon and Lady Sackville as flower collectors.[9] It was clearly something of a risk to send these precious objects all the way to England to be sold in the London branch, given their fragility; even Birbaum seems surprised that they survived the journey. Only two flowers are recorded in the London ledgers as having been purchased by members of the royal family: a raspberry bush bought by Queen Alexandra on 27 June 1909 (cat. 124) and a Japanese pine by the Prince of Wales in 1908 (cat. 121). This confirms that many of the flowers were presented as gifts, mainly to Queen Alexandra. They were also purchased as gifts for others, for example a cactus bought by King George V and Queen Mary on 13 December 1915 was clearly intended as a Christmas present as there is no trace of it in the collection today. The Royal Collection contains the largest surviving group of Fabergé's flowers: twenty-six from the total of approximately eighty that is believed to have been made. Queen Elizabeth made the last additions in the late 1940s when she acquired two charming studies of cornflowers and oats (cat. 132) and cornflowers and buttercups (cat. 133).

1 Muntian 1997, p. 328.
2 Fersmann & Vlodavets 1921, p. 25.
3 Habsburg & Lopato 1993, p. 458.
4 Ibid., p. 458.
5 Bainbridge 1942a, p. 937.
6 RA GV/CC 55/242.
7 Muntian 1997, p. 328.
8 Habsburg & Lopato 1993, p. 58.
9 Bainbridge 1938.

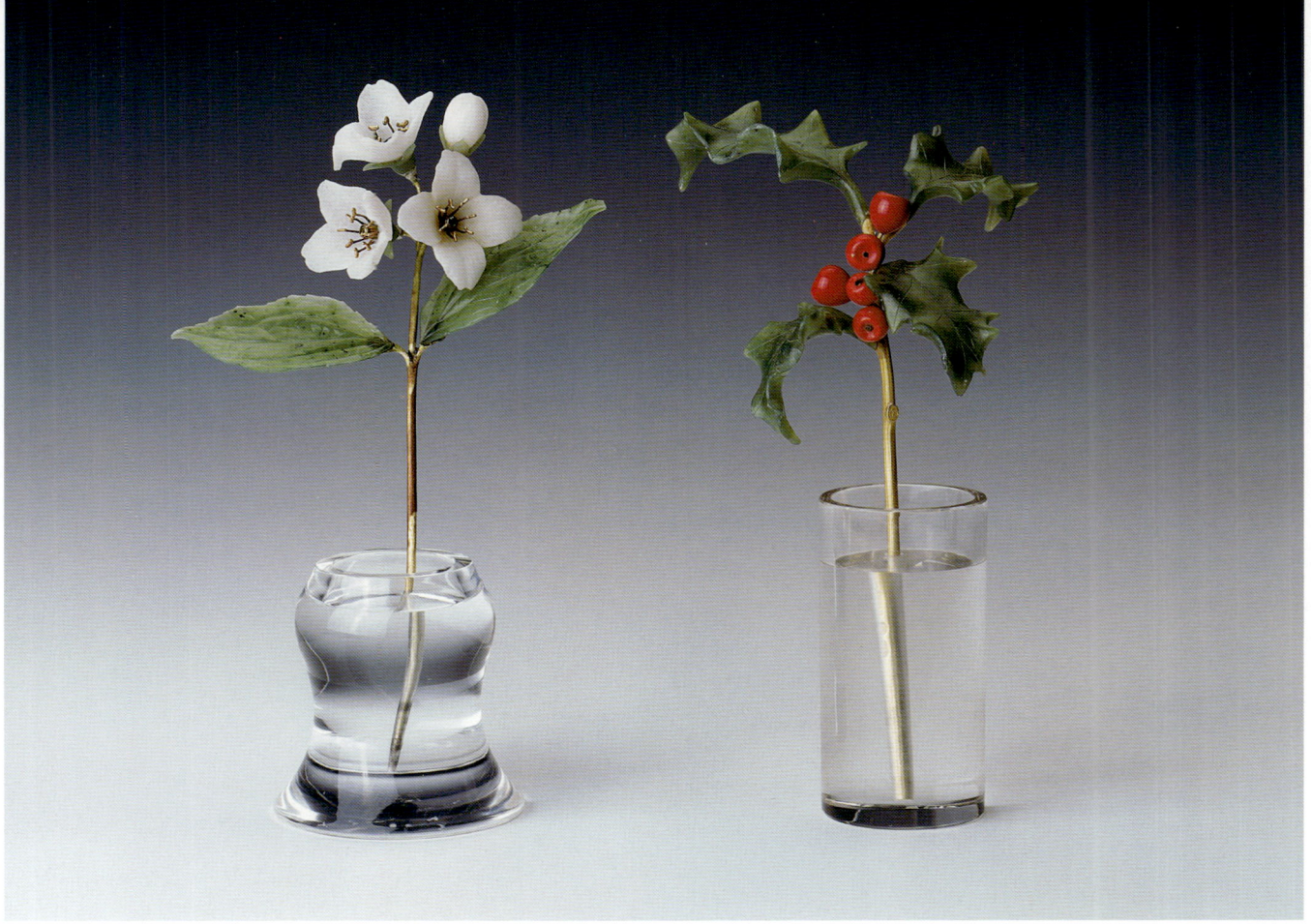

116   PHILADELPHUS, *c.*1900

While the majority of Fabergé's flowers have enamelled petals, this study differs in having carved hardstone flower heads. Another example of the use of hardstone to replicate petals is the study of bleeding heart (cat. 131). A drawing for a study of philadelphus, closely related to this one, exists in an unpublished album of designs from Henrik Wigström's workshop (see p. 104).

Vase of rock crystal, gold, nephrite, quartzite, olivines, 14.2 x 7 x 9 cm (15⁹/₁₆ x 2³/₄ x 3⁹/₁₆")
Marked *FABERGÉ* in Cyrillic characters
RCIN 40252
PROVENANCE: Acquired by Queen Alexandra, date unknown
REFERENCES: Bainbridge 1949, p. 95
EXHIBITIONS: London 1953, no. 48; London 1977, no. E16; New York 1983, no. 2; QG 1985-6, no. 4;
QG 1995–6, no. 121; QG 2002–3, no. 252

117   HOLLY SPRIG, *c.*1908

Of the eight flowers in the Royal Collection which are marked, six bear Wigström's mark. This holly plant was purchased by Mrs George Keppel on a visit to Fabergé's London branch with King Edward VII in 1908.

Rock crystal, gold, nephrite, purpurine, 14.1 x 8 x 8 cm (5⁹/₁₆ x 3¹/₈ x 3¹/₈")
Mark of Henrik Wigström; gold mark of 72 *zolotniks* (1896–1908); *FABERGÉ* in Cyrillic characters
RCIN 40501
PROVENANCE: Bought by the Hon. Mrs George Keppel from Fabergé's London branch, 1908 (£43); apparently given to Queen Alexandra
REFERENCES: Bainbridge 1949, p. 95
EXHIBITIONS: London 1953, no. 39; London 1977, no. E21; New York 1983, no. 15; QG 1985–6, no. 7;
QG 1995–6, no. 210; QG 2002–3, no. 240

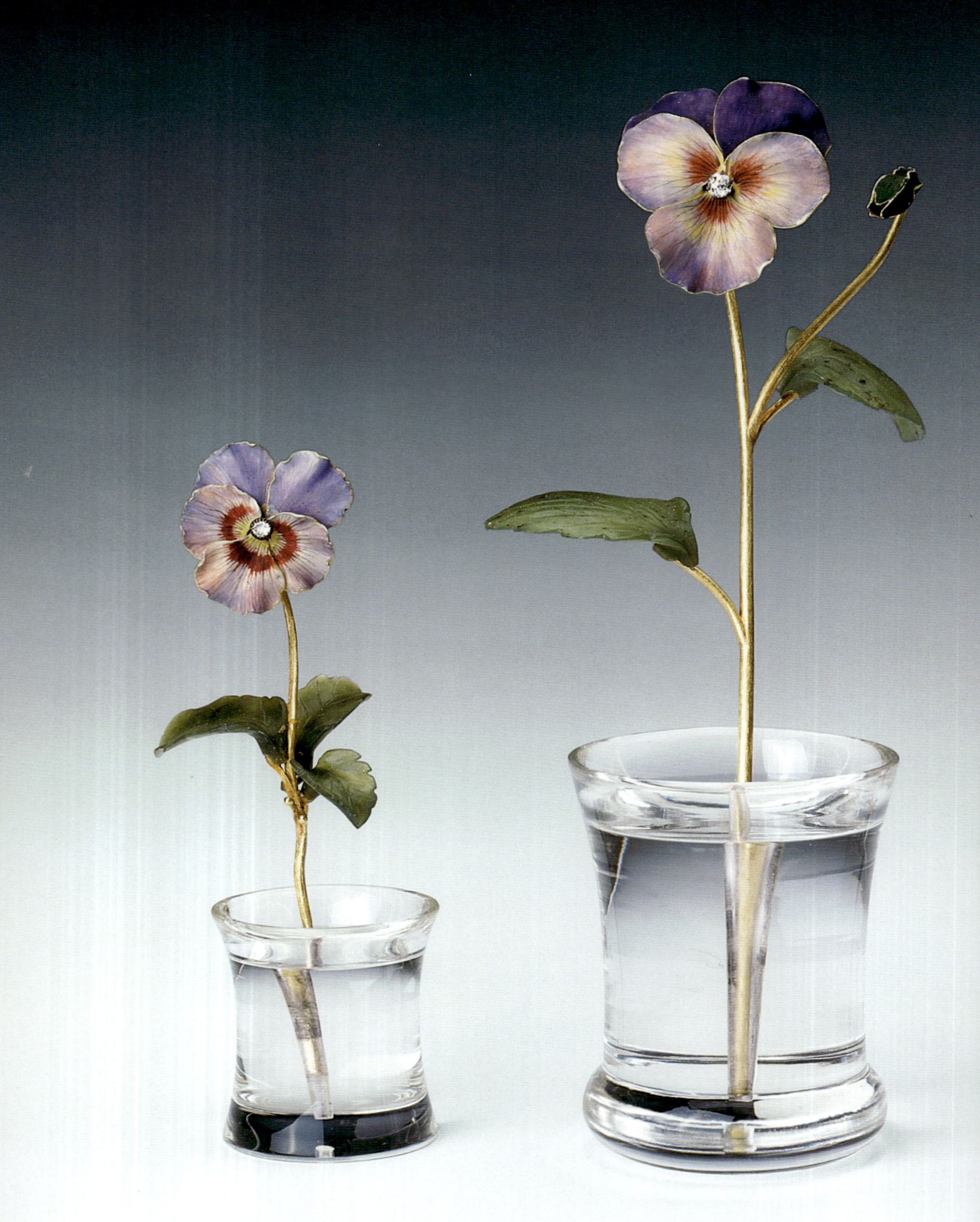

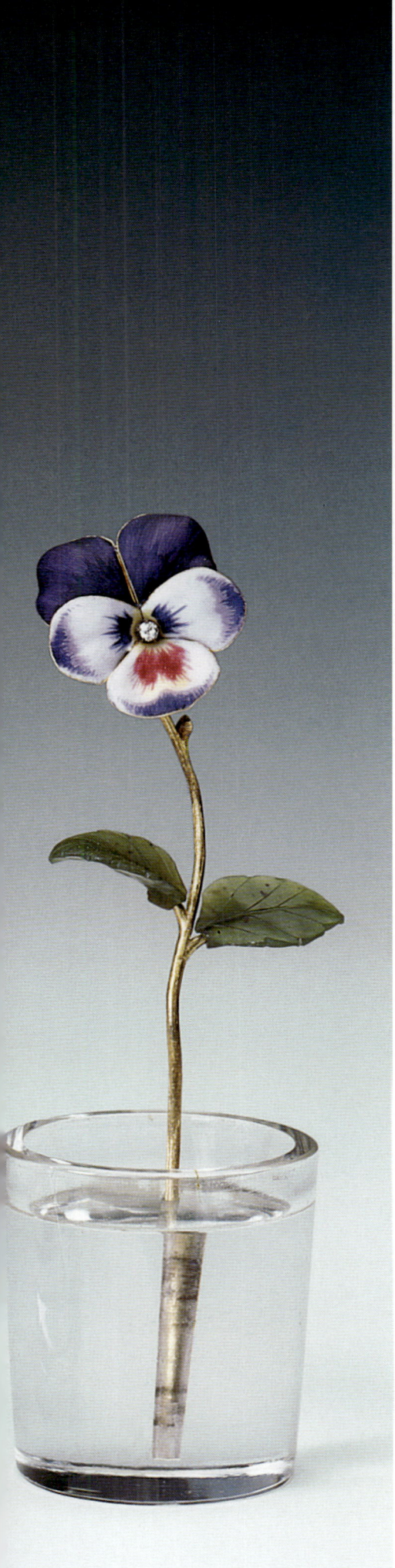

118 PANSY, c. 1900

All three of the pansy flower groups in the Royal Collection combine the same purple and yellow colours of enamel. The similar treatment of the petals, with variations in tone and combination of matt and polished enamel, would seem to indicate that the enamelling was completed in the same workshop. Indeed, Bainbridge asserts that all the flowers were enamelled by Alexander and Nicholas Petrov and by Boitzov, the main enamellers working for Fabergé. A drawing for a similar pansy exists in an unpublished album of designs from Wigström's workshops (see p. 104).

Rock crystal, gold, enamel, nephrite, brilliant diamond, 10.2 x diameter 3.3 cm (4 x 1⁵/₁₆")
Unmarked
RCIN 40210
PROVENANCE: Probably acquired by Queen Alexandra; Royal Collection before 1953
REFERENCES: Bainbridge 1942a
EXHIBITIONS: London 1953; London 1992; QG 1995–6, nc. 132; QG 2002–3, no. 246

119 PANSY, c. 1900

Rock crystal, gold, enamel, nephrite, brilliant diamond, 10.7 x 5.5 x 4 cm (4³/₁₆ x 2³/₁₆ x 1⁹/₁₆")
Unmarked
RCIN 40505
PROVENANCE: Probably acquired by Queen Alexandra; Royal Collection before 1953
EXHIBITIONS: London 1953, no. 31; London 1977, no. E14; QG 1985–6, no. 3; QG 1995–6, no. 126; QG 2002–3, no. 245

120 PANSY, 1903–1908

A drawing exists (on pl. 77) in the design books of Wigström's workshop for a pansy flower head which was executed in April 1912, some years after this flower. Michael Perchin had earlier produced the art nouveau-style Imperial Pansy Egg of 1899, and in 1903 he designed a miniature frame in the form of a pansy flower. This has a mechanism which, when released, opens the petals to reveal miniature portraits of the five children of Tsar Nicholas II and Tsarina Alexandra Feodorovna (Moscow Kremlin Armoury Museum).

Rock crystal, nephrite, gold, enamel, rose diamond, 10.1 x 5.3 x 5 cm (4 x 2¹/₁₆ x 1¹⁵/₁₆")
Mark of Henrik Wigström; gold mark of 72 *zolotniks* (1896–1908); *FABERGÉ* in Cyrillic characters
RCIN 40180
PROVENANCE: Probably acquired by Queen Alexandra; Royal Collection before 1953
REFERENCES: Tillander-Godenhielm *et al.* 2000, pl. 77
EXHIBITIONS: London 1953, no. 36; London 1977, no. E15; New York 1983, no. 24; QG 1985–6, no.1; QG 1995–6, no.130; QG 2002–3, no. 244

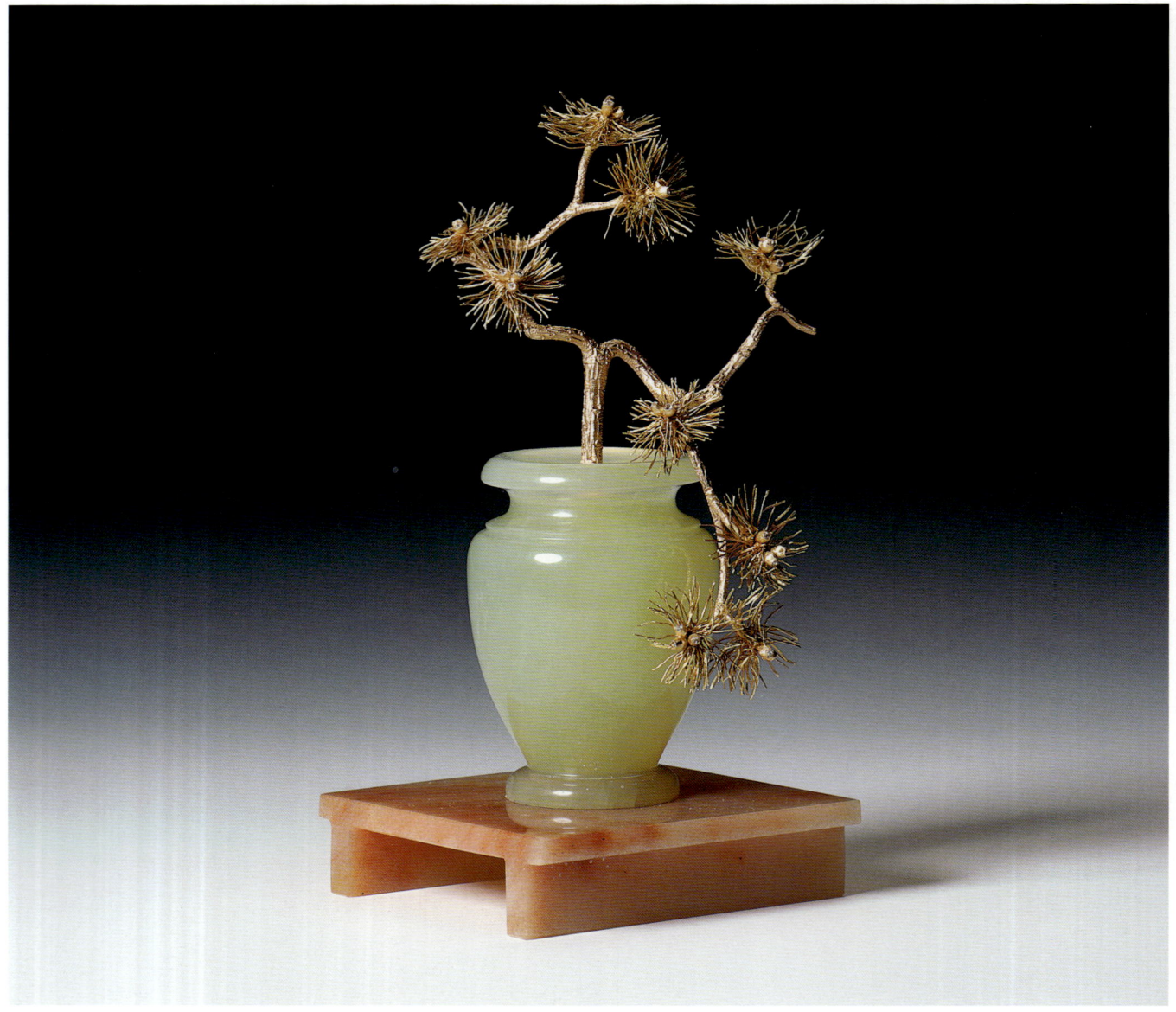

121 PINE TREE, *c.*1908

This Japanese-style pine tree was modelled from nature at Sandringham, presumably as part of King Edward VII's commission. A similar but not identical study of a gold pine tree in a bowenite vase exists, apparently marked by Perchin.

This model plant and cat. 122 and 123 are unusual in Fabergé's output of botanical works as they are displayed not in rock crystal pots but in carved hardstone or metal containers.

Bowenite, aventurine-quartz, gold, brilliant diamonds, 12.3 x 6.2 x 5.8 cm (4^{13}/$_{16}$ x 2^{7}/$_{16}$ x 2^{5}/$_{16}$")
Unmarked
RCIN 40186
PROVENANCE: Commissioned by King Edward VII, 1907; bought by the Prince of Wales (later King George V) from Fabergé's London branch, 14 December 1908 (£52)
REFERENCES: Bainbridge 1949, p. 95; Christie's, 24 October 2002b, lot 114
EXHIBITIONS: London 1953, no. 43; London 1977, no. E13; New York 1983, no. 28; QG 1985–6, no. 162; QG 1995–6, no. 528; QG 2002–3, no. 235

122 FIELD DAISIES, 1903–1908

Silver, gold, enamel, rose diamonds, nephrite, 7.5 x diameter 5.5 cm (2¹⁵/₁₆ x 2³/₁₆")
Mark of Henrik Wigström; silver mark of 88 *zolotniks* (1896–1908); *FABERGÉ* in Cyrillic characters
RCIN 40211
PROVENANCE: Probably acquired by Queen Alexandra; Royal Collection by 1953
EXHIBITIONS: London 1953, no. 51; London 1977, no. E19; New York 1983, no. 5; QG 1985–6, no. 127;
QG 1995–6, no. 154; QG 2002–3, no. 234

123 CONVOLVULUS, *c.*1900

This miniature of one of the gardener's greatest enemies, the bindweed, formerly belonged to the doyenne
of twentieth-century English garden writers, Vita Sackville-West (the Hon. Mrs Harold Nicolson,
1892–1962). Photographs of this flower at the time of its acquisition by Queen Mary show it mounted
on a hardstone base described as being of white jade. Bainbridge also illustrates the piece with the
base still intact, but it no longer survives. This flower was also owned by Sir Bernard Eckstein and
after his death was sold at Sotheby's, on 8 February 1949.

Bowenite, gold, nephrite, enamel, rose diamond, 11.1 x 6.5 x 2.5 cm (4³/₈ x 2⁹/₁₆ x 1")
Unmarked
RCIN 8943
PROVENANCE: Bought by [–] Sackville-West from Fabergé's London branch, 30 March 1908 (£35); the Hon. Mrs
Harold Nicolson; Sir Bernard Eckstein; Sotheby's 1949, lot 119; presented by the royal family to Queen Mary on
her birthday, 26 May 1949
REFERENCES: QMPP, XI, no. 71; Sotheby's, Sir Bernard Eckstein Collections, 8 February 1949, lot 199; Bainbridge
1949, pl. 78
EXHIBITIONS: London 1977, no. E3; New York 1983, no. 49; London QG 1985–6, no. 161; London 1995–6,
no. 213; QG 2002–3, no. 236

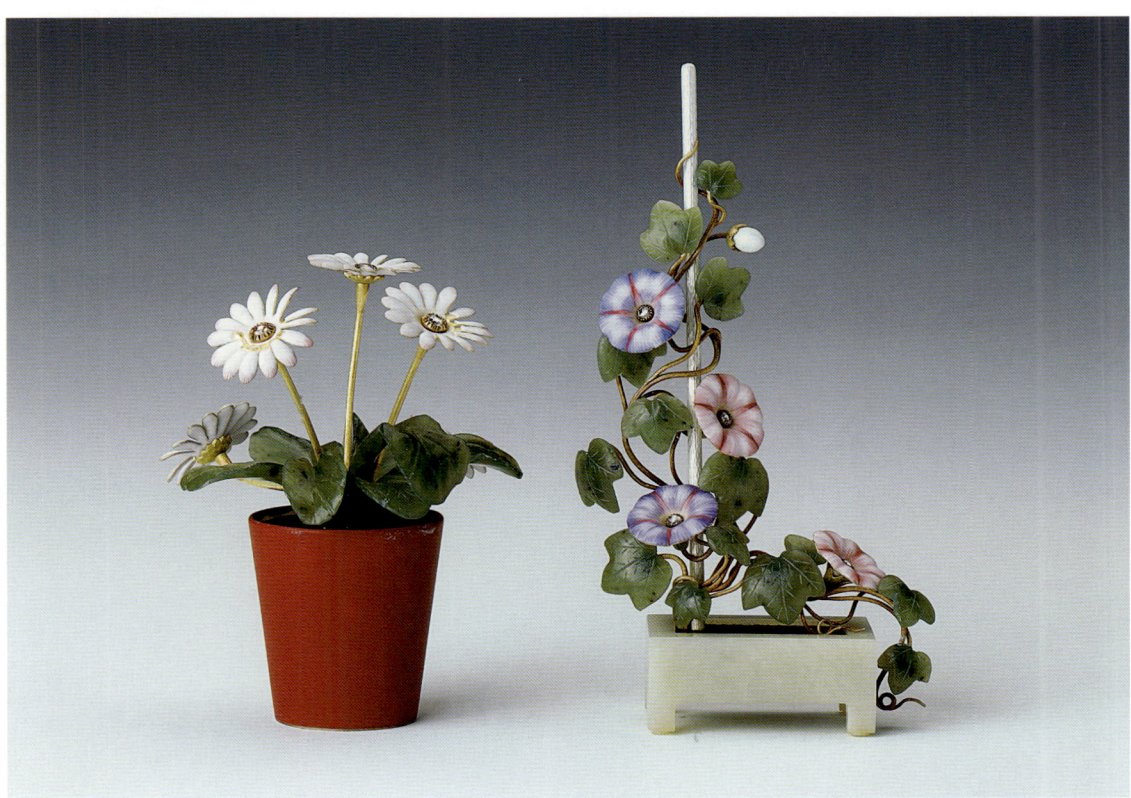

124 RASPBERRY, *c.*1900

Rock crystal, gold, nephrite, rhodonite, 9 x 4 x 4 cm (3⁹/₁₆ x 1⁹/₁₆ x 1⁹/₁₆")
Unmarked
RCIN 40176
PROVENANCE: Probably acquired by Queen Alexandra; Royal Collection by 1953
EXHIBITIONS: London 1953, no. 41; London 1977, no. E10; QG 1985–6, no. 16; QG 1995–6, no. 211

125 RASPBERRY, *c.*1900

One of two Fabergé raspberries in the Royal Collection (see cat. 124). According to a note in an inventory of Queen Mary's Fabergé collection, dated 1949, a raspberry flower was given to Queen Victoria in 1894 by Lord Carrington (1843–1928), her Lord Chamberlain from 1892 to 1895.

Rock crystal, gold, nephrite, rhodonite, 15.9 x 7.8 x 6.7 cm (6¹/₄ x 3¹/₁₆ x 2⁵/₈")
Unmarked
RCIN 40251
PROVENANCE: Probably acquired by Queen Alexandra; Royal Collection by 1953
REFERENCES: Bainbridge 1949, p. 95; RA GV/CC 55/242
EXHIBITIONS: London 1953, no. 37; London 1977, no. E9; QG 1985–6, no. 17; QG 1995–6, no. 129; QG 2002–3, no. 238

126 WILD STRAWBERRY, *c.*1900

As already noted, Fabergé on rare occasions made more than one version of some of the flower studies, and an almost identical version of this group exists in the Wernher Collection.

Rock crystal, gold, nephrite, enamel, pearl, 11.5 x 6 x 4.3 cm (4¹/₂ x 2³/₈ x 1¹¹/₁₆")
Unmarked
RCIN 9123
PROVENANCE: Probably acquired by Queen Alexandra; Royal Collection by 1953
EXHIBITIONS: QG 1995–6, no. 208; QG 2002–3, no. 237

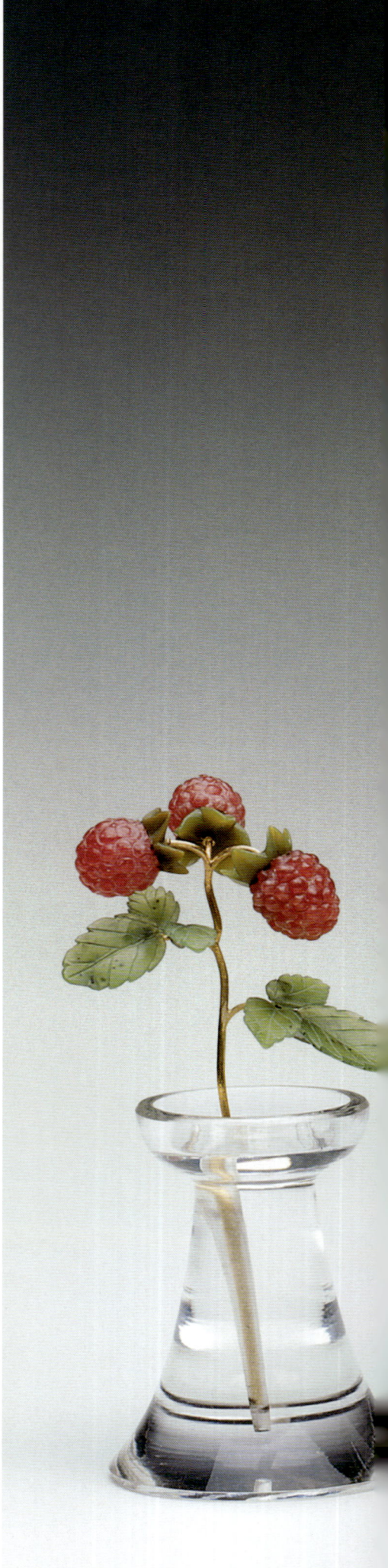

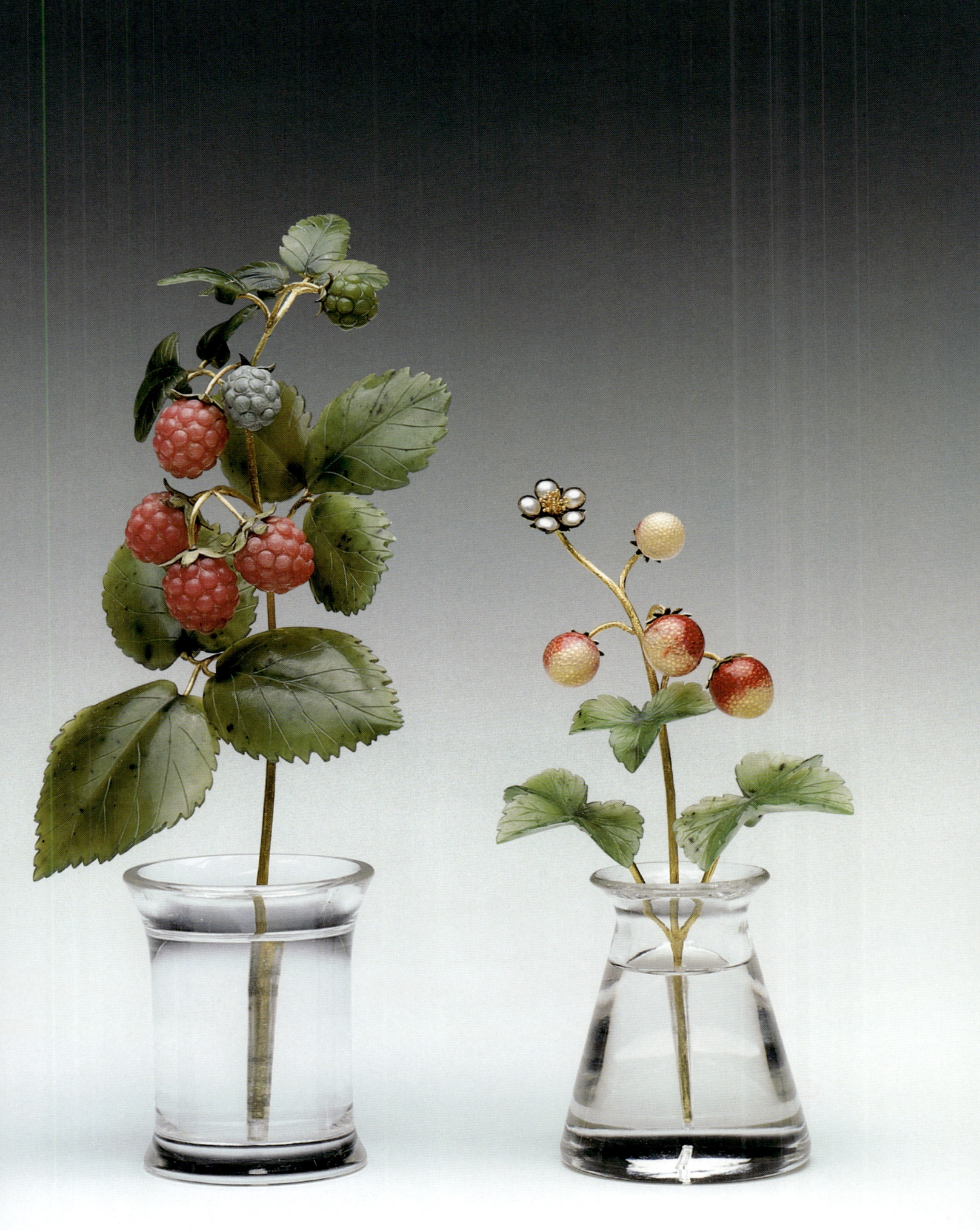

127 ROSEBUDS, *c.*1900

Gold, enamel, nephrite, rock crystal, 12.3 x 7.7 x 4.5 cm (4¹³/₁₆ x 3¹/₁₆ x 1³/₄")
Unmarked
RCIN 40216
PROVENANCE: Acquired by Queen Alexandra, date unknown
REFERENCES: Bainbridge 1949, p. 95
EXHIBITIONS: London 1953, no. 47; London 1977, no. E12; New York 1983, no. 39; QG 1985–6, no. 11;
QG 1995–6, no. 133; QG 2002–3, no. 253

128 WILD ROSES, *c.*1900

A similar realistically modelled study exists in the India Early Minshall Collection, Cleveland Museum
of Art. A previously unpublished drawing from an album of designs executed by Henrik Wigström relates
closely to this flower study (see p. 104).

Rock crystal, gold, enamel, brilliant diamonds, nephrite, 14.8 x 7.8 x 6.4 cm (5¹³/₁₆ x 3¹/₁₆ x 2¹/₂")
Unmarked
RCIN 8958
PROVENANCE: Probably acquired by Queen Alexandra; Royal Collection by 1953
EXHIBITIONS: QG 1995–6, no. 123; QG 2002–3, no. 258

129 WILD ROSE, *c.*1900

Rock crystal, gold, nephrite, enamel, diamonds, 14.6 x 5.9 x 4 cm (5³/₄ x 2⁵/₁₆ x 1⁹/₁₆")
RCIN 40223
PROVENANCE: Probably acquired by Queen Alexandra; Royal Collection by 1953
EXHIBITIONS: London 1977, no. E18; QG 1995–6, no. 125; QG 2002–3, no. 257

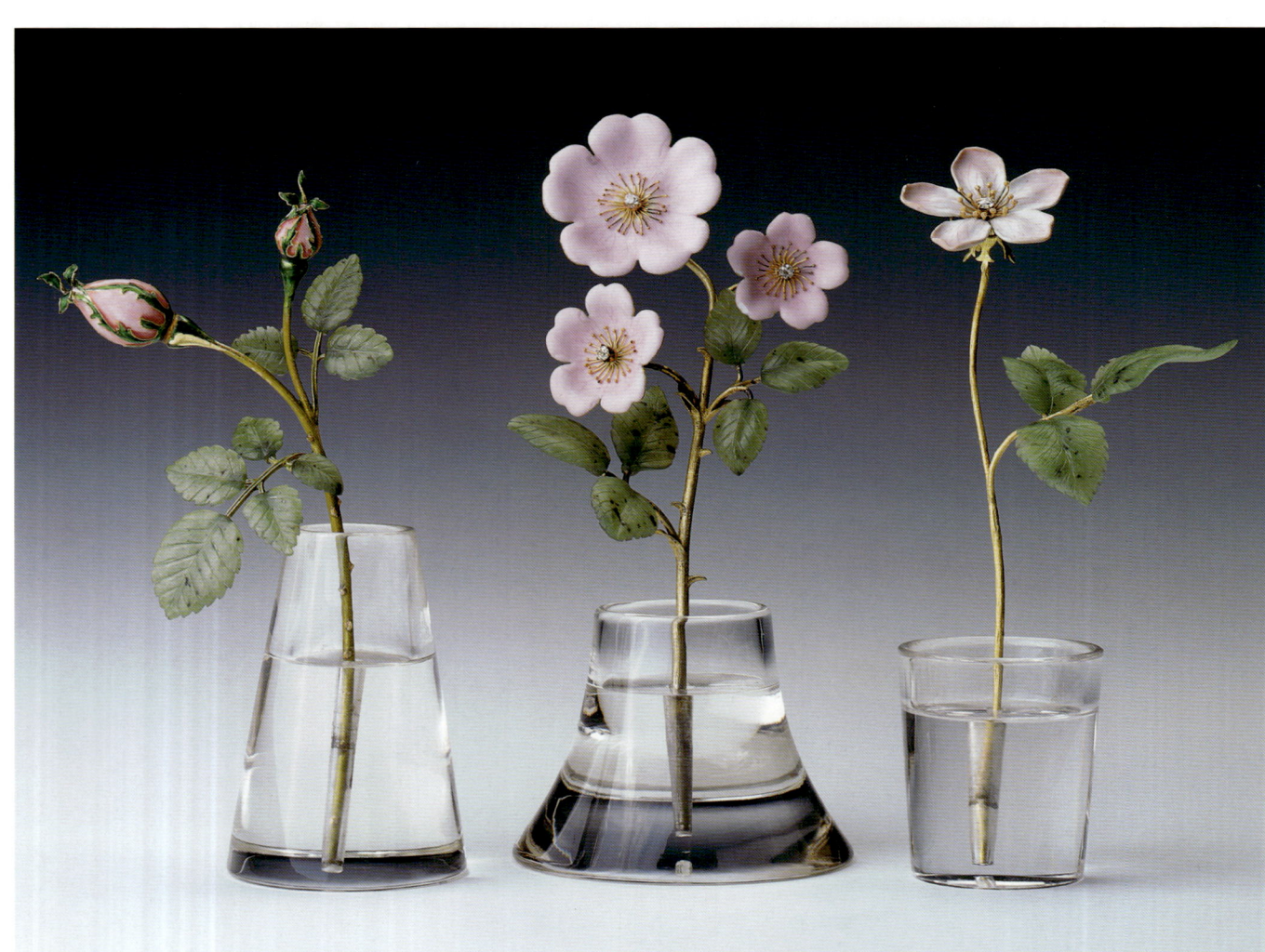

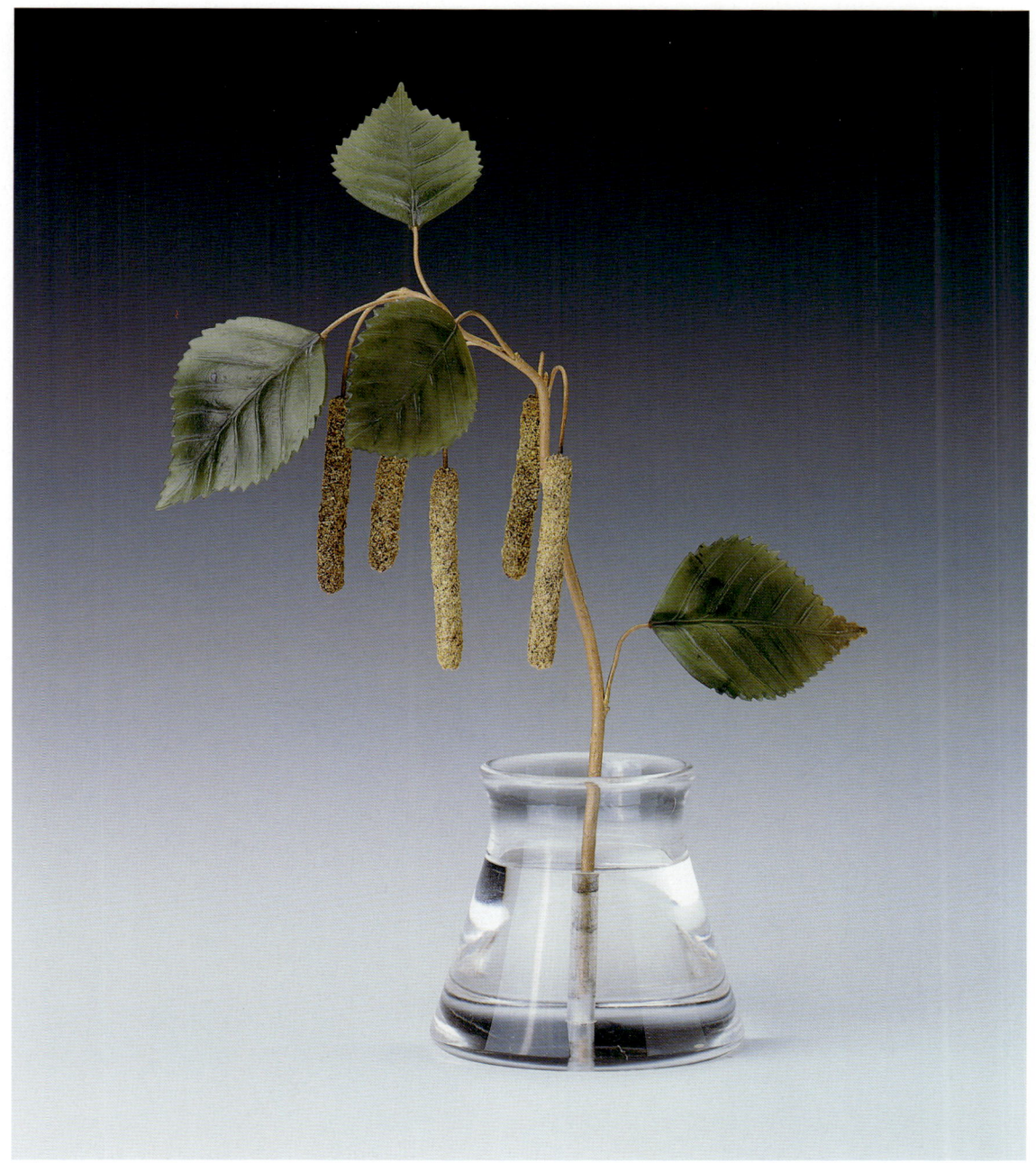

130 CATKIN, *c.*1900

This flower was made in the workshop of Feodor Afanassiev, who specialised in producing small *objets d'art* such as miniature Easter eggs and picture frames. It is an interesting example of the use of different coloured golds, the matt red gold of the stems contrasting with the powdery yellow spun gold of the flowers.

Rock crystal, two-colour gold, nephrite, 13.2 x 11.7 x 5 cm (5³/₁₆ x 4⁵/₈ x 1¹⁵/₁₆")
Mark of Feodor Afanassiev; gold mark of 56 *zolotniks*
RCIN 40507
PROVENANCE: Acquired by Queen Alexandra, date unknown
REFERENCES: Bainbridge 1949, p. 95
EXHIBITIONS: London 1953, no. 38; London 1977, no. E11; New York 1983, no. 17; QG 1985–6, no. 14; London 1992; QG 1995–6, no. 128; QG 2002–3, no. 251

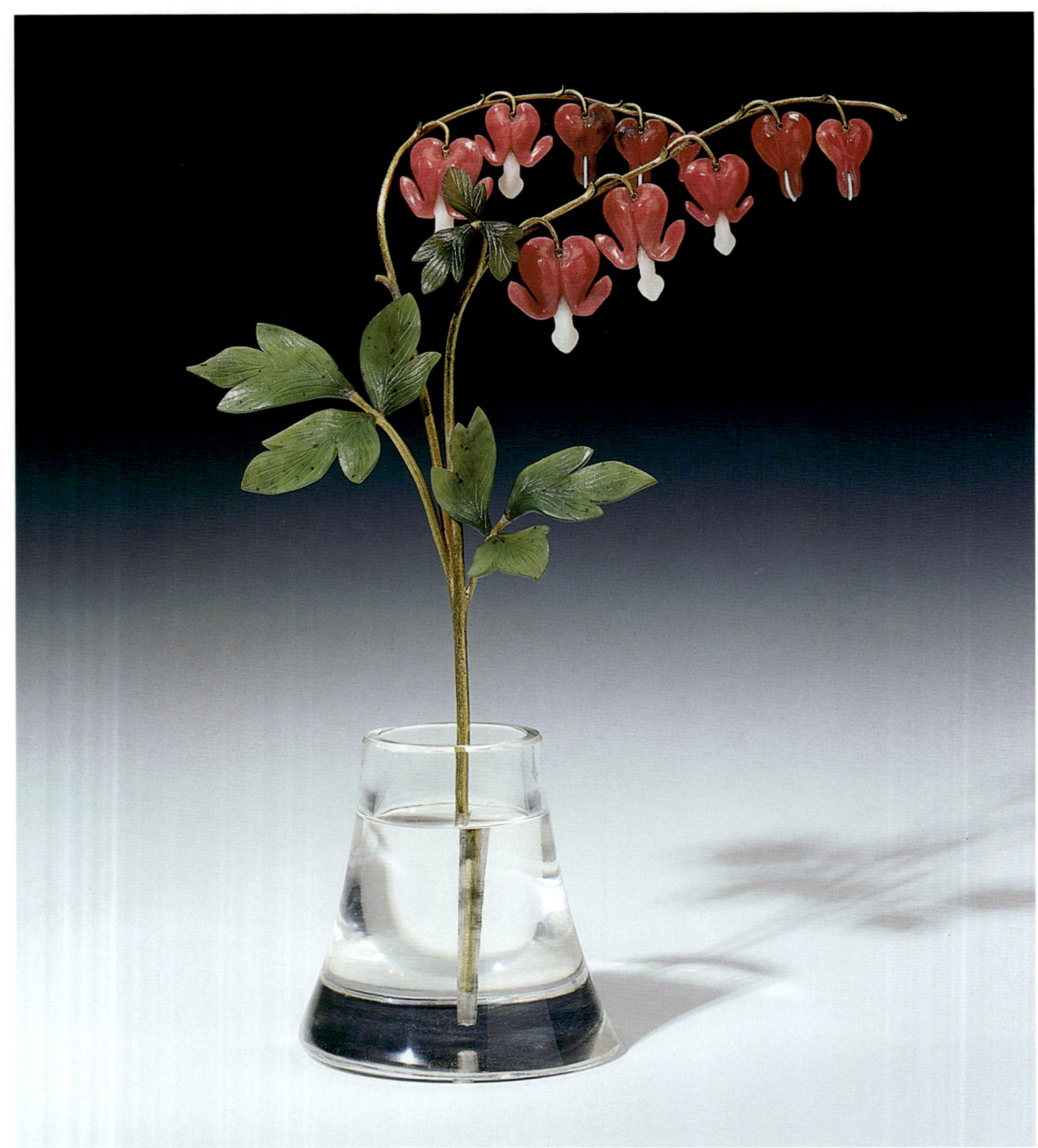

131 BLEEDING HEART, *c*. 1900

Queen Mary's taste in Fabergé extended beyond the bibelots and Imperial Easter Eggs, with which she has been closely associated, to include flowers. In the late 1920s and 1930s, she was actively seeking to purchase enamel flowers and this piece appears in a list of items obtained by her in 1934. Curiously, Bainbridge appears to have been mistaken about its provenance, noting in 1949 that it had been in Queen Alexandra's collection.

Rock crystal, gold, nephrite, rhodonite, quartzite, 19 x 15.3 x 6.2 cm (7¹/₂ x 6 x 2⁷/₁₆")
Unmarked
RCIN 40502
PROVENANCE: Acquired by Queen Mary, 1934
REFERENCES: Archives of Princess George Galitzine; QMB III, no. 220; QMPP VIII, no. 103
EXHIBITIONS: London 1953, no. 32; London 1977, no. E6; New York 1983, no. 1; QG 1985–6, no. 18;
QG 1995–6, no. 118; QG 2002–3, no. 256

132   CORNFLOWERS AND OATS, *c.*1900

In 1944 Queen Mary contributed to the purchase of 'a pretty Fabergé cornflower' for Queen Elizabeth to cheer up her shelter room at Buckingham Palace. Queen Elizabeth was delighted with the present
and described it as 'a charming thing, and so beautifully unwarlike'. The oats are particularly well
modelled and the husks are attached in such a way as to allow movement, thereby adding to their
realistic quality. A similar but not identical group was acquired by the Hermitage Museum in 1922
from the Yusopov Collection.

Rock crystal, engraved gold, enamel, brilliant and rose-cut diamonds, 18.5 x 12.3 x 8.5 cm (7⁵/₁₆ x 4¹³/₁₆ x 3³/₈")
Unmarked
RCIN 100010
PROVENANCE: Bought by Queen Mary and Queen Elizabeth from Wartski, 27 June 1944 (£145)
REFERENCES: RA GV/CC 13/93 and 97
EXHIBITIONS: London 1949, no. 4; London 1971, no. 141; London 1977, no. F8; New York 1983, no. 26;
QG 1985–6, no. 12; Munich 1986–7, no. 399; London 1987; QG 1995–6, no. 135; QG 2002–3, no. 255

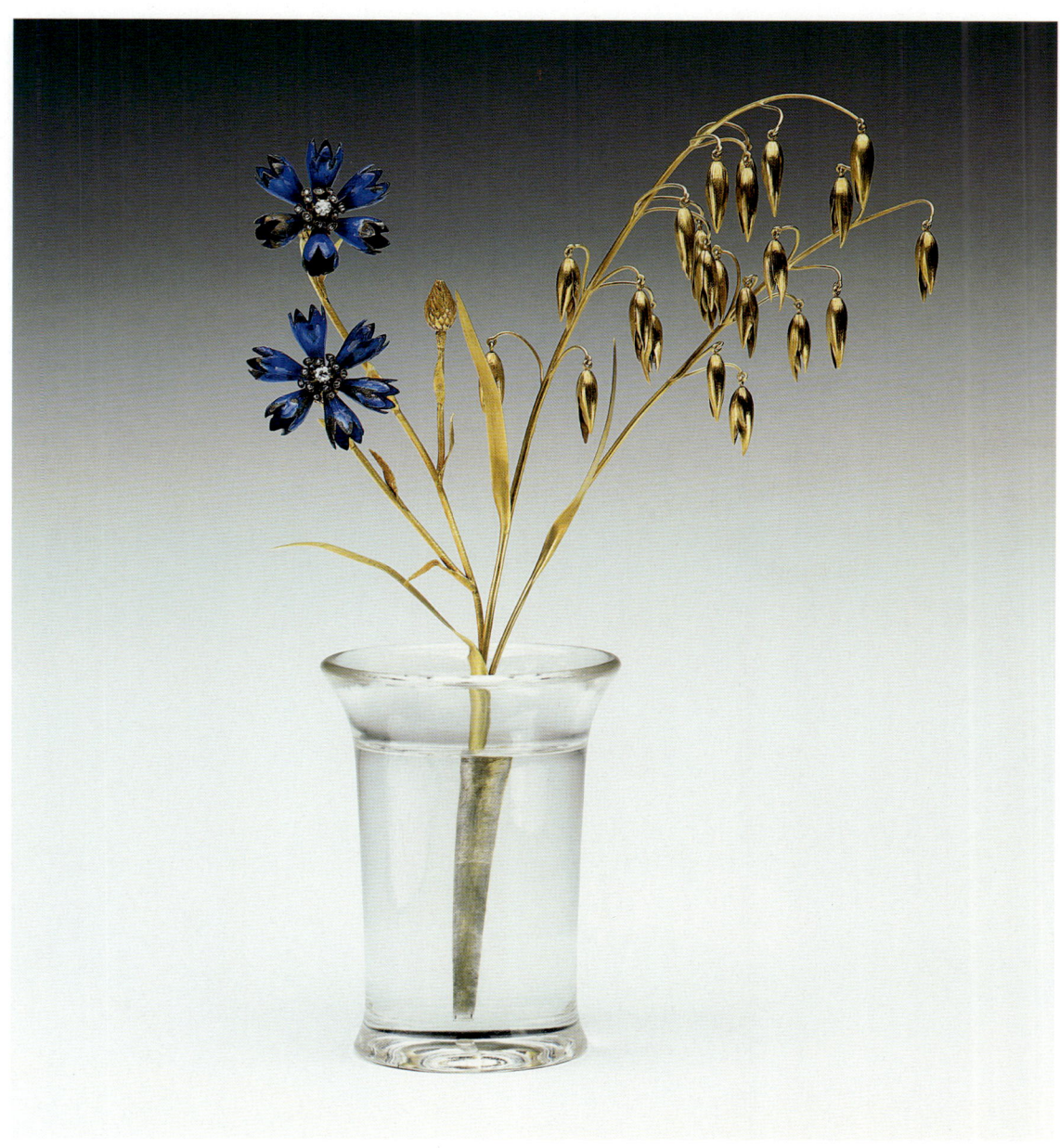

133 CORNFLOWERS AND BUTTERCUPS, *c.*1900

Fabergé produced flower studies of both cornflowers and ranunculus individually. In this example they are combined and, unusually, a jewelled enamel bee is added to the group.

Rock crystal, gold, enamel, rose diamonds, rubies, 22.3 x 14 x 8 cm (8³/₄ x 5¹/₂ x 3¹/₈")
Unmarked
RCIN 100011
PROVENANCE: Bought by Queen Elizabeth from Wartski, 2 February 1947 (£375)
EXHIBITIONS: London 1953, no. 123; London 1971, no. 139; London 1977, no. F9; New York 1983, no. 27;
QG 1985–6, no. 13; Munich 1986–7, no. 394; London 1987; QG 1995–6, no.137; QG 2002–3, no. 254

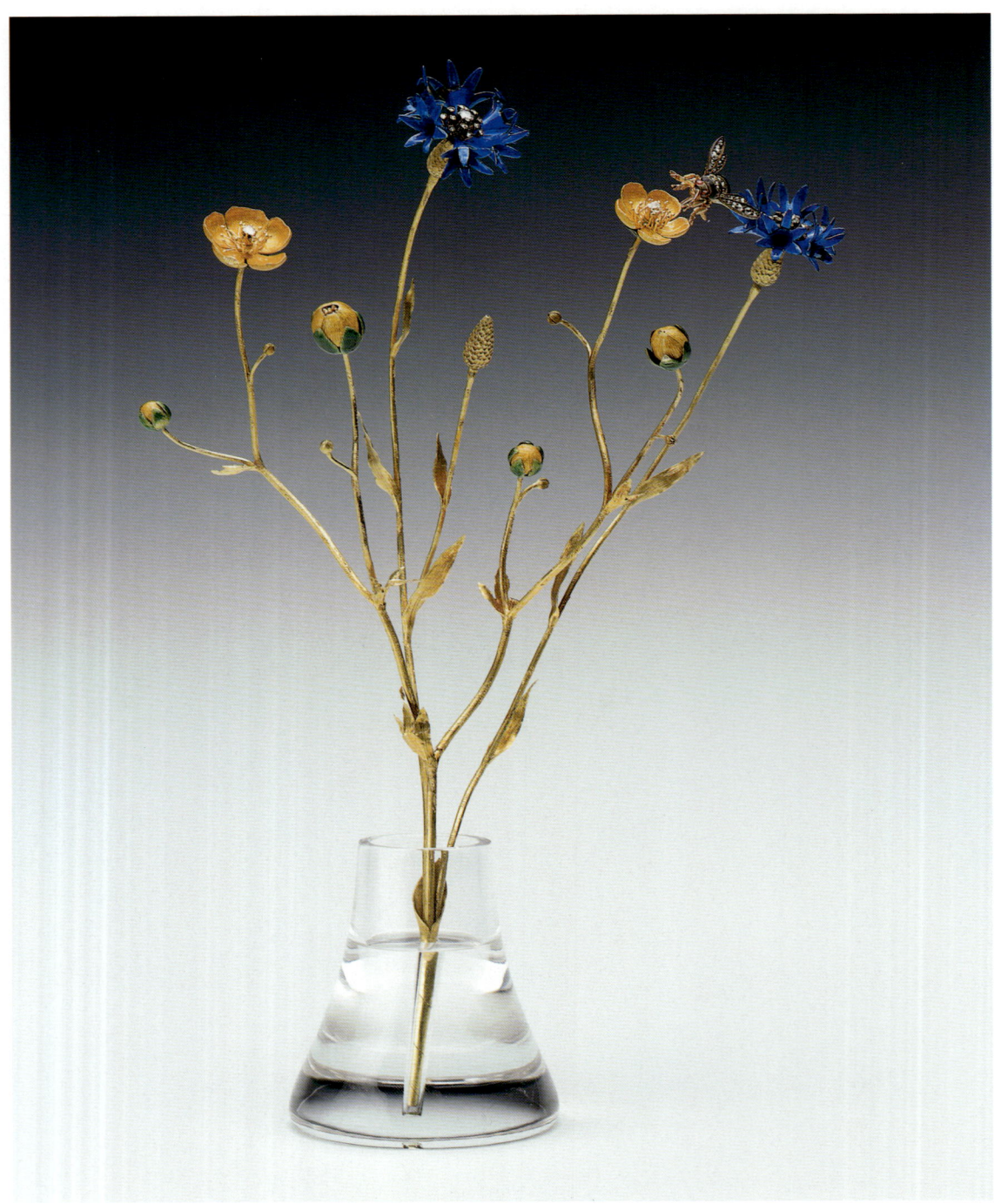

134 REDCURRANT, *c.*1900

Rock crystal, gold, enamel, nephrite, 8 x 5.5 x 5 cm (3^1/$_8$ x 2^3/$_{16}$ x 1^{15}/$_{16}$")
Unmarked
RCIN 8953
PROVENANCE: Probably acquired by Queen Alexandra; Royal Collection by 1953
EXHIBITIONS: QG 1995–6, no. 124; QG 2002–3, no. 243

135 LINGONBERRY, *c.*1900

In this study of lingonberry, the use of cornelian and chalcedony evokes the translucent quality of the berries. A similar study is held in the India Early Minshall Collection, Cleveland Museum of Art.

Rock crystal, gold, nephrite, cornelian, chalcedony, 12.2 x 6.2 x 4 cm (4^{13}/$_{16}$ x 2^7/$_{16}$ x 1^9/$_{16}$")
Unmarked
RCIN 40250
PROVENANCE: Acquired by Queen Alexandra, date unknown
EXHIBITIONS: London 1953, no. 30; London 1977, no. E20; New York 1983, no. 62; QG 1985–6, no. 8; QG 1995–6, no. 209; QG 2002–3, no. 242

136 ROWAN TREE, *c.*1900

The berries of purpurine and the leaves of nephrite are particularly realistic in this example of a rowan spray. This is one of the few models which Fabergé is known to have repeated.

Rock crystal, gold, nephrite, purpurine, 22.5 x 20.5 x 7.5 cm (8^7/$_8$ x 8^1/$_{16}$ x 2^{15}/$_{16}$")
Unmarked
RCIN 40508
PROVENANCE: Queen Alexandra; by whom bequeathed to Princess Victoria (1868–1935); King George V
REFERENCES: Bainbridge 1949, p.95
EXHIBITIONS: London 1953, no. 50; London 1977, no. E4; New York 1983, no. 16; QG 1985–6, no. 9; London 1992; QG 1995–6, no. 119; QG 2002–3, no. 241

137 WILD CHERRIES, *c.*1900

These incredibly delicate and highly fragile objects are held together with great precision by stalks and stamens of finely engraved and chased dull gold. While their realism is remarkable, it is clear that in this instance Fabergé considered decorative quality more important than botanical accuracy – this piece, for example, features both blossom and fruit.

Rock crystal, gold, nephrite, purpurine, enamel, brilliant diamonds, 13.5 x 9.2 x 4.8 cm (5^5/$_{16}$ x 3^5/$_8$ x 1^7/$_8$")
Unmarked
RCIN 40218
PROVENANCE: Acquired by Queen Alexandra, date unknown
REFERENCES: Bainbridge 1949, p. 95
EXHIBITIONS: London 1953, no. 45; London 1977, no. E17; New York 1983, no. 4; QG 1985–6, no. 10; London 1992; QG 1995–6, no. 122; QG 2002–3, no. 239

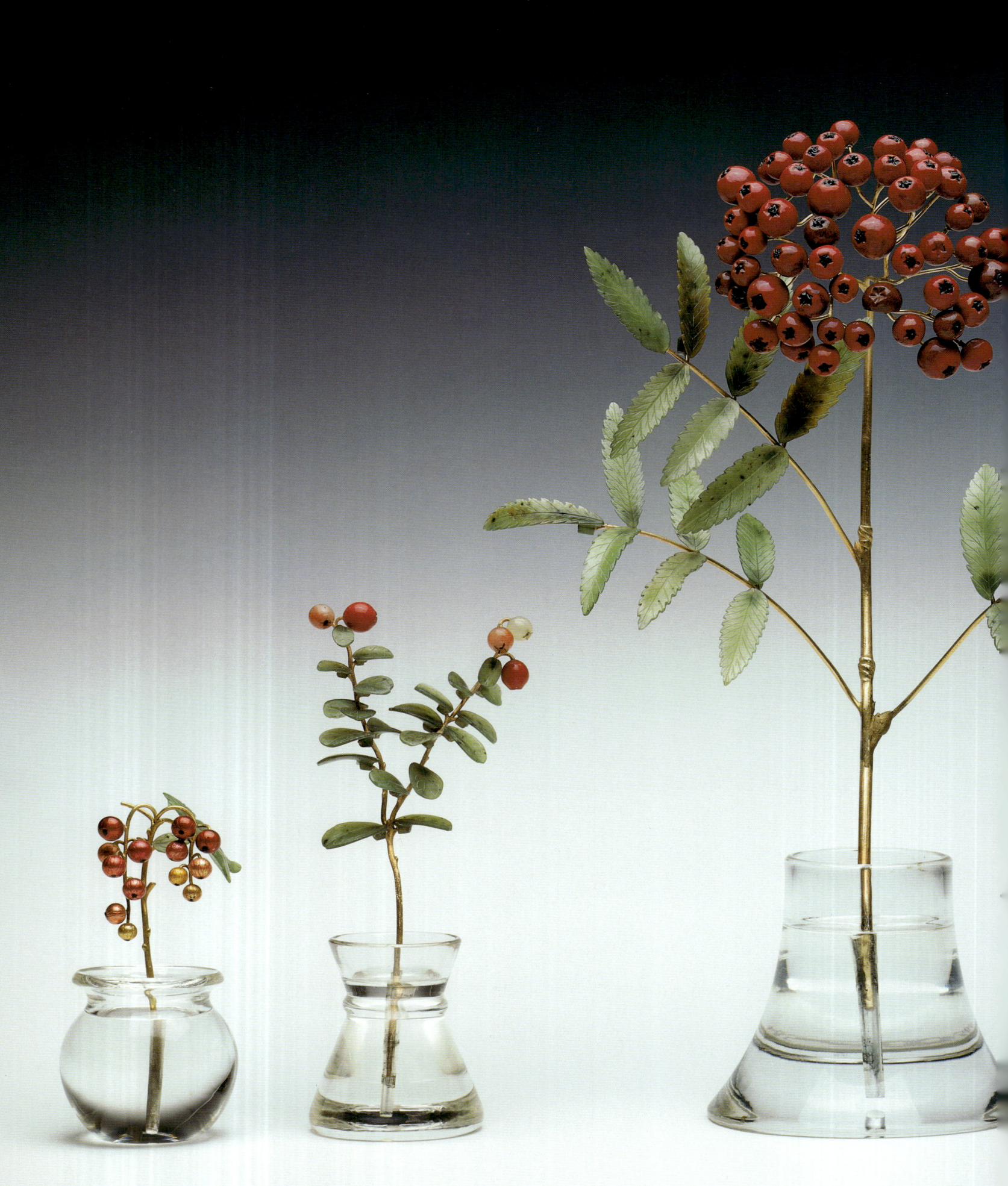

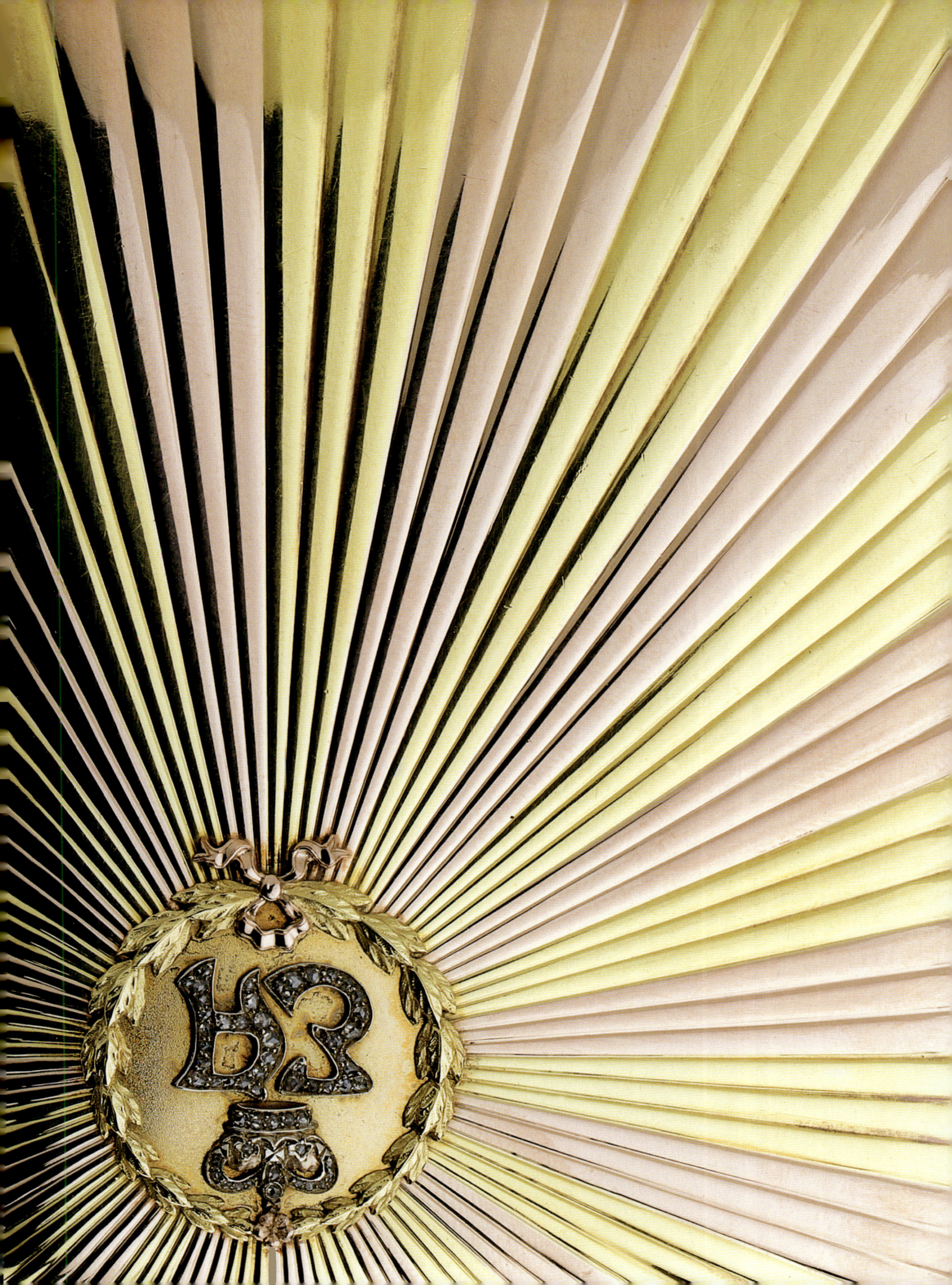

139 JAPONICA, c.1907

According to Bainbridge, Stanislas Poklewski-Koziell – who purchased this flower model and cat. 140 – was 'perhaps the most prolific present giver the world has ever seen'. He was a councillor at the Russian Embassy in London and a great friend of King Edward VII. It is assumed that this flower was a gift from him to Queen Alexandra.

Gold, nephrite, enamel, rose diamonds, 16.8 x 9 x 5.5 cm (6⁵/₈ x 3⁹/₁₆ x 2³/₁₆")
Mark of Henrik Wigström; gold mark of 72 *zolotniks* (1896–1908); FABERGÉ in Cyrillic characters
RCIN 40504
PROVENANCE: Purchased by Stanislas Poklewski-Koziell from Fabergé's London branch, October 1907 (£52 5s); by whom presented to Queen Alexandra
REFERENCES: Bainbridge 1949, p. 83
EXHIBITIONS: London 1953, no. 49; New York 1983, no. E2; QG 1985–6, no. 55; QG 1995–6, no. 134; QG 2002–3, no. 248

140 CHRYSANTHEMUM, c.1908

This was the most expensive flower study purchased at the London branch.

Rock crystal, gold, nephrite, enamel, 24.6 x 11.3 x 7 cm (9¹¹/₁₆ x 4⁷/₁₆ x 2³/₄")
Mark of Henrik Wigström; gold mark of 72 *zolotniks* (1908–17); FABERGÉ in Cyrillic characters
RCIN 40506
PROVENANCE: Bought by Stanislas Poklewski-Koziell from Fabergé's London branch, 27 December 1908 (£117); by whom given to Queen Alexandra.
REFERENCES: Bainbridge 1949, p. 95
EXHIBITIONS: London 1953, no. 42; New York 1983, no. E7; QG 1985–6, no. 3; QG 1995–6, no. 133; London 1992, QG 1995–6, no. 127; QG 2002–3, no. 249

141 CARNATION, c.1903

This remarkably realistic study illustrates the painstaking work involved in achieving exactly the right combination of colour, shape, translucence and opaque sheen for the papery petals. The stem, unusually, is marked and indicates that the flower was produced in Wigström's workshop.

Rock crystal, gold, enamel, 17.7 x 7.5 x 5.7 cm (6¹⁵/₁₆ x 2¹⁵/₁₆ x 2¹/₄")
Mark of Henrik Wigström; date marks illegible; FABERGÉ in Cyrillic characters
RCIN 40503
PROVENANCE: Probably acquired by Queen Alexandra; Royal Collection by 1953
EXHIBITIONS: London 1953, no. 44; London 1977, no. E1; New York 1983, no. 38; QG 1985–6, no. 6; QG 1995–6, no. 131; QG 2002–3, no. 250

138 LILY OF THE VALLEY, *c.*1900

Fabergé made several studies of lily of the valley, reputed to have been the favourite flower of Tsarina Alexandra Feodorovna. These range from the basket of lily of the valley presented to the Tsarina in 1896 to the Lily of the Valley Imperial Easter Egg of 1898. At least two other groups in rock crystal vases are known, but of a different composition (one in the India Early Minshall Collection, Cleveland Museum of Art). This group was in the collection of Princess Victoria, second daughter of King Edward VII and Queen Alexandra, who inherited her parents' love of Fabergé and collected several Fabergé flowers (see cat. 136). She owned or inherited many pieces, notably flowers but also animals, parasol handles, letter openers and photograph frames.

Rock crystal, gold, nephrite, pearls, rose diamonds, 14.5 x 7.8 x 5.5 cm (5^{11}/$_{16}$ x 3^{1}/$_{16}$ x 2^{3}/$_{16}$")
Unmarked
RCIN 40217
PROVENANCE: Queen Alexandra; by whom bequeathed to Princess Victoria (1868–1935); King George V
EXHIBITIONS: London 1953, no. 33; London 1977, no. E8; New York 1983, no. 66; QG 1985–6, no. 15; QG 1995–6, no. 120; QG 2002–3, no. 247

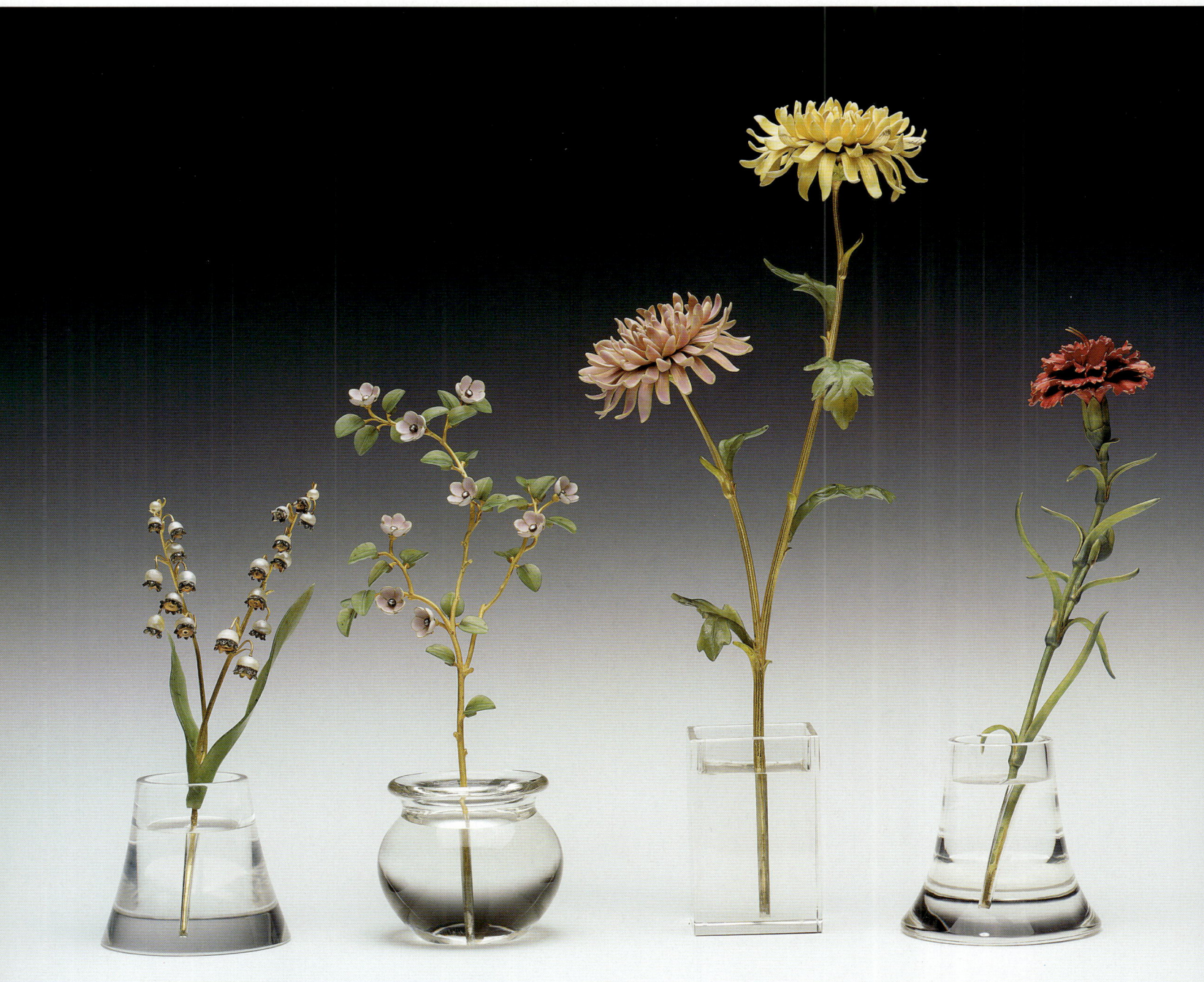

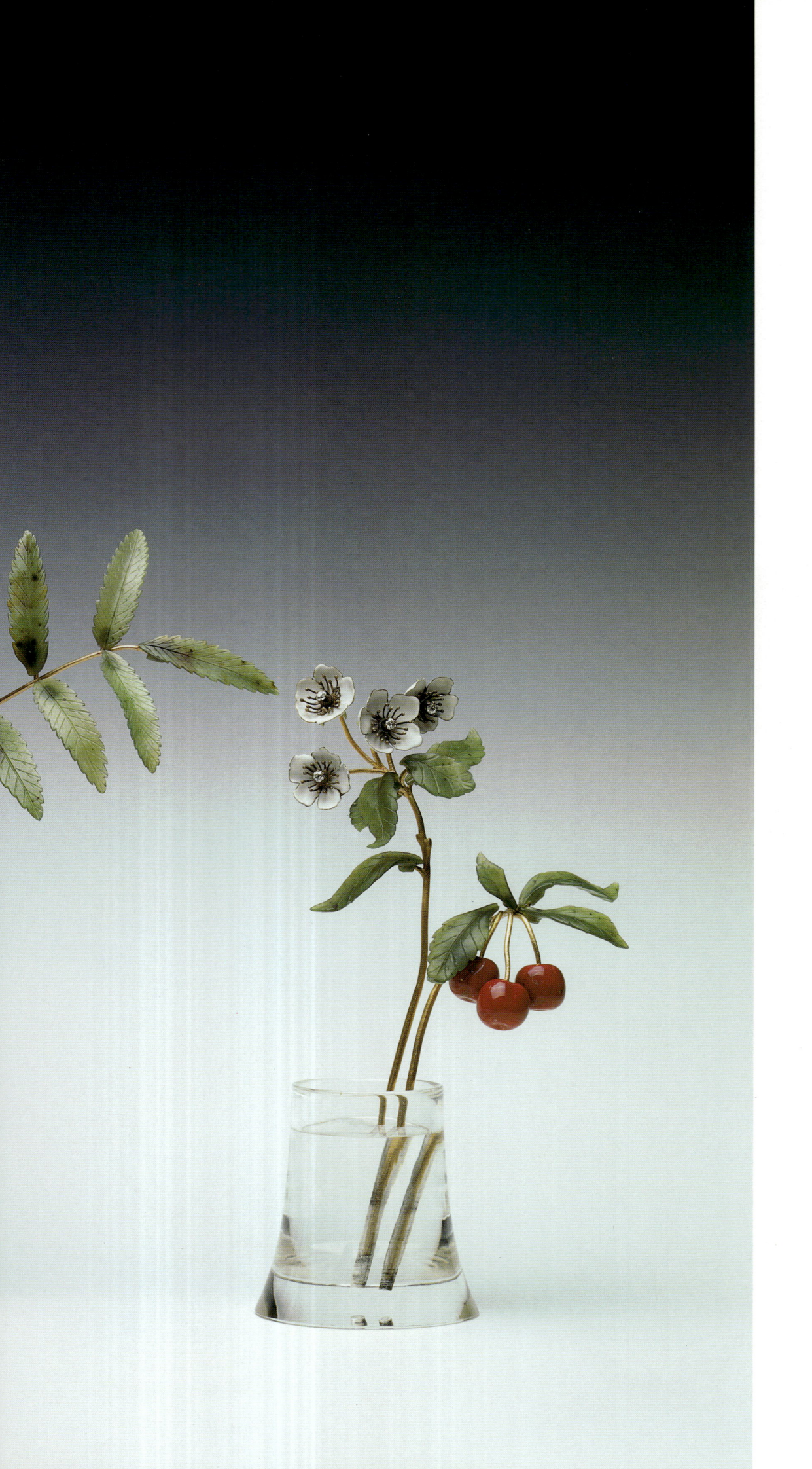

BOXES

THE BOXES PRODUCED by Fabergé range from the most lavish imperial presentation pieces commissioned by the Imperial Cabinet, costing over 2,000 roubles, to the simplest wooden cigarette cases costing as little as 85 roubles, which were bought in scores by Fabergé's clientele. Fabergé boxes of all types are well represented in the Royal Collection, owing to the exchange of gifts between the Russian and English royal families and to purchases made by King George V, Queen Mary and King George VI.

There are four imperial presentation boxes by Fabergé in the Royal Collection, all made during the reign of Tsar Nicholas II. Two bear a miniature portrait of the Tsar (cat. 143 and 144), one his cypher set in diamonds (cat. 145) and the fourth the imperial eagle (cat. 142). The hierarchy of official gifts presented by the Tsar was strictly organised according to the intended recipient's ranking in society. The table of ranks had been established in 1722 during the reign of Peter the Great and continued to be used throughout Tsar Nicholas II's period of rule. Gifts from the Imperial Cabinet included boxes, which had a long tradition as official presentation gifts. Those with the portrait miniature of the Tsar (or the imperial couple) were presented to ranks two and three, which included very high-ranking officials at home and abroad. In total during Nicholas II's reign fifty-six boxes with the miniature portrait were bestowed: twenty-two

to Russian subjects and thirty-four to foreign dignitaries. None was given to a member of the British royal family as more personal gifts were exchanged between the families. The four boxes now in the Royal Collection were acquired from the 1930s onwards.

Presentation boxes with the diamond-set cypher of the Tsar were of a lower category than those with the Tsar's portrait and were presented to ranks four and five. During Nicholas II's reign, 370 such boxes were commissioned, of which 100 were presented to foreign dignitaries and the remainder to Russian recipients. Of these boxes, 150 were made by Fabergé and the remainder were made by the other court jewellers and goldsmiths such as Hahn, Köchli and Bolin.[1] A Nicholas II presentation box by Hahn with the Tsar's cypher was acquired by Queen Mary in 1934 (cat. 354).

The imperial presentation boxes are the most richly decorated of all Fabergé's boxes. The use of coloured gold and guilloché enamel, together with precious stones and portrait miniatures, results in a dazzling combination of techniques. These boxes are among the best demonstrations of Fabergé's use of guilloché enamel. This was a revival by Fabergé of a French eighteenth-century technique which he succeeded in bringing to a new level of sophistication by improving the range of patterns and colours and by ensuring a very high level of finish through hours of hand polishing. The range of enamel colours and guilloché patterns was demonstrated in a chart which hung in Fabergé's workshops. This showed eighty translucent enamel colours and shades

LEFT: *Cigarette case, 1903 (cat. 163, detail).*

fused over a similarly wide variety of engine-turned patterns.[2] The opalescent pinks and 'oyster' whites were particularly fine, giving a mixture of hues as an object was rotated. The moiré, sunburst and wave designs seen on the presentation boxes were achieved by cutting patterns into the gold or silver base metal with a machine called a *tour à guilloché* (rose-engine). The coloured enamel was then fused to the metal in five or six separate layers, each fired at temperatures in excess of 750 degrees Centigrade. Curved and lightly cut patterns enhanced the delicate appearance of pale tints, while radiating straight lines and geometric patterns increased the apparent depth and richness of darker translucent enamels. The four presentation boxes in the Royal Collection demonstrate these techniques particularly well.

There is also a large group of cigarette cases, snuff boxes and match cases in the Royal Collection in a wide variety of styles. By the nineteenth century cigarettes were in widespread use and cigarette cases became increasingly fashionable as the taste for snuff-taking declined. Dr Marina Lopato has identified the increase in orders placed by the imperial court for cigarette cases as opposed to snuff boxes from the 1890s into the new century.[3] The more elaborate cases were made as presentation objects in connection with important events, for example Nicholas II's coronation in 1896 and the Romanov tercentenary in 1913. Simpler cases in plain silver were routinely given by the imperial family as gifts. In London, Fabergé's cigarette cases sold in hundreds. As with all Fabergé's products, a range of styles is represented in the design of the cases, from Egyptian-inspired (cat. 165) and Louis XVI (cat. 176) to art nouveau (cat. 187). Some of the most successful designs were the multi-coloured gold cases engraved with wave, sunburst and radiating lines. According to a note in Queen Mary's hand, one such cigarette case now in the Royal Collection was a favourite of Tsar Nicholas II (cat. 188). The cigarette cases in the Royal Collection were acquired by King Edward VII, King George V and King George VI, the last two monarchs making the most additions to the collection. All the cases were used at one time or another; Bainbridge recalls how King George VI received him at Buckingham Palace on 1 November 1948 and showed him a selection of his cigarette cases by Fabergé: 'With the exception of four, all of them are suitable for daily use and His Majesty tells me he gives each one of them a turn.'[4]

1   These figures were established by the archival research of Valentin Skurlov. See Tillander-Godenhielm *et al.* 2000, p. 153.
2   The chart is illustrated in the catalogue *Carl Fabergé 1846–1920*, London 1977.
3   Lopato, 1998, pp. 161–4.
4   Bainbridge 1949, pp. 109–10.

142 IMPERIAL PRESENTATION BOX, BEFORE 1896

The imperial provenance of this box is clearly indicated by the Romanov double-headed eagle and by the colour yellow – yellow and black being the colours of the imperial mantle. It was purchased by the Maharaja of Bikanir, a good client of Fabergé's London branch.

Gold, guilloché enamel, brilliant and rose diamonds, 1.7 x 8.2 x 4.5 cm ($^{11}/_{16}$ x 3$^{1}/_{4}$ x 1$^{3}/_{4}$")
Mark of Michael Perchin; gold mark of 72 *zolotniks* (before 1896); *FABERGÉ* in Cyrillic characters
RCIN 8999
PROVENANCE: Bought from Wartski by the Maharaja of Bikanir, 15 May 1937 (£95); by whom presented to Queen Mary for her birthday, 26 May 1937
REFERENCES: QMB III, no. 338; QMPP IX, no. 73; Bainbridge 1949, pl. 5
EXHIBITIONS: QG 1985–6, no. 74; QG 1995–6, no. 151; QG 2002–3, no. 268

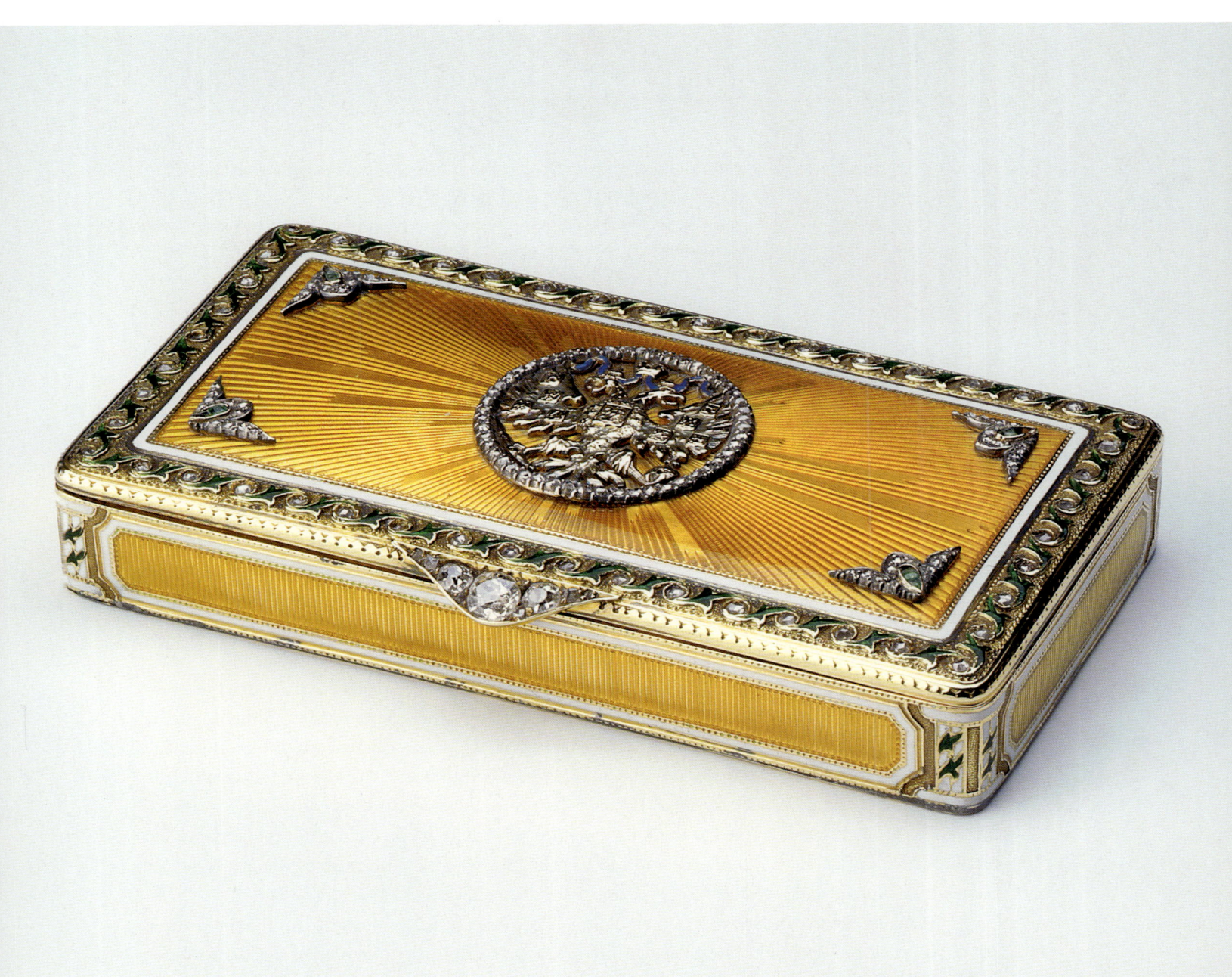

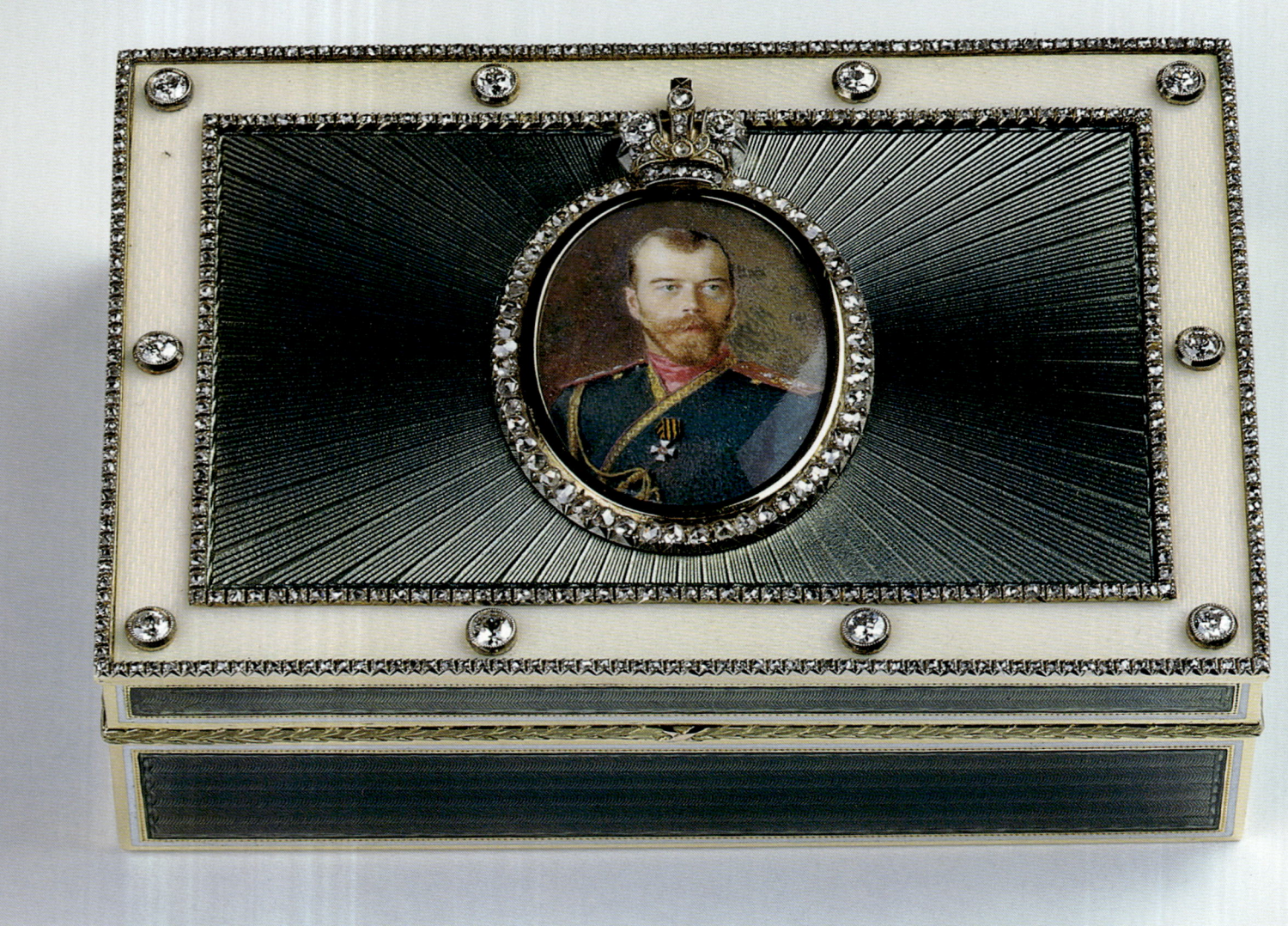

143 IMPERIAL PRESENTATION BOX, 1916

In the hierarchy of state gifts presented by the Tsar, gem-set presentation boxes with miniature portraits of the Tsar or the imperial couple were reserved for monarchs, non-royal heads of state and, very selectively, high-ranking officials at home and abroad.

The original watercolour drawing of this box, exactly as made, has been discovered recently in an unpublished album from Wigström's workshop. It shows that the box was completed on 30 September 1916. The box would have been sent to the Imperial Cabinet stock with a space for the miniature portrait of the Tsar, or his diamond-set cypher, to be incorporated at the time of presentation. It is mounted with a miniature of Tsar Nicholas II, painted by the court miniaturist Vassily Zuiev (1870–*c*.1917). This miniature is almost identical to that on a nephrite presentation box formerly in the Forbes Collection which is signed by Zuiev and dated 1916. The Tsar wears the uniform of the 4th Imperial Family Rifle Guards and the Order of St George, which he received on 25 October 1915.

Queen Mary acquired this box in 1934 as a present for King George V for his sixty-ninth birthday and made a note of its provenance, which states that the box was presented by the Tsar to 'General Trepoff' [*sic*]. A box of this importance would have been presented to a senior Russian official, and three members of the Trepov family rose to prominence during the reign of Nicholas II: Vladimir

Feodorovich Trepov (1860–1918), a member of the state council; Dimitri F. Trepov (1855–1906), Governor-General of St Petersburg in 1905, and Palace Commandant, 1905–6; and Alexander F. Trepov (1862–1926), who joined the civil service after a distinguished military career, becoming Minister of Communications, 1915–17, and Prime Minister from November 1916 to January 1917. It seems most likely that the last named would have merited the presentation of such a gift. The Imperial Cabinet Archives however, contain no evidence that any member of the Trepov family was the recipient of a presentation box during Nicholas II's reign.

The Cabinet ledgers in the Imperial Cabinet Archives do reveal that the miniature on this presentation box, from Cabinet stock, was allocated to it on 5 May 1917, almost two months after the Tsar's abdication. The accounts further state that the recipient was a member of the French Academy, Gabriel Hanotaux, to whom the box was presented on behalf of Tsar Nicholas II by the former Grand Duke Nicholas (1859–1919), first cousin once removed of Nicholas II. There were often delays in the presentation of imperial gifts. It is notable that, in spite of the political situation in Russia, this box managed to reach its intended recipient; it is one of the last imperial presentation boxes ever to have been given on behalf of the Tsar. The Trepov provenance was evidently erroneously attached to the box prior to its acquisition by Queen Mary and can now be discounted.

Two-colour gold, guilloché enamel, brilliant and rose-cut diamonds, watercolour, 3.2 x 9.5 x 6.4 cm (1¼ x 3¾ x 2½")
Mark of Henrik Wigström; gold mark of 72 *zolotniks* (1908–17); FABERGÉ in Cyrillic characters
RCIN 19128
PROVENANCE: Presented on behalf of Tsar Nicholas II to Gabriel Hanotaux by the former Grand Duke Nicholas of Russia, 1917; acquired by Queen Mary and given to King George V on his birthday, 3 June 1934
REFERENCES: Habsburg & Lopato 1993, pp. 280–81; Christie's 2002a, lot 128; de Guitaut 2002
EXHIBITIONS: London 1977, no. K22; New York 1983, no. 193; QG 1985–6, no. 77; Munich 1986–7, no. 518; St Petersburg/Paris/London 1993–4, no. 148; QG 1995–6, no. 253; QG 2002–3, no. 266

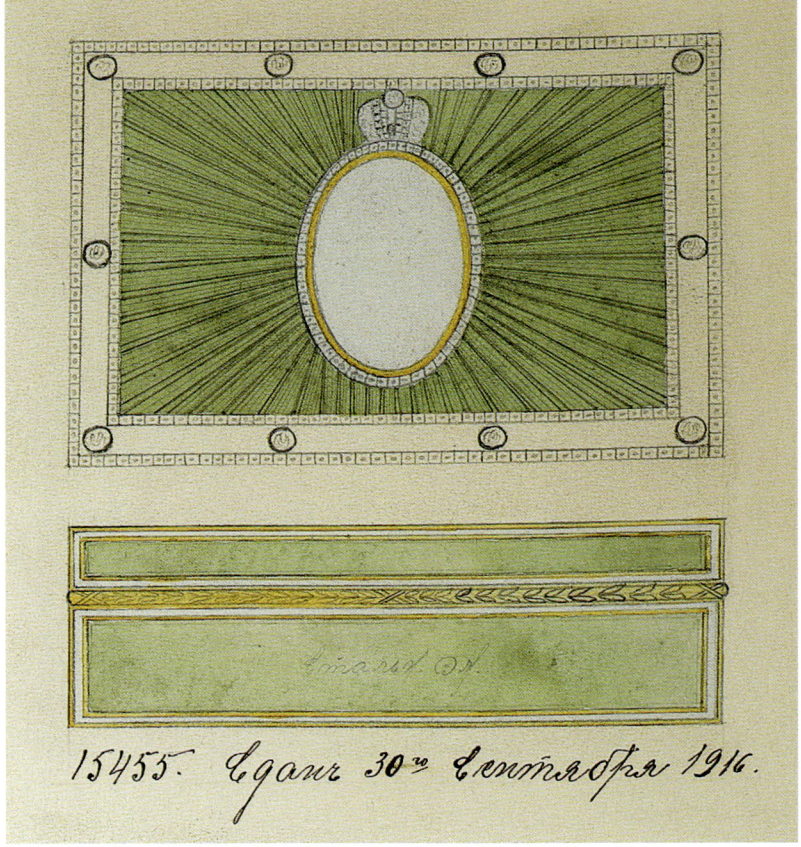

Watercolour design for the imperial presentation box (cat. 143) in an unpublished album from the workshop of Henrik Wigström, 1916.

144 IMPERIAL PRESENTATION BOX, 1914

The combination of patterns of moiré and concentric circles forming the guilloché enamelling on this box constitutes one of the finest examples of Fabergé's enamelling. The provenance of the box, one of four imperial presentation boxes in the Royal Collection, is intriguing.

From the Imperial Cabinet Accounts it can be established that this box was completed on 18 May 1914 and one year later it was presented by Tsar Nicholas II to serving Privy Councillor Artur Germanovich Raffalovich. The accounts record that at the time of completion the box was not mounted with the miniature portrait that it now bears, but with the diamond-set cypher of the Tsar. Boxes applied with the cypher were of a lower category than those bearing his miniature portrait and were certainly more numerous; during Nicholas II's reign the Imperial Cabinet commissioned 370 snuff boxes bearing the cypher of the Tsar. During his long career, Raffalovich had been presented with two boxes set with the Tsar's cypher: one in 1898 and one in 1913.

The Cabinet Accounts show that on 11 April 1915 this box was sent back to Fabergé's workshops, where the cypher was removed and exchanged for the miniature portrait; the number in the ledgers matches perfectly the inventory number marked on the miniature on this box. The miniature, which shows Tsar Nicholas II in the uniform of the Preobrazhensky Regiment and wearing the Russian Orders of St Andrew and St Vladimir and the Danish Order of Dannebrog amongst other medals, was again painted by Vassily Zuiev.

The recent discovery of a watercolour drawing in an unpublished design album from Henrik Wigström's workshop shows the box with the cypher as it was originally supplied by Fabergé in 1914. The box was supplied for Imperial Cabinet stock, from which suitable gifts were selected and appropriately prepared for the intended recipient. In this instance the decision was made to present Raffalovich with a box of the higher category and accordingly the cypher was removed and replaced by the portrait miniature. It is therefore certain that the design (see opposite) is for the box now in the Royal Collection.

It was not uncommon for presentation boxes to be returned by Russian recipients to the Imperial Cabinet, where they were exchanged for money. The box would then be recycled and re-presented. Boxes were also altered, cleaned and repaired, usually in the workshop of the court supplier Hahn.

Three-colour gold, guilloché enamel, rose and brilliant diamonds, watercolour, 2.8 x 9.8 x 6.7 cm (1¹⁄₈ x 3⁷⁄₈ x 2⁵⁄₈")
Mark of Henrik Wigström; gold mark of 72 *zolotniks* (1908–17)
RCIN 100338
PROVENANCE: Presented by Tsar Nicholas II to Artur Germanovich Raffalovich, 1915; bought by Queen Elizabeth from Wartski, 8 January 1947 (£1,045)
REFERENCES: de Guitaut 2002
EXHIBITIONS: London 1977, no. F7; QG 1985–6, no. 76; St Petersburg/Paris/London 1993–4, no. 150

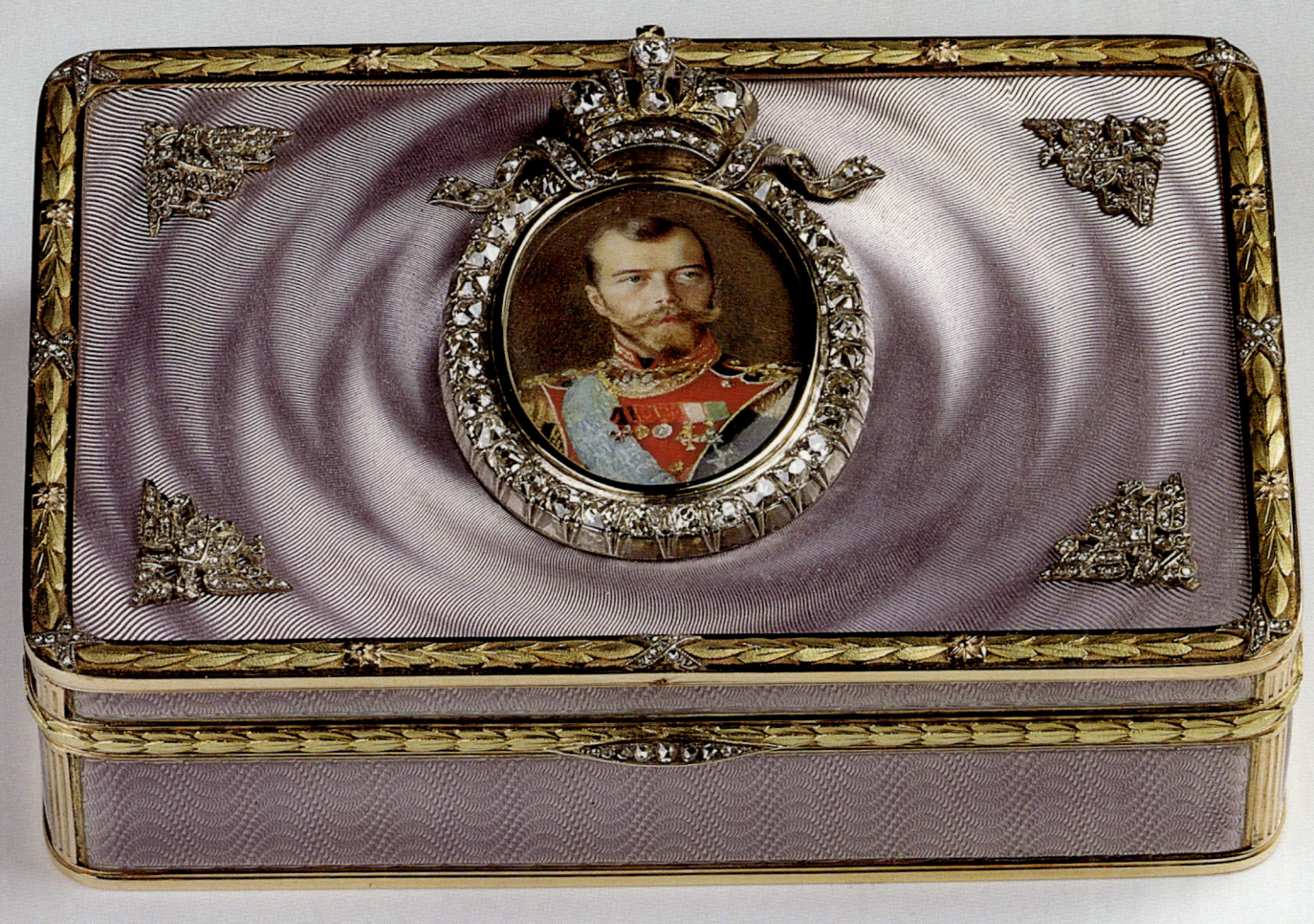

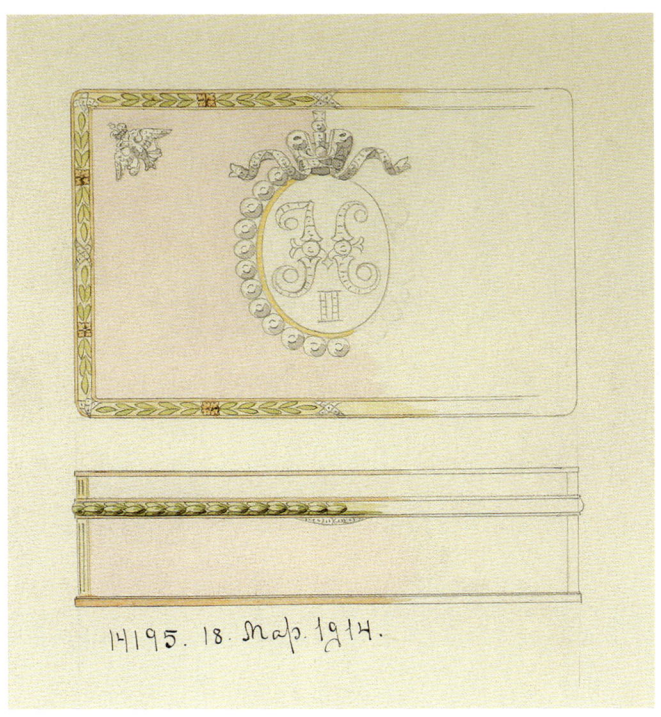

Watercolour design believed to be for a box (cat. 144) by Henrik Wigström, inscribed with the date 18 May 1914.

145 IMPERIAL PRESENTATION BOX, 1896–1908

Of the 370 snuff boxes with the cypher of the Tsar commissioned by the Imperial Cabinet during the reign of Tsar Nicholas II, 150 were made by Fabergé and the remainder by the other court suppliers, Hahn, Köchli and Bolin (see cat. 354). These boxes were intended for presentation to ambassadors, aides-de-camp and other prominent officials in the service of foreign heads of state and to officials in Russia of the appropriate rank. This box is an example of one of the grandest types of presentation box produced by Fabergé. A number of these, similarly mounted with the Tsar's cypher in diamonds, were made at the time of Nicholas II's coronation in 1896. These boxes are usually in the colours of the imperial mantle and some are also decorated with the Romanov two-headed eagle.

The very fine guilloché enamelling combines a concentric circle and sunburst design. Fabergé's enamellers did not mark their work, but the importance of their contribution to Fabergé's success cannot be overestimated. A separate workshop entirely devoted to enamelling was run by Alexander Petrov and his son Nicholas. Birbaum states in his memoirs that the fame of the firm's enamelling was mainly due to Nicholas Petrov.

Gold, enamel, diamonds, 3.1 x 8.3 x 8.3 cm (1¼ x 3¼ x 3¼")
Mark of August Hollming; gold mark of 56 *zolotniks* (1896–1908); *FABERGÉ* in Cyrillic characters
RCIN 100012
PROVENANCE: Bought by Queen Elizabeth from Wartski, 27 June 1944 (£475)
REFERENCES: Bainbridge, 1949, pl. 103
EXHIBITIONS: London 1949, no. 5; QG 1962–3, no. 61; London 1977, no. F10; New York 1983, no. 192;
QG 1985–6, no. 75; Munich 1986–7, no. 511; St Petersburg/Paris/London 1993–4, no. 106; QG 1995–6, no. 147;
Stockholm 1997, no. 58; QG 2002–3, no. 265

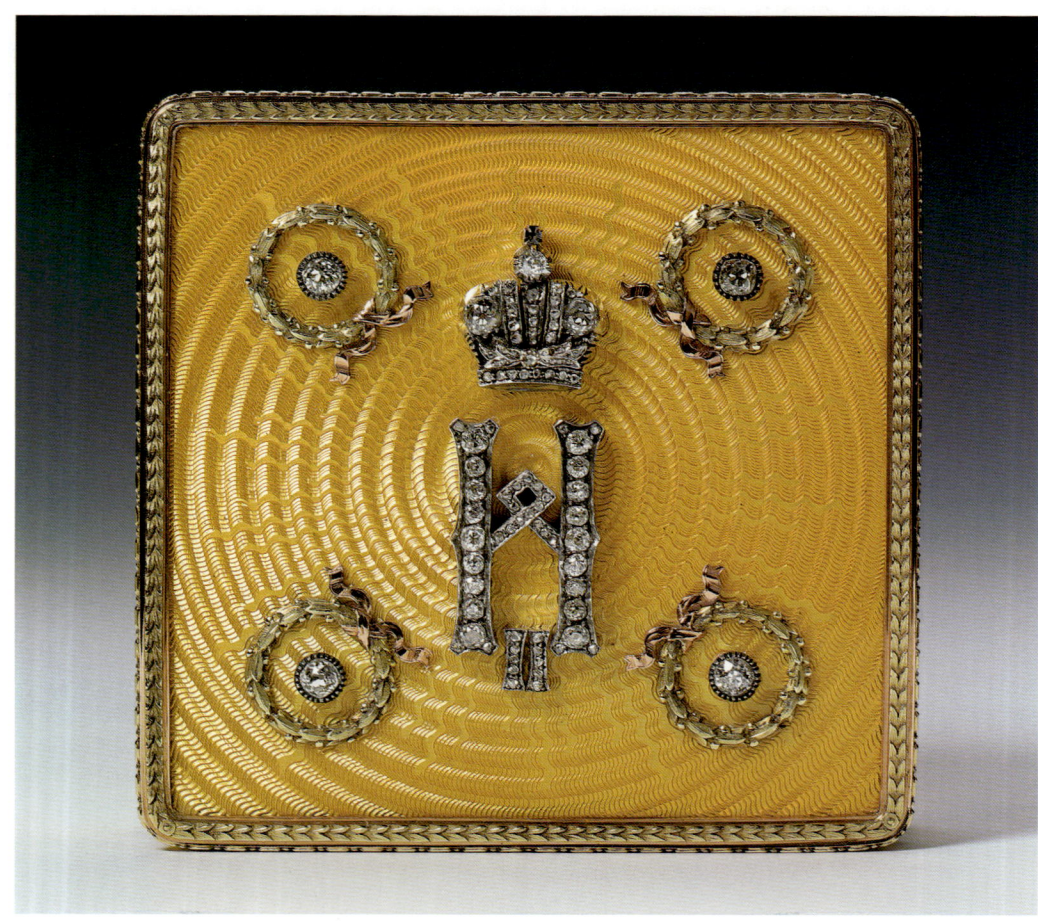

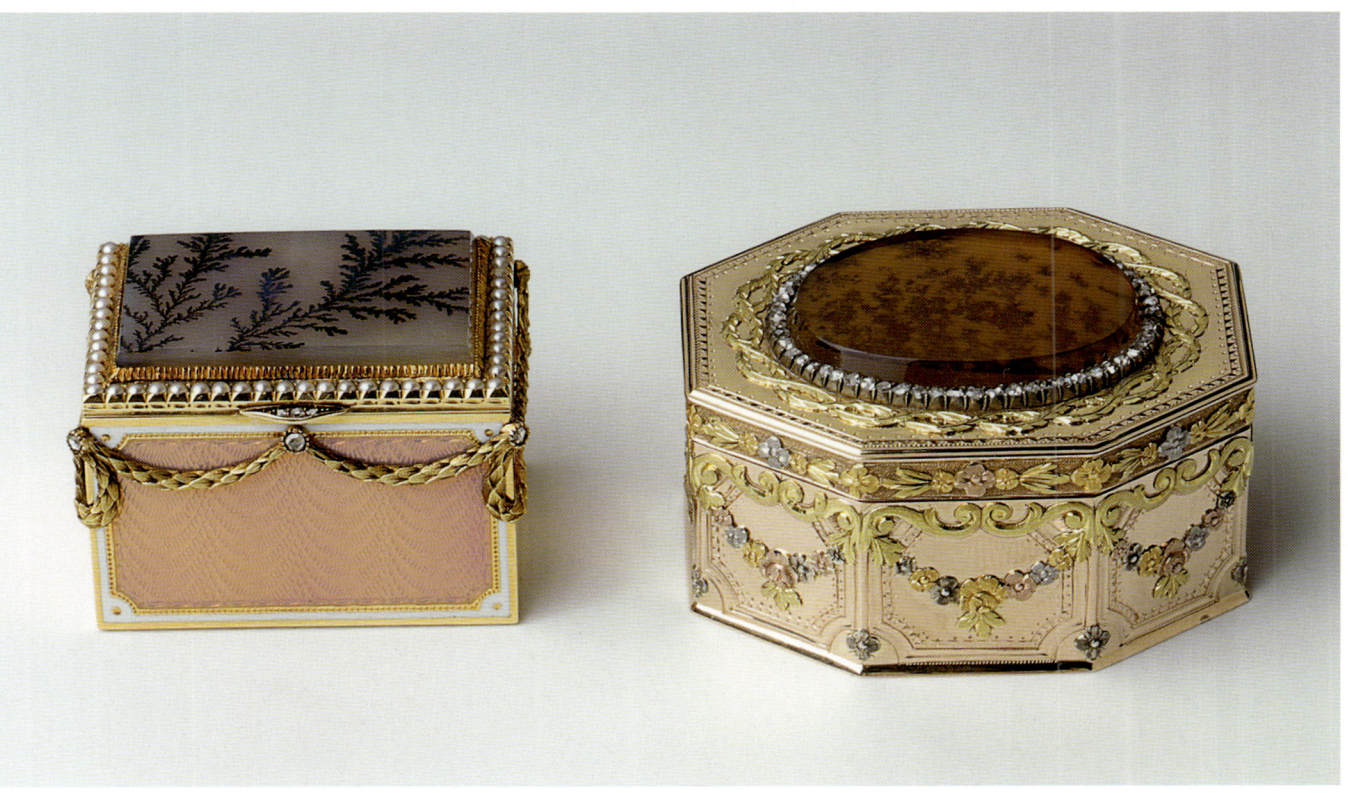

146 BOX WITH MOSS AGATE PANEL, 1903–1908

By including moss agate in mounted jewellery and boxes, Fabergé was continuing a long tradition. Originally mined in India, these agates were known as mocha stones after the town on the Red Sea from which they were imported to Europe. The term 'moss' agate came about because deposits of ferrous and manganese oxides infiltrated the stone, thereby forming dendritic or tree- and moss-like patterns.

In the eighteenth century moss agate was discovered in Germany and it became much sought after in Europe, both for collectors of natural history specimens and for incorporating into snuff boxes and jewellery. Fabergé's source of the material was Siberia. His craftsmen also produced enamel with patterns simulating moss agate, as seen in cat. 4.

Two-colour gold, guilloché enamel, rose diamonds, moss agate, 2.6 x 3.5 x 2.7 cm (1 x 1³/₈ x 1¹/₁₆")
Mark of Henrik Wigström; gold mark of 72 *zolotniks* (1896–1908); *FABERGÉ* in Cyrillic characters; Fabergé's initials in Roman letters; English import marks for 1911
RCIN 40155
PROVENANCE: Acquired by Queen Alexandra, date unknown
REFERENCES: Scarisbrick 1981
EXHIBITIONS: London 1953, no. 64; London 1977, no. J6; QG 1985–6, no. 141; QG 1995–6, no. 250

147 PATCH BOX, 1894

Four-colour gold, moss agate, rose diamonds, 4.6 x 4.1 x 2.5 cm (1¹³/₁₆ x 1⁵/₈ x 1")
Mark of Michael Perchin; gold mark of 56 *zolotniks* (before 1896); *FABERGÉ* in Cyrillic characters
RCIN 9133
PROVENANCE: Presented to the Duchess of York (later Queen Mary) by Tsar Nicholas II and Tsarina Alexandra Feodorovna, Christmas 1894
REFERENCES: QMB I, no. 607; QMPP I, no. 182
EXHIBITIONS: QG 1985–6, no. 59; QG 1995–6, no. 255

148 DISPLAY BOX, 1908–1917

Fabergé used different woods to make cigarette and match cases and, as here, for a small number of other practical objects. This display box of birch wood was made in the workshop of Karl Armfelt (1873–1959).

Birch wood, glass, two-colour gold, 4.2 x 20.6 x 9.1 cm (1⅝ x 8⅛ x 3⁹⁄₁₆")
Mark of Karl Armfelt; gold mark of 56 *zolotniks* (1908–17); *FABERGÉ* in Cyrillic characters
RCIN 14743
PROVENANCE: Royal Collection by 1953
EXHIBITIONS: QG 1995–6, no. 229

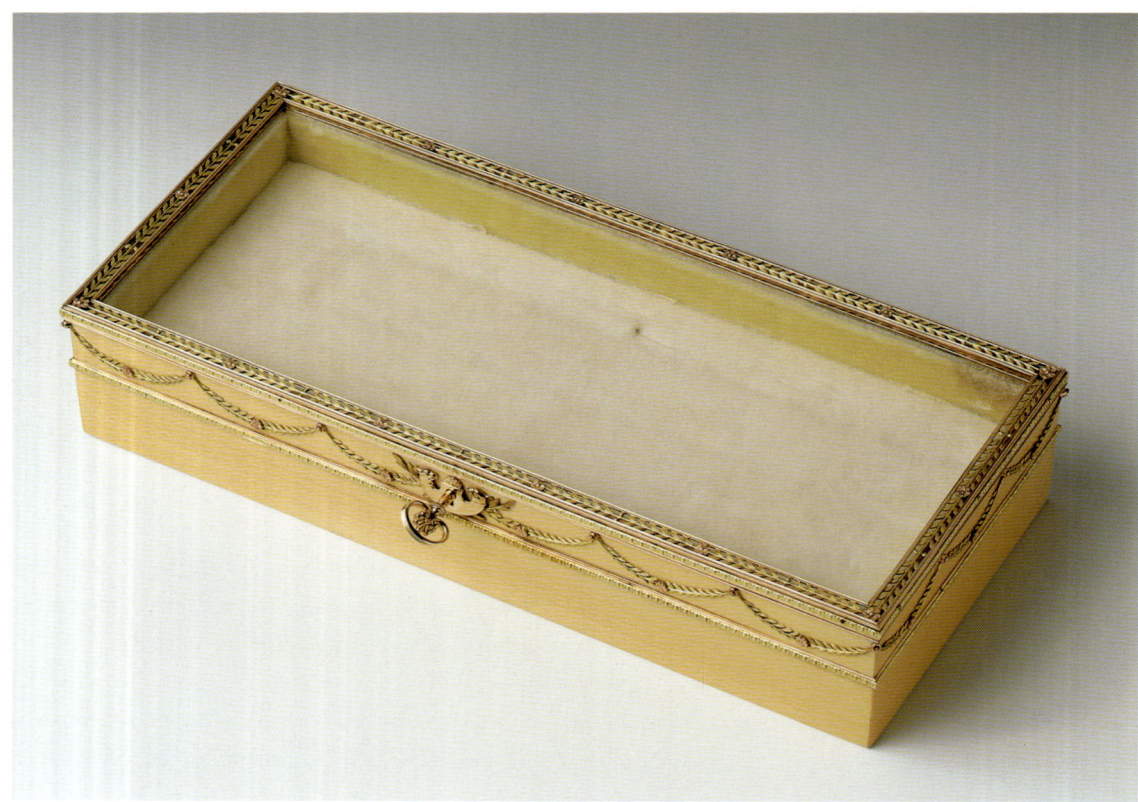

149 BOX, 1894

Major-General Sir Arthur Ellis (1837–1907) served King Edward VII when both Prince of Wales and King, first as an Equerry and later as Comptroller. He accompanied the Prince and Princess of Wales on their visit to Moscow and St Petersburg in November 1894 to attend the funeral of Tsar Alexander III and the wedding of Tsar Nicholas II to Princess Alix of Hesse. Earlier that year, in August, he had accompanied the Princess of Wales to St Petersburg for the marriage of Grand Duchess Xenia to Grand Duke Alexander, when this box was presented to him by Marie Feodorovna.

Nephrite, gold, guilloché enamel, rose diamonds forming crowned Cyrillic *F*, 3.4 x 14 x 8 cm (1⁵⁄₁₆ x 5½ x 3⅛")
Mark of Michael Perchin; gold mark of 56 *zolotniks* (before 1896); *FABERGÉ* in Cyrillic characters; engraved *ARTHUR ELLIS* in Roman letters, *PETERHOF* in Cyrillic characters, *AUGUST 1894* in Roman letters
RCIN 40810
PROVENANCE: Given by Tsarina Marie Feodorovna to Sir Arthur Ellis, 1894; by whom bequeathed to Queen Alexandra, June 1907
EXHIBITIONS: QG 1995–6, no. 476

150 FIVE-SIDED BOX, *c.*1912

A drawing for an almost identical box appears in a design album from Henrik Wigström's workshop.

Nephrite, gold, rose diamonds, cabochon rubies, 2.8 x 6.3 x 4.9 cm (1¹/₈ x 2¹/₂ x 1¹⁵/₁₆")
FABERGÉ in Cyrillic characters
RCIN 22937
PROVENANCE: Bought by the Dowager Tsarina Marie Feodorovna, 7 December 1912 (275 roubles) by whom given to Queen Mary for Christmas 1912
REFERENCES: QMB I, no. 269; QMPP I, no. 277; Tillander-Godenhielm *et al.* 2000, p. 161, pl. 203
EXHIBITIONS: QG 1995–6, no. 416

151 SEGMENTAL-SHAPED BOX, BEFORE 1896

Nephrite, gold, rose diamonds, cabochon ruby, 2.5 x 3.6 x 3.8 cm (1 x 1⁷/₁₆ x 1¹/₂")
Mark of Michael Perchin; gold mark of 56 *zolotniks* (before 1896)
RCIN 40154
PROVENANCE: Bought by Tsarina Marie Feodorovna 12 January 1898 (150 roubles); by whom given to Queen Alexandra
EXHIBITIONS: London 1977, no. G20; QG 1985–6, no. 22; QG 1995–6, no. 483

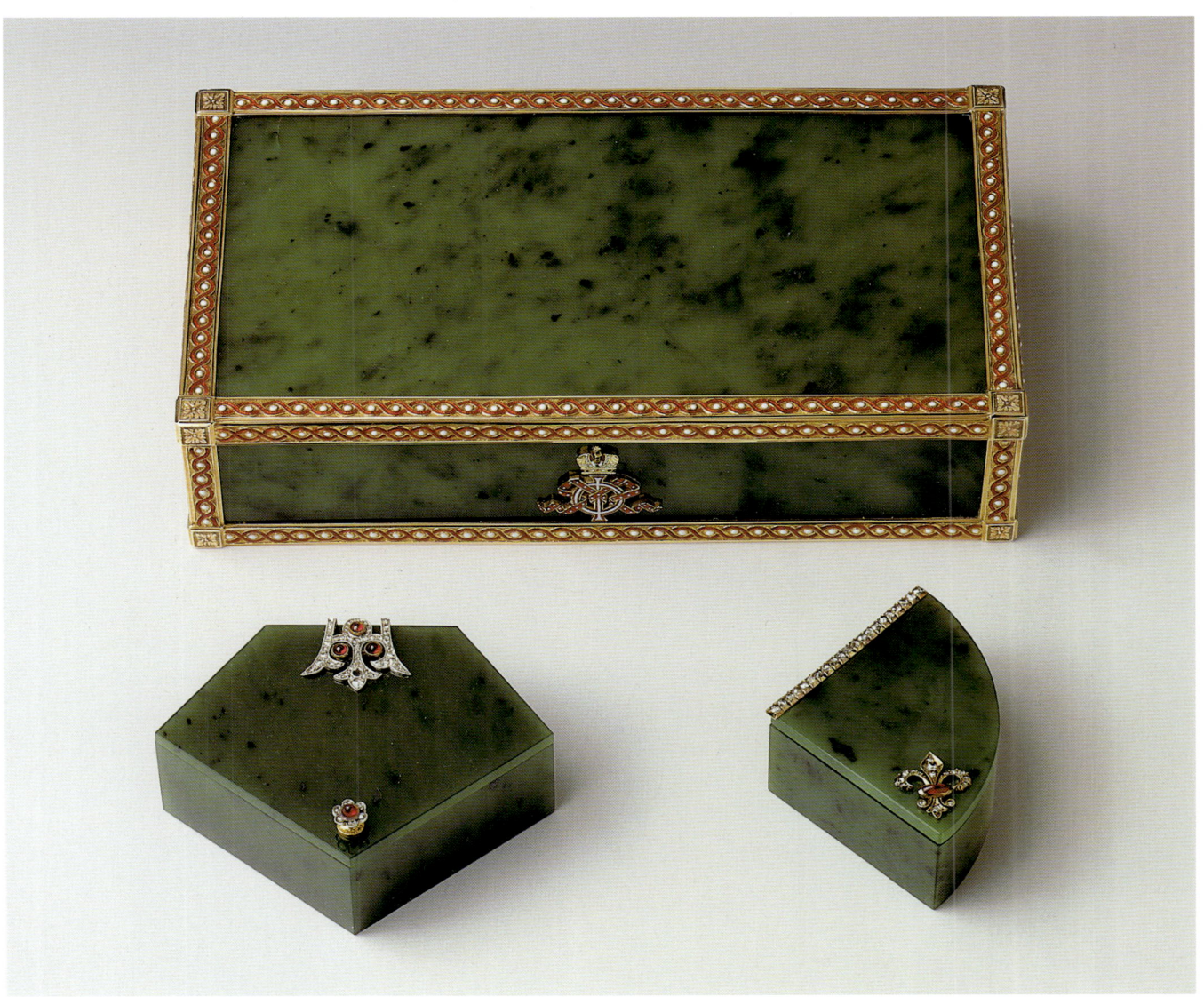

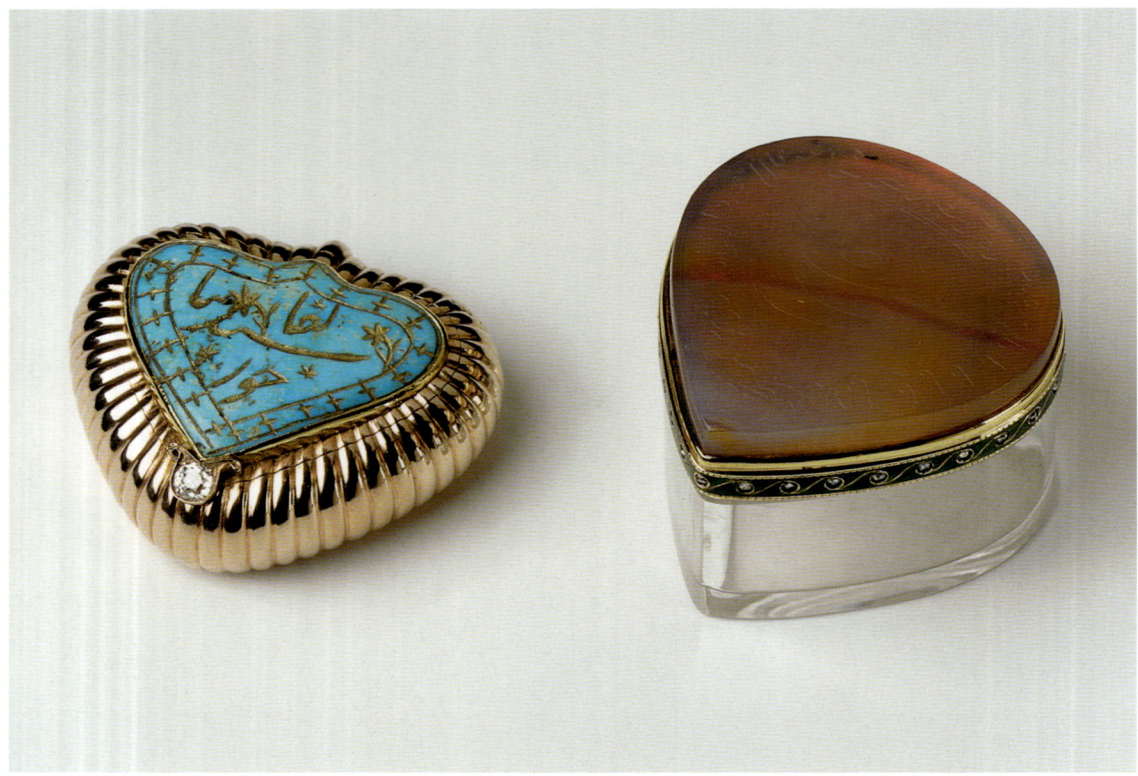

152 HEART-SHAPED BOX, BEFORE 1896

One of two objects in the collection (see cat. 153) incorporating an Arabic inscription. In this box it is engraved in gold on a piece of turquoise set into the lid. In an inventory of Princess Victoria's effects at Buckingham Palace made in 1936, this box is described as 'heart-shaped gold box, with ribbed sides, the lid inset with a scarab'.

Gold, turquoise, rose diamond, 1.5 x 4 x 3.6 cm (⁹/₁₆ x 1⁹/₁₆ x 1⁷/₁₆")
Mark of Erik Kollin; gold mark of 56 *zolotniks* (before 1896); inscribed inside lid *From Lavinia 1894*
RCIN 38211
PROVENANCE: Princess Victoria; King George V
REFERENCES: RA PP/BIR/50/2

153 HEART-SHAPED BOX, BEFORE 1896

Fabergé encouraged his designers and craftsmen to seek out sources of inspiration from areas as diverse as Greek, Roman, Gothic, Moorish, Renaissance and Asian art. This eclectic mixture of styles is evident in pieces produced throughout the lifetime of his business and greatly contributed to the success of the firm. The objects that resulted from this trawl through the history of design were skilfully conceived by the designers and exquisitely made by the craftsmen, not as slavish copies but incorporating references to earlier styles or traditions (see also cat. 152). This box was inspired by oriental designs and incorporates an Arabic inscription.

Rock crystal, enamel, rose diamonds, engraved mecca stone, 2.7 x 4 x 3.6 cm (1¹/₁₆ x 1⁹/₁₆ x 1⁷/₁₆")
Mark of Michael Perchin; gold mark of 56 *zolotniks* (before 1896); *FABERGÉ* in Cyrillic characters
RCIN 40151
EXHIBITIONS: London 1977, no. J5; QG 1985–6, no. 164; QG 1995–6, no. 468

154 CIRCULAR BOX, 1908–1917

The design for this box has recently come to light in the published album from Henrik Wigström's workshop.

Rhodonite, two-colour gold, guilloché enamel, 3.5 x diameter 6.5 cm (1⅜ x 2⁹/₁₆")
Gold mark of 72 *zolotniks* (1908–17); *FABERGÉ* in Roman letters; English import marks
RCIN 22924
PROVENANCE: Queen Alexandra; by whom given to Queen Mary
REFERENCES: Snowman 1962, p. XII; Tillander-Godenhielm *et al.* 2000, p. 161, pl. 203
EXHIBITIONS: QG 1995–6, no. 464

155 RECTANGULAR BOX, 1910

Rhodonite, two-colour gold, enamel, 3.9 x 7.3 x 5.3 cm (1⁹/₁₆ x 2⅞ x 2¹/₁₆")
Mark of Henrik Wigström
RCIN 9170
PROVENANCE: Bought by the Duchess of Roxburghe from Fabergé's London branch, 28 November 1910 (£35 5s); by whom presented to Queen Mary, Christmas 1910
REFERENCES: QMPP II, no. 65
EXHIBITIONS: QG 1985–6, no. 120; QG 1995–6, no. 53

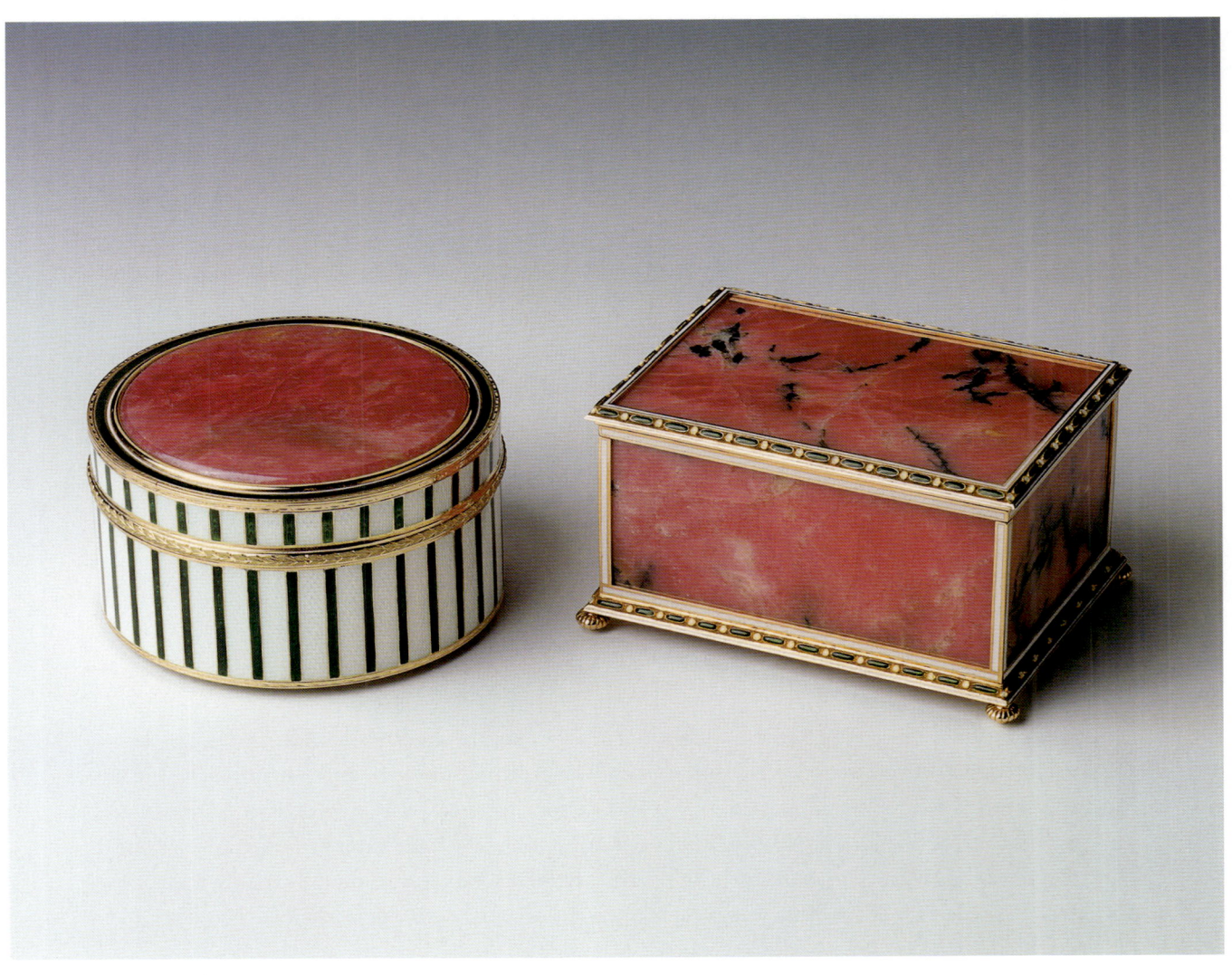

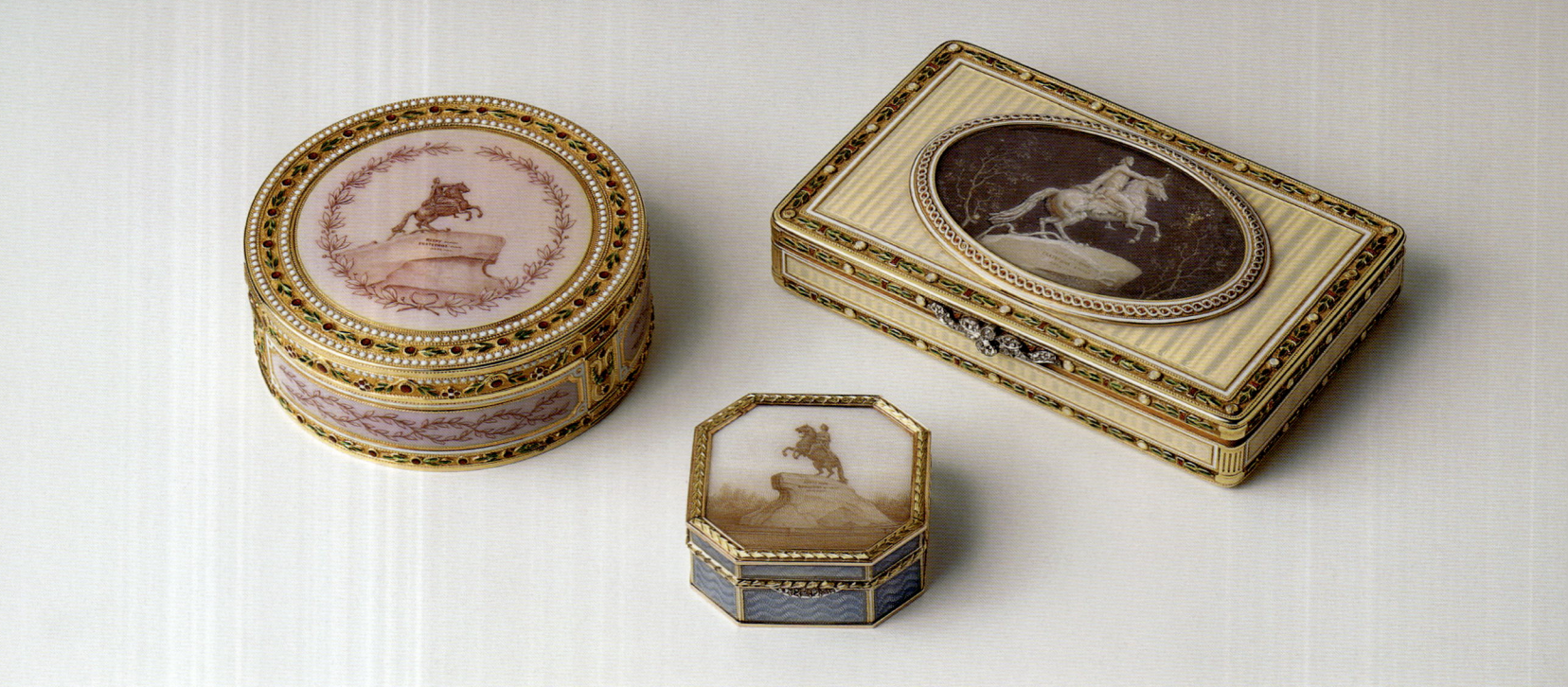

156 CIRCULAR BOX WITH MINIATURES OF PETER THE GREAT'S MONUMENT AND THE PETER AND PAUL FORTRESS, 1903–1908

This box has views in enamel of two monuments in St Petersburg: the monument to Peter the Great (1672–1725), and the Peter and Paul Fortress (on the underside).

The monument was commissioned by Catherine the Great from the French sculptor Etienne Falconet (1716–91) to glorify Peter the Great's absolutism and was completed in 1782. It was placed beside the Neva river on a massive rock pedestal which had been brought from the village of Lakhta, outside St Petersburg.

Erected at the command of Peter the Great in 1703, the Peter and Paul Fortress marks the foundation of St Petersburg as the new capital of Russia. It is the burial site of Peter the Great and all subsequent tsars. This box was probably made in 1903 to coincide with the two hundredth anniversary of St Petersburg.

Gold, enamel and sepia enamel, 2.6 x diameter 6.8 cm (1 x 2¹¹/₁₆")
Mark of Henrik Wigström; gold mark of 72 *zolotniks* (1896–1908)
RCIN 40489
PROVENANCE: Probably acquired by King Edward VII and Queen Alexandra, date unknown
EXHIBITIONS: London 1953, no. 95; London 1977, no. H9; QG 1985–6, no. 69; QG 1995–6, no. 276

157 BOX WITH A MINIATURE OF PETER THE GREAT'S MONUMENT, *c.*1913

This is the largest of three boxes in the Royal Collection that feature images of Falconet's monument to Peter the Great.

Images of the city of St Petersburg began to appear in the Russian decorative arts with greater frequency during the nineteenth and twentieth centuries on silver and papier-mâché boxes and on objects produced by the Imperial Porcelain Factory. Fabergé's designers continued this tradition and many of the objects with views of the city (including two of the three boxes in the Royal Collection) were produced in Wigström's workshop. The miniature on this box was painted by Vassily Zuiev and is dated 1913, the year of the Romanov tercentenary. A design for a similar box appears on plate 135 of an album from Wigström's workshop.

Gold, guilloché enamel, rose and brilliant diamonds, miniature *en grisaille*, 2 x 9.3 x 6.2 cm ($^{13}/_{16}$ x $3^{11}/_{16}$ x $2^{7}/_{16}$")
Mark of Henrik Wigström; gold mark of 56 *zolotniks* (1908–17); *FABERGÉ* in Cyrillic characters.
RCIN 19126
PROVENANCE: Prince Vladimir Galitzine; from whom purchased by Queen Mary, 10 September 1934 (£178); given to King George V, Christmas 1934
REFERENCES: GV Boxes, vol. V, no. 366; Tillander-Godenhielm *et al.* 2000, pp. 135, 159
EXHIBITIONS: London 1977, no. K24; New York 1983, no. 195; QG 1985–6, no. 297; St Petersburg/Paris/London 1993–4, no. 149; QG 1995–6, no. 254

158   OCTAGONAL BOX WITH A MINIATURE OF PETER THE GREAT'S MONUMENT, 1908–1917

Two-colour gold, silver-gilt, guilloché and sepia enamel, rose diamonds, 1.7 x 3.9 x 3.9 cm ($^{11}/_{16}$ x $1^{9}/_{16}$ x $1^{9}/_{16}$")
Mark of Feodor Afanassiev; silver mark of 88 *zolotniks* (1908–17); *FABERGÉ* in Cyrillic characters
RCIN 40488
PROVENANCE: Royal Collection by 1953
EXHIBITIONS: London 1977, no. H10; QG 1985–6, no. 60; QG 1995–6, no. 256

159   LOUIS XV STYLE BOX, BEFORE 1896

Formerly owned by Grand Duchess Xenia of Russia (1875–1960), whose initials are applied to the top of the box. Grand Duchess Xenia was the sister of Tsar Nicholas II and wife of Grand Duke Alexander (1866–1933), a first cousin of Tsar Alexander III.

Aventurine quartz, gold, rose diamonds, olivines, 9 x 6.4 x 4.7 cm ($3^{9}/_{16}$ x $2^{1}/_{2}$ x $1^{7}/_{8}$")
Mark of Michael Perchin; gold mark of 56 *zolotniks* (before 1896); *FABERGÉ* in Cyrillic characters
RCIN 9126
PROVENANCE: Grand Duchess Xenia Alexandrovna; Queen Mary's collection
REFERENCES: Snowman 1962, pl. XII
EXHIBITIONS: QG 1985–6, no. 144; QG 1995–6, no. 219

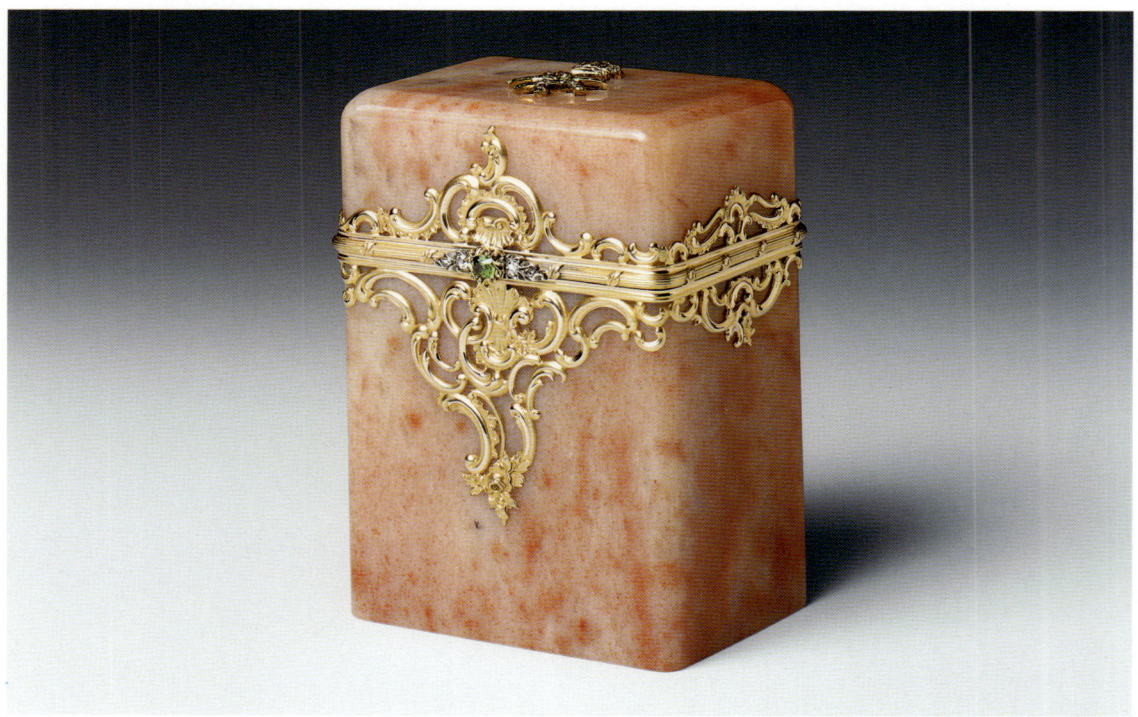

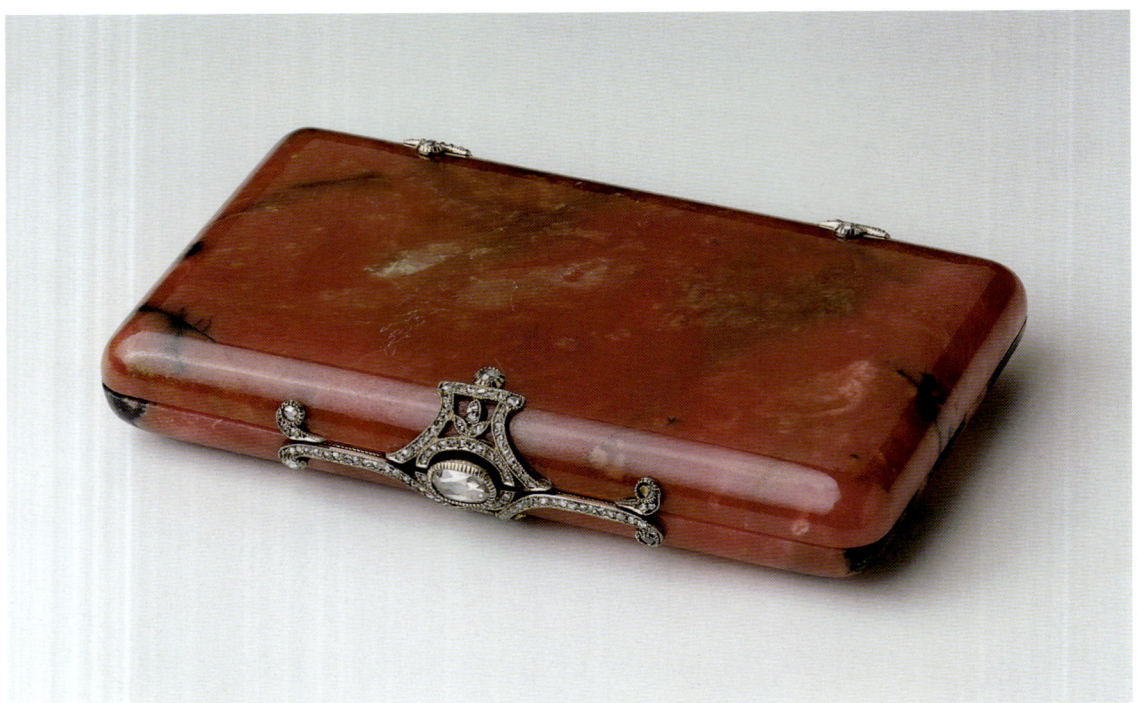

160 CIGARETTE CASE, 1911

Rhodonite, gold, rose diamonds, 1.6 x 8.7 x 5.5 cm ($^5/_8$ x 3$^7/_{16}$ x 2$^3/_{16}$")
Mark of Henrik Wigström; gold mark (numbers illegible; 1908–17); *FABERGÉ* in Cyrillic characters
RCIN 4065
PROVENANCE: Bought by Grand Duke Michael of Russia from Fabergé's London branch, 6 July 1911 (£64);
King George V's collection
REFERENCES: GV Cigarette Cases, no. 6; Bainbridge 1949, pl. 117
EXHIBITIONS: London 1949, no. 3; London 1977, no. K19; QG 1985–6, no. 121; QG 1995–6, no. 56

161 CIGARETTE CASE, BEFORE 1896

This *samorodok* (hammered gold) cigarette case was made in the workshop of Eduard Schramm. Of German origin, Schramm supplied Fabergé with gold objects such as this.

Gold, brilliant diamonds, cabochon sapphires, 1.6 x 8.5 x 5.3 cm ($^5/_8$ x 3$^3/_8$ x 2$^1/_{16}$")
Mark of Eduard Schramm; gold mark of 56 *zolotniks* (before 1896)
RCIN 4320
PROVENANCE: Given to King George V by Queen Alexandra
REFERENCES: GV Cigarette Cases, no. 49
EXHIBITIONS: QG 1985–6, no. 307; QG 1995–6, no. 511

162 CIGARETTE CASE, BEFORE 1903

Fitted with a pencil and a match compartment.

Gold, cabochon sapphire, 1.7 x 9.9 x 6.1 cm ($^{11}/_{16}$ x 3$^3/_8$ x 2$^3/_8$")
Mark of August Holmström; gold mark of 56 *zolotniks*
RCIN 100305
PROVENANCE: Bought by Queen Elizabeth, date unknown

163 CIGARETTE CASE, 1903

The crowned *EA* cypher on one side and dates inscribed in diamonds – *10 March 1903 XL 1863–1903* – on the other indicate that this case was made to celebrate the fortieth wedding anniversary of King Edward VII and Queen Alexandra.

Three-colour gold, rose diamonds, cabochon ruby, 1.4 x 9.4 x 6.8 cm (⁹⁄₁₆ x 3¹¹⁄₁₆ x 2¹¹⁄₁₆")
Moscow gold mark of 56 *zolotniks* (1896–1908); *C. FABERGÉ* in Cyrillic characters
RCIN 4344
PROVENANCE: Given to King Edward VII by Marie Feodorovna as a fortieth wedding anniversary gift
REFERENCES: GV Cigarette Cases, no. 43; Bainbridge 1949, pl. 121
EXHIBITIONS: QG 1995–6, no. 486

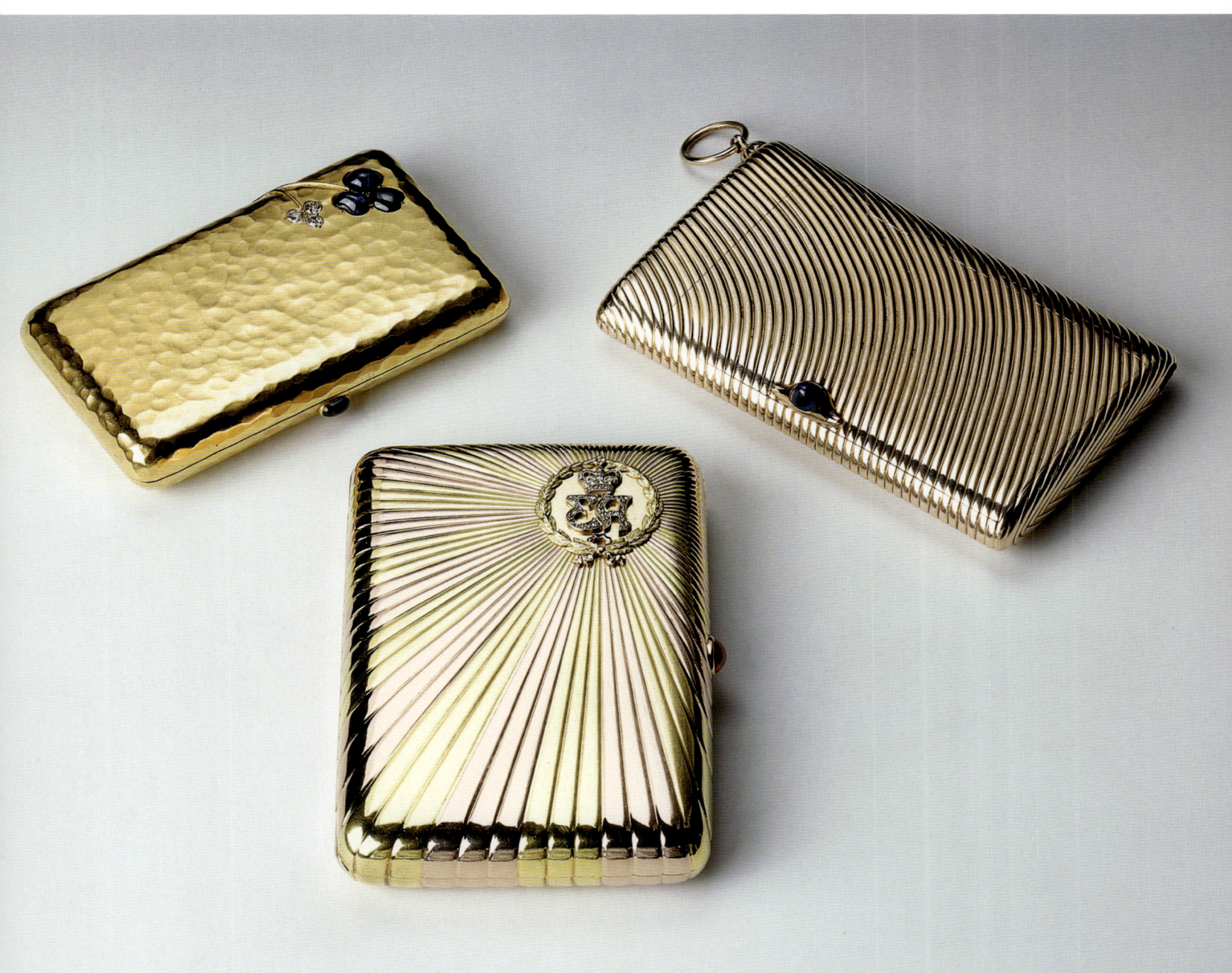

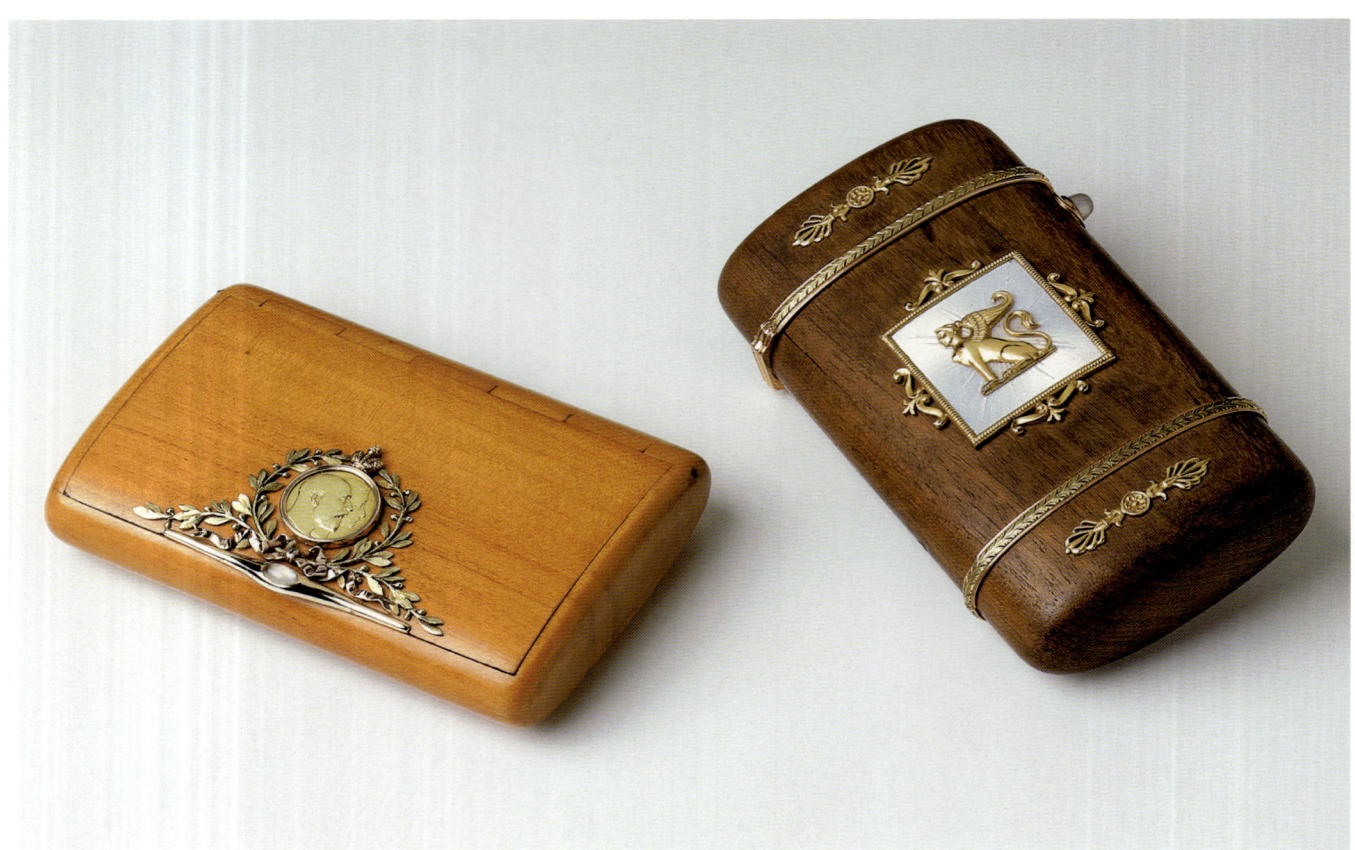

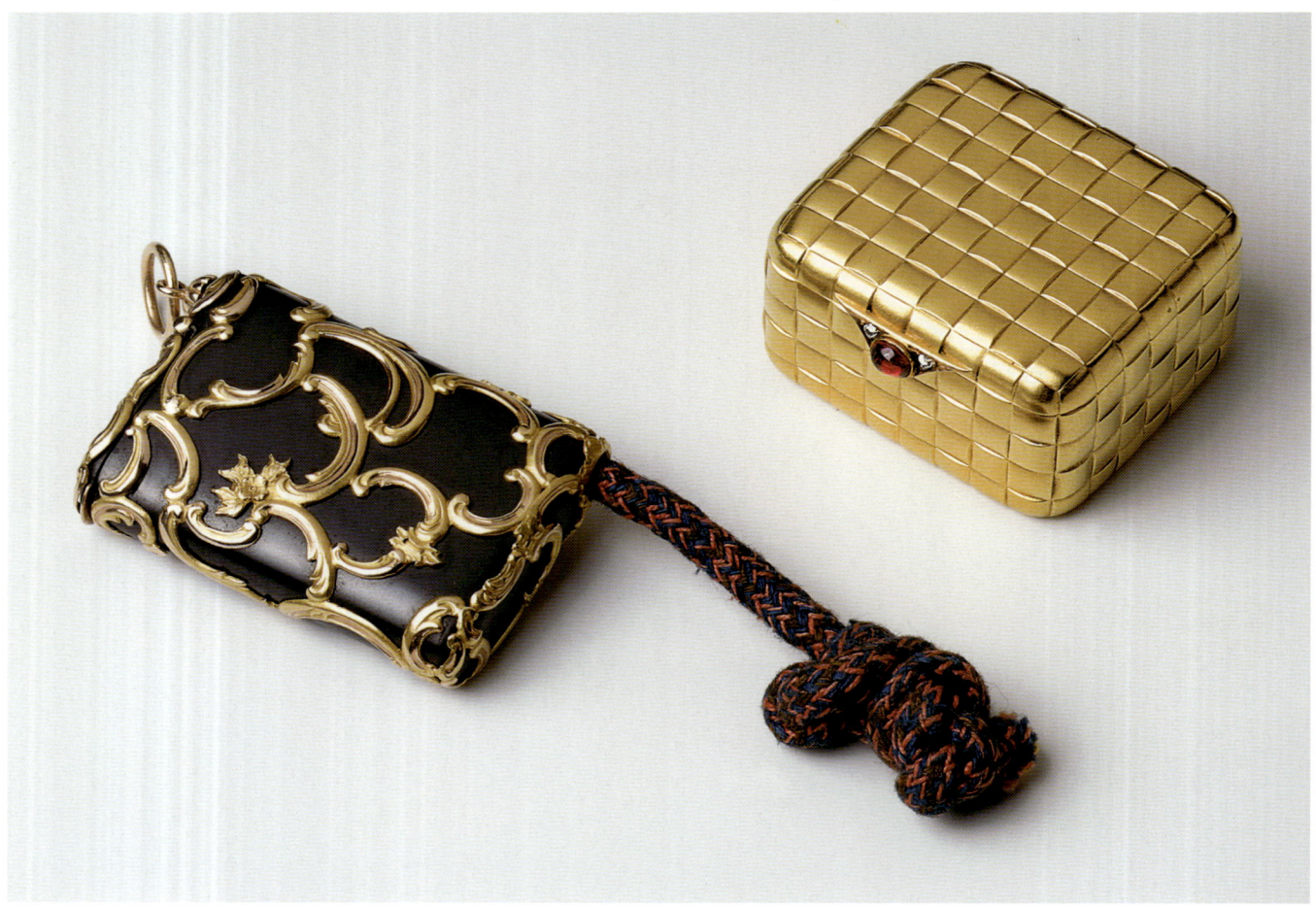

164   CIGARETTE CASE, 1896–1908

Fabergé used a variety of different woods to make the simpler and less expensive cigarette cases in his range. This example incorporates a profile portrait medallion of King Edward VII and Queen Alexandra.

Birch wood, three-colour gold, moonstone, 2.2 x 9 x 6.1 cm (⁷/₈ x 3⁹/₁₆ x 2³/₈")
Gold mark of 56 *zolotniks* (1896–1908); FABERGÉ in Cyrillic characters
RCIN 4067
PROVENANCE: Presumably acquired by King Edward VII; given to King George V by Queen Alexandra
REFERENCES: GV Cigarette Cases, no. 29
EXHIBITIONS: QG 1995–6, no. 506

165   CIGARETTE CASE, 1896–1903

This cigarette case demonstrates the range of sources from which Fabergé's designers sought inspiration. Michael Perchin, whose period as head workmaster is generally acknowledged to have been the most inventive in terms of design, chose the Egyptian sphinx and classical anthemions (ornamental motifs based on honeysuckle) to decorate this case. A palisander wood case with a similar applied sphinx in gold, but made in Wigström's workshop, was sold at Christie's in 1976.

Palisander wood, two-colour gold, guilloché enamel, moonstone, 3.1 x 10.1 x 6 cm (1¹/₄ x 4 x 2³/₈")
Mark of Michael Perchin; gold mark of 56 *zolotniks* (1896–1908); FABERGÉ in Cyrillic characters
RCIN 4069
PROVENANCE: The Duke of Gloucester; by whom given to King George V
REFERENCES: GV Cigarette Cases, no. 1; Christie's, 9 March 1976, The Robert Strauss Collection, lot 11
EXHIBITIONS: London 1977, no. K18; QG 1985–6, no. 312; QG 1995–6, no. 509

166   MATCH CASE, BEFORE 1896

Fabergé occasionally used non-precious metals for certain objects, such as this match case made of gunmetal. The application of rococo scrolls in two-colour gold results in a far from mundane object. A cigarette case of similar design is in the State Hermitage Museum, St Petersburg.

Gunmetal, two-colour gold, with tinder cord, 5.2 x 3.2 x 1.2 cm (2¹/₁₆ x 1¹/₄ x ¹/₂")
Mark of Michael Perchin; gold mark of 56 *zolotniks* (before 1896)
RCIN 13940
PROVENANCE: Probably acquired by the Prince of Wales (later King Edward VII)
REFERENCES: Habsburg & Lopato 1993, p. 176
EXHIBITIONS: QG 1995–6, no. 508

167   SQUARE BOX, BEFORE 1896

Produced in the workshop of Fabergé's first head workmaster, Erik Kollin, this box is engraved to resemble basket weave.

Gold, rose diamond, cabochon ruby, 2.2 x 3.9 x 3.9 cm (⁷/₈ x 1⁹/₁₆ x 1⁹/₁₆")
Mark of Erik Kollin; gold mark of 56 *zolotniks* (before 1896)
RCIN 22961
PROVENANCE: Presented to Queen Mary by the Nawab of Bahamalpour, before 1949
EXHIBITIONS: QG 1995–6, no. 59

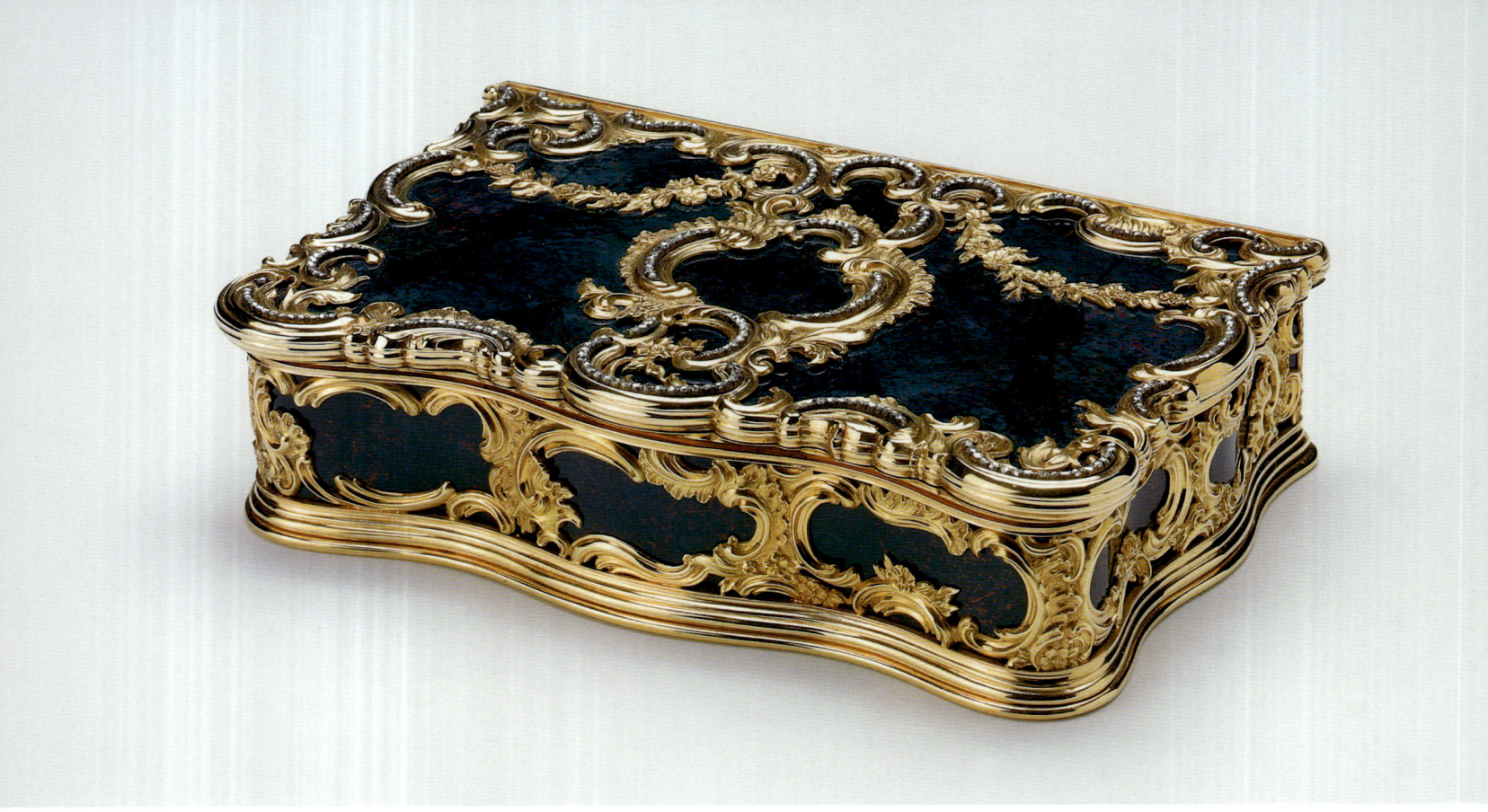

168 BLOODSTONE BOX, BEFORE 1896

Fabergé's workshops, particularly that of Michael Perchin – his chief workmaster from 1886 to 1903 – produced many neo-rococo pieces, a style that was very popular in St Petersburg in the 1880s. Notable among them is the Imperial Easter Egg known as the Memory of Azov Egg, dated 1891, which features the combination of bloodstone and gold mounts set with diamonds used here. Henrik Wigström, who took over as chief workmaster in 1903, continued neo-rococo ornament in some of his work (as seen in a drawing in his design books for a nephrite and gold cigarette case), but his style was lighter and more restrained than Perchin's. The neo-rococo was quickly subsumed by the neo-classical in Wigström's designs.

The flamboyant rococo design of this box, mounted in gold and set with rose diamonds, is similar to a green jasper carnet in the Wernher Collection, made between 1896 and 1899, also by Michael Perchin. Another Russian carnet of similar design, dating from the late nineteenth century, exists in the Thyssen-Bornemisza Collection, although it is not marked by Fabergé.

Bloodstone, gold, rose diamonds, 3.8 x 13.7 x 9.3 cm (1½ x 5⅜ x 3¹¹/₁₆")
Mark of Michael Perchin; gold mark of 72 *zolotniks* (before 1896); *FABERGÉ* in Cyrillic characters
RCIN 9314
PROVENANCE: Marie, Duchess of Saxe-Coburg-Gotha (d.1920); presented by her daughter to King George V
REFERENCES: Somers Cocks & Truman 1984, pp. 308–9; Tillander-Godenhielm *et al.* 2000, p. 36
EXHIBITIONS: QG 1985–6, no. 310; QG 1995–6, no. 220; QG 2002–3, no. 267

169 BOX, 1896–1903

Silver, two-colour gold, guilloché enamel, rose diamond, 2.2 x 4 x 4 cm (⅞ x 1⁹/₁₆ x 1⁹/₁₆")
Mark of Michael Perchin; silver mark of 88 *zolotniks* (1896–1908); *FABERGÉ* in Cyrillic characters
RCIN 40184
PROVENANCE: Probably acquired by Queen Alexandra; Royal Collection by 1953
EXHIBITIONS: London 1977, no. J11; QG 1985–6, no. 303; QG 1995–6, no. 269

170 CIGARETTE CASE, 1906

The enamelling on this cigarette case is unusual because it has been applied to an undecorated surface and is both opaque and matt, rather than the highly polished, translucent guilloché enamel more familiar in Fabergé's work.

Two-colour gold, silver-gilt, enamel, rose diamonds, 8.6 x 5.6 x 2.3 cm (3³/₈ x 2³/₁₆ x ⁷/₈")
Mark of Henrik Wigström; gold mark of 56 *zolotniks*; silver mark of 88 *zolotniks* (1896–1908); *FABERGÉ* in Cyrillic characters
RCIN 4062
PROVENANCE: Bought by Queen Alexandra from Fabergé's London branch, 29 October 1906 (£31 5s);
King George VI's collection
REFERENCES: GV Cigarette Cases, no. 50; Bainbridge 1949, pl. 120
EXHIBITIONS: London 1949, no. 2; London 1977, no. K1; QG 1985–6, no. 309; QG 1995–6, no. 510

171 CIRCULAR BOX, 1908–1917

Feodor Afanassiev, the workmaster who produced this box bearing the imperial eagle, specialised in making small objects in gold and enamel.

Two-colour gold, silver-gilt, guilloché enamel, rose diamonds, 2.2 x 5.4 x 4.9 cm (⁷/₈ x 2¹/₈ x 1¹⁵/₁₆")
Mark of Feodor Afanassiev; silver mark of 88 *zolotniks* (1908–17); *FABERGÉ* in Cyrillic characters
RCIN 22983
PROVENANCE: Probably acquired by Queen Alexandra; Royal Collection by 1953
EXHIBITIONS: QG 1995–6, no. 245

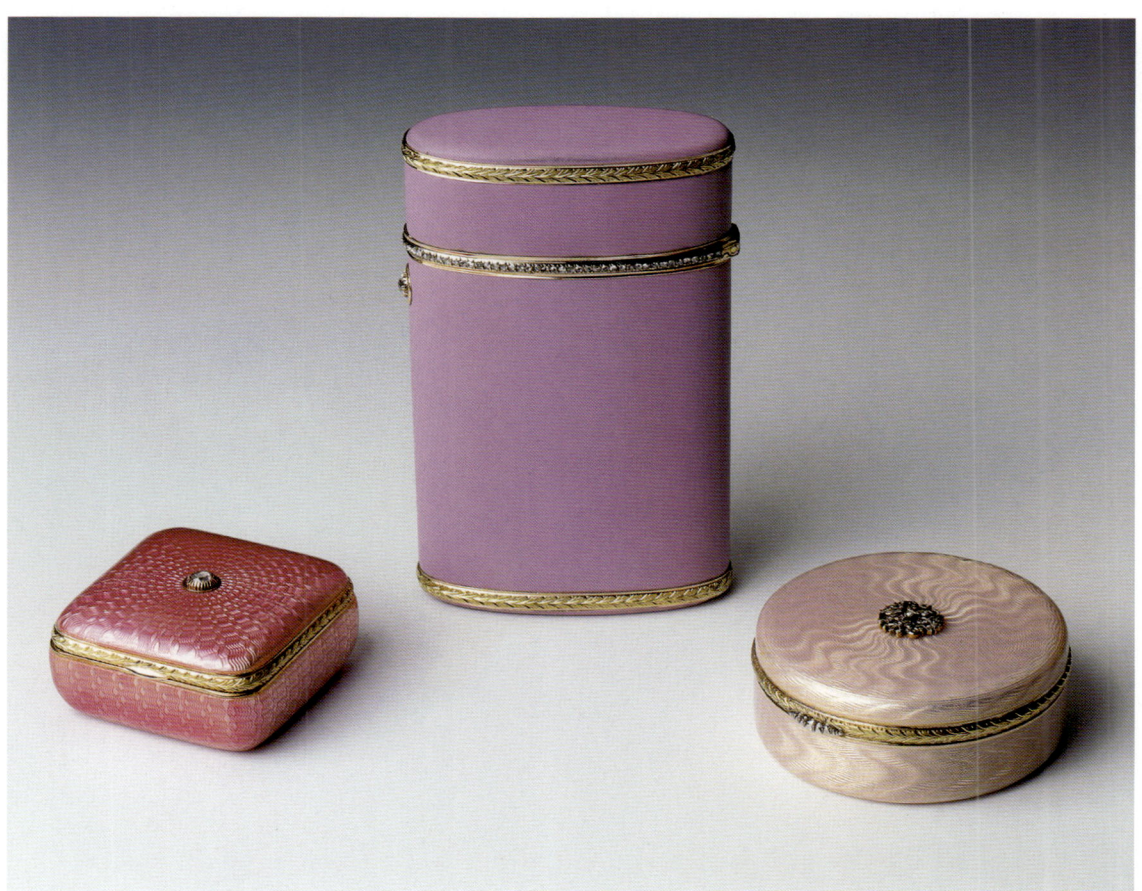

172 ROCOCO BOX, BEFORE 1896

Nephrite, gold, cabochon ruby, rose diamonds, 3.4 x 3.8 x 3.8 cm (1⁵/₁₆ x 1¹/₂ x 1¹/₂")
Mark of Erik Kollin; gold mark of 56 *zolotniks* (before 1896)
RCIN 9150
PROVENANCE: Acquired by Queen Mary before 1913
REFERENCES: QMB I, no. 351; QMPP I, no. 245
EXHIBITIONS: QG 1995–6, no. 484

173 CIGARETTE CASE, *c.*1902

This case in the shape of a suitcase, the gold 'straps' with buckles, was presented by King Edward VII to his close friend Sir Michael Bass (1837–1909). Created Lord Burton in 1886, he ran his family's brewing company and became a Liberal MP. King Edward frequently visited him at his London home, Chesterfield House, his Scottish seat of Glen Quoich and his estate, Rangemore, near Burton-upon-Trent.

Nephrite, gold, 2.5 x 9.1 x 5.6 cm (1 x 3⁹/₁₆ x 2³/₁₆")
Mark of Michael Perchin; gold mark of 56 *zolotniks* (1896–1908); *FABERGÉ* in Cyrillic characters
RCIN 40114
PROVENANCE: Presented to Lord Burton by King Edward VII, 24 February 1902; sold Christie's 25 November 1958 lot 135; Wartski; from whom purchased for the Royal Collection
REFERENCES: Christie's 1958
EXHIBITIONS: London 1977, no. G1; QG 1985–6, no. 299; QG 1995–6, no. 480

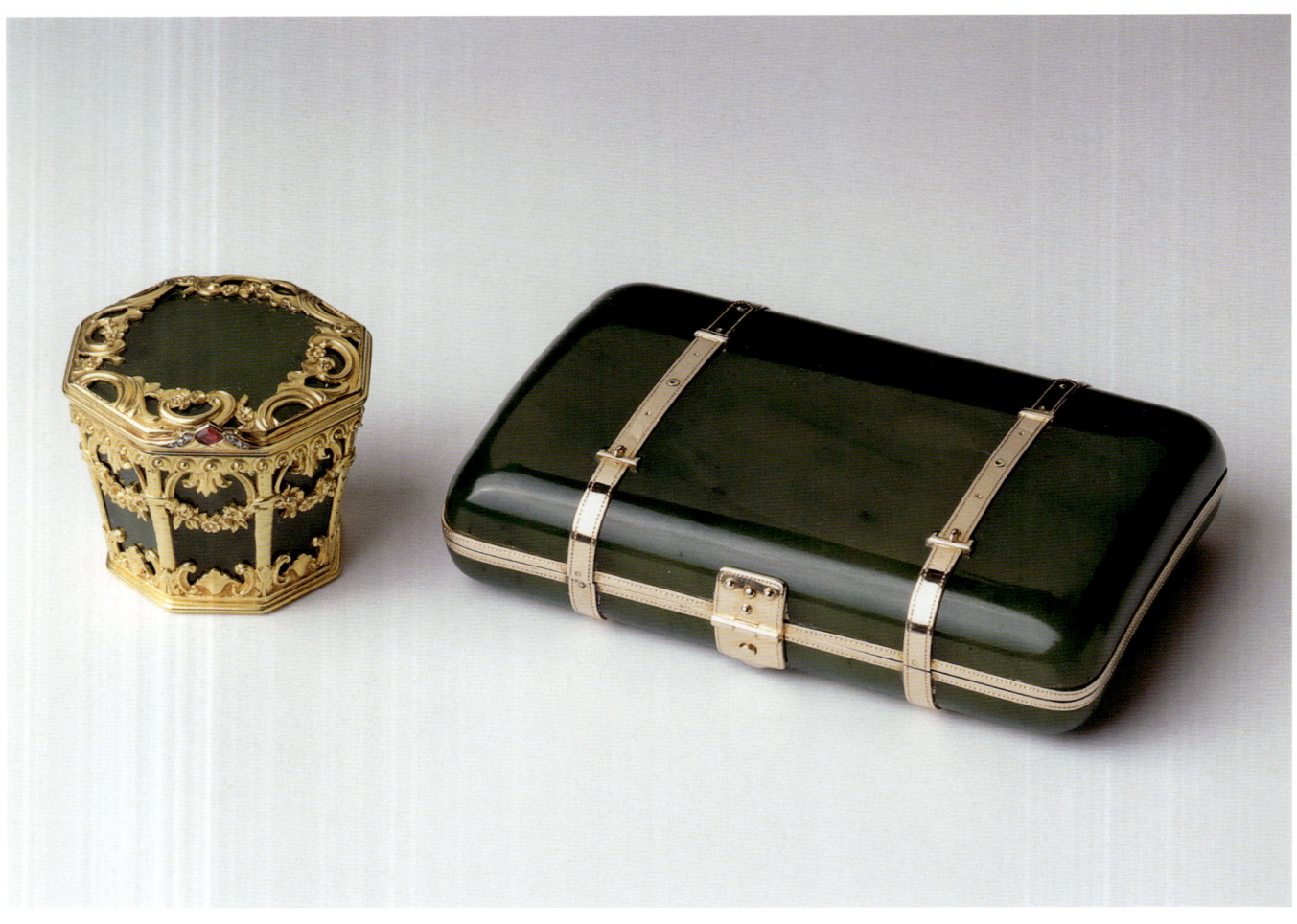

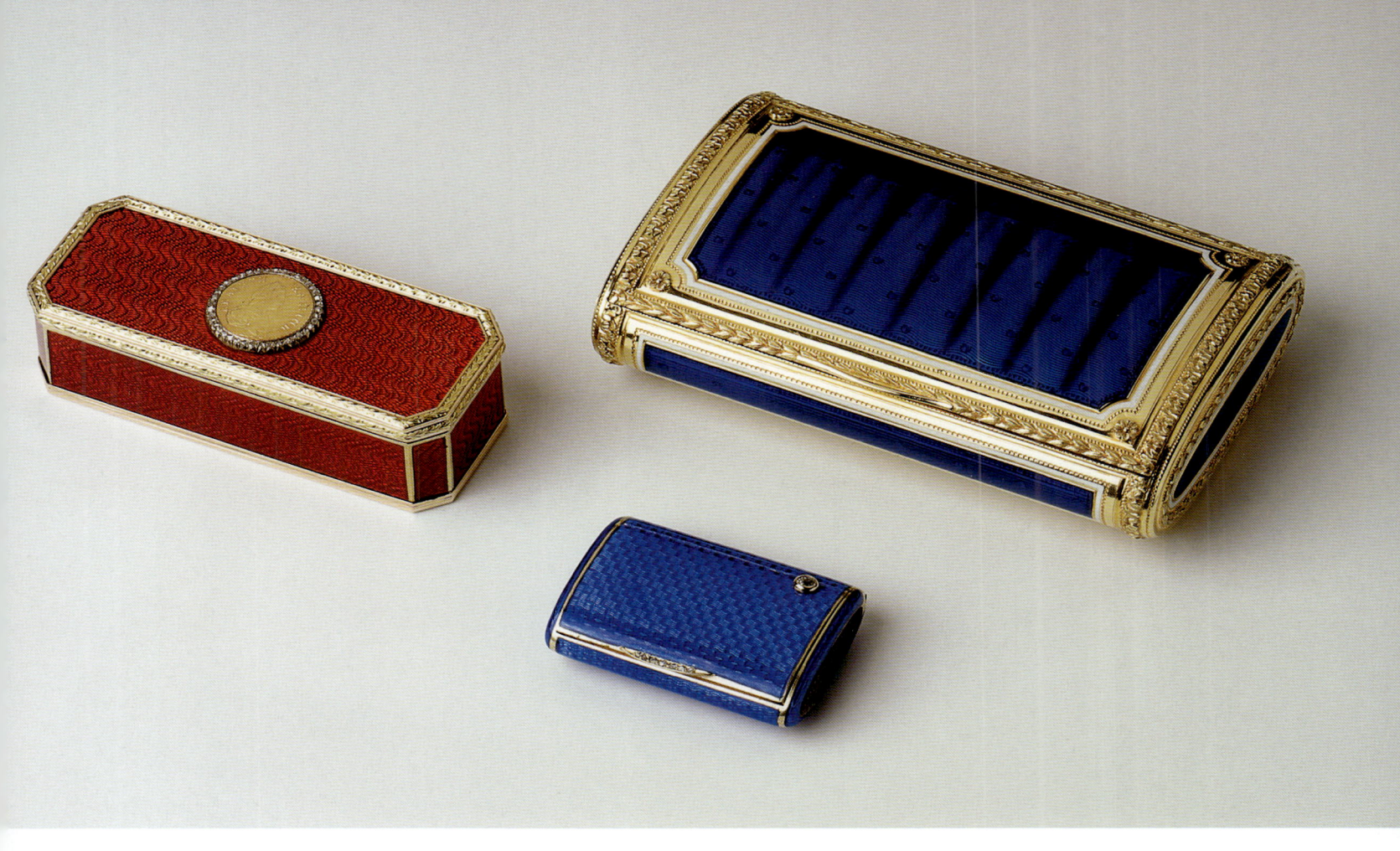

174 SNUFF BOX, 1896–1903

Silver-gilt, two-colour gold, red guilloché enamel, the lid set with a gold Catherine the Great rouble within a circle of rose diamonds, 1.9 x 6.4 x 2.7 cm (³/₄ x 2¹/₂ x 1¹/₁₆")
Mark of Michael Perchin; silver mark of 88 *zolotniks* (1896–1908); FABERGÉ in Cyrillic characters
RCIN 40168
PROVENANCE: Probably acquired by Queen Alexandra; Royal Collection by 1953
EXHIBITIONS: London 1977, no. J2; QG 1985–6, no. 305; QG 1995–6, no. 475

175 MATCH CASE, 1896–1903

Silver-gilt, guilloché enamel, rose diamonds, 0.5 x 3.5 x 2.5 cm (³/₁₆ x 1³/₈ x 1")
Mark of August Holmström; silver mark of 88 *zolotniks* (1896–1908); FABERGÉ in Cyrillic characters
RCIN 15131
PROVENANCE: Probably acquired by King Edward VII; Royal Collection by 1953
EXHIBITIONS: QG 1995–6, no. 504

176 CIGARETTE CASE, 1903–1908

Designed in the Louis XVI style.

Gold, guilloché enamel, 2.2 x 8.4 x 8.5 cm (⁷/₈ x 3⁵/₁₆ x 3³/₈")
Mark of Henrik Wigström; gold mark of 72 *zolotniks* (1896–1908); FABERGÉ in Cyrillic characters
RCIN 9339
PROVENANCE: Acquired by Queen Mary before 1936
REFERENCES: QMPP VIII, no. 50
EXHIBITIONS: QG 1995–6, no. 492

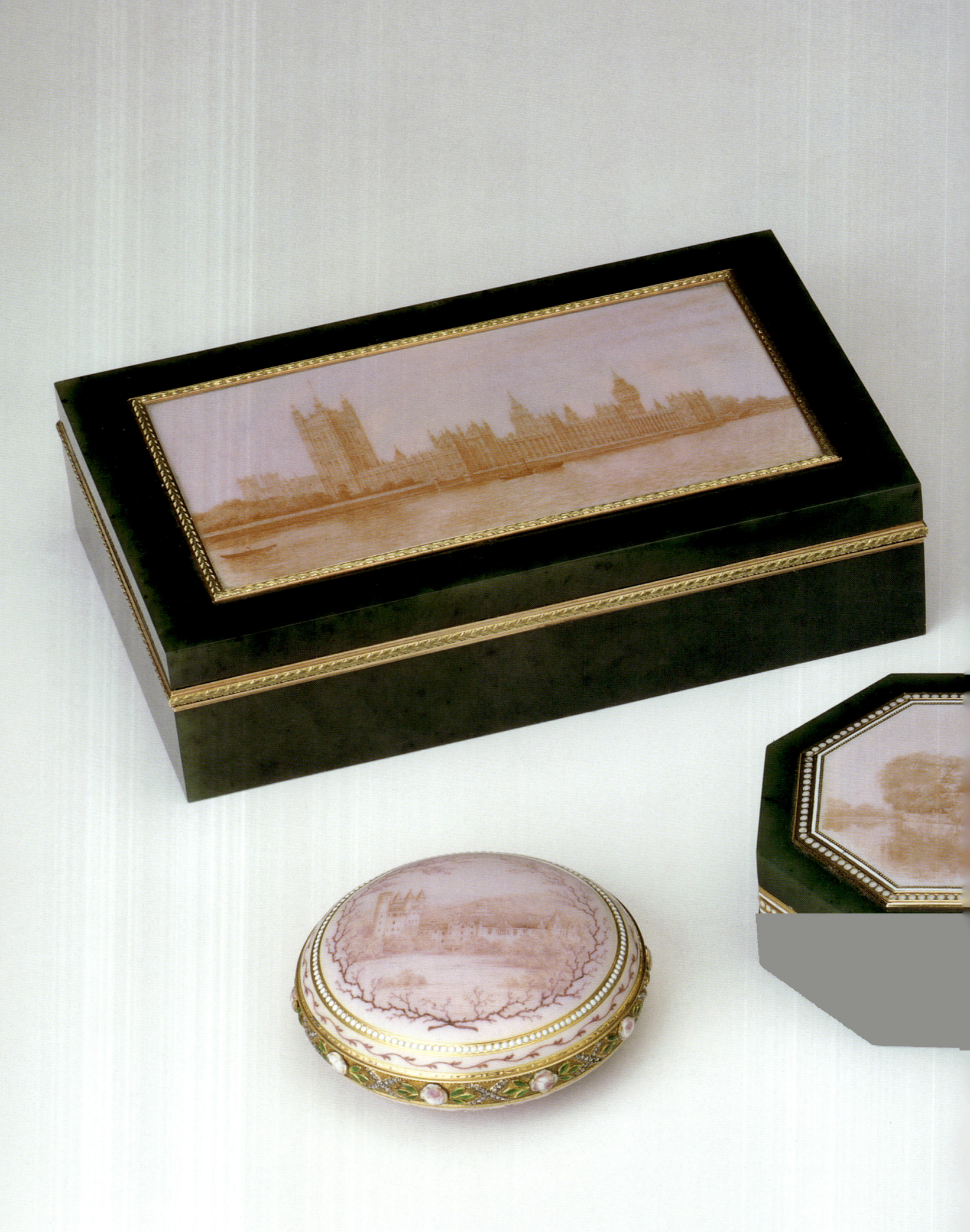

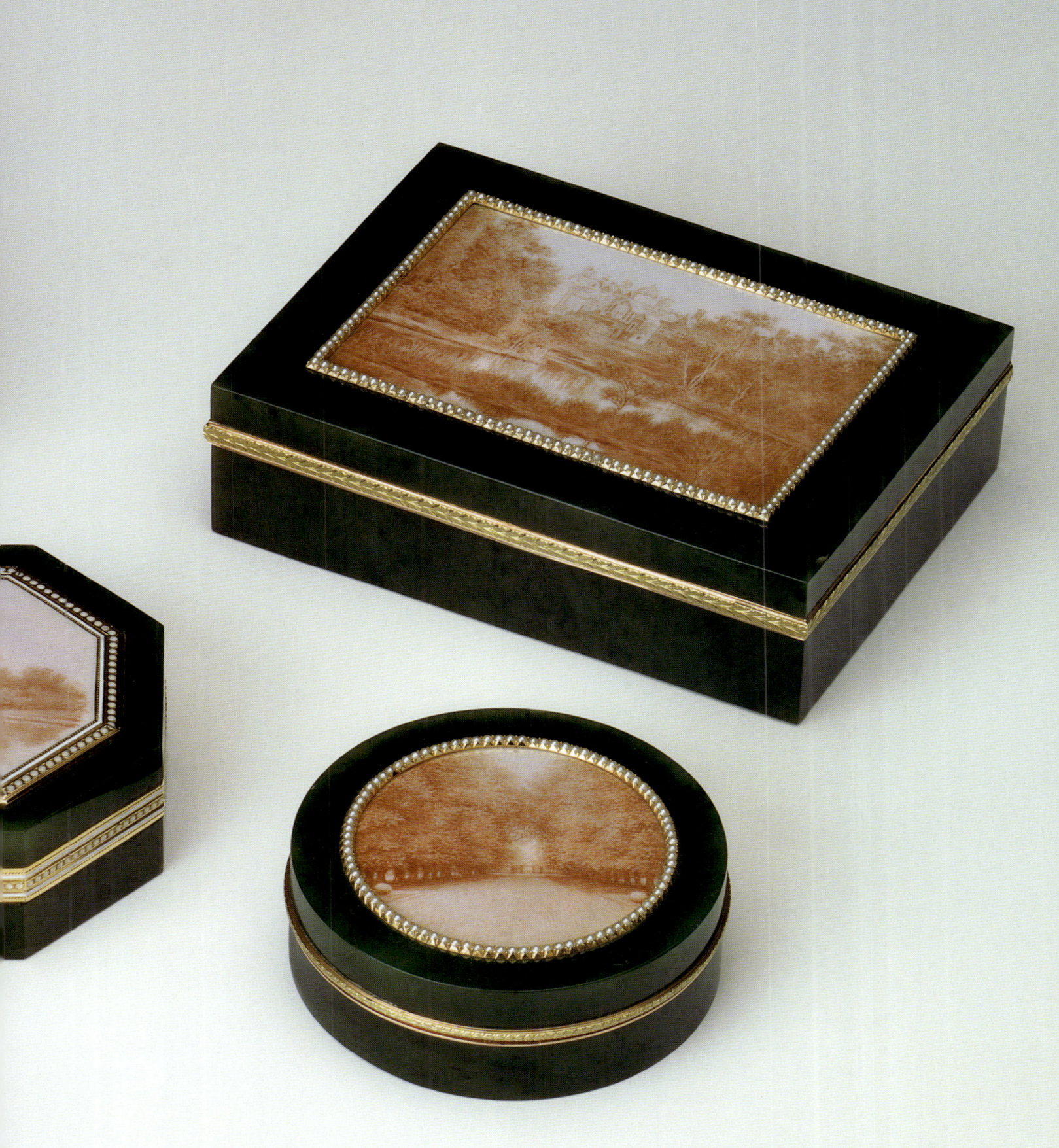

177 BONBONNIÈRE WITH A VIEW OF BALMORAL CASTLE, 1907

The range of boxes with enamelled views of monuments and buildings in Russia, which included some special commissions (for example the Yusopov music box now in the Hillwood Collection, Washington, DC), was complemented by boxes and frames decorated with enamelled views of buildings and places in England. The Royal Collection contains five boxes, three of them featuring royal residences. The Princess of Wales (later Queen Mary) had much admired the first example to return from St Petersburg and this, Bainbridge records, inspired him to suggest that Fabergé made boxes or frames with views of all the royal residences which 'would be enough to keep Fabergé going until the end of King Edward's reign and well into King George's'. However, the Princess of Wales suggested to Bainbridge that it would be appropriate to include views of the private residences such as Balmoral and Sandringham only. Even so, this box includes on the reverse a view of Windsor Castle, and Bainbridge states that both Buckingham Palace and Hampton Court Palace were made as enamelled plaques framed in nephrite (see cat. 225–228).

Gold, enamel and sepia enamel, rose diamonds, 2.5 x diameter 5.7 cm (1 x 2¹/₄")
Mark of Henrik Wigström; gold mark of 72 *zolotniks* (1896–1908); *FABERGÉ* in Cyrillic characters
RCIN 40490
PROVENANCE: Bought by Sir Ernest Cassel from Fabergé's London branch, 4 November 1907 (£81 5s); Sir Philip Sassoon; by whom given to Queen Mary for her birthday, 26 May 1934
REFERENCES: Bainbridge 1949, p. 98; Habsburg & Lopato 1993, p. 311, cat. 190
EXHIBITIONS: London 1953, no. 63; London 1977, no. H8; QG 1985–6, no. 70; QG 1995–6, no. 277

178 CIGAR BOX WITH A VIEW OF THE HOUSES OF PARLIAMENT, 1908

Encouraged by the Princess of Wales's enthusiasm for a box with a view of Sandringham House owned by Queen Alexandra (cat. 179), Bainbridge records how he envisaged 'all of England' in 'warm sepia enamel: the Palaces, the Cathedrals, Waterfalls, the Houses of Parliament'. Queen Alexandra purchased a box with views of Chatsworth from Fabergé's London branch in 1909; it now forms part of the Chatsworth Collection.

Nephrite, two-colour gold, sepia enamel, 3.8 x 13.4 x 9 cm (1¹/₂ x 5¹/₄ x 3⁹/₁₆")
Mark of Henrik Wigström; gold mark of 56 *zolotniks* (1908–17); *FABERGÉ* in Cyrillic characters
RCIN 40498
PROVENANCE: Bought by Grand Duke Michael of Russia from Fabergé's London branch, November 1908 (£160); by whom presumably given to King Edward VII
REFERENCES: Bainbridge 1949, p. 98
EXHIBITIONS: London 1977, no. H1; QG 1985–6, no. 317; QG 1995–6, no. 419

179 BOX WITH A VIEW OF SANDRINGHAM HOUSE, 1908–1910

Bainbridge describes how, in his constant search for possible new pieces to add to Queen Alexandra's collection, he sent photographs of Sandringham House to Fabergé. A little while later a box arrived with an enamelled view of Sandringham House and grounds on its lid. In spite of Bainbridge's claim to be the inspiration behind the design of the boxes and frames with views of royal residences, such a scheme would undoubtedly have involved the King and possibly the Queen. This box was purchased by King George V a few months after his father's death.

Nephrite, two-colour gold, half pearls, sepia enamel, 3.2 x 10.3 x 7.6 cm (1¼ x 4¹/₁₆ x 3")
Mark of Henrik Wigström; gold mark of 56 *zolotniks* (1908–17); *FABERGÉ* in Cyrillic characters
RCIN 40493
PROVENANCE: Bought by King George V from Fabergé's London branch, 7 November 1910 (£96 10s)
REFERENCES: Bainbridge 1949, p. 98
EXHIBITIONS: London 1977, no. H5; QG 1985–6, no. 320; QG 1995–6, no. 361

180 BOX WITH A VIEW OF SANDRINGHAM ALLEY, 1908

The view on this box is of Sandringham Alley, an avenue of elm trees that used to lead to the Mews, which was built in 1870.

Nephrite, two-colour gold, half pearls, sepia enamel, 2.4 x diameter 6.7 cm (¹⁵/₁₆ x 2⅝")
Mark of Henrik Wigström; gold mark of 56 *zolotniks* (1908–17); *FABERGÉ* in Cyrillic characters
RCIN 40496
PROVENANCE: Bought by Queen Alexandra from Fabergé's London branch, November 1908 (£52 10s)
EXHIBITIONS: London 1977, no. H6; QG 1985–6, no. 319; QG 1995–6, no. 360

181 BOX WITH A VIEW OF STRATFORD CHURCH, 1903–1908

The church of Holy Trinity at Stratford-upon-Avon, Durham Cathedral (cat. 228) and the Houses of Parliament (cat. 178) are three of the places featured in Fabergé frames or on Fabergé boxes in the Royal Collection in addition to those bearing images of royal residences.

Nephrite, gold, enamel and sepia enamel, rose diamond, ruby, 2.8 x 6.8 x 7 cm (1⅛ x 2¹¹/₁₆ x 2¾")
Mark of Henrik Wigström; gold mark of 72 *zolotniks* (1896–1908); *FABERGÉ* in Cyrillic characters and Carl Fabergé's initials in Roman letters; English import marks for 1911
RCIN 40497
PROVENANCE: Bought by Mrs Leeds from Fabergé's London branch, 12 December 1915 (£65); bought by Queen Mary, 1934
REFERENCES: QMB III, no. 168
EXHIBITIONS: London 1953, no. 14; London 1977, no. H4; QG 1985–6, no. 316; QG 1995–6, no. 359

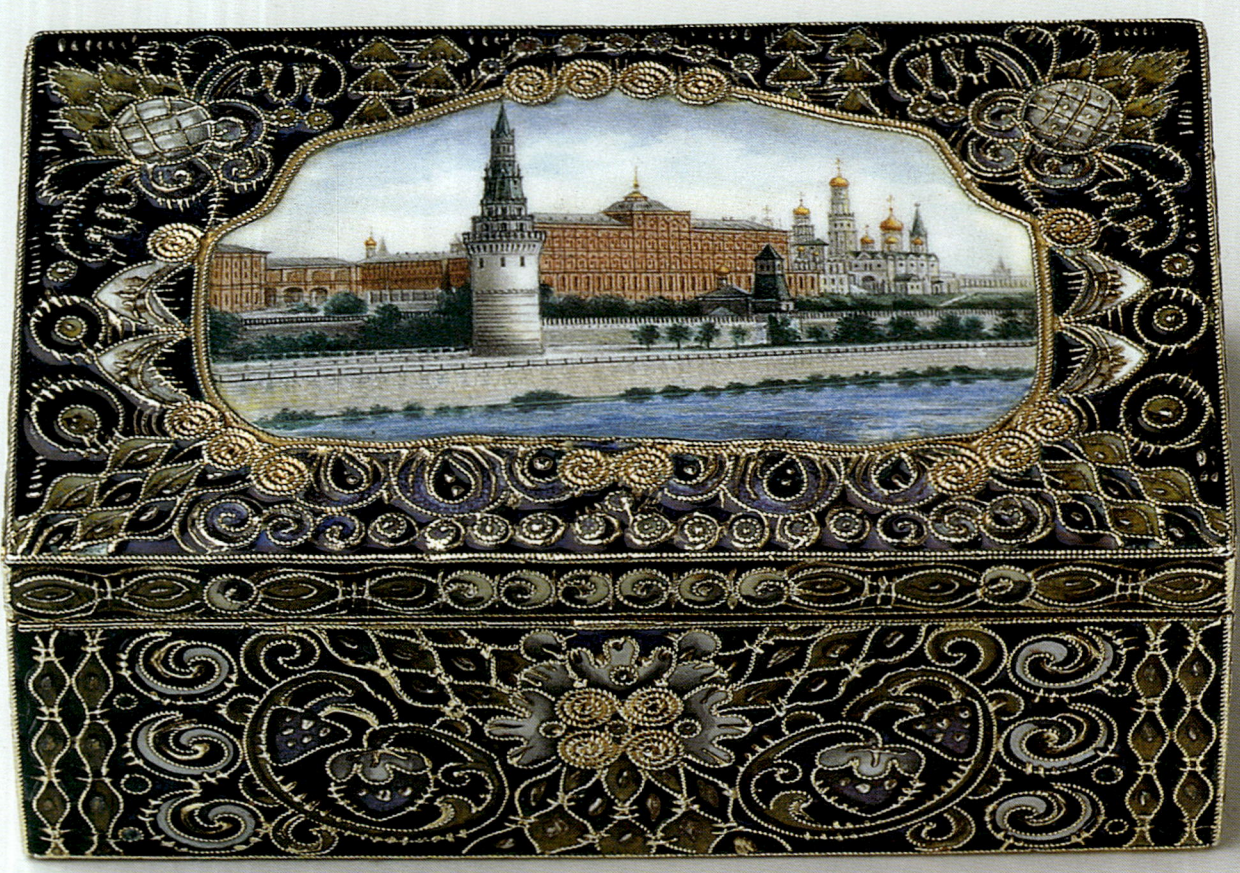
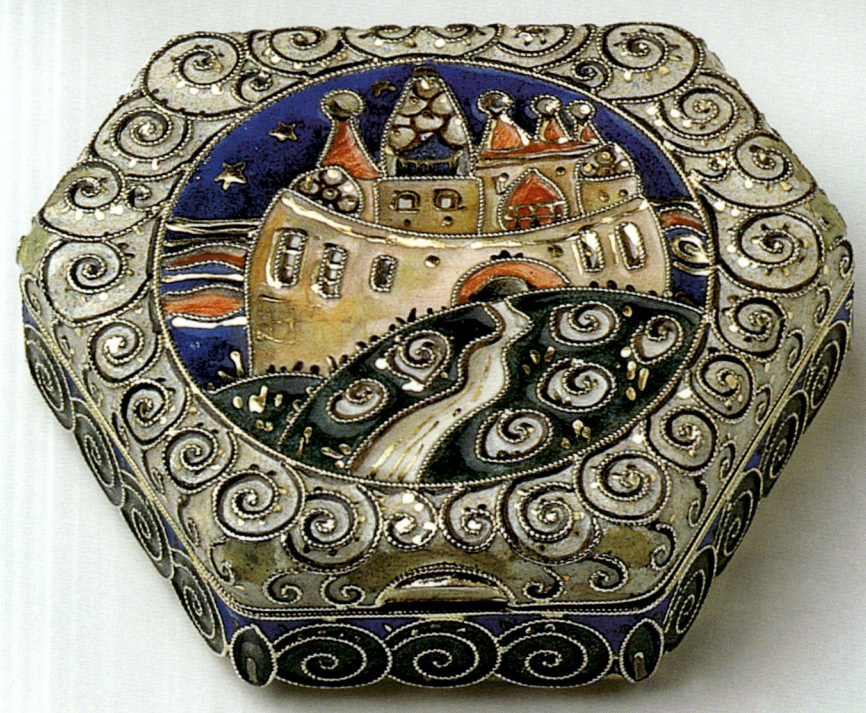

182 BOX WITH A VIEW OF THE KREMLIN, 1908–1917

The Moscow workshops where this box was made specialised in objects in the Old Russian or Pan-Slavic style, often with cloisonné decoration. See cat. 323, 324 and 325 for other pieces in the Old Russian style.

Silver-gilt, cloisonné enamel, enamelled miniature, 3.1 x 7.9 x 5 cm (1¹/₄ x 3¹/₈ x 1¹⁵/₁₆")
Moscow silver mark of 88 *zolotniks* (1908–17); *FABERGÉ* in Cyrillic characters
RCIN 32474
PROVENANCE: Marie, Duchess of Saxe-Coburg-Gotha (d.1920); given by her daughter to King George V, October 1920
EXHIBITIONS: QG 1985–6, no. 114; QG 1995–6, no. 43

183 BOX WITH A RUSSIAN SCENE, *c.*1908

Feodor Rückert, who made this box, was Fabergé's main enamellist in the Russian style. He began an association with Fabergé at the time of the opening of the Moscow branch in 1887 but he also worked for other jewellery and silversmithing businesses in Moscow, such as Khlebnikov and Ovchinnikov (see cat. 364). According to Anne Odom, most of the pieces Rückert produced for Fabergé were made after 1908, by which time the colours of his enamelling had changed from pastels to dark blues, greens, greys and browns and he had begun to use intricate wirework patterns in his cloisonné enamelling, particularly in coils, as seen on this box.

The scene on this box is from the Tale of Tsar Sultan, taken from a poem by Alexander Pushkin (1799–1837), and depicts the walled city which miraculously appeared to Tsar Sultan's wife and his son, Prince Gvidon.

Silver, cloisonné enamel, 1.9 x 5.1 x 4.4 cm (³/₄ x 2 x 1³/₄")
Mark of Feodor Rückert; silver mark of 88 *zolotniks*; *C.FABERGÉ* in Cyrillic characters; *STERLING RUSSIA* in Roman letters
RCIN 100306
PROVENANCE: Wartski; given to Queen Elizabeth, May 1979
REFERENCES: Snowman 1979, p. 57

184 PUMPKIN-SHAPED BOX, BEFORE 1896

This charming box is entirely carved from a piece of cornelian, one section having been cut out to form the 'lid'.

Cornelian, gold, enamel, rose diamonds, 2.5 x diameter 5.2 cm (1 x 2$^1/_{16}$")
Gold mark of 72 *zolotniks* (before 1896); *FABERGÉ* in Cyrillic characters
RCIN 40175
PROVENANCE: Royal Collection by 1953
EXHIBITIONS: London 1953, no. 105; London 1977, no. J10; Zurich 1989, no. 3; QG 1995–6, no. 214

185 BOX, BEFORE 1896

The cypher engraved on this box indicates that it belonged to Tsarina Alexandra Feodorovna.

Rock crystal, gold, guilloché enamel, topaz, ruby, 3 x 4 x 3.4 cm (1$^3/_{16}$ x 1$^9/_{16}$ x 1$^5/_{16}$")
Mark of Michael Perchin; gold mark of 56 *zolotniks* (before 1896)
RCIN 22955
PROVENANCE: Tsarina Alexandra Feodorovna; acquired by Queen Mary between 1922 and 1931
REFERENCES: QMB II, no. 439; QMPP V, no. 231
EXHIBITIONS: QG 1995–6, no. 471

186 BOX, 1908–1911

On her birthday in 1934 Queen Mary recorded in her diary 'the family gave me a cornelian & enamel Russian Fabergé box'. It is believed that this is the box.

Gold, enamel, jasper, rose diamonds, 1.7 x 7.5 x 2.8 cm ($^{11}/_{16}$ x 2$^{15}/_{16}$ x 1$^1/_8$")
Mark of Henrik Wigström; gold mark of 56 *zolotniks* (1908–17); initials of Carl Fabergé in Roman letters; *FABERGÉ* in Roman letters; English import marks for 1911
RCIN 9163
PROVENANCE: Given to Queen Mary by the royal family on her birthday, 26 May 1934
REFERENCES: QMB III, no. 169; QMPP VIII, no. 95; RA GV/QMD: 26 May 1934
EXHIBITIONS: QG 1995–6, no. 215

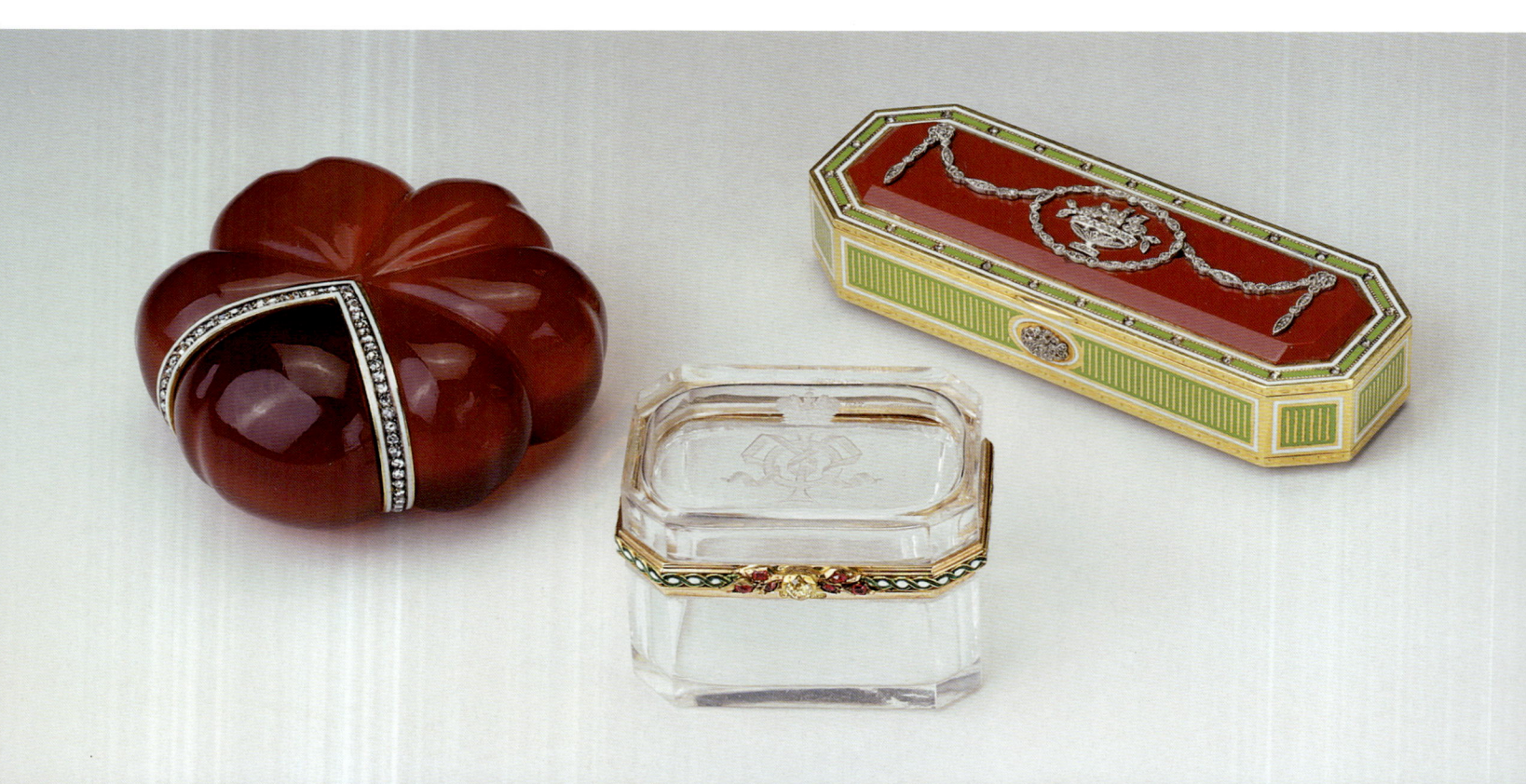

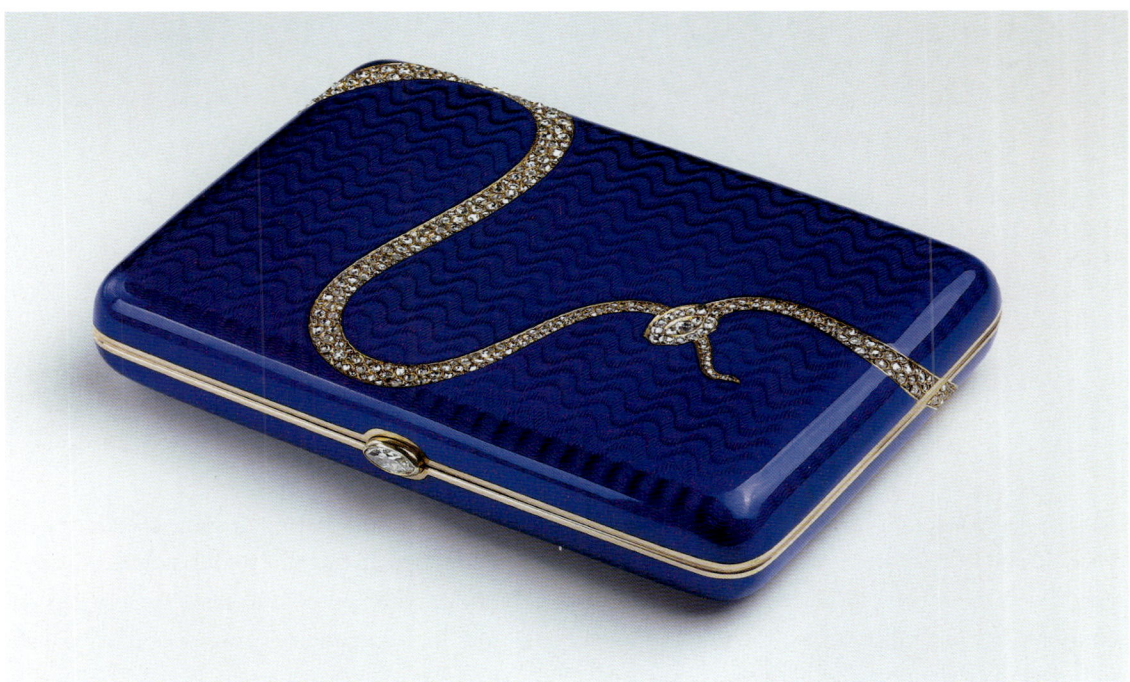

187 CIGARETTE CASE, 1908

The art nouveau style of this case, arguably one of Fabergé's most successful designs, is something of a departure from the restrained Louis XVI classicism of the majority of Fabergé's output. Fabergé was criticised at the time of the 1900 Exposition Universelle in Paris for his neo-classical designs, which the French felt compared unfavourably with the popular organic 'modern style' or art nouveau of the early 1890s. Probably in response to this, Fabergé produced pieces in the art nouveau style, notably three Imperial Easter Eggs as well as a number of smaller pieces.

In spite of the criticisms of his designs there was universal praise for Fabergé's workmanship. Here, the skilfully recessed hinge allows the edges of the case to be simplified and the design of the snake to be integrated on both sides. This cigarette case demonstrates Fabergé's brilliant handling of guilloché enamelling, the geometric moiré wave pattern being one of his favourite designs. The remarkably vivid colour of the enamel is one example from the rainbow of colours which Fabergé used.

The cigarette case was presented to King Edward VII by Mrs George Keppel, who was also an avid collector of Fabergé and encouraged the King to commission portraits of the animals at Sandringham. She became the King's mistress and confidante in the late 1890s and remained close to him until his death. Both the King and Mrs Keppel shared an admiration for Carl Fabergé's work and both used cigarette cases made by him. Following the King's death in 1910, Queen Alexandra returned the case to Mrs Keppel as a souvenir. She in turn gave it to Queen Mary in 1936. It still contains the stub of one of King Edward VII's cigars.

Two-colour gold, guilloché enamel, brilliant and rose-cut diamonds, 1.7 x 9.6 x 7 cm (¹¹/₁₆ x 3³/₄ x 2³/₄")
Moscow gold mark of 56 *zolotniks* (1896–1908)
RCIN 40113
PROVENANCE: Presented by the Hon. Mrs George Keppel to King Edward VII, 1908; returned by Queen Alexandra to Mrs Keppel, 1911; given by Mrs Keppel to Queen Mary, 1936
REFERENCES: Bainbridge 1949, p. 83; Habsburg & Lopato 1993, pp. 116–23
EXHIBITIONS: London 1977, no. K2; New York 1983, no. 203; QG 1985–6, no. 298; Munich 1986–7, no. 468; Zurich 1989, no. 117; St. Petersburg/Paris/London 1993–4, no. 165; QG 1995–6, no. 502; Stockholm 1997, no. 101; Cardiff 1998, no. 148; QG 2002–3, no. 269

188   CIGARETTE CASE, 1896–1908

This is believed to have been a favourite cigarette case of Tsar Nicholas II. It was made in the work-shop of August Hollming (1854–1913), who specialised in gold objects and jewellery.

Gold, brilliant diamond, cabochon sapphire, 1.8 x 9.3 x 6.3 cm ($^{11}/_{16}$ x 3 $^{11}/_{16}$ x 2$^1/_2$")
Mark of August Hollming; gold mark of 56 *zolotniks* (1896–1908); *FABERGÉ* in Cyrillic characters
RCIN 4355
PROVENANCE: Tsar Nicholas II; King George VI's collection
REFERENCES: Bainbridge 1949, p. 118
EXHIBITIONS: London 1977, no. K16; QG 1985–6, no. 296; QG 1995–6, no. 487

189   CIGARETTE CASE, 1900

Fabergé's coloured gold cigarette cases with striped, sunburst and radiating designs are among the most elegant of their kind. Usually fitted with a compartment for matches and tinder, these cases were regarded as the most stylish accessories of their day. Bainbridge commented that cases such as this one would always appeal to men of taste and that they felt and looked good because they had 'just the right weight of precious metal to measurements'. This particular case was given to Tsar Nicholas II by his mother Marie Feodorovna on his Saint's Day.

Two-colour gold, cabochon ruby, 1.5 x 9.6 x 6.6 cm ($^9/_{16}$ x 3$^3/_4$ x 2$^5/_8$")
Mark of August Hollming; gold mark of 56 *zolotniks* (1896–1908); *FABERGÉ* in Cyrillic characters; inscribed in Cyrillic characters *Greetings from Gatchina to my dear Niki 6 December 1900 from Mama*
RCIN 4309
PROVENANCE: Given to Tsar Nicholas II by Dowager Tsarina Marie Feodorovna, 6 December 1900; King George VI's collection
REFERENCES: GV Cigarette Cases, no. 39; Bainbridge 1949, p. 135
EXHIBITIONS: London 1977, no. K17; QG 1985–6, no. 295; QG 1995–6, no. 488

190   CIGARETTE CASE, 1896–1908

Two-colour gold, cabochon sapphire, 1.7 x 10 x 6.8 cm ($^{11}/_{16}$ x 3$^{15}/_{16}$ x 2$^{11}/_{16}$")
Mark of August Hollming; gold mark of 56 *zolotniks* (1896–1908)
RCIN 100304
PROVENANCE: Bought by Queen Elizabeth from Wartski, 7 April 1949 (£120)

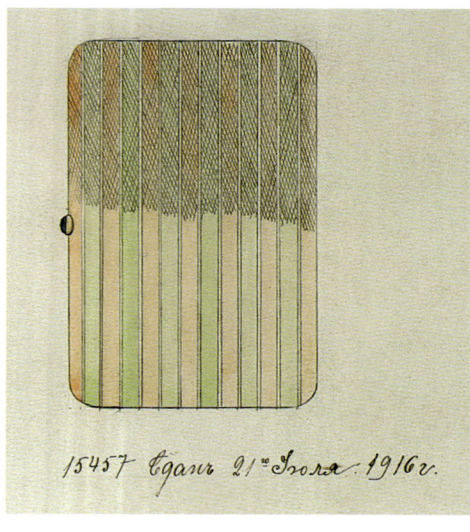

A plate from a previously unpublished album of watercolour designs by Henrik Wigström, including the design for a gold cigarette case similar to cat. 190.

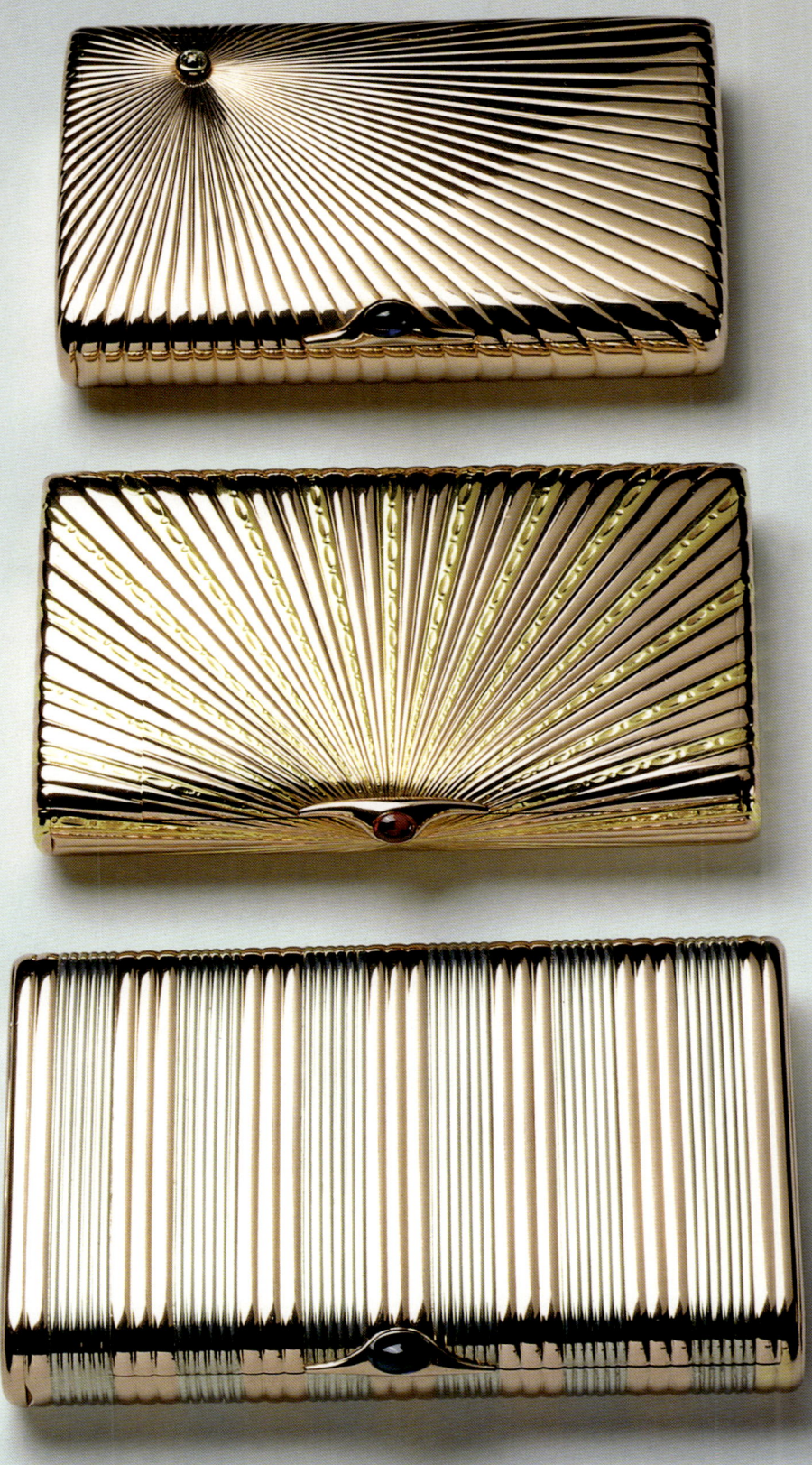

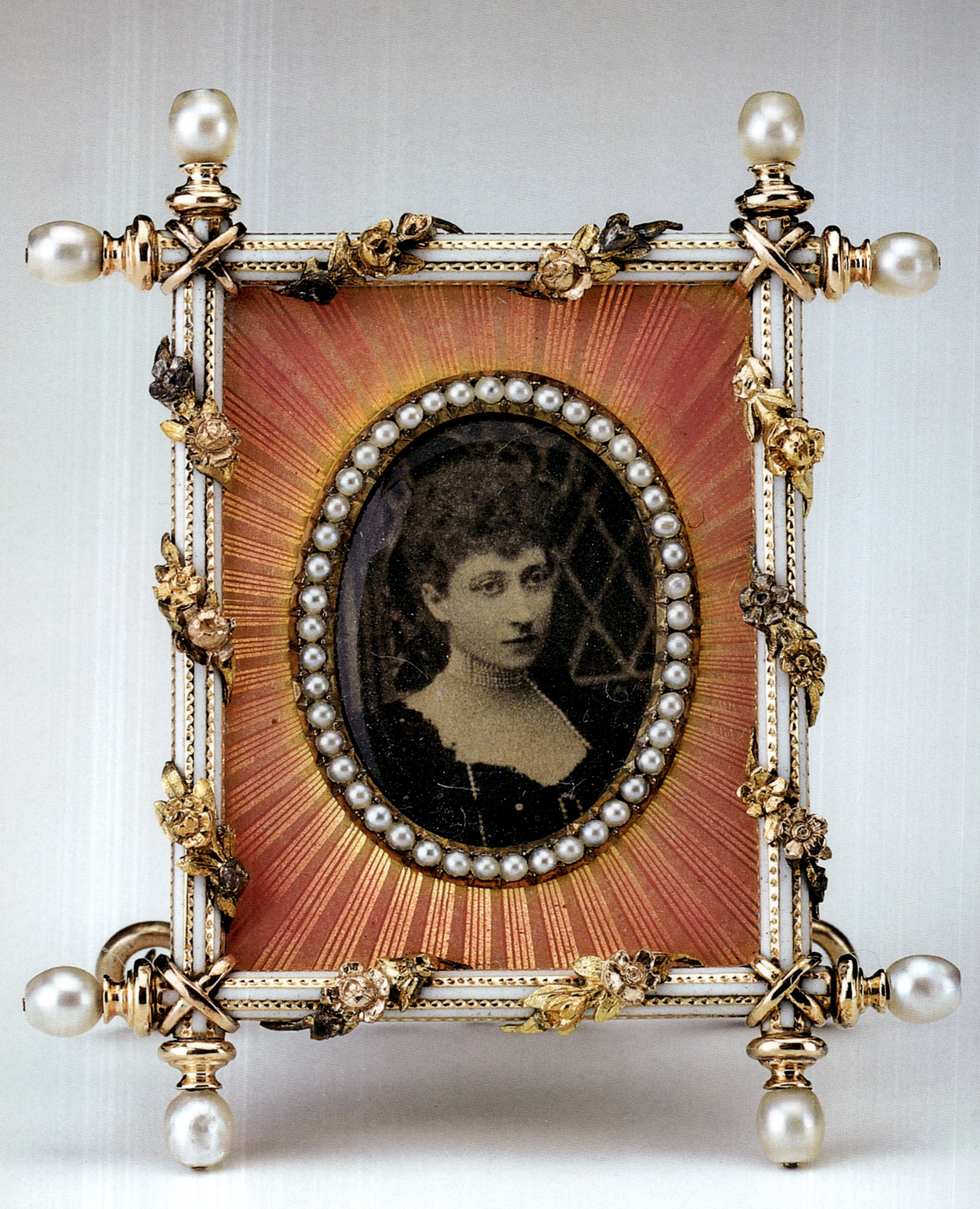

FRAMES

THE FABERGÉ FRAMES in the Royal Collection not only illustrate the close links between the Russian, Danish and English royal families but underline the unique way in which the collection was formed. Many were received as gifts from various members of these families, containing photographs or miniatures of each other. Their innately personal nature gives many of the images contained in the frames a great poignancy.

The demand for Fabergé's frames must have been very great, judging by the large number known today. This demand was undoubtedly stimulated by the increased importance of photography during the late nineteenth and early twentieth centuries. The drawing rooms and desks of the royal residences at Buckingham Palace, Sandringham House and Marlborough House from King Edward VII's reign onwards were filled with frames of all shapes and sizes, many of them by Fabergé. Those of the Russian imperial family were similarly arranged. Tsarina Alexandra Feodorovna is known to have owned hundreds of miniature Fabergé frames which were set out in rows in her private apartments at Tsarkoë Selo and in the Alexander Palace.

Many of the frames included in this exhibition contain contemporary photographs of members of the royal family by a range of photographers, including W. & D. Downey

and Alice Hughes. Several of the frames contain miniatures, for example cat. 204 of Princess Mary, the Princess Royal. The frames from the Russian and Danish relatives contain the same mixture of photographs and miniatures, for example cat. 222 of King Christian IX and Queen Louise (parents of Queen Alexandra) and cat. 213 of Marie Feodorovna, painted by the Danish-born Johannes Zehngraf (1857–1908), one of Fabergé's chief miniaturists. Other miniatures feature views of royal residences and other buildings (cat. 225–8). These are closely linked to the boxes decorated with similar views (see pp. 148–51) and represent particularly fine examples of opalescent and sepia enamelling. Like the boxes, it seems likely that they were commissioned by King Edward VII or Queen Alexandra. One frame that was certainly commissioned is that enamelled in the racing colours of King Edward and containing a photograph of Persimmon, his most successful racehorse (cat. 224).

The range of styles and materials used on the frames is extensive, incorporating the work of almost all of Fabergé's workmasters. Those represented here include Perchin, Wigström, Nevalainen and Armfelt. In addition there are fourteen frames by the workmaster Viktor Aarne, who specialised in miniature frames which feature guilloché enamelling and delicate coloured gold decoration in the form of ribbon-cresting, beading, acanthus leaves, and floral and foliate swags. The coloured gold was achieved by the addition of silver, copper and platinum – which produced green, red and white gold respectively. This was a revival of a French eighteenth-century technique, seen particularly on snuff boxes of that period. However, as with his use of guilloché enamelling, Fabergé surpassed his eighteenth-century precursors by juxtaposing all four colours of gold in complicated applied decoration. This is well illustrated by cat. 213. In addition to the enamel frames, Fabergé used a variety of other materials including wood, silver, hardstone and lacquer.

A very small number of Fabergé's frames formed part of the hierarchy of official gifts presented by the Tsar. During Nicholas II's reign twenty-two such frames were presented to recipients of the qualifying rank.[1] They were elaborately decorated with precious stones and the Romanov crown, and featured the Tsar's miniature portrait. Curiously, there are very few examples in the Royal Collection of frames surmounted by the imperial crown, which were ordered as semi-official commissions.[2] Many more frames, some of very elaborate design, were ordered by the imperial family as semi-official commissions. These were intended as gifts for birthdays, christenings, weddings and anniversaries for their circle of family and friends. Large orders were placed with Fabergé before Marie Feodorovna's annual trips to London and Copenhagen.[3] It is likely that the frames with photographs or miniatures of Marie Feodorovna and Alexander III now in the Royal Collection were received as gifts by King Edward VII and Queen Alexandra following such visits. The royal family also purchased frames from Fabergé's London branch which were to be given away. Several that are not now part of the Royal Collection are noted in the London ledgers.

One of the most unusual portrait frames in the Royal Collection is the cameo carved from smoky topaz of the Prince of Wales (later King Edward VIII) at the time of his investiture as Prince of Wales in 1911 (cat. 220). The cameo is suspended from an easel frame of silver. It was commissioned by King George V from Fabergé's London branch and given by him to Queen Mary on her birthday on 26 May 1912.

1   According to the research of Ulla Tillander-Godenhielm.
2   Tillander-Godenhielm *et al*. 2000, p. 47.
3   According to the research of Dr Marina N. Lopato; see Habsburg & Lopato, 1993, p. 58.

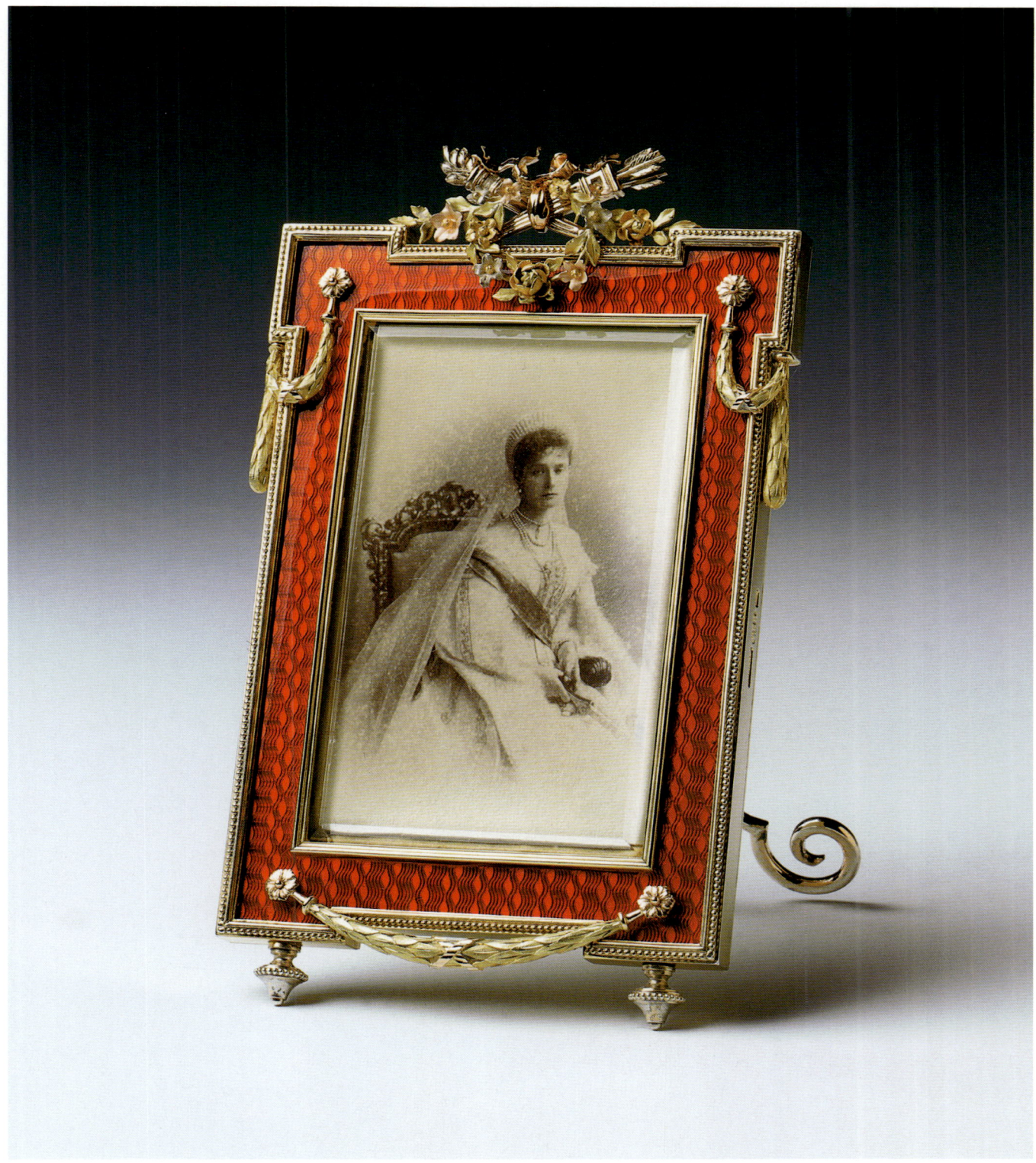

191 FRAME WITH A PHOTOGRAPH OF TSARINA ALEXANDRA FEODOROVNA, FRAME BEFORE 1896, PHOTOGRAPH 1899

Silver-gilt, guilloché enamel, four-colour gold, ivory, 11 x 6.8 x 1.5 cm (4⁵/₁₆ x 2¹¹/₁₆ x ³/₁₆")
Mark of Viktor Aarne; silver mark of 88 *zolotniks* (before 1896); *FABERGÉ* in Cyrillic characters
RCIN 8560
PROVENANCE: Bought by Tsar Nicholas II and Tsarina Alexandra Feodorovna, 11 August 1898 (135 roubles)

192   FRAME WITH A MINIATURE OF QUEEN ALEXANDRA, FRAME 1896–1908, MINIATURE 1913

Produced in the workshop of Anders Nevalainen (1858–1933), who specialised in enamelled objects and frames, this example is unusual in that it incorporates lacquer decoration, a relatively rare technique in Fabergé's *oeuvre*. The miniature is unsigned.

Silver, lacquer, miniature in watercolour, 12.9 x 9 x 0.7 cm (5¹/₁₆ x 3⁹/₁₆ x ¹/₄")
Mark of Anders Nevalainen; silver mark of 88 *zolotniks* (1896–1908)
RCIN 9215
PROVENANCE: Acquired by Queen Alexandra, date unknown
EXHIBITIONS: QG 1985–6, no. 413

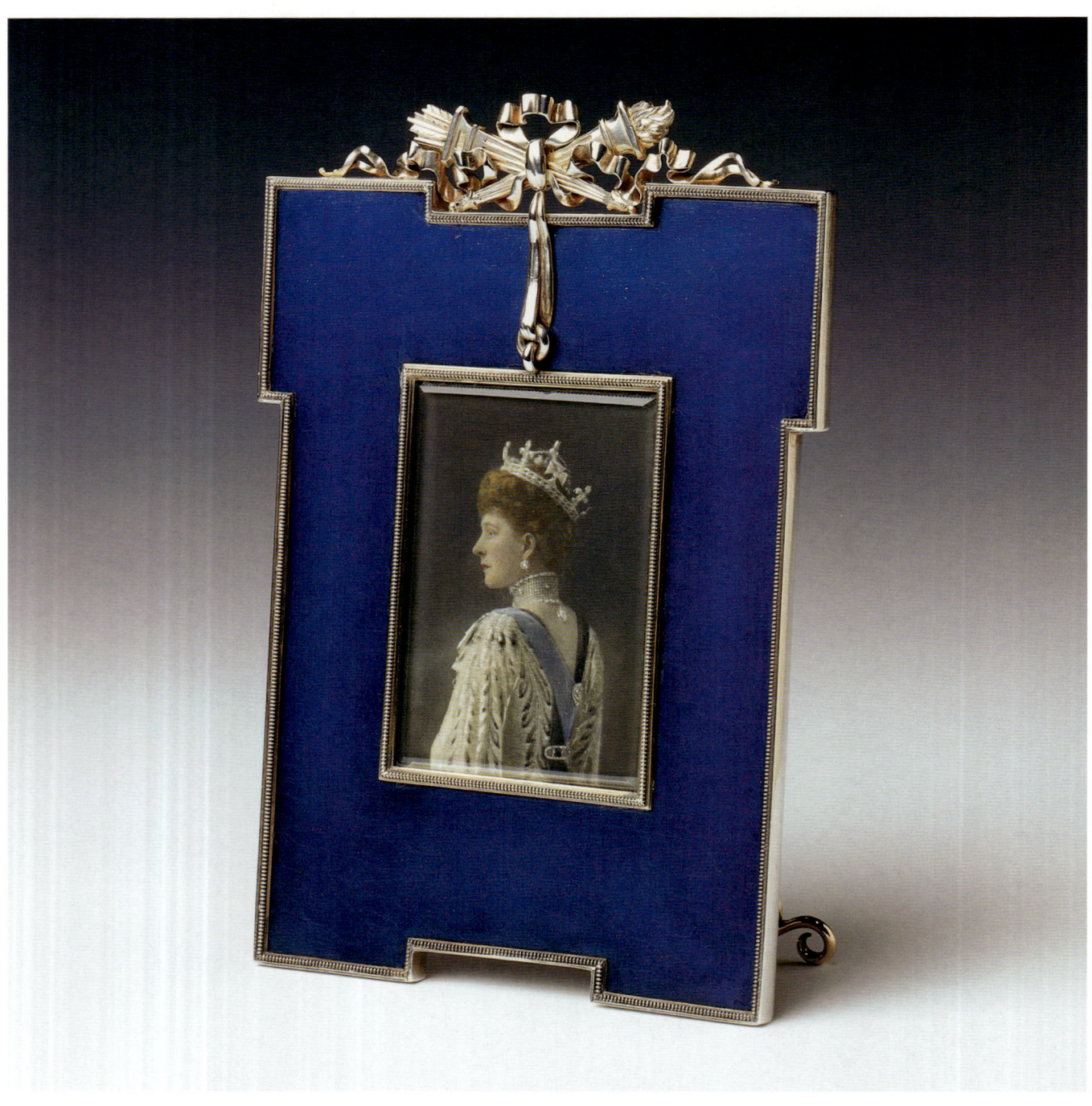

193   FRAME WITH A PHOTOGRAPH OF PRINCESS PATRICIA
OF CONNAUGHT, *c.*1905

Princess Patricia (1886–1974), daughter of Arthur, Duke of Connaught, and granddaughter of Queen Victoria, married the Hon. Sir Alexander Ramsay in 1919.

Two-colour gold, silver-gilt, guilloché enamel, brilliant diamonds, ivory, 7.6 x 8.1 x 5.5 cm (3 x 3³/₁₆ x 2³/₁₆")
Mark of Karl Armfelt; gold mark of 56 *zolotniks* and silver mark of 88 *zolotniks* (1896–1908); *FABERGÉ* in Cyrillic characters
RCIN 32469
PROVENANCE: Bought by Tsar Nicholas II and Tsarina Alexandra Feodorovna, 14 July 1907 (185 roubles); by whom given to King Edward VII and Queen Alexandra
EXHIBITIONS: QG 1985–6, no. 47; QG 1995–6, no. 496

194   FRAME WITH A PHOTOGRAPH OF MARIE,
CROWN PRINCESS OF ROMANIA, *c.*1908

Princess Marie of Edinburgh (1875–1938), daughter of Alfred, Duke of Edinburgh, and granddaughter of Queen Victoria, married Ferdinand, Crown Prince of Romania, in 1893. He succeeded to the throne in 1914. Both cat. 193 and this frame were made in the workshop of Karl Armfelt, who specialised in producing frames.

Silver-gilt, guilloché enamel, ivory, 7.4 x 7.2 x 4.3 cm (2¹⁵/₁₆ x 2¹³/₁₆ x 1¹¹/₁₆")
Mark of Karl Armfelt; silver mark of 91 *zolotniks* (1896–1908); *FABERGÉ* in Cyrillic characters
RCIN 32470
PROVENANCE: Bought by the Dowager Tsarina Marie Feodorovna, 19 July 1908 (100 roubles)
EXHIBITIONS: QG 1985–6, no. 129; QG 1995–6, no. 469

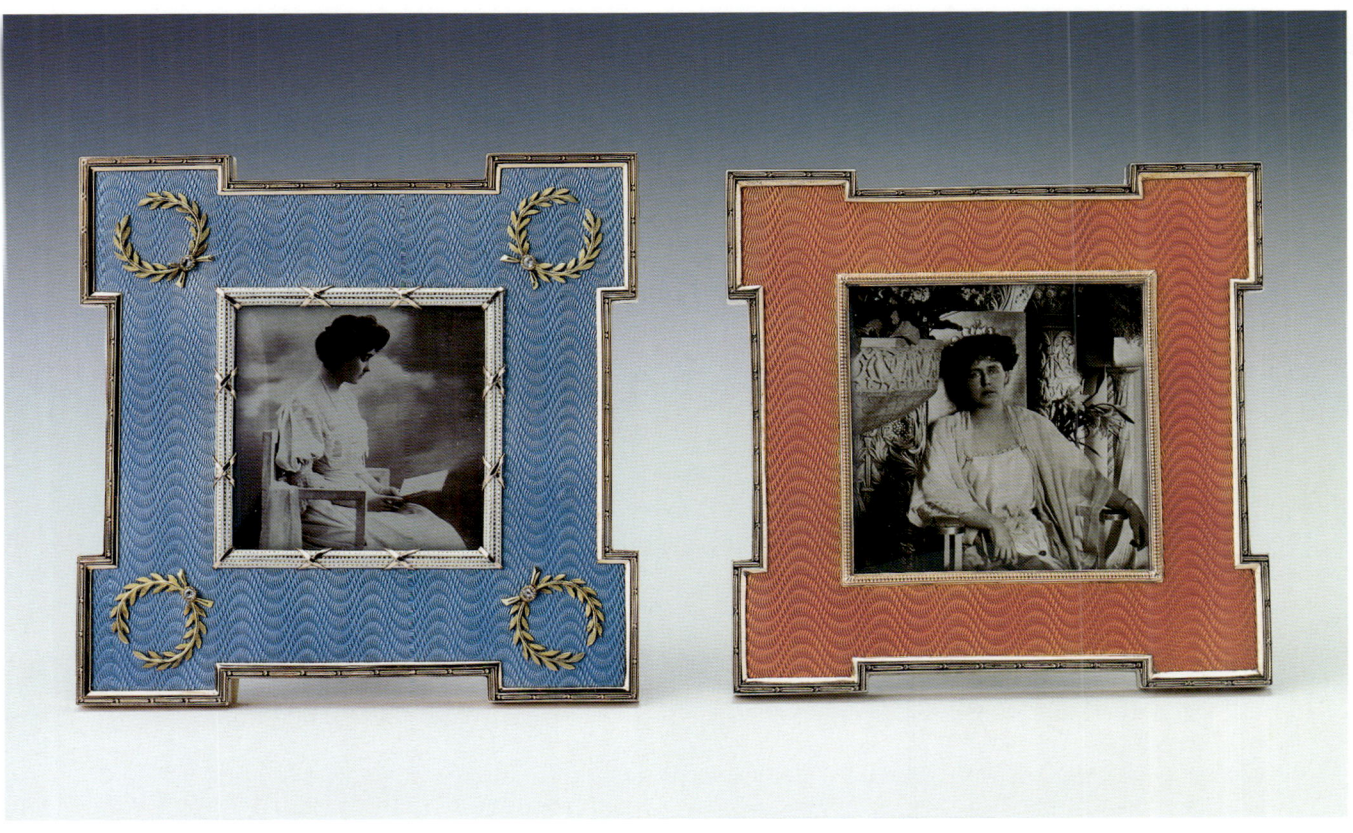

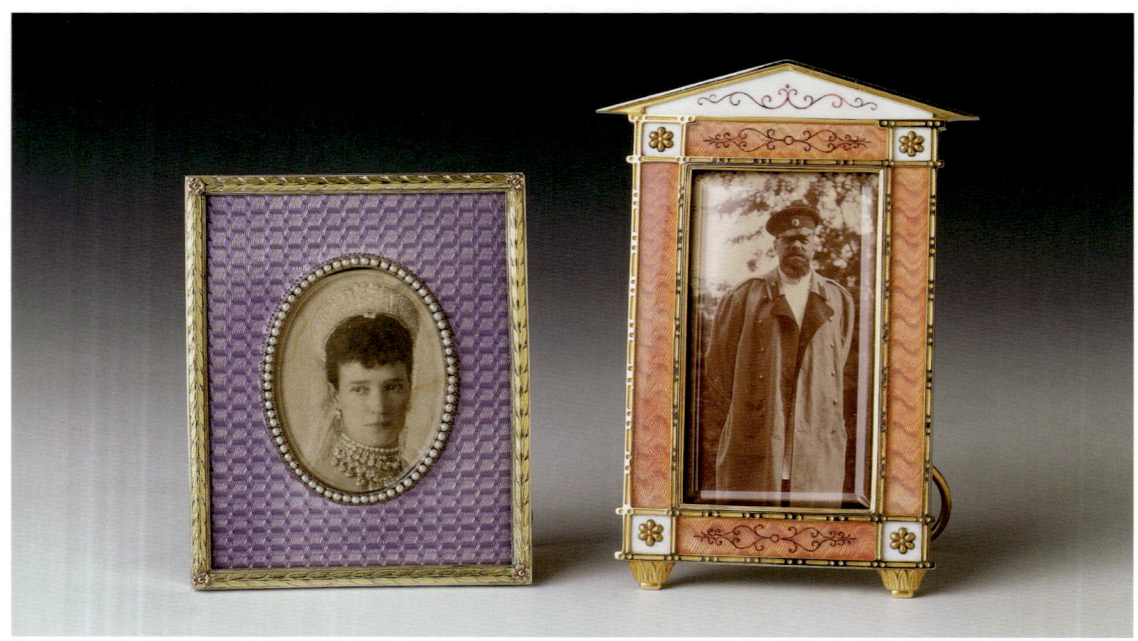

195   FRAME WITH A PHOTOGRAPH OF TSARINA MARIE FEODOROVNA, *c.* 1890

Silver, two-colour gold, guilloché enamel, half pearls, ivory, 6.9 x 6 x 6.6 cm (2¹¹/₁₆ x 2³/₈ x 2⁵/₈")
Mark of Viktor Aarne, silver mark of 88 *zolotniks* (before 1896); *FABERGÉ* in Cyrillic characters
RCIN 9183
PROVENANCE: Probably acquired by Queen Alexandra; Royal Collection by 1953
EXHIBITIONS: QG 1985–6, no. 51; QG 1995–6, no. 260

196   FRAME WITH A PHOTOGRAPH OF TSAR ALEXANDER III, *c.* 1896

Alexander III (1845–94) was the second son of Alexander II, whom he succeeded in 1881 following the death of his older brother Tsarevitch Nicholas, from whom he also inherited his bride-to-be, Princess Dagmar. She was known as Marie Feodorovna following her conversion to the Russian Orthodox faith. They were married on 10 November 1866. A stern and hard-working ruler, he was devoutly religious and generally lived with his family in the country at Gatchina Palace, returning to St Petersburg only for the winter social season. The one departure from his rather austere lifestyle seems to have been his taste for elaborate Easter eggs ordered from Fabergé, whose work probably first came to the Tsar's personal attention at the 1882 Pan-Russian exhibition in Moscow. Fabergé was formally appointed Supplier to the Court of Tsar Alexander III in 1885.

This photograph was taken very shortly before the Tsar's death on 1 November 1894. The informality of the photograph is complemented by the small decorative frame, which emphasises its very personal nature. The frame was made a few years after the Tsar's death.

Silver, gold, guilloché enamel, ivory, 9 x 6.9 x 6.4 cm (3⁹/₁₆ x 2¹¹/₁₆ x 2¹/₂")
Illegible workmaster's mark; Moscow gold mark of 56 *zolotniks* and silver mark of 84 *zolotniks* (1896–1908);
C. FABERGÉ in Cyrillic characters
RCIN 32473
PROVENANCE: Acquired by King Edward VII and Queen Alexandra, date unknown
EXHIBITIONS: QG 1985–6, no. 49; QG 1995–6, no. 173; QG 2002–3, no. 259

197   FRAME WITH A PHOTOGRAPH OF QUEEN MARY WHEN DUCHESS OF YORK, FRAME BEFORE 1896, PHOTOGRAPH *c.*1897

Two-colour gold, guilloché enamel, ivory, 5.3 x 5.3 x 4.8 cm (2^{1}/$_{16}$ x 2^{1}/$_{16}$ x 1^{7}/$_{8}$")
Mark of Michael Perchin; gold mark of 56 *zolotniks* (before 1896); *FABERGÉ* in Cyrillic characters
RCIN 9187
PROVENANCE: Queen Mary's collection
EXHIBITIONS: QG 1985–6, no. 134; QG 1995–6, no. 165

198   FRAME WITH A PHOTOGRAPH OF QUEEN ALEXANDRA IN CORONATION ROBES, 1902

Four-colour gold, silver-gilt, guilloché enamel, rose diamonds, mother-of-pearl, 5.5 x 3.6 x 4.4 cm (2^{3}/$_{16}$ x 1^{7}/$_{16}$ x 1^{3}/$_{4}$")
Mark of Viktor Aarne; gold mark of 56 *zolotniks* and silver mark of 88 *zolotniks* (1896–1908); *FABERGÉ* in Cyrillic characters; photograph by W. & D. Downey
RCIN 23308
PROVENANCE: Given to the Princess of Wales (later Queen Mary) by the Prince of Wales (later King George V), 1906
REFERENCES: QMB I, no. 252; QMPP I, no. 251
EXHIBITIONS: QG 1995–6, no. 158

199   FRAME WITH A PHOTOGRAPH OF QUEEN ALEXANDRA WHEN PRINCESS OF WALES, FRAME BEFORE 1896, PHOTOGRAPH 1898

Gold, guilloché enamel, ivory, 6.5 x 5.4 x 5.2 cm (2^{9}/$_{16}$ x 2^{1}/$_{8}$ x 2^{1}/$_{16}$")
Mark of Michael Perchin; gold mark of 56 *zolotniks* (before 1896); photograph by Alice Hughes
RCIN 23306
PROVENANCE: Probably acquired by Queen Alexandra, date unknown
EXHIBITIONS: QG 1995–6, no. 174; Cardiff 1998, no. 149

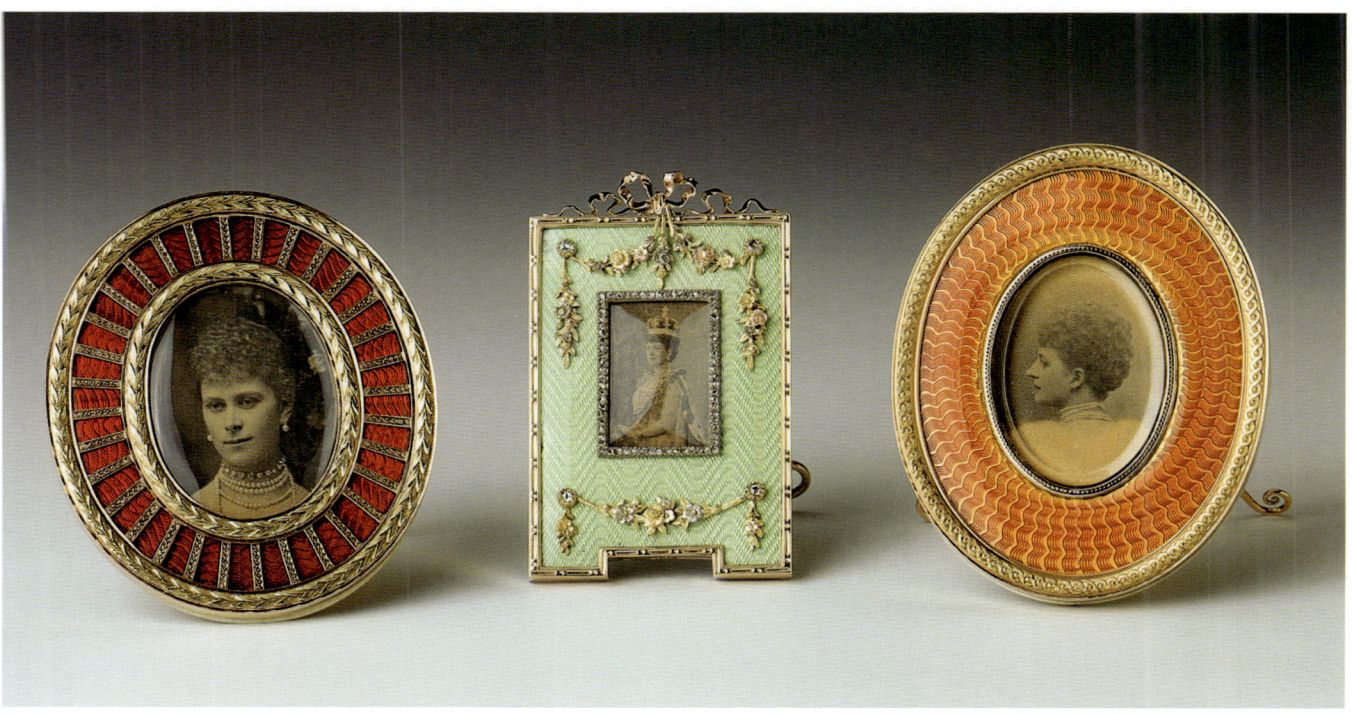

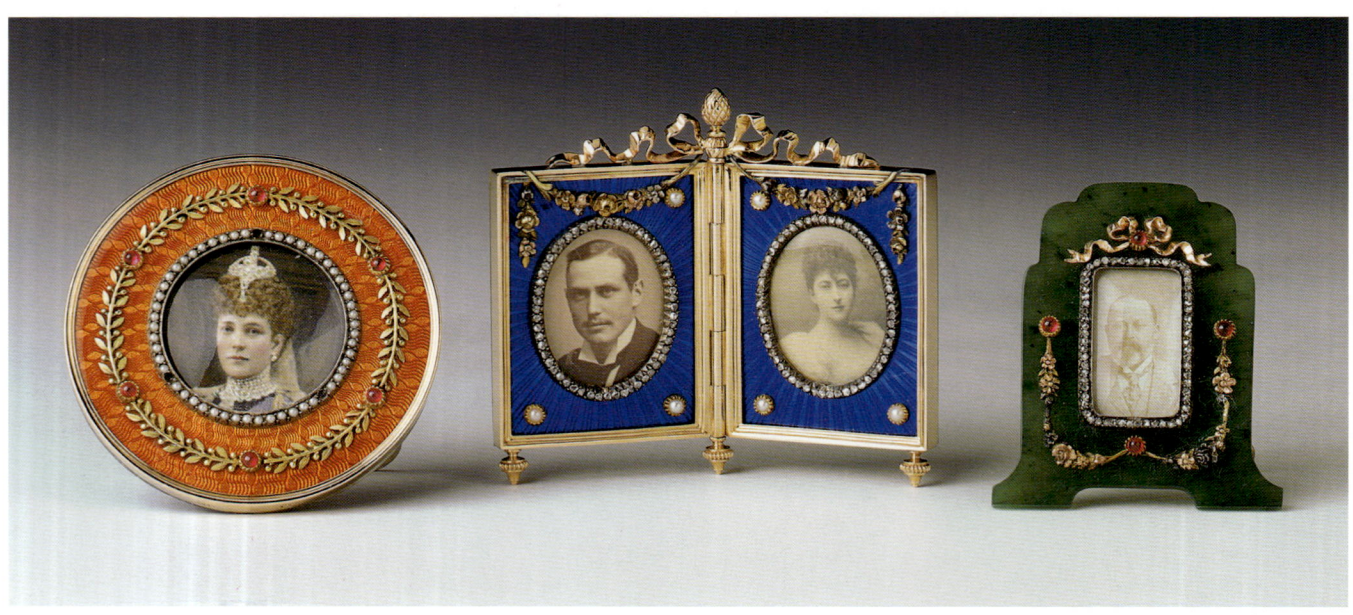

200 FRAME WITH A PHOTOGRAPH OF QUEEN ALEXANDRA, *c.*1907–1908

Two-colour gold, silver-gilt, guilloché enamel, cabochon rubies, mother-of-pearl, 4.4 x 4.4 x 2.7 cm (1³/₄ x 1³/₄ x 1¹/₁₆")
Mark of Victor Aarne; silver mark of 88 *zolotniks* (1896–1908); FABERGÉ in Cyrillic characters; coloured photograph by Alice Hughes
RCIN 23312
PROVENANCE: Probably acquired by Queen Alexandra, date unknown
EXHIBITIONS: QG 1995–6, no. 163

201 DOUBLE FRAME WITH PHOTOGRAPHS OF PRINCE CHARLES OF DENMARK AND PRINCESS MAUD OF WALES, FRAME 1896–1901, PHOTOGRAPHS 1896 AND 1895

Princess Maud (1869–1938) was the youngest daughter of King Edward VII and Queen Alexandra. She married Prince Charles of Denmark (from 1905 King Haakon of Norway) in 1896.

Three-colour gold, guilloché enamel, half pearls, rose diamonds, ivory, 5 x 5.6 x 0.4 cm (1¹⁵/₁₆ x 2³/₁₆ x ³/₁₆")
Mark of Viktor Aarne; gold mark of 56 *zolotniks* (1896–1908); FABERGÉ in Cyrillic characters
RCIN 40227
PROVENANCE: Bought by the Dowager Tsarina Marie Feodorovna, 3 January 1901 (160 roubles)
EXHIBITIONS: London 1977, no. K11; QG 1985–6, no. 62; St Petersburg/Paris/London 1993–4, no. 81; QG 1995–6, no. 157

202 FRAME WITH A PHOTOGRAPH OF KING EDWARD VII WHEN PRINCE OF WALES, *c.*1896

Nephrite, three-colour gold, silver-gilt, cabochon rubies, rose diamonds, mother-of-pearl, 3.3 x 3.5 x 3.6 cm (1⁵/₁₆ x 1³/₈ x 1⁷/₁₆")
Mark of Viktor Aarne; silver mark of 88 *zolotniks* (1896–1908)
RCIN 40237
PROVENANCE: Acquired by Queen Alexandra, date unknown
EXHIBITIONS: London 1977, no. K14; QG 1985–6, no. 131; QG 1995–6, no. 347; Cardiff 1998, no. 152

203   FRAME WITH A PHOTOGRAPH OF GRAND DUCHESS ELIZABETH FEODOROVNA, BEFORE 1896

Elizabeth Feodorovna (1864–1918), daughter of Princess Alice of Hesse and granddaughter of Queen Victoria, married Grand Duke Sergei, brother of Tsar Alexander III, in 1884. See also cat. 216.

Rock crystal, gold, rose diamonds, guilloché enamel, 6.3 x 6.7 x 2.7 cm (2¹/₂ x 2⁵/₈ x 1¹/₁₆")
Mark of Michael Perchin; gold mark of 56 *zolotniks* (before 1896)
RCIN 40126
PROVENANCE: Probably acquired by Queen Alexandra, date unknown
EXHIBITIONS: London 1977, no. K7; QG 1995–6, no. 241

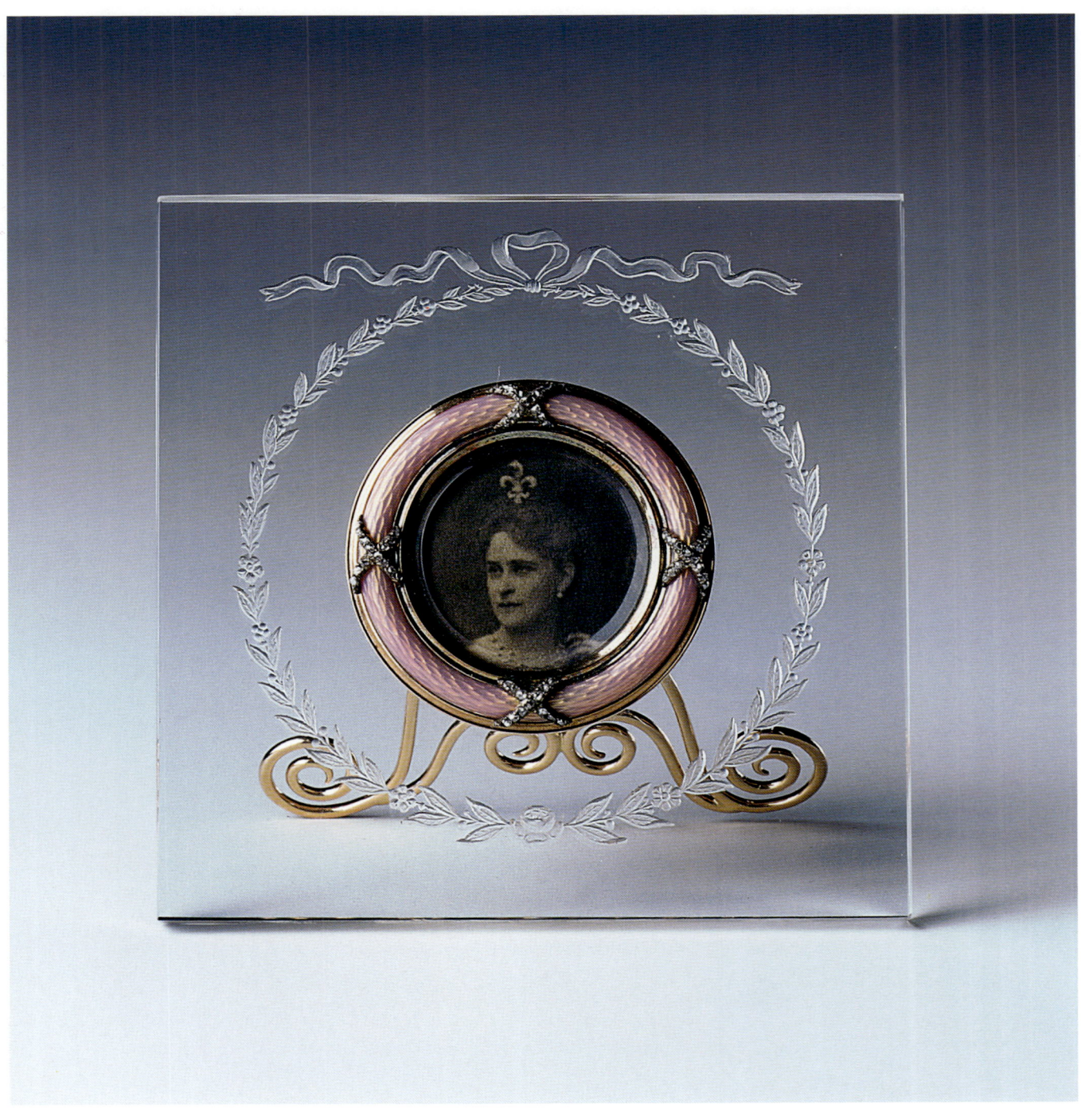

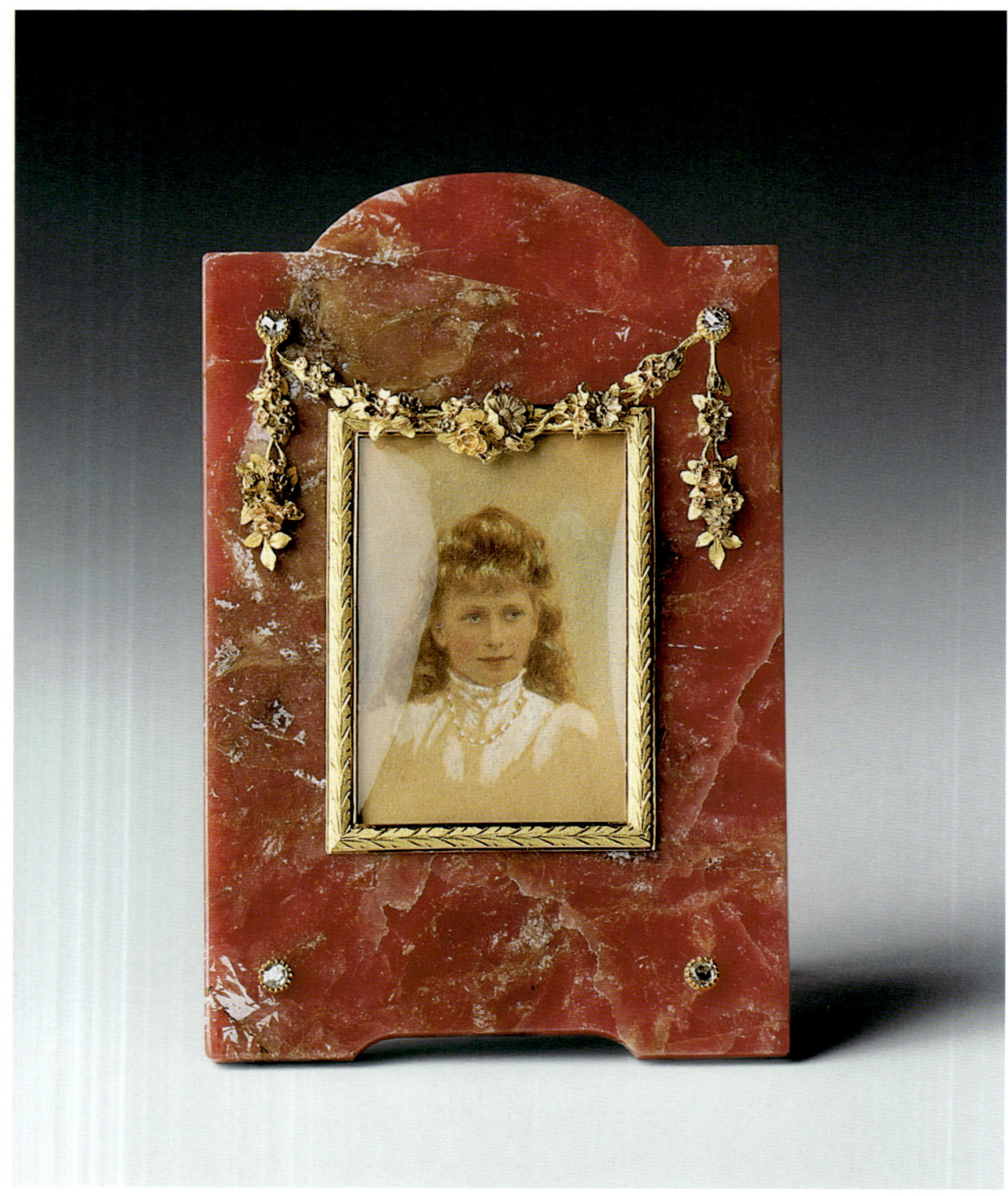

204 FRAME WITH A MINIATURE OF PRINCESS MARY
(THE PRINCESS ROYAL), *c.*1906

Princess Mary (1897–1965), only daughter of King George V and Queen Mary, married Viscount Lascelles (later 6th Earl of Harewood) in 1922.

Rhodonite, four-colour gold, silver-gilt, rose diamonds, mother-of-pearl, watercolour, 7.9 x 4.8 x 3.9 cm (3¹/₈ x 1⁷/₈ x 1⁹/₁₆")
Silver mark of 88 *zolotniks* (1896–1908); *FABERGÉ* in Cyrillic characters
RCIN 23310
PROVENANCE: Bought by the Prince of Wales (later King George V) from Fabergé's London branch, December 1909 (£14 15s)
EXHIBITIONS: QG 1995–6, no. 54

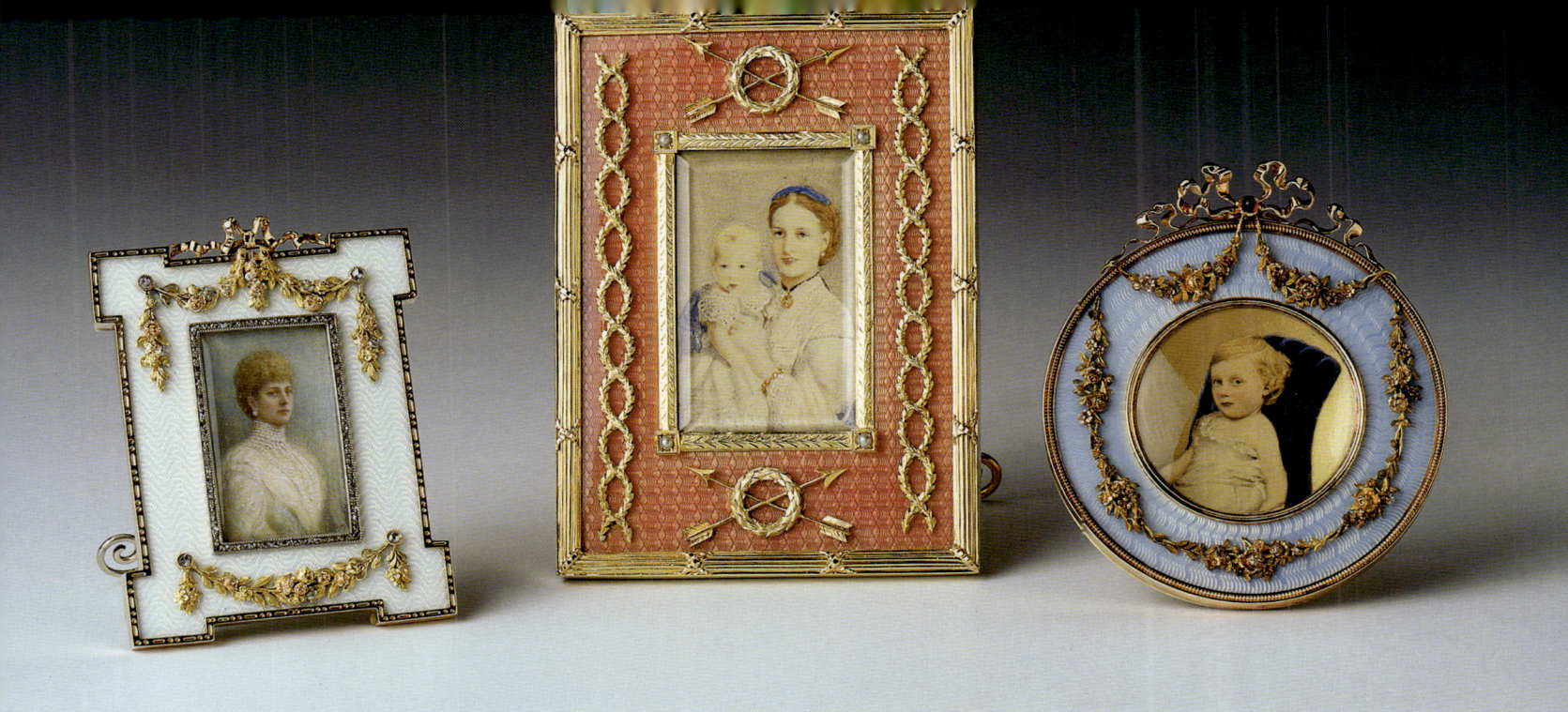

205 FRAME WITH A PHOTOGRAPH OF
QUEEN ALEXANDRA, *c.*1902–1903

Four-colour gold, silver-gilt, guilloché enamel, rose diamonds, ivory, 5.5 x 5 x 6.5 cm (2³/₁₆ x 1¹⁵/₁₆ x 2⁹/₁₆")
Unmarked
Tinted photograph by Downey
RCIN 9049
PROVENANCE: Queen Alexandra; by whom given to Queen Mary for her birthday, 26 May 1911
REFERENCES: QMB I, no. 749; QMPP I, no. 85
EXHIBITIONS: QG 1985–6, no. 48; QG 1995–6, no. 168

206 FRAME WITH A PHOTOGRAPH OF QUEEN ALEXANDRA,
WHEN PRINCESS OF WALES, WITH HER SON
PRINCE ALBERT VICTOR, DUKE OF CLARENCE, BEFORE 1896

Silver-gilt, two-colour gold, guilloché enamel, half pearls, ivory, 8.5 x 6.6 x 6.2 cm (3³/₈ x 2⁵/₈ x 2⁷/₆")
Mark of Michael Perchin; silver mark of 88 *zolotniks* (before 1896); *FABERGÉ* in Cyrillic characters; coloured
photograph by Lock & Whitfield
RCIN 40106
PROVENANCE: Bought by Tsar Nicholas II and Tsarina Alexandra Feodorovna, 19 December 1896 (110 roubles)
REFERENCES: Bainbridge 1949, pl. 88
EXHIBITIONS: QG 1995–6, no. 240

207 FRAME WITH A PHOTOGRAPH OF GEORGE,
DUKE OF YORK, LATER KING GEORGE V, BEFORE 1896

Silver-gilt, four-colour gold, guilloché enamel, 6.8 x 6.1 x 3 cm (2¹¹/₁₆ x 2³/₈ x 1³/₁₆")
Mark of Victor Aarne; gold mark of 56 *zolotniks* and silver mark of 88 *zolotniks*; *FABERGÉ* in Cyrillic characters;
coloured photograph by Hills & Saunders, November 1867
RCIN 40127
PROVENANCE: Acquired by Queen Alexandra, date unknown
EXHIBITIONS: QG 1995–6, no. 155

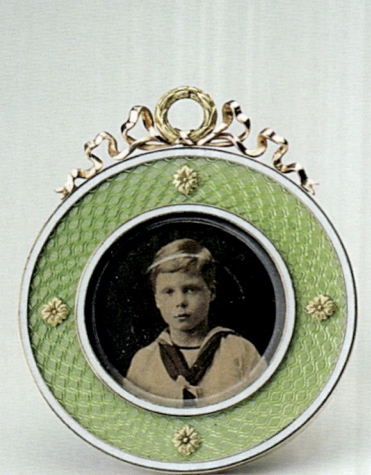
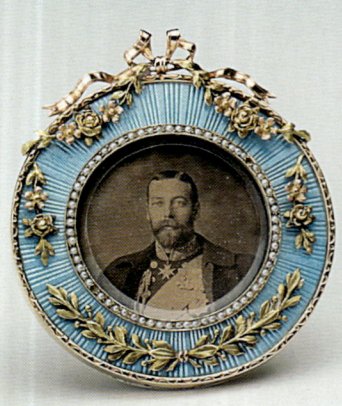
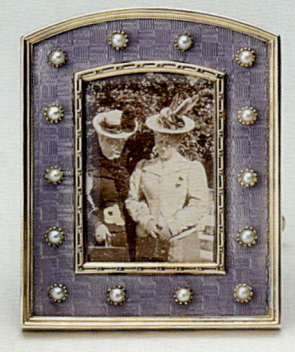
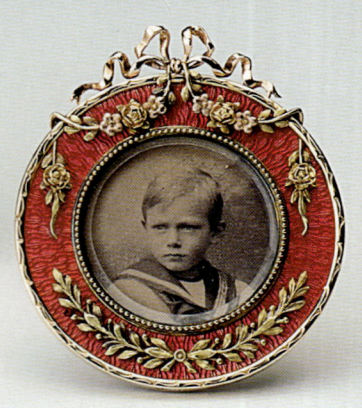

208 FRAME WITH A PHOTOGRAPH OF PRINCE HENRY OF WALES (LATER DUKE OF GLOUCESTER, 1900–1974), *c.*1905–1906

Three-colour gold, guilloché enamel, ivory, 4.3 x 4 x 3.3 cm (1¹¹/₁₆ x 1⁹/₁₆ x 1⁵/₁₆")
Gold mark of 56 *zolotniks* (1896–1908); initials of Carl Fabergé in Cyrillic characters
RCIN 9047
PROVENANCE: Royal Collection by 1953
EXHIBITIONS: QG 1995–6, no. 172

209 FRAME WITH A PHOTOGRAPH OF KING GEORGE V, FRAME 1896–1908, PHOTOGRAPH *c.*1911–1913

Three-colour gold, guilloché enamel, half pearls, ivory, 4.1 x 4 x 3.9 cm (1⁵/₈ x 1⁹/₁₆ x 1⁹/₁₆")
Gold mark of 56 *zolotniks* (1896–1908); FABERGÉ in Cyrillic characters
RCIN 9056
PROVENANCE: Queen Mary's collection
EXHIBITIONS: QG 1985–6, no. 46; QG 1995–6, no. 162

210 FRAME WITH A PHOTOGRAPH OF PRINCESS MAUD OF WALES AND PRINCESS MARIE OF GREECE, LATE 1890s

Princess Maud was the youngest daughter of King Edward VII and Queen Alexandra (see cat. 201). Princess Marie (1876–1940) was the younger daughter of King George I and Queen Olga of Greece. She married Grand Duke George of Russia.

Gold, silver-gilt, guilloché enamel, half pearls, mother-of-pearl, 4 x 3.9 x 3.5 cm (1⁹/₁₆ x 1⁹/₁₆ x 1³/₈")
Mark of Viktor Aarne; gold mark of 56 *zolotniks* and silver mark of 88 *zolotniks* (1896–1908); FABERGÉ in Cyrillic characters
RCIN 40232
PROVENANCE: Probably acquired by Queen Alexandra, date unknown
EXHIBITIONS: London 1977, no. K13; QG 1985–6, no. 137; QG 1995–6, no. 243

211 FRAME WITH A PHOTOGRAPH OF PRINCE EDWARD OF WALES (LATER KING EDWARD VIII), *c.* 1901–1902

Two-colour gold; guilloché enamel, ivory, 4.8 x diameter 4 x 3.9 cm (1⁷/₈ x 1⁹/₁₆ x 1⁹/₁₆")
Gold mark of 56 *zolotniks* (1896–1908); initials of Carl Fabergé in Cyrillic characters; photograph by
W. & D. Downey
RCIN 23313
PROVENANCE: Probably acquired by King George V and Queen Mary, date unknown
EXHIBITIONS: QG 1995–6, no. 169

212 FRAME WITH A PHOTOGRAPH OF GLADYS, MARCHIONESS OF RIPON, 1896–1903

Constance Gladys Herbert was the niece of the 12th Earl of Pembroke. In 1878 she married St George,
4th Earl of Lonsdale, who died in 1882. In 1885 she married Frederick, Earl de Grey, who became
the 2nd Marquess of Ripon. She died in 1916.

Two-colour gold, silver-gilt, guilloché enamel, 11.3 x 8.4 x 5.3 cm (4⁷/₁₆ x 3⁵/₁₆ x 2¹/₁₆")
Mark of Michael Perchin; silver mark of 88 *zolotniks* (1896–1908); *FABERGÉ* in Cyrillic characters
RCIN 32471
PROVENANCE: Royal Collection by 1953
EXHIBITIONS: QG 1995–6, no. 490

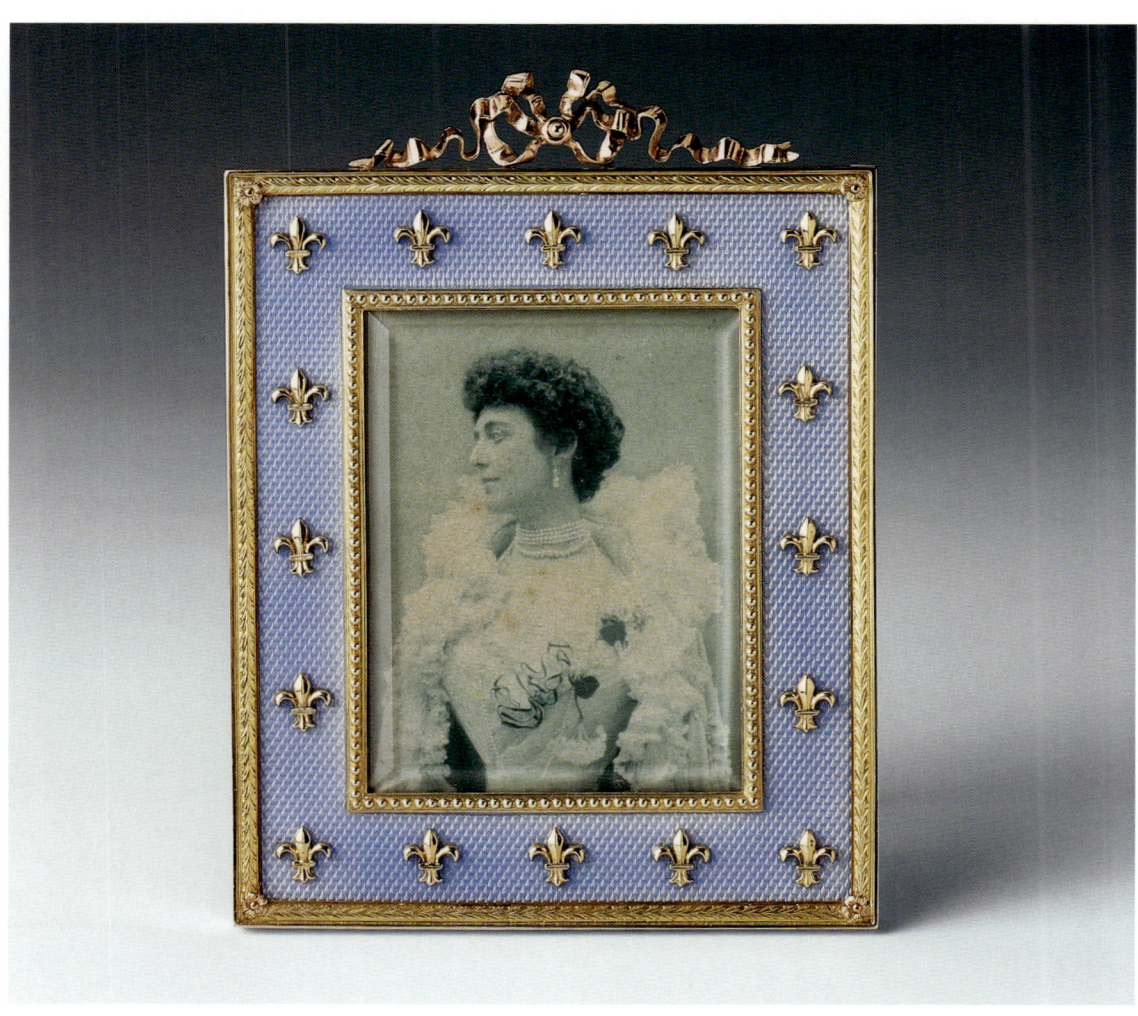

213 FRAME WITH A MINIATURE OF TSARINA MARIE FEODOROVNA, *c.*1895

This portrait miniature of Marie Feodorovna was painted by Johannes Zehngraf and is based on a photograph by Pasetti of 1894.

Marie Feodorovna (1847–1928), born Princess Dagmar of Denmark, married the future Tsar Alexander III in 1866. In contrast to the Tsar, she enjoyed the excitement and extravagance of court life in St Petersburg. She had great admiration for Fabergé and his artistry and in 1882 she personally endorsed his work by purchasing a pair of gold cuff links in neo-Greek style from the Pan-Russian exhibition in Moscow. Following her husband's death in 1894, her son Nicholas II continued the tradition of presenting her with a Fabergé Easter egg. In a letter dated 8 April 1914 to her sister Queen Alexandra, she describes how on receipt of the egg for that year she told Fabergé 'vous êtes un génie incomparable'.

Even during the first decade of the twentieth century, in a period of particularly difficult political relations between England and Russia, Marie Feodorovna visited England several times, notably in 1902 for the coronation of King Edward VII and Queen Alexandra. Following the Revolution in 1917, the Dowager Tsarina escaped to the Crimea and was eventually rescued by a British cruiser sent at King George V's insistence. After a brief stay with her sister and nephew at Sandringham, she returned to Denmark, moving finally to Hvidøre, the villa outside Copenhagen that was shared with Queen Alexandra. Even at Hvidøre, where she was to spend the remainder of her life, she was not without objects by Fabergé, having earlier had seals made for use there; of these there is an example in the Royal Collection (not shown, RCIN 40249).

Four-colour gold, guilloché enamel, ivory, watercolour, 9 x 7.8 x 7.3 cm (3⁹/₁₆ x 3¹/₁₆ x 2⁷/₈")
Mark of Michael Perchin; gold mark of 56 *zolotniks* (before 1896); *FABERGÉ* in Cyrillic characters; miniature signed *Zehngraf*
RCIN 40107
PROVENANCE: Acquired by King Edward VII and Queen Alexandra, *c.*1895
REFERENCES: Bainbridge 1949, pp. 95–6; Habsburg & Lopato 1993, p. 179
EXHIBITIONS: London 1977, no. K3; New York 1983, no. 174; QG 1985–6, no. 135; Munich 1986–7, no.524; Zurich 1989, no. 89; St Petersburg/Paris/London 1993–4; no. 248; Cardiff 1998, no. 150; QG 2002–3, no. 260

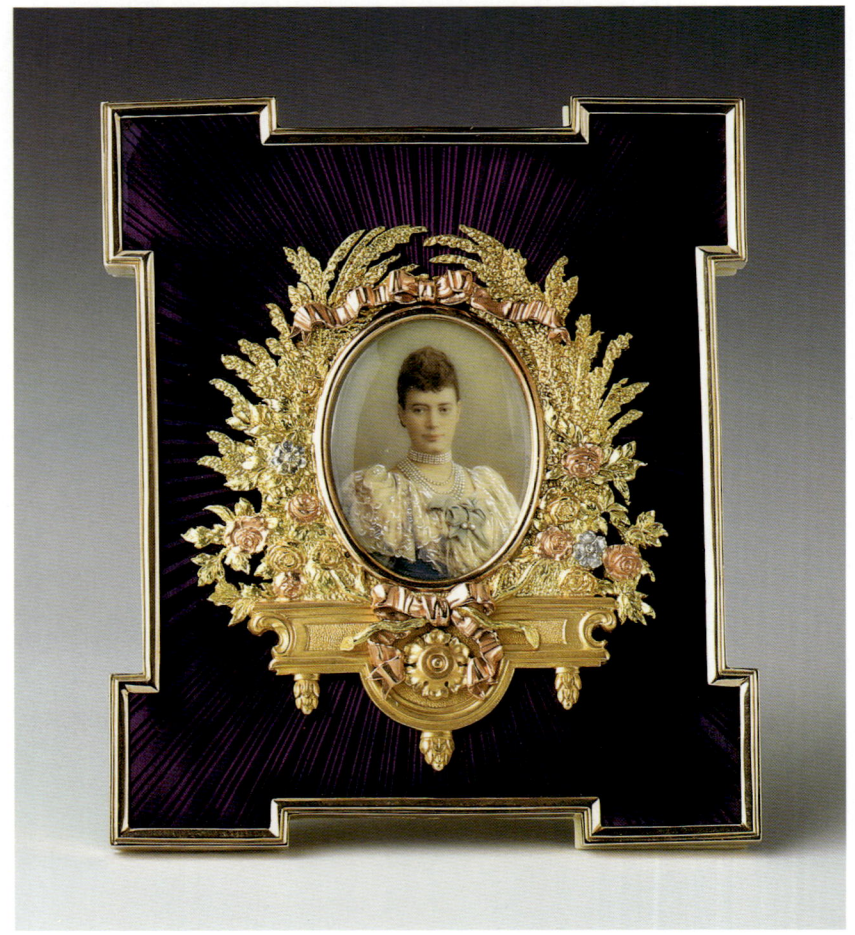

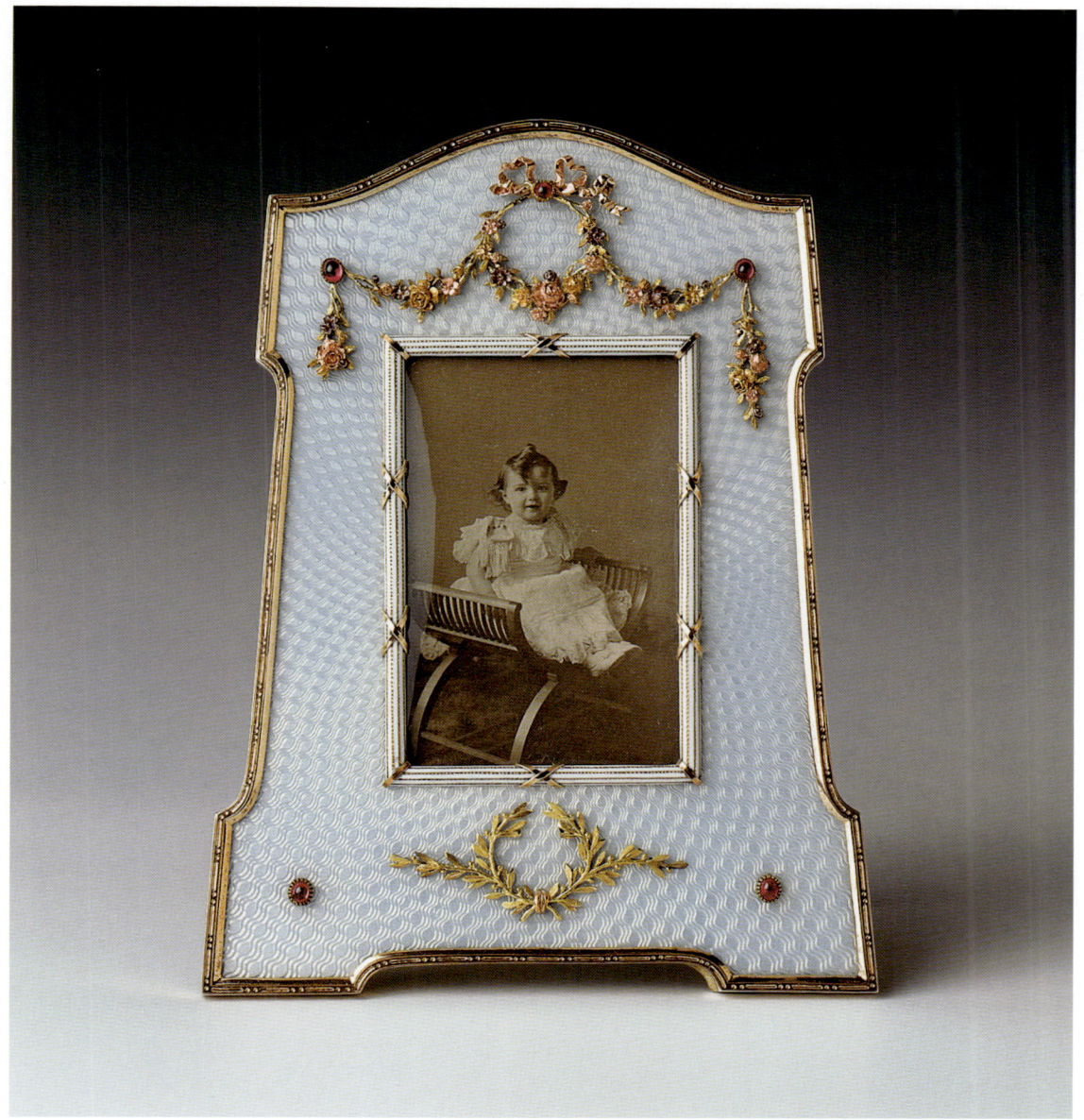

214 FRAME WITH A PHOTOGRAPH OF
TSAREVITCH ALEXIS, *c.*1905

The Tsarevitch Alexis (1904–18) was the fifth child and only son of Tsar Nicholas II and Tsarina Alexandra Feodorovna. The imperial family is symbolically represented in the Colonnade Egg (cat. 2) of 1910, which is surmounted by a putto representing the long-awaited heir to the throne. The Tsar and Tsarina's joy at Alexis's birth was short lived; within a few months Alexis developed the first signs of haemophilia. The Tsarevitch almost died in 1911 and in desperation the Tsarina asked for the help of Gregori Rasputin, the peasant monk, to cure her son. Following the Revolution in 1917, the imperial family were taken to Ekaterinburg in Siberia where the Tsarevitch and his sisters and parents were shot on 17 July 1918.

Silver-gilt, four-colour gold, guilloché enamel, rubies, ivory, 10.2 x 8.4 x 5 cm (4 x 3⁵/₁₆ x 1¹⁵/₁₆")
Mark of Viktor Aarne; silver mark of 88 *zolotniks* (1896–1908); *FABERGÉ* in Cyrillic characters
RCIN 40105
PROVENANCE: Bought by Tsar Nicholas II and Tsarina Alexandra Feodorovna, 21 June 1906 (165 rcubles)
EXHIBITIONS: QG 1985–6, no. 138; QG 1995–6, no. 501; QG 2002–3, no. 262

215 FRAME WITH A PHOTOGRAPH OF KING GEORGE V AND QUEEN MARY, WHEN PRINCE AND PRINCESS OF WALES, 1905

Two-colour gold, silver-gilt, guilloché enamel, seed pearls, rose diamond, cabochon ruby, mother-of-pearl, 6.1 x 4.8 x 2.7 cm (2³⁄₈ x 1⁷⁄₈ x 1¹⁄₁₆")
Mark of Viktor Aarne; gold mark of 56 *zolotniks* and silver mark of 88 *zolotniks* (1896–1908); *FABERGÉ* in Cyrillic characters; photograph by W. & D. Downey
RCIN 23305
PROVENANCE: Given to the Princess of Wales (later Queen Mary) by the Prince of Wales (later King George V), August 1905
REFERENCES: QMB I, no. 251; QMPP I no. 250
EXHIBITIONS: QG 1995–6, no. 164

216 FRAME WITH A PHOTOGRAPH OF GRAND DUCHESS SERGEI, FRAME 1896–1903, PHOTOGRAPH *c.*1916

Grand Duchess Sergei (Elizabeth Feodorovna) served as a nursing sister during the First World War.

Two-colour gold, silver-gilt, guilloché enamel, pearls, mother-of-pearl, 4 x 3 x 2.9 cm (1⁹⁄₁₆ x 1³⁄₁₆ x 1¹⁄₈")
Mark of Viktor Aarne; gold mark of 56 *zolotniks* and silver mark of 88 *zolotniks* (1896–1908); *FABERGÉ* in Cyrillic characters
RCIN 40234
PROVENANCE: Bought by Tsar Nicholas II and Tsarina Alexandra Feodorovna, 30 March 1903 (150 roubles)
EXHIBITIONS: London 1977, no. K9; QG 1985–6, no. 132; QG 1995–6, no. 175

217 FRAME WITH A PHOTOGRAPH OF PRINCE ALBERT OF YORK (LATER KING GEORGE VI), *c.*1899

Three-colour gold, guilloché enamel, ivory, 4.3 x 4.6 x 4.5 cm (1¹¹⁄₁₆ x 1¹³⁄₁₆ x 1³⁄₄")
Gold mark of 56 *zolotniks* (1896–1908); initials of Carl Fabergé in Cyrillic characters
RCIN 23304
PROVENANCE: Royal Collection by 1953
EXHIBITIONS: QG 1995–6, no. 156

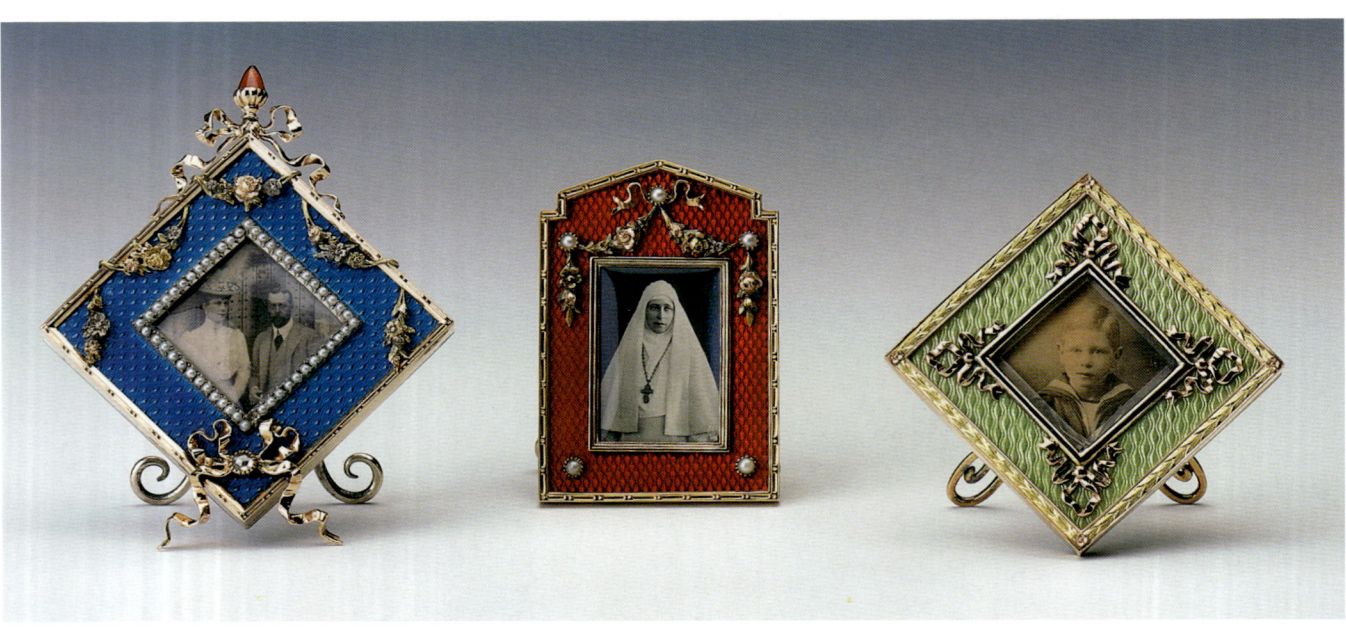

218 FRAME WITH A PHOTOGRAPH OF CHARLES, PRINCE OF WALES, FRAME BEFORE 1896, PHOTOGRAPH *c.*1955

Bowenite, two-colour gold, enamel, 12 x 11.4 x 1 cm (4³/₄ x 4¹/₂ x ³/₈")
Mark of Michael Perchin; gold mark of 56 *zolotniks* (before 1896); *FABERGÉ* in Cyrillic characters
RCIN 100310
PROVENANCE: Bought by Queen Elizabeth from Wartski

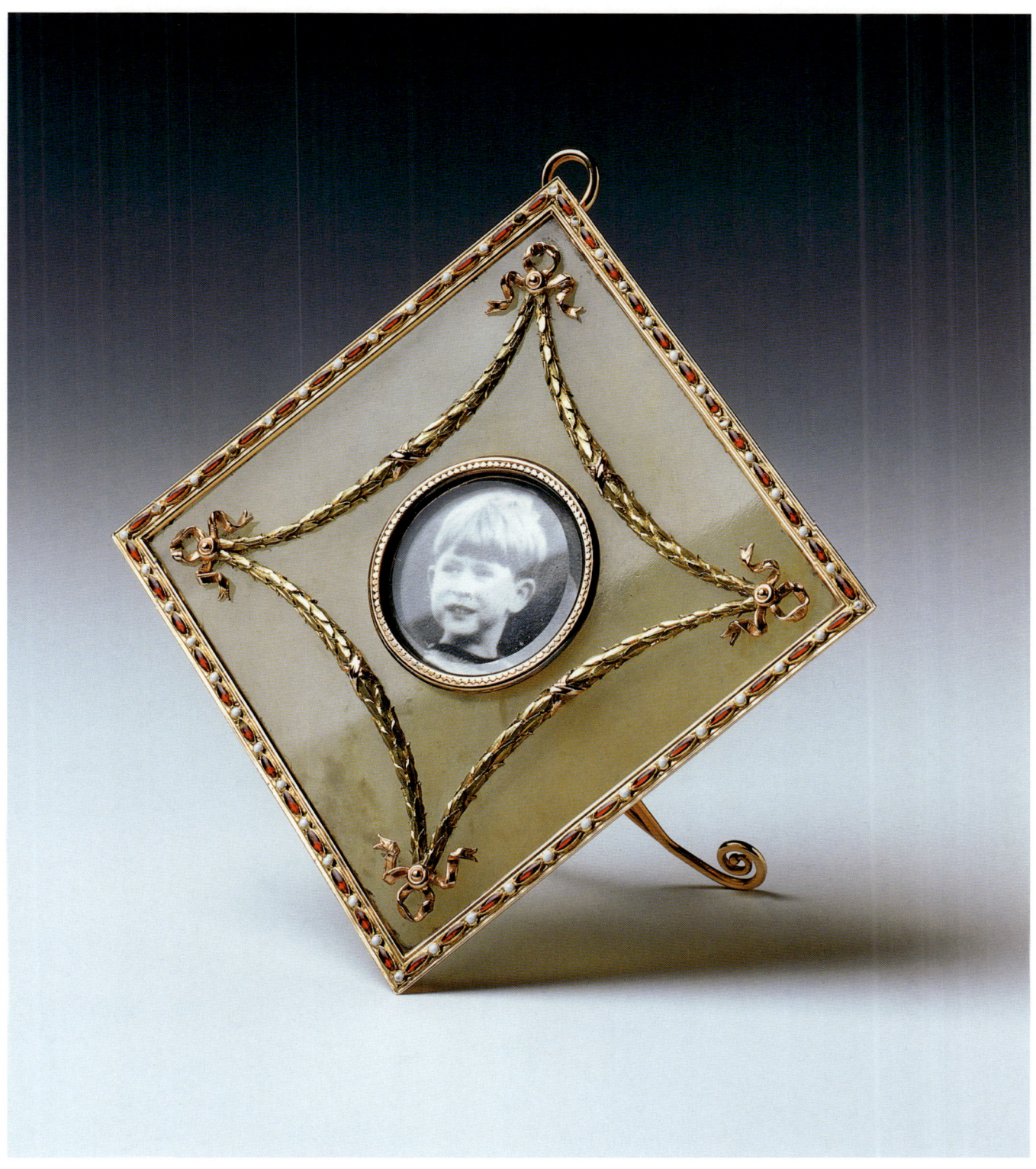

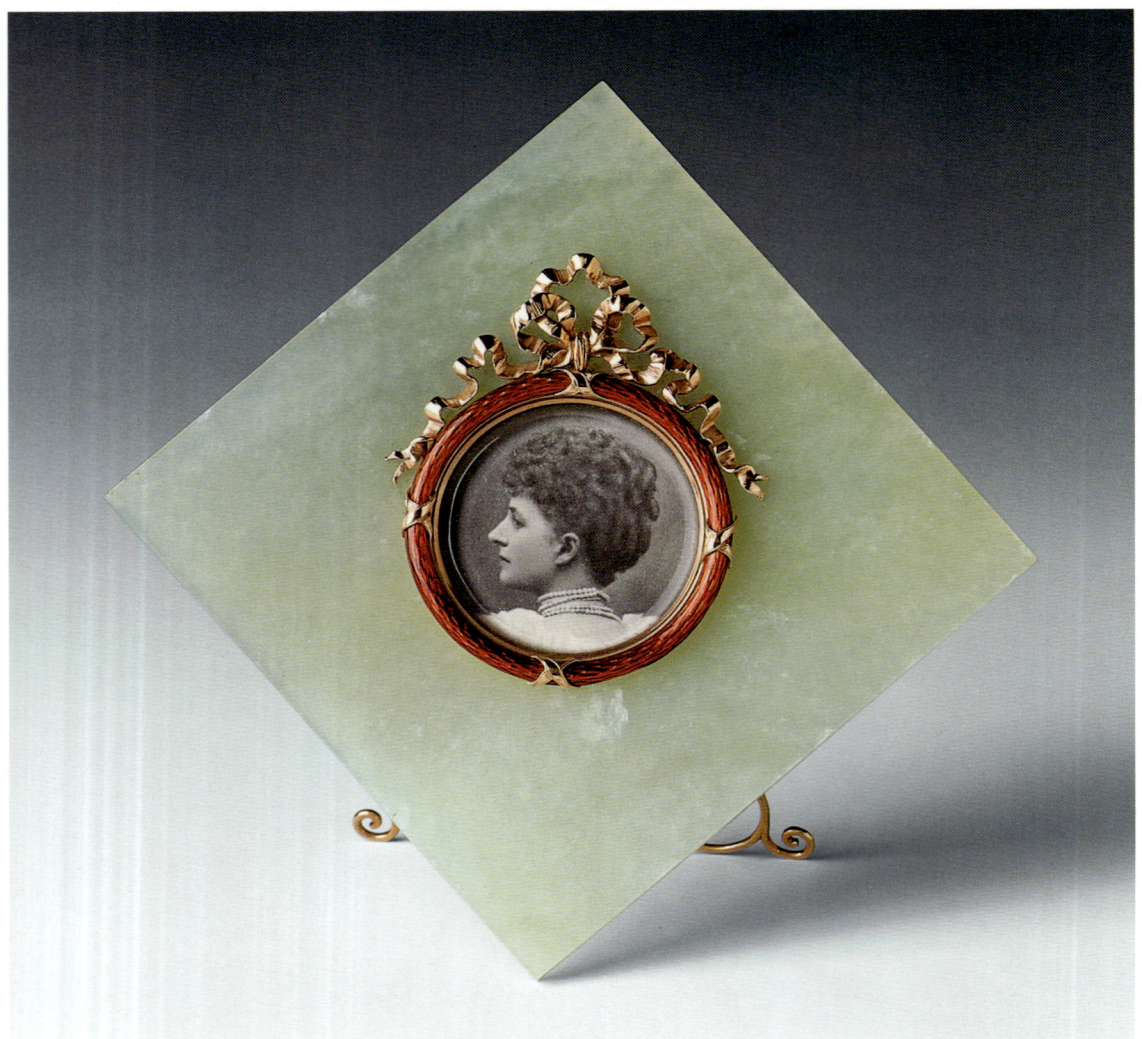

219 FRAME WITH A PHOTOGRAPH OF QUEEN ALEXANDRA WHEN PRINCESS OF WALES, FRAME 1896–1903, PHOTOGRAPH 1898

Bowenite, guilloché enamel, gold, rose diamonds, 11.8 x 11.9 x 0.5 cm (4⁵/₈ x 4¹¹/₁₆ x ³/₁₆")
Mark of Michael Perchin; gold mark of 56 *zolotniks* (1896–1908); *FABERGÉ* in Cyrillic characters
RCIN 38808
PROVENANCE: Acquired by Queen Alexandra, date unknown

220 CAMEO PORTRAIT OF EDWARD, PRINCE OF WALES (LATER KING EDWARD VIII), 1911

This unusual cameo portrait, carved from smoky quartz, was made in the workshop of Henrik Wigström and commissioned by King George V. The drawing for the cameo appears on plate 319 of a design album from Wigström's workshop. The cameo depicts the Prince wearing the mantle worn at his investiture as Prince of Wales in 1911.

Smoky quartz, gold, rose diamonds, chased silver, 10.2 x 4.5 x 6 cm (4 x 1³⁄₄ x 2³⁄₈")
Mark of Henrik Wigström; silver mark of 88 *zolotniks* (1908–17); *FABERGÉ* in Roman letters; the cameo signed *C.T. 1911*
RCIN 23314
PROVENANCE: Bought by King George V from Fabergé's London branch, 27 April 1912 (£67 10s); by whom presented to Queen Mary for her birthday, 26 May 1912
REFERENCES: QMB I, no. 809; Tillander-Godenhielm *et al.* 2000, p. 164, pl. 319
EXHIBITIONS: QG 1985–6, no. 117; QG 1995–6, no. 166

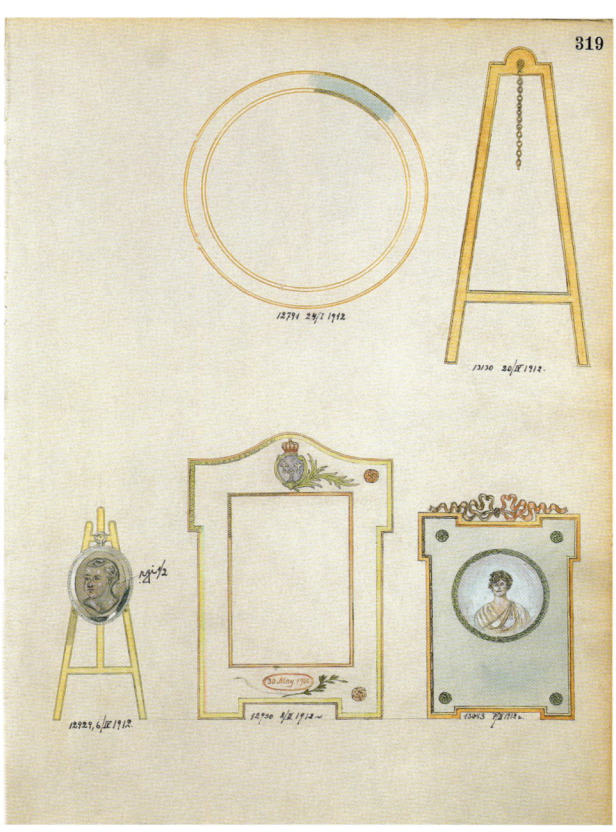

Plate 319 from the design book of Henrik Wigström, showing the cameo portrait of King Edward VIII and easel (cat. 220).

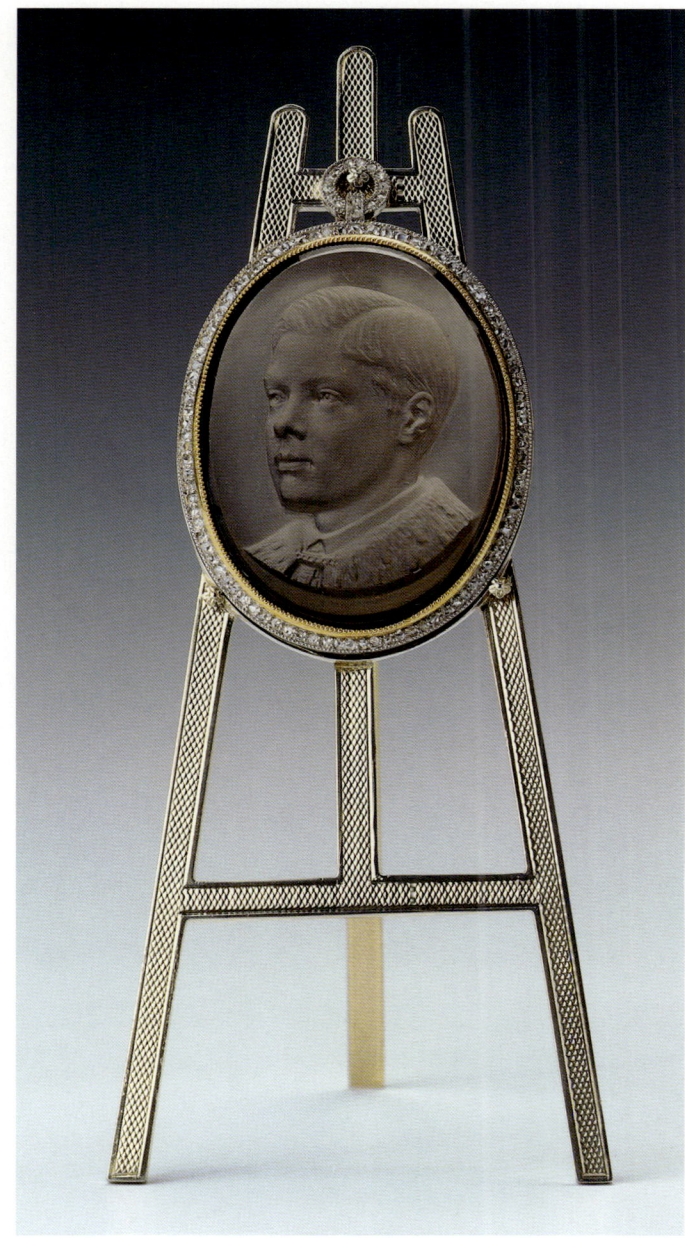

221 FRAME WITH A PHOTOGRAPH OF QUEEN VICTORIA'S PORTRAIT BY WINTERHALTER, FRAME BEFORE 1896

The photograph is a detail from the full-length portrait of Queen Victoria by Franz Xaver Winterhalter (1805–73), dated 1843, which hangs in the Garter Throne Room at Windsor Castle.

Silver, guilloché enamel, gold, ivory, 13.2 x 9.4 x 1 cm (5³/₁₆ x 3¹¹/₁₆ x ³/₈")
Mark of Michael Perchin; silver mark of 88 *zolotniks* (before 1896)
RCIN 100307
PROVENANCE: Queen Mary's collection; Queen Elizabeth
EXHIBITIONS: QG 1995–6, no. 53

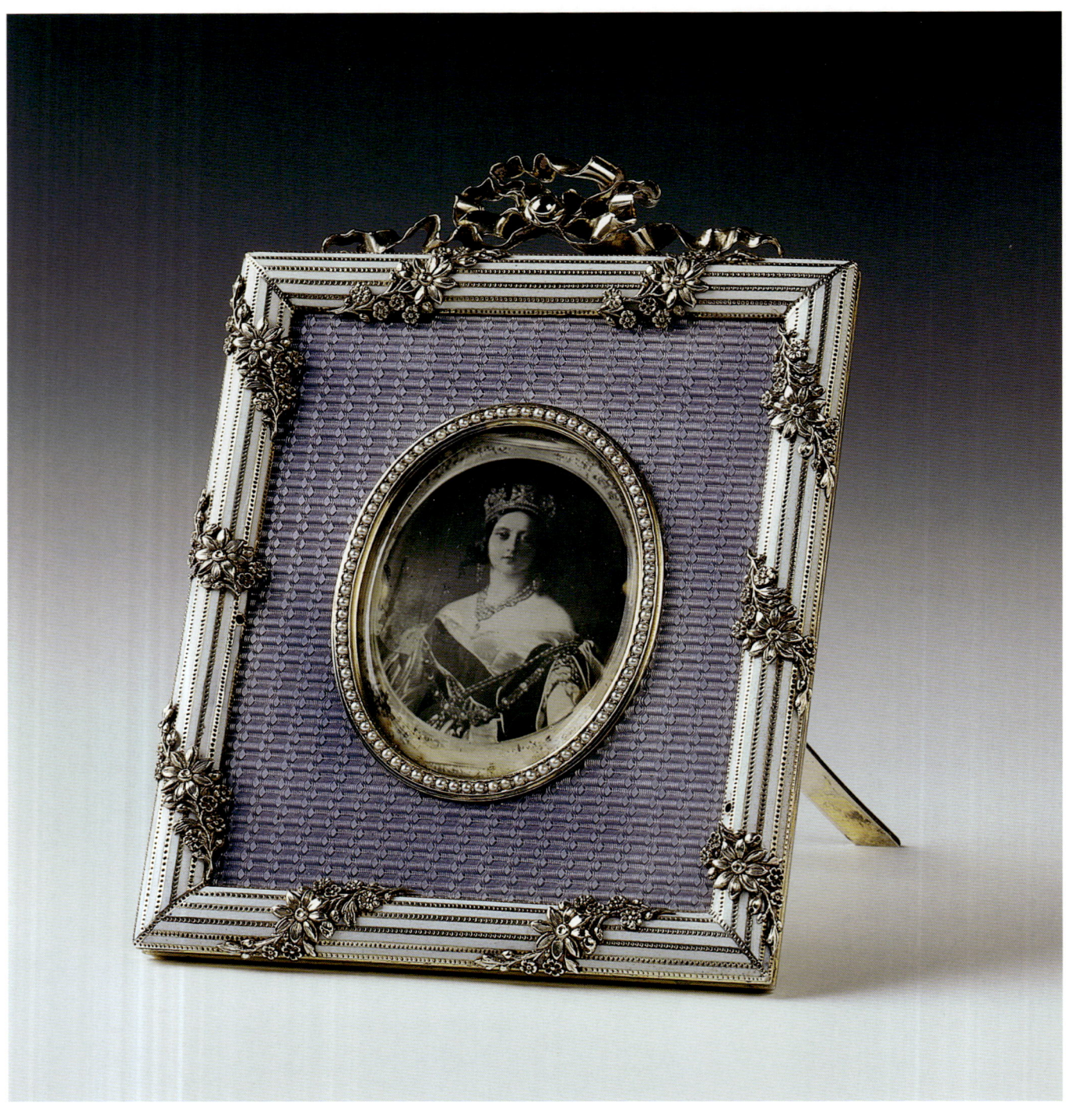

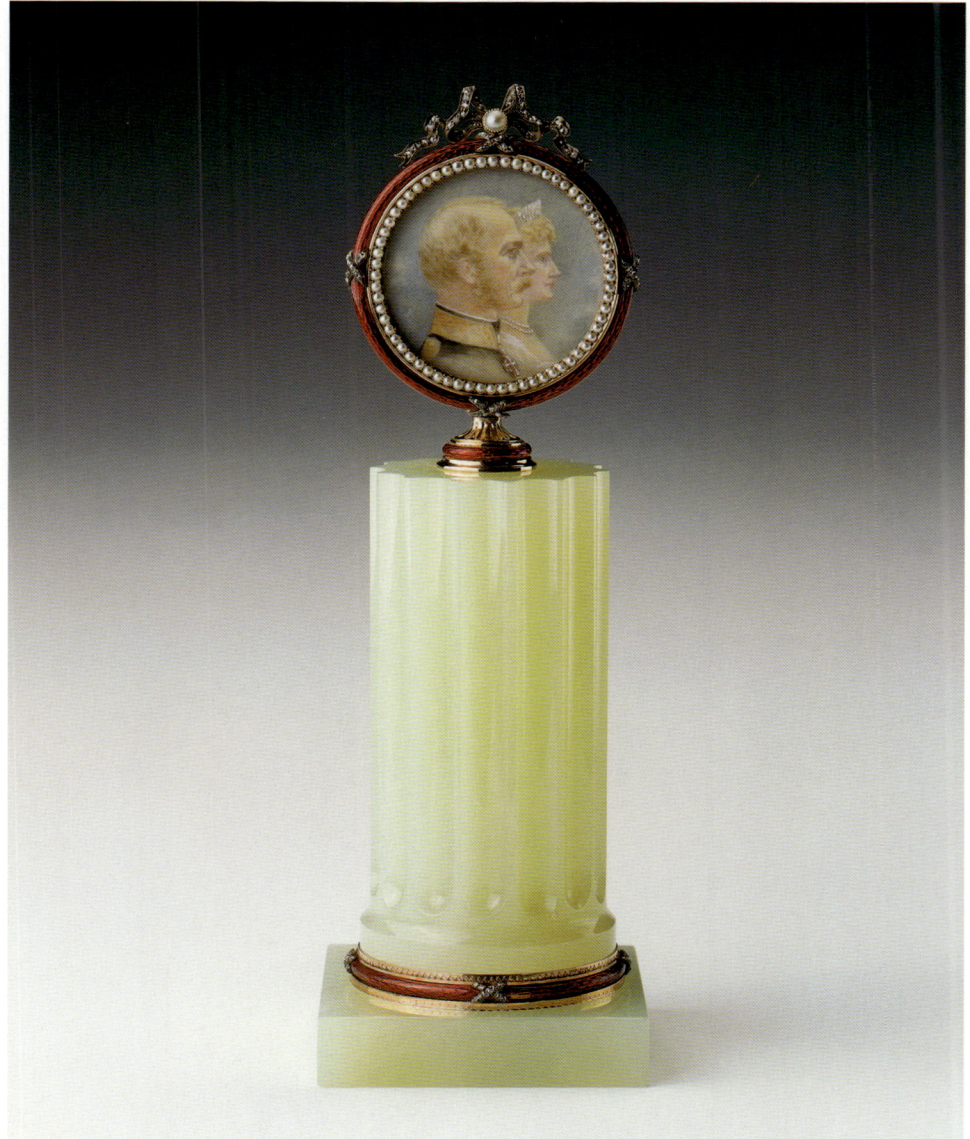

222 COLUMN SURMOUNTED BY A FRAMED MINIATURE OF KING CHRISTIAN IX AND QUEEN LOUISE OF DENMARK, *c.*1900

Frames mounted on columns first appeared as official gifts from the Imperial Cabinet for presentation to high-ranking officials at home and abroad. The prototype was developed by Fabergé and Tsar Nicholas II liked it so much that he purchased two for himself. Fabergé continued to produce the model for other customers. This example bears the double portrait miniature of Queen Alexandra's parents King Christian IX and Queen Louise of Denmark. The frame is unmarked, but was probably made in the late 1890s or in the early years of the new century. It might have been a present to the British royal couple at the time of King Edward VII's accession to the throne on 22 January 1901 or perhaps for the coronation, which took place on 9 August 1901.

Bowenite, guilloché enamel, pearls, rose diamonds, watercolour 16.3 x 5.3 x 5.3 cm (6^{7}/₁₆ x 2^{1}/₁₆ x 2 /₁₆")
Unmarked
RCIN 40097
PROVENANCE: Acquired by King Edward VII and Queen Alexandra, *c.*1901
EXHIBITIONS: QG 1995–6, no. 61

223 FRAME WITH A PHOTOGRAPH OF PRINCESS LOUISE, DUCHESS OF FIFE, *c.*1896

Princess Louise (1867–1931) was the eldest daughter of King Edward VII and Queen Alexandra and in 1889 she married the 1st Duke of Fife. She was created Princess Royal in 1905.

Three-colour gold, silver-gilt, guilloché enamel, pearls, mother-of-pearl, 4.6 x 4.2 x 2.8 cm (1¹³/₁₆ x 1⅝ x 1⅛")
Mark of Viktor Aarne; gold mark of 56 *zolotniks* and silver mark of 88 *zolotniks* (1896–1908); *FABERGÉ* in Cyrillic characters
RCIN 40231
PROVENANCE: Bought by Tsar Nicholas II and Tsarina Alexandra Feodorovna, 25 December 1900 (130 roubles)
EXHIBITIONS: London 1977, no. K12; QG 1985–6, no. 50; QG 1995–6, no. 170

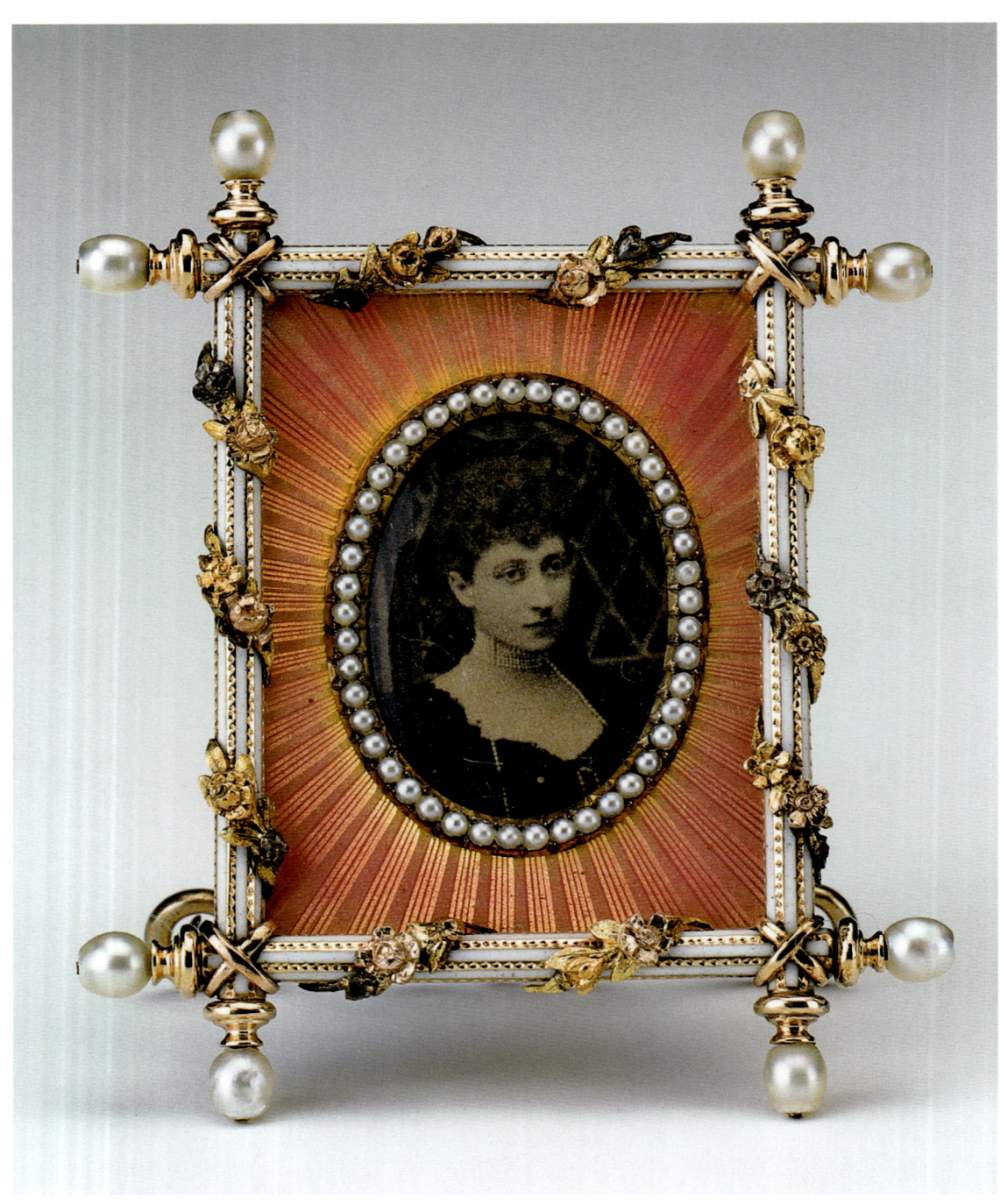

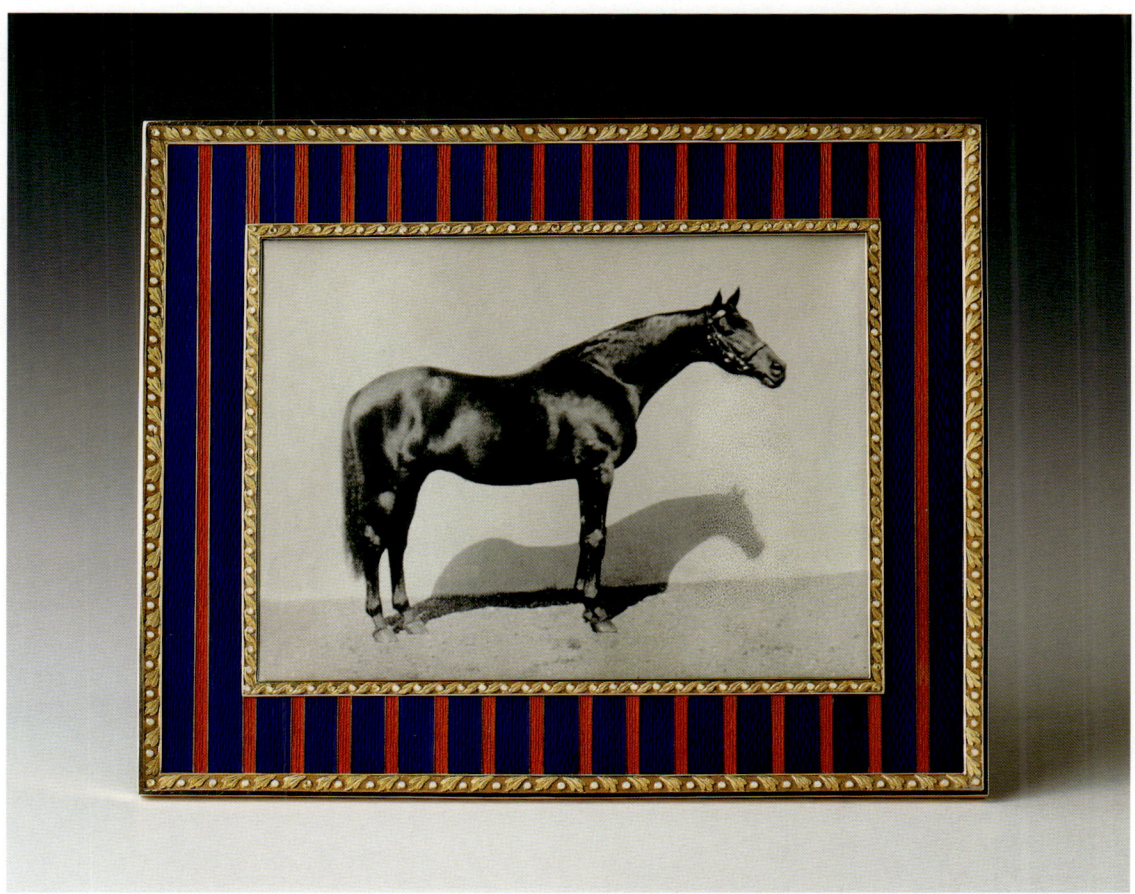

224 FRAME WITH A PHOTOGRAPH OF PERSIMMON, *c.*1908

This frame contains a photograph of King Edward VII's most successful racehorse, Persimmon, who won the Derby and St Leger in 1896 and the Ascot Gold Cup and Eclipse Stakes in 1897. Persimmon was among the animals modelled from life during the Sandringham commission in 1907. The sculptor Boris Frödman-Cluzel prepared the wax model from which a silver statuette was made by Henrik Wigström in 1908 (see cat. 18). Lord Knutsford describes how, during a visit to Sandringham in 1900, the guests were given an opportunity to admire the horse: 'such a splendid bay, and in grand condition. We all took snapshots at him. The Princess promised to send me hers.' This photograph differs from those in the Royal Photograph Collection, which are known to have been taken by Queen Alexandra. The groom appears to have been deliberately faded out of the print.

The frame itself is enamelled in the racing colours of King Edward VII, who probably commissioned it from Fabergé. This idea of personalising the colours of frames met with the approval of Fabergé's customers; Bainbridge reported that Leopold de Rothschild also had photograph frames and other items made in his racing colours.

Two-colour gold, guilloché red and blue enamel, moonstones, silver-gilt, 12 x 15.8 x 10.1 cm (4³/₄ x 6¹/₄ x 4")
Mark of Henrik Wigström; gold mark of 56 *zolotniks* and silver mark of 91 *zolotniks* (1908–17); FABERGÉ in Cyrillic characters
RCIN 15168
PROVENANCE: King Edward VII (recorded as being purchased by the Queen – probably Queen Alexandra – for £70 from Fabergé's London branch; date of purchase unknown)
REFERENCES: Bainbridge 1949, p. 84
EXHIBITIONS: QG 1995–6, no. 197; QG 2002–3, no. 264

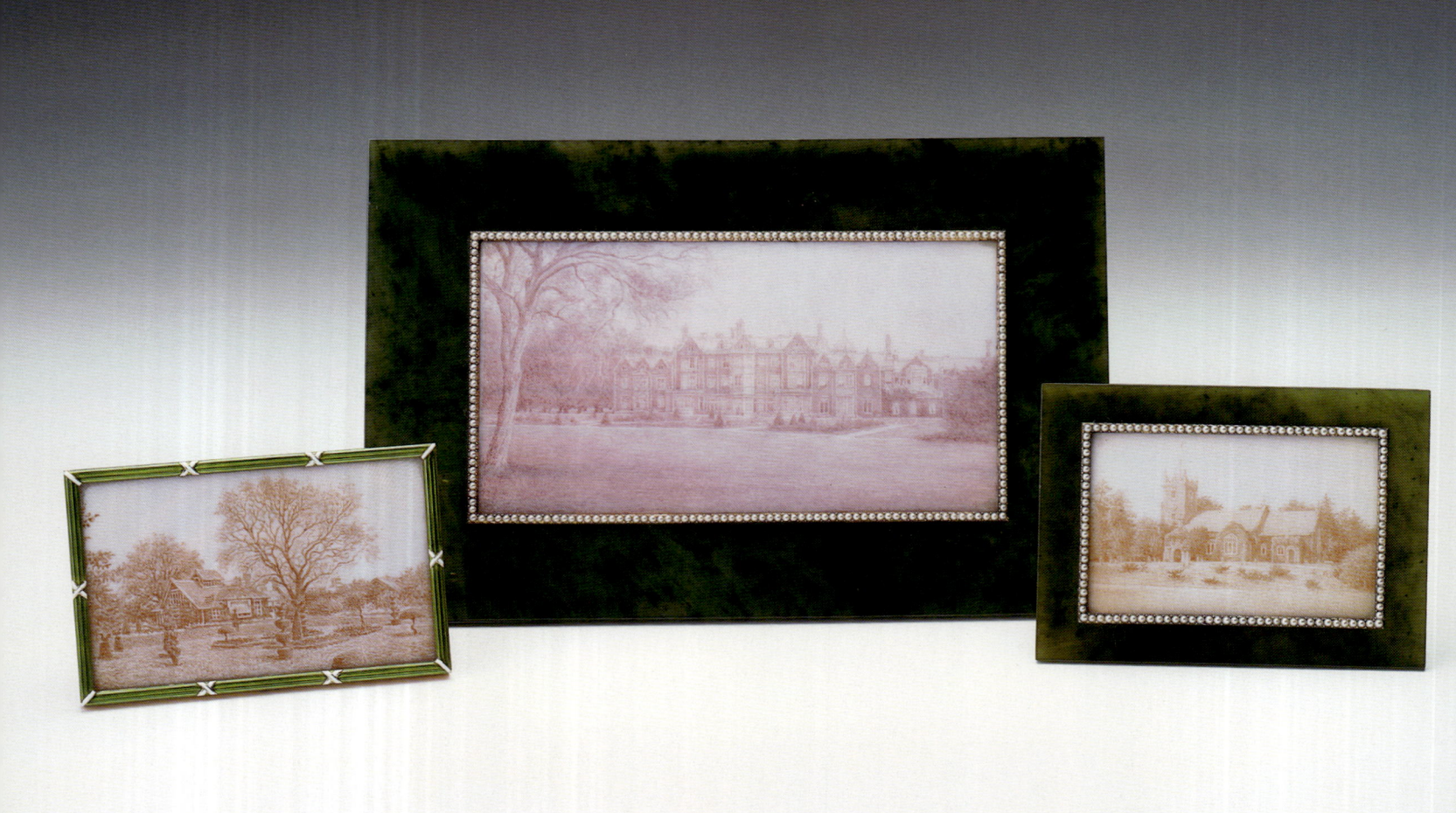

225 FRAME WITH AN ENAMELLED VIEW OF SANDRINGHAM DAIRY, *c*.1911

In addition to the boxes which Fabergé made with views of Russia and England (cat. 156–8, 177–82), he supplied frames containing sepia enamel plaques. This is one of three Fabergé frames in the Royal Collection with views of Sandringham (see cat. 226, 227). All three were made in the workshop of Henrik Wigström. Other frames containing enamelled plaques of royal residences were also made by Fabergé. Bainbridge states that two held images of Buckingham Palace and Hampton Court Palace. The latter is probably that now in the India Early Minshall Collection, Cleveland Museum of Art. The whereabouts of the former is not known. The London ledgers reveal that Queen Alexandra purchased a frame with an enamelled view of Windsor Castle in 1909 but this is not to be found in the Royal Collection. Like the boxes similarly applied with sepia enamel views of royal residences, some of these frames may have been commissioned by King Edward VII and Queen Alexandra.

The Dairy at Sandringham, known during King Edward VII's occupation of the estate as 'the Queen's Dairy', was a working dairy supplying the royal household at Sandringham with milk, butter and cream. It consisted of a dairy, butter room and can room and was decorated inside with Minton tiles. It was here that the wax models of the Sandringham animals prepared by Fabergé's sculptors were laid out for examination by the King in 1907.

Gold, enamel, sepia enamel, ivory, 4.6 x 7.1 x 2.1 cm (1¹³/₁₆ x 2¹³/₁₆ x ¹³/₁₆")
Mark of Henrik Wigström; gold mark of 56 *zolotniks* (1908–17); *FABERGÉ* in Cyrillic characters
RCIN 40495
PROVENANCE: Bought by Princess Victoria from Fabergé's London branch, 14 November 1911 (£32)
REFERENCES: Bainbridge 1949, pl. 89
EXHIBITIONS: London 1977, no. H7; New York 1983, no. 139; QG 1985–6, no. 321; St Petersburg/Paris/London 1993–4, no. 83; QG 1995–6, no. 342

226   FRAME WITH AN ENAMELLED VIEW OF SANDRINGHAM HOUSE, 1908

Nephrite, gold, half pearls, sepia enamel, ivory, 9 x 15.2 x 7.1 cm ($3^9/_{16}$ x 6 x $2^{13}/_{16}$")
Mark of Henrik Wigström; gold mark of 56 *zolotniks* (1896–1908); *FABERGÉ* in Cyrillic characters
RCIN 40492
PROVENANCE: Bought by King Edward VII from Fabergé's London branch, November/December 1908 (£67);
Princess Victoria's collection
REFERENCES: Bainbridge 1949, p. 98
EXHIBITIONS: London 1935; London 1977, no. H3; QG 1995–6, no. 344

227   FRAME WITH AN ENAMELLED VIEW OF SANDRINGHAM CHURCH, *c.*1908

Nephrite, gold, half pearls, sepia enamel, ivory, 4.7 x 7.8 x 3 cm ($1^7/_8$ x $3^1/_{16}$ x $1^3/_{16}$")
Mark of Henrik Wigström; gold mark of 56 *zolotniks*
RCIN 40494
PROVENANCE: Bought by Earl Howe from Fabergé's London branch, 24 December 1908 (£35)
EXHIBITIONS: QG 1995–6, no. 343

228   FRAME WITH AN ENAMELLED VIEW OF DURHAM CATHEDRAL, 1909

This frame was purchased by Dr Emanuel Nobel (1859–1932), one of Fabergé's best customers, and
is presumed to have been given to King Edward VII or Queen Alexandra.

Bowenite, two-colour gold, sepia enamel, 11 x 15.8 x 6.5 cm ($4^5/_{16}$ x $6^1/_4$ x $2^9/_{16}$")
Mark of Henrik Wigström; gold mark of 56 *zolotniks* (1908–17); *FABERGÉ* in Cyrillic characters
RCIN 40491
PROVENANCE: Bought by Dr Emanuel Nobel from Fabergé's London branch, 16 April 1909 (£70); presumed to
have been given to King Edward VII and Queen Alexandra
REFERENCES: Bainbridge 1949, p. 98
EXHIBITIONS: London 1953, no. 62; London 1977, no. I5; QG 1985–6, no. 315; QG 1995–6, no. 421

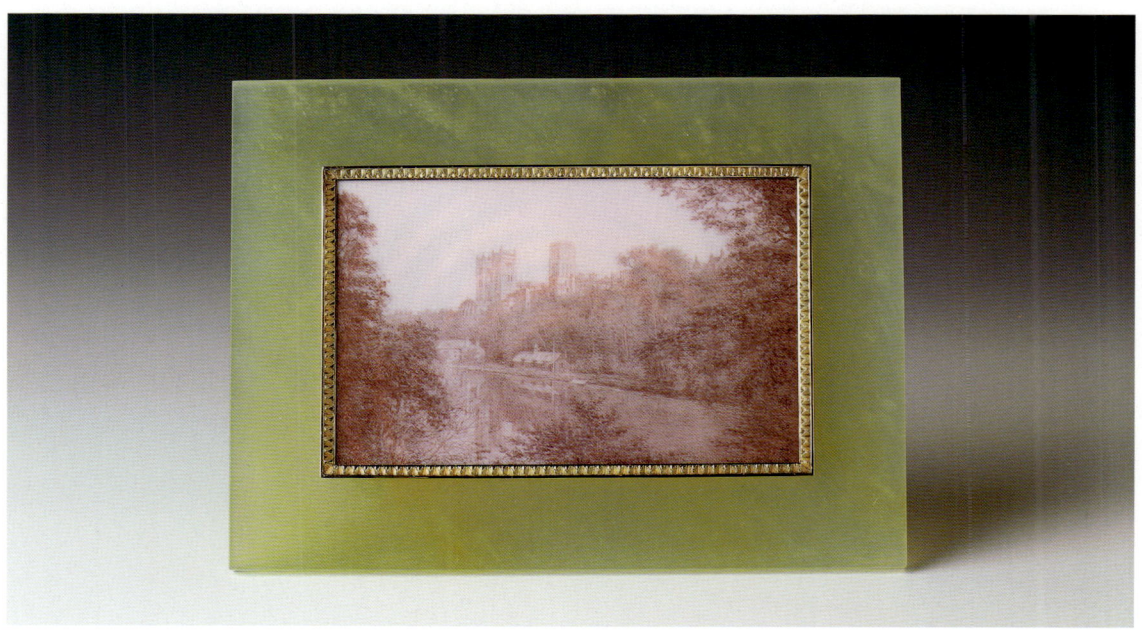

229 COLUMN SURMOUNTED BY FRAMED MINIATURES OF PORT SCENES, 1896–1908

One of a small number of frames that belonged to Princess Victoria. The watercolour maritime scene shows the Peter and Paul Fortress in the background.

Four-colour gold, guilloché enamel, miniatures in watercolour, 10.3 x 4.4 x 4 cm (4¹/₁₆ x 1³/₄ x 1⁹/₁₆")
Mark of Karl Armfelt; gold mark of 56 *zolotniks* (1896–1908)
RCIN 40109
PROVENANCE: Bought by Princess Victoria from Fabergé's London branch, November/December 1909 (£22)
EXHIBITIONS: QG 1995–6, no. 251

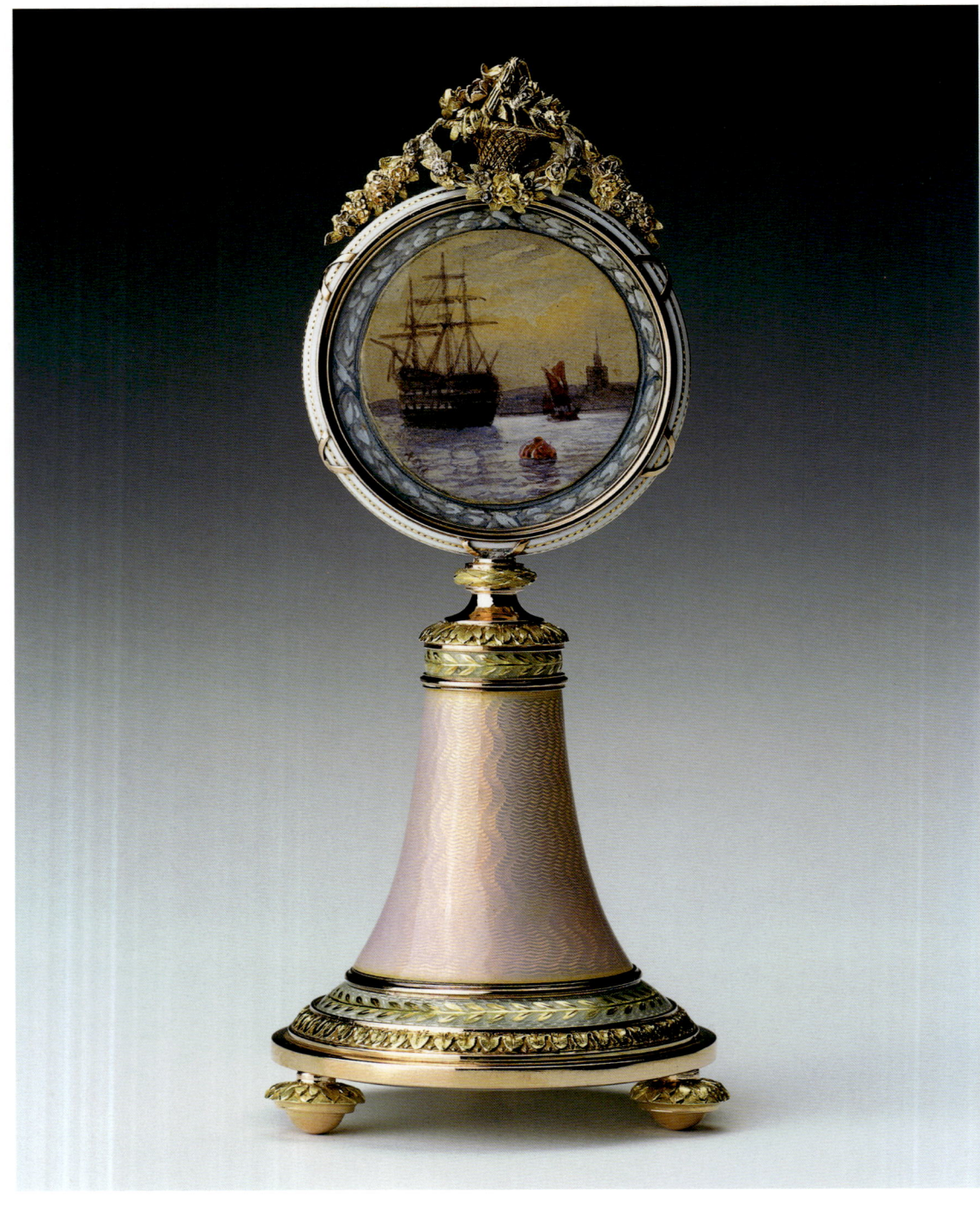

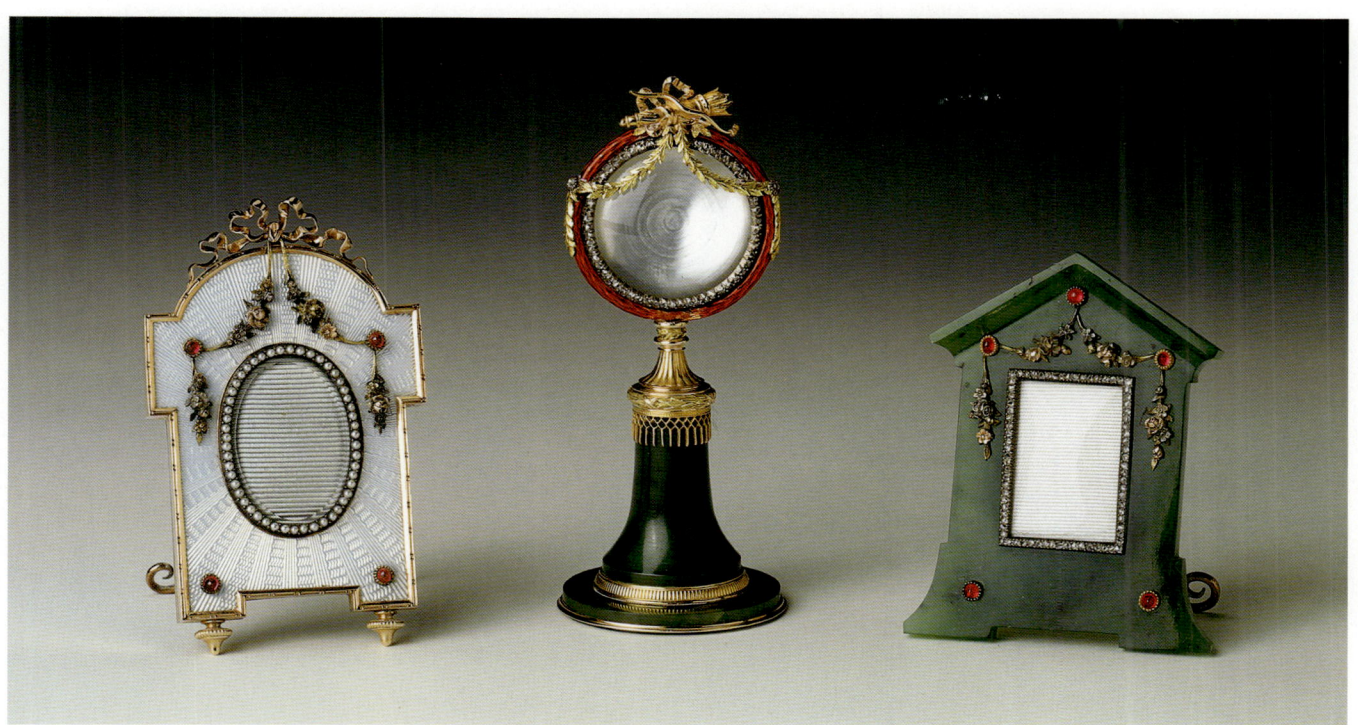

230 FRAME, 1896–1908

Four-colour gold, guilloché enamel, seed pearls, cabochon rubies, mother-of-pearl, 6.7 x 4.1 x 5 cm (2⁵/₈ x 1⁵/₈ x 1¹⁵/₁₆")
Mark of Viktor Aarne; gold mark of 56 *zolotniks* (1896–1908); *FABERGÉ* in Cyrillic characters
RCIN 100308
PROVENANCE: Acquired by Queen Elizabeth before 1962
REFERENCES: Snowman 1962, pl. 193

231 COLUMN SURMOUNTED BY CIRCULAR FRAME, *c.*1900

Fabergé's range of frames included a number surmounted on pedestals or columns. There are two other examples in the Royal Collection (cat. 222 and 229). This frame was a birthday present to Queen Mary from Queen Elizabeth in 1946.

Nephrite, two-colour gold, guilloché enamel, rose diamonds, mother-of-pearl, 8.7 x diameter 3.4 cm (3⁷/₁₆ x 1⁵/₁₆")
Unmarked
RCIN 9016
PROVENANCE: Given to Queen Mary by Queen Elizabeth, 26 May 1946
REFERENCES: QMPP XI, no. 2
EXHIBITIONS: QG 1995–6, no. 479

232 FRAME, 1896–1908

Nephrite, silver-gilt, four-colour gold, cabochon rubies, rose diamonds, mother-of-pearl, 5.8 x 4.5 x 0.6 cm
(2⁵/₁₆ x 1³/₄ x ¹/₄")
Mark of Viktor Aarne; silver mark of 88 *zolotniks* (1896–1908); *FABERGÉ* in Cyrillic characters
RCIN 100309
PROVENANCE: Bought by Queen Elizabeth from Wartski, 2 February 1947 (£65)
REFERENCES: Snowman 1962, pl. 193
EXHIBITIONS: Munich 1986–7, no. 251

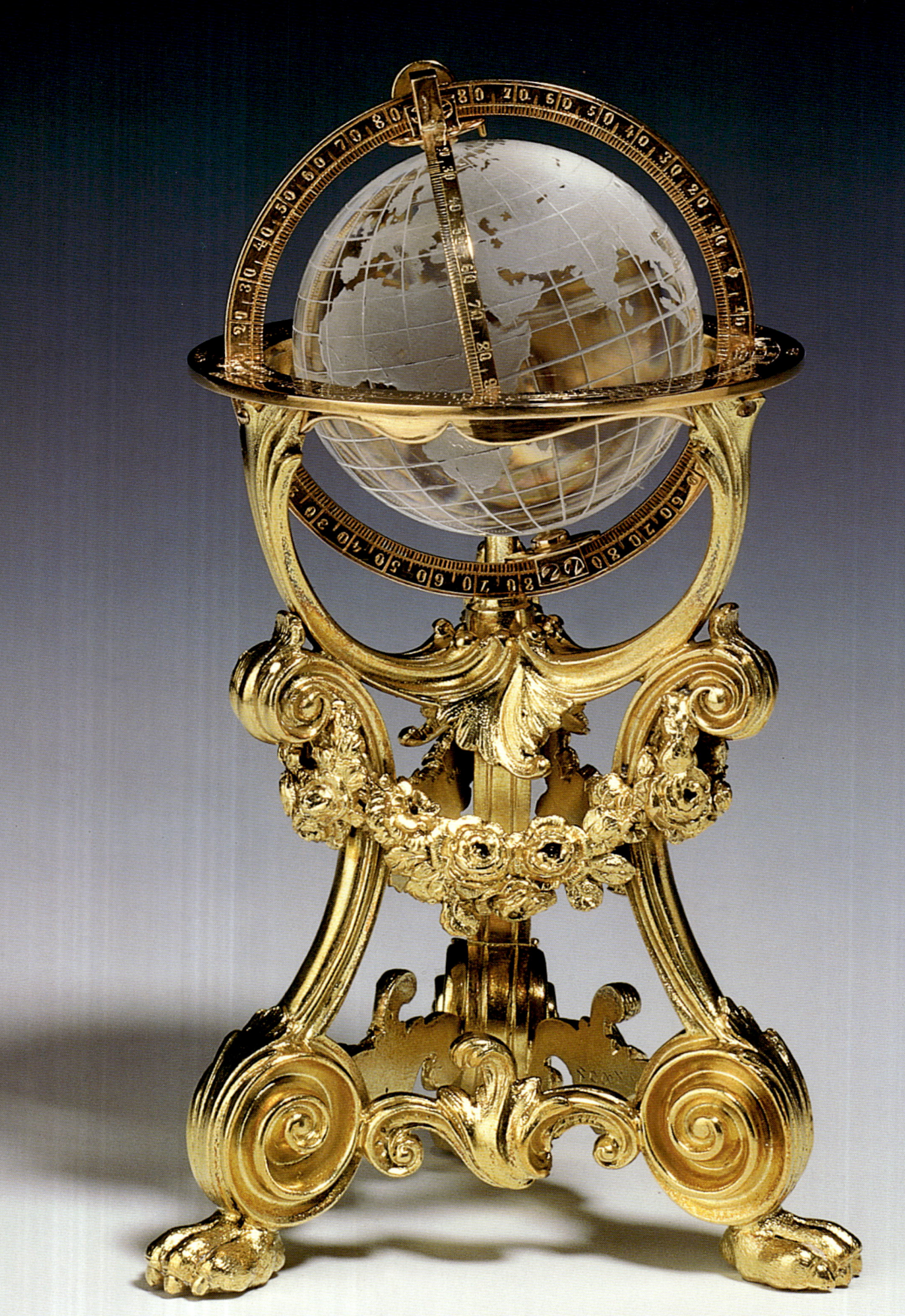

BIBELOTS AND JEWELLERY

FABERGÉ PRODUCED some objects of a whimsical nature, including carved hardstone figures, miniature objects such as furniture, scientific instruments and automata. All were made in relatively small numbers. The Royal Collection contains a group assembled principally by King Edward VII and Queen Alexandra, and by King George V and Queen Mary.

The hardstone figure of a Chelsea pensioner (cat. 234) in the Royal Collection is one of a small number of figures of English types made by Fabergé. In total Fabergé made approximately sixty individual figures, primarily of traditional Russian types. He would have been aware of earlier examples, notably those from the 'Peoples of Russia' series taken from models by J.D. Rachette (1744–1809) and made by the Imperial Porcelain Factory in 1780. Examples are in the Hermitage Museum, St Petersburg. Fabergé's figures appear to be the first made in Russian hardstone. According to Birbaum, they were modelled by Savitski and Frödman-Cluzel.[1]

There are five pieces of miniature furniture in the Royal Collection: two tables, a piano, a desk and a globe. They afforded Fabergé's workmasters the opportunity to experiment with different styles, notably interpretations of Louis XV and Louis XVI designs. These pieces are extraordinary for their attention to detail – especially the desk (cat. 246), with a miniature key opening its drop front to reveal mother-of-pearl compartments, and the rock crystal globe, perfectly engraved with a geographically accurate map of the world. These pieces appear to have been made purely to bring delight to their owners, although some of them served as bonbonnières. Other miniature objects include

a finely carved portrait bust in smoky topaz of Tsar Alexander III, surmounting a nephrite column.

There are few pieces of Fabergé jewellery in the Royal Collection for, unlike their Russian relatives, the British royal family placed no commissions with Fabergé for jewellery. Large amounts of fine jewellery ranging from tiaras, necklaces and rings were produced for the imperial family and other Russian clients in August Holmström's workshop – Holmström was Fabergé's chief jeweller until 1903. Bolin, Russian court jewellers from the 1860s, retained most jewellery commissions for the imperial family until the Revolution, but Fabergé fulfilled many important commissions, including a pearl and diamond necklace given by Nicholas II to his bride Princess Alix of Hesse.[2] In addition Fabergé made a series of pieces of jewellery in gold inspired by antiquities – notably the Scythian treasure unearthed at Kerch in the Crimea, but there are no pieces of jewellery in this style in the Royal Collection. Such jewellery as exists is of a modest nature and includes pendants, brooches, cuff links and stick pins enamelled and set with semi-precious stones. Many of these objects were purchased from Fabergé's London branch, but almost all were given away.

There are three Fabergé fans in the Royal Collection, two of which are included here. They are a good example of the type of accessory which Fabergé designed for his female clientele; this included evening purses, lorgnettes, compacts and scent bottles.

1   Habsburg & Lopato 1993, p. 459.
2   Op. cit., p. 24.

233 BUST OF TSAR ALEXANDER III, *c.*1900

There is another miniature portrait bust of Tsar Alexander III in the Forbes Collection, New York. It too is carved from smoky quartz and is mounted on a nephrite column. It was made in Henrik Wigström's workshop in 1912 and was therefore a commemorative piece (the Tsar having died in 1894), possibly in connection with the Romanov dynasty's tercentenary, which was celebrated in 1913.

The bust in the Royal Collection shows Alexander III in uniform wearing full decorations. It is a more detailed carving than that in the Forbes Collection and bears the Romanov eagles on the column instead of Alexander III's cypher.

Smoky quartz, nephrite, two-colour gold, 17.6 x 7.5 x 5.3 cm (6^{15}/$_{16}$ x 2^{15}/$_{16}$ x 2^{1}/$_{16}$")
Unmarked
RCIN 40512
PROVENANCE: Queen Alexandra; Princess Victoria's collection
REFERENCES: Tillander-Godenhielm *et al.* 2000, p. 76
EXHIBITIONS: London 1935; London 1977, no H2; QG 1985–6, no. 116; QG 1995–6, no. 159

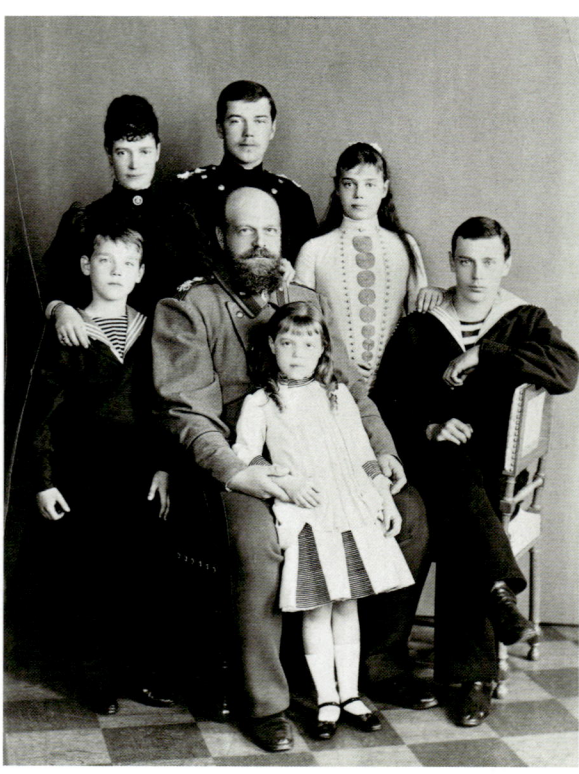

Tsar Alexander III with his family, c.1888

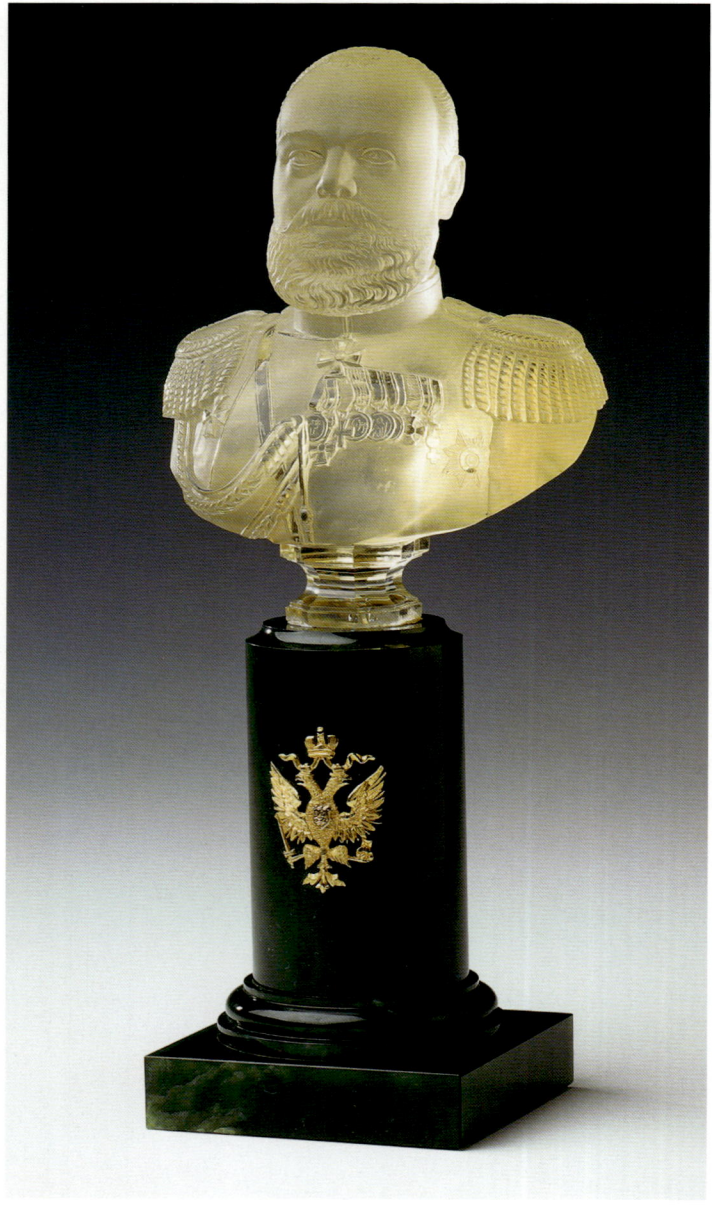

234 CHELSEA PENSIONER, 1909

Carl Fabergé utilised the wealth of naturally occurring hardstones and the expert skill of his craftsmen to produce a vast number of hardstone carvings. These were principally of birds, animals and flowers, as well as functional items, but included a small number of figurines. According to Bainbridge, it was Grand Duke Nicholas (1856–1929), the grandson of Tsar Nicholas I, who first suggested to Fabergé that he should make figurines. Sixteen were paid for by Tsar Nicholas II and others were purchased by Emanuel Nobel and the King of Siam.

It appears that sixty figurines at most were made in Fabergé's workshops; the precise number has not been established. Birbaum explains in his memoirs that the reason for this small output was the lack of experienced masters due to the outbreak of the First World War. Technically, the figures required a great deal of skill in the designing, carving and combining of different stones and metals. The names of the modellers are known only in a few cases, for example Georgi Konstantinovich Savitski (1887–1947) and Boris Frödman-Cluzel.

The figurines were modelled by the sculptors, then cut, carved and polished by the stonecarvers. Finally the silver and gold parts were added. The majority of the figurines are of traditional Russian types such as soldiers and ice-carriers. In addition actual portraits were made, for example of the Dowager Tsarina Marie Feodorovna's *kamer-kazak* (personal bodyguard). This was assembled in Wigström's workshop. Bainbridge mentions that Fabergé made models of a few English types, such as a policeman and Alice in Wonderland. He also refers to a 'Yeoman of the Guard' in the Sandringham collection; this is presumably the Chelsea pensioner, being the only example of a figure in the Royal Collection. According to Bainbridge, Lord Revelstoke, one of Fabergé's best customers – who travelled a great deal between St Petersburg and London – was the first to bring figurines to London.

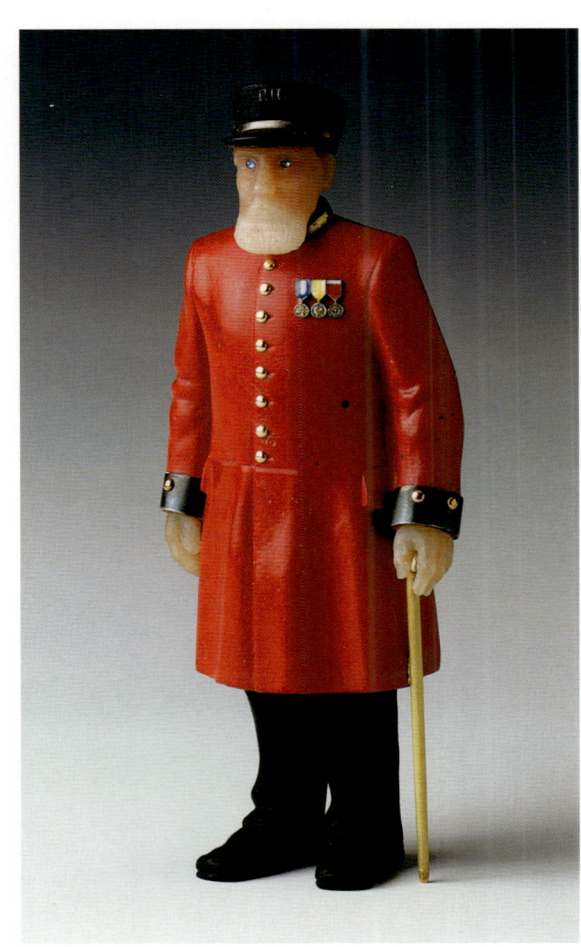

The term 'Chelsea pensioner' is derived from the in-pensioners of the Royal Hospital, Chelsea, established by Charles II in 1682. These veteran soldiers of meritorious service are housed in Sir Christopher Wren's building on the Chelsea Embankment.

Purpurine, aventurine quartz, jasper, gunmetal, gold, enamel, cabochon sapphires, 11.2 x 4.5 x 2 cm (4⁷⁄₁₆ x 1³⁄₄ x ¹³⁄₁₆")
Unmarked
RCIN 40485
PROVENANCE: Bought by King Edward VII on his last visit to Fabergé's London branch, 22 November 1909 (£49 15s)
REFERENCES: Skurlov 1997, pp. 33–8
EXHIBITIONS: London 1953, no. 94; London 1967, no. 188; London 1977, no. K5; New York 1983, no. 197; QG 1985–6, no. 115; Munich 1986–7, no. 385; QG 1995–6, no. 212; QG 2002–3, no. 208

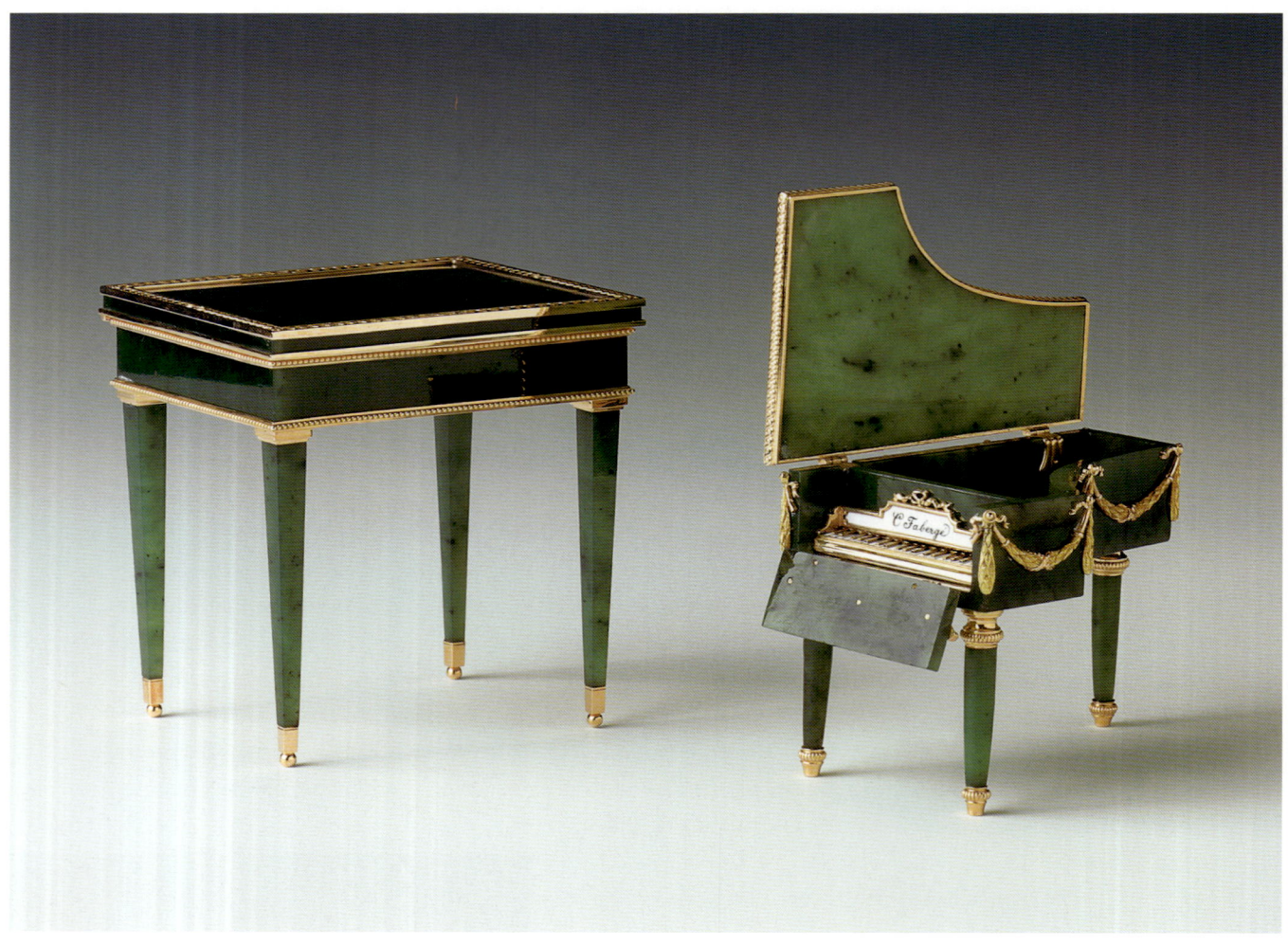

235 MINIATURE TABLE IN THE LOUIS XVI STYLE, 1896–1903

Fabergé produced a number of bibelots in the form of miniature furniture. Some, like this table, were intended to be used as bonbonnières.

Nephrite, gold, 7.4 x 7.1 x 5.8 cm (2¹⁵/₁₆ x 2¹³/₁₆ x 2⁵/₁₆")
Mark of Michael Perchin; gold mark of 56 *zolotniks* (1896–1908); *FABERGÉ* in Cyrillic characters
RCIN 9021
PROVENANCE: Presented to Queen Mary by Lord Revelstoke, Christmas 1921
REFERENCES: QMB I, no. 25; QMPP IV, no. 28
EXHIBITIONS: QG 1985–6, no. 19; QG 1995–6, no. 370

236 MINIATURE PIANO IN THE LOUIS XVI STYLE, BEFORE 1896

The lid of the piano opens and the front drops down to reveal the keyboard, which is enamelled *C. Fabergé*.

Nephrite, two-colour gold, enamel, 5.5 x 7.3 x 4.5 cm (2³/₁₆ x 2⁷/₈ x 1³/₄")
Mark of Michael Perchin; gold mark of 56 *zolotniks* (before 1896); enamelled above the keyboard *C. Fabergé* in Roman letters
RCIN 9030
PROVENANCE: Queen Mary's collection, acquired between 1922 and 1931
REFERENCES: QMB II, no. 437; QMPP V, no. 180
EXHIBITIONS: London 1954; London 1977, no. K23; QG 1985–6, no. 28; QG 1995–6, no. 374

237   MINIATURE PENCIL, 1908–1917

Two-colour gold, guilloché enamel, 4.2 x diameter 0.7 cm (1⅝ x ¼")
Mark of Karl Armfelt; gold mark of 56 *zolotniks* (1908–17)
RCIN 18643
PROVENANCE: Probably acquired by Queen Alexandra, *c*.1910

238   MINIATURE PATCH BOX, 1896–1908

An almost identical box enamelled in turquoise is in the Forbes Collection.

Gold, guilloché enamel, rose diamonds, 0.8 x 2.1 x 1.4 cm (⁵⁄₁₆ x ¹³⁄₁₆ x ⁹⁄₁₆")
Moscow gold mark of 56 *zolotniks* (1896–1908); label inscribed *From Xenia*
RCIN 18644
PROVENANCE: Grand Duchess Xenia of Russia (1875–1960); by whom given to Queen Mary
REFERENCES: Forbes & Tromeur-Brenner 1999, pp. 166–7
EXHIBITIONS: QG 1995–6, no. 230

239   MINIATURE MAGNIFYING GLASS, *c*.1900

Even for the most minute and barely functional objects, Fabergé's level of craftsmanship and quality of finish was always of an extremely high standard.

Gold, guilloché enamel, glass, 6.9 x 2.3 x 0.5 cm (2¹¹⁄₁₆ x ⅞ x ³⁄₁₆")
RCIN 18642
PROVENANCE: Probably acquired by Queen Alexandra, *c*.1900
EXHIBITIONS: QG 1995–6, no. 247

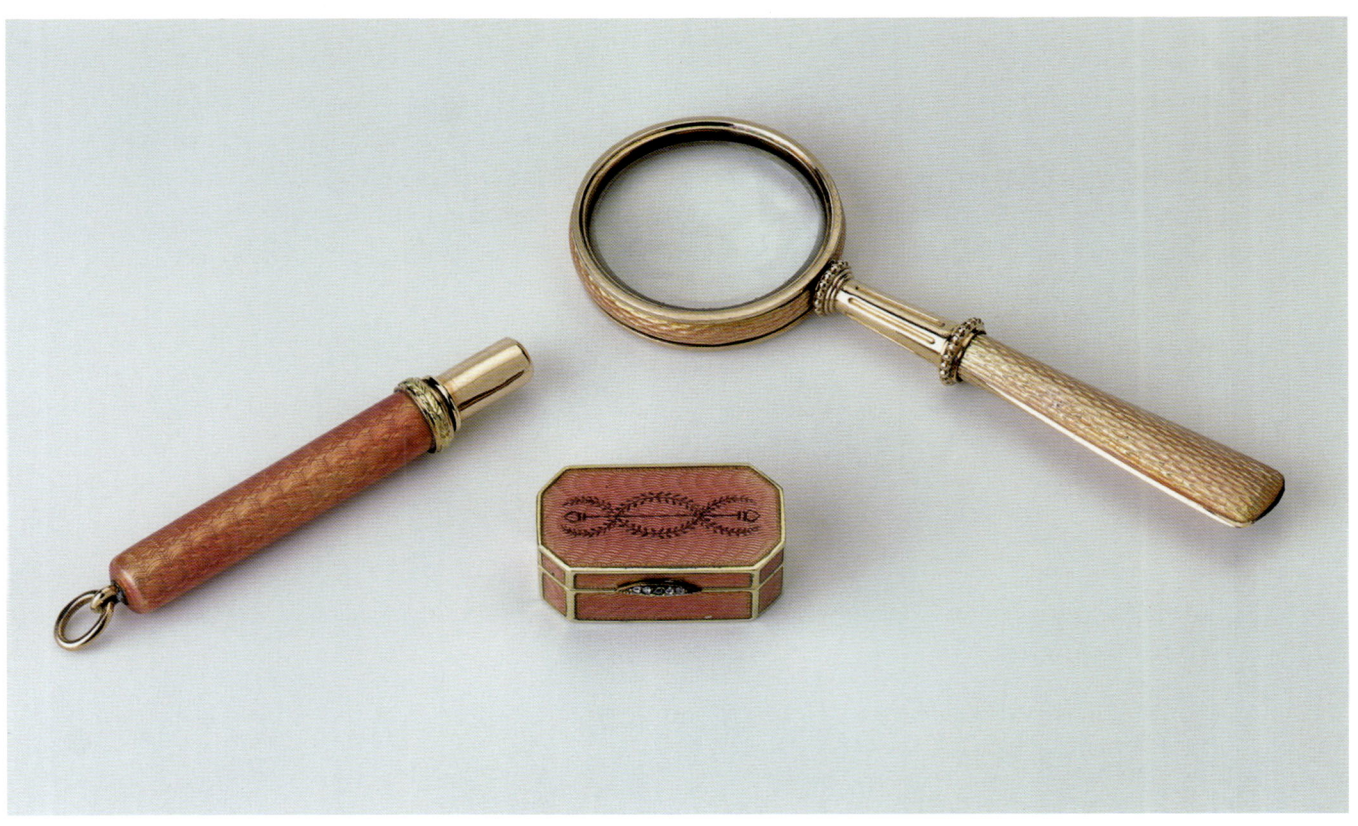

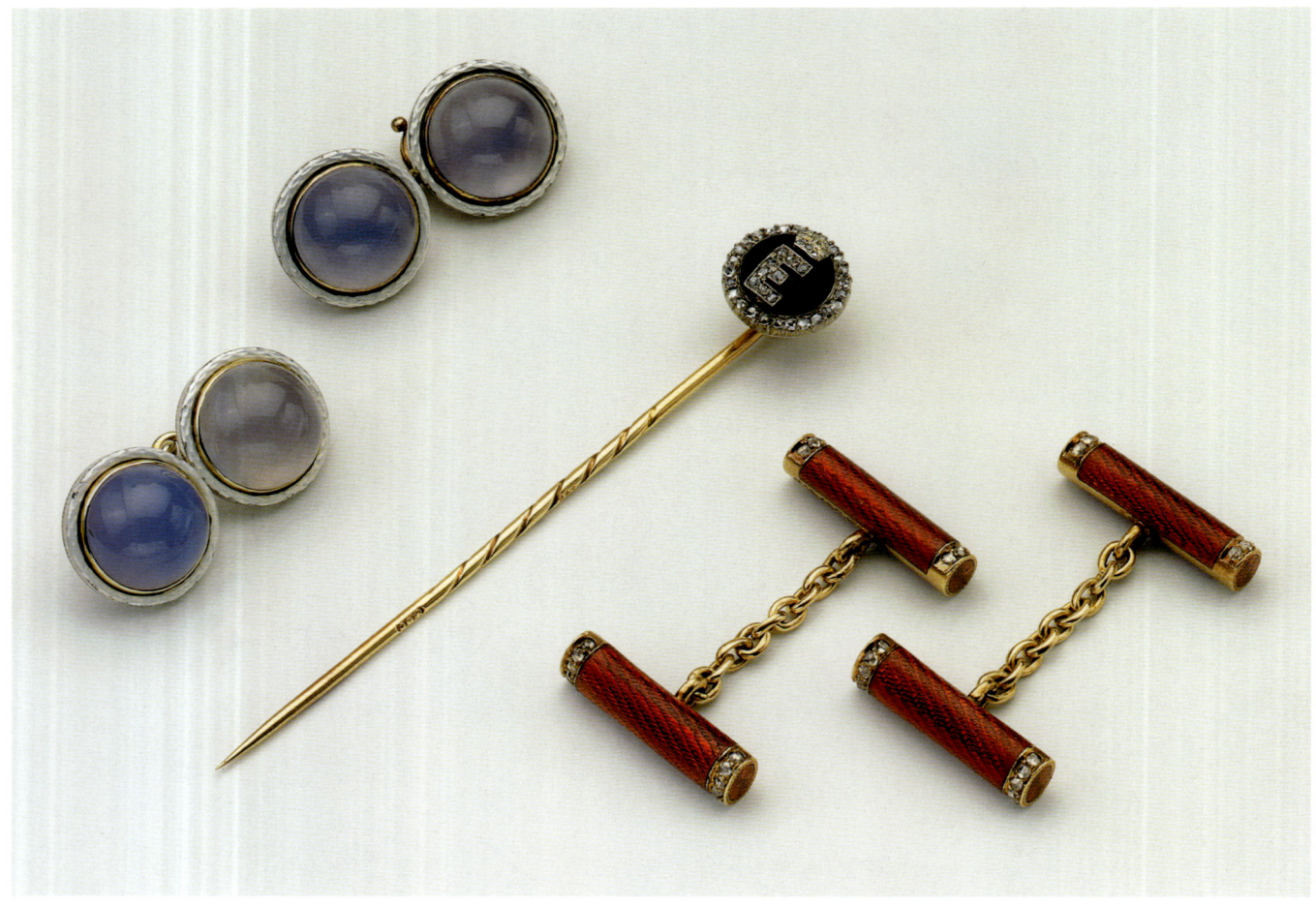

240 CUFF LINKS, *c.*1908

Fabergé's London branch supplied numerous pairs of cuff links to its royal customers. These ranged in price from £10 to the most expensive at £36. Together with brooches, pendants, tie-pins, studs and buttons in enamel set with semi-precious rather than precious stones, they made relatively inexpensive presents. This pair was made in the workshop of Alfred Thielemann, who was head of Fabergé's second jewellery workshop from 1880, specialising in small jewels, trinkets and decorations.

Gold, enamel, cabochon chalcedony, 0.8 x diameter 1.4 cm (⁵/₁₆ x ⁹/₁₆")
Mark of Alfred Thielemann; gold mark of 56 *zolotniks*
RCIN 43593
PROVENANCE: Bought by Queen Alexandra from Fabergé's London branch, November 1908 (£11 15s)
EXHIBITIONS: QG 1995–6, no. 237

241 TIE-PIN, *c.*1900

Made in the workshop of Eduard Schramm, this pin bears a crowned *E* cypher and was therefore made for King Edward VII.

Gold, enamel, brilliant diamonds, 7.5 x 1 x 0.9 cm (2¹⁵/₁₆ x ³/₈ x ³/₈")
Mark of Eduard Schramm; gold mark of 56 *zolotniks*
RCIN 43669
PROVENANCE: Acquired by King Edward VII, *c.*1900

242   CUFF LINKS, BEFORE 1896

Gold, guilloché enamel, rose diamonds, 0.5 x diameter 1.9 cm ($^3/_{16}$ x $^3/_4$")
Mark of Michael Perchin; gold mark of 56 *zolotniks* (before 1896)
RCIN 43594
PROVENANCE: Probably acquired by Edward, Prince of Wales (later King Edward VII), date unknown
EXHIBITIONS: QG 1995–6, no. 234

243   BROOCH, *c.*1900

Numerous brooches were purchased from Fabergé's London branch by the royal family, but none of the
descriptions matches this one. The central stone is a cabochon chalcedony.

Silver-gilt, chalcedony, enamel, rose diamonds, rubies, 3.7 x 3.7 x 1.9 cm (1$^7/_{16}$ x 1$^7/_{16}$ x $^3/_4$")
Engraved *FABERGÉ* in Cyrillic characters
RCIN 23461
PROVENANCE: Probably acquired by Queen Alexandra, *c.*1900
EXHIBITIONS: QG 1995–6, no. 236

244   OVAL PENDANT, *c.*1900

Of art nouveau style, decorated with irises, this pendant does not bear a workmaster's mark. Much of
Fabergé's jewellery was produced in Holmström's workshop but this pendant is quite different in
style and design from his pieces.

Gold, *pliqué-a-jour* enamel, rose diamonds, 2.6 x 1.5 x 0.3 cm (1 x $^9/_{16}$ x $^1/_8$")
Engraved *FABERGÉ* in Cyrillic characters
RCIN 14584
PROVENANCE: Acquired by Queen Alexandra, date unknown
EXHIBITIONS: QG 1995–6, no. 231

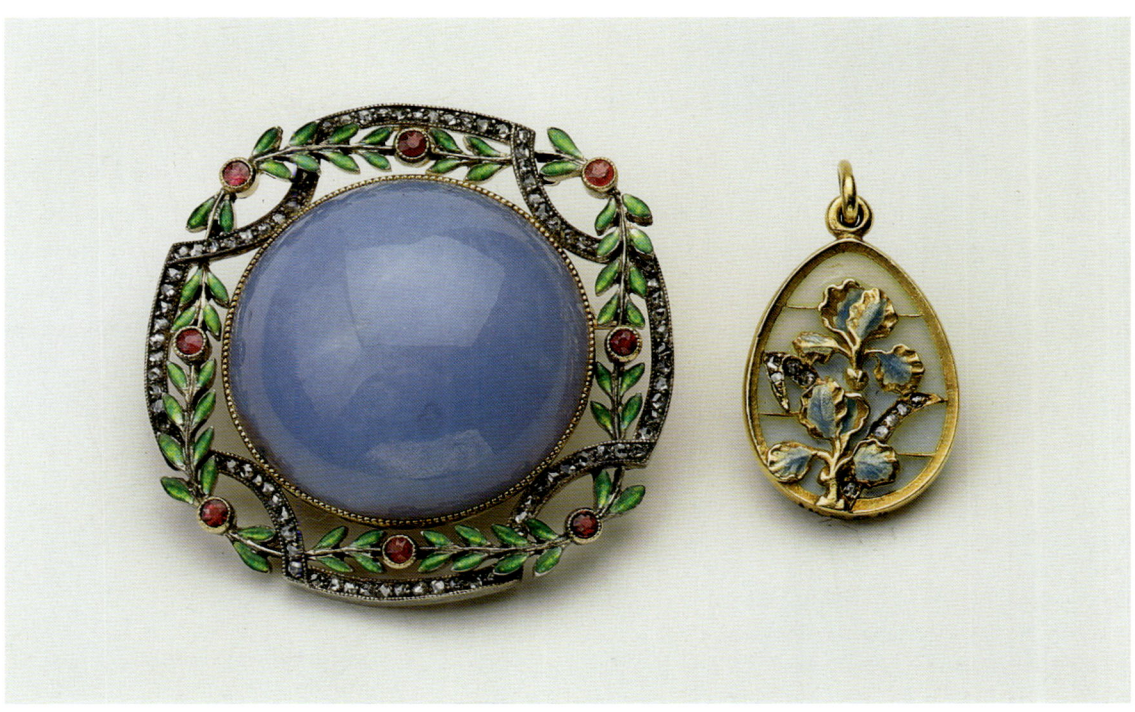

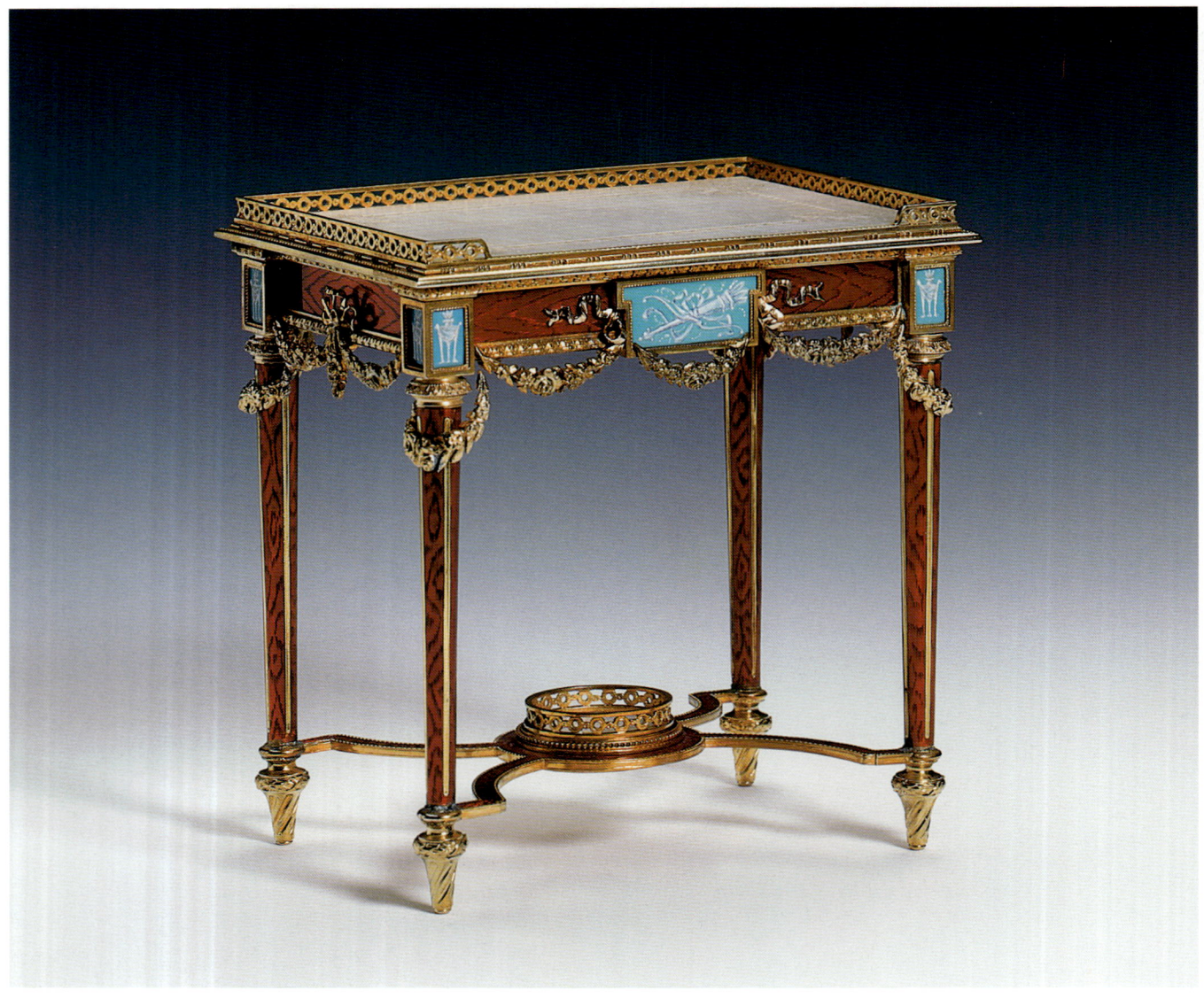

245 MINIATURE TABLE, 1896–1903

This, the second Louis XVI-style table in the Royal Collection, is also from Perchin's workshop (see cat. 235). The clever use of materials includes red guilloché enamel to imitate wood veneer, two-coloured gold mounts to imitate gilt-bronze and blue-and-white enamel plaques to imitate Sèvres porcelain. The eight plaques above the legs have been described previously as incorporating the cypher of Tsarina Marie Feodorovna, but this is not obvious on close examination. The mother-of-pearl top, in imitation of marble, is engraved with the Romanov eagles and the central shelf joining the legs is lined with mother-of-pearl. A very similar table, also by Perchin, is in the Forbes Collection and a further Louis XVI-style table by Perchin, but of a different form, is in the Hermitage.

Gold, mother-of-pearl, guilloché enamel, 8.9 x 8.4 x 6.1 cm (3½ x 3⁵⁄₁₆ x 2³⁄₈")
Mark of Michael Perchin; gold mark of 56 *zolotniks* (1896–1908); *FABERGÉ* in Cyrillic characters
RCIN 9142
PROVENANCE: Bought by Queen Mary from Wartski, 22 November 1947 (£650)
REFERENCES: QMPP XI, no. 45; Snowman 1962, pl. LIV
EXHIBITIONS: London 1948; London 1977, no. K4; New York 1983, no. 182; QG 1985–6, no. 80; Munich 1986–7, no. 527; QG 1995–6, no. 244; Stockholm 1997, no. 148; QG 2002–3, no. 270

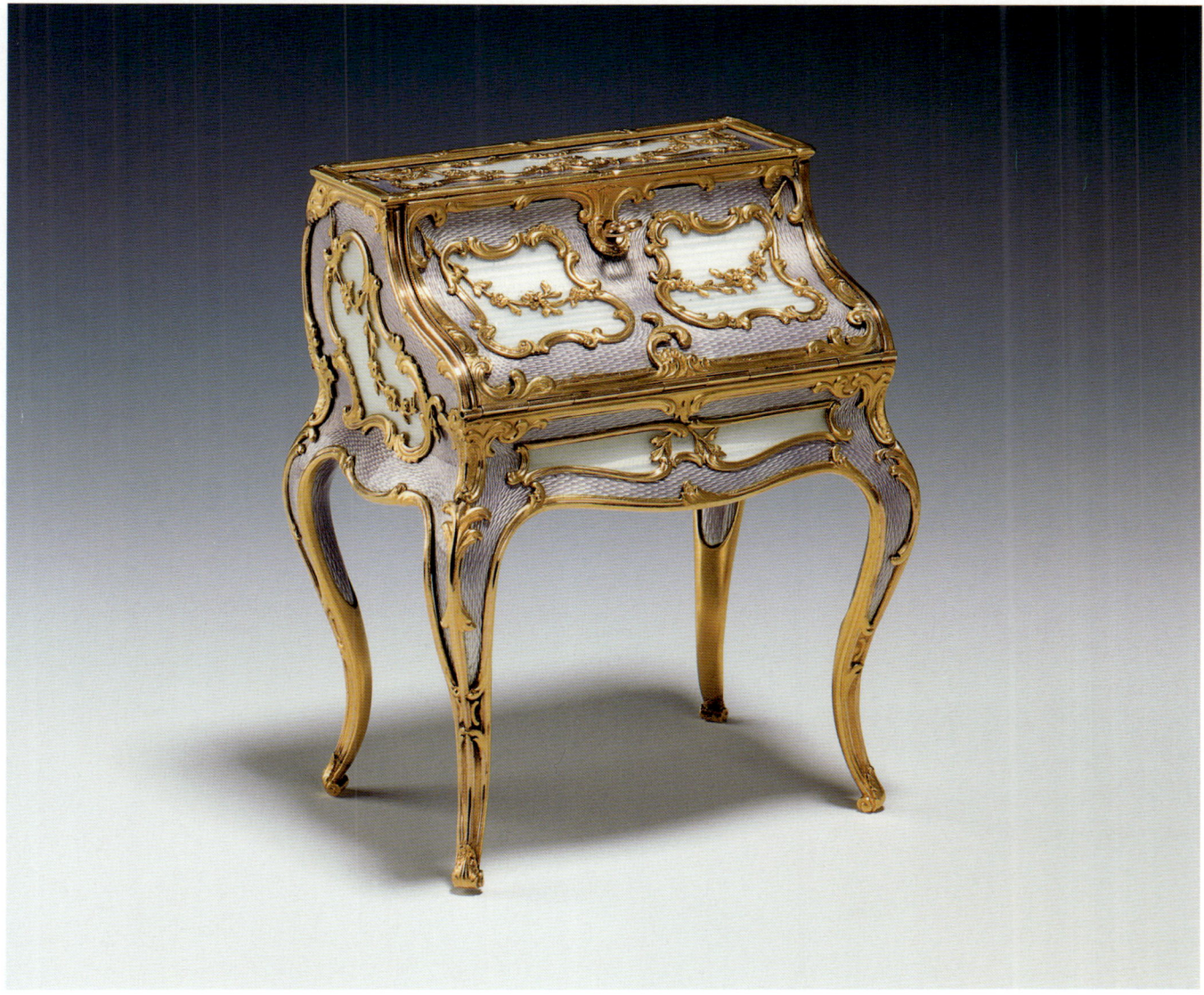

246 MINIATURE DESK, 1896–1908

The drop front of this Louis XV-style roll-top desk with rococo mounts opens by means of a miniature gold key to reveal an interior lined with engraved mother-of-pearl and divided into compartments.
Although the workmaster's mark is now illegible, the neo-rococo design is reminiscent of the objects produced in Perchin's workshop. The attention to detail, particularly in the fine mauve and opalescent white
enamel on a minute scale, exemplifies Fabergé's exacting standards of workmanship.

Two-colour gold, guilloché enamel, engraved mother-of-pearl, 11 x 8.7 x 6.5 cm (4⁵/₁₆ x 3⁷/₁₆ x 2⁹/₁₆")
Illegible workmaster's mark; gold mark of 56 *zolotniks* (1896–1908); *FABERGÉ* in Cyrillic characters
RCIN 100013
PROVENANCE: Bought by Leopold de Rothschild at Fabergé's London branch, 12 July 1909 (£150 15s); acquired by
Queen Elizabeth, date unknown
REFERENCES: Snowman 1962, p. 165
EXHIBITIONS: London 1953, no. 122; London 1977, no. F6; QG 1985–6, no. 78; Munich 1986–7, no. 526;
QG 1995–6, no. 262; Stockholm 1997, no. 147; QG 2002–3, no. 272

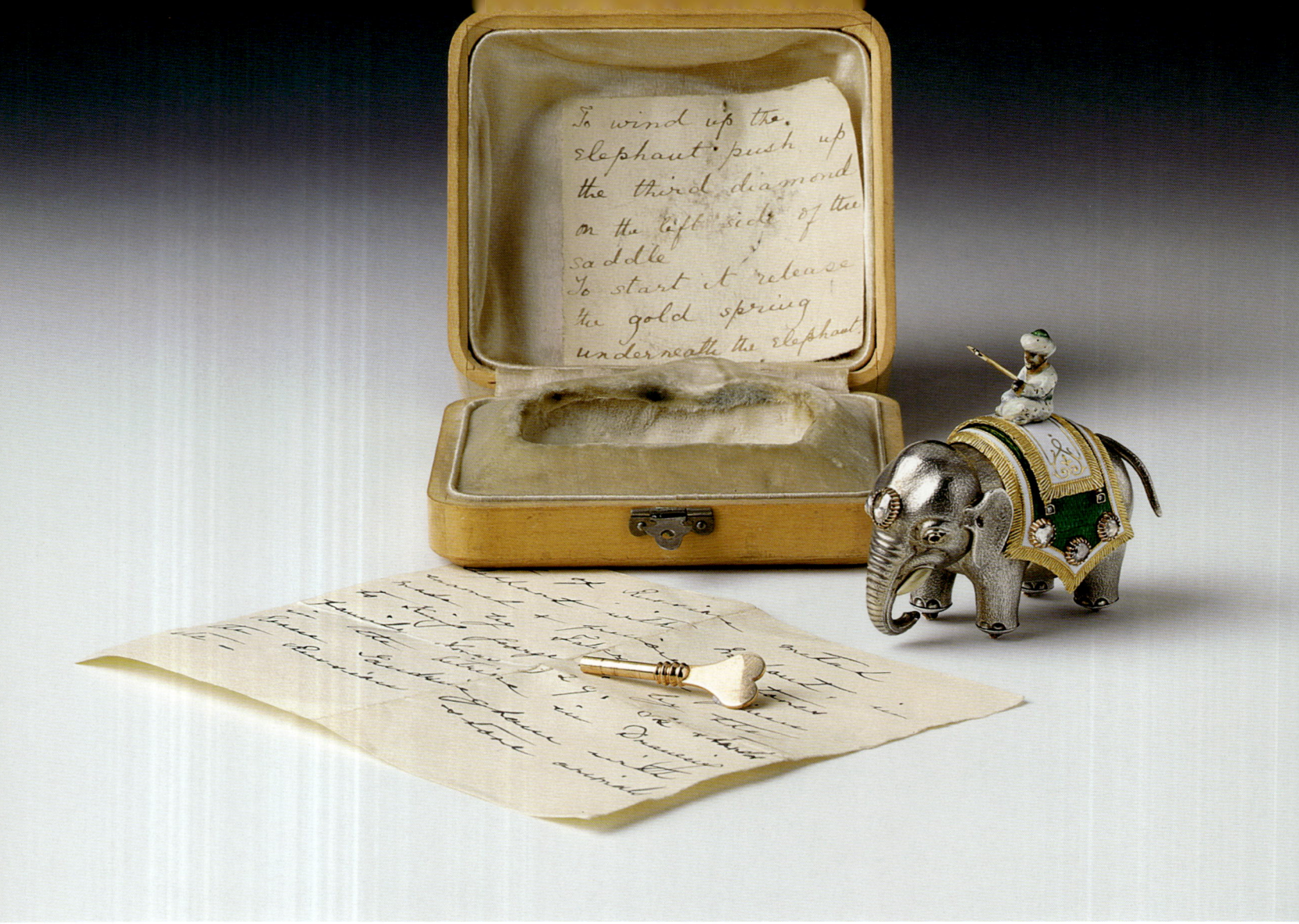

247 ELEPHANT AUTOMATON, *c.*1900

Fabergé produced several automata, usually as the 'surprises' in his Imperial Easter Eggs. The automated sedan chair from the Grisaille Egg of 1914 is one example and an elephant automaton of almost identical design to this one serves as the surprise in the Pine Cone Egg of 1900, one of the seven eggs commissioned by Alexander and Barbara Kelch to rival those of the imperial family (see cat. 4).

     The date of production and original purchaser of this automaton are not known. Like many of Fabergé's automata, the mechanism is wound with a key. When released, the elephant walks, swinging its head and trunk. The tail is also articulated. Queen Mary, who with her family gave this elephant to King George V for Christmas 1929, made a note about its provenance which, together with instructions for its operation, is kept in the original fitted case supplied by Fabergé. According to Queen Mary's note, the automaton was kept in a vitrine in the Drawing Room at Sandringham with the other Fabergé animals.

Silver, gold, guilloché enamel, rose diamonds, cabochon rubies, ivory, 4.8 x 5.1 x 3.2 cm (1⁷⁄₈ x 2 x 1¼")
RCIN 40486
PROVENANCE: Presented to King George V by his family, Christmas 1929
REFERENCES: Fabergé, Proler, Skurlov 1997, p. 73
EXHIBITIONS: London 1953, no. 18; London 1977, no. C21; QG 1985–6, no. 148; QG 1995–6, no. 148

248 TERRESTRIAL GLOBE, BEFORE 1896

This globe was produced in the workshop of Erik Kollin. It is an early example of Fabergé's characteristic use of different coloured golds in combination with silver-gilt. Another terrestrial globe by Fabergé is now in the Lillian Thomas Pratt Collection, Virginia Museum of Fine Arts, Richmond. The rock crystal globe is geographically accurate and is an exemplary demonstration of the carving skills of the craftsmen concerned. A further, similarly engraved globe surmounts a nephrite clock, now in the Forbes Collection.

Rock crystal, gold, silver-gilt, 10.5 x diameter 6 cm (4¹⁄₈ x 2³⁄₈")
Mark of Erik Kollin; gold mark of 56 *zolotniks* and silver mark of 88 *zolotniks* (before 1896); *FABERGÉ* in Cyrillic characters
RCIN 40484
PROVENANCE: Bought by Tsar Nicholas II, 31 December 1897 (350 roubles); Prince Vladimir Galitzine; from whom bought by Queen Mary, 16 December 1928 (£25 2s; archives of Princess George Galitzine)
REFERENCES: Snowman 1962, p. 164; Habsburg 2000; Forbes & Tromeur-Brenner 1999, p. 72
EXHIBITIONS: London 1953, no. 108; London 1977, no. 19; New York 1983, no. 21; QG 1985–6, no. 119; QG 1995–6, no. 258; Stockholm 1997, no. 146; QG 2002–3, no. 271

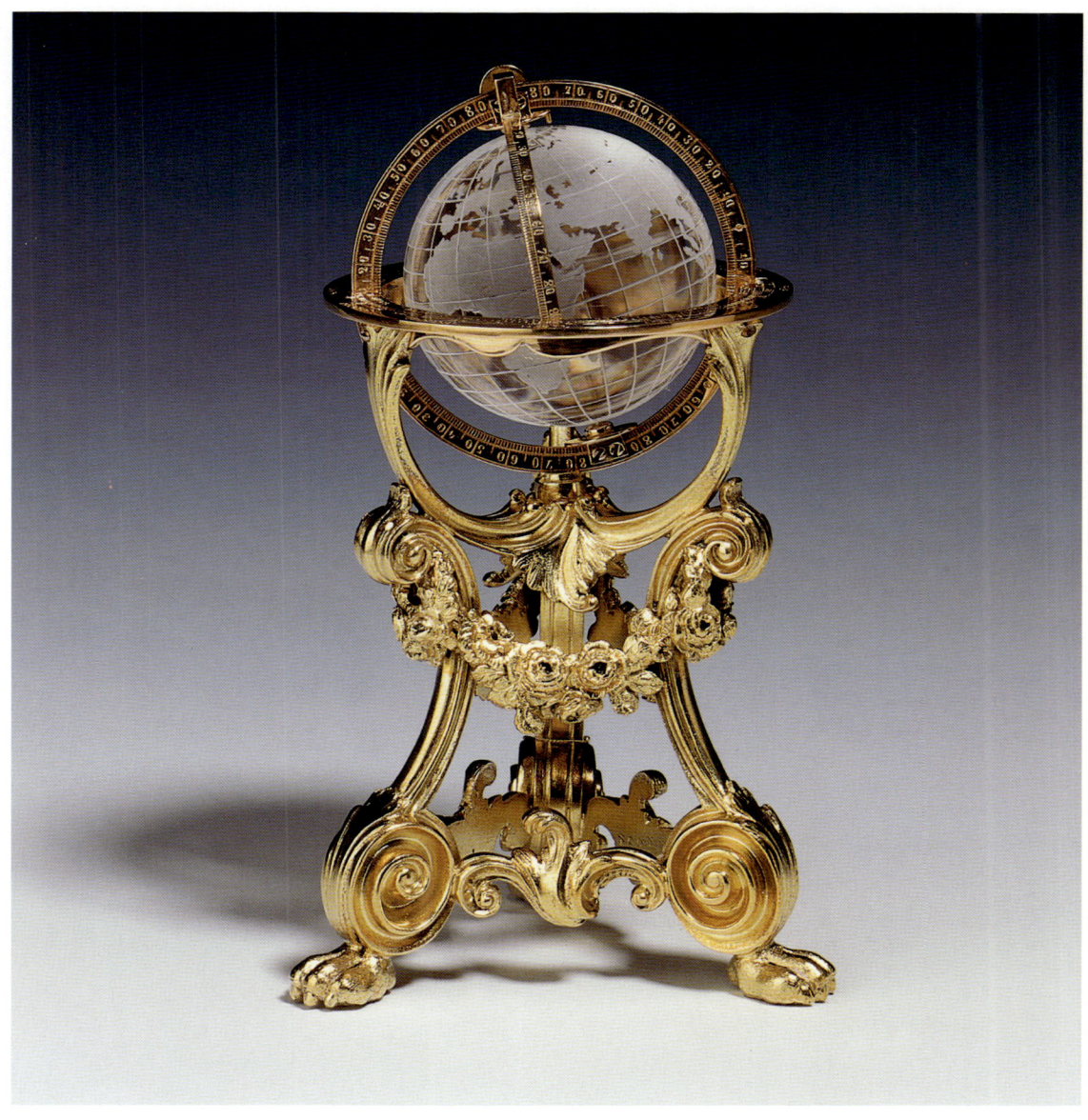

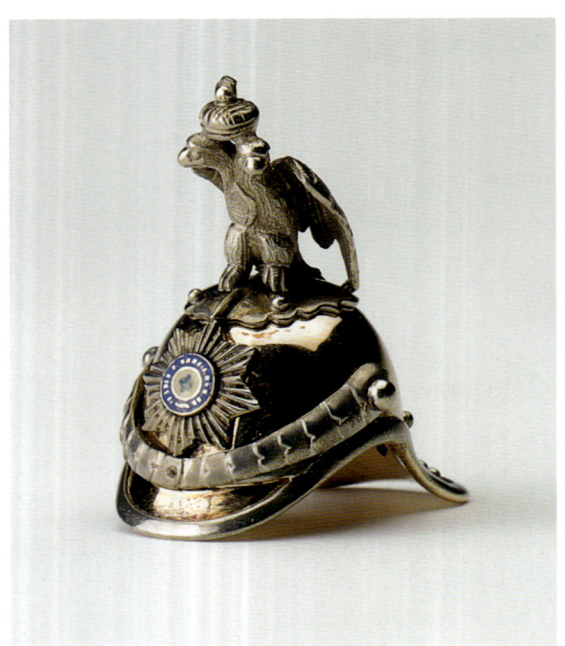

249 MINIATURE HELMET, BEFORE 1896

Fabergé made numerous objects with military associations, often as presentation pieces. Helmets were produced as drinking vessels, although this miniature version is far too small to have been intended as a functional object. It is a helmet of the Imperial Chevalier Guard and is enamelled on the front with the star of the Order of St Andrew. The helmet is surmounted by the imperial eagle. Queen Mary purchased a miniature helmet by Fabergé in 1934 but it is slightly different in design from this one.

Two-colour gold, enamel, 2.3 x 2.3 x 1.5 cm ($^7/_8$ x $^7/_8$ x $^9/_{16}$")
Mark of Erik Kollin; gold mark of 56 *zolotniks* (before 1896)
RCIN 24599
PROVENANCE: Royal Collection by 1953
EXHIBITIONS: QG 1995–6, no. 203

250 FAN, *c*.1912

There are three Fabergé fans in the Royal Collection. This one was made in Henrik Wigström's workshop. The silk is painted with eighteenth-century-style scenes and flowers.

Three-colour gold, guilloché enamel, silk, mother-of-pearl, cabochon rubies, 23 (with ring) x 40.5 x 2.8 cm ($9^1/_{16}$ x $15^{15}/_{16}$ x $1^1/_8$")
Mark of Henrik Wigström; gold mark of 56 *zolotniks* (1908–17); *FABERGÉ* in Cyrillic characters
RCIN 25136
PROVENANCE: Bought by Queen Alexandra from Fabergé's London branch, 24 December 1912 (£26 10s); by whom given to Queen Mary for Christmas
EXHIBITIONS: QG 1995–6, no. 235

251 FAN, *c*.1904

This fan by Henrik Wigström is of mother-of-pearl with gold sequin decoration on silk. It was bought by Tsarina Marie Feodorovna for her sister Queen Alexandra and later given by Queen Mary to Her Majesty The Queen when Princess Elizabeth of York.

Two-colour gold, guilloché enamel, mother-of-pearl, gold sequins, silk, cabochon rubies, rose diamonds, 23.7 (with ring) x 42 x 3.2 cm ($9^5/_{16}$ x $16^9/_{16}$ x $1^1/_4$")
Mark of Henrik Wigström; gold mark of 56 *zolotniks* (1896–1908)
RCIN 25219
PROVENANCE: Bought by the Dowager Tsarina Marie Feodorovna, 25 December 1904 (325 roubles); by whom given to Queen Alexandra; Queen Mary; by whom given to Her Majesty The Queen, when Princess Elizabeth of York, 1932

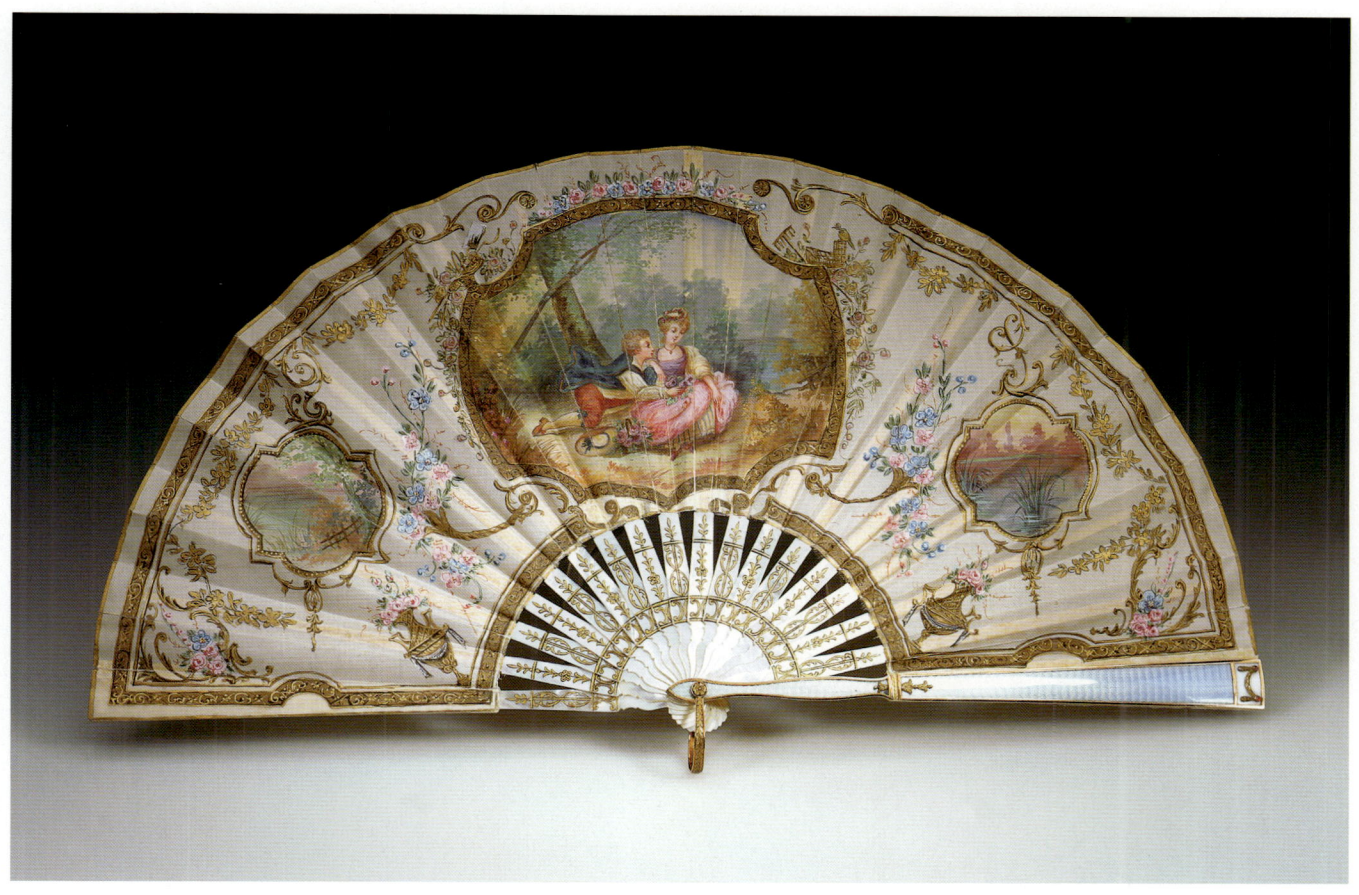

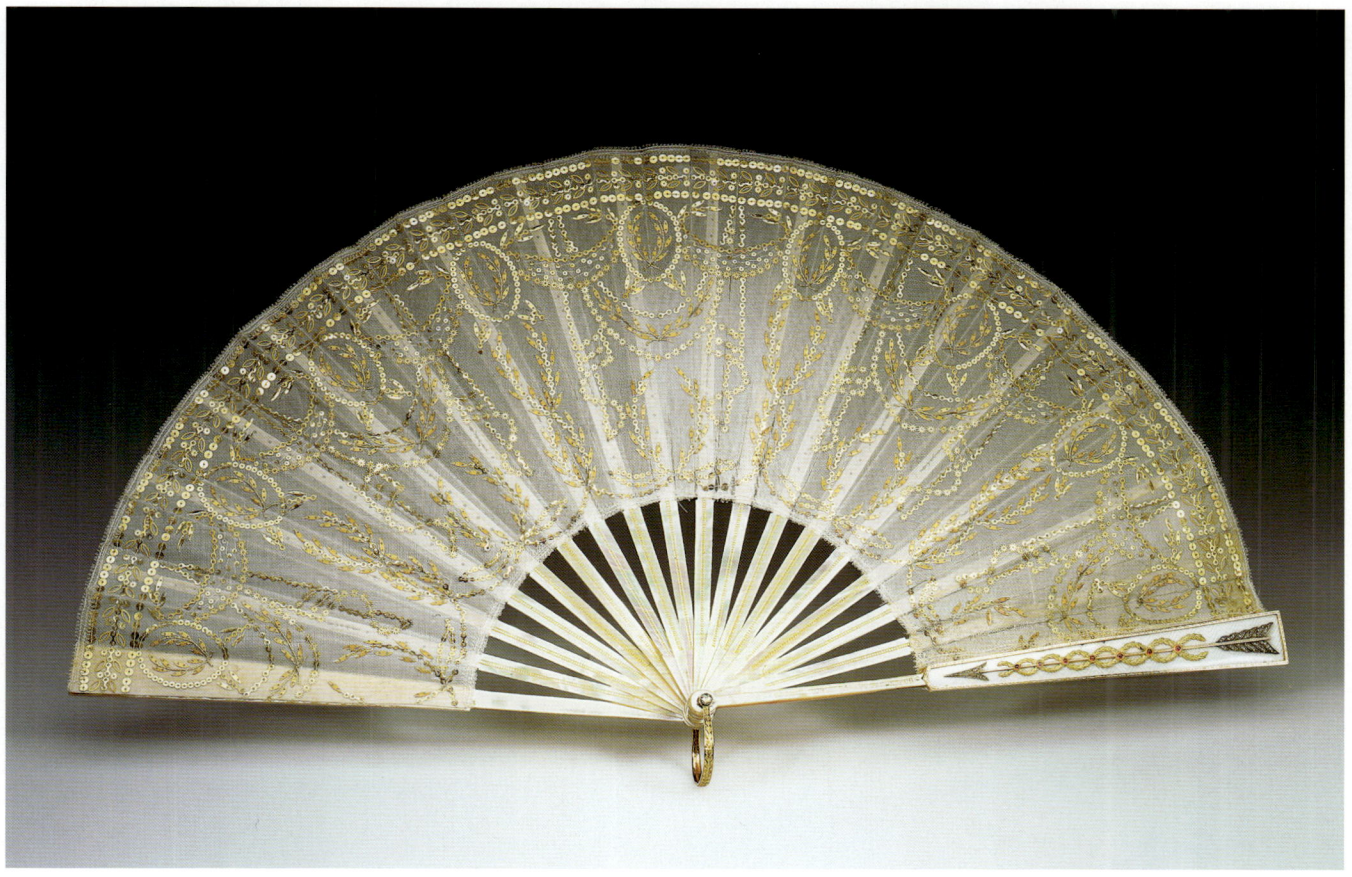

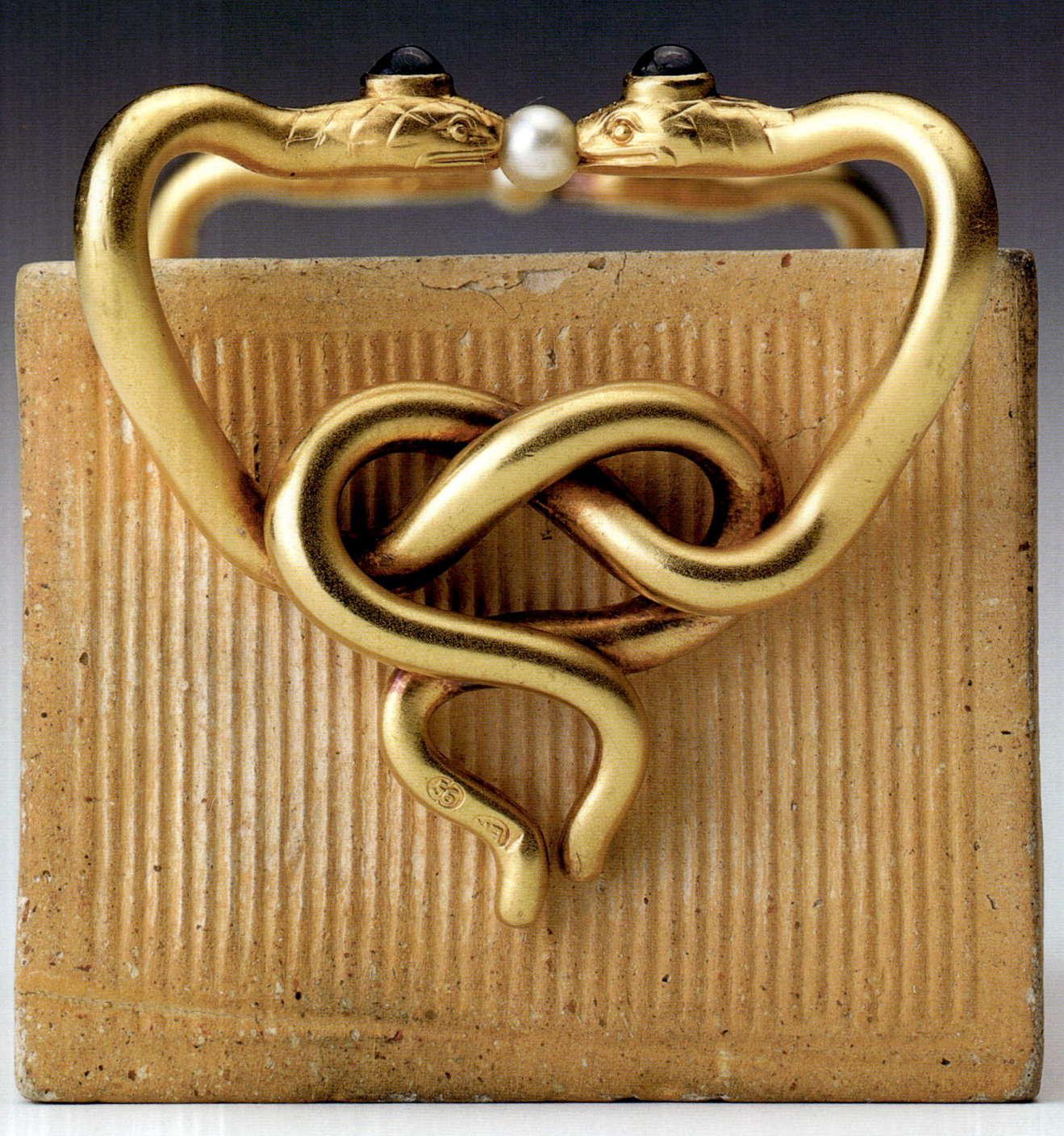

DESK ITEMS AND PRACTICAL OBJECTS

A LARGE PART OF FABERGÉ'S business was based on the supply of silverware, mainly produced in his Moscow workshops. It included tea services, flatware, trays, jugs, vases and bowls. There are several pieces of silver of this kind in the Royal Collection, but they lack the originality of design and technique seen in the objects of a practical nature included here. Many grand silver services were made for the imperial family by Fabergé, including one ordered by Alexander III and completed after his death for Tsar Nicholas II in 1894,[1] but there are no such pieces in the Royal Collection. Orders of this kind would have been commissioned from the British crown jewellers, Garrard. What the Royal Collection does contain, however, is a remarkable variety of practical objects, in an amazing range of designs – cups and beakers, Russian *kovshes* and *tcharki* (small vodka cups), bowls, scent bottles, candlesticks, clocks and every conceivable type of desk accessory.

Fabergé managed to turn the production of desk accessories into an art form, extending his ingenious designs and techniques to all manner of seemingly mundane objects such as stamp boxes, bell pushes, pen rests, seals and paperknives. Some of the most elaborate and charming objects that he made fall into the category of desk accessories. They include a bell push decorated with an elephant (cat. 275), a gum pot in the form of an apple (cat. 314) and an exquisitely enamelled visitor's book (cat. 331). All the objects, however small, incorporate the finest materials and techniques. As already mentioned, Fabergé's designers drew on an extensive range of sources, including earlier Russian artistic traditions.

Of all the groups of objects shown here, the practical objects show the widest variety of styles. There are traditional Russian *kovshes* and *tcharki* in Pan-Slavic (Old Russian) style enamel, many of which were made in the Moscow workshops by Feodor Rückert (cat. 324); nephrite candlesticks with Baroque-style silver mounts (cat. 335); a pen rest and beaker in art nouveau style (cat. 271 and 272) and a scent flacon and snuff bottle of oriental design (cat. 258 and 259). The art nouveau style, or *style moderne* as it was known in Russia, started to appear in Fabergé's work as his designers and craftsmen broke free of the conventional Old Russian style which was officially approved under the reign of Tsar Alexander III. It was also a departure from the rigid and yet elegant nec-classical designs seen in many of Fabergé's objects, notably those from the workshop of Henrik Wigström.[2] There are examples of a workmaster's particular skills and predilections, for example the vase made by Michael Perchin as part of a group of Renaissance-style objects (cat. 330); an extraordinary purpurine and silver-gilt *kovsh* in Russian style by Julius Rappoport, who specialised in producing silver-mounted objects (cat. 329); and a gold-mounted agate cup of antique inspiration by Erik Kollin, which is in keeping with the type of gold objects he favoured (cat. 264). Among the most practical of Fabergé's objects were his clocks, which were made in relatively large numbers. While they demonstrate a variety of styles, the type he most often produced was the enamelled strut clock with plain white enamel dial and ivory back, of which there are several examples in the Royal Collection.

This section also includes a number of presentation objects, notably a large nephrite vase (cat. 326) presented to King Edward VII by Tsar Nicholas II and a silver *kovsh*, also presented to King Edward, at the coronation of Tsar Nicholas II (cat. 317).

1   Habsburg & Lopato 1993, p. 51.
2   Biryukova 1976, pp. 516–23.

252 PARASOL HANDLE, 1896–1908

Queen Elizabeth purchased three enamel umbrella handles in 1947 from Wartski. This one is in its original fitted case.

Gold, guilloché enamel, cabochon sapphires, rose diamonds, pearls, 5.3 x 7.4 x 2.4 cm (2¹/₁₆ x 2¹⁵/₁₆ x ¹⁵/₁₆")
Mark of Feodor Afanassiev; gold mark of 56 *zolotniks* (1896–1908)
RCIN 100312
PROVENANCE: Acquired by Queen Elizabeth, 1947

253 DESK CLOCK, 1909

Gold, silver-gilt, guilloché enamel, 6.2 x 6.3 x 3.7 cm (2⁷/₁₆ x 2¹/₂ x 1⁷/₁₆")
Mark of Henrik Wigström; gold mark of 56 *zolotniks* and silver mark of 91 *zolotniks* (1908–1917); *FABERGÉ* in Cyrillic characters
RCIN 40125
PROVENANCE: Bought by Queen Alexandra from Fabergé's London branch, 29 October 1909 (£29)
EXHIBITIONS: London 1977, no. G8; QG 1995–6, no. 272

254 POWDER BOX (AND SPATULA), 1896–1903

Silver-gilt, two-colour gold, guilloché enamel, rose diamond, moonstone, 2 x 10 x 4.5 cm (¹³/₁₆ x 3¹⁵/₁₆ x 1³/₄")
Mark of August Holmström; silver mark of 88 *zolotniks* (1896–1908); *FABERGÉ* in Cyrillic characters
RCIN 40115
PROVENANCE: Presented to Queen Mary by the Marquess and Marchioness of Cholmondeley, 1936
EXHIBITIONS: London 1977, no. J3; QG 1995–6, no. 275

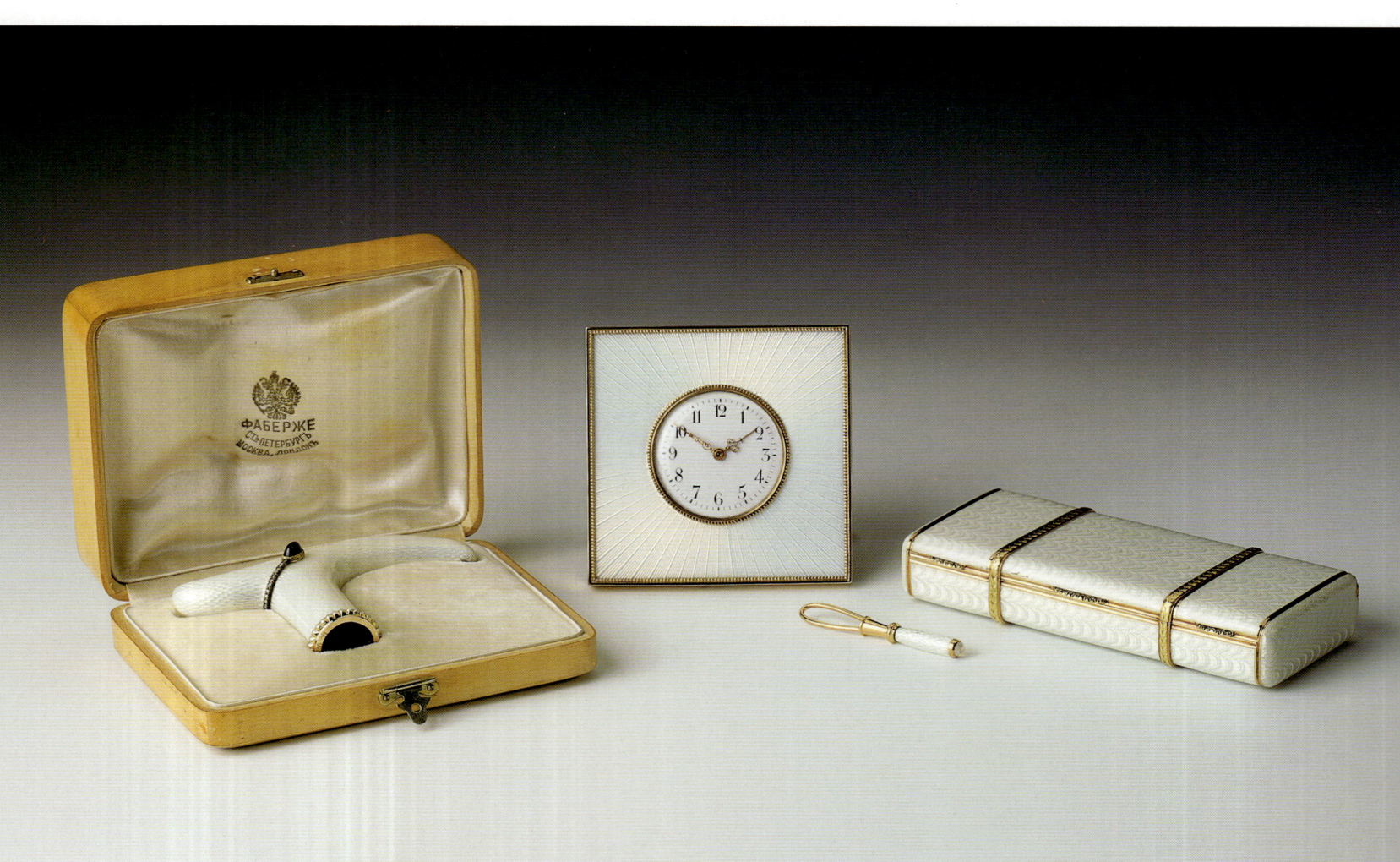

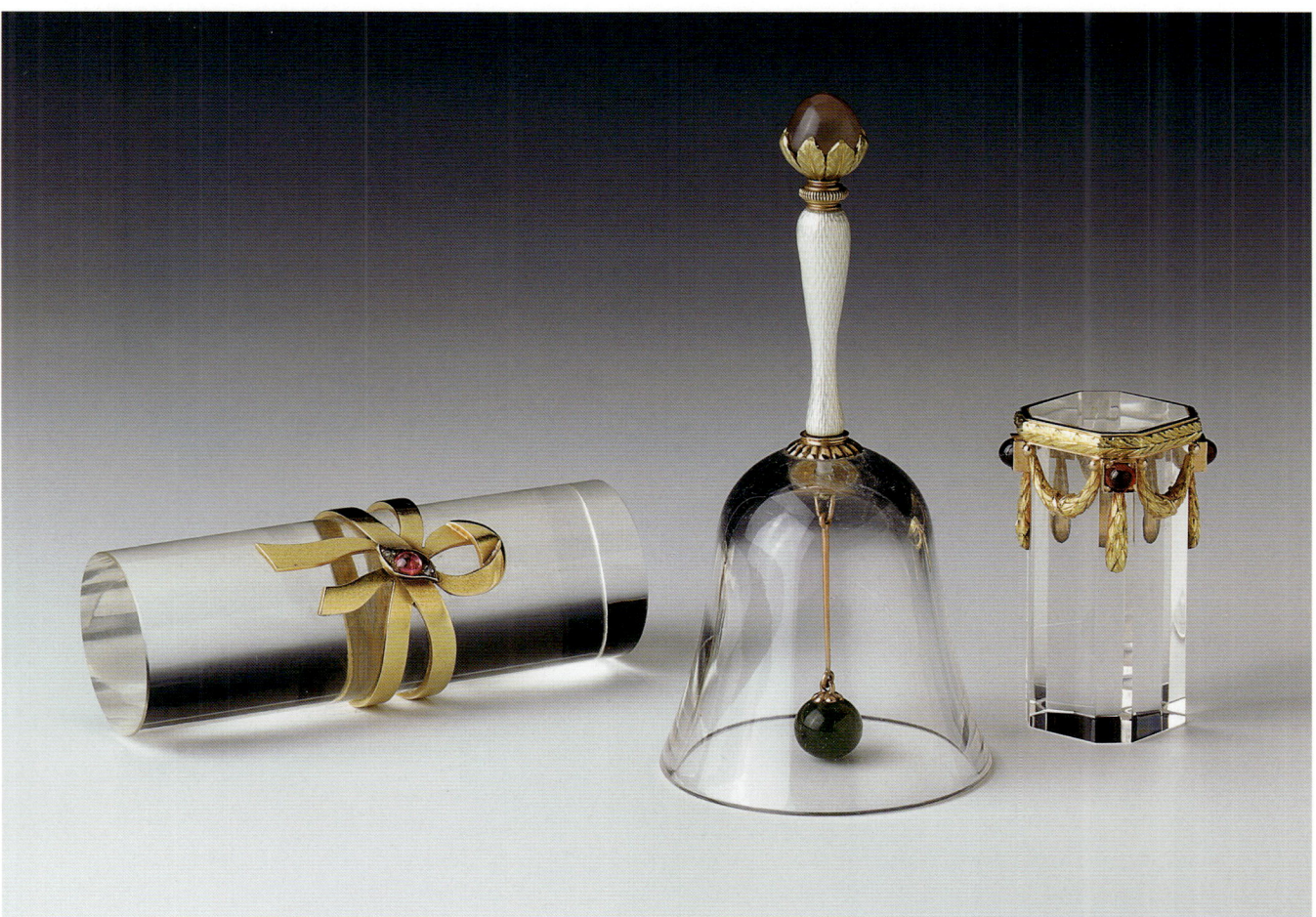

255   SEAL, BEFORE 1896

Rock crystal, gold, cabochon ruby, rose diamonds, 6.7 x diameter 2.3 cm (2⁵/₈ x ⁷/₈")
Mark of Erik Kollin; gold mark of 56 *zolotniks* (before 1896)
RCIN 100323
PROVENANCE: Acquired by Queen Elizabeth, before 1962
REFERENCES: Snowman 1962, pl. 285

256   BELL, BEFORE 1896

Rock crystal, gold, guilloché enamel, mecca stone, 8.3 x diameter 4 cm (3¹/₄ x 1⁹/₁₆")
Unmarked
RCIN 100322
PROVENANCE: Acquired by Queen Elizabeth, date unknown

257   SEAL, *c.*1900

Rock crystal, two-colour gold, cabochon rubies, 4 x 2 x 2 cm (1⁹/₁₆ x ¹³/₁₆ x ¹³/₁₆")
Unmarked
RCIN 40159
PROVENANCE: Probably acquired by King Edward VII, date unknown
REFERENCES: Snowman 1962, pl. 285
EXHIBITIONS: QG 1995–6, no. 466

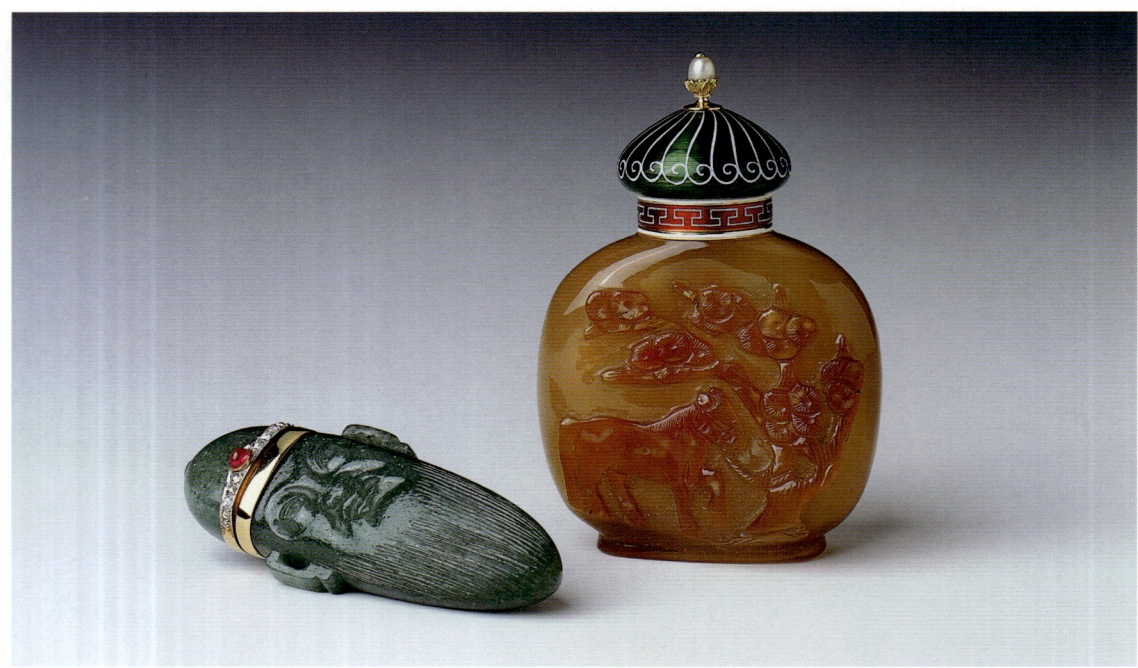

258   SCENT FLACON, c.1900

Several scent flacons in this form, imitating earlier Chinese carving, were made in Fabergé's workshops. A Fabergé scent flacon in jade was purchased by Queen Alexandra at Lady Paget's charity
bazaar in 1904.

Aventurine quartz, gold, rose diamonds, cabochon ruby, 6.2 x 2.5 x 1.5 cm (2$^7/_{16}$ x 1 x $^9/_{16}$")
Unmarked
RCIN 40221
PROVENANCE: Probably acquired by Queen Alexandra, c.1904
EXHIBITIONS: London 1977, no. J17; QG 1995–6, no. 518

259   SNUFF BOTTLE, 1908–1913

An extremely rare example of Fabergé's re-use of a Chinese snuff bottle, to which he has applied a
gold and enamel cover.

Chinese agate, gold, enamel, pearl, 7.3 x 4.8 x 2.2 cm (2$^7/_8$ x 1$^7/_8$ x $^7/_8$")
Gold mark of 72 *zolotniks* (1908–17); *FABERGÉ* in Roman letters
RCIN 23841
PROVENANCE: Presented to Queen Mary by the Dowager Tsarina Marie Feodorovna, Christmas 1913
REFERENCES: QMB I, no. 385; QMPP I, no. 286; Habsburg 1987, p. 157, no. 182
EXHIBITIONS: QG 1995–6, no. 516

260   BELL PUSH, 1903–1908

Bowenite, two-colour gold, guilloché enamel, mecca stone, 3.3 x 5.4 x 5.1 cm (1$^5/_{16}$ x 2$^1/_8$ x 2")
Mark of Henrik Wigström; gold mark of 56 *zolotniks* (1896–1908)
RCIN 9153
PROVENANCE: Probably acquired by King Edward VII and Queen Alexandra, date unknown
EXHIBITIONS: QG 1995–6, no. 62

261 DESK CLOCK, BEFORE 1896

Bowenite, two-colour gold, silver-gilt, half pearls, rose diamond, 8.5 x diameter 9.9 cm (3⅜ x 3⅞")
Mark of Michael Perchin; silver mark of 88 *zolotniks* (before 1896); *FABERGÉ* in Cyrillic characters
RCIN 40104
EXHIBITIONS: London 1977, no. I4; QG 1995–6, no. 422

262 BELL PUSH, 1896– *c*.1900

Bell pushes of every conceivable design are well represented in the Royal Collection. This example
has push pieces at both ends.

Bowenite, gold, guilloché enamel, cabochon rubies, 6 x diameter 2.7 cm (2⅜ x 1¹/₁₆")
Mark of Michael Perchin, gold mark of 56 *zolotniks* (1896–1908)
RCIN 9122
PROVENANCE: Probably acquired by King Edward VII and Queen Alexandra, *c*.1900
EXHIBITIONS: QG 1995–6, no. 406

263 PAPER-CUTTER, 1896–1903

Bowenite, two-colour gold, guilloché enamel, 8.1 x 1.6 x 0.4 cm (3³/₁₆ x ⅝ x ³/₁₆")
Mark of Michael Perchin; gold mark of 56 *zolotniks* (1896–1908); *FABERGÉ* in Cyrillic characters
RCIN 40162
EXHIBITIONS: QG 1995–6, no. 390

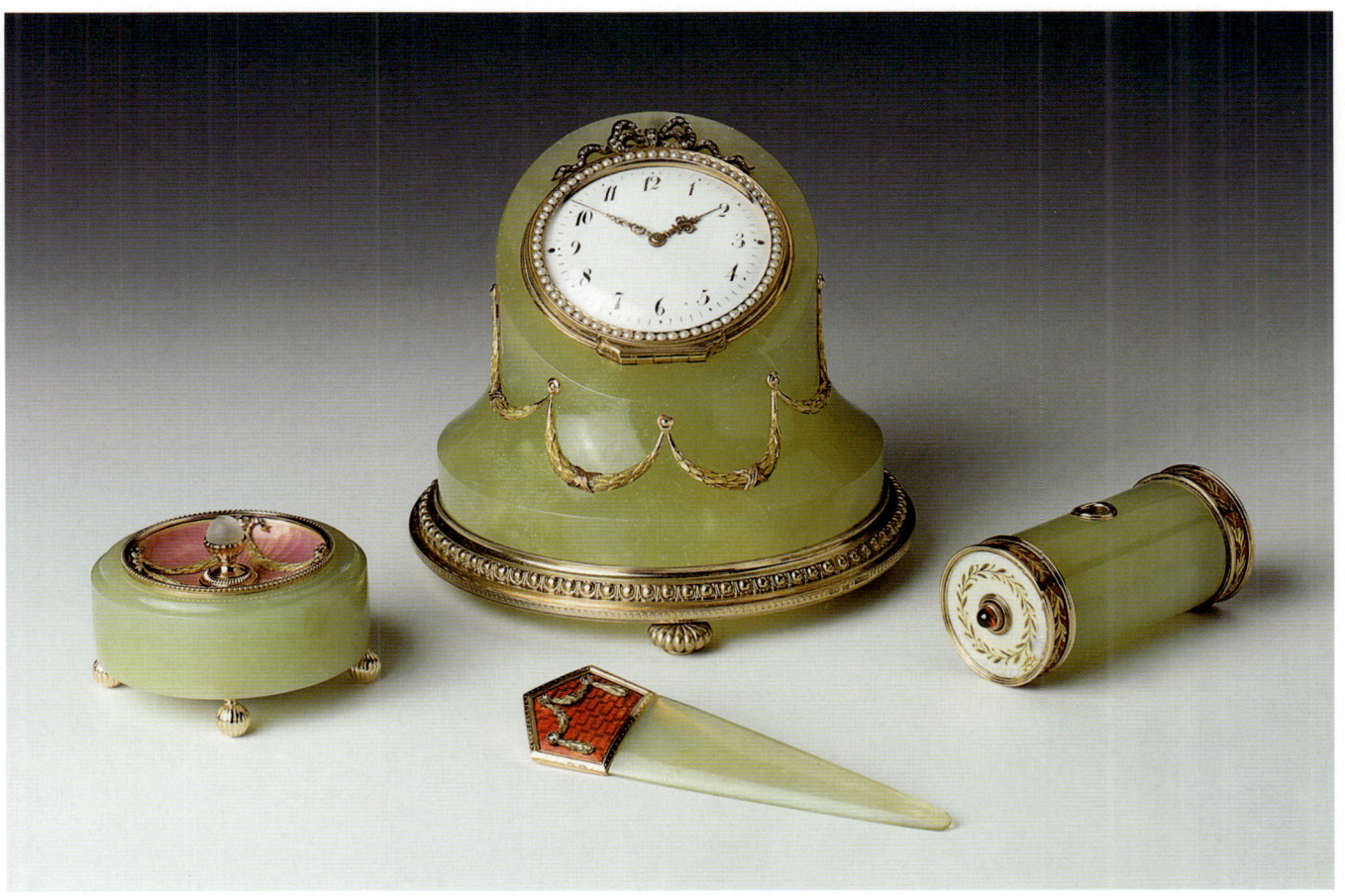

264 CUP, BEFORE 1896

Carved from a piece of banded agate, this cup has mounts in the form of a bird's leg.

Agate, gold, cabochon sapphires, 6.2 x 7.3 x 5.3 cm (2⁷/₁₆ x 2⁷/₈ x 2¹/₁₆")
Mark of Erik Kollin; gold mark of 56 *zolotniks* (before 1896)
RCIN 23090
PROVENANCE: From the collection of Princess Mary Adelaide, Duchess of Teck (1833–97); her daughter
Queen Mary by 1920
REFERENCES: QMB I, no. 267; QMPP I, no. 252
EXHIBITIONS: QG 1995–6, no. 41

265 KOVSH, BEFORE 1896

The handle of the *kovsh* is formed by a pair of entwined serpents.

Bloodstone, gold, 5.3 x 9.8 x 6.1 cm (2¹/₁₆ x 3⁷/₈ x 2³/₈")
Mark of Erik Kollin; gold mark of 56 *zolotniks* (before 1896)
RCIN 23103
EXHIBITIONS: QG 1995–6, no. 40

266 CUP, 1874

This is one of the earliest pieces by Fabergé in the Royal Collection and was made just two years after
Erik Kollin had become the firm's first head workmaster. Kollin specialised in revivalist gold pieces.
The hatched surface of the cup, which seems to imitate woven cloth, is in keeping with the trend in
Russia in the 1860s and 1870s to use motifs from weaving and embroidery in metalwork. The handle
of the cup is set with a Catherine the Great rouble dated 1777. According to a note in Queen Mary's
inventory, this cup always stood on King George V's dressing table and contained a pin cushion.

Two-colour gold, cabochon sapphires, 4.6 x 7.6 x 5 cm (1¹³/₁₆ x 3 x 1¹⁵/₁₆")
Mark of Erik Kollin; gold mark of 56 *zolotniks* (before 1896)
RCIN 23083
PROVENANCE: Given to Prince George of Wales (later King George V) by Marie Duchess of Saxe-Coburg-Gotha
(d.1920) in 1874
REFERENCES: QMPP IX; State Hermitage 1996, p. 160
EXHIBITIONS: QG 1995–6, no. 60

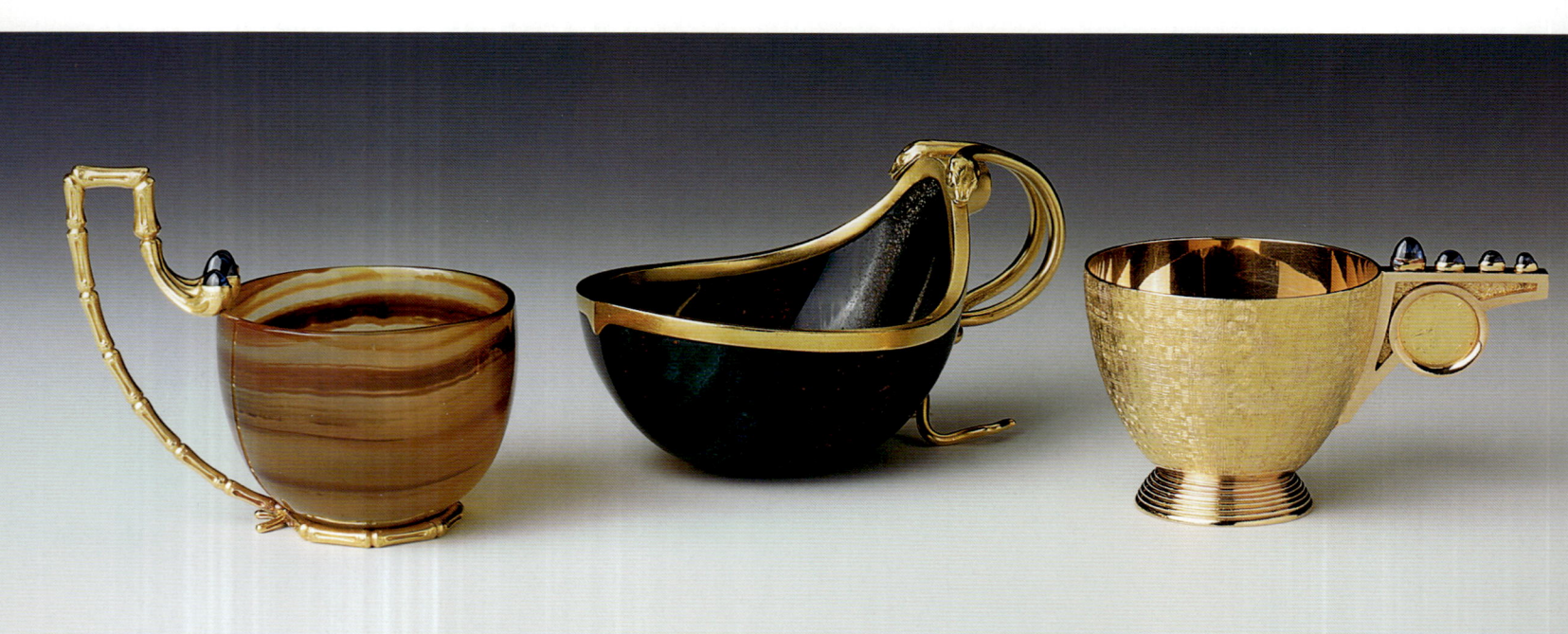

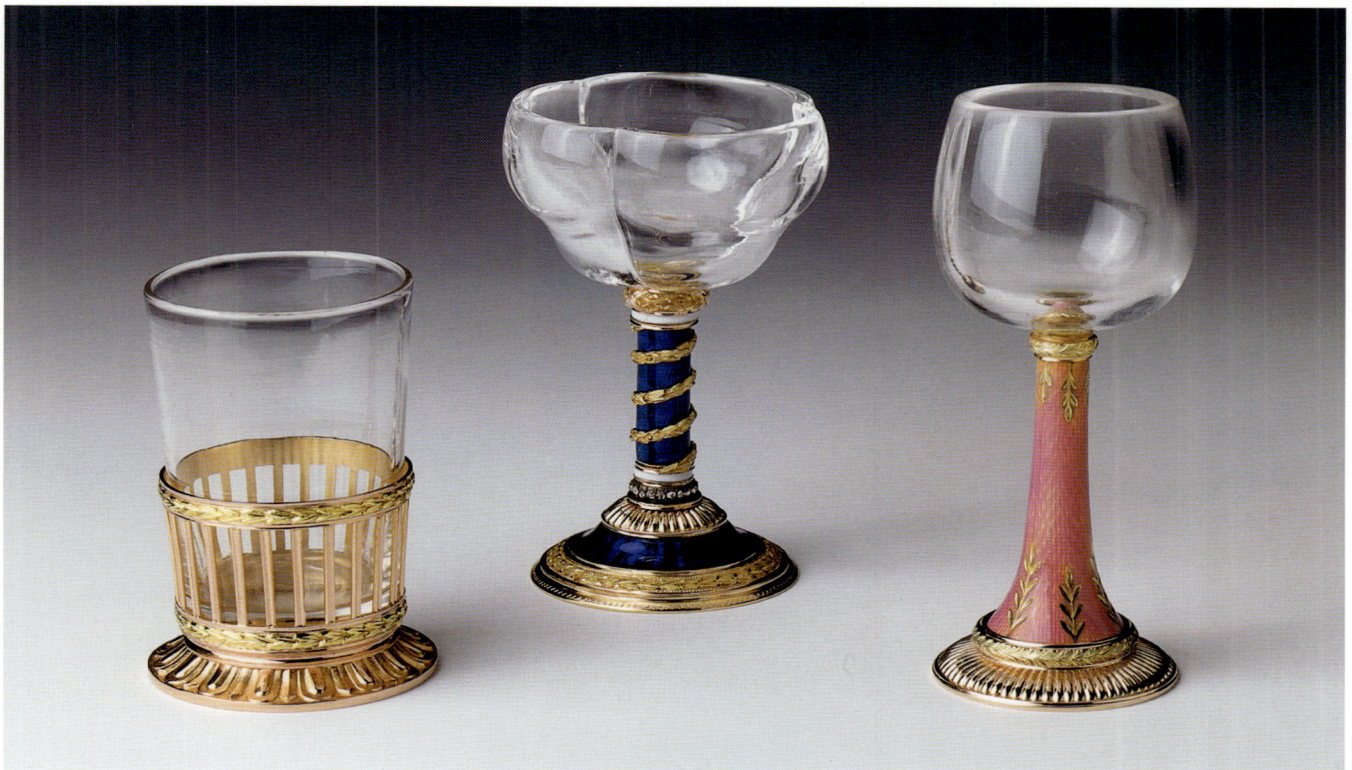

267 TEA GLASS, BEFORE 1896

All manner of drinking vessels were produced in Fabergé's workshops, from traditional Russian *kovshes* and *tcharki* to tea glasses and goblets.

Glass, two-colour gold, 5.4 x diameter 3.8 cm (2¹/₈ x 1¹/₂")
Mark of Michael Perchin; gold mark of 56 *zolotniks* (before 1896)
RCIN 9195
PROVENANCE: Probably acquired by Alexandra, Princess of Wales (later Queen Alexandra), *c.*1896
EXHIBITIONS: QG 1995–6, no. 202

268 GOBLET, 1895

Rock crystal, two-colour gold, guilloché enamel, rose diamonds, 6.8 x diameter 4.3 cm (2¹¹/₁₆ x 1¹¹/₁₆")
Mark of Michael Perchin; gold mark of 56 *zolotniks* (before 1896); *FABERGÉ* in Cyrillic characters
RCIN 9039
PROVENANCE: Given to the Duchess of York (later Queen Mary) by the Dowager Tsarina Marie Feodorovna, Christmas 1895
REFERENCES: QMB I, no. 417; QMPP I, no. 248
EXHIBITIONS: QG 1995–6, no. 503

269 MINIATURE WINE GLASS, 1896–1903

Rock crystal, two-colour gold, guilloché enamel, 7.6 x diameter 2.3 cm (3 x ⁷/₈")
Mark of Michael Perchin; gold mark of 56 *zolotniks* (1896–1908); *FABERGÉ* in Cyrillic characters
RCIN 40248
PROVENANCE: Royal Collection by 1953
EXHIBITIONS: London 1977, no. I1; QG 1995–6, no. 267

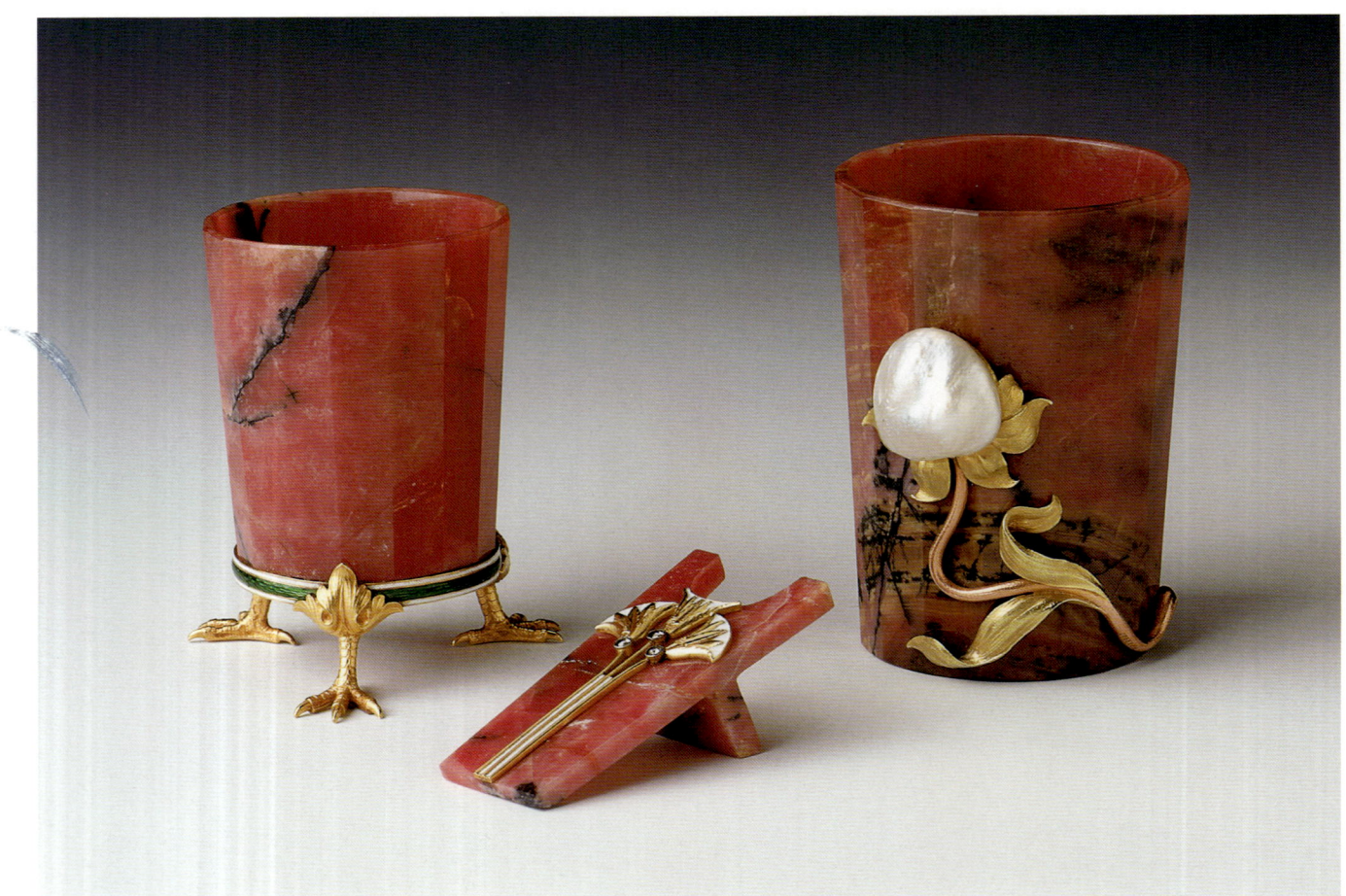

270 BEAKER, 1908–1917

A drawing for a very similar beaker, also with bird's feet mounts, appears in a design album from Henrik Wigström's workshop, dated 1911. This beaker does not, however, bear Wigström's mark. It is one of the very few objects in the Royal Collection to retain the original Fabergé fitted box in which it was sold.

Rhodonite, gold, guilloché enamel, 5.7 x 4 x 4.2 cm (2¼ x 1⁹⁄₁₆ x 1⁵⁄₈")
Gold mark of 72 *zolotniks*; FABERGÉ in Cyrillic characters
RCIN 23106
PROVENANCE: Presented to Queen Mary by the royal family, Christmas 1948
REFERENCES: QMPP XI, no. 59; Tillander-Godenhielm *et al.* 2000, p. 116, pl. 253
EXHIBITIONS: QG 1995–6, no. 57

271 PEN REST, 1896–1908

This elaborately decorated pen rest is one of a small group of pieces in the Royal Collection in the art nouveau style.

Rhodonite, gold, enamel, rose diamonds, 1.8 x 2.3 x 4.4 cm (¹¹⁄₁₆ x ⁷⁄₈ x 1³⁄₄")
Gold mark of 56 *zolotniks* (1896–1908); initials of Carl Fabergé in Cyrillic characters
RCIN 23253
PROVENANCE: Royal Collection by 1953
EXHIBITIONS: QG 1995–6, no. 384

272   BEAKER, 1896–1908

The beaker is in the art nouveau style, the stylised flower head formed by a baroque pearl.

Rhodonite, two-colour gold, pearl, 6 x 5.1 x 4.1 cm (2⁵⁄₈ x 2 x 1⁵⁄₈")
Mark of Viktor Aarne; gold mark of 56 *zolotniks* (1896–1908); *FABERGÉ* in Cyrillic characters
RCIN 9116
PROVENANCE: Royal Collection by 1953
EXHIBITIONS: QG 1995–6, no. 55

273   WALKING STICK, 1893

The nephrite handle is inscribed *Alix 24 May 1893*, indicating that this walking stick originally belonged to Tsarina Alexandra Feodorovna, consort of Tsar Nicholas II.

Nephrite, gold, malacca cane, handle 6 x 9.7 x 2.7 cm (2⁵⁄₈ x 3¹³⁄₁₆ x 1¹⁄₁₆")
Mark of Michael Perchin; gold mark of 56 *zolotniks* (before 1896)
RCIN 35953
PROVENANCE: Tsarina Alexandra Feodorovna
EXHIBITIONS: QG 1995–6, no. 337

274   PARASOL HANDLE, BEFORE 1896

The handle, in the form of a parrot's head, is now mounted as a paperweight.

Chalcedony, gold, enamel, brilliant diamonds, 6 x 9 x 3 cm (2⁵⁄₈ x 3⁹⁄₁₆ x 1³⁄₁₆")
Mark of Michael Perchin; gold mark of 56 *zolotniks* (before 1896)
RCIN 9164
PROVENANCE: Probably acquired by Alexandra, Princess of Wales (later Queen Alexandra)
EXHIBITIONS: QG 1995–6, no. 362

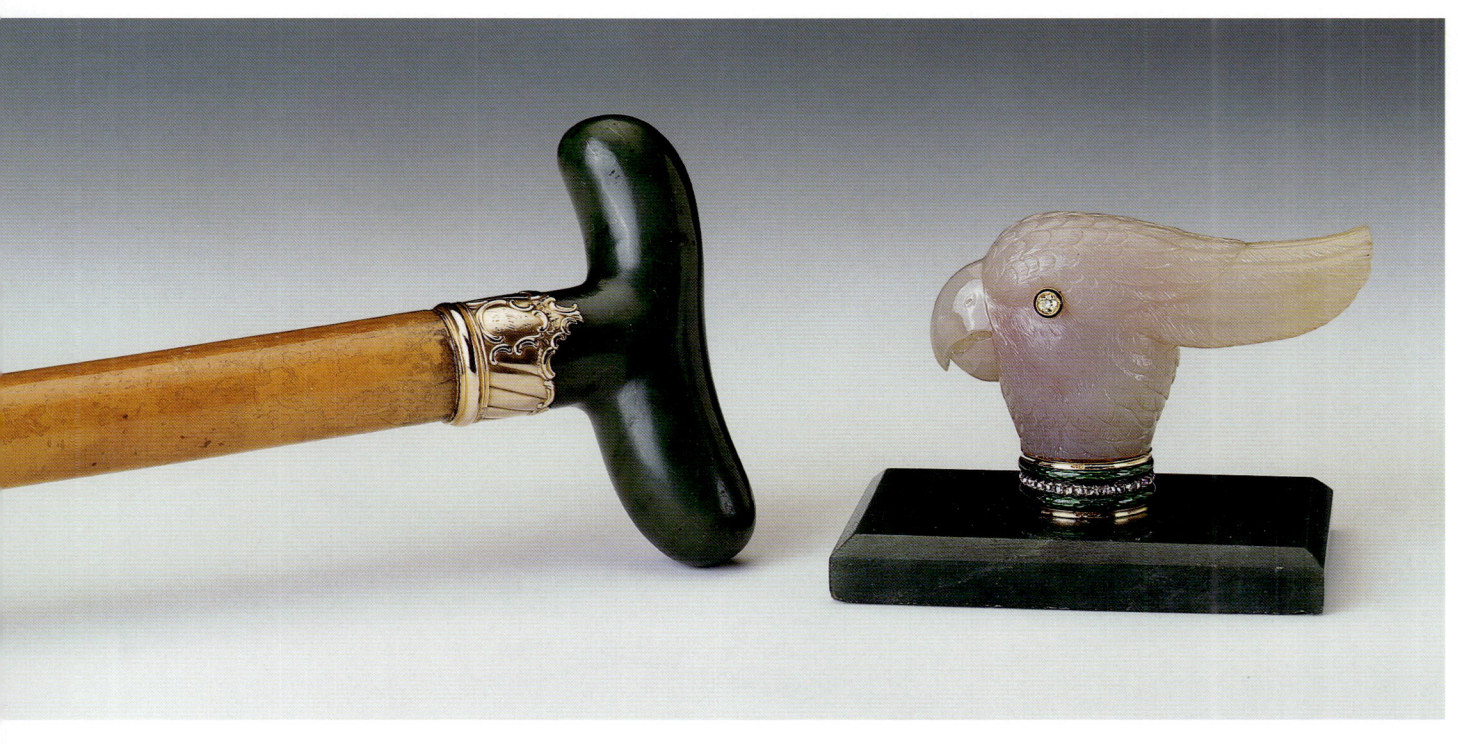

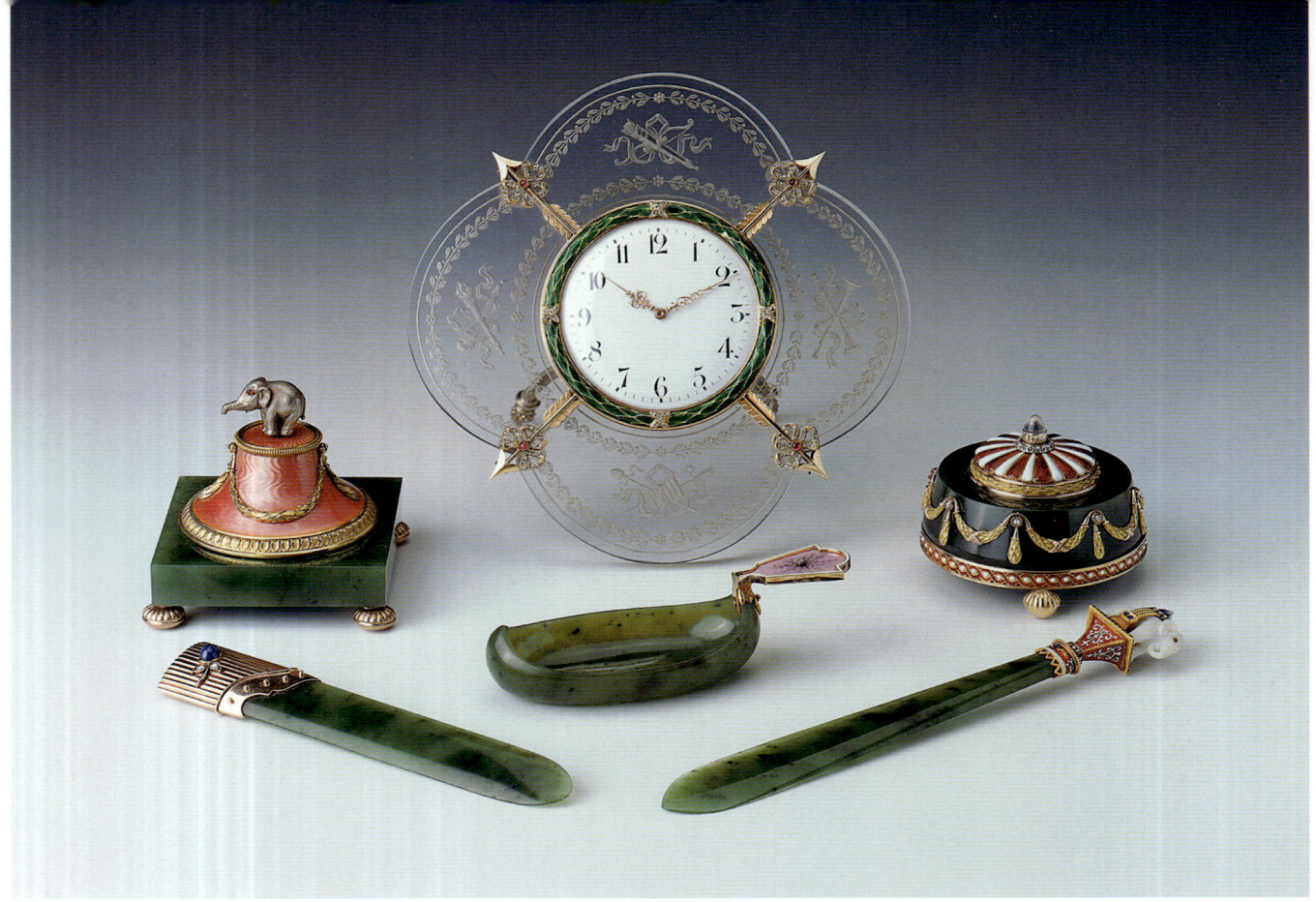

275 BELL PUSH, 1896– c.1900

Nephrite, silver, guilloché enamel, 5.2 x 5.8 x 5.8 cm (2¹/₁₆ x 2⁵/₁₆ x 2⁵/₁₆")
Mark of Karl Armfelt; silver mark of 88 *zolotniks* (1896–1908); *FABERGÉ* in Cyrillic characters
RCIN 40124
PROVENANCE: Probably acquired by Queen Alexandra, *c.*1900
EXHIBITIONS: QG 1995–6, no. 382

276 CLOCK, 1896– c.1900

The four lobes engraved with trophies are of rock crystal, a naturally occurring stone that Fabergé
used extensively for both functional and decorative objects. The panels are divided by diamond and ruby-
set arrows of red gold. The reverse of the movement has two fixed keys with folding handles and is
engraved in Russian, indicating an eight-day movement.

Fabergé's clocks, however extravagantly decorated, were designed to be functional and easy
to use. The majority of the desk clocks have opaque white enamelled dials with Arabic numerals and the
bezels are usually of chased or enamelled gold laurel or acanthus, sometimes set with seed pearls.

The design of cat. 276 is unusual in Fabergé's repertoire; the model most frequently produced was the enamelled strut clock, of which there are several examples in the Royal Collection.
One of only three pieces of Fabergé known to have belonged to Queen Victoria, this clock was later
placed by King George V on his desk at Buckingham Palace.

Rock crystal, gold, silver-gilt, enamel, rose diamonds, rubies, 11.6 x 12.5 x 9.9 cm (4⁹/₁₆ x 4¹⁵/₁₆ x 3⁷/₈")
Mark of Michael Perchin; silver mark of 88 *zolotniks* (1896–1908)
RCIN 40100
PROVENANCE: Presented to Queen Victoria by Tsarina Alexandra Feodorovna, *c.*1900
EXHIBITIONS: London 1953, no. 13; London 1967, no. 188; London 1977, no. I2; New York 1983, no. 10;
QG 1985–6, no. 66; Zurich 1989, no. 103; St Petersburg/Paris/London 1993–4, no. 20; QG 1995–6, no. 401;
QG 2002–3, no. 275

277 BELL PUSH, 1896–1903

This elaborately decorated bell push appears to have once formed part of a large desk set. Designs for the entire set – which included a calendar frame, desk pad, blotter, gum pot, photograph frame, inkwell, candlestick, pen tray, seal and pen holder, as well as the bell push – were sold at Christie's in 1989. The bell push is the only piece from the desk set in the Royal Collection. The whereabouts of the other components is unknown.

Nephrite, three-colour gold, guilloché enamel, moonstone, 3.9 x 5.8 x 5.3 cm (1⁹/₁₆ x 2⁵/₁₆ x 2¹/₁₆")
Mark of Michael Perchin; gold mark of 56 *zolotniks* (1896–1908); *FABERGÉ* in Cyrillic characters
RCIN 23190
REFERENCES: Christie's 1989, p. 97
EXHIBITIONS: QG 1995–6, no. 418

278 PAPER-KNIFE, BEFORE 1886

This paper-knife was produced in the workshop of Erik Kollin, Fabergé's chief workmaster between 1872 and 1886. Kollin's workshop specialised in producing gold objects and jewellery inspired by archaeological finds.

Nephrite, gold, rose diamonds, cabochon sapphire, 0.8 x 10.8 x 1.7 cm (⁵/₁₆ x 4¹/₄ x ¹¹/₁₆")
Mark of Erik Kollin; gold mark of 56 *zolotniks* (before 1896)
RCIN 23239
PROVENANCE: Princess Mary Adelaide, Duchess of Teck (1833–97); her daughter Queen Mary
REFERENCES: QMB II, no. 271; QMPP I, no. 225
EXHIBITIONS: QG 1995–6, no. 420; QG 2002–3, no. 279

279 KOVSH, 1896–1908

Nephrite, gold, guilloché enamel, rose diamond, 2.2 x 8.5 x 3.5 cm (⁷/₈ x 3³/₈ x 1³/₈")
Gold mark of 56 *zolotniks* (1896–1908); initials of Carl Fabergé in Cyrillic characters
RCIN 23089
EXHIBITIONS: QG 1995–6, no. 46

280 PAPER-KNIFE, BEFORE 1896

The elephant on the handle probably refers obliquely to Denmark; an elephant and castle is incorporated in the design of all Danish royal insignia and Queen Alexandra and Tsarina Marie Feodorovna were the daughters of King Christian IX and Queen Louise of Denmark. Fabergé made miniature elephants and castles for Marie Feodorovna; similar miniature elephants also exist in the Royal Collection, probably acquired by Queen Alexandra (see cat. 114 and 115).

Nephrite, gold, quartzite, enamel, rose diamonds, sapphire, 1 x 14.5 x 1.9 cm (³/₈ x 5¹¹/₁₆ x ³/₄")
Mark of Michael Perchin; gold mark of 56 *zolotniks* (before 1896)
RCIN 40204
PROVENANCE: Probably acquired by Queen Alexandra, date unknown
EXHIBITIONS: London 1953, no. 61; London 1977, no. J19; New York 1983, no. 41; QG 1985–6, no. 23; QG 1995–6, no. 386; QG 2002–3, no. 280

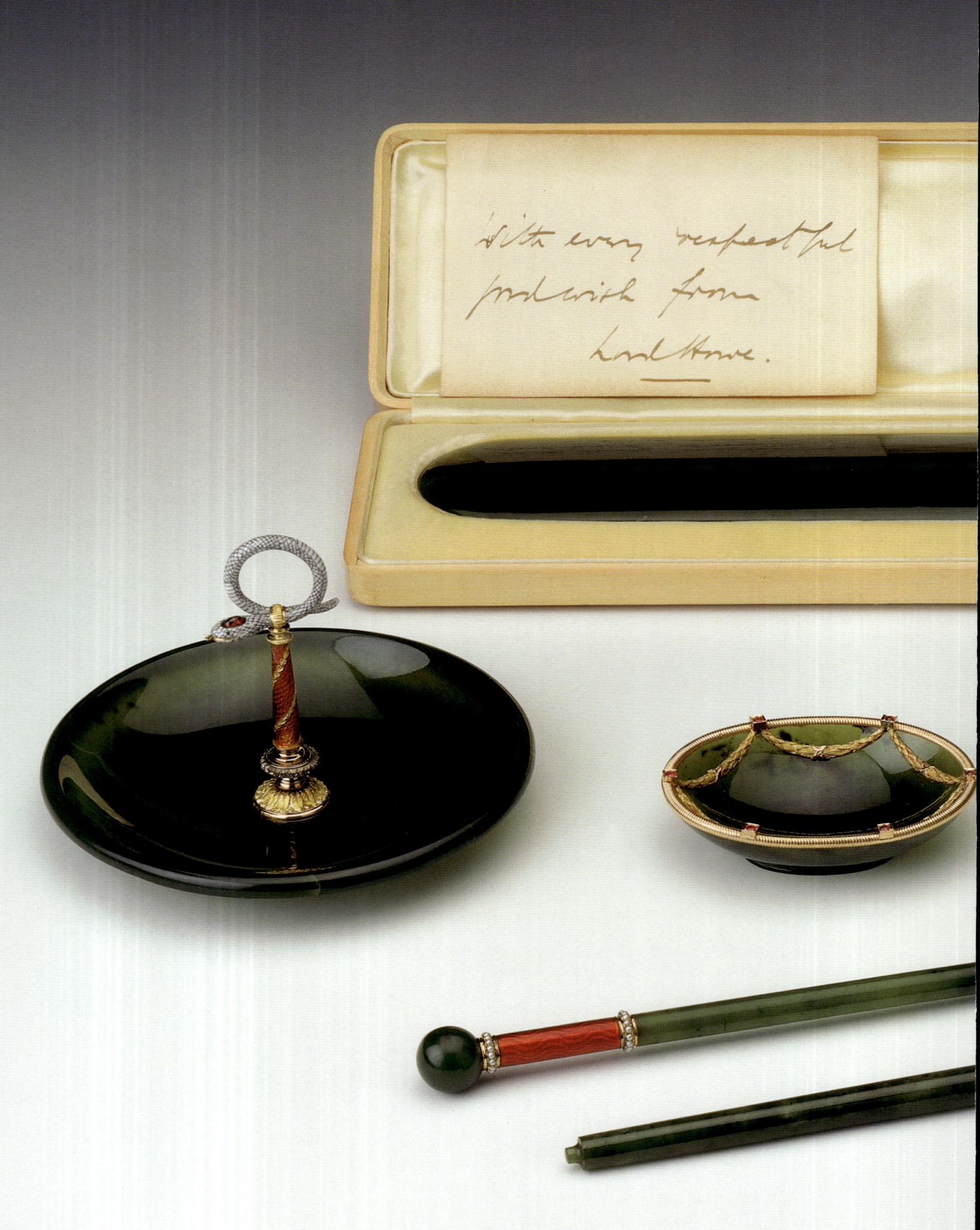

With every respectful
good wish from
Lord Howe.

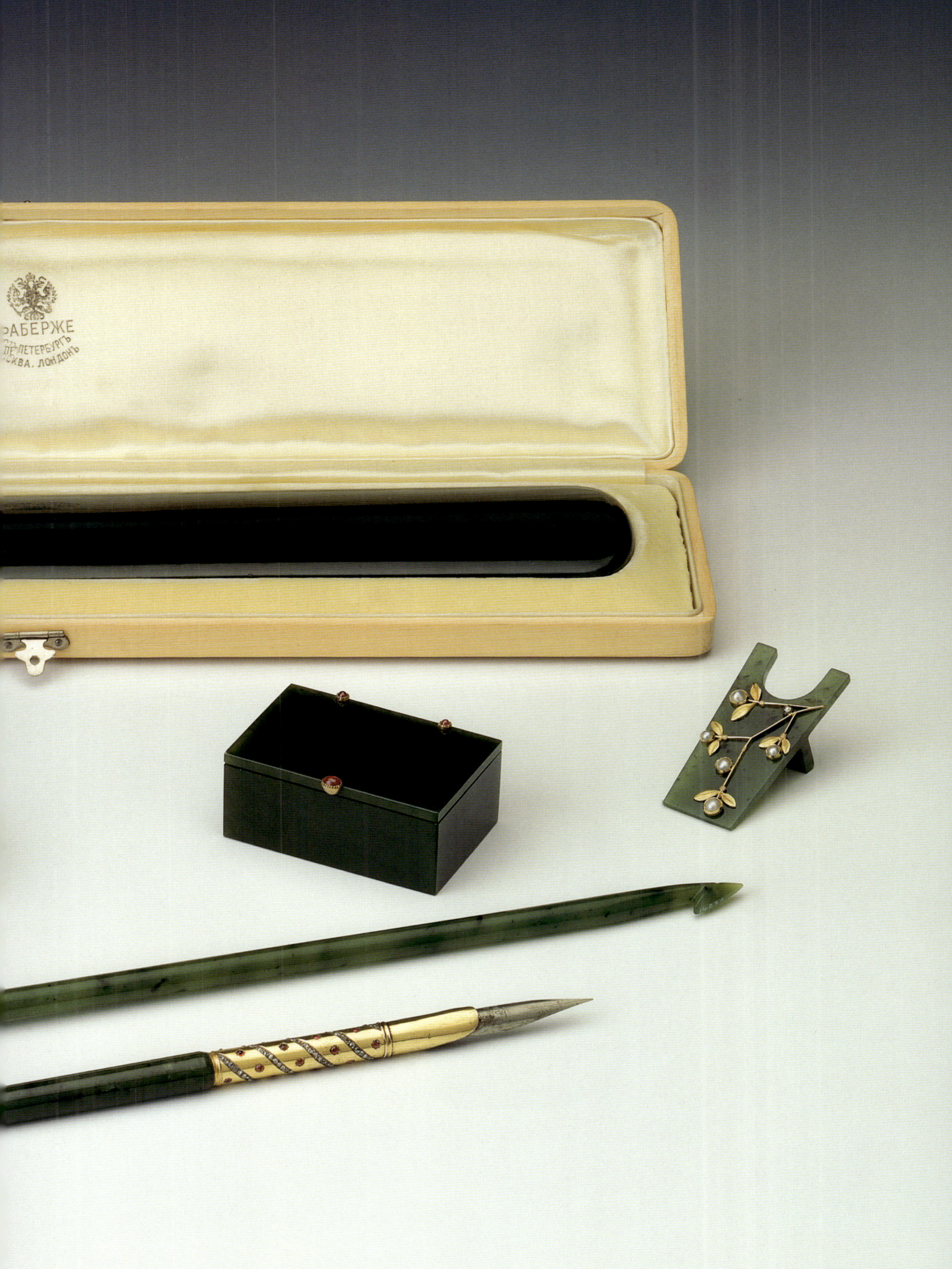

281 PAPER-KNIFE, *c.*1900

This plain nephrite paper-knife was in the collection of Queen Elizabeth but its original fitted box contains a label explaining that it was presented by Lord Howe. Richard Curzon, 4th Earl Howe, served as Queen Alexandra's Lord Chamberlain from 1903 to 1925 and it is therefore assumed that the paper-knife was originally presented to her and later passed to Queen Elizabeth.

Nephrite, 26.4 x 3.8 x 0.7 cm (10³/₈ x 1¹/₂ x ¹/₄")
RCIN 100326
PROVENANCE: Lord Howe; by whom presented to Queen Alexandra; Queen Elizabeth

282 DISH, 1896–1908

Nephrite, two-colour gold, guilloché enamel, cabochon rubies, rose diamonds, 6.2 x diameter 9.5 cm (2⁷/₁₆ x 3³/₄")
Gold mark of 56 *zolotniks* (1896–1908)
RCIN 23084
EXHIBITIONS: QG 1995–6, no. 369

283 DISH, 1896–1901

The drawing for this dish, or one identical to it, has now been traced (see below).

Nephrite, two-colour gold, rubies, 1.6 x 6 x 4.5 cm (⁵/₈ x 2³/₈ x 1³/₄")
Mark of Erik Kollin; gold mark of 56 *zolotniks* (1896–1908)
RCIN 23096
PROVENANCE: Given to Queen Mary by the Duke and Duchess of Gloucester, Easter 1937
REFERENCES: QMB III, no. 389; QMPP IX, no. 32; Christie's 1989, p. 26
EXHIBITIONS: QG 1995–6, no. 49

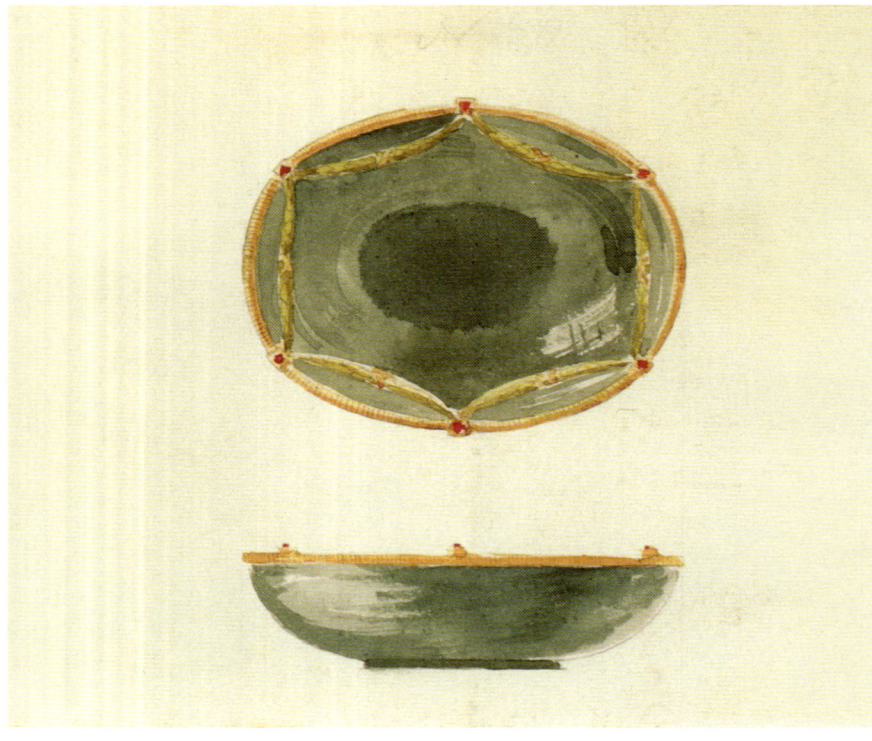

Pencil and watercolour design from a Fabergé design book for a nephrite dish identical to cat. 283.

284   STAMP BOX, *c.*1900

This is a good example of a beautifully designed yet practical object. The nephrite lid, decorated at the hinge and fastening with rubies, opens to reveal two compartments with sloping bases to enable the stamps to be removed easily.

Nephrite, gold, cabochon rubies, 2.4 x 4.9 x 3.2 cm ($^{15}/_{16}$ x $1^{15}/_{16}$ x $1^{1}/_{4}$")
FABERGÉ in Cyrillic characters
RCIN 22935
EXHIBITIONS: QG 1995–6, no. 417

285   PEN REST, 1896–1908

Bainbridge describes how no one appreciated both the practical value and the delicacy of design and materials used in Fabergé's work more than King George V. He adds that the King always kept this nephrite pen rest, which is decorated with mistletoe, on his writing table.

Nephrite, gold, rose diamonds, pearls, 1.9 x 4.3 x 2.3 cm ($^{3}/_{4}$ x $1^{11}/_{16}$ x $^{7}/_{8}$")
Gold mark (1896–1908); Carl Fabergé's initials in Cyrillic characters
RCIN 23254
PROVENANCE: Acquired by King George V, date unknown
REFERENCES: Bainbridge 1949, pp. 108–9
EXHIBITIONS: QG 1995–6, no. 375

286   CROCHET HOOK, *c.*1900

A crochet hook was purchased from the London branch by Queen Alexandra in 1909, but its description does not match this example. Knitting needles and thimbles were also made by Fabergé.

Nephrite, gold, guilloché enamel, seed pearls, 27 x diameter 1.2 cm (10$^{5}/_{8}$ x $^{1}/_{2}$")
RCIN 14832
EXHIBITIONS: QG 1995–6, no. 221

287   PEN, BEFORE 1896

Many of Fabergé's desk sets came complete with pens. A similar example is known in the Forbes Collection.

Nephrite, gold, rose diamonds, cabochon rubies, length 17.9 cm (8")
Mark of Michael Perchin; gold mark of 56 *zolotniks* (before 1896)
RCIN 100315
PROVENANCE: Acquired by Queen Elizabeth, date unknown

288 DESK CLOCK, 1903–1908

This clock is an excellent example of two of the key techniques which Fabergé derived from eighteenth-century France: refined guilloché enamelling and the use of applied coloured gold decoration. The ribbon-tied laurel swags and flower heads are typical of Fabergé's decoration and the white enamelled clock face with a seed-pearl bezel is the type that appears most frequently in his clock designs. A design for a similar clock (see below) appears in an unpublished album from Henrik Wigström's workshop, where this clock was made.

Three-colour gold, silver-gilt, guilloché enamel, seed pearls, rose diamonds, ivory, 12.8 x 9.2 x 0.7 cm (5¹/₁₆ x 3⁵/₈ x ¹/₄")
Mark of Henrik Wigström; silver mark of 88 *zolotniks* (1896–1908)
RCIN 100316
PROVENANCE: Acquired by Queen Elizabeth, date unknown
REFERENCES: Snowman 1962, pl. 193
EXHIBITIONS: London 1999, no. 3

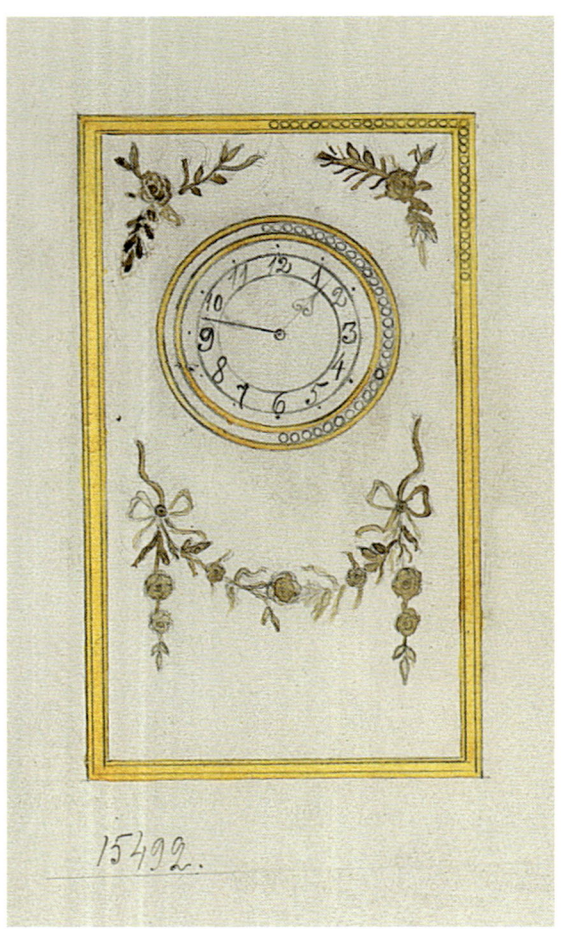

A plate from a previously unpublished album of watercolour designs by Henrik Wigström, which includes a design for a clock of very similar form to cat. 288.

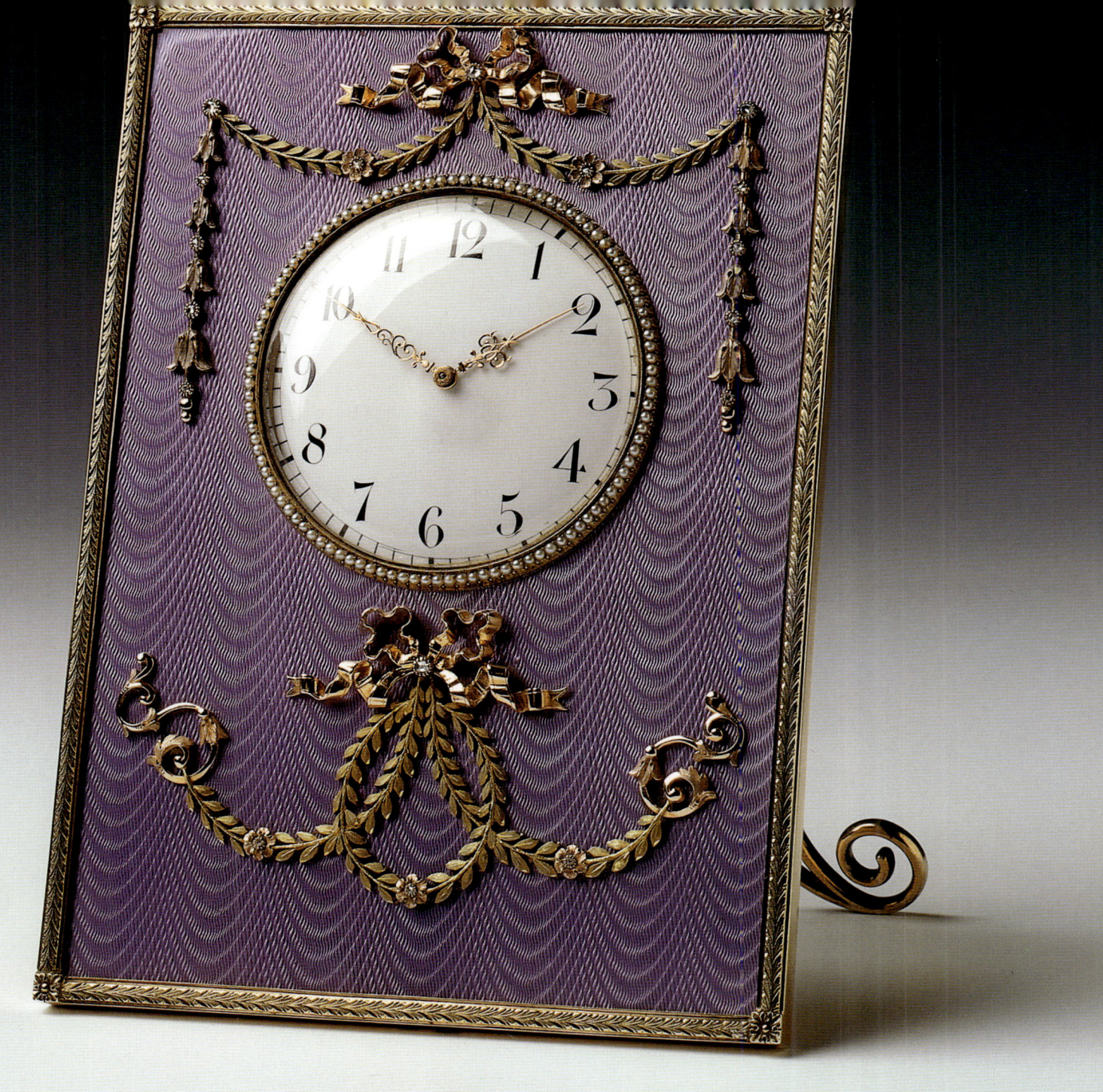

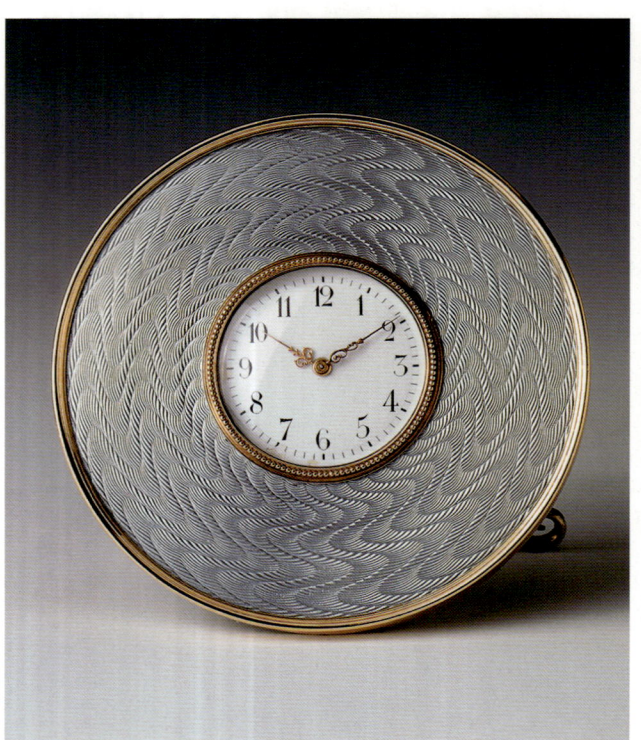

289 DESK CLOCK, 1908–1910

The restrained combination of Louis XVI design with moiré grey guilloché enamel makes this clock one of the best examples of Fabergé's work in this idiom.

Gold, guilloché enamel, silver-gilt, ivory, 7.7 x diameter 7.7 cm (3^{1}/$_{16}$ x 3^{1}/$_{16}$")
Mark of Henrik Wigström; gold mark of 56 *zolotniks* and silver mark of 91 *zolotniks* (1908–17)
RCIN 100321
PROVENANCE: Bought by the Prince de la Moscova from Fabergé's London branch, 14 December 1910 (£24 10s); Queen Elizabeth's collection

290 DESK CLOCK, 1910

Gold, silver-gilt, guilloché enamel, 7.8 x 5.4 x 6 cm (3^{1}/$_{16}$ x 2^{1}/$_{8}$ x 2^{3}/$_{8}$")
Mark of Henrik Wigström; gold mark of 56 *zolotniks* and silver mark of 91 *zolotniks* (1908–17); *FABERGÉ* in Cyrillic characters
RCIN 22745
PROVENANCE: Dowager Tsarina Marie Feodorovna; by whom given to Queen Mary, Christmas 1910
REFERENCES: QMB I, no. 553; QMPP II, no. 61
EXHIBITIONS: QG 1995–6, no. 238

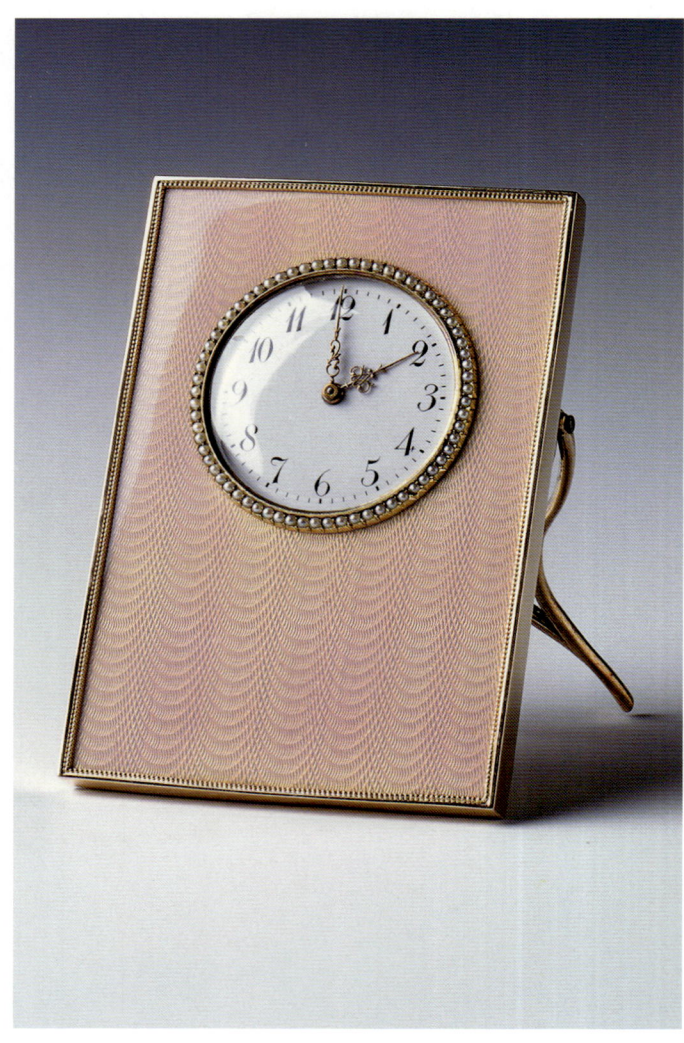

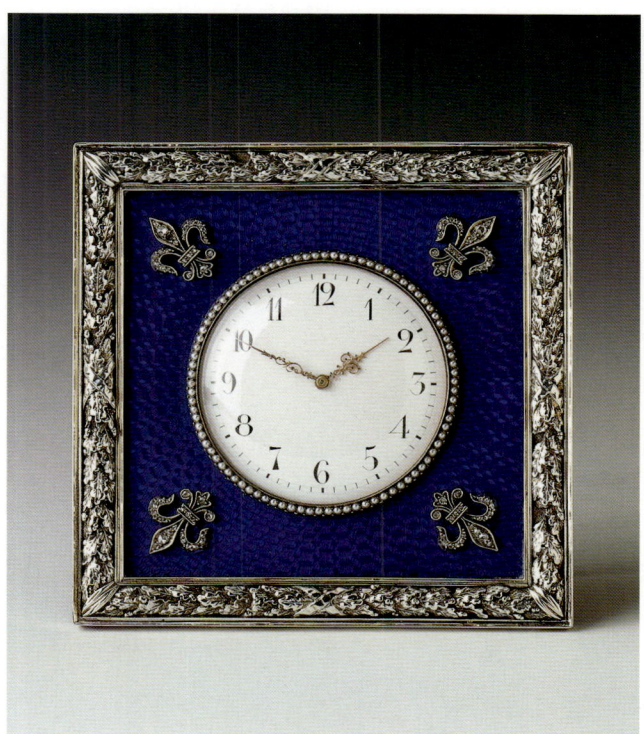
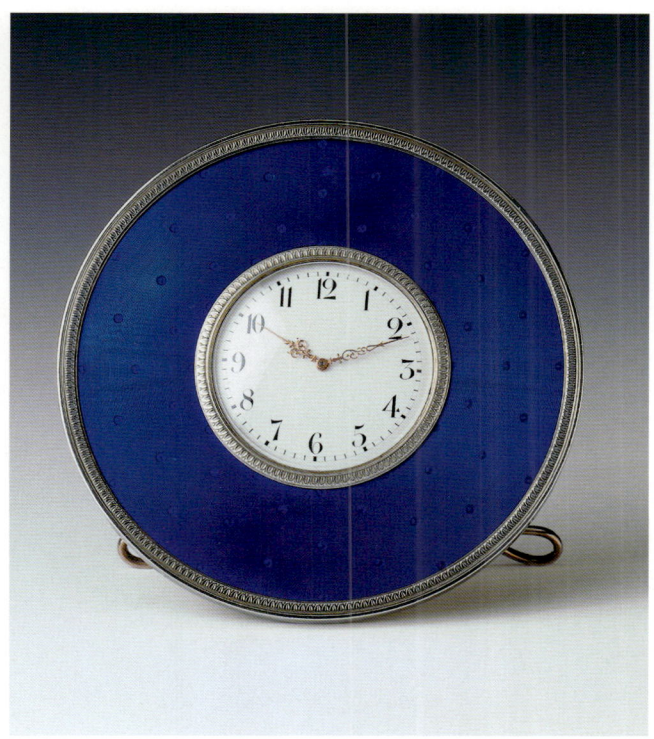

291 DESK CLOCK, BEFORE 1896

It has been suggested that the diamond-set fleurs-de-lis applied to this clock indicate that it was originally intended to be a gift for a member of the French royal family. A clock of very similar design, although designed to lie flat, was formerly in the Forbes Collection.

Silver, guilloché enamel, rose diamonds, pearls, 9.9 x 9.8 x 2.5 cm (3⁷/₈ x 3⁷/₈ x 1")
Mark of Michael Perchin; silver mark of 88 *zolotniks* (before 1896); *FABERGÉ* in Cyrillic characters
RCIN 100313
PROVENANCE: Acquired by Queen Elizabeth, date unknown
EXHIBITIONS: London 1999, no. 5

292 DESK CLOCK, 1903–1908

Silver, guilloché enamel, 11.8 x 11.8 x 0.9 cm (4⁵/₁₆ x 4⁵/₁₆ x ³/₈")
Mark of Henrik Wigström; silver mark of 91 *zolotniks* (1896–1908); *FABERGÉ* in Cyrillic characters
RCIN 100325
PROVENANCE: Bought by the Prince of Wales (later King George V) from Fabergé's London branch, 25 May 1908 (£23 5s); Queen Elizabeth
EXHIBITIONS: London 1999, no. 4

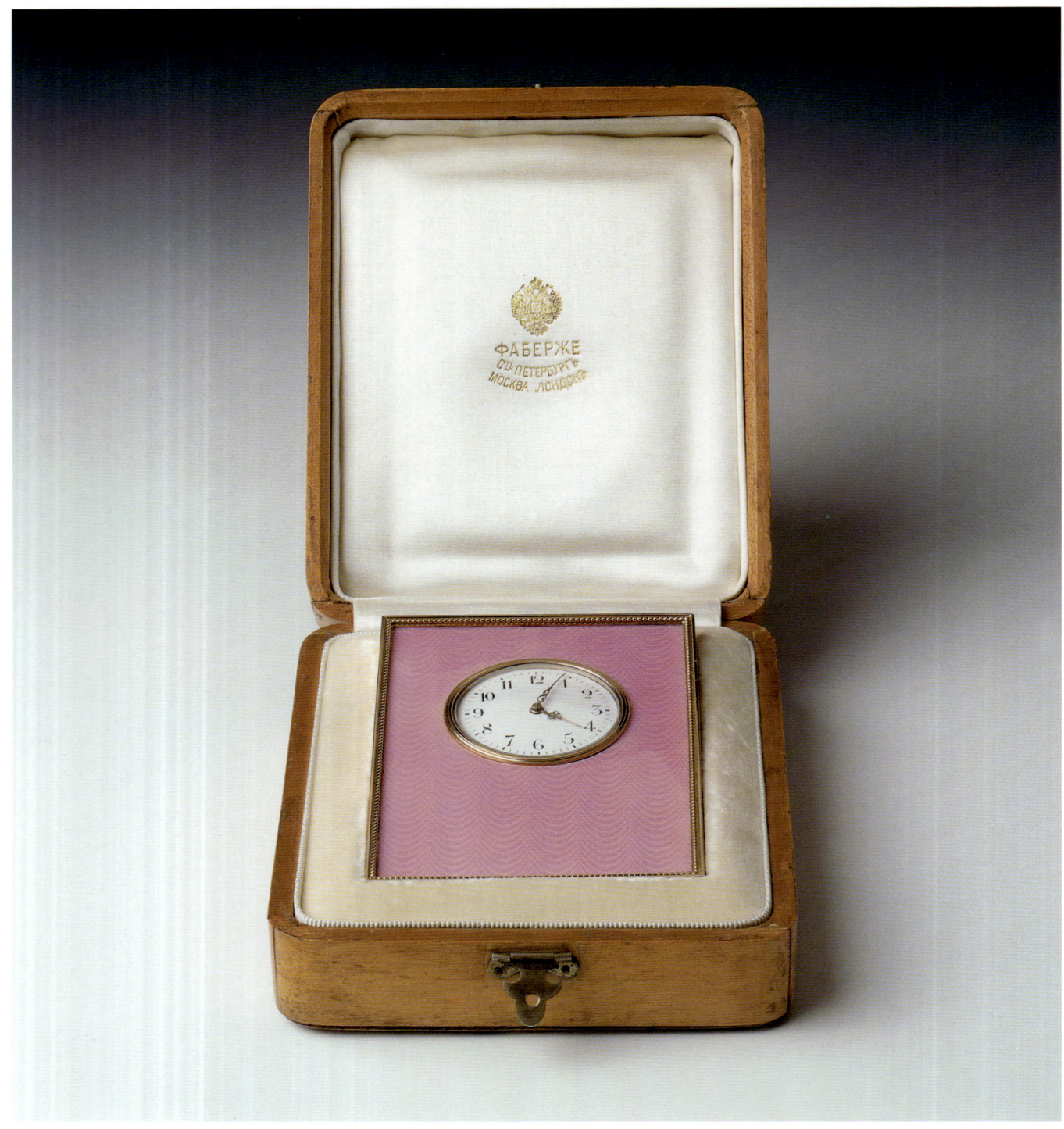

293 DESK CLOCK, 1908–1913

This clock retains its original holly wood box, lined in silk and velvet.

Gold, silver-gilt, guilloché enamel, ivory, 8 x 6.1 x 4.7 cm (3¹⁄₈ x 2³⁄₈ x 1⁷⁄₈")
Mark of Henrik Wigström; gold mark of 56 *zolotniks* and silver mark of 88 and 91 *zolotniks* (1908–17); *FABERGÉ* in Cyrillic characters
RCIN 32646
PROVENANCE: Bought from Fabergé's London branch by Sir E. Hambro, 29 October 1913 (£29 10s)
EXHIBITIONS: QG 1995–6, no. 265

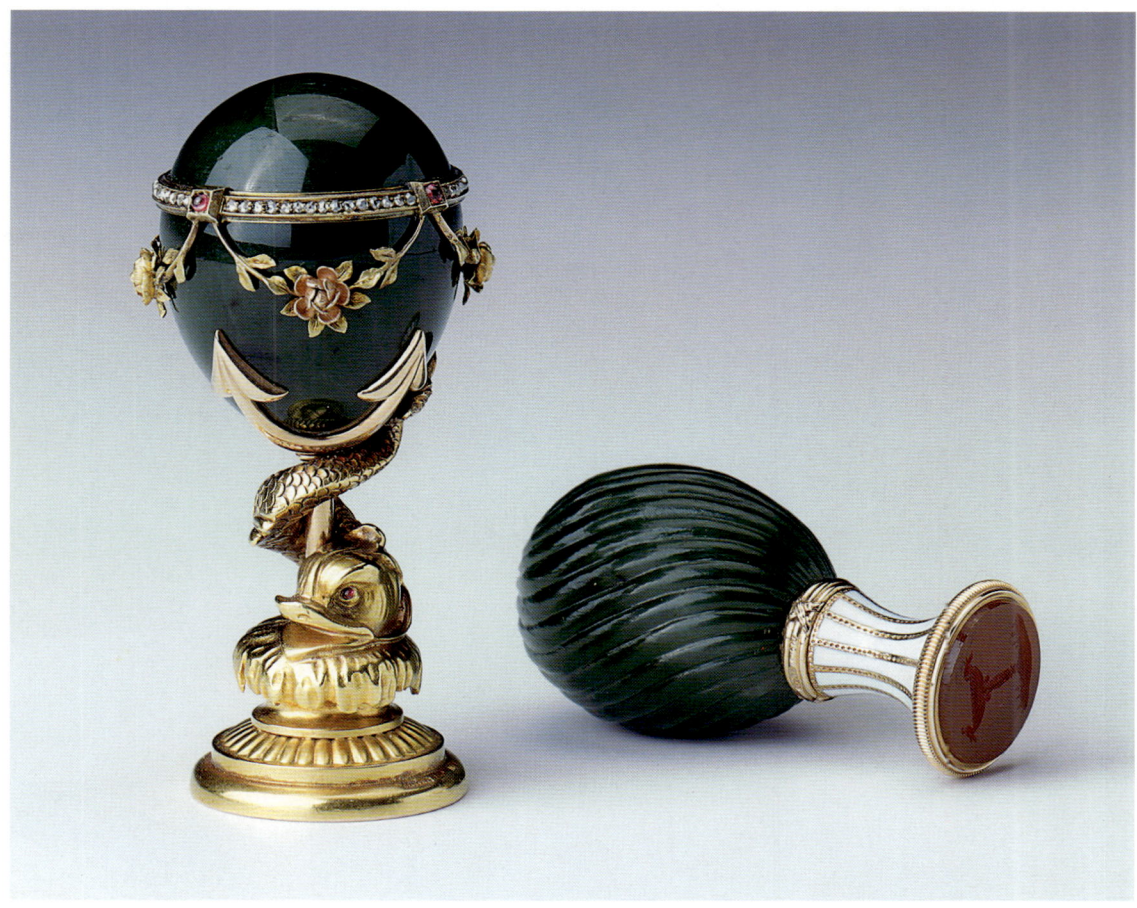

294 SEAL, *c.*1900

This nephrite hand seal is engraved with the crowned cypher of King George V. The egg-shaped handle supported on a dolphin is elaborately decorated with three-coloured gold floral swags and a band of diamonds and rubies.

Nephrite, three-colour gold, rose diamonds, rubies, 6.4 x 2.8 cm (2¹/₂ x 1¹/₈")
Mark of Michael Perchin; FABERGÉ in Cyrillic characters
RCIN 9258
PROVENANCE: Probably the nephrite and gold seal acquired by King George V from Fabergé's London branch, 28 October 1912 (£19)
EXHIBITIONS: QG 1995–6, no. 373; QG 2002–3, no. 276

295 SEAL, 1896–1903

The agate seal stone is engraved on the matrix with two birds perched on the rim of a classical bird-bath. There are several Fabergé hand seals in the Royal Collection, most of them engraved with the cyphers of their owners.

Nephrite, enamel, gold, agate, 4.8 x diameter 2.3 cm (1⁷/₈ x ⁷/₈")
Mark of Michael Perchin; gold mark of 56 *zolotniks* (1896–1908)
RCIN 40161
EXHIBITIONS: London 1977, no. G14; New York 1983, no. 45; QG 1985–6, no. 330; QG 1995–6, no. 378; QG 2002–3, no. 273

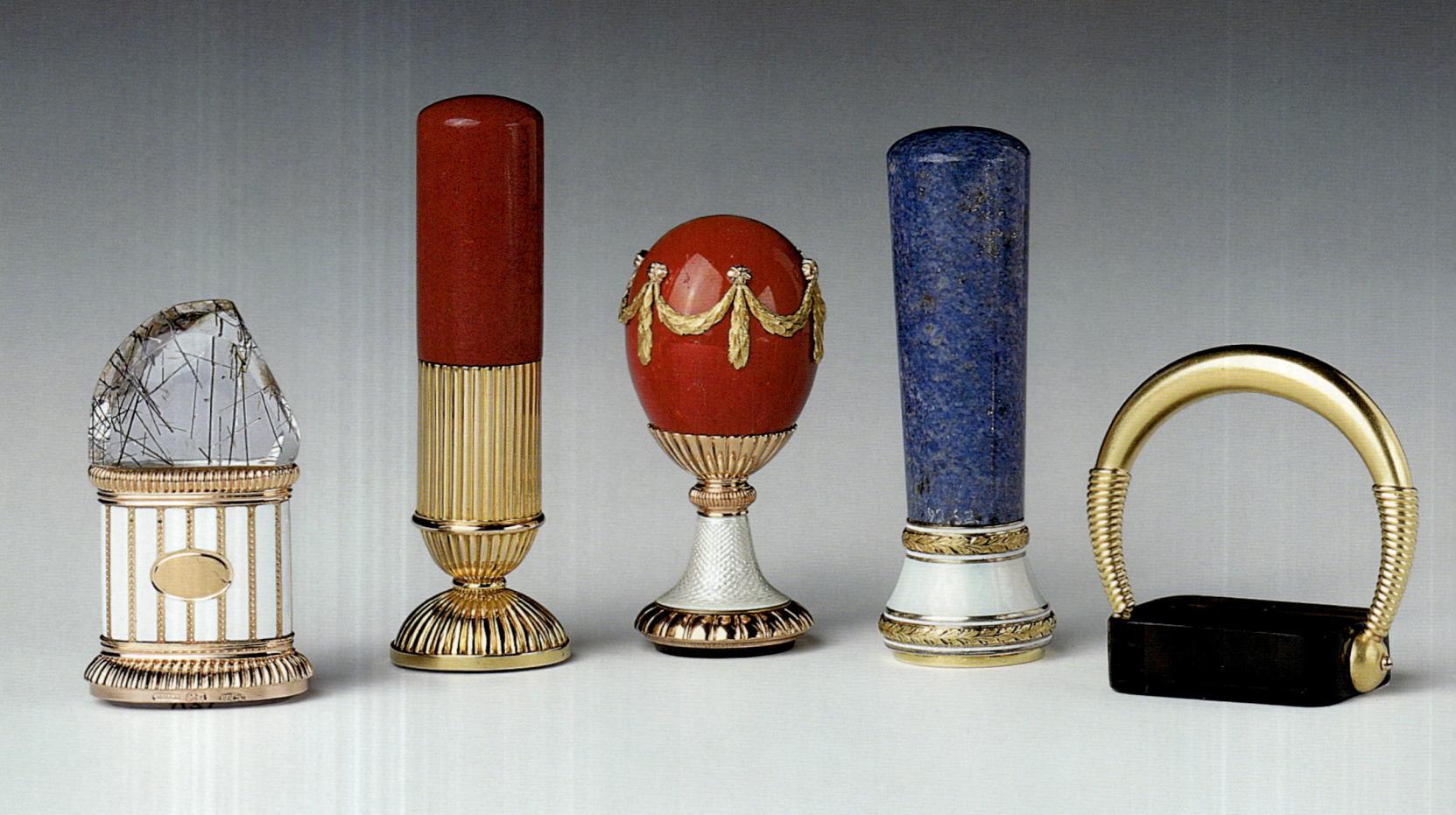

296 SEAL, 1896–1903

The handle of the seal is formed of rutilated quartz, which is rock crystal containing rutile – a mineral which occurs in columnar-shaped crystals.

Rutilated quartz, gold, enamel, 5 x 2.7 x 1.8 cm (1¹⁵/₁₆ x 1¹/₁₆ x ¹¹/₁₆")
Mark of Michael Perchin; gold mark of 56 *zolotniks* (1896–1908); *FABERGÉ* in Cyrillic characters
RCIN 9137
PROVENANCE: Prince and Princess Nicholas of Greece; by whom given to Queen Mary for her birthday, 26 May 1935
REFERENCES: QMPP VIII, no. 200
EXHIBITIONS: QG 1995–6, no. 463

297 SEAL, 1903–1908

Purpurine, two-colour gold, guilloché enamel, agate, 5.6 x diameter 2.5 cm (2³/₁₆ x 1")
Mark of Henrik Wigström; gold mark of 56 *zolotniks* (1896–1908); the cypher engraved *LN*
RCIN 9037
PROVENANCE: Acquired by Queen Mary; Royal Collection by 1953
EXHIBITIONS: QG 1995–6, no. 206

298 SEAL, BEFORE 1896

Purpurine, gold, cornelian, 7.2 x 2.2 x 2 cm (2¹³/₁₆ x ⁷/₈ x ¹³/₁₆")
Mark of Michael Perchin; gold mark of 56 *zolotniks* (before 1896); seal engraved *MM*
RCIN 43735
PROVENANCE: Acquired by Queen Mary; Royal Collection by 1953
EXHIBITIONS: QG 1995–6, no. 207

299 SEAL, *c.*1900

Lapis lazuli, two-colour gold, guilloché enamel, 6.7 x diameter 2.2 cm (2⅝ x ⅞")
Engraved with the crowned cypher of King George V
Unmarked
RCIN 9262
PROVENANCE: Acquired by King George V, *c.*1900
EXHIBITIONS: QG 1995–6, no. 410

300 SEAL, BEFORE 1896

A blank swivel seal in revivalist style, inspired by Scythian goldwork. A second example of this model is known.

Smoky quartz, gold, 4.2 x 4.3 x 2 cm (1⅝ x 1¹¹⁄₁₆ x ¹³⁄₁₆")
Mark of Erik Kollin; gold mark of 56 *zolotniks* (before 1896)
RCIN 13955
REFERENCES: Habsburg 1987, p. 140
EXHIBITIONS: QG 1995–6, no. 42

301 SEAL, 1903–1917

This amusing hand seal mounted with a nephrite frog was repeated by Fabergé, but in a slightly different model. A version mounted with a chameleon in nephrite exists in the Matilda Geddings Gray Collection, New Orleans Museum of Art. There are also two other versions with frogs, but in serpentine and agate, in the De Grigné Collection.

Silver, two-colour gold, guilloché enamel, nephrite, height 9.5 cm (3¾")
Mark of Henrik Wigström
RCIN 100339
PROVENANCE: Acquired by The Prince of Wales, 1981
EXHIBITIONS: QG 1985–6, no. 20; London 1992a, no. 5; London 1999, no. 25

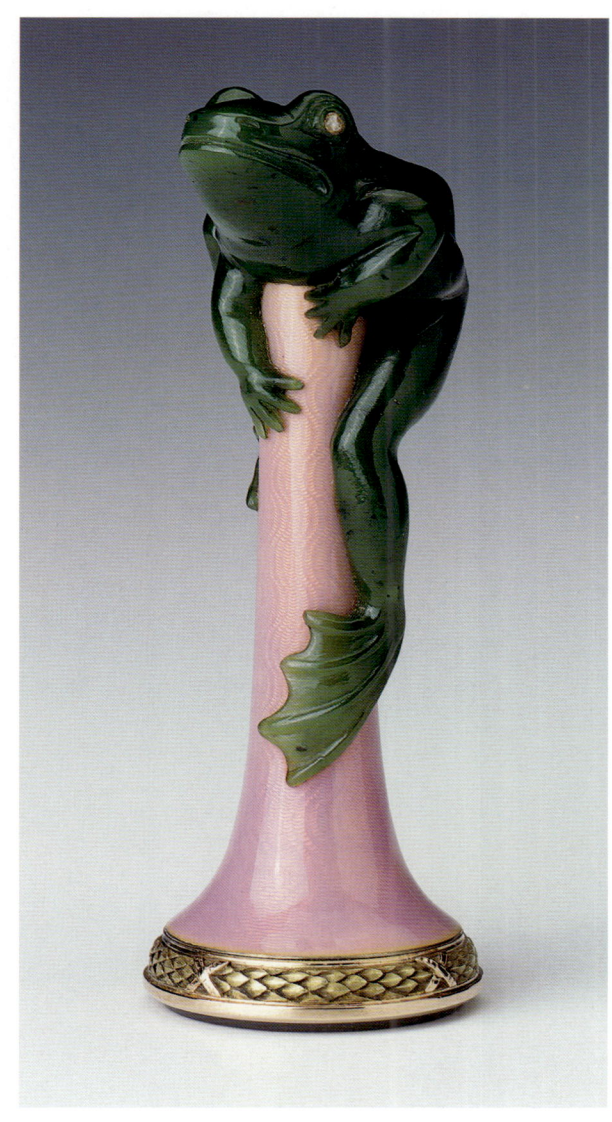

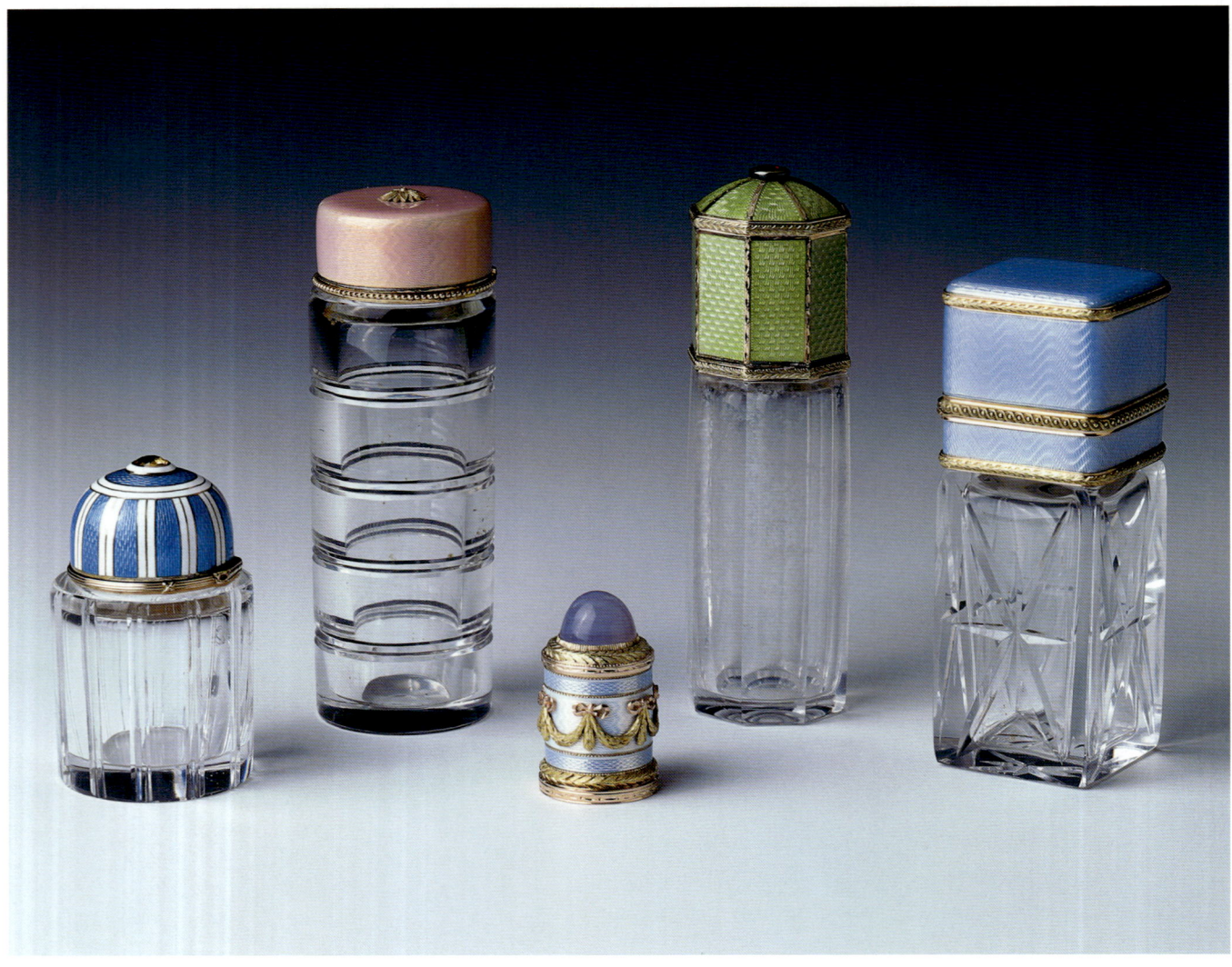

302 SCENT BOTTLE, 1908–1910

Scent bottles, powder boxes and compacts, menthol cases and parasol handles are among the accessories for women that Fabergé made. His elegant designs were keenly sought by society ladies, both in Russia and in England.

Rock crystal, gold, guilloché enamel, brilliant topaz, 5.4 x diameter 3.4 cm (2¹/₈ x 1⁵/₁₆")
Mark of Feodor Afanassiev; gold mark of 56 *zolotniks* (1908–17)
RCIN 8990
PROVENANCE: Bought by the Dowager Tsarina Marie Feodorovna, 11 April 1910 (80 roubles); by whom given to Queen Mary
EXHIBITIONS: QG 1985–6, no. 43; QG 1995–6, no. 138

303 SCENT BOTTLE, 1908–1917

Rock crystal, gold, silver-gilt, guilloché enamel, 9.1 x diameter 3.3 cm (3⁹/₁₆ x 1⁵/₁₆")
Mark of Feodor Afanassiev; gold mark of 56 *zolotniks* and silver mark of 88 *zolotniks* (1908–17); *FABERGÉ* in Cyrillic characters
RCIN 8985
EXHIBITIONS: QG 1985–6, no. 39; QG 1995–6, no. 266

304   MENTHOL CASE, 1908

Two-colour gold, guilloché enamel, moonstones, 3.2 x diameter 1.9 cm   (1¼ x ¾")
Mark of Henrik Wigström; gold mark of 56 *zolotniks* (1896–1908)
RCIN 9114
PROVENANCE: Given by the Duchess of Roxburghe to the Princess of Wales (later Queen Mary), Christmas 1908
REFERENCES: QMB I, no. 247; QMPP I, no. 239
EXHIBITIONS: QG 1995–6, no. 145

305   SCENT BOTTLE, *c.*1900

Glass, gold, guilloché enamel, silver-gilt, garnet, 9.5 x diameter 2.5 cm   (3¾ x 1")
Silver mark of 88 *zolotniks*
RCIN 100318
PROVENANCE: Bought by Lady Eckstein from Fabergé's London branch, 24 December 1908 (£14 10s); Queen
Elizabeth's collection

306   SCENT BOTTLE, 1908

Rock crystal, two-colour gold, guilloché enamel, 8.1 x 2.9 x 2.9 cm   (3³⁄₁₆ x 1⅛ x 1⅛")
Mark of Henrik Wigström; gold mark of 56 *zolotniks* (1896–1908)
RCIN 9007
PROVENANCE: Lord Revelstoke; by whom given to the Princess of Wales (later Queen Mary), 1909
REFERENCES: QMB I, no. 428; QMPP I, no. 209
EXHIBITIONS: QG 1985–6, no. 42; QG 1995–6, no. 139

307   CIGARETTE HOLDER, BEFORE 1896

Amber, two-colour gold, rose diamonds, rubies, 14.4 x diameter 1.8 cm   (5¹¹⁄₁₆ x ¹¹⁄₁₆")
Mark of Michael Perchin; gold mark of 56 *zolotniks* (before 1896); *FABERGÉ* in Cyrillic characters
RCIN 13941
PROVENANCE: Bought by Tsar Nicholas II and Tsarina Alexandra Feodorovna, 6 December 1895 (155 roubles); by
whom given to the Prince of Wales (later King Edward VII)
EXHIBITIONS: QG 1995–6, no. 364

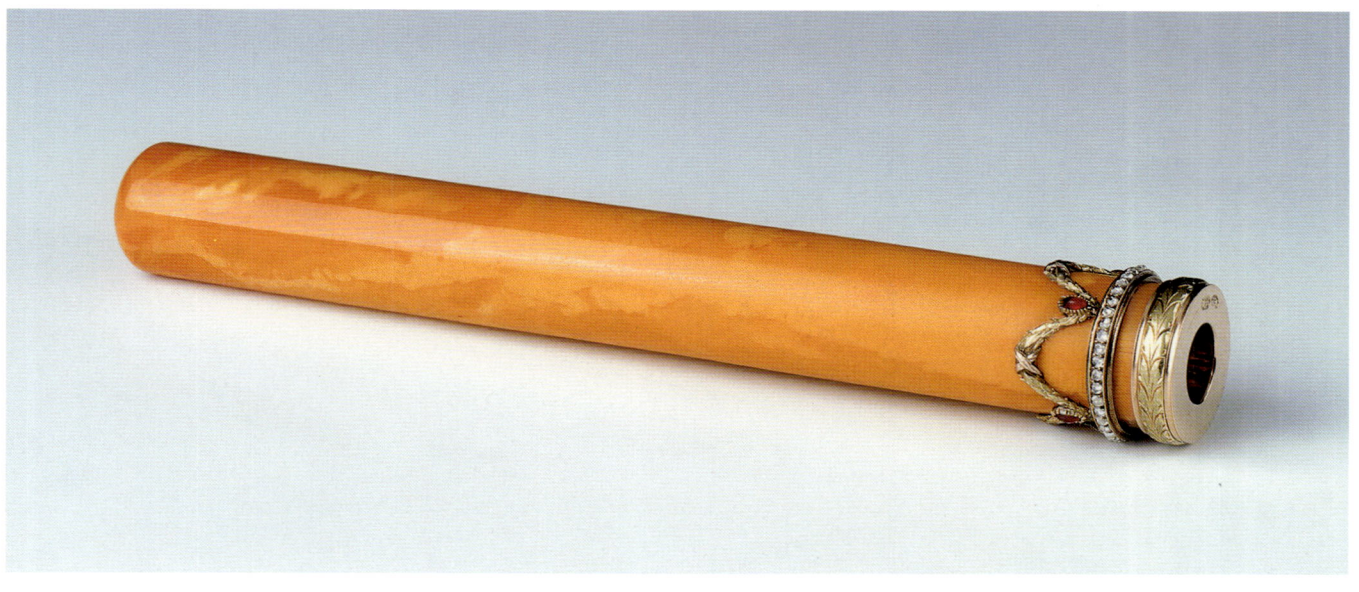

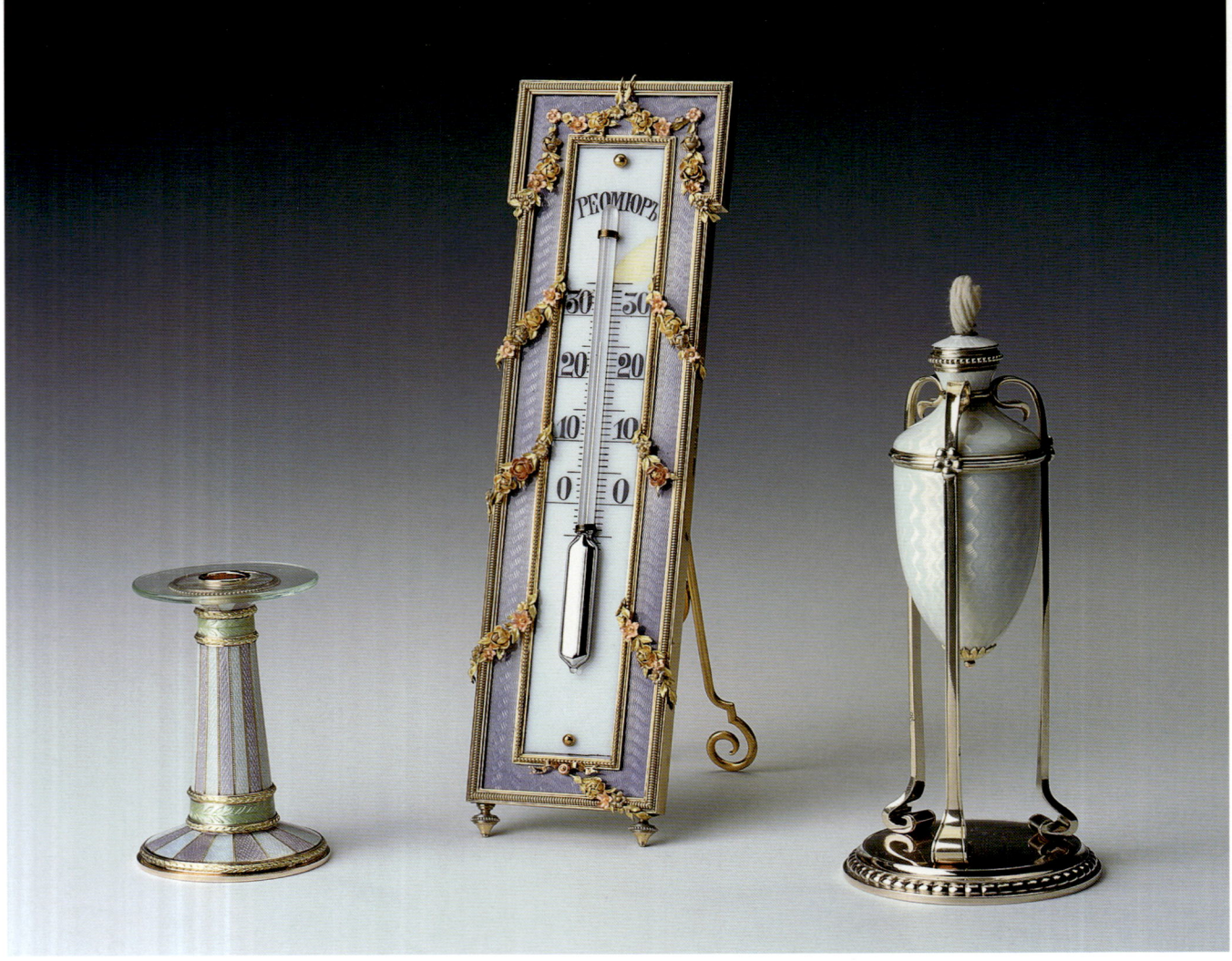

308 TAPER-STICK HOLDER, 1908–1917

Two-colour gold, rock crystal, guilloché enamel, 7.2 x diameter 4.7 cm (2¹³/₁₆ x 1⁷/₈")
Mark of Feodor Afanassiev; silver mark of 88 *zolotniks* (1908–17); *FABERGÉ* in Cyrillic characters
RCIN 40477
EXHIBITIONS: QG 1995–6, no. 273

309 THERMOMETER, BEFORE 1896

Fabergé's practical objects included highly decorative thermometers; he even produced clinical thermometers. Examples fitted with strut supports are known, including one also enamelled in mauve and made by Viktor Aarne.

Silver-gilt, guilloché enamel, ivory, 19.7 x 5.6 x 1.2 cm (7³/₄ x 2³/₁₆ x ½")
Mark of Viktor Aarne; silver mark of 88 *zolotniks* (before 1896)
RCIN 32448
PROVENANCE: Bought by Tsar Nicholas II, 1 July 1898 (145 roubles)
REFERENCES: Christie's 2000, pp. 64–5, lot 106

310 LAMP, 1896–1903

Silver-gilt, guilloché enamel, 13.3 x diameter 6 cm (5¹/₄ x 2³/₈")
Mark of Michael Perchin; silver mark of 88 *zolotniks* (1896–1908); *FABERGÉ* in Cyrillic characters
RCIN 40803
EXHIBITIONS: QG 1995–6, no. 402

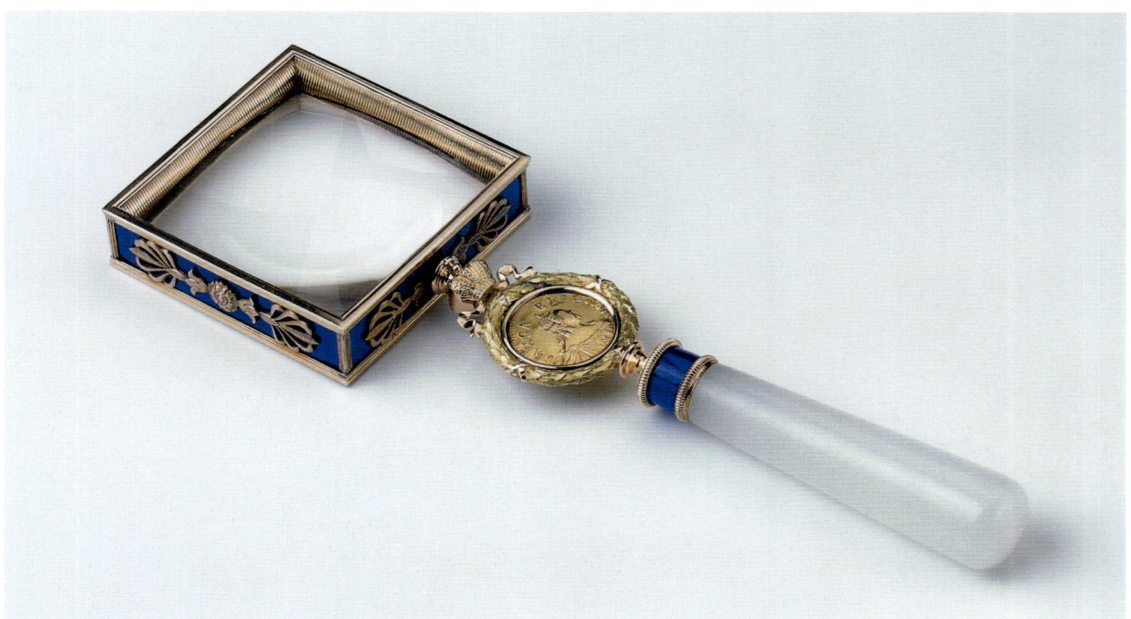

311 MAGNIFYING GLASS, 1896–1903

The gold mounts are in neo-classical style and the handle is set with a gold rouble of Tsarina Elizabeth Feodorovna, dated 1750.

Chalcedony, two-colour gold, guilloché enamel, 11.4 x 3.8 x 0.9 (4³/₈ x 1¹/₂ x ³/₈")
Mark of Michael Perchin; gold mark of 56 *zolotniks* (1896–1908); *FABERGÉ* in Cyrillic characters
RCIN 40165
PROVENANCE: Royal Collection by 1953
EXHIBITIONS: QG 1995–6, no. 411

312 MAGNIFYING GLASS, 1903–1905

Two-colour gold, nephrite, 20.5 x 9.1 x 2 cm (8¹/₁₆ x 3⁹/₁₆ x ¹³/₁₆")
Mark of Henrik Wigström; gold mark of 56 *zolotniks* (1896–1908); *FABERGÉ* in Cyrillic characters
RCIN 38805
PROVENANCE: Bought by Tsarina Alexandra Feodorovna, 12 November 1905 (275 roubles)

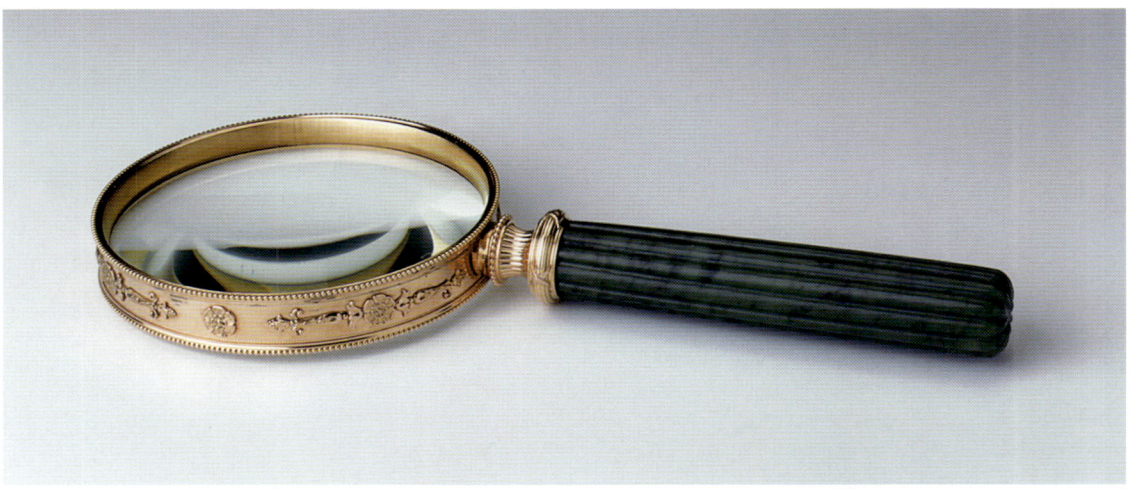

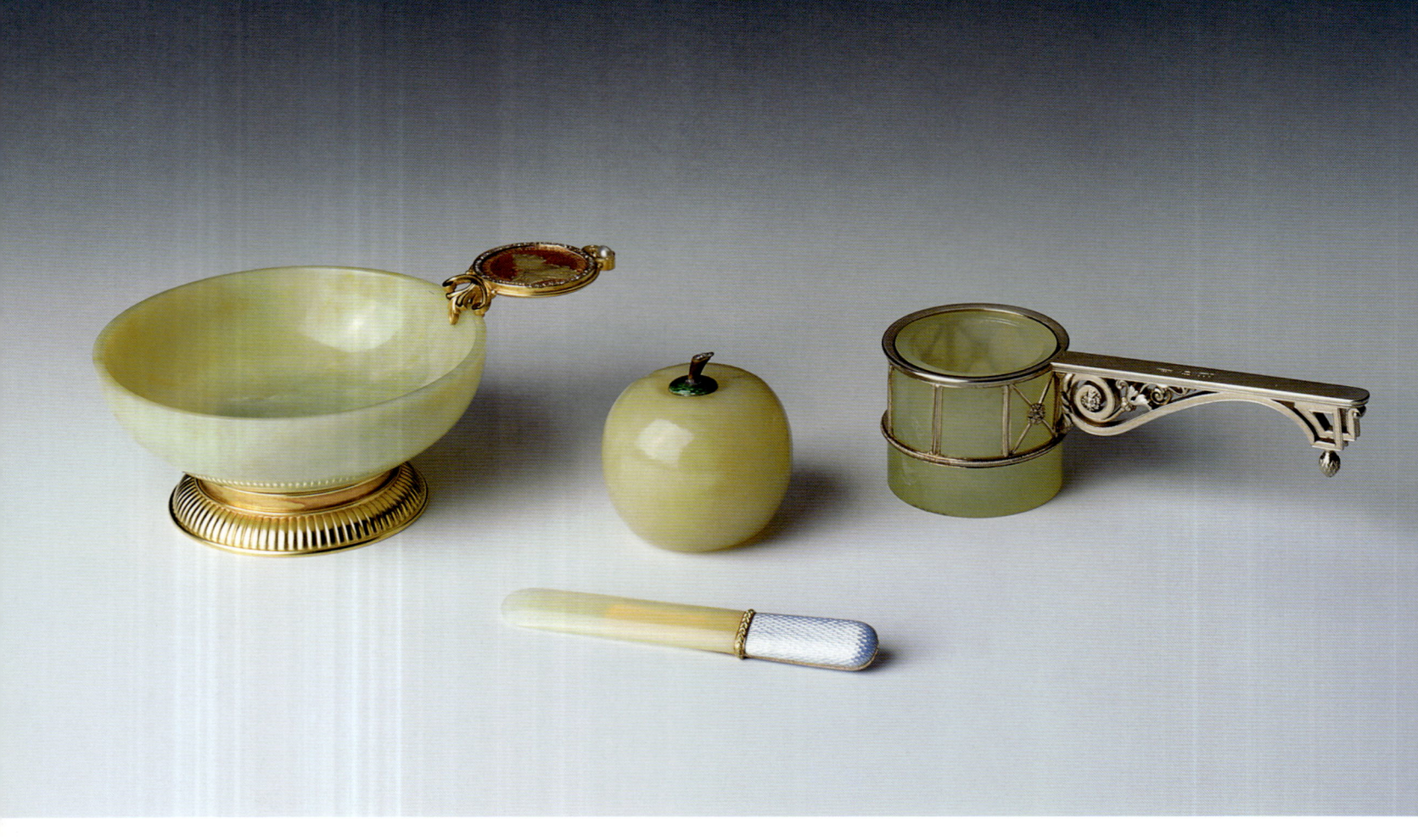

313 KOVSH, BEFORE 1896

The handle is inset with a Catherine the Great rouble of 1766.

Bowenite, gold, rose diamonds, pearl, enamel, 4.5 x 12.2 x 8.5 cm (1³/₄ x 4¹³/₁₆ x 3⅜")
Mark of Erik Kollin; gold mark of 56 *zolotniks* (before 1896)
RCIN 40108
PROVENANCE: Royal Collection by 1953
EXHIBITIONS: London 1953, no. 90; London 1977, no. I6; QG 1985–6, no. 24; QG 1995–6, no. 65

314 GUM POT IN THE FORM OF AN APPLE, 1896–1903

One of two examples in the Royal Collection of gum pots in the form of fruit. This was a popular shape for Fabergé's gum pots and several other examples are known.

Bowenite, gold, guilloché enamel, rose diamonds, 4.1 x diameter 4.1 cm (1⅝" x 1⅝")
Mark of Michael Perchin; gold mark of 56 *zolotniks* (1896–1908)
RCIN 100324
PROVENANCE: Acquired by Queen Elizabeth, date unknown

315 WINE TASTER, BEFORE 1896

Bowenite, silver-gilt, 3.8 x 11.2 x 4.1 cm (1½ x 4⁷/₁₆ x 1⅝")
Mark of Michael Perchin; silver mark of 88 *zolotniks* (before 1896); *FABERGÉ* in Cyrillic characters
RCIN 40804
PROVENANCE: Royal Collection before 1953
EXHIBITIONS: QG 1995–6, no. 64

316 PAPER-KNIFE, BEFORE 1896

Bowenite, two-colour gold, guilloché enamel, rose diamonds, 8.4 x 2.2 x 0.4 cm (3⁵⁄₁₆ x ⁷⁄₈ x ³⁄₁₆")
Mark of Michael Perchin; gold mark of 56 *zolotniks* (before 1896); *FABERGÉ* in Cyrillic characters
RCIN 23237
PROVENANCE: Given to Queen Mary by Dowager Tsarina Marie Feodorovna before 1918
REFERENCES: QMB I, no. 376; QMPP I, no. 219
EXHIBITIONS: QG 1995–6, no. 397

317   PRESENTATION KOVSH, 1894

This *kovsh* was presented to the Prince of Wales (later King Edward VII) on the occasion of the coronation of Tsar Nicholas II on 9 May 1896 at Uspensky Cathedral in the Kremlin, where all the tsars of the House of Romanov had been crowned.

Silver, 13 x 30.5 x 15 cm (5¹⁄₈ x 12 x 5⁷⁄₈")
Presentation inscription in Cyrillic
RCIN 40801
PROVENANCE: Presented to the Prince of Wales (later King Edward VII) on the occasion of the coronation of Tsar Nicholas II, 9 May 1896
EXHIBITIONS: QG 1995–6, no. 357

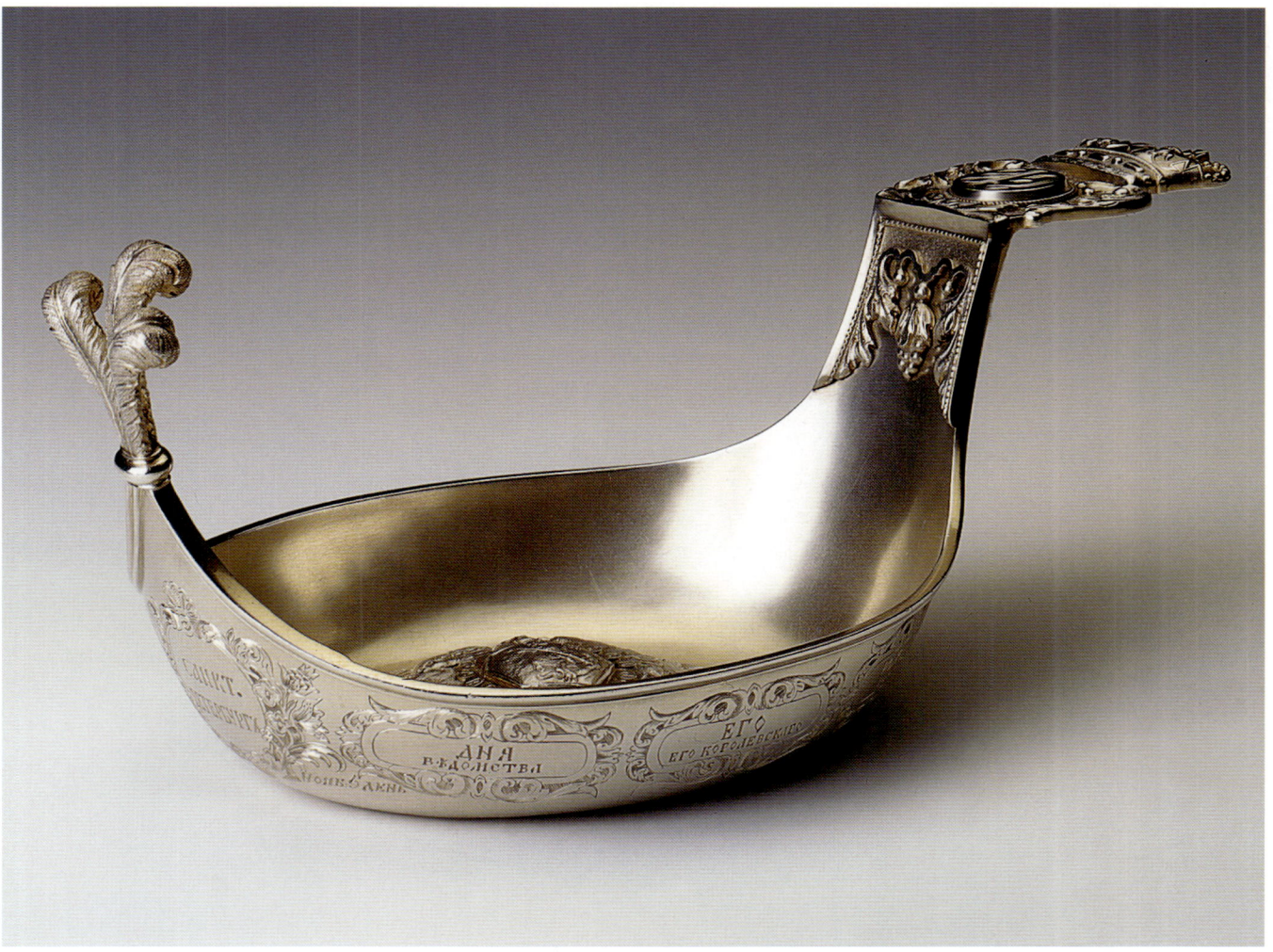

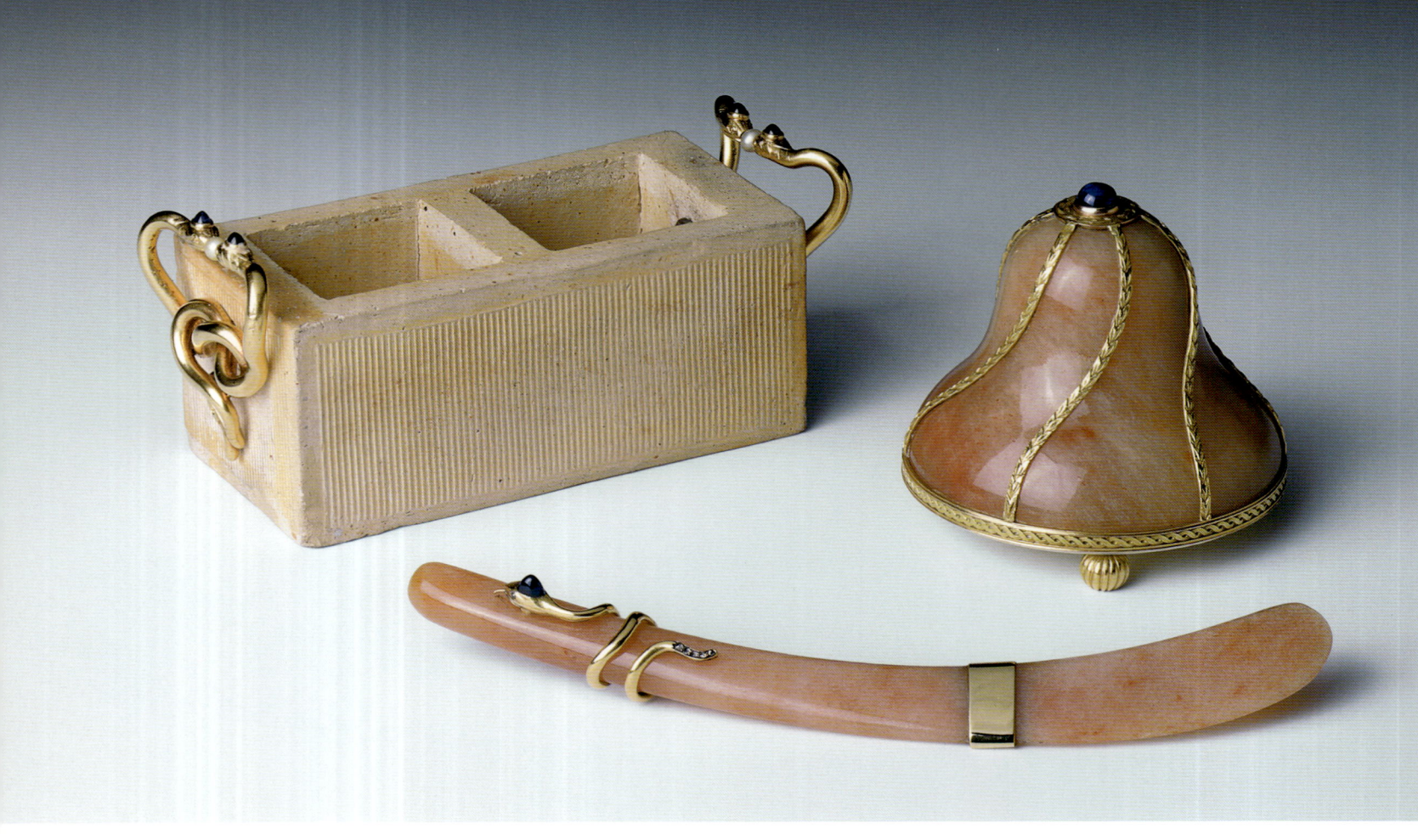

318 MATCH HOLDER, BEFORE 1896

This is one of three match holders formed of bricks made by the Gusareva factory in Moscow and now in the Royal Collection, two of which are by Fabergé. This example is mounted with handles in the form of pairs of entwined serpents. The serpent motif was used with great regularity by Fabergé's designers whether for mounted objects such as the *kovsh* (cat. 265) or as an integral part of the design of an object such as the cigarette case (cat. 187).

The Gusareva factory supplied the bricks to build the German cemetery at Vedenskuga, Moscow. Nicholas Kelch, brother of Alexander (see cat. 4); Henrik Bolin, one of the founders of Fabergé's competitor Bolin (see p. 25); and Oscar Pihl, one of Fabergé's workmasters and the father of Alma Pihl (see cat. 3) are buried there.

Brick, gold, cabochon sapphires, pearls, 5.3 x 11.3 x 4.9 cm (2¹/₁₆ x 4⁷/₁₆ x 1¹⁵/₁₆")
Mark of Erik Kollin; gold mark of 56 *zolotniks* (before 1896); brick stamped A. GUSAREV, MOSCOW in Cyrillic characters
RCIN 8337
PROVENANCE: Acquired by King Edward VII, date unknown
EXHIBITIONS: QG 1995–6, no. 58

319 PAPER-KNIFE, BEFORE 1896

Of scimitar form, this paper-knife features a gold mount in the form of a serpent.

Aventurine quartz, gold, rose diamonds, cabochon sapphire, 14.2 x 1.7 x 1.5 cm (5⁹/₁₆ x ¹¹/₁₆ x ⁹/₁₆")
Mark of Michael Perchin; gold mark of 56 *zolotniks* (before 1896)
RCIN 100320
PROVENANCE: Acquired by Queen Elizabeth, date unknown

320   BELL PUSH, BEFORE 1896

Gold, aventurine quartz, cabochon sapphire, ivory, 6 x diameter 6.3 cm (2⅜ x 2½")
Mark of Michael Perchin; gold mark of 56 *zolotniks* (before 1896)
RCIN 100314
PROVENANCE: Acquired by Queen Elizabeth, date unknown

321   KOVSH, 1896–1907

The handle of this *kovsh* is fitted with a Catherine the Great rouble of 1781.

Silver, moonstones, 6.2 x 14.5 x 5.8 cm (2⁷/₁₆ x 5¹¹/₁₆ x 1⁵/₁₆")
Mark of Anders Nevalainen; Moscow silver mark of 88 *zolotniks* (1896–1908)
RCIN 32419
PROVENANCE: Bought by Dowager Tsarina Marie Feodorovna, 14 December 1907 (70 roubles)
EXHIBITIONS: QG 1995–6, no. 45

322   MATCH HOLDER, *c.*1900

Julius Rappoport (1864–1916), who made this match holder, specialised in silver-mounted objects. His putto mount elevates the brick from a mundane to a sophisticated object. A similar silver-mounted brick match holder was formerly in the Forbes Collection.

Brick, silver, 10 x 10.1 x 6.1 cm (3¹⁵/₁₆ x 4 x 2³/₈")
Mark of Julius Rappoport; *FABERGÉ* in Cyrillic characters; brick stamped *A GUSAREV FACTORY, MOSCOW* in Cyrillic characters
RCIN 8338
PROVENANCE: Acquired by King Edward VII, date unknown
REFERENCES: Forbes & Tromeur-Brenner 1999, pp. 238–9
EXHIBITIONS: QG 1995–6, no. 199

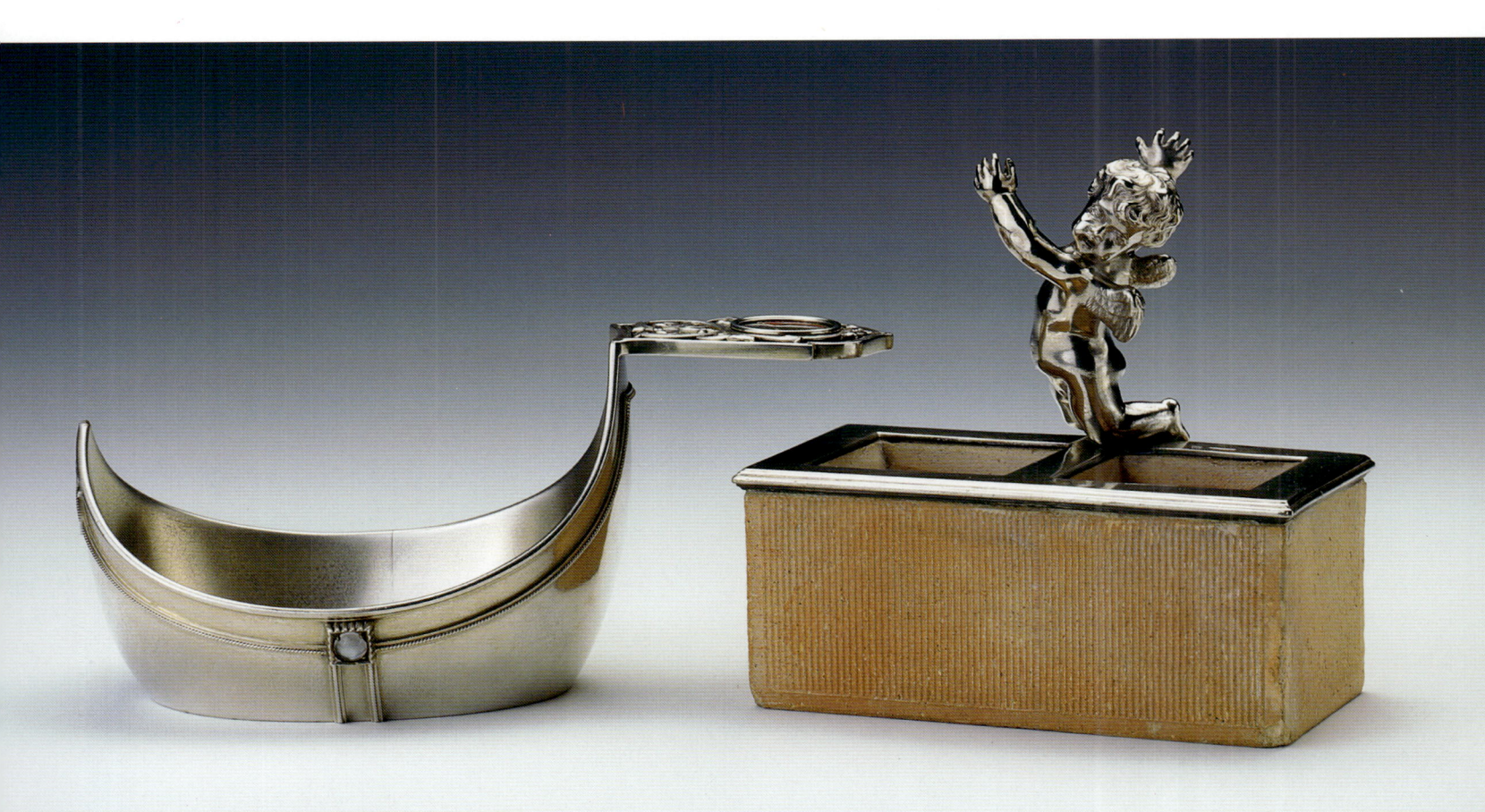

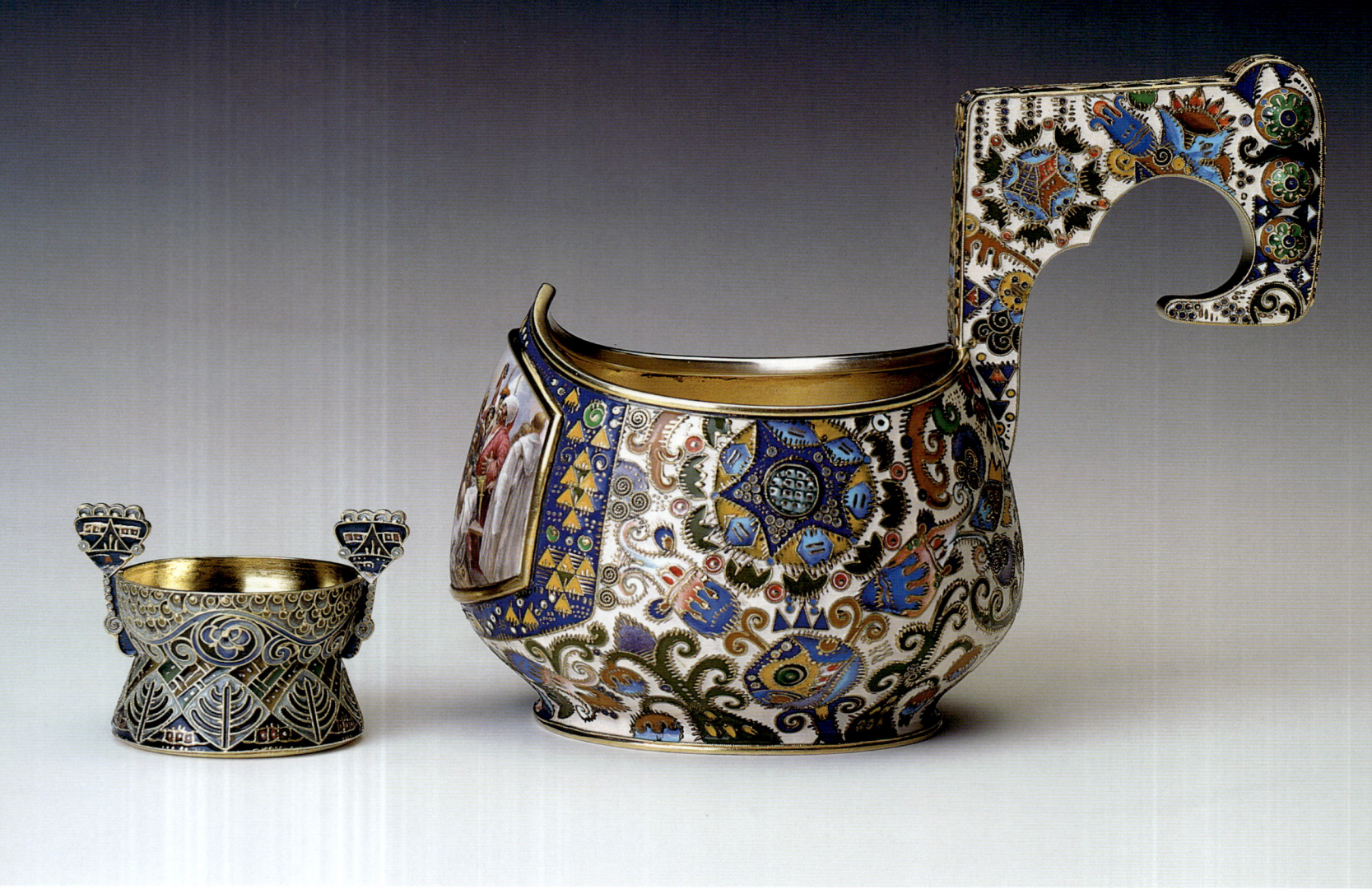

323 BRATINA, 1908–1917

This dish has cloisonné enamel decoration of geometric shapes in a restrained palette of browns, blues and greens. It was made in Feodor Rückert's workshop in Moscow and is consistent with his style of enamelling from 1908 onwards.

Silver-gilt, cloisonné enamel, 5.2 x 7.2 x 5.3 cm (2¹/₁₆ x 2¹³/₁₆ x 2¹/₁₆")
Mark of Feodor Rückert; Moscow silver mark of 88 *zolotniks* (1908–17)
RCIN 100311
PROVENANCE: Acquired by Queen Elizabeth, date unknown

324 KOVSH, 1908–1913

This *kovsh* in traditional Russian style is enamelled *en plein* with a scene of the Zaporozhye Cossacks after the painting by Ilya Repin (1844–1930). It was made in the Moscow workshop of Feodor Rückert and incorporates brightly coloured cloisonné enamelling on the body and high hooked handle.

Silver-gilt, cloisonné and *en plein* enamel, cabochon emeralds, 15.5 x 18.7 x 11.4 cm (6¹/₈ x 7³/₈ x 4¹/₂")
Mark of Feodor Rückert; Moscow silver mark of 88 *zolotniks* (1908–17); C. FABERGÉ in Cyrillic characters; English import marks for 1913
RCIN 100327
PROVENANCE: Acquired by Queen Elizabeth, date unknown

325   KOVSH, *c*.1911

This *kovsh*, in the traditional Russian style, was made in Fabergé's Moscow branch by Feodor Rückert.

Silver-gilt, cloisonné enamel, 14.4 x 18.2 x 11 cm (5¹¹/₁₆ x 7³/₁₆ x 4³/₈")
Mark of Feodor Rückert; Moscow silver mark of 91 *zolotniks* (1908–17); *C. FABERGÉ* in Cyrillic characters;
initials of Carl Fabergé in Roman letters; English import marks for 1911
RCIN 32475
EXHIBITIONS: QG 1995–6, no. 44

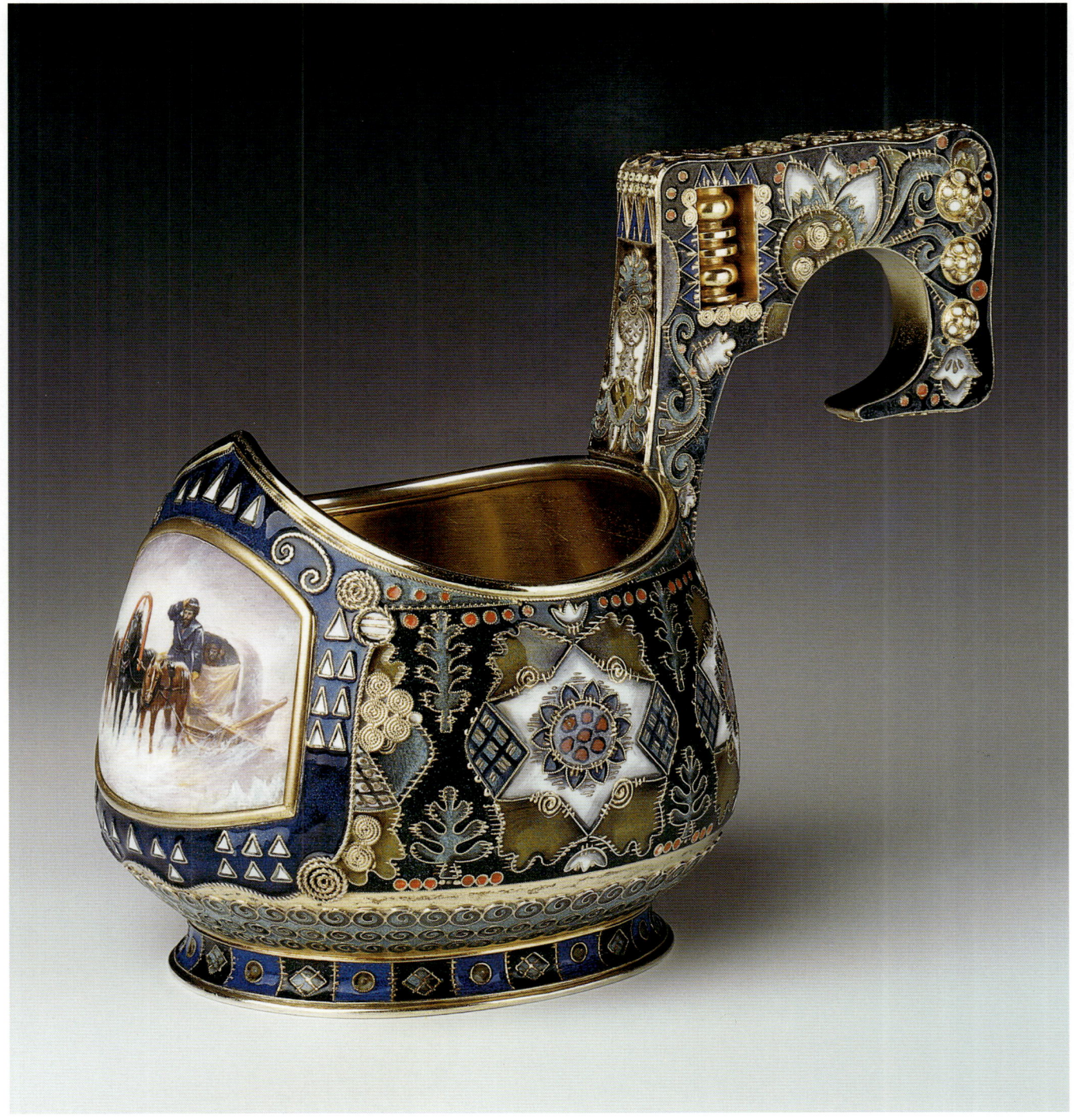

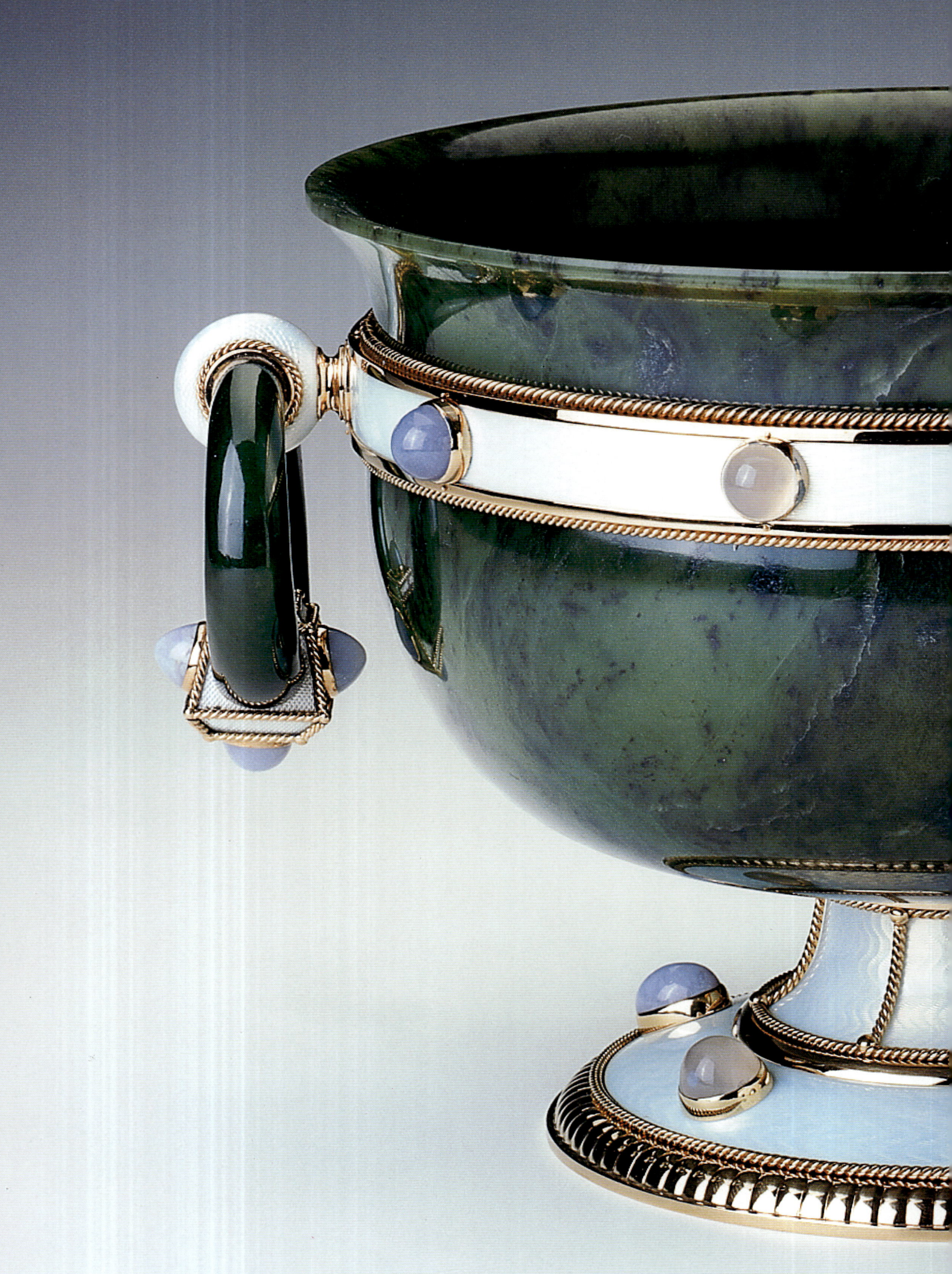

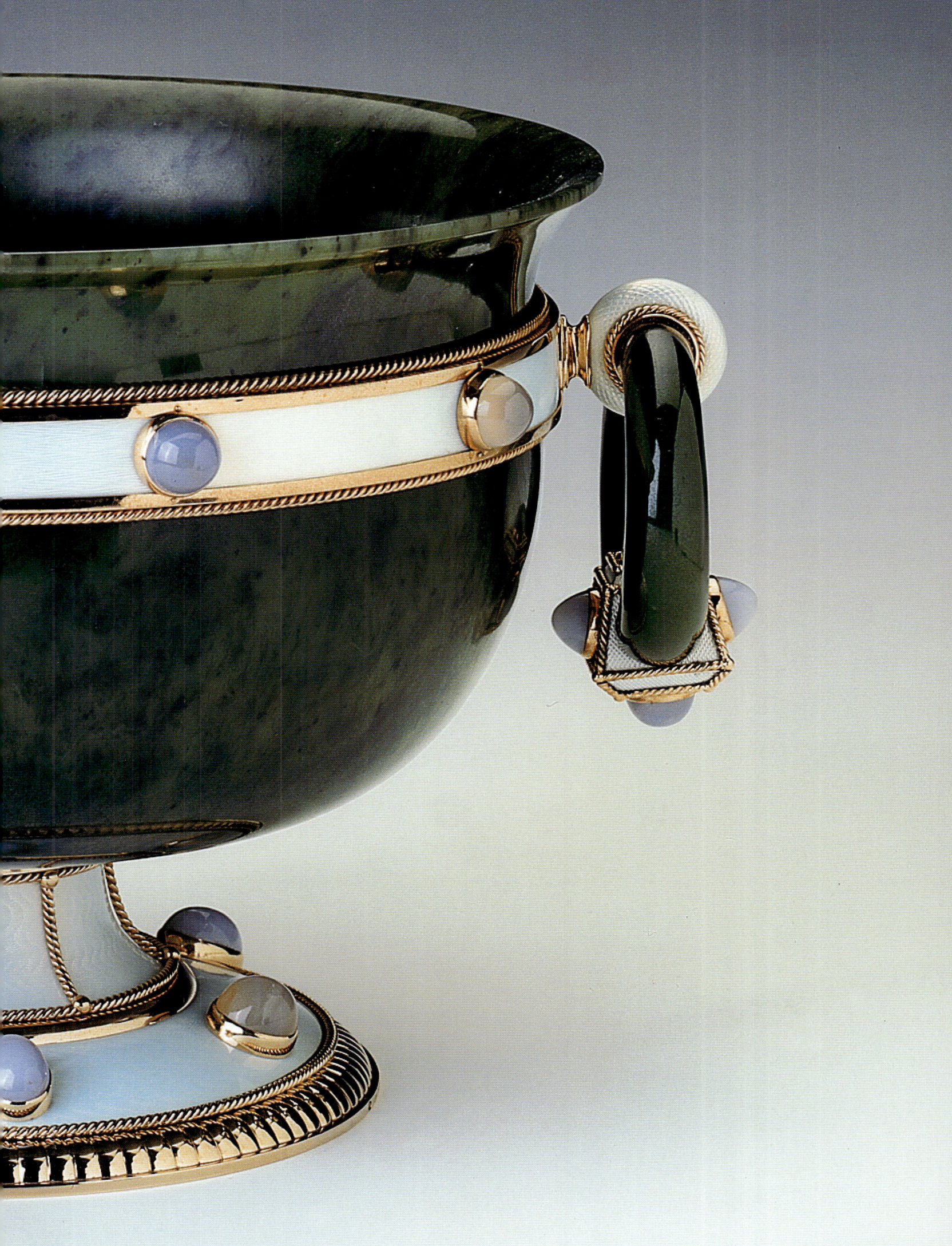

326 VASE, 1908

This urn-shaped nephrite vase was presented by Tsar Nicholas II to King Edward VII when the King visited Reval (now Tallinn in Estonia) in June 1908. King Edward VII was accompanied on his visit by Queen Alexandra and Princess Victoria. They departed on the royal yacht *Victoria and Albert* and passed through the Kiel Canal, where they were greeted by Prince Henry of Prussia and a large contingent from the German navy. On 9 June King Edward was met by the Tsar and most of the imperial family on their yachts the *Standart* and the *Pole Star*. During the two-day meeting diplomatic discussions, banquets and balls were held on the yachts but neither the King nor the Tsar went ashore. The King's gift to his nephew to mark the occasion was a naval sword made by Wilkinson and inscribed *For His Imperial Majesty Emperor of All Russia Nicholas II from His Loving Uncle Edward Reval 1908*. The sword is now in the museum at Tsarskoë Selo, outside St Petersburg.

Nephrite, guilloché enamel, silver-gilt, gold, moonstones, cabochon chalcedony, 15.7 x 24.9 x 20.3 cm
(6³/₁₆ x 9¹³/₁₆ x 8")
Mark of Henrik Wigström; silver mark of 88 *zolotniks* (1896–1908); *FABERGÉ* in Cyrillic characters
RCIN 49821
PROVENANCE: Bought by Tsar Nicholas II, 23 May 1908 (2,500 roubles); by whom presented to King Edward VII, 9 June 1908
REFERENCES: Bainbridge 1949, pl. 92; Magnus 1964, pp. 407–8

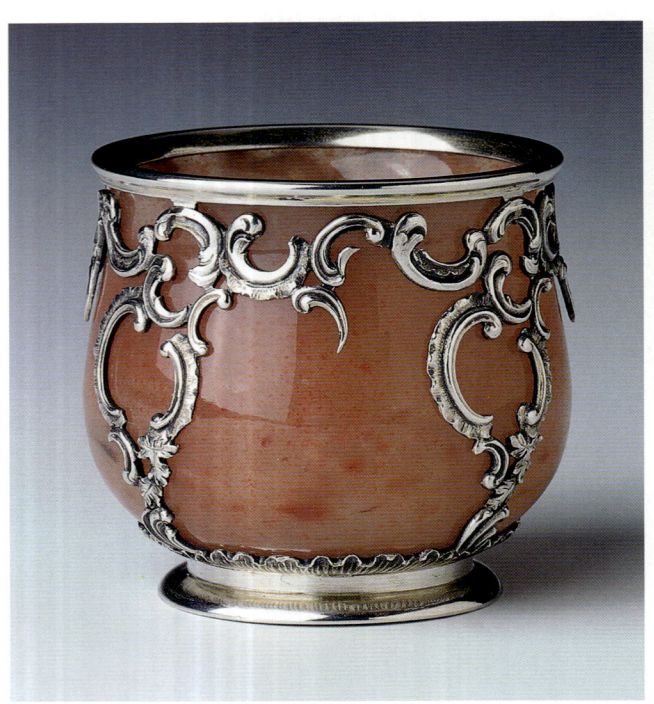

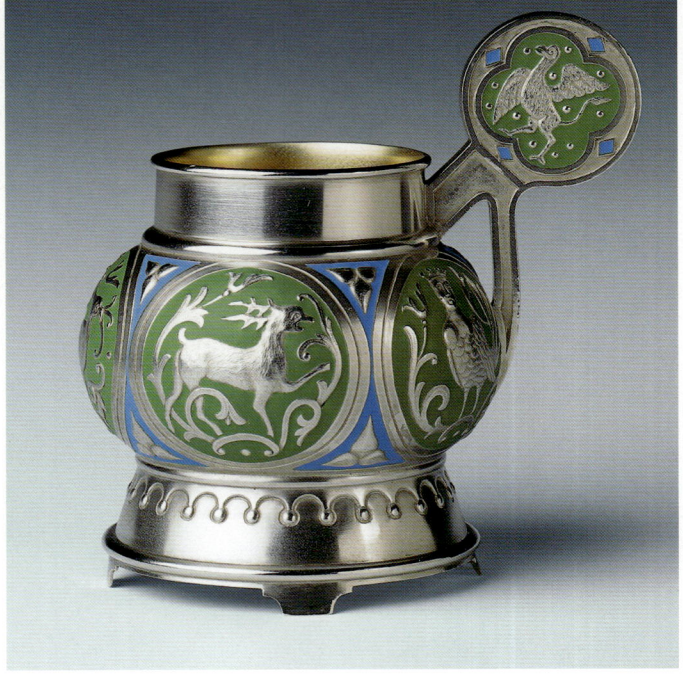

327 VASE, BEFORE 1896

This silver-mounted aventurine quartz vase is a further example of the neo-rococo style often used by Fabergé's designers.

Aventurine quartz, silver, 4.6 x diameter 4.9 cm (1¹³/₁₆ x 1¹⁵/₁₆")
Mark of Julius Rappoport; silver mark of 88 *zolotniks* (before 1896)
RCIN 100317
PROVENANCE: Acquired by Queen Elizabeth, date unknown

328 TCHARKA, 1896–1908

The design of this *tcharka* is derived from the Old Russian style, but the combination of repoussé decoration of birds and stags with the matt blue and green enamel gives the cup a very modern feel. It was made in the Moscow workshops.

Silver, silver-gilt, enamel, 10.6 x 10.5 x 8 cm (4³/₁₆ x 4¹/₈ x 3¹/₈")
Moscow silver mark of 84 *zolotniks* (1896–1908); *C. FABERGÉ* in Cyrillic characters
RCIN 100319
PROVENANCE: Acquired by Queen Elizabeth, date unknown

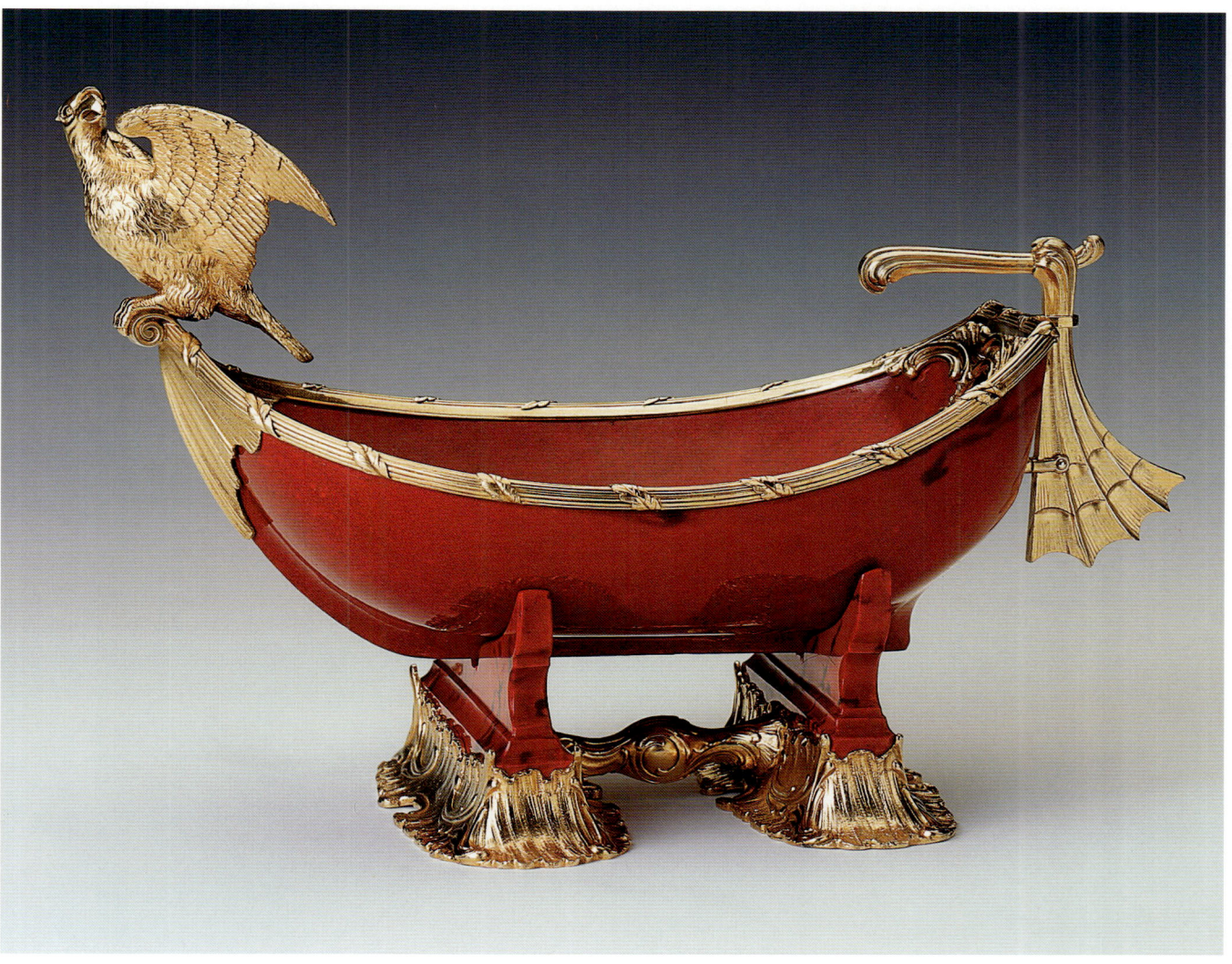

329 KOVSH, BEFORE 1896

This large-scale *kovsh* is in the form of a boat with rococo mounts.

Purpurine, silver-gilt, 17.8 x 28.3 x 13.7 cm (7 x 11¹/₈ x 5³/₈")
Mark of Julius Rappoport; silver mark of 84 *zolotniks* (before 1896); *FABERGÉ* in Cyrillic characters
RCIN 32537
EXHIBITIONS: QG 1995–6, no. 460

330 VASE, 1896–1903

This vase was bought by Leopold de Rothschild as a coronation present for King George V and Queen Mary in 1911. It is one of several gold-mounted, jewelled and enamelled rock crystal pieces in the Renaissance style produced by Perchin. The enamel includes stylised polychrome foliate decoration set with cabochon precious stones. Leopold de Rothschild presented the vase, filled with orchids grown in his hot-houses at Gunnersbury Park, to the King and Queen on coronation day.

Rock crystal, gold, enamel, cabochon rubies, emeralds, sapphires, 16.5 x diameter 13.5 cm (6½ x 5⁵⁄₁₆")
Mark of Michael Perchin; gold mark of 72 *zolotniks* (1896–1908); *FABERGÉ* in Cyrillic characters
RCIN 8949
PROVENANCE: Bought by Leopold de Rothschild from Fabergé's London branch, 1911 (£430); by whom presented to King George V and Queen Mary on their coronation day, 22 June 1911
REFERENCES: QMB I, no. 423; QMPP I, no. 271; Bainbridge 1949, p. 84
EXHIBITIONS: London 1954; London 1977, no. F4; QG 1985–6, no. 118; St Petersburg/Paris/London 1993–4, no. 168; QG 1995–6, no. 39

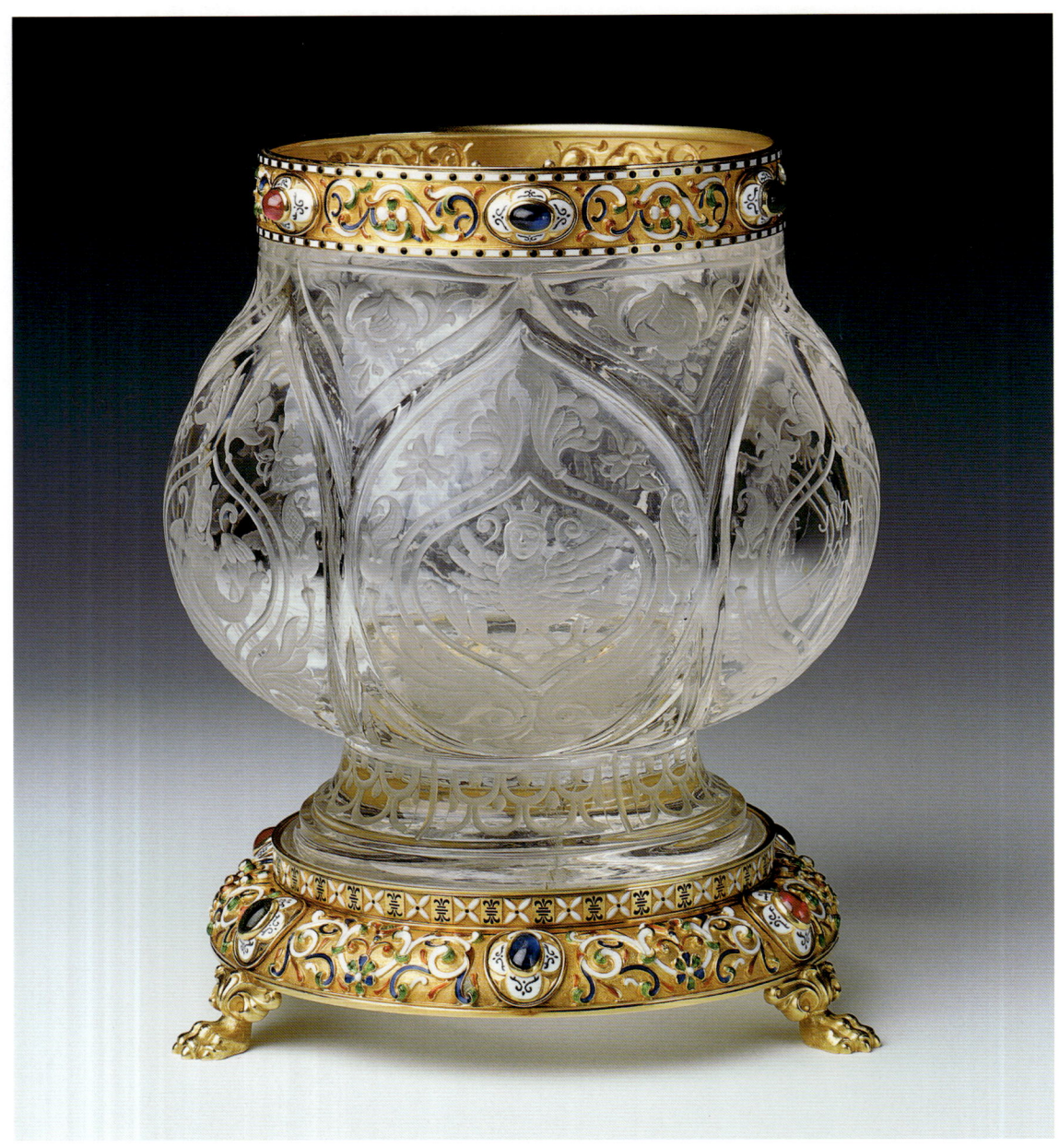

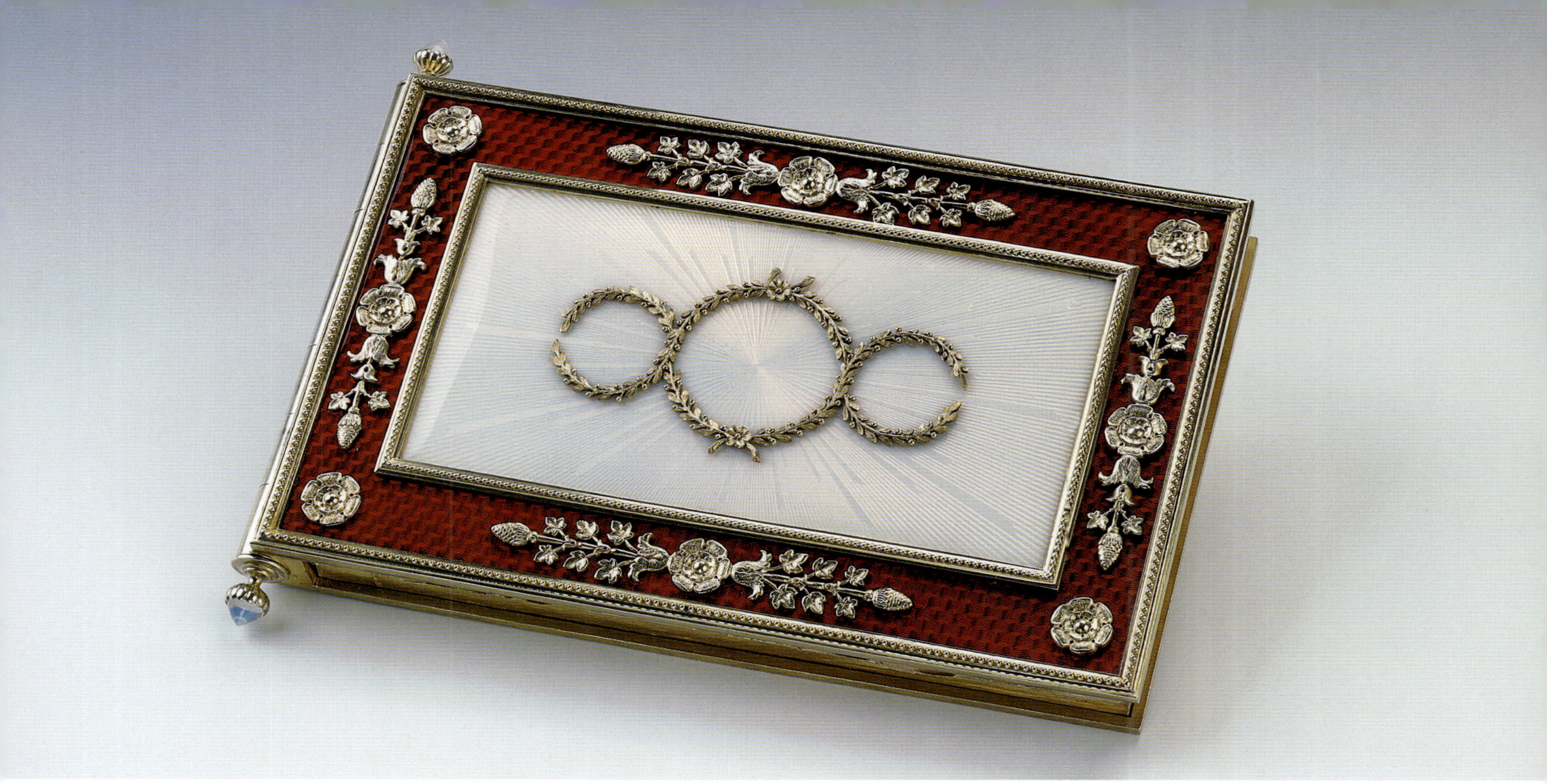

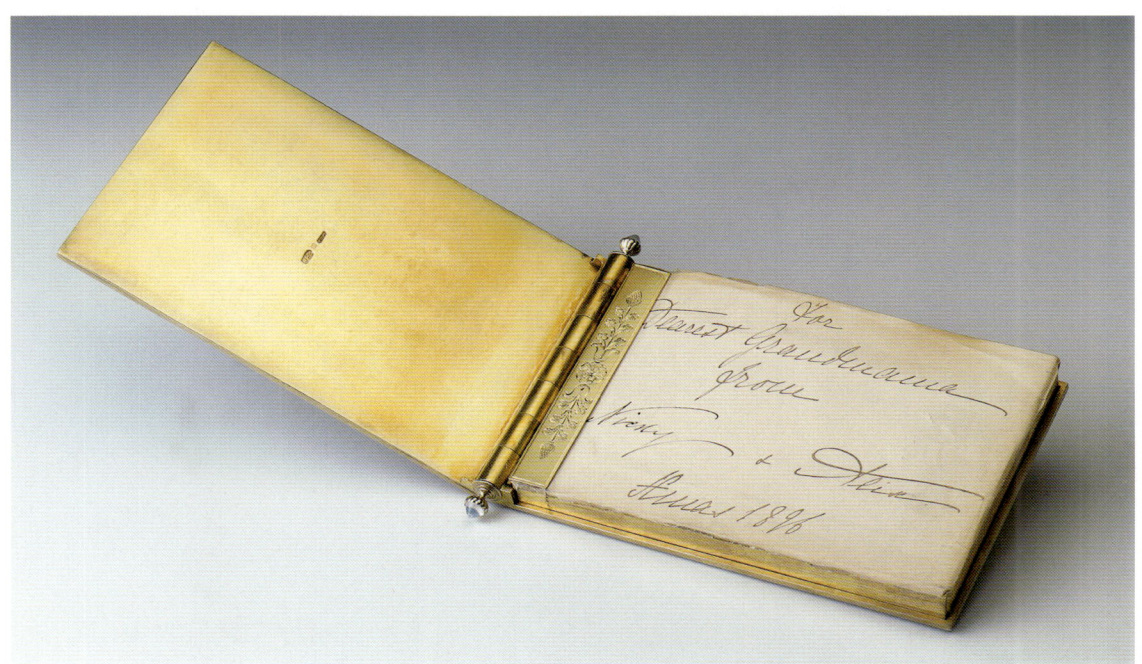

331 NOTEBOOK, BEFORE 1896

This beautifully enamelled notebook was a present from Tsar Nicholas II and Tsarina Alexandra Feodorovna to Queen Victoria for Christmas 1896. Its pages were later signed by visitors to Queen Victoria's Diamond Jubilee celebration on 22 June 1897.

Silver-gilt, guilloché enamel, moonstones, 1.8 x 16.2 x 12.6 cm ($^{11}/_{16}$ x 6$^3/_8$ x 4$^{15}/_{16}$")
Mark of Viktor Aarne; silver mark of 88 *zolotniks* (before 1896); *FABERGÉ* in Cyrillic characters
RCIN 4819
PROVENANCE: Bought jointly by Tsar Nicholas II and Tsarina Alexandra Feodorovna, December 1896 (250 roubles); by whom given to Queen Victoria, Christmas 1896
EXHIBITIONS: QG 1995–6, no. 467

332 NOTEBOOK CASE, 1903–1907

Members of the royal family were always accompanied on their visits to Fabergé's London branch and on the occasion of the purchase of this notebook case in 1907, King Edward VII visited with Mrs Keppel and a Mrs Hartman, the last named being the purchaser.

Leather, two-colour gold, enamel, rose diamonds, moonstone, 1.7 x 7.5 x 11 cm (¹¹/₁₆ x 2¹³/₁₆ x 4⁵/₁₆")
Mark of Henrik Wigström; gold mark of 56 *zolotniks* (1896–1908)
RCIN 40112
PROVENANCE: Bought by Mrs Hartman from Fabergé's London branch, 29 November 1907 (£26 5s); by whom given to Queen Alexandra
EXHIBITIONS: London 1953, no. 23; London 1977, no. K21; QG 1995–6, no. 264

333 EXTENDING PENCIL HOLDER, BEFORE 1896

Gold, guilloché enamel, rose diamonds, 7.1 x diameter 0.8 cm (2¹³/₁₆ x ⁵/₁₆")
Mark of Michael Perchin; gold mark before 1896
RCIN 23245
PROVENANCE: Given to Queen Mary by the Prince of Wales (later King Edward VIII) before 1920
REFERENCES: QMB I, no. 244; QMPP I, no. 240
EXHIBITIONS: QG 1995–6, no. 385

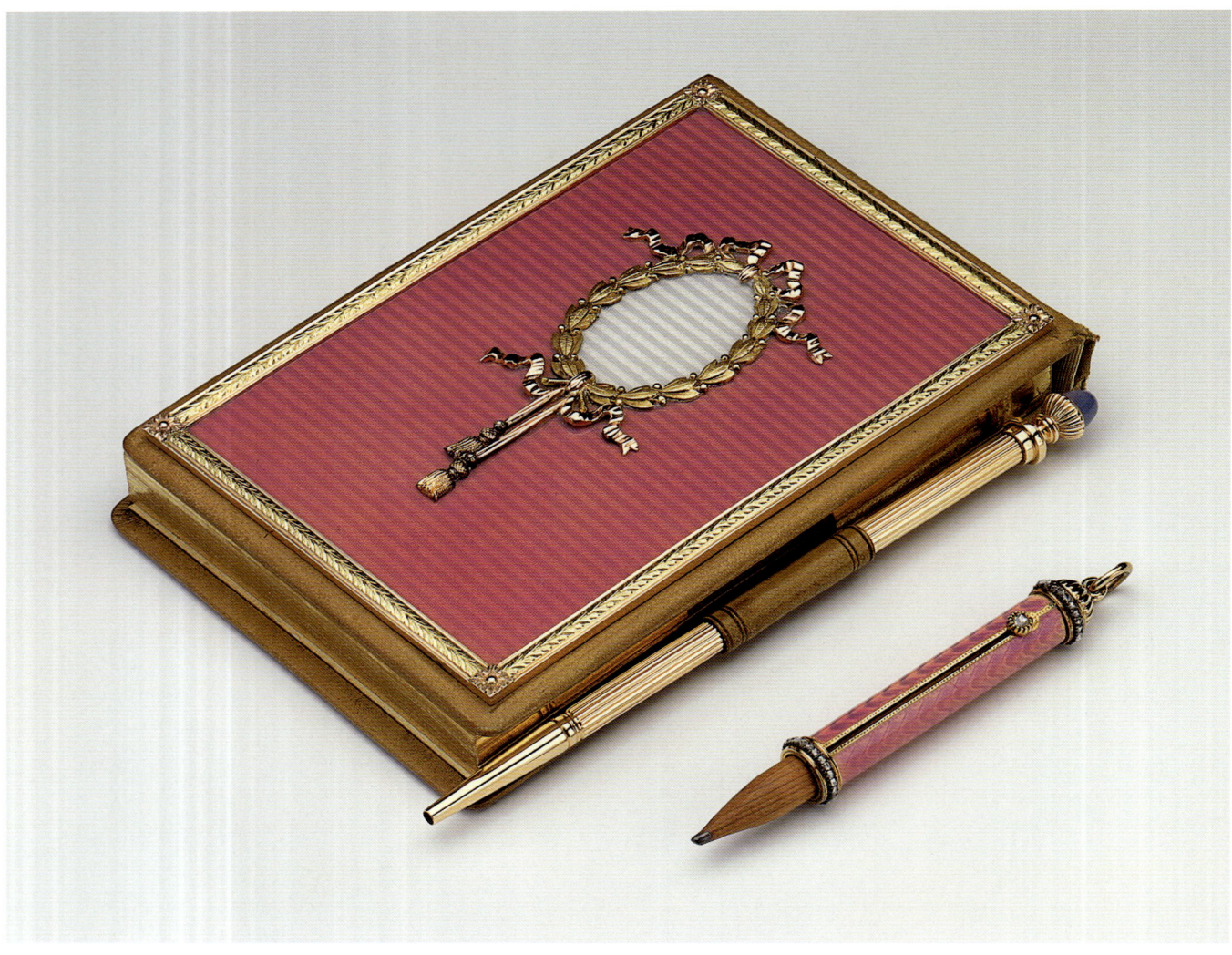

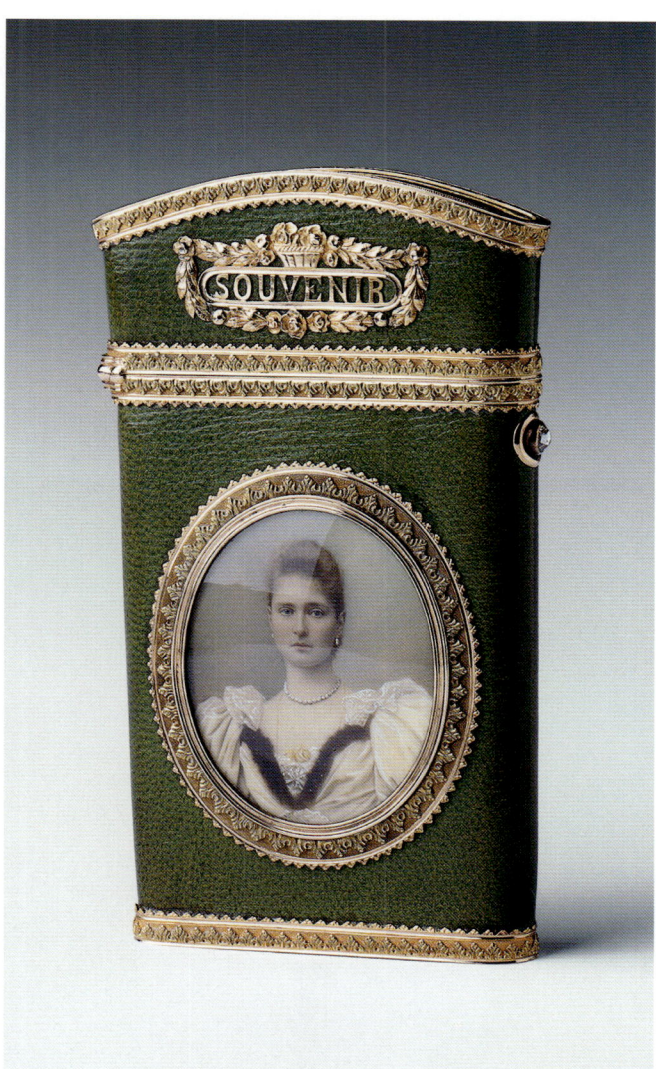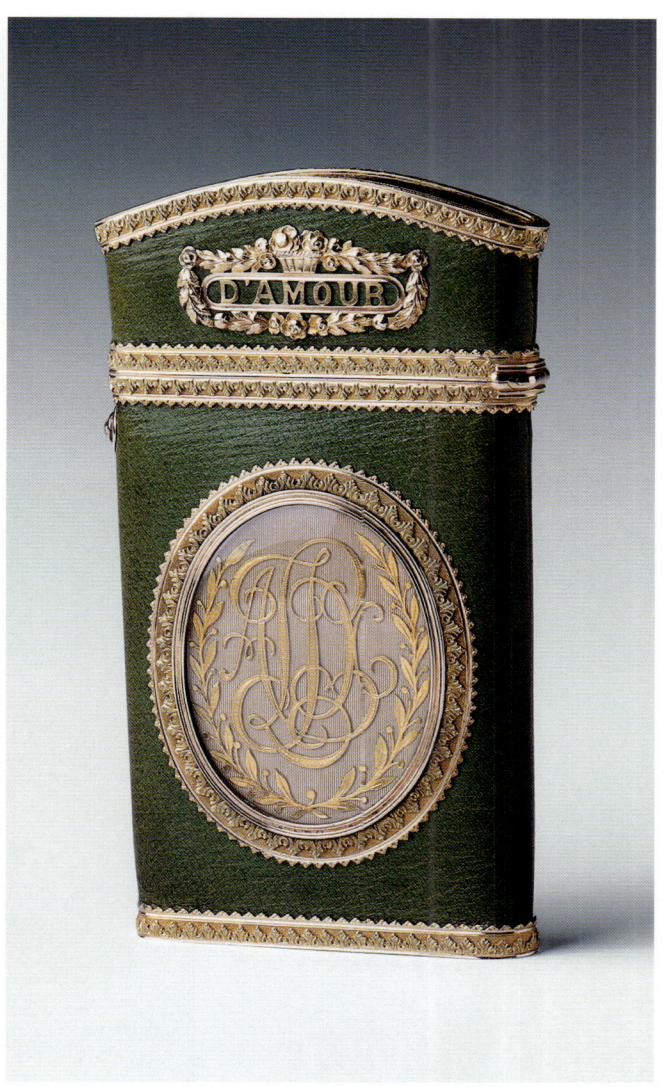

334 CARNET, *c.*1894–1895

It is extremely rare to find objects by Fabergé which are made in leather; only a handful of such pieces are known. This case, inspired by eighteenth-century French design, bears a miniature of Tsarina Alexandra Feodorovna by Zehngraf. It formed part of Queen Mary's collection and contains a note written by Agathon Fabergé (1876–1951), Carl's second son. It explains that the case was made in 1894 or 1895 at the time when Agathon joined his father's business in St Petersburg. Agathon considered the case to be one of his father's finest pieces, largely because the chiselling of the gold is so fine and such a good re-creation of the French eighteenth-century pieces that inspired it. The note is dated 12 September 1937. The case was previously in the possession of Dr James Hasson. An almost identical French eighteenth-century case was acquired by Queen Mary in 1928.

Leather, gold, watercolour, 10.1 x 6 x 1.2 cm (4 x 2⅜ x ½")
Mark of Michael Perchin; gold mark of 56 *zolotniks* (before 1896); *FABERGÉ* in Cyrillic characters; miniature signed by Zehngraf; case marked *SOUVENIR D'AMOUR* and *ALIX* in gold
RCIN 9141
PROVENANCE: Dr James Hasson; acquired by Queen Mary by 1949
REFERENCES: Bainbridge 1949, pl. 9; QMPP XI, no. 83
EXHIBITIONS: London 1954; QG 1985–6, no. 308; QG 1995–6, no. 405

335 PAIR OF CANDLESTICKS, BEFORE 1896

Julius Rappoport produced several objects, including a further pair of candlesticks, using a combination of nephrite and silver. These candlesticks in overtly baroque style have mounts that incorporate winged putti.

Nephrite, silver, 21 x 8.8 x 8.5 cm (8¼ x 3⁷⁄₁₆ x 3⅜")
Mark of Julius Rappoport; silver mark of 88 and 84 *zolotniks* (before 1896); *FABERGÉ* in Cyrillic characters
RCIN 32444
PROVENANCE: Probably acquired by King Edward VII and Queen Alexandra, date unknown
REFERENCES: Habsburg & Lopato 1993, pp. 372–3
EXHIBITIONS: QG 1995–6, no. 349

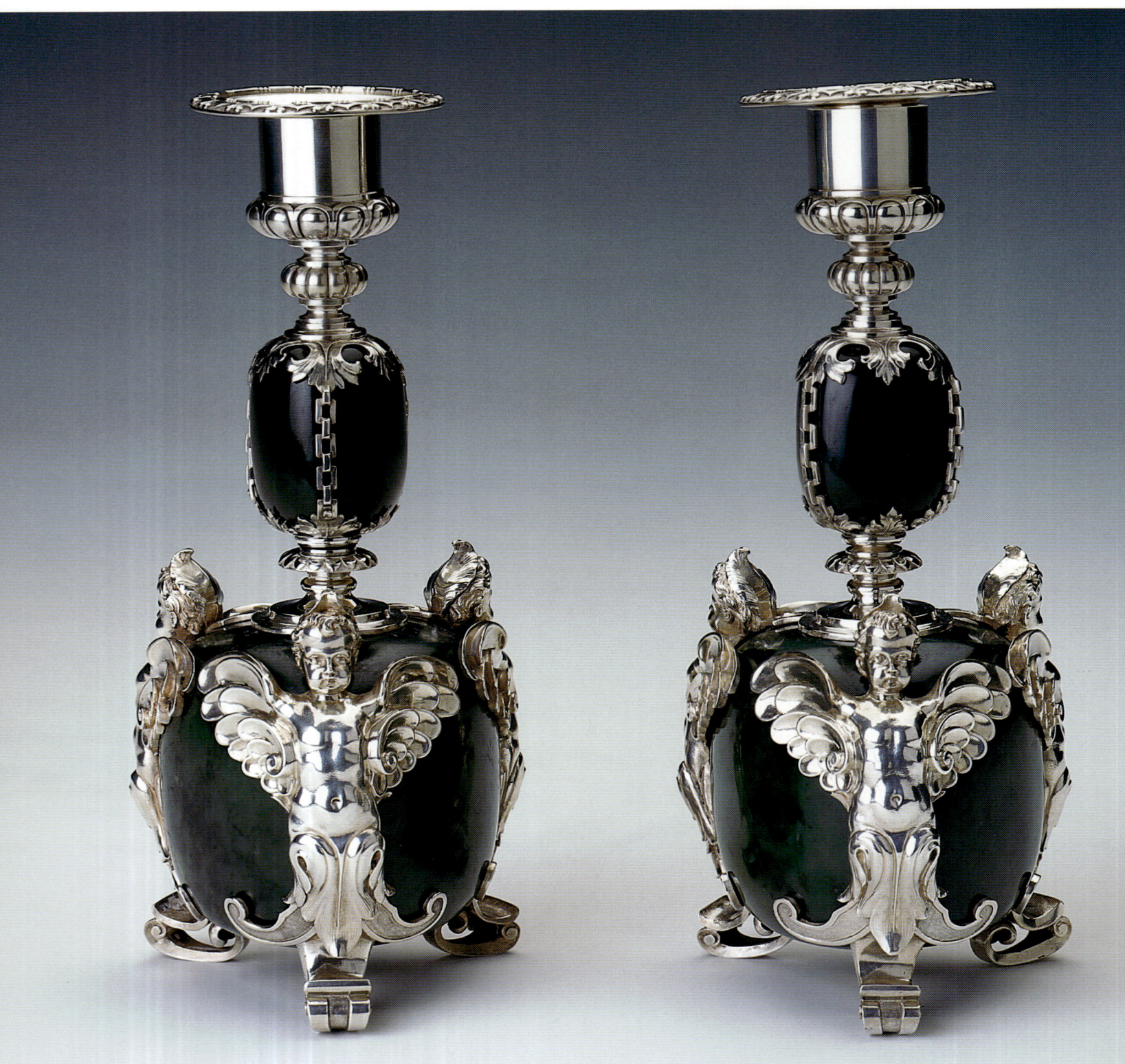

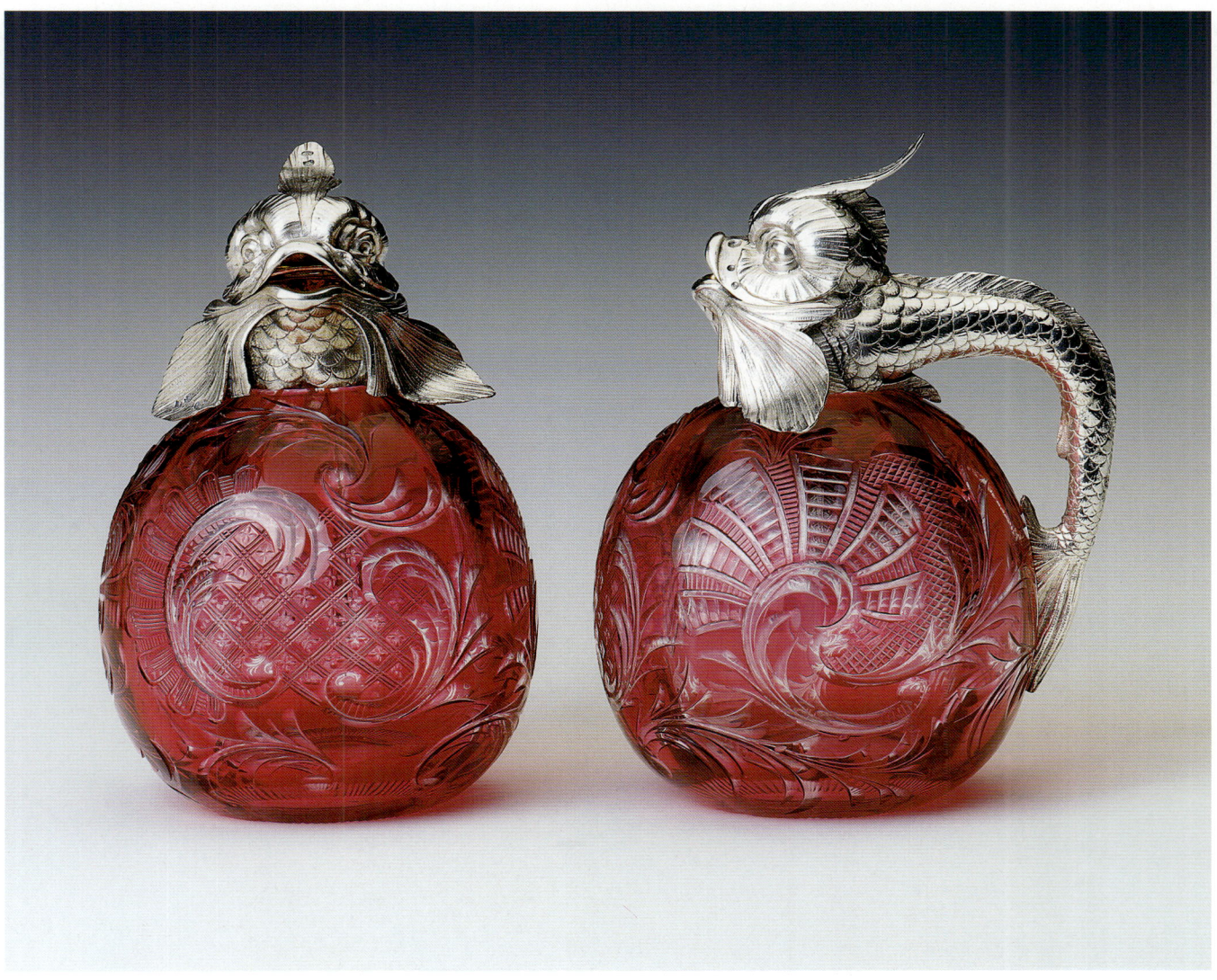

336   PAIR OF DECANTERS, BEFORE 1896

Mounted glass and porcelain objects were produced in Fabergé's workshops in both St Petersburg and Moscow. There are a small number of pieces of glass and porcelain by other makers – such as glass by Gallé and Tiffany and porcelain by Royal Doulton and the Rørstrand Manufactory – to which Fabergé applied silver mounts.

These pieces are notable not only for the combination of firms involved, but as good examples of the evolution of Fabergé's style towards art nouveau.

Glass, silver, 15.8 x 10 x diameter 12 cm (6¼ x 3¹⁵/₁₆ x 4³/₄")
Moscow silver mark of 84 *zolotniks* (before 1896); *C. FABERGÉ* and Carl Fabergé's initials in Cyrillic characters
RCIN 100337
PROVENANCE: Bought by Queen Elizabeth, September 1973 (£1,815)
REFERENCES: Habsburg & Lopato 1993, pp. 199–201, 212–15
EXHIBITIONS: QG 1995–6, no. 204

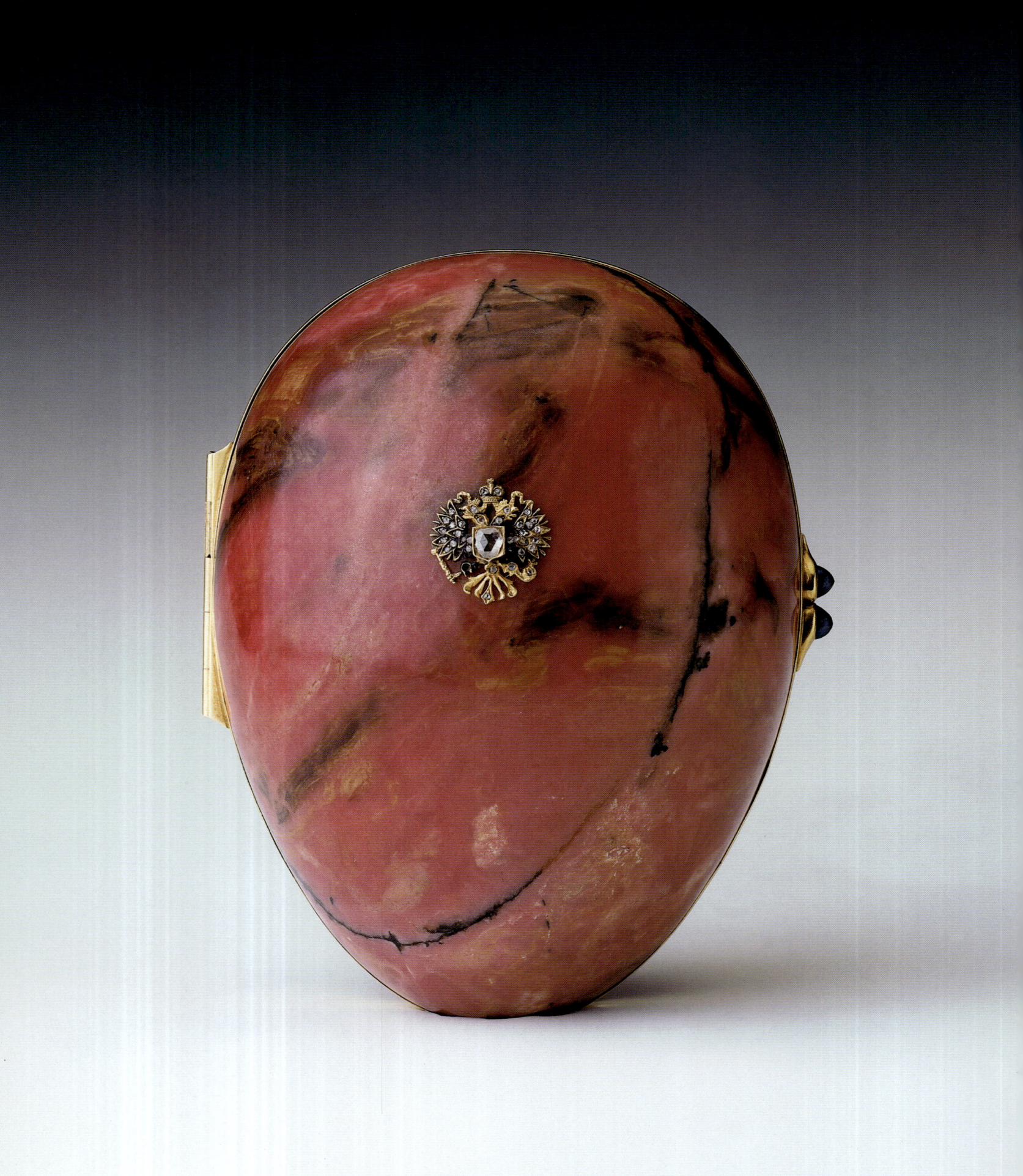

WORKS BY
CONTEMPORARIES
AND COMPETITORS

337 EGG, BEFORE 1896

This rhodonite egg was made by the firm of Köchli, who supplied the Dowager Tsarina Marie Feodor-ovna and who also produced presentation boxes and cigarette cases during the reign of Tsar Nicholas II. This is the only known hardstone egg produced by the firm. While of considerably simpler design than any of the large eggs that Fabergé made, it is nonetheless applied with the imperial eagle.

Although the egg was correctly sold by Emanuel Snowman as a work by Köchli, Queen Mary had recorded it in her list of bibelots as being by Fabergé. The error was only rectified when Wartski's sales ledgers were checked at Queen Mary's request by Emanuel Snowman's son Kenneth, following a visit to Marlborough House in the early 1950s.

Rhodonite, gold, diamonds, cabochon sapphires, 11.3 x diameter 8.4 cm (4⁷/₁₆ x 3⁵/₁₆")
Mark of Friedrich Köchli; gold mark of 56 *zolotniks* (before 1896); English import marks of Stockwell and Co. Ltd for 1928–9
RCIN 9048
PROVENANCE: Bought by Queen Mary from Wartski, 1947
REFERENCES: QMPP XI, no. 46; Von Solodkoff 1984, pp. 128–9

338 FLAMINGO, 1907

One of the many types of object that Cartier produced in imitation of Fabergé was hardstone animal carvings. Cartier used several different Russian suppliers for these including Svietchnikov, Sourovi and Karl Wöerffel – from the last of these Fabergé also acquired hardstone objects. Nadelhoffer claims that in 1910 Cartier purchased two animals directly from Fabergé. The most popular animals sold by Cartier included owls, storks, elephants and pigs; none of these is represented in the Royal Collection.

In spite of Cartier's imitation of Fabergé's animals and use of some of the same suppliers, this flamingo is fundamentally different in character from Fabergé's carvings in form, style and choice of material. The differences are particularly apparent when it is compared with the Fabergé flamingo (cat. 79). Fabergé's flamingo is in proportion, and realistically carved with details of the feathers, the head, legs and the pose closely observed from nature; Cartier's flamingo is, by contrast, almost a caricature of the bird with the neck and legs accentuated and out of proportion. The use of rose quartz, while alluding to the flamingo's natural colour, is much less subtle than Fabergé's agate. The other notable difference is that Cartier's flamingo requires a base to give it stability, whereas Fabergé's is carefully balanced so that the gold legs are exactly the right length to support the weight of the agate body. Given these overwhelming differences it is interesting to note that Bainbridge nonetheless attributed cat. 338 to Fabergé.

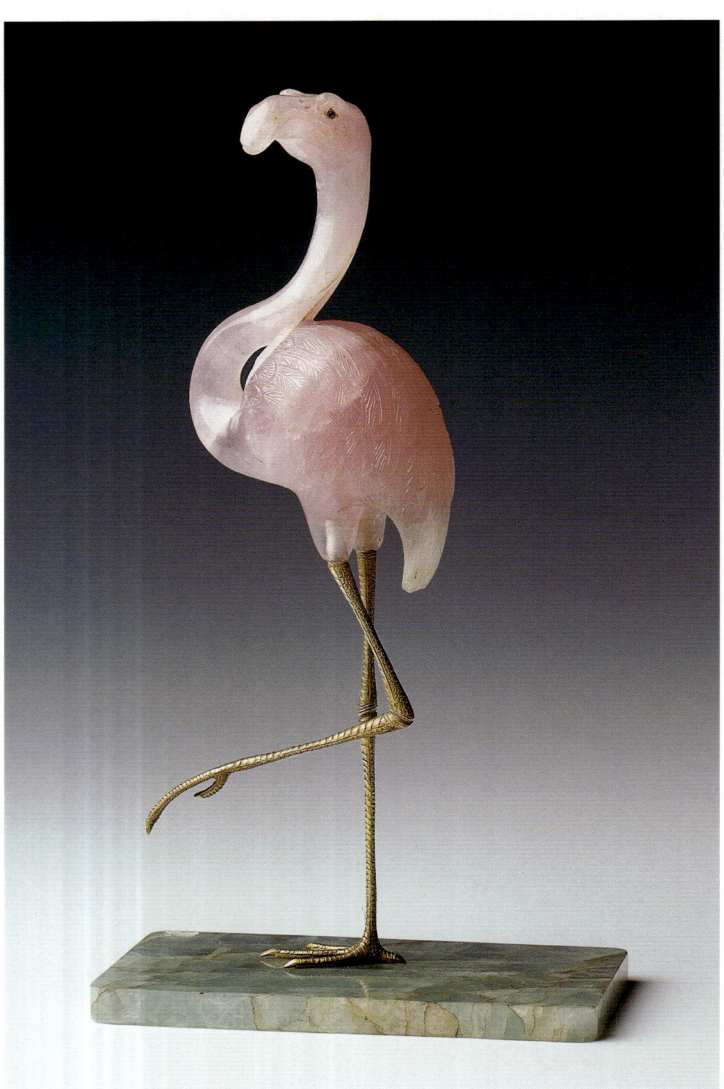

Rose quartz, gold, fluorspar, diamonds, 18 x 9.5 x 6.1 cm (7¹/₁₆ x 3³/₄ x 2³/₈")
Maker's mark illegible; French hallmarks, date illegible
RCIN 13754
PROVENANCE: Bought from Cartier by Mrs Whitelaw-Reid, 25 September 1908 (£32)
REFERENCES: Bainbridge 1949, pl. 74; Nadelhoffer 1984

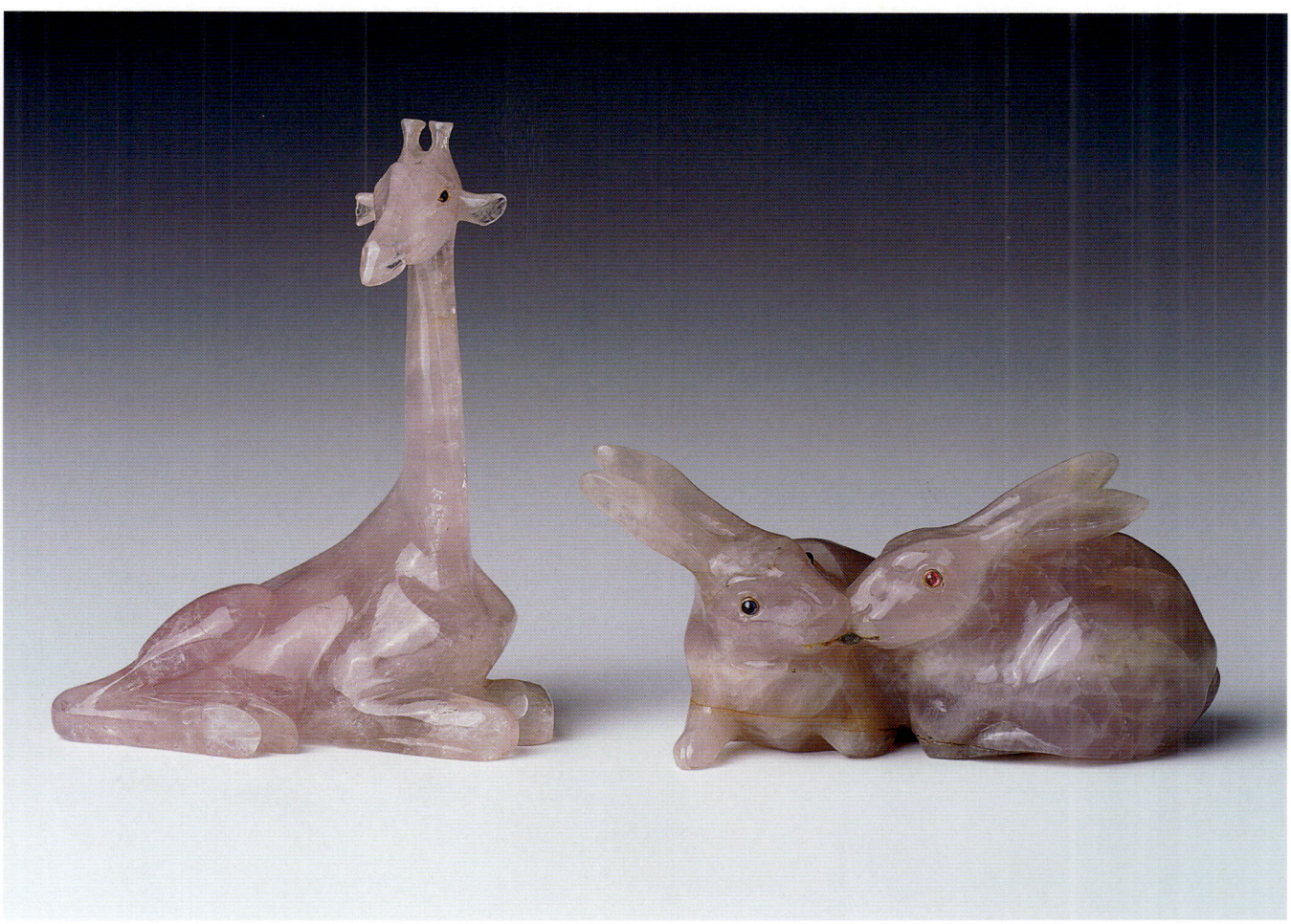

339 GIRAFFE, *c.*1900

Like the flamingo (cat. 338), this giraffe carved from rose quartz has a caricature quality. It is believed to be by Cartier although it is unmarked and cannot be traced in the Cartier Archives.

Rose quartz, cabochon sapphires, 10.8 x 8.5 x 4.8 cm (4¼ x 3⅜ x 1⅞")
Unmarked
RCIN 13735
PROVENANCE: Probably acquired by Queen Alexandra; Royal Collection by 1953

340 PAIR OF RABBITS, *c.*1900

Fabergé made several animal carvings which were formed of pairs or groups of a particular species (see cat. 49, 61 and 104). This pair of rabbits was probably inspired by those groups and it was almost certainly made by Cartier. The use of rose quartz is consistent with other animals known to have been made by Cartier, who also copied Fabergé's technique of using chips of precious stones for the eyes, which helps to animate the sculptures.

Rose quartz, cabochon sapphires and rubies, 5.3 x 10.1 x 5.2 cm (2¹/₁₆ x 4 x 2¹/₁₆")
Unmarked
RCIN 13746
PROVENANCE: Probably acquired by Queen Alexandra; Royal Collection by 1953

341 PEKINESE, *c.*1900

Although originally thought to be one of Fabergé's animal carvings, this dog is more in the style of Cartier's animals – particularly in the use of rose quartz, a stone not favoured by Fabergé. The Pekinese was one of Queen Alexandra's favourite breeds of dog and this model undoubtedly formed part of her collection at Sandringham. A similar Pekinese exists in the Cartier Collection; carved in jade, it was made for Cartier New York *c.*1925.

Rose quartz, cabochon sapphires, 4.3 x 5.8 x 3 cm (1^{11}/$_{16}$ x 2^{5}/$_{16}$ x 1^{3}/$_{16}$")
Unmarked
RCIN 40433
PROVENANCE: Acquired by Queen Alexandra; Royal Collection by 1953
REFERENCES: Rudoe 1997, p. 115, no. 54

342 PUG, *c.*1900

This dog is believed to be by Cartier, although no reference to this model can be traced in the Cartier Archives. The style of carving is quite different from that of Fabergé's animals. The hardstone carvings made by the Berquin-Varangoz workshop, by Fourrier and by Cartier's Russian suppliers tend to have a more consistent colouring through the piece of hardstone, rather than using the stone's natural striations to describe the markings of the animal.

Bowenite, cabochon rubies, 3 x 5 x 2.3 cm (1^{3}/$_{16}$ x 1^{15}/$_{16}$ x ^{7}/$_{8}$")
Unmarked
RCIN 19164
PROVENANCE: Probably acquired by King Edward VII; Royal Collection by 1953

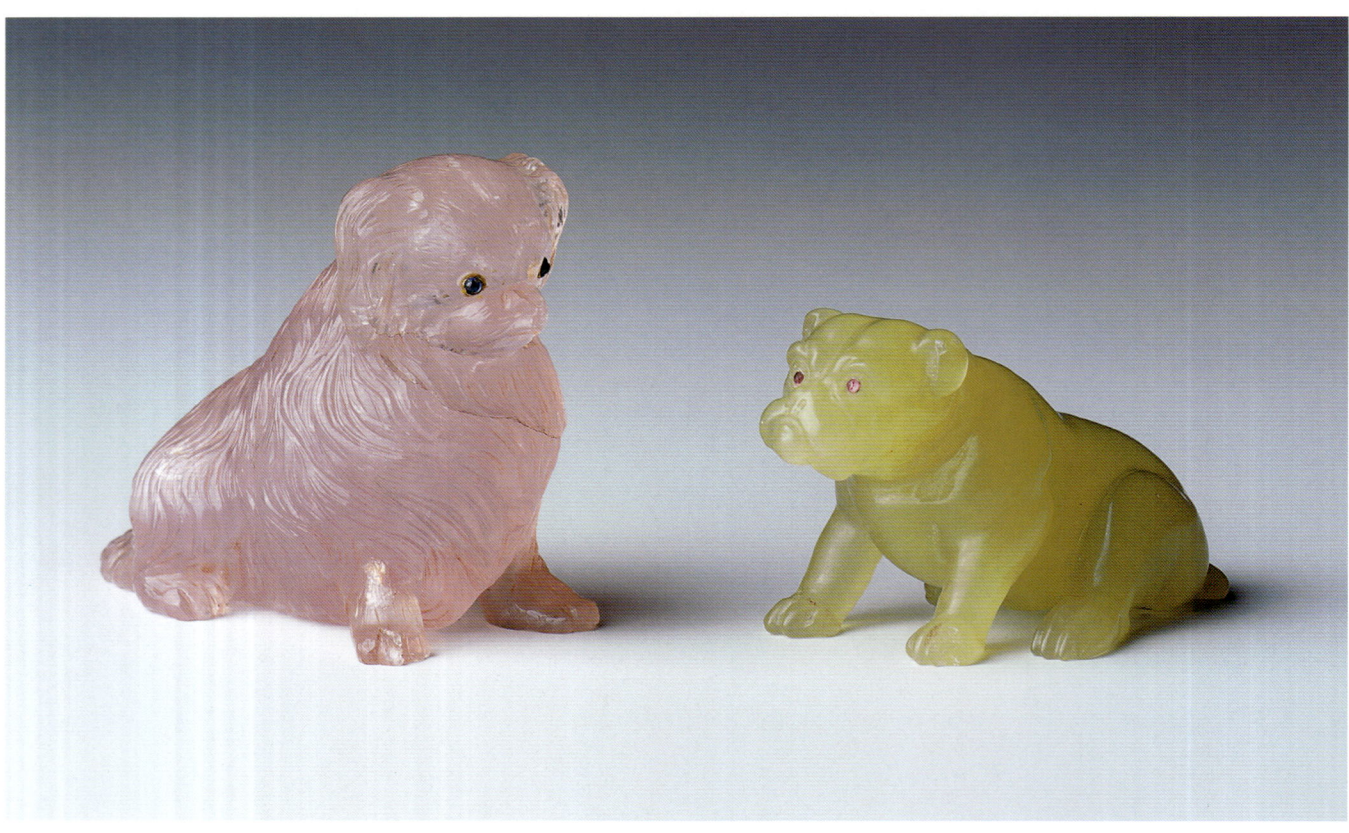

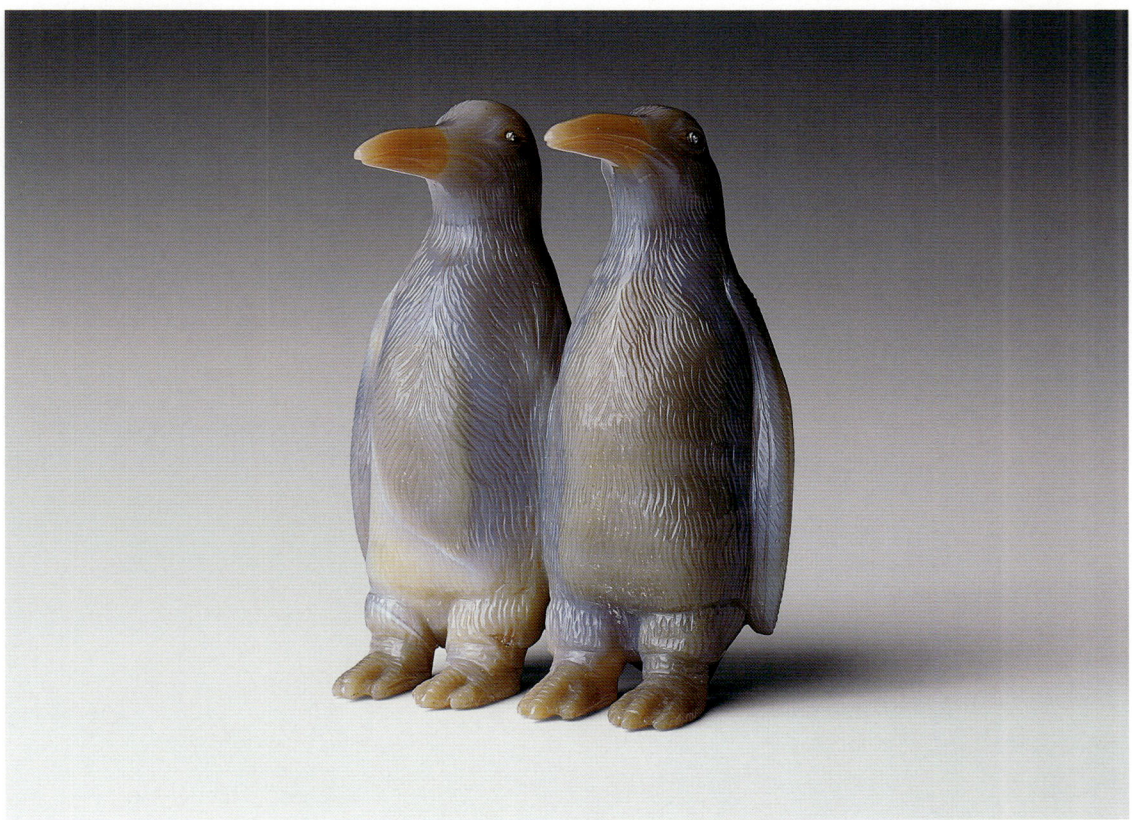

343   PAIR OF PENGUINS, *c.*1900

This pair of agate penguins is very similar to a model produced by Cartier, now in the Cartier Collection. The Cartier Collection penguins are of brown agate with ruby eyes and were probably made by the Fourrier workshop around 1923–4. Two other similar models were made by Cartier in the same period.

Agate, rose diamonds, 7.8 x 6.5 x 4.6 cm (3$^1/_{16}$ x 2$^9/_{16}$ x 1$^{13}/_{16}$")
Unmarked
RCIN 19637
PROVENANCE: Probably acquired by Queen Alexandra; Royal Collection by 1953
REFERENCES: Rudoe 1997, p. 115, cat. 53

344   LILAC FLOWER, *c.*1900

Although Cartier's flowers were inspired by Fabergé's, they were of a quite different character and style. They show the influence of Japanese flower arranging known as *ikebana*, together with characteristics of French jewelled bouquets of the eighteenth and nineteenth centuries of the kind that would have been seen in the Louvre by Cartier's designers.

The most significant difference between Cartier's and Fabergé's flowers is that Cartier's are placed inside glass cases imitating miniature hot-houses, whereas Fabergé's are all freestanding. Cartier's flowers are usually contained in porcelain or stone containers, often with hardstones to imitate earth; Fabergé's are usually in rock crystal vases cut to give the impression that they are filled with water. Cartier's range of flowers was quite extensive but based on different species from Fabergé's and included rare and exotic examples of orchids and lilies rather than Fabergé's more familiar lily of the valley, buttercups, berries, carnations and wild flowers.

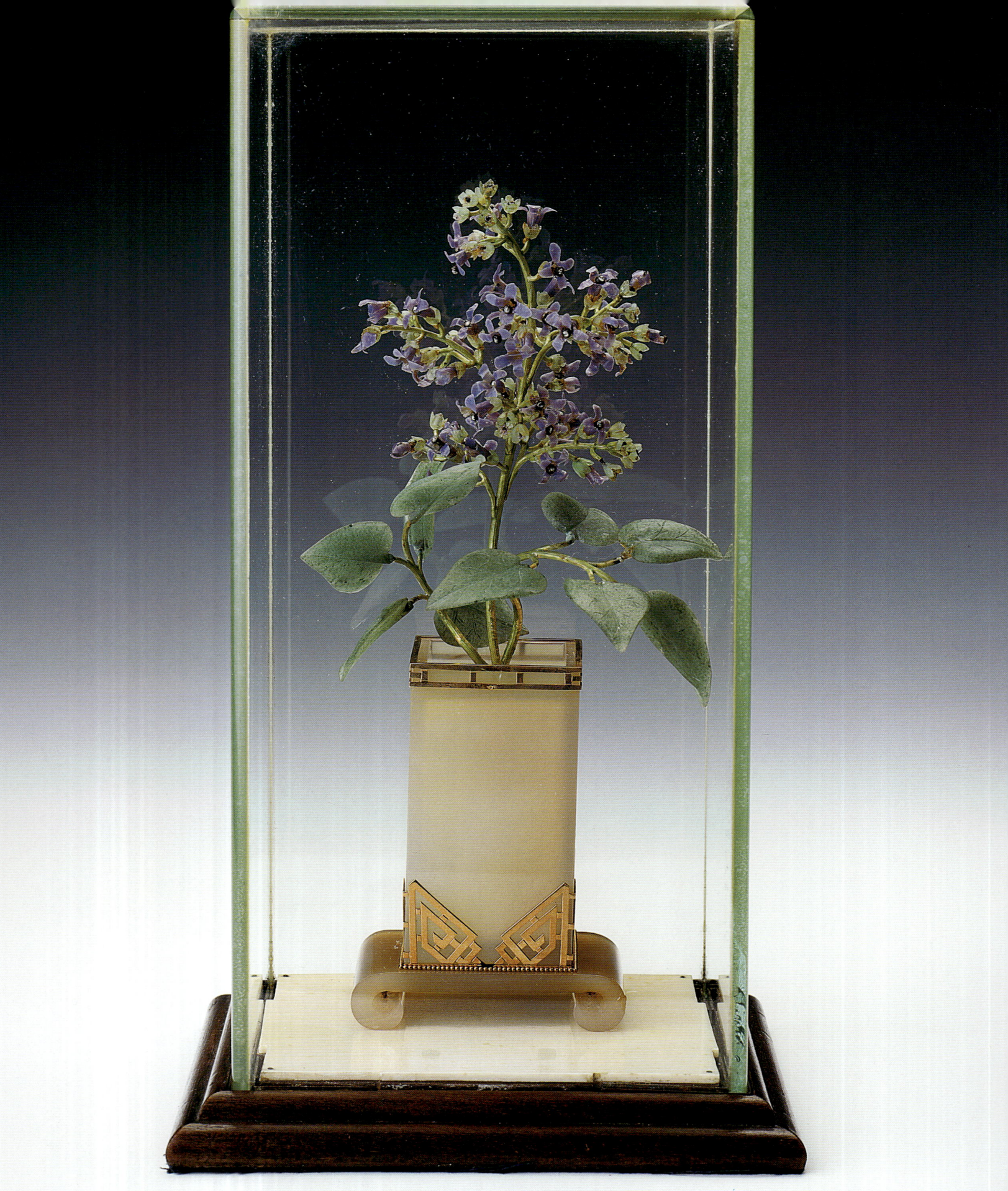

Cartier's flowers were initially commissioned from the Berquin-Varangoz workshop based in Saint-Siméon in Seine-et-Marne. In 1918 the workshop was bought out by Aristide Fourrier, who continued to supply Cartier. Fourrier apparently claimed that Fabergé was the only inspiration for his flowers but he continued to produce floral pieces in the same distinctive style as his predecessor.

This lilac displays all the characteristics of one of Cartier's flowers, notably the glass hot-house, the ivory base, the *ikebana*-style arrangement on a plinth and the use of glass for the flower heads, but it is nonetheless unmarked.

Glass, wood, ivory, gemstones, gilt metal, 25.5 x 13.4 x 13.4 cm (10¹/₁₆ x 5¹/₄ x 5¹/₄")
RCIN 3272
PROVENANCE: Acquired by Queen Mary, 1924
REFERENCES: QMB II, no. 31; QMPP IV, no. 180; Nadelhoffer 1984; New Orleans Museum of Art 1988, p. 100

345 BOX, *c.*1910

This hardstone box mounted with enamel and gem set was probably inspired by Fabergé's work. The familiar plain white enamel bands, seen on many of Cartier's *objets d'art* and practical objects, here enclose cabochon sapphires. The use of jade with the blue sapphires was a colour combination Cartier often employed, particularly for jewellery from 1913 onwards.

Jade, gold, enamel, cabochon sapphires, 7.8 x 4.3 x 2.5 cm (3¹/₁₆ x 1¹¹/₁₆ x 1")
Unmarked
RCIN 40120
REFERENCES: Rudoe 1997, p. 208

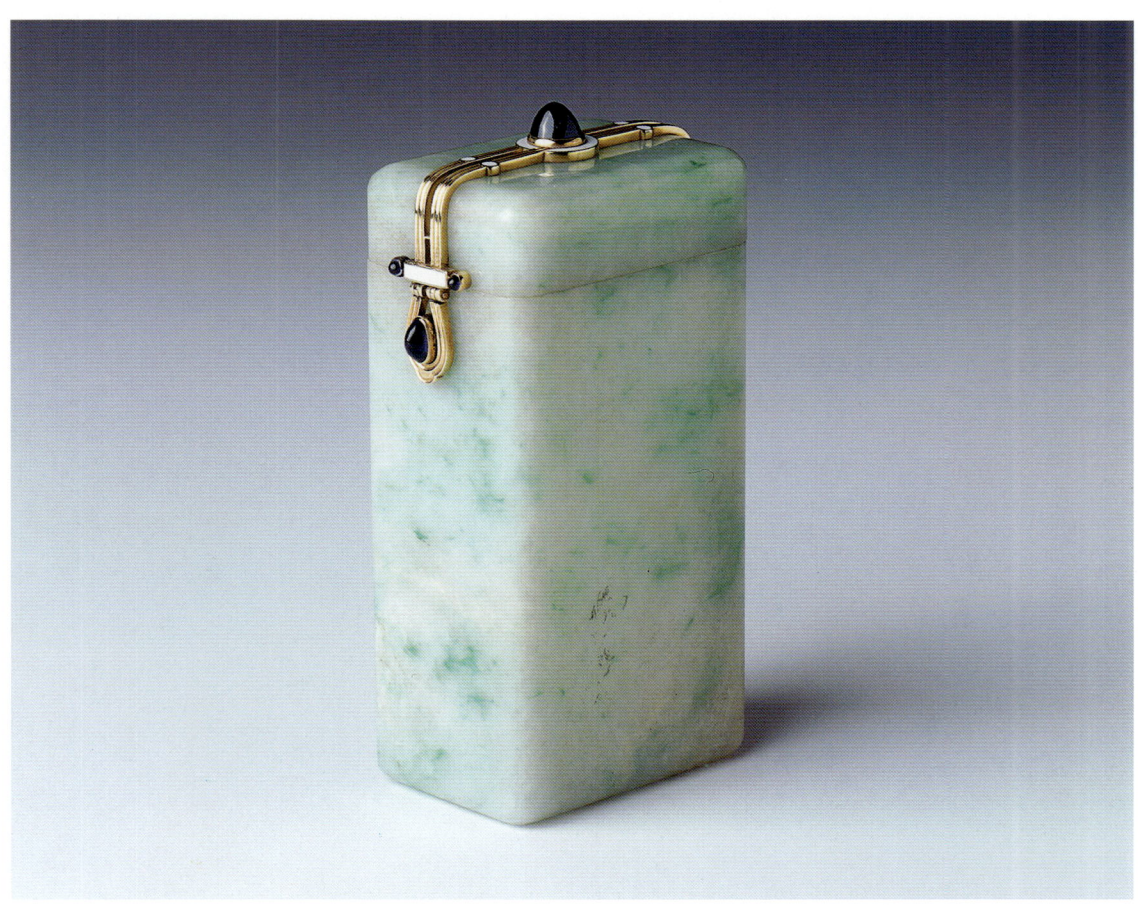

346 VESTA CASE, *c.*1902

Like Fabergé, Cartier produced commemorative objects mounted with coins. In this example the sides of the match case are formed from a gold coronation crown with the portrait of King Edward VII on the obverse and St George and the Dragon and the date *1902* on the reverse.

Gold, guilloché enamel, rose diamond, 4.3 x 4.4 x 0.8 cm (1¹¹/₁₆ x 1¾ x ⁵/₁₆")
Inscribed *Cartier Paris*; French hallmarks, date illegible; illegible maker's mark
RCIN 14764
PROVENANCE: Probably acquired by King Edward VII and Queen Alexandra, 1902

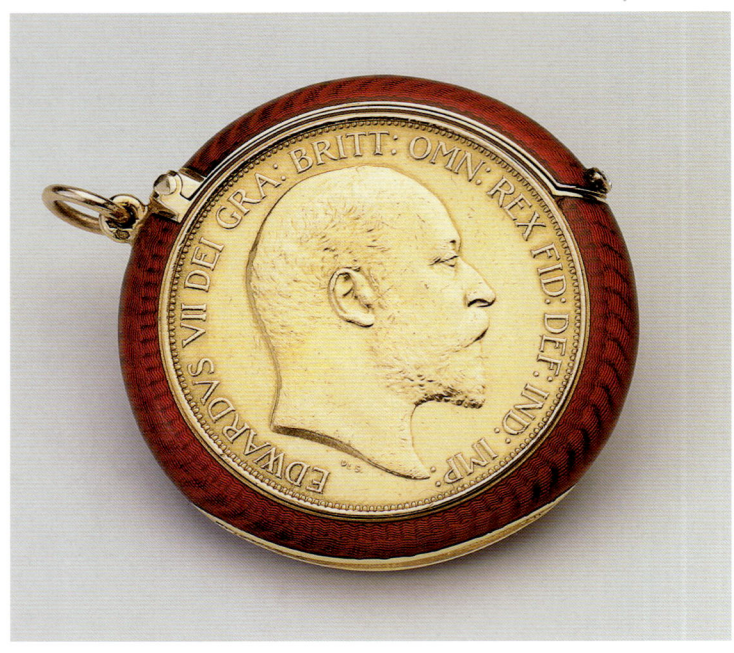

347 FRAME WITH A MINIATURE OF KING EDWARD VII WHEN PRINCE OF WALES, *c.*1900

This oval frame combines hardstone with enamel. Although the materials are familiar from Fabergé's work, their combination is unlike his. The border of white enamel is a distinctive feature on many of Cartier's enamelled items from this period; it is also seen on the dish (cat. 353). The miniature portrait is of King Edward VII and the frame has an ivory back and silver-gilt strut in the manner of Fabergé's frames.

Agate, gold, enamel, ivory, silver-gilt, watercolour, 7.5 x 6.4 x 0.2 cm (2¹⁵/₁₆ x 2½ x ¹/₁₆")
Inscribed *Cartier Paris*; French hallmarks, date illegible
RCIN 100332
PROVENANCE: Acquired by Queen Elizabeth, date unknown

348 FRAME, 1908–1917

The white guilloché enamelling of this frame is characteristic of Ivan Britsin's work and is marked by him. The style and materials used are very much in the manner of Fabergé, for whom, according to Snowman, Britsin worked before establishing his own business.

Silver, guilloché enamel, wood, 11.4 x 8.7 x 1.1 cm (4½ x 3⁷/₁₆ x ⁷/₁₆")
Mark of Ivan Britsin; silver mark of 88 *zolotniks* (1908–17)
RCIN 100333
PROVENANCE: Acquired by Queen Elizabeth, date unknown
REFERENCES: Snowman 1962, no. 128

349 FRAME WITH A PHOTOGRAPH OF TSAR NICHOLAS II, c.1900

Although of guilloché enamel, the gold surround of this miniature frame is heavy and crudely finished. Little is known about the maker, whose mark *OB* is stamped on the frame, but his work was clearly inspired by that of Fabergé. Other works by the same maker are known and include a silver niello box.

Two-colour gold, guilloché enamel, 5 x 3.5 x 3.6 cm (1^{15}/$_{16}$ x 1^{3}/$_{8}$ x 1^{7}/$_{16}$")
Maker's mark *OB*; gold mark of 56 *zolotniks*
RCIN 40238
PROVENANCE: Acquired by the Prince and Princess of Wales (later King Edward VII and Queen Alexandra), c.1900

350 FRAME WITH A PHOTOGRAPH OF TSARINA MARIE FEODOROVNA, c.1900

This Russian enamelled frame by an unknown maker is in Fabergé's style but crudely made by comparison with his work. It contains a photograph of Tsarina Marie Feodorovna. The back is of wood rather than Fabergé's usual ivory and the strut is of plain design unlike Fabergé's elegant scrolled supports in gold or silver-gilt.

Silver, guilloché enamel, 1.1 x diameter 10 cm (^{7}/$_{16}$ x 3^{15}/$_{16}$")
Unmarked
RCIN 100336
PROVENANCE: Acquired by Queen Elizabeth, date unknown

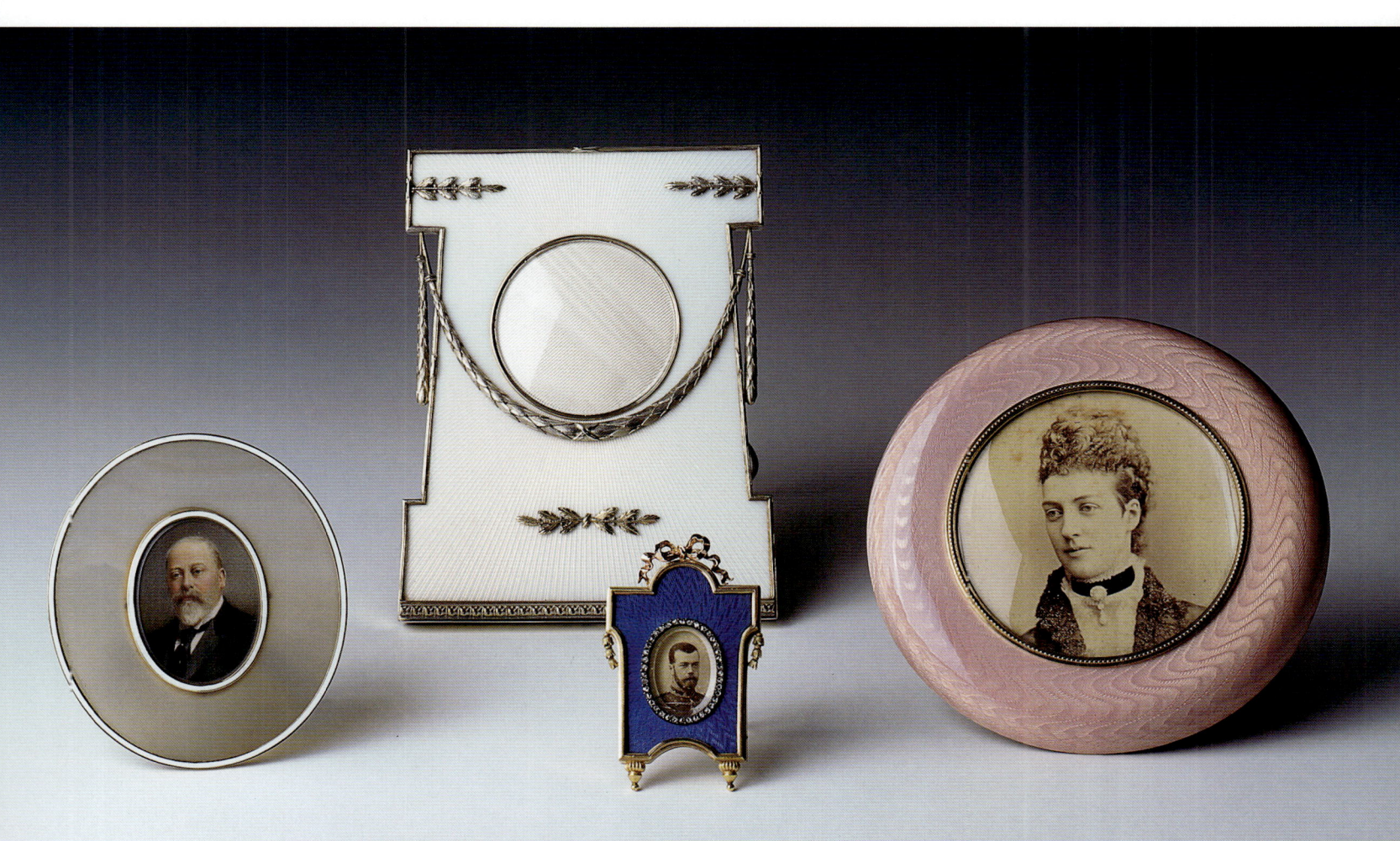

351 BUDDHA, *c.*1900–1920

Fabergé's interest in oriental works of art is illustrated in many of his *objets d'art*, such as Japanese netsuke-inspired animal carvings, mounted Chinese snuff bottles, hardstone flowers and scent flacons carved in the form of oriental figures (see cat. 258 and 259). He also produced one or two Buddha-type figures, notably one carved from nephrite for the King of Siam, now in a private collection, which was copied from an oriental design. Fabergé had been appointed court jeweller and enameller to King Chulalongkorn of Siam in 1908. Two further Buddha figures are known, one illustrated by Bainbridge, in jade with rubies, the other sold by Parke Bernet Galleries, New York, in 1966. The latter was apparently marked by Perchin; the former appears to have been unmarked.

This figure appears to have been inspired by the two last-mentioned Buddhas, both of which had nodding heads and moveable hands and tongues. Bainbridge asserts that this Buddha is by Fabergé, although the use of a mixture of different stones is more in keeping with the Buddha figures made by Cartier in the period 1900–20.

Cartier also made other Buddha-like figures which the firm referred to as Billikens, supposedly representing the Anglo-Saxon god of happiness. According to Nadelhoffer, Queen Alexandra acquired such a figure although no specific date or further reference is given. This Buddha is believed to be by Cartier and was given to Queen Mary in 1939.

Rose quartz, agate, fluorspar, rubies, rose diamonds, gold, enamel, 16 x 13 x 13 cm (6⁵/₁₆ x 5¹/₈ x 5¹/₈")
RCIN 9026
PROVENANCE: Given by the Dowager Viscountess Harcourt to Queen Mary on her birthday, 26 May 1939
REFERENCES: QMPP X, no. 18; Bainbridge 1949, pl. 72; *Apollo*, April 1967, vol. 62, p. 313; Nadelhoffer 1984; Tillander-Godenhielm *et al.* 2000, p. 89
EXHIBITIONS: QG 1962–3, no. 4; London 1977, no. F2; QG 1985–6, no. 163

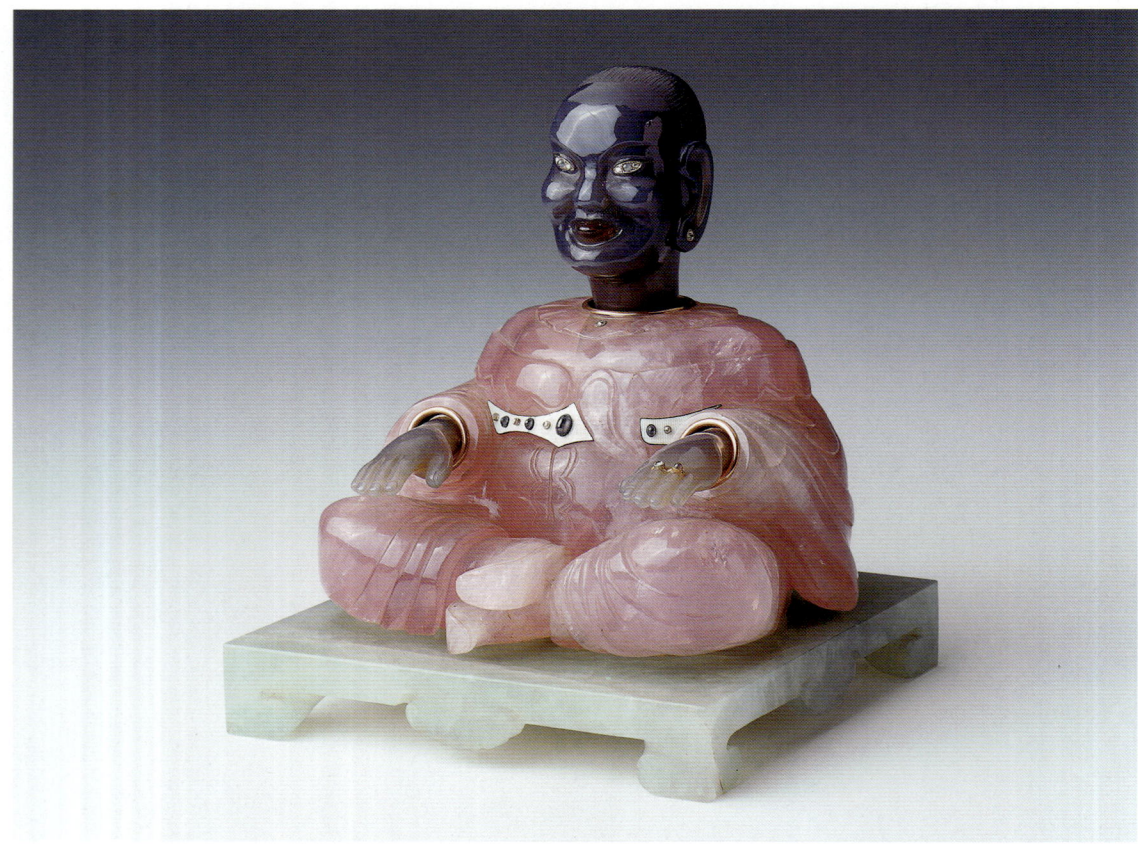

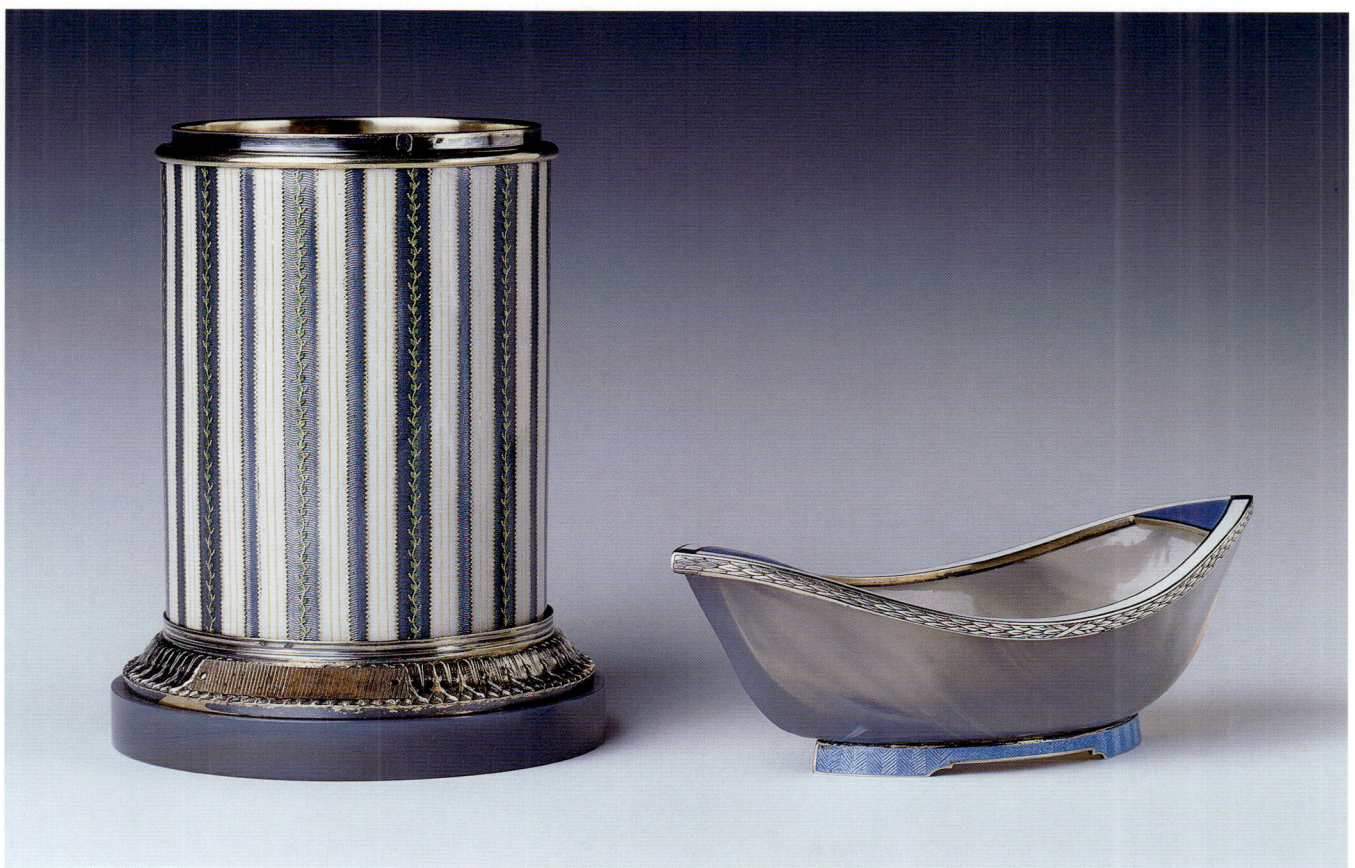

352 TAPER HOLDER, *c.*1910

Cartier's palette of enamels was much less extensive than that of Fabergé, although Cartier did create some new colour combinations such as blue and green and mauve and green. Here the enamel is in alternate white and guilloché grey stripes which incorporate gold and green foliate bands. Some enamelled objects were acquired by Cartier from the Moscow workshop of the firm Yahr in 1904, although this piece seems to be later in date. The grey stone base is fitted with a striking plate.

Agate, silver, enamel, 10.4 x diameter 8.1 cm (4¹/₈ x 3³/₁₆")
Stamped *Cartier Paris Londres*; French hallmarks, date illegible
RCIN 18090
PROVENANCE: Probably acquired by King Edward VII, *c.*1910
REFERENCES: Nadelhoffer 1984, pp. 90–91

353 DISH, *c.*1909

Cartier's distinctive style is evident in this unusual dish. While the guilloché enamel decoration and use of hardstone hint at the influence of Fabergé's work, the finished product is quite different from anything he would have produced.

Agate, enamel and guilloché enamel, gold, 3.8 x 1 x 5.2 cm (1¹/₂ x ³/₈ x 2¹/₁₆")
Maker's mark illegible; inscribed *Cartier Paris Londres*; stamped *1764*
RCIN 3544
PROVENANCE: Given by the Duchess of Roxburghe to Queen Mary, 1909
REFERENCES: QMB I, no. 274; QMPP I, no. 215

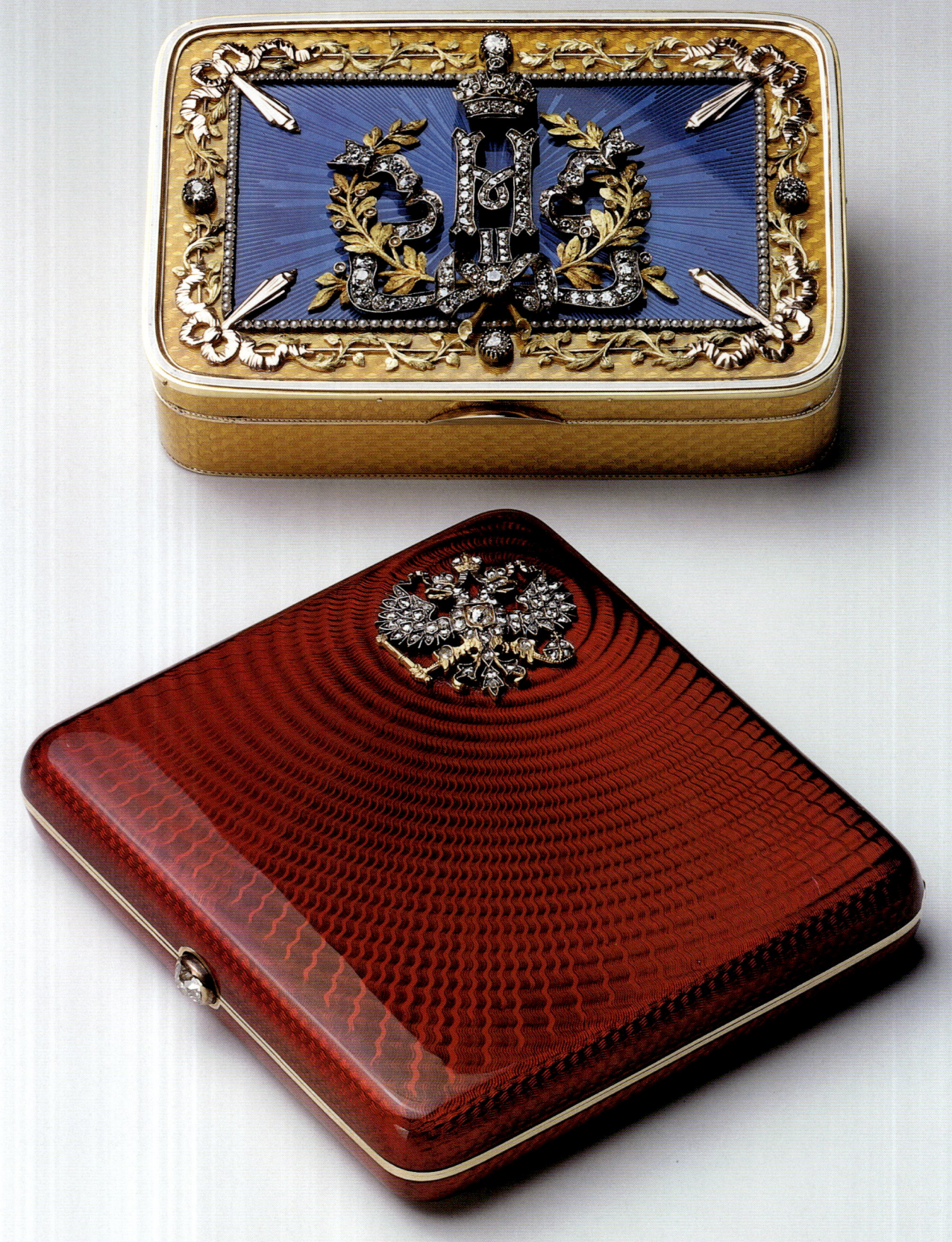

354 IMPERIAL PRESENTATION BOX, *c.*1900

Hahn was one of Fabergé's main competitors for imperial commissions and specialised in producing presentation boxes. Many of the finest boxes produced by the firm bear the mark of Carl Blank, who was employed by Hahn from around 1892 and became a partner from 1911. He also established his own workshop, making objects independently of Hahn which bear his own mark (*CB*). Those produced while he worked at the firm of Hahn bear both his mark and that of Hahn.

Hahn made approximately 50 of the 370 snuff boxes set with the diamond cypher of Tsar Nicholas II ordered during his reign, whereas Fabergé made 150 out of the total. The familiar techniques of guilloché enamelling and coloured gold decoration are included in Hahn's presentation boxes and the finished products are both grand and elegant, befitting such an important state gift. However, the combination of enamel colours is often much less refined than in Fabergé's work and in general his mounts – whether of gold or precious stones – are more fussy than Fabergé's elegant and restrained decoration. Nonetheless, this box is a very fine example of Hahn and Blank's best work, and even Queen Mary recorded it as a work by Fabergé when she acquired it in 1934. It has not been possible to establish from the Imperial Cabinet Archives the identity of the original recipient.

Two-colour gold, guilloché enamel, rose diamonds, seed pearls, 9.2 x 6.5 x 3 cm (3⁵/₈ x 2⁹/₁₆ x 1³/₁₆")
Mark of K. Hahn; mark of Carl Blank; gold mark of 56 *zolotniks* (1896–1908)
RCIN 19121
PROVENANCE: Tsar Nicholas II; Queen Mary; by whom given to King George V, 3 June 1934
REFERENCES: GV Boxes, vol. IV, no. 358
EXHIBITIONS: QG 1962–3, no. 61

355 CIGARETTE CASE, BEFORE 1896

This cigarette case is an example of the excellent enamelling Carl Blank produced, either in conjunction with the firm of Hahn or independently. Here the sunburst design is combined with a basketweave pattern on the sides of the case. The imperial eagle mount indicates that this was an official presentation cigarette case. Cigarette cases with the Romanov crown or the imperial eagle were given to junior civil servants of ranks 6 to 14 and to the corresponding rank of non-Russian recipient.

According to the inscription engraved inside this case, it was originally presented by Tsar Nicholas II to Turkhan Pasha. Born in Tirhala, Turkey, in 1846, Turkhan Pasha trained as a civil servant in the translation office at the Babiali, an Ottoman institution that included the Ministry of Foreign Affairs. He became Chargé d'Affaires at the Turkish Embassy in St Petersburg in 1873 and – after postings in Berlin, Vienna, Rome and Madrid – returned to St Petersburg as Ambassador between 1908 and 1913. It is therefore likely that an official gift of this kind would have been given to him by the Tsar. Unfortunately, the official records relating to the date of presentation have not been traced.

Gold, guilloché enamel, diamonds, 8.9 x 8.3 x 1.5 cm (3¹/₂ x 3¹/₄ x ⁹/₁₆")
Mark of Carl Blank; gold mark of 56 *zolotniks* (before 1896); inside engraved: *Given to Turkhan Pasha by Emperor Nicholas II Acquired by Queen Mary Given to King George in 1928*
RCIN 4058
PROVENANCE: Presented by Tsar Nicholas II to Turkhan Pasha between 1908 and 1913; Queen Mary; by whom given to King George V, 1928

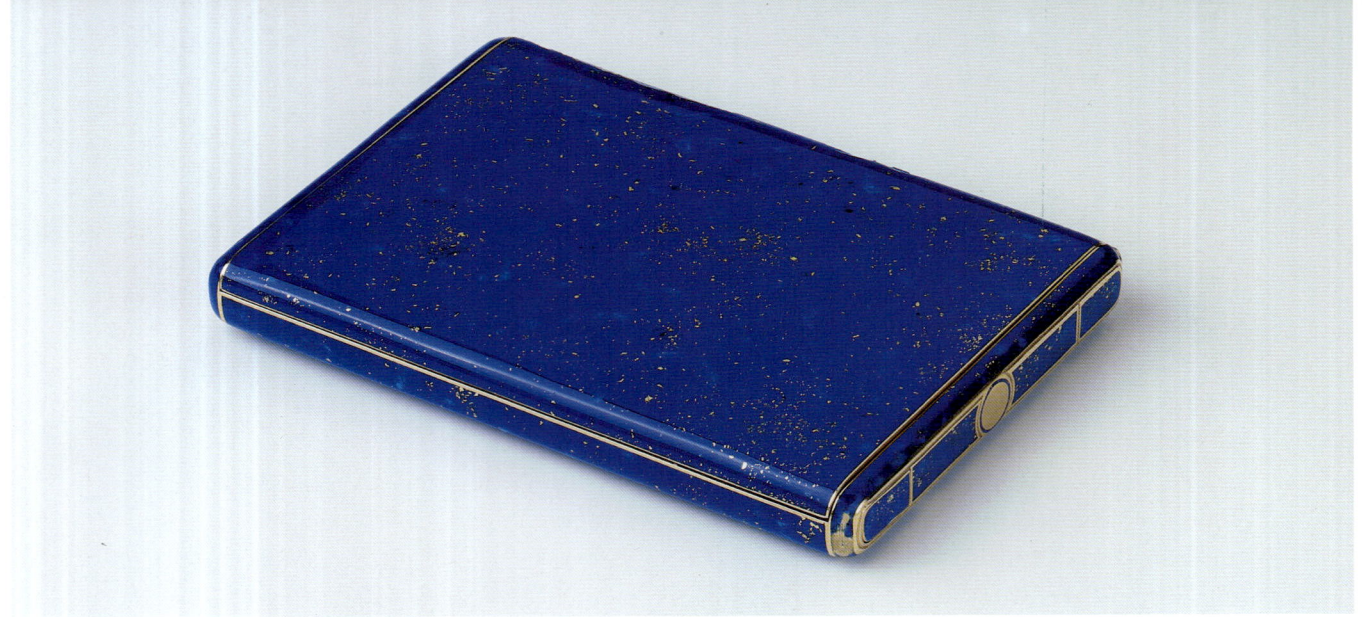

356 CIGARETTE CASE, *c.* 1920

Boucheron established a branch in Moscow in 1893. Mainly producing jewellery, Boucheron also included cigarette cases such as this and other small Fabergé-like enamel objects in its range of products.

Gold, enamel, 8.4 x 5.9 x 1.1 cm (3⁵/₁₆ x 2⁵/₁₆ x ⁷/₁₆")
French hallmarks, date illegible
RCIN 9178
PROVENANCE: Given to King George V by Queen Mary, 6 July 1928
REFERENCES: GV Boxes, vol. VI no. 487

357 CIGARETTE CASE, *c.* 1912

The style and quality of this box suggest that it was made in Fabergé's workshops, but it is unmarked. Several other firms produced good-quality cigarette cases in guilloché enamel and gold. Those who supplied the imperial family included Hahn, Köchli, Britsin and Bolin. The box was a gift to Queen Mary from Grand Duchess Xenia of Russia for Christmas 1912.

Silver-gilt, gold, guilloché enamel, rhodonite, garnet, 1.6 x 9.1 x 5.5 cm (⁵/₈ x 3⁹/₁₆ x 2⁵/₁₆")
Silver mark of 88 *zolotniks* (1908–17); engraved *Xenia 1912*
RCIN 4061
PROVENANCE: Grand Duchess Xenia; by whom given to Queen Mary, Christmas 1912

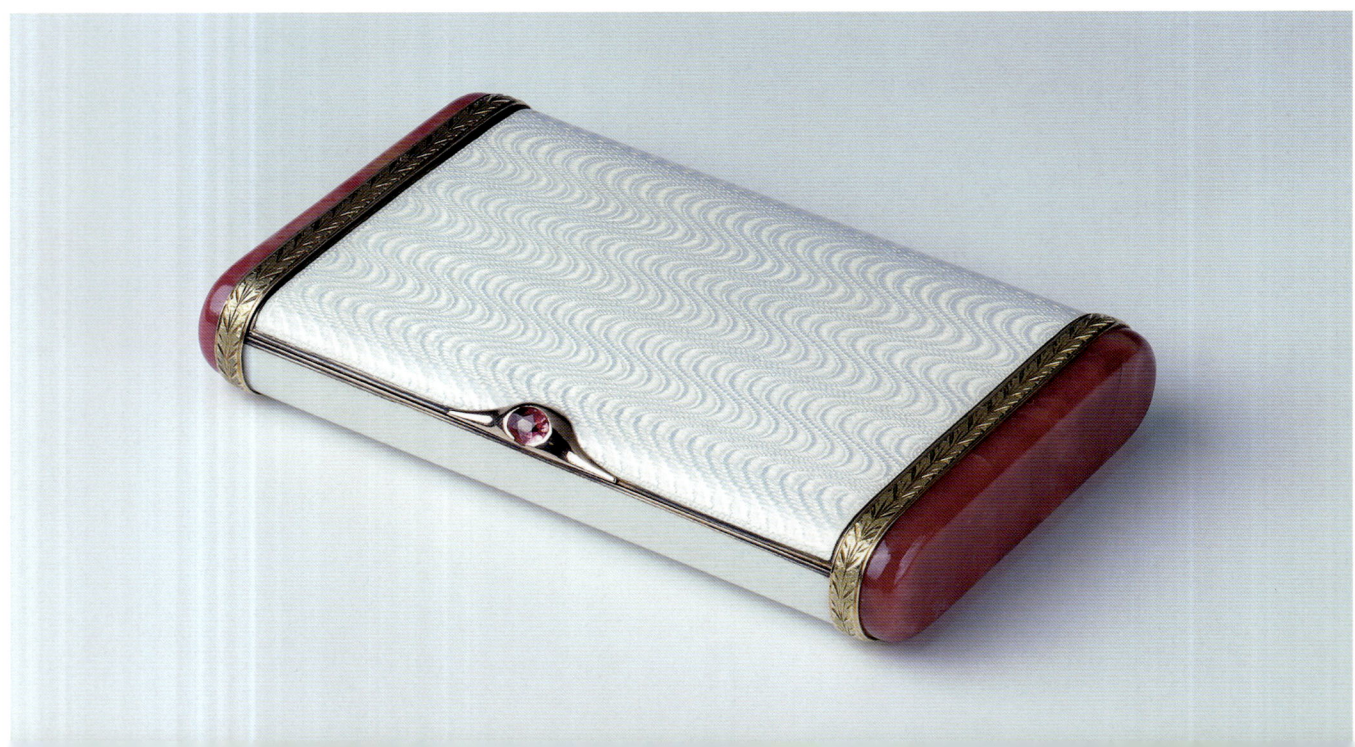

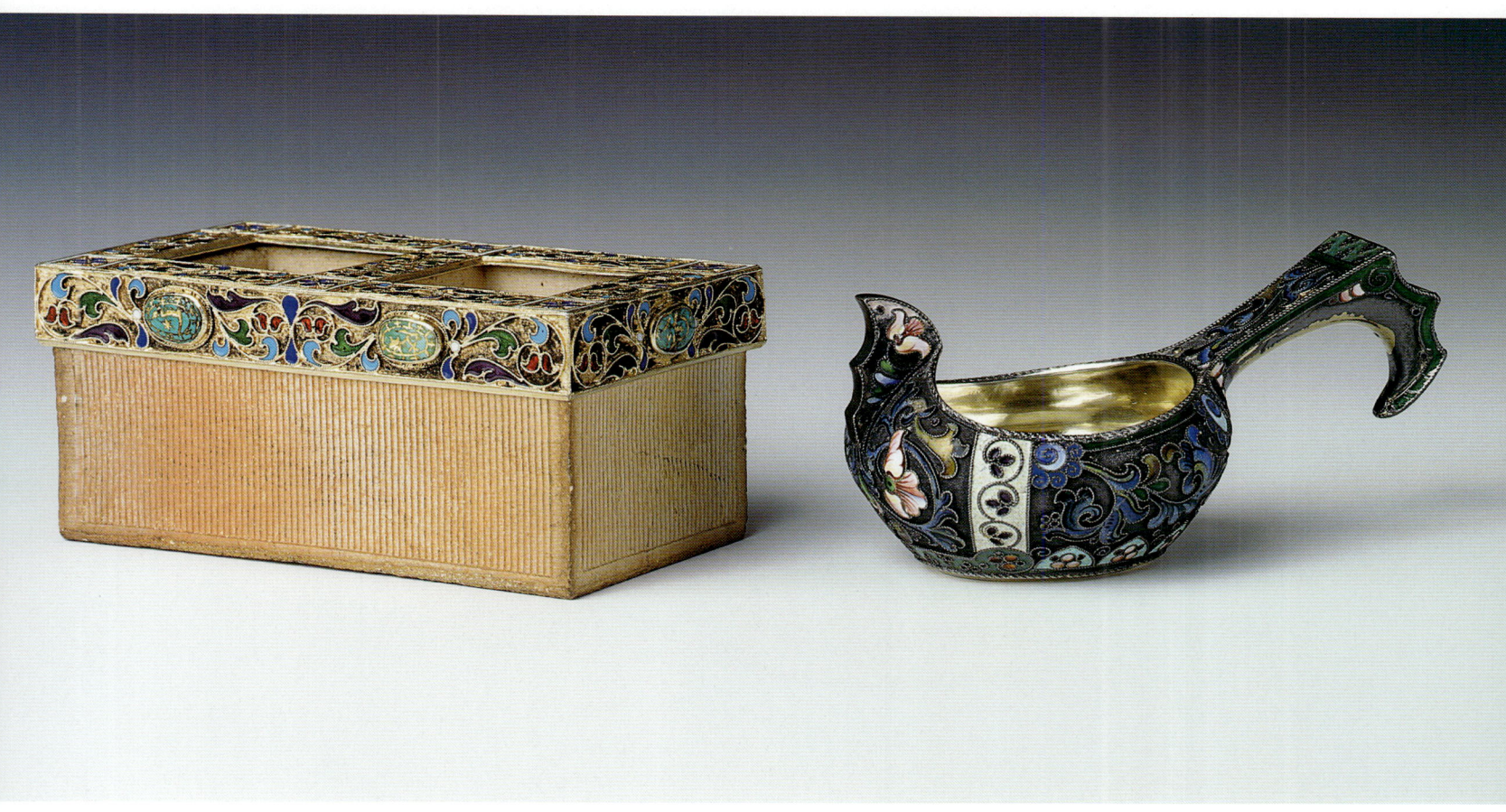

358 MATCH HOLDER, *c.*1900

Fabergé used bricks, which he had mounted with silver or gold to turn them into elegant match holders (see cat. 318 and 322). Here a brick from the factory that supplied Fabergé – Gusareva in Moscow – is mounted with traditional Old Russian-style cloisonné enamelling incorporating incised turquoises. Although the enamelled silver-gilt bears no marks, the match holder is quite likely to have been produced by one of Fabergé's Russian competitors in Moscow.

Brick, silver, cloisonné enamel, turquoise, 4.2 x 10.1 x 5.5 cm (1⁵/₈ x 4 x 2³/₁₆")
Brick stamped *A. GUSAREVA MOSCOW*
RCIN 50723
PROVENANCE: Probably acquired by the Prince of Wales (later King Edward VII)

359 KOVSH, 1908–1917

This small cloisonné enamel *kovsh* was made in the workshop of the Eleventh Artel in Moscow. The Eleventh Artel was founded in the 1890s (see p. 27) and specialised in cloisonné-enamelled objects, often showing an art nouveau influence. This influence is particularly apparent on the white bands with trefoils, which divide the more traditional Old Russian-style flower panels.

Silver, cloisonné enamel, 4.6 x 5.4 x 9.7 cm (1¹³/₁₆ x 2¹/₈ x 3¹³/₁₆")
Mark of the Eleventh Artel; Moscow silver mark of 84 *zolotniks* (1908–17)
RCIN 100328
PROVENANCE: Acquired by Queen Elizabeth, date unknown

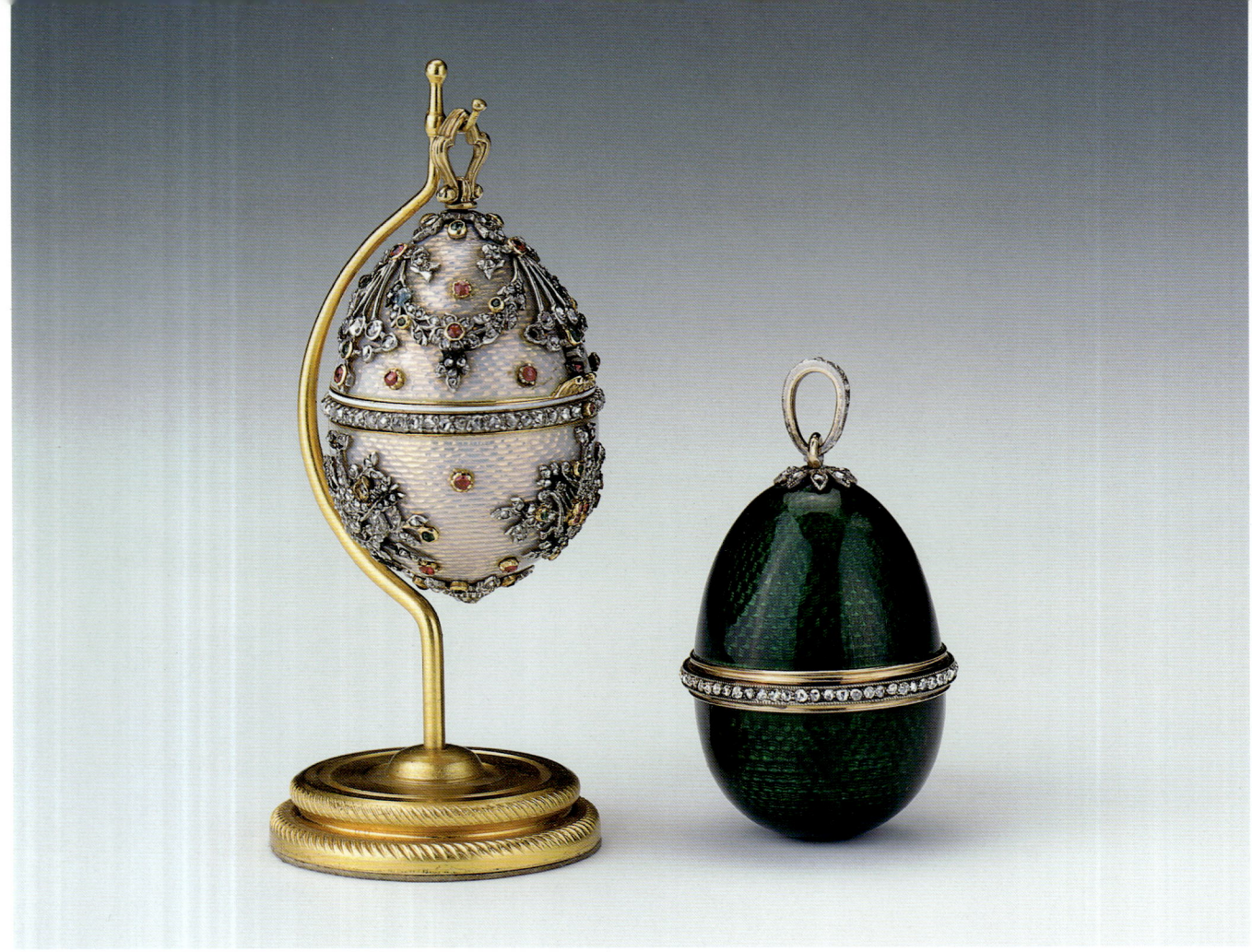

360 EGG-SHAPED BOX, *c.*1900

The retailer Edouard Henry Dreyfous, based in London, sold antiques and furniture as well as *objets d'art*, some of which were marked with the firm's stamp (see cat. 362). This egg appears to have been inspired by Fabergé's miniature decorated eggs. The guilloché enamelling and gem-set ribboned swags are reminiscent of his work. Both Queen Alexandra and Queen Mary patronised Dreyfous.

Gold, guilloché enamel, diamonds, emeralds, rubies, 4.6 x diameter 2.7 cm (1¹³⁄₁₆ x 1¹⁄₁₆")
Stamped *E. DREYFOUS*
RCIN 8941
PROVENANCE: Given to Queen Mary by her children, Christmas 1927
REFERENCES: QMB II, no. 155; QMPP V, no. 152

361 MINIATURE EGG, *c.*1900

Although this miniature egg is very much in Fabergé's style and is described in Queen Mary's inventory as being by Fabergé, it bears no marks and may have been produced by a rival firm. It contains a small figure of an angel in silver-gilt; some of Fabergé's small eggs contained figures or other objects in the same manner as the 'surprises' in the Imperial Easter Eggs. The maker has not been identified.

Gold, guilloché enamel, diamonds, silver-gilt, 4.5 x diameter 2.7 cm (1¾ x 1¹⁄₁₆")
Unmarked
RCIN 8947
PROVENANCE: Acquired by Queen Mary before 1933
REFERENCES: QMPP VI, no. 8
EXHIBITIONS: QG 1985–6, no. 72

362 ROSE, *c.*1900

In spite of the fact that this rose is quite different from Fabergé's flowers, it was included in an early Fabergé exhibition at Wartski (1953) and again in the major Fabergé exhibition held at the Victoria and Albert Museum in 1977. It was also included in the Royal Collection's first exhibition devoted to the Fabergé collection, held at The Queen's Gallery in 1985–6. The vase is of rock crystal, the stems of gold and the flowers of enamel – all techniques used by Fabergé for his flowers – but the quality of the enamelling is unlike that of Fabergé's flowers, being much less naturalistic, especially when compared to the Fabergé roses in the Royal Collection (see cat. 128 and 129). A diamond forms a dew drop on one of the petals.

Rock crystal, gold, enamel, rose diamond, 8.7 x diameter 3.5 cm (3⁷/₁₆ x 1³/₈")
Engraved *E. Dreyfous*
RCIN 40179
PROVENANCE: Presumably acquired by Queen Alexandra or Queen Mary, date unknown
REFERENCES: Snowman 1962, pl. 303
EXHIBITIONS: London 1953, no. 34; London 1977, no. E5; QG 1985–6, no. 2

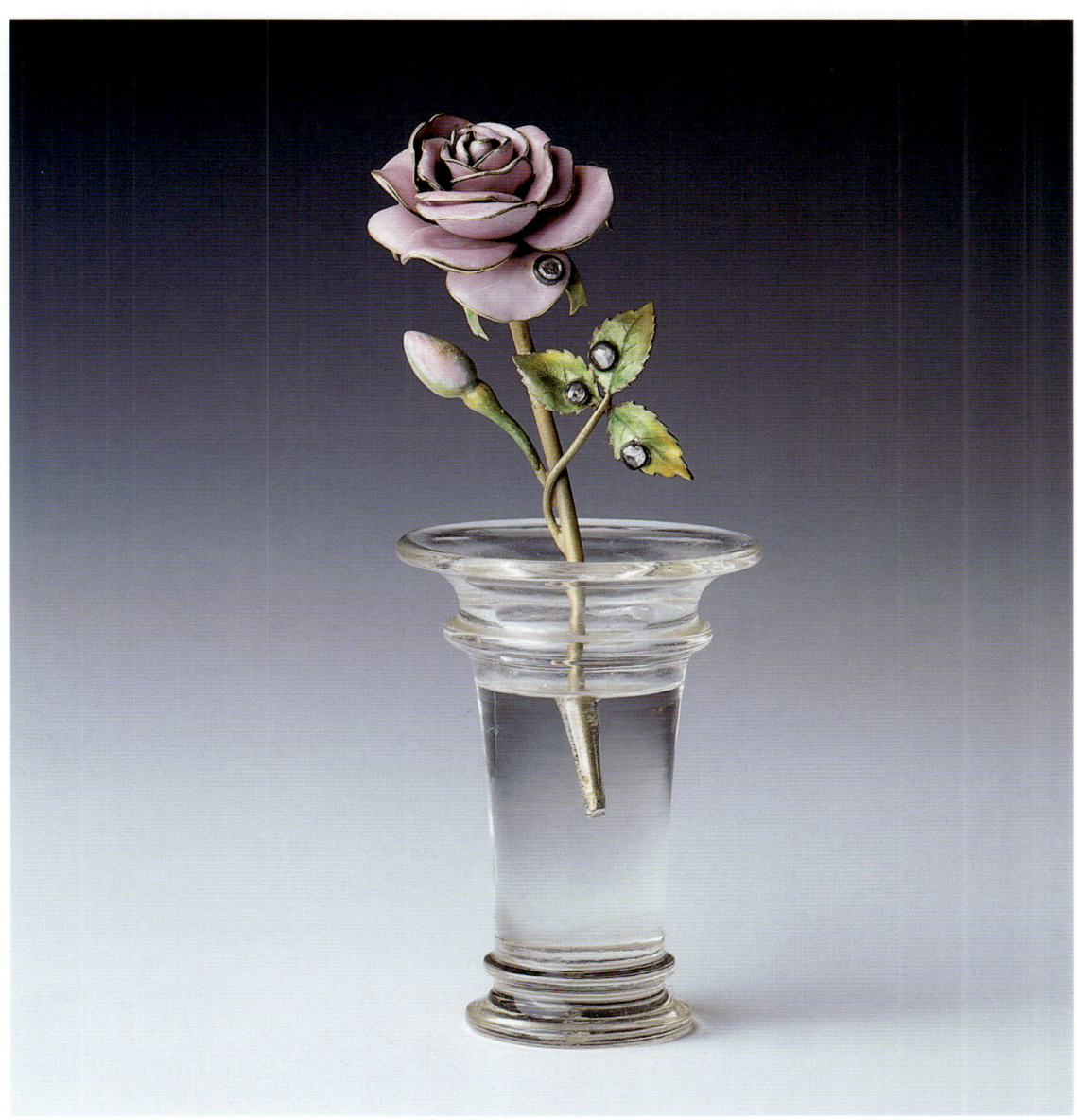

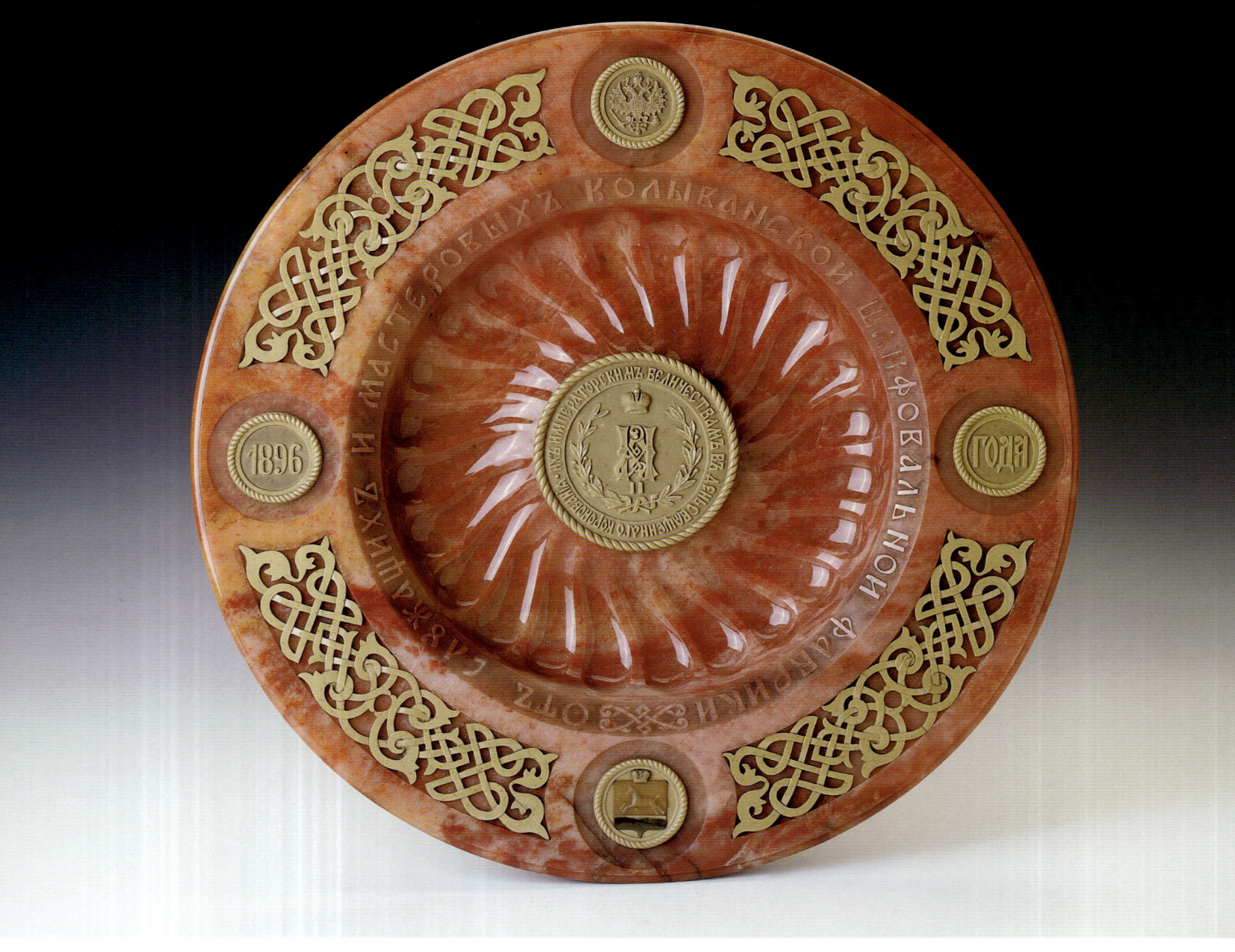

363 CORONATION PRESENTATION DISH, 1896

This dish was presented to Tsar Nicholas II and Tsarina Alexandra Feodorovna on the day of their coronation, 9 May 1896, by the employees and workers of the lapidaries of Kolyvan. Kolyvan, together with Ekaterinburg and Peterhof, was the traditional centre for lapidary workshops in Russia. In the early twentieth century Fabergé's use of Russian hardstones helped to revitalise the lapidary industry. He acquired most of his stone from the Wöerffel workshops in St Petersburg and the Stern workshops in Idar Oberstein, Germany. Occasionally stone articles were acquired from the Ekaterinburg workshops. According to Birbaum, 'a whole series of small objects from the Kolyvan factory' was acquired around 1914; this appears to be because many craftsmen from the Ekaterinburg workshops had been called up to serve in the First World War. Birbaum recorded that the ready-made objects from Kolyvan were technically well made but old-fashioned. The style of carving on this dish is similar to that on Russian carved wooden presentation dishes from the 1870s to 1890s, now in the Hermitage.

The dish was acquired by Queen Mary in 1938. The circumstances under which it left Russia are unclear.

Rhodonite, stone, 4.5 x diameter 42.6 cm (1³/₄ x 16³/₄")
Applied with inscription in Cyrillic characters: *To Their Imperial Majesties on the day of the holy Coronation. From the employees and workers of the lapidaries of Kolyvan 1896*; applied with the imperial eagles, crowned cypher of Nicholas II and the arms of the lapidaries of Kolyvan
RCIN 49799
PROVENANCE: Presented to Tsar Nicholas II and Tsarina Alexandra Feodorovna, 9 May 1896; acquired by Queen Mary, 1938
REFERENCES: QMPP IX, no. 131; Habsburg & Lopato 1993, p. 460; St Petersburg 1996, pp. 168–9

364 SET OF SIX SALTS, c.1896

These salts, in their original box, were made in the workshops of Pavel Ovchinnikov in Moscow, famous for silver and cloisonné enamel objects and competing directly with Fabergé in this market. Ovchinnikov often sold his articles and *objets d'art* in wooden boxes similar to those used by Fabergé. The former's work became known in the West after being exhibited at the 1900 Exposition Universelle in Paris.

Silver-gilt, cloisonné enamel, wood, silk, velvet, salt cellar 2.5 x diameter 4.6 cm (1 x 1¹³/₁₆"), spoon 6.5 x 1.9 x 0.7 cm (2⁹/₁₆ x ³/₄ x ¹/₄")
Mark of Pavel Ovchinnikov; Moscow silver mark of 88 *zolotniks* (before 1896)
RCIN 46526
PROVENANCE: Probably acquired by the Prince and Princess of Wales (later King Edward VII and Queen Alexandra), c.1896

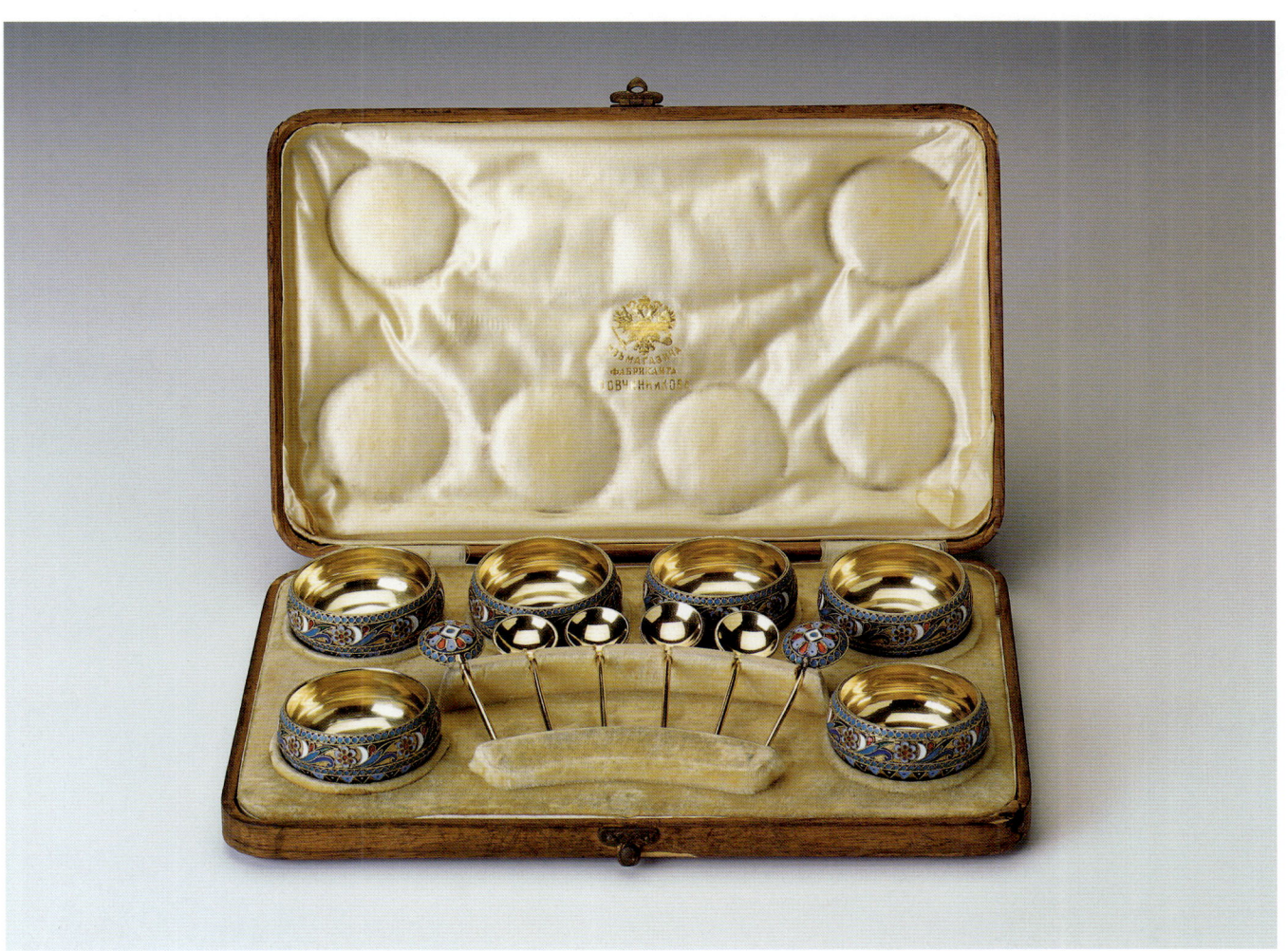

365 PAPER-KNIFE AND PENCIL HOLDER, *c.*1900

This combined paper-knife and pencil holder is of a shape typically produced by Fabergé. The metal is unmarked and it could have been made in one of several Russian workshops at the end of the nineteenth century. The pencil is stamped with the name Johann Faber.

Two-colour gold, guilloché enamel, 9.5 x 2.1 x 1.1 cm (3³/₄ x ¹³/₁₆ x ⁷/₁₆")
Pencil marked *Johann Faber*
RCIN 100335
PROVENANCE: Acquired by Queen Elizabeth, date unknown
REFERENCES: Habsburg 1987, p. 224

366 SEAL, 1908–1911

Britsin exported his work to England and the United States from 1900 to 1917 and this seal bears English import marks for 1911. The shape of the seal, with an amethyst forming the finial and with gold at the waist and around the matrix, is very close to Fabergé's work. The pale blue guilloché enamel is in keeping with Britsin's apparently limited palette of colours.

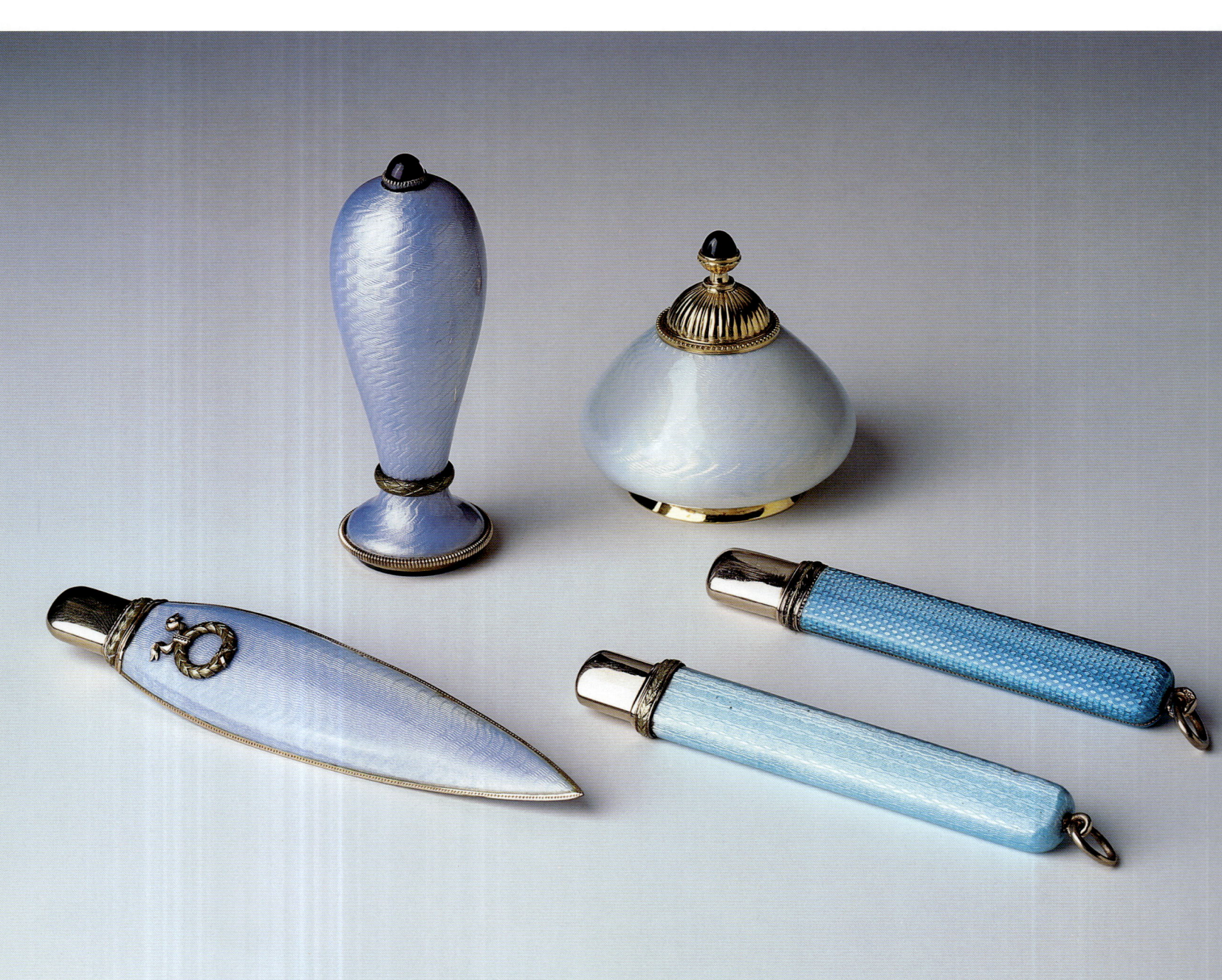

Gold, silver, guilloché enamel, amethyst, nephrite, 6.9 x diameter 2.5 cm (2^{11}/$_{16}$ x 1")
Mark of Ivan Britsin; silver mark of 88 *zolotniks* (1908–17); English import marks for 1911
RCIN 100334
PROVENANCE: Acquired by Queen Elizabeth, date unknown

367   GUM POT, 1908–1917

This gum pot is extremely close in design and quality to Fabergé's own work. It was made by the Third Artel, a goldsmiths' co-operative which consisted of more than ten craftsmen (including some who had worked for Fabergé) and which had premises at 48 Ekaterinskii Canal in St Petersburg. In addition to competing directly with Fabergé, particularly in the field of small guilloché enamelled objects (such as clocks, frames and miniature eggs), the Third Artel also supplied Fabergé with pieces which he sold.

Silver, gold, guilloché enamel, cabochon amethyst, 4.7 x diameter 4.3 cm (1^{7}/$_{8}$ x 1^{11}/$_{16}$")
Mark of the Third Artel; gold mark of 56 *zolotniks* and silver mark of 88 *zolotniks* (1908–17)
RCIN 40178
PROVENANCE: Royal Collection by 1953
REFERENCES: Habsburg 1987, p. 294, nos. 600–602
EXHIBITIONS: London 1977, no. G6; QG 1985–6, no. 58; QG 1995–6, no. 403

368   PENCIL HOLDER, 1908–1917

The mark on this gold and guilloché enamel pencil holder reveals that it was made by A. Astreyden. Little is known about this maker except that he was active in St Petersburg in the early twentieth century and specialised in producing small enamelled objects. His guilloché enamelling was of fine quality, as seen on a cigarette case made by him.

Two-colour gold, guilloché enamel, 8.3 x 1.2 x 0.5 cm (3^{1}/$_{4}$ x ^{1}/$_{2}$ x ^{3}/$_{16}$")
Mark of A. Astreyden; gold mark (1908–17)
RCIN 100329
PROVENANCE: Acquired by Queen Elizabeth, date unknown
REFERENCES: Habsburg 1987, p. 293, no. 594

369   PENCIL HOLDER, 1896–1908

Although this pencil holder is almost identical to cat. 368, it was made by a different workmaster – known only by his mark of *AR*. Unfortunately the maker's mark has been struck on the gold underneath the guilloché enamel and thus shows through the translucent layers. The combination of guilloché enamel and of coloured gold was inspired directly by Fabergé's work but this St Petersburg maker also produced silver-mounted objects, of which an example is included in this exhibition (see cat. 370).

Two-colour gold, guilloché enamel, 8.1 x 1.1. x 0.5 cm (3^{3}/$_{16}$ x ^{7}/$_{16}$ x ^{3}/$_{16}$")
Mark of workmaster *AR*; gold mark (1896–1908)
RCIN 100330
PROVENANCE: Acquired by Queen Elizabeth, date unknown

370 MOUNTED PORCELAIN BOWL, 1896–1908

This is the only piece of mounted porcelain by one of Fabergé's workmasters in the Royal Collection. The bowl itself is unmarked but the silver-gilt mounts are marked by the Russian workmaster *AR*, about whom very little is known. His mark is very occasionally found in conjunction with Fabergé's mark, but on this piece it is alone. Other pieces by the same workmaster include the pencil holder (cat. 369).

Porcelain, silver-gilt, 5 x diameter 8 cm (1 ¹⁵/₁₆ x 3⅛")
Mark of workmaster *AR*; silver mark of 88 *zolotniks* (1896–1908)
RCIN 100331
PROVENANCE: Given to Queen Elizabeth by Wartski, 1977

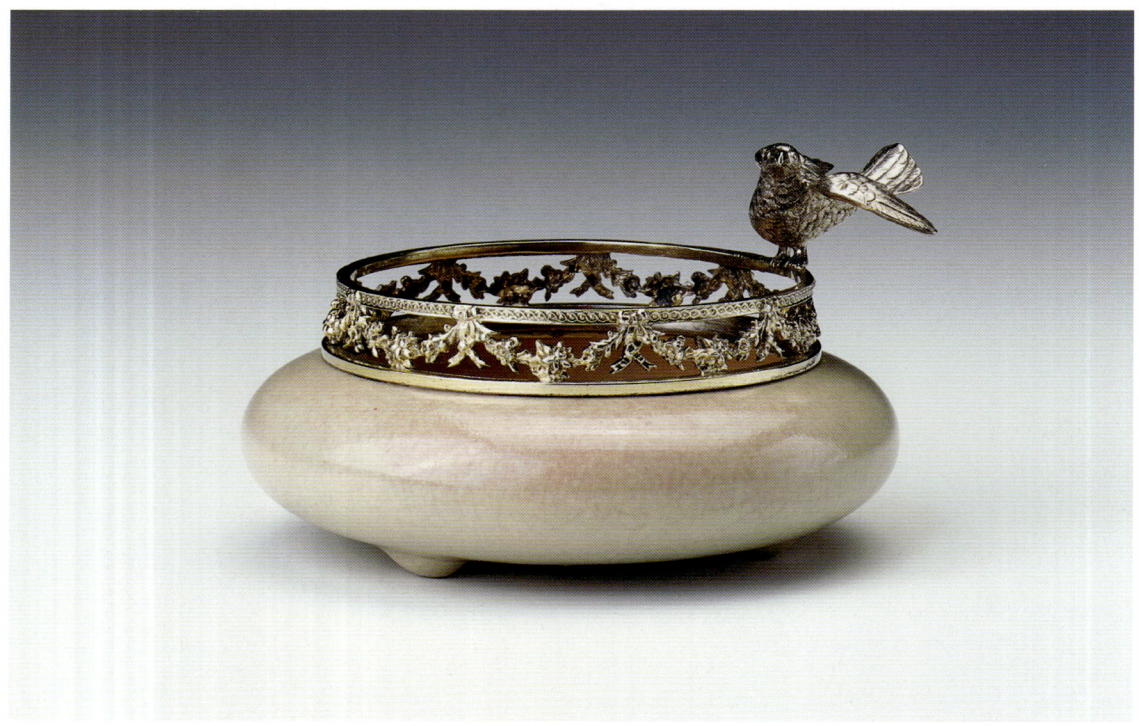

FAMILY TREE

The British, Danish and Russian royal families

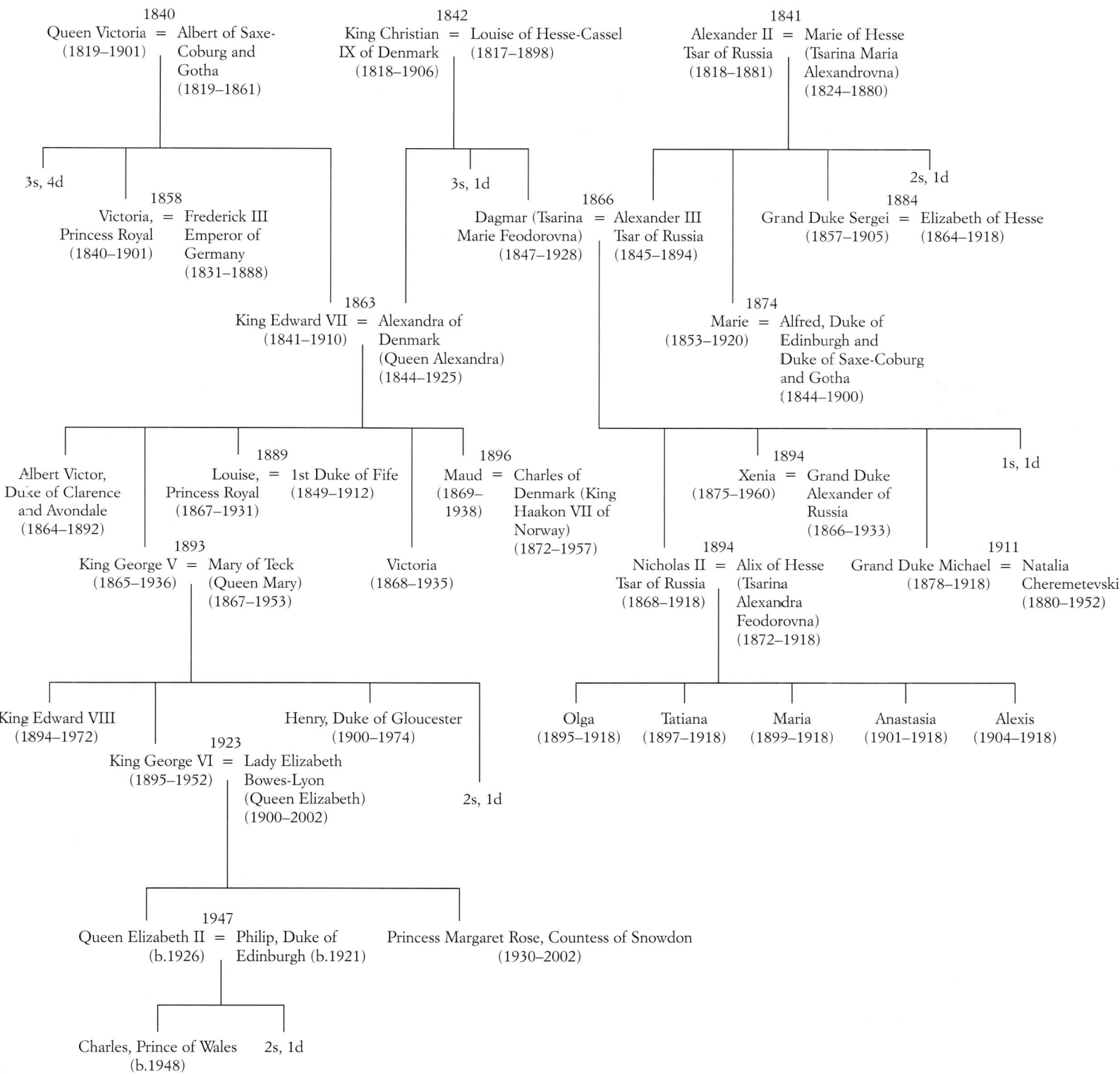

1840
Queen Victoria = Albert of Saxe-
(1819–1901)   Coburg and
                 Gotha
                 (1819–1861)

1842
King Christian = Louise of Hesse-Cassel
IX of Denmark   (1817–1898)
(1818–1906)

1841
Alexander II = Marie of Hesse
Tsar of Russia (Tsarina Maria
(1818–1881)   Alexandrovna)
                (1824–1880)

3s, 4d

1858
Victoria, = Frederick III
Princess Royal Emperor of
(1840–1901)   Germany
                (1831–1888)

3s, 1d

Dagmar (Tsarina = Alexander III
Marie Feodorovna) Tsar of Russia
(1847–1928)   (1845–1894)
1866

2s, 1d
1884
Grand Duke Sergei = Elizabeth of Hesse
(1857–1905)   (1864–1918)

1863
King Edward VII = Alexandra of
(1841–1910)   Denmark
                  (Queen Alexandra)
                  (1844–1925)

1874
Marie = Alfred, Duke of
(1853–1920) Edinburgh and
             Duke of Saxe-Coburg
             and Gotha
             (1844–1900)

Albert Victor,
Duke of Clarence
and Avondale
(1864–1892)

1889
Louise, = 1st Duke of Fife
Princess Royal (1849–1912)
(1867–1931)

1896
Maud = Charles of
(1869– Denmark (King
1938)   Haakon VII of
        Norway)
        (1872–1957)

1894
Xenia = Grand Duke
(1875–1960) Alexander of
             Russia
             (1866–1933)

1s, 1d

1893
King George V = Mary of Teck
(1865–1936)   (Queen Mary)
                (1867–1953)

Victoria
(1868–1935)

1894
Nicholas II = Alix of Hesse
Tsar of Russia (Tsarina
(1868–1918)   Alexandra
                Feodorovna)
                (1872–1918)

1911
Grand Duke Michael = Natalia
(1878–1918)   Cheremetevski
                     (1880–1952)

King Edward VIII
(1894–1972)

Henry, Duke of Gloucester
(1900–1974)

Olga
(1895–1918)

Tatiana
(1897–1918)

Maria
(1899–1918)

Anastasia
(1901–1918)

Alexis
(1904–1918)

1923
King George VI = Lady Elizabeth
(1895–1952)   Bowes-Lyon
                 (Queen Elizabeth)
                 (1900–2002)

2s, 1d

1947
Queen Elizabeth II = Philip, Duke of
(b.1926)   Edinburgh (b.1921)

Princess Margaret Rose, Countess of Snowdon
(1930–2002)

Charles, Prince of Wales   2s, 1d
(b.1948)

BIOGRAPHIES OF FABERGÉ'S WORKMASTERS

This section includes only those whose work is represented in this book.

HEAD WORKMASTERS

Erik Kollin (1836–1901)
Erik August Kollin was born in Finland, where he completed his apprenticeship before travelling to St Petersburg. In 1858 he obtained a position in the workshop of the goldsmith August Holmström, who had been appointed principal jeweller by Gustav Fabergé in 1857. In 1870 Kollin opened his own workshop. He was made head workmaster by Fabergé two years later and held that post until 1886. Kollin is famous for his gold work, particularly jewellery inspired by Scythian archaeological finds.

Michael Perchin (1860–1903)
Born in Petrosavodsk, Michael Perchin worked initially as a journeyman in the workshop of Erik Kollin. In 1884 he qualified as a master craftsman. His artistic potential must have been obvious to Fabergé, who appointed him head workmaster in 1886. Many new objects in gold and enamel that were elegant yet functional were produced in his workshop. All the important commissions of the time, including some of the Imperial Easter Eggs, were made in his workshop. His period as head workmaster is generally acknowledged to be the most artistically innovative, with a huge range of styles from neo-rococo to Renaissance.

Henrik Wigström (1862–1923)
Born in Tammisaari, Finland, Henrik Wigström was apprenticed to a local silversmith, Petter Madsen. He travelled to St Petersburg and in 1884 was taken on by Perchin as a journeyman, becoming his most valued assistant. When Perchin died in 1903 his workshop passed to Wigström and Fabergé appointed him head workmaster. The workshop continued to produce important commissions and some of the best examples of cigarette cases and boxes which the firm ever made, in Wigström's largely neo-classical style. Many of the hardstone animals and figures, together with the flowers, were produced in his workshop.

OTHER WORKMASTERS

Johan Viktor Aarne (1863–1934)
Born in Finland, Viktor Aarne qualified as a journeyman before moving to St Petersburg and working with Fabergé. He produced a wide range of objects in a variety of styles and is particularly noted for his miniature frames with vari-coloured gold decoration.

Karl Armfelt (1873–1959)
In 1904 Aarne sold his workshop to Karl (Hjalmar) Armfelt, who had come from Finland to St Petersburg in 1886 and served under Nevalainen (see below) as a workmaster. He trained at the German Art School and the Baron Stieglitz Central School of Technical Drawing in St Petersburg, but in spite of his ambitions as an artist his workshop continued to supply Fabergé with objects in the same style as Aarne.

August Hollming (1854–1913)
August Hollming was apprenticed to a goldsmith in Helsinki and in 1876 became a journeyman in St Petersburg. Hollming manufactured jewellery as well as decorative and functional objects for Fabergé in gold and silver.

Albert Holmström (1876–1925)
Albert Holmström was apprenticed to his father August and took over his workshop in 1903. He was a talented craftsman and produced many pieces of jewellery in elegant settings for Fabergé.

August Holmström (1829–1903)
Born in Helsinki, August Holmström was apprenticed to the jeweller Herold in 1850 and became a master in 1857. In the same year he was appointed principal jeweller by Fabergé, a post he held until his death. His workshop produced a wide range of jewelled objects from exclusive jewellery to miniature Easter eggs. Of the important commissions which his workshop undertook, the miniature replicas of the Russian imperial regalia, exhibited at the Exposition Universelle in Paris in 1900 and now in the State Hermitage Museum, St Petersburg, are perhaps the most famous.

Anders Nevalainen (1858–1933)
Born in Finland, Anders Nevalainen gained his master's certificate in St Petersburg in 1885. He worked in August Holmström's workshop initially and then independently, producing small gold and silver objects such as frames and cigarette cases exclusively for Fabergé.

Julius Rappoport (1864–1916)
Trained in Berlin, Julius Rappoport opened his own workshop in St Petersburg in 1883, becoming Fabergé's most important supplier of silver objects. His range of products included large silver dinner services, silver-mounted functional objects and silver animals.

Alfred Thielemann (active c.1840–c.1900)
Of German origin, Alfred Thielemann qualified as a master craftsman in 1858 and from 1880 ran Fabergé's second jewellery workshop. In addition to jewellery he also made small gold items, such as jettons.

Stefan Wakeva (1833–1910)
Stefan Wakeva arrived in St Petersburg in 1843, becoming a master silversmith in 1856. He worked for Fabergé from his own workshop, producing silver tableware and small decorative objects in the neo-classical style.

GLOSSARY

Gold is measured in 56 and 72 *zolotniks*, the equivalent to 14 and 18 carats.

Silver is measured in 84, 88 and 91 *zolotniks*, the equivalent to 21, 22 and 22³/₄ carats.

Agate: A form of chalcedony in which iron oxide causes varying shades of brown

Aventurine quartz: A quartz containing mica, iron oxides or pyrite crystals which give it a range of colours

Bowenite: A pale green serpentine named after its discoverer, G.T. Bowen

Cabochon: Dome-shaped unfaceted stone

Chalcedony: A fine-grained mineral of silicic acid, usually of a white or milky hue

Coloured gold: Achieved by the eighteenth-century technique of dyeing gold with other metals:
    yellow = gold in its purest form
    red = mixed with copper
    green = mixed with silver
    white = mixed with nickel or palladium

Cornelian: A variety of chalcedony, usually a warm orange colour

Diamond
brilliant: Circular-cut diamond with a flat top
portrait: A thin diamond cut with two large, flat, parallel surfaces, so that a viewer can see through it to an object beneath
rose: Diamond with the top cut into triangular facets

Enamel: A glass capable of being fused to metal.
cloisonné: Enamel technique in which a design is drawn with strips of wire or *cloisons* which are shaped to form a network of cells. The cells are then filled with enamels
en camaieu: A delicate form of grisaille enamel painting, seen particularly in the decoration of snuff boxes
en grisaille: Monochrome or toned grey effects produced by fusing white enamel over a dark ground
guilloché: Translucent enamel is fused over a geometric pattern incised into gold or silver by engine-turning
pliqué a jour: Technique in which translucent or opalescent enamel is fused across a network of cells with no backing under the glazed areas

Jasper: An opaque chalcedony ranging from brown to green in colour

Lapis lazuli: A dark blue stone with gold deposits, found in Siberia

Mecca stone: Dyed cabochon chalcedony

Moonstone: A blue variety of icespar

Moss agate: A variety of chalcedony with dendritic inclusions

Mother-of-pearl: The strongly iridescent inner layer of shells

Nephrite: A dark green jade found in Siberia

Netsuke: Japanese toggle used to fasten *inros* (boxes) to belts

Obsidian: A dark grey or black volcanic glass found in Siberia

Olivine: A pale green mineral, also called peridot

Purpurine: A dark red, man-made, vitreous substance first produced in the seventeenth century and introduced to Russia by the Imperial Glass Factory. Reinvented by Fabergé and his contemporaries

Quartzite: A form of quartz

Rhodonite: A pink manganese silicate with black inclusions, found in the Urals

Rock crystal: The purest form of quartz, found in the Ukraine and the Urals

Rutilated quartz: A quartz (usually rock crystal) containing columnar-shaped crystals with a metallic lustre

Samorodok: Gold or silver heated to just below melting point then cooled rapidly, giving a nugget-like finish

Tiger's eye quartz: A yellow quartz with an iridescent quality found in western Germany

Topaz: An aluminium silicate ranging in colour from pale blue to yellow, orange, brown and pink

EXHIBITION ABBREVIATIONS

ST PETERSBURG 1902
Artistic Objects and Miniatures by Fabergé, Baron von Dervis mansion

LONDON 1935
Exhibition of Russian Art, Belgrave Square

LONDON 1948
Antique Dealers' Fair and Exhibition, Grosvenor House

LONDON 1949
Fabergé, A Loan Exhibition of the Works of Carl Fabergé Jeweller and Goldsmith to the Imperial Court of Russia, Wartski

LONDON 1953
Carl Fabergé Special Coronation Exhibition, Wartski

LONDON 1954
Queen Mary's Art Treasures, Victoria and Albert Museum

QG 1962–3
Treasures from the Royal Collection, The Queen's Gallery, Buckingham Palace

LONDON 1967
Great Britain USSR, Victoria and Albert Museum

LONDON 1971
A Thousand Years of Enamel, Wartski

AUSTRALIA 1977
The Royal Silver Jubilee Exhibition, in four carriages of a special train, travelling 11,250 km (6,986 miles) in four months, with numerous stops on a route Sydney–Brisbane–Melbourne–Adelaide–Perth–Sydney

LONDON 1977
Fabergé 1846–1920, Goldsmith to the Imperial Court of Russia, Victoria and Albert Museum

LONDON RA 1977
Derby Day 200, Royal Academy

MELBOURNE 1979–80
The Kangaroo in Decorative Art, National Gallery of Victoria, Melbourne

LONDON 1981
Exhibition for a Charity Auction for the RNID, Christie's

NEW YORK 1983
Fabergé, Jeweller to Royalty, Cooper Hewitt Museum

QG 1985–6
Fabergé, The Queen's Gallery, Buckingham Palace

MUNICH 1986–7
Fabergé Hofjuwelier der Zaren, Kunsthalle der Hypo-Kulturstiftung, Hirmer Verlag

LONDON 1987
Burlington House Fair, Royal Academy

ZURICH 1989
Carl Fabergé, Museum Bellerive

SAN DIEGO/MOSCOW 1989–90
Fabergé. The Imperial Eggs, San Diego Museum of Art 1989; Armoury Museum, Kremlin 1989-90

LONDON 1991
Grosvenor House Antiques Fair

LONDON 1992
Sovereign: EIIR. A Celebration of Forty Years Service, Victoria and Albert Museum

LONDON 1992a
Fabergé from Private Collections, Wartski

ST PETERBURG/PARIS/LONDON 1993–4
Fabergé Imperial Jeweller, State Hermitage Museum 1993; Musée des Arts Decoratifs 1993; Victoria and Albert Museum 1993–4

QG 1995–6
Fabergé, The Queen's Gallery, Buckingham Palace

STOCKHOLM 1997
Carl Fabergé Goldsmith to the Tsar, Nationalmuseum

CARDIFF 1998
Princes as Patrons. The Art Collections of the Princes of Wales from the Renaissance to the Present Day, National Museum of Wales

LONDON 1999
Countdown to the Millennium: Fabergé, Tessier

QG 2002–3
Royal Treasures. A Golden Jubilee Celebration, The Queen's Gallery, Buckingham Palace

BIBLIOGRAPHY AND ABBREVIATIONS

Published sources

BAINBRIDGE 1933
    H.C. Bainbridge, *Twice Seven. The Autobiography*, London

BAINBRIDGE 1938
    H.C. Bainbridge, 'Fabergé Flowers Naturalistic', *The New York Sun*, 17 December

BAINBRIDGE 1942a
    H.C. Bainbridge, 'Fabergé Flowers at Sandringham', *Country Life*, 13 November

BAINBRIDGE 1942b
    H.C. Bainbridge, 'Fabergé Animals at Sandringham', *Country Life*, 20 November

BAINBRIDGE 1949
    H.C. Bainbridge, *Peter Carl Fabergé. His Life and Work 1846–1920*, London

BEVAN 1896
    H. Bevan, *Marlborough House and its Occupants*, London

BIRYUKOVA 1976
    N. Biryukova, 'Art Nouveau at the Hermitage', *Apollo*, vol. 103, no. 172

CATHCART 1964
    H. Cathcart, *Sandringham, The Story of a Royal Home*, London

CHRISTIE'S 1958
    Objects of Art and Vertu and Works by Carl Fabergé, London, 25 November

CHRISTIE'S 1976
    The Robert Strauss Collection, London, 9 March

CHRISTIE'S 1989
    Designs from the House of Carl Fabergé, London, 27 April

CHRISTIE'S 2000
    Important Silver, Objects of Vertu and Russian Works of Art, New York, 23 October

CHRISTIE'S 2002a
    Important Works of Art by Carl Fabergé from the Forbes Collection, New York, 19 April

CHRISTIE'S 2002b
    Important Silver, Objects of Vertu and Russian Works of Art, New York, 24 October

DAVEY 1982
    N.K. Davey, *Netsuke – A Comprehensive Study*, London

DUTT 1904
    W.A. Dutt, *The King's Homeland, Sandringham and North West Norfolk*, London

FABERGÉ, PROLER, SKURLOV 1997
    T. Fabergé, L.G. Proler and V.V. Skurlov, *The Fabergé Imperial Easter Eggs*, London

FERSMANN & VLODAVETS 1921
    A.E. Fersmann and H.I. Vlodavets, *State Peterhof Lapidary Works: Past, Present and Future*, Petrograd

FORBES & TROMEUR-BRENNER 1999
    C. Forbes and R. Tromeur-Brenner, *Fabergé The Forbes Collection*, New York

DE GUITAUT 2002
    C. de Guitaut, 'Two Fabergé Imperial Presentation Boxes', *Apollo*, vol. 155, no. 468

HABSBURG 1987
    G. von Habsburg, *Fabergé*, Munich

HABSBURG 1996
    G. von Habsburg, *Fabergé in America*, New York

HABSBURG 2000
    G. von Habsburg, *Fabergé Imperial Craftsman*, New York

HABSBURG & LOPATO 1993
    G. von Habsburg and M. Lopato, *Fabergé: Imperial Jeweller*, Washington

HOUGH 1992
    R. Hough, *Edward and Alexandra. Their Public and Private Lives*, London

JONES 1883
    H. Jones, *A Guide to Sandringham Past and Present*, London

LOPATO 1998
    M. Lopato, untitled (pp. 161–4), in J. Traina, *The Fabergé Case: From the Private Collection of John Traina*, New York

MAGNUS 1964
    P. Magnus, *King Edward the Seventh*, London

MUNN 1987
    G. Munn, 'Fabergé and Japan', *The Antique Collector*, vol. 58, no. 1

MUNTIAN 1997
    T. Muntian, 'The Kremlin Collection of the Empress's Personal Belongings', in *Marie Feodorova Empress of Russia*, Copenhagen

NADELHOFFER 1984
    Cartier Jewellers Extraordinary, London

NATIONALMUSEUM STOCKHOLM 1997
    Carl Fabergé Goldsmith to the Tsar

NERET 1988
    G. Neret, *Boucheron – Four Generations of a World Renowned Jeweler*, New York

NEW ORLEANS MUSEUM OF ART 1988
    Reflections of Elegance. Cartier Jewels from the Lindemann Collection, New Orleans

PATTERSON 1996
    S. Patterson, *Royal Insignia: British and Foreign Orders of Chivalry from the Royal Collection*, London

RUDOE 1997
    J. Rudoe, *Cartier 1900–1939*, London

ST PETERSBURG 1996
    Historicism in Russia: Style and Epoch in the Decorative Arts 1820s–1890s, St Petersburg

SCARISBRICK 1981
    D. Scarisbrick, 'From Pliny to Fabergé. The Story of Moss Agate', *Country Life*, 4 June

SCHAFFER 1984
    P. Schaffer, 'A La Vielle Russie's Fabergé', in *Masterpieces from the House of Fabergé*, ed. A. von Solodkoff, New York

SKURLOV 1997
    V.V. Skurlov, 'Boris Frödman-Cluzel, Fabergé Firm Artist', in *Carl Fabergé Goldsmith to the Tsar*, ed. E. Welander-Berggren, Stockholm

SNOWMAN 1955
    A.K. Snowman, 'The English Royal Collection at Sandringham House, Norfolk', *Connoisseur*, June

SNOWMAN 1962
    A.K. Snowman, *The Art of Carl Fabergé*, London

SNOWMAN 1979
    A.K. Snowman, *Carl Fabergé: Goldsmith to the Imperial Court of Russia*, London

SNOWMAN 1984
   A.K. Snowman, 'Wartski and
   Fabergé', in *Masterpieces from the
   House of Fabergé*, ed. A. von
   Solodkoff, New York
SNOWMAN 1987
   A.K. Snowman, 'Two Books of
   Revelations: The Fabergé Stock
   Books', *Apollo*, vol. 126, p. 150
SOMERS COCKS & TRUMAN 1984
   A. Somers Cocks and C. Truman,
   *The Thyssen-Bornemiza Collection:
   Renaissance Jewels, Gold Boxes and
   Objets de Vertu*, London
TILLANDER-GODENHIELM *et al.* 2000
   U. Tillander-Godenhielm *et al.*,
   *Golden Years of Fabergé: Drawings
   and Objects from the Wigström
   Workshop*, Paris

VON SOLODKOFF 1984
   A. von Solodkoff, *Masterpieces
   from the House of Fabergé*, New
   York

Unpublished sources
(RA – Royal Archives, Windsor Castle)

GV BOXES
   Inventory of Snuff, Patch and
   Other Boxes in the Collections
   of Queen Victoria, King Edward
   VII and King George V, 6 vols,
   1929–35 (typescript; RCIN
   1112523, 1114513, 1114515–18)
GV CIGARETTE CASES
   Inventory of Cigarette Cases etc.
   in the Collection of King George V,
   1936

QMB
   Catalogue of Bibelots, Miniatures
   and Other Valuables. The Property
   of HM Queen Mary, 4 vols: I,
   1920; II, 1921–31; III, 1932–7;
   IV, 1938–45 (illustrated typescript;
   RCIN 114504–09)
QMPP
   Inventory of the Private Property of
   HM The Queen [Mary], 11 vols:
   I–VI, 1912–32(?); VII, 1933;
   1912–33; VIII, 1936; IX, 1936–8;
   XI, 1946–8 (illustrated typescript;
   RCIN 1114193–503)

ACKNOWLEDGEMENTS

In the preparation of this book I have received the assistance of many colleagues both in the Royal Collection and elsewhere. In the Royal Collection and Royal Archives I would like to thank Julia Bagguley, Paul Briggs, Stephen Chapman, Pamela Clark, Jacky Colliss Harvey, Frances Dimond, Frances Dunkels, Henrietta Edwards, Gemma Entwistle, Kathryn Jones, Jill Kelsey, Karen Lawson, Jonathan Marsden, Elaine Pammenter, Shruti Patel, David Rankin-Hunt, Hugh Roberts, Jane Roberts, Lucy Scherer, David Wheeler and Matthew Winterbottom. In the Royal Household I would like to thank Edward Griffiths, Stephen Murray and Stuart Stacey.

I am grateful to the many experts on Fabergé whom I have consulted and who have generously shared their knowledge. I would particularly like to thank Ulla Tillander–Godenhielm for allowing me to illustrate previously unpublished designs. I would like to thank Kieran McCarthy, Geoffrey Munn and Katherine Purcell at Wartski. I gratefully acknowledge the help of Tatiana Fabergé and Valentin Skurlov for sharing their research. The support of Alice Milicia Ilich has been greatly appreciated, as has the help of the following people: Lyudmila Bakayutova, Christian Bolin, Paul Bulatov, Linda Kramer, Galina Gabriel, Elena Goldberg, Joyce Lasky Reed, Bernard Matthews, Marina Lopato, Anya Piotrovski, Emma Roberts, Peter Schaffer and Kevin Stayton. Finally, I would like to thank my husband and my parents for their support and encouragement.

INDEX